Roman Law for Scots Law Students

Roman Law for Scots Law Students

Craig Anderson, LL.B. Ph.D.

EDINBURGH
University Press

Edinburgh University Press is one of the leading university presses in the UK. We publish academic books and journals in our selected subject areas across the humanities and social sciences, combining cutting-edge scholarship with high editorial and production values to produce academic works of lasting importance. For more information visit our website: edinburghuniversitypress.com

© Craig Anderson, 2021

Edinburgh University Press Ltd
The Tun – Holyrood Road
12(2f) Jackson's Entry
Edinburgh EH8 8PJ

Typeset in 11/13 Baskerville by
IDSUK (DataConnection) Ltd, and
printed and bound in Great Britain.

A CIP record for this book is available from the British Library

ISBN 978 1 4744 5018 8 (hardback)
ISBN 978 1 4744 5019 5 (paperback)
ISBN 978 1 4744 5020 1 (webready PDF)
ISBN 978 1 4744 5021 8 (epub)

The right of Craig Anderson to be identified as the author of this work has been asserted in accordance with the Copyright, Designs and Patents Act 1988, and the Copyright and Related Rights Regulations 2003 (SI No. 2498).

Contents

Preface viii
Note on Online Resources x
Table of Cases xi
Table of Statutes xvi
List of Illustrations xix
List of Abbreviations xx

PART ONE THE HISTORICAL AND CONSTITUTIONAL CONTEXT OF ROMAN LAW
1 Historical Introduction to Roman Governance and Society 3
2 The Legal Process 29
3 Development of Roman Law 46
4 Reception of Roman Law 72

PART TWO THE LAW OF PERSONS
5 Categories of Person 95
6 Slavery 103
7 Parents and Guardians 116
8 Husband and Wife 134
9 Liability for Another 149

PART THREE THE LAW OF THINGS: PROPERTY
10 Ownership and Possession 161
11 Acquisition of Ownership: Derivative Acquisition 194
12 Acquisition of Ownership: Original Acquisition 216
13 Praedial Servitudes 244
14 Usufruct and Related Rights 259
15 Rights in Security 269

PART FOUR THE LAW OF THINGS: SUCCESSION
16 Succession 283

PART FIVE THE LAW OF THINGS: OBLIGATIONS

17	Introduction to the Law of Obligations and the Law of Contracts	321
18	Verbal Contracts	339
19	Real Contracts	344
20	Consensual Contracts	352
21	Other Contractual Arrangements	379
22	The Law of Delicts and the *Lex Aquilia*	385
23	Liability for Insulting Behaviour: The *Actio Iniuriarum*	405
24	Other Delicts	417
25	Quasi-Contractual Liability	428
26	Quasi-Delictual Liability	437

Appendix 1: Finding and Citing Roman Sources — 445
Appendix 2: Timeline of Major Events from the Foundation of Rome to Justinian I — 460
Index — 463

UXORI OPTIMAE

Preface

This book is aimed primarily at students of law in Scottish universities, who are either studying Roman law for its own sake, or who are exploring the connections between Roman and modern law. The experienced reader may ask why such a book is necessary. After all, there exist already student textbooks on Roman law that are of undoubted excellence. It must be said, though, that the existing textbooks that are available in English tend not to have much to say about Scotland. Where they talk about modern law, this is much more likely to be English law than Scots law. However, the much greater importance of Roman law in the development of the Scottish legal tradition, compared with that south of the border, means that students of Scots law have special needs in this regard. While we are fortunate to live in a time when there is a growing body of first-class scholarly literature on Scots law and its history – a greater body than at any previous time – most of this is at an advanced level. There is very little for the beginner or for the non-expert. It has seemed to me since I was an undergraduate law student that there has been an urgent need for a textbook on Roman law written with the Scots law student in mind. When Edinburgh University Press expressed a willingness to consider publishing such a book, I was therefore delighted to take up this task. I have been very grateful for their patient support through the whole process of writing the book.

This book attempts to do two things. First, it gives an account of Roman private law as it developed through the Roman period. Second, I have attempted to show how that law influenced later law, and in particular Scots law. In pursuance of this, there are references to Scots law (and, to a lesser extent, other legal systems) throughout. In doing this, I have tried to avoid interrupting the flow of the discussion of Roman law too much, in the hope that those interested only in the Roman law will be able to skip over discussion of later law without excessive difficulty.

In writing this book, I have benefited from the expertise of many others. I remain grateful to my own teachers. In addition, a number of my fellow teachers of Roman law gave generously of their time to read and comment on draft versions of parts of the book. I am grateful for their comments, which have greatly improved the final result. In this regard, I am particularly grateful to

Dr Jonathan Brown of the University of Strathclyde and to Gordon Cameron of the University of Dundee. None of these people, of course, bears any responsibility for remaining errors or obscurities. My greatest debt of gratitude, however, is to my wife, Dr Katherine Anderson. In addition to being my great support through twenty years of marriage, she has also read and commented on the whole book in draft.

References to Scots law are intended to be correct as at 29 February 2020.

Craig Anderson
Aberdeen
Ides of March, ab urbe condita *2773*
(15 March 2020)

Note on Online Resources

This book is supported by online resources, to be found at <https://edinburghuniversitypress.com/book-roman-law-for-scots-law-students.html>. These include:

- sample essay and problem questions, together with guidance on answering those questions
- short biographies of selected jurists
- a glossary of commonly used Latin terms and
- a timeline of major events from the foundation of Rome to the reign of Justinian I.

Table of Cases

Aberdeenshire County Council v Lord Glentanar 1999 SLT 1456 248
Alba Homes Ltd v Duell 1993 SLT (Sh Ct) 49 254
Armour v Thyssen Edelstahlwerke AG 1986 SLT 452 (Outer House), 1989 SLT 182
    (Inner House), 1990 SLT 891 (House of Lords) 205, 234
Assessor for Argyll v Broadland Properties Ltd 1973 SC 152 221

Bain v Carrick 1983 SLT 675 174
Barbour v Halliday (1840) 2 D 1279 .... 224, 225
Barclays Bank v O'Brien [1994] 1 AC 180 121
Barnett v Chelsea and Kensington Hospital Management Committee [1969] 1 QB 428 394
Baronetcy of Pringle of Stichill [2016] UKPC 16, 2016 SC (PC) 1 122
Bartonshill Coal Co v Reid (1858) 3 Macq 266 .... 88, 400
Beattie v Lord Napier (1831) 9 S 639 224
Berry v Berry (No 2) 1989 SLT 292 172
Binning v Brotherstones (1676) Mor 13401 .... 185, 224
Black v Incorporation of Bakers, Glasgow (1867) 6 M 136 234
Boskabelle v Laird 2006 SLT 1079 223
Brand's Trs v Brand's Trs (1876) 3 R (HL) 16 224
Brock v Hamilton (1852) 19 D 701 172
Brogan v O'Rourke Ltd 2005 SCLR 337 51
Brown v Marr (1880) 7 R 427 .... 337, 381
B's Executor v Keeper of the Registers and Records of Scotland 1935 SC 745 294
Burnett's Trustee v Grainger 2004 SC (HL) 19 .... 163, 202

C v Chief Constable of the Police Service of Scotland [2019] CSOH 48, 2019 SLT 875
    (Outer House); [2019] CSIH 61 (Inner House) 415
Campbell v Campbell (1866) 4 M 867 141
Cantiere San Rocco, SA v Clyde Shipbuilding & Engineering Co Ltd 1923 SC (HL) 105 432
Charleston v News Group Newspapers Ltd [1995] 2 AC 65 414
Chief Constable, Strathclyde Police v Sharp 2002 SLT (Sh Ct) 95 191
Chowan v Associated Motor Holdings (Pty) Ltd 2018 (4) SA 145 385
Christie v Smith's Executrix 1949 SC 572 222
Clark v Lindale Homes Ltd 1994 SC 210 360
Clydesdale Bank plc v Black 2002 SC 555 99
Cochrane v Stevenson (1891) 18 R 1208 222
Compugraphics International Ltd v Nikolic 2011 SLT 955 249

Costello v Chief Constable of Derbyshire Constabulary [2001] EWCA Civ 381,
  [2001] WLR 1437 173
Cowan v Bennett 2012 GWD 37–738... 412
Crown Estate Commissioners v Fairlie Yacht Slip Ltd 1979 SC 156 197

Dean v Lord Advocate [2019] HCJAC 31 87
Donoghue v Stevenson 1932 SC (HL) 31 .... 399–400, 401, 402, 403
Dorion v Les Ecclésiastiques du Séminaire de St Sulpice de Montréal (1880) 5 App Cas 362 246
Douglas v Douglas (1876) 4 R 105 291
Douglas v Duke of Hamilton (1769) 2 Pat 143... 122
Dowall v Milne (1874) 1 R 1180 223
Drake v Dow 2006 SCLR 456.. 444
Duke of Hamilton v Johnston (1877) 14 SLR 298 224
Duke of Roxburghe v Duchess Dowager of Roxburghe 19 Jan 1816, FC................. 263
Dumbreck v Robert Addie & Sons (Collieries) Ltd 1929 SC (HL) 51 401
Duncan v MFV Marigold PD145 2006 SLT 975... 377

Eadie v Young (1815) Hume 705 212
English v Thomas Sanderson Ltd [2008] EWCA Civ 1421, [2009] 2 CMLR 18.................. 413

Fairchild v Glenhaven Funeral Services Ltd [2003] 1 AC 32............................. 397, 403
Faulds v Townsend (1861) 23 D 437 183
Fernie v Robertson (1871) 9 M 437 435
Ferrier v Walker (1832) 10 S 317 256
Fife Assessor v Hodgson 1966 SC 30.. 223
Franklin v Lawson 2013 SLT (Lands Tr) 81 249

Gibbs v Ruxton 2000 JC 258.. 29
Grant v Henry (1894) 21 R 358 196
Gray v Dunlop 1954 SLT (Sh Ct) 75... 440

Hedley Byrne & Co Ltd v Heller & Partners Ltd [1964] AC 465 328
Henderson v Chief Constable, Fife Police 1988 SLT 361... 415
Hetherington v Galt (1905) 7 F 706... 223
Hogg v Gow 27 May 1812, FC 137
Howie's Trs v McLay (1902) 5 F 214... 223
Hughes v Lord Advocate 1963 SC (HL) 31.. 394

Innes v Magistrates of Edinburgh (1798) Mor 13189 .... 195, 400
International Banking Corporation v Ferguson, Shaw & Sons 1910 SC 182 ..... 234, 235
Irvine Knitters Ltd v North Ayrshire Co-operative Society Ltd 1978 SC 109.......... 247

J L Cohen Motors SWA (Pty) Ltd v Alberts 1985 (2) SA 427..................................... 238
Johnson, Thomas and Thomas (A Firm) v Smith 2016 GWD 25–456...................... 250
Joint Liquidators of Scottish Coal v Scottish Environmental Protection Agency 2014 SC 372 221

Keith v Texaco Ltd 1977 SLT (Lands Tr) 16.. 254
Kerr v Brown 1939 SC 140 248
Kerr v Martin (1840) 2 D 752 126
Khaliq v HM Advocate 1984 JC 23 395
Khan v Minister of Law and Order 1991 (3) SA 439 229

Kidson v Jimspeed Enterprises CC 2009 (5) SA 246 267
Kinloch Damph Ltd v Nordvik Salmon Farms Ltd 30 June 1999 Outer House 236
Kirkpatrick v Murray (1856) 19 D 91 256
Knight v Wedderburn (1778) Mor 14545 103
Kolbin & Sons v Kinnear & Co 1930 SC 724 435

Le Roux v Dey [2011] ZACC 4, 2011 (3) SA 274 414
Leitch v Fairy (1711) Mor 13946 439
Lewars v Hay (1712) 4 Bro Sup 894 439
Lockhart v Cunninghame (1870) 8 SLR 151 391
Lord Advocate v Aberdeen University 1963 SC 533 238

McCaig v University of Glasgow 1907 SC 231 294
McCaig's Trustees v Kirk Session of United Free Church of Lismore 1915 SC 426 294
Macdonald v Aberdeenshire Council [2013] CSIH 83, 2014 SC 114 .... 195, 403
McDonald v Provan (of Scotland Street) Limited 1960 SLT 231 234
Macdonald v Watson (1830) 8 S 584 256
McDyer v The Celtic Football and Athletic Co Ltd 2000 SC 379 .... 440, 441
Mackenzie v Mackenzie's Trs 1916 1 SLT 349 141
Mackenzie v Maclean 1981 SLT (Sh Ct) 40 .... 220, 418
Mackie v Mackie 1917 SC 276 140
McLaren, Sons & Co Ltd v Mann, Byars & Co Ltd (1935) 51 Sh Ct Rep 57 234
Macleod v Kerr 1965 SC 253 .... 207, 330
McTaggart v Macdouall (1867) 5 M 534 247
Maloy v McCosh (1885) 12 R 431 140
Marjandi Ltd v Bon Accord Glass Ltd 15 October 2007, Aberdeen Sheriff Court 366
Martin v McGuinness 2003 SLT 1424 415
Matheson v Stewart (1872) 10 M 704 181
May v Wingate (1694) Mor 9236 443
Miller v HM Advocate [2019] HCJAC 7 103
Milligan v Ross 1994 SCLR 430 214
Moncrieff v Jamieson 2008 SC (HL) 1 .... 248, 250, 252
More v Boyle 1967 SLT (Sh Ct) 38 167
Morgan Guaranty Trust Co of New York v Lothian Regional Council 1995 SC 151 432–3
Morrisson v Robertson 1908 SC 332 .... 205, 207, 330
Muirhead & Turnbull v Dickson (1905) 7 F 686 331
Mullen v Barr & Co; McGowan v Barr & Co 1929 SC 461 401
Mustard v Paterson 1923 SC 142 443

Nacap Ltd v Moffat Plant Ltd 1987 SLT 221 398
Nisbet's Creditors v Robertson (1791) Mor 9554 270

O'Keeffe v Argus Printing and Publishing Co Ltd 1954 (3) SA 244 413
Oliver & Boyd v The Marr Typefounding Co Ltd (1901) 9 SLT 170 .... 232, 235
Ord v Mashford 2006 SLT (Lands Tr) 15 249
Orr's Trustee v Tullis (1870) 8 M 936 214

Pert v McCaffrey [2020] CSIH 5, 2020 SLT 225 434
Petrie v Petrie 1911 SC 360 140
PMP Plus Ltd v Keeper of the Registers of Scotland 2009 SLT (Lands Tr) 2 207

R v Mafohla 1958 (2) SA 373 221

Raffles v Wichelhaus (1864) 159 ER 375 328
Reid v Scott of Harden (1687) Mor 9505 .... 103, 105
Roscorla v Thomas (1842) 3 QB 234 327
Royal Bank of Scotland plc v Etridge (No 2) [2002] 2 AC 773 99

S v Mnomiya 1970 (1) SA 66 228
S v S 2006 SLT 471 141
Safeway Stores plc v Tesco Stores Ltd 2004 SC 29 174
Satchwell v McIntosh 2006 SLT (Sh Ct) 117 434
Scammell v Scottish Sports Council 1983 SLT 462 196
Scot v Forbes (1755) Mor 8278 .... 264, 267
Scott v Everitt (1853) 15 D 288 221
Scott v Yates (1800) Hume 207 443
Scottish Transit Trust Ltd v Scottish Land Cultivators Ltd 1955 SC 254 214
Scrimgeour v Scrimgeour 1988 SLT 590 172
Shields v Donnelly 2000 JC 46 29
Shilliday v Smith 1998 SC 725 433
Simmons v British Steel plc 2004 SC (HL) 94 394
Simpson v Duncanson's Creditors (1786) Mor 14204 228
Sloans Dairies Ltd v Glasgow Corporation 1977 SC 223 357
Smith v Bank of Scotland 1997 SC (HL) 111 99
Sneddon v Durant 1982 SLT (Sh Ct) 39 355
Stevens v Yorkhill NHS Trust [2006] CSOH 143, 2006 SLT 889 415
Stewart v Kennedy (1890) 17 R (HL) 25 331
Stewart v Sinclair (1694) 4 Bro Sup 195 439
Stichting Crediteurenbelangen Hollander's v Coöperatieve Raiffeissenbank 'Domburg'
    24 March 1995, Hoge Raad (Netherlands) 236
Stilk v Meyrick (1809) 170 ER 851 327
Stirling v Bartlett 1993 SLT 763 226
Stove v Colvin (1831) 9 S 633 221
Stronach's Executors v Robertson 2002 SC 540 265
Sutter v Aberdeen Arctic Co (1861) 23 D 465 (Court of Session), (1862) 4 Macq 355
    (House of Lords) 221

Thomson v Clarkson's Trustees (1892) 20 R 59 298
Tolley v J S Fry & Sons Ltd [1931] AC 333 413
Trotter v Trotter 2001 SLT (Sh Ct) 42 270

Valentine v Kennedy 1985 SCCR 89 221
Vincent v Lake Erie Transportation Company (1910) 109 Minn. 456, 124 N.W. 221 392

W S Karoulias SA v Drambuie Liqueur Co Ltd (No 2) 2005 SLT 813 332–3
Walker v Milne (1823) 2 S 379 332
Wardlaw v Wardlaw's Trs (1875) 2 R 368 263
Watling v McDowall (1825) 4 S 83 443
Watt v Jamieson 1954 SC 56 167
Welsh v Russell (1894) 21 R 769 359
Williamson v White 21 June 1810, FC 443
Williamson v Williamson 1997 SC 94 295
Wills' Trustees v Cairngorm Canoeing and Sailing School Ltd 1976 SC (HL) 30 196
Wilson v Dykes (1872) 10 M 444 221

Wilson & McLellan v Sinclair (1830) 4 W & S 398 433
Wylie & Lochhead v Mitchell (1870) 8 M 552 .... 231, 236

X v Y 1921 1 SLT 79 140

Zahnrad Fabrik Passau GmbH v Terex 1985 SC 364 231

Table of Statutes

Primary Legislation

Abolition of Feudal Tenure etc (Scotland) Act 2000 192
    s. 67 192
Age of Legal Capacity (Scotland) Act 1991
    s. 1(1)(a) 131
    s. 1(1)(b) 131
    s. 2 131
    s. 3(1) 131
    s. 3(3)(h) 131
    s. 4(1) 131
Animals (Scotland) Act 1987 425

Bankruptcy and Diligence etc (Scotland) Act 2007
    s. 208(3) 276
    s. 208(5) 276
Bankruptcy (Scotland) Act 1913 42
Bürgerliches Gesetzbuch (Germany) 81
    s. 930 212

Carriers Act 1830
    s. 1 443
Children (Scotland) Act 1995
    s. 7 129
    s. 11(2)(h) 129
Code civil (France) 60, 80, 81, 88
    art. 2276 166
    art. 2521 191
Consumer Credit Act 1974
    s. 8 274
    s. 121 274
    s. 189 274
Consumer Rights Act 2015
    s. 29 357
Contracts (Rights of Third Parties) Act 1999 328
Contract (Scotland) Act 1997
    s. 3 364

Contract (Third Party Rights) (Scotland) Act 2017 328
Conveyancing and Feudal Reform (Scotland) Act 1973
    s. 9(3) 271

Family Law (Scotland) Act 2006
    s. 3 141
    s. 28 434

Hotel Proprietors Act 1956
    s. 1(1) 444
    s. 1(3) 444
    s. 2 444
Human Trafficking and Exploitation (Scotland) Act 2015
    s. 4(1)(a) 103

Island of Rockall Act 1972 226

Land Registration etc (Scotland) Act 2012 199
    s. 66 225
    s. 86 .... 166, 203
Law Reform (Contributory Negligence) Act 1945
    s. 1(1) 398
Law Reform (Husband and Wife) (Scotland) Act 1984
    s. 1(1) 137
Law Reform (Personal Injuries) Act 1948
    s. 1(1) 401
Leases Act 1449 .... 84, 167, 367
Liferent Caution Act 1491 265
Liferent Caution Act 1535 265

Marriage (Scotland) Act 1939 140
Mercantile Law Amendment Act (Scotland) 1856
    s. 8 278

Occupiers' Liability Act 1957 401
Occupiers' Liability (Scotland) Act 1960
    ss. 1–2 401

Partnership Act 1890 376
    s. 1(1) 376
    s. 4(2) 376
    s. 5 376
    s. 29(1) 374
    s. 38 377
Prescription Act 1617 242
Prescription and Limitation (Scotland) Act 1973 242
    s. 1 360
    s. 3 252
    Part II 322
Protection from Harassment Act 1997
    s. 8 412

Requirements of Writing (Scotland) Act 1995
  s. 1(2) 379
  s. 3(4)(e) 299

Sale and Supply of Goods Act 1994
  s. 1(1) 363
Sale of Goods Act 1893 .... 214, 363
Sale of Goods Act 1979 214
  s. 12 363
  s. 14 363
  s. 14(2) 363
  s. 18 rule 4 337
  s. 20 357
  s. 24 .... 166, 203
  s. 25 .... 166, 203
  s. 53A(2) 364
Subscription of Deeds Act 1681 299
Succession (Scotland) Act 1964 171
  s. 2 291
  s. 8 291
  s. 9 291

Tenements (Scotland) Act 2004 166
Title Conditions (Scotland) Act 2003 246
  ss. 76–7 250
  s. 79 246

Union with England Act 1707
  s. XVIII 87
  s. XIX 87

Secondary Legislation

Commercial Agents (Council Directive) Regulations 1993 (SI 1993/3053) 366

Others

European Convention for the Protection of Human Rights and Fundamental Freedoms,
  as amended by Protocols Nos 11 and 14, 4 November 1950
  art. 8 415

Illustrations

Figures

4.1 Trends in references to Roman law 90
4.2 References to Ulpian, Papinian and Modestinus 91

Table

6.1 The rules on manumissions by will under the *lex Fufia Caninia* 111

Abbreviations

Birks, *New Perspectives*	P Birks ed, *New Perspectives in the Roman Law of Property* (Oxford University Press 1989)
Birks, *Obligations*	P Birks, *The Roman Law of Obligations* (E Descheemaeker ed, Oxford University Press 2014)
Borkowski, *Textbook*	P du Plessis, *Borkowski's Textbook on Roman Law* 5th edn (Oxford University Press 2015)
Buckland, *Textbook*	W W Buckland, *A Text-Book of Roman Law from Augustus to Justinian* 3rd edn by P Stein (Cambridge University Press 1963)
Burrows and Rodger, *Mapping the Law*	A Burrows and Lord Rodger of Earlsferry eds, *Mapping the Law: Essays in Memory of Peter Birks* (Oxford University Press 2006)
Cairns and du Plessis, *Beyond Dogmatics*	J W Cairns and P J du Plessis eds, *Beyond Dogmatics: Law and Society in the Roman World* (Edinburgh University Press 2007)
Daube, *Studies in Sale*	D Daube ed, *Studies in the Roman Law of Sale: Dedicated to the Memory of Francis de Zulueta* (Oxford University Press 1959)
DCFR	Study Group on a European Civil Code, *Principles, Definitions and Model Rules of European Private Law: Draft Common Frame of Reference (DCFR)* (6 vols, Sellier 2009)
Du Plessis, *New Frontiers*	P du Plessis ed, *New Frontiers: Law and Society in the Roman World* (Edinburgh University Press 2013)
Evans-Jones, *Civil Law Tradition*	R Evans-Jones ed, *The Civil Law Tradition in Scotland* (Stair Society 1995)
Grotius	H Grotius, *The Jurisprudence of Holland* (R W Lee trans, Oxford University Press 1926–36)
History of Private Law in Scotland, vol I	R Zimmermann and K Reid eds, *A History of Private Law in Scotland, Volume I: Introduction and Property* (Oxford University Press 2000)

History of Private Law in Scotland, vol II	R Zimmermann and K Reid eds, *A History of Private Law in Scotland, Volume II: Obligations* (Oxford University Press 2000)
Johnston, *Roman Law in Context*	D Johnston, *Roman Law in Context* (Cambridge University Press 1999)
Jolowicz and Nicholas, *Historical Introduction*	H J Jolowicz and B Nicholas, *Historical Introduction to the Study of Roman Law* 3rd edn (Cambridge University Press 1972)
Judge and Jurist	A S Burrows, D Johnston and R Zimmermann eds, *Judge and Jurist: Essays in Memory of Lord Rodger of Earlsferry* (Oxford University Press 2013)
Lewis and Ibbetson, *Roman Law Tradition*	A D E Lewis and D J Ibbetson, *The Roman Law Tradition* (Cambridge University Press 1994)
Metzger, *Companion*	E Metzger ed, *A Companion to Justinian's Institutes* (Duckworth 1998)
Nicholas, *Introduction*	B Nicholas, *An Introduction to Roman Law* (Oxford University Press 1962)
Robinson, *Sources*	O F Robinson, *The Sources of Roman Law: Problems and Methods for Ancient Historians* (Routledge 1997)
Robinson, Fergus and Gordon, *European Legal History*	O F Robinson, T D Fergus and W M Gordon, *European Legal History: Sources and Institutions* 3rd edn (Oxford University Press 2000)
Simpson and Wilson, *Scottish Legal History, vol 1*	A R C Simpson and A L M Wilson, *Scottish Legal History, Volume One: 1000–1707* (Edinburgh University Press 2017)
Stein, *Regulae Iuris*	P Stein, *Regulae Iuris: From Juristic Rules to Legal Maxims* (Edinburgh University Press 1966)
Stein and Lewis, *Studies in Justinian's Institutes*	P G Stein and A D E Lewis eds, *Studies in Justinian's Institutes in Memory of J A C Thomas* (Sweet and Maxwell 1983)
Thomas, *Textbook*	J A C Thomas, *Textbook of Roman Law* (North-Holland 1976)
Watson, *Law Making*	A Watson, *Law Making in the Later Roman Republic* (Oxford University Press 1974)
Watson, *Obligations*	A Watson, *The Law of Obligations in the Later Roman Republic* (Oxford University Press 1965)
Watson, *Property*	A Watson, *The Law of Property in the Later Roman Republic* (Oxford University Press 1968)
Watson, *Roman Law & Comparative Law*	A Watson, *Roman Law & Comparative Law* (University of Georgia Press 1991)

Watson, *Succession*	A Watson, *The Law of Succession in the Later Roman Republic* (Oxford University Press 1971)
Zimmermann, *Obligations*	R Zimmermann, *The Law of Obligations: Roman Foundations of the Civilian Tradition* (Oxford University Press 1996)
Zimmermann, Visser and Reid, *Mixed Legal System*s	R Zimmermann, D Visser and K Reid, *Mixed Legal Systems in Comparative Perspective: Property and Obligations in Scotland and South Africa* (Oxford University Press 2004)

PART ONE

The Historical and Constitutional Context of Roman Law

In the study of any system of law, there is a certain amount of background material which is often assumed in legal writing, but which is essential in order to understand that writing fully. Included here are matters such as: who makes the law? Who is responsible for interpreting and enforcing it? How is the law to be found? These are the kinds of thing that, in an undergraduate law degree, are typically covered in an introductory course called Legal Systems, or something similar. They are part of the common stock of knowledge that any lawyer can reasonably be assumed to be familiar with. A lawyer writing about a court decision, for example, needs to be able to assume that his or her readers understand that the court's function is to interpret the law rather than to make the law, without having to explain that to readers.

The need for this kind of background material is particularly great when studying a historical legal system, such as Roman law. When modern law is under consideration, a reasonably educated non-lawyer can be assumed to have at least some outline understanding of how Parliament works or how the courts work, and of the different roles of such groups as lawyers and the police. When studying the law of a past society, this outline understanding cannot be assumed. Roman society was, in many ways, profoundly different from our own. The purpose of this first part of the book is to provide this context to the study of Roman law.

First, Chapter 1 provides an overview of Roman history, from the beginnings of the city of Rome up to the end of the Roman Empire. A particular focus here is the governance of Rome, and how this changed over time.

Next, in Chapter 2 we look at the legal process. We will see here how litigation worked in Roman law. Of particular interest here is the role of the public official with the title of urban praetor, who was responsible for civil justice.

In Chapter 3, we will see how Roman law developed, from earliest times through to the sixth-century emperor Justinian's compilation of legal materials known as the *Corpus Iuris Civilis*, or 'Body of the Civil Law', from which we derive most of our knowledge of Roman law. In this chapter we will also meet the class of legal writers known as jurists, who had a major influence on the development of Roman law, both directly and indirectly.

Although this book has been written with students of Scots law particularly in mind, we will not see much of Scotland in these first three chapters. We will see more of Scotland in Chapter 4, which considers the influence of Roman law on later law, up to the modern day.

There is one final point to note. Throughout this book, there is extensive reference to Roman legal literature. It is likely that most readers of this book will not, at the outset, be familiar with standard referencing styles for these texts. However, if much headway is to be made with the study of Roman law, it is essential to be familiar with these. Accordingly, readers are referred to Appendix 1 at the end of this book, where there is a list of all Roman texts referred to in this book, together with guidance on how they are to be found and cited.

CHAPTER ONE

Historical Introduction to Roman Governance and Society

A. Introduction

Any course of study of Roman law is pulled in two directions. On the one hand, the study of Roman law is an important part of the study of the historical civilisation of Rome more generally. The law of the Romans is among their greatest cultural and intellectual achievements, and it is perhaps even the greatest of these, and this fact alone would make it worth studying. To understand Roman law in this context requires deep study of how the Romans themselves thought about law and how they developed and applied it. On the other hand, Roman law is also worth studying, not just for its own sake, but because of its continuing importance in modern law. For that purpose, it is more important to understand the process by which Roman law came to influence modern law and its continuing importance to modern law. These two elements – Roman law as historical legal system and Roman law as a source of modern law – are not always entirely compatible.

However the conflict is to be resolved, though, a proper study of Roman law must involve both of these elements. Throughout this book, we will be spending a lot of time looking at Roman law from the standpoint of its importance to modern law. At the same time, though, it is necessary to understand Roman law in its own terms as well. We begin in this chapter, then, by considering the historical, political and constitutional context within which Roman law developed, because to study Roman law without this is not really to study Roman law at all. Roman law, like any system of law, was a product of the society that gave birth to it. The subject matter of this chapter is, then, a historical account of the Roman world and how it was governed.

B. The Pre-Roman Background (to 753 BC)

In the study of any period of history, the limitations of the evidence available are an inescapable fact. For the history of a particular place, whole periods may be shrouded in mystery, and the earliest history of the Romans is one such period. Archaeology can teach us much about how people lived and died in a particular time and place, but it can only go so far. In the case of the city of Rome itself, there is the added difficulty that what remains of the earliest settlement is covered by the remains of all the later centuries, with the modern city on top.

Beyond archaeology, we must look to written accounts. Here, Rome presents us with a further problem. The more prominent a city is, the more likely people are to write about it, and the more likely it is that such writings will survive to be read by us. For centuries after its founding, however, Rome was a place of only local significance. All written accounts of the Romans' early history were composed centuries after the events described. As a result, while these accounts undoubtedly contain fragments of some genuine historical events, there is no agreement about the extent to which that is the case, and in any event the genuine history is mixed together with myth and legend. It may be better to think of these stories, not as historical events which can be tied to any specific point in time, but rather as part of the mythological background to the Romans' understanding of themselves, with events happening simply 'once upon a time'.

With those warnings in place, we can turn to the Romans' own accounts of their earliest history. Even if we cannot rely on these as historically accurate accounts, nonetheless there is value in understanding what the Romans believed of their origins if we wish to understand the Romans themselves.

The Romans told various stories about their origins. The story of their earliest origins, however, reached what we might call its canonical form in the late first century BC, in an epic poem called the *Aeneid*, written by a poet called Publius Vergilius Maro ('Virgil' or 'Vergil' in English). When reading this account, it is important to bear in mind that this is an artistic work rather than a historical account, and it also had political motives.[1] In the story as told by Vergil, the founder of the Roman people was a Trojan prince by the name of Aeneas. The Trojans were the people of Troy, a city in the west of what is now Turkey. In approximately the twelfth century BC, Troy was destroyed by an invading Greek force after a ten-year siege.[2] Aeneas escaped with a band of followers and, on the instructions of the gods, sailed west to Italy.[3] There he founded a city. This was not Rome, which was not established until some centuries later. Instead, the city he founded was called Lavinium.[4]

---

[1] Part of its purpose was to legitimise the rule of the first emperor, Augustus. We will meet Augustus below. For an interesting discussion of some of the themes in the *Aeneid*, see W Fitzgerald, *How to Read a Latin Poem if You Can't Read Latin Yet* (Oxford 2013) 156–80.

[2] The invasion was provoked by the abduction, by a Trojan prince named Paris, of Helen, wife of King Menelaus of the Greek city-state of Sparta. The siege was brought to an end by a famous trick. The Greeks pretended to depart, leaving behind a giant wooden horse, supposedly as a gift to honour the Trojans. The Trojans took the horse into the city, unaware that it was in fact filled with Greek soldiers who, in the night, sneaked out and opened the gates of the city for their comrades.

[3] Aeneas and his followers had numerous adventures on the way. The best known of these was his brief romance with Dido, Queen of Carthage in North Africa. After he abandoned her, she committed suicide, swearing eternal enmity between their peoples. We shall meet the Carthaginians again, below.

[4] This, at least, was a real place. Its ruins lie near the sea, to the south of Rome. It is said to have been named for Aeneas' wife, Lavinia, daughter of King Latinus of the Latins. Aeneas married Lavinia after his arrival in Italy. See Ursula K Le Guin's novel, *Lavinia* (Harcourt 2008), for the story told from her point of view.

This is as far as Vergil takes the story. The rest is to be found in other writers, whose accounts are broadly consistent, though differing on points of detail. Following the death of Aeneas, he was succeeded by his son, Ascanius. Ascanius founded the city of Alba Longa, south-east of the later site of Rome, to settle part of the growing population of Lavinium. The founders of Rome, Romulus and Remus, were born of the royal line of Alba Longa approximately 400 years after its foundation.[5] Romulus and Remus were the twin sons of Rhea Silvia, a Vestal Virgin,[6] and (reputedly) the god Mars. Rhea Silvia was the daughter of Numitor, king of Alba Longa, who had been deposed by his brother, Amulius. Fearing them as potential rivals, Amulius ordered that the twins be killed. They were abandoned to die on the banks of the River Tiber, but were kept alive by a she-wolf, who allowed them to suckle. They were then found by a shepherd called Faustulus, who adopted them. When they grew up and learned their true identity, they returned to Alba Longa and helped to restore their grandfather to the throne. They themselves, however, decided to found a new city by the Tiber, near where they had been abandoned.

The twins, though, were unable to agree on which hill to establish their city. Romulus favoured the Palatine Hill, Remus the nearby Aventine Hill. It was decided that the disagreement would be settled through augury, which is the art of determining the will of the gods by observing the flight of birds. Each went to his preferred hill and awaited a sign. This attempt to resolve the disagreement was unsuccessful, however: while Remus was the first to see the necessary birds, he only saw six while Romulus saw twelve. The two were unable to agree which had had the stronger omen. In the ensuing dispute, Remus was killed.

The city was therefore established by Romulus alone, along with his followers. This was the city of Rome. To grow the population of the new city, Romulus established another nearby hill, the Capitoline Hill, as a place of refuge (called an *asylum*) where individuals from other cities could settle and to whom Roman citizenship could be given. The major problem, though, was a shortage of women. The Romans' approaches to nearby communities to provide them with wives having been rejected, the Romans' next idea was to hold games and, during the festivities, to kidnap the marriageable women among their guests. This act led to war with the neighbouring Sabines, one of the communities from which women had been taken. This war was brought to an end when the women interposed themselves between the two armies and prevailed on their fathers and brothers, on one side, and their husbands, on the other, not to make war on each other. In the ensuing peace, the Romans and the Sabines merged into a single community, under the joint rule of Romulus and Titus Tatius, the king of the Sabines. After the subsequent death of Titus Tatius, Romulus ruled alone.

---

[5] It is very likely that this part of the history was invented to fill in the gap between Aeneas and Romulus.
[6] Vestal Virgins were priestesses of the goddess Vesta, and had to take an oath of celibacy. In Rhea Silvia's case, she was compelled to become a Vestal Virgin to prevent her producing rival claimants to the kingship.

In reality, it is likely that the establishment of Rome was much less dramatic. Modern historians tend to give little credence to much of the story. It is likely that, at most, only fragments of the story are founded in any kind of genuine historical event. Indeed, few settlements have any kind of specific, identifiable foundation at all. Instead, they develop gradually as people settle in a particular place, to exploit that place's resources, natural defences or trading potential. The most that can be said is that the traditional date of Rome's foundation, 753 BC, probably lies within the period during which Rome was forming from a group of individual villages.

Roman history is traditionally divided into a number of distinct periods, as the form of Roman government changed. The first stage is the Monarchy (753–509 BC), when Rome was ruled by a series of kings. Next comes the Republic (509–27 BC). Finally, there is the Empire (from 27 BC), when a republican form of government was replaced by what was, in effect, a new monarchy, with power ultimately in the hands of an emperor. The Empire can be subdivided into an earlier phase, the Principate, during which republican institutions were formally preserved; and a later phase, the Dominate, during which the monarchical power of the emperor was more openly asserted. The change from Principate to Dominate can be dated to AD 284. We will follow this system of dividing up Roman history, but will add a further subdivision. Below, the period of the Republic will be divided into two. In the earlier Republic (up to 264 BC), Rome was merely a regional power within Italy, though one with growing authority and influence. From 264 BC, Roman power is increasingly felt beyond the Italian peninsula.

C. The Monarchy (753–509 BC)

(1) The Situation of Rome under the Monarchy

Rome developed on a promising site by the River Tiber, in central Italy. The river gave it easy access to the sea, and the city's position at a convenient crossing-point made it strategically important. Rome was also built on higher ground, which aided defence.[7] The river was also a cultural boundary. Italy at this time was highly fragmented, both politically and culturally. Rome was part of Latium, which was occupied by the Latins, who were loosely allied and who spoke related languages. The Romans' language, Latin, is part of this language group. To the north, on the other side of the Tiber, lay Etruria, centred on modern Tuscany. Etruria was the home of the Etruscans, a confederation of independent city states. During this period, the Etruscans were the dominant culture in much of

---

[7] There were seven hills on which Rome was built: Quirinal, Viminal, Esquiline, Caelian, Aventine, Capitoline and Palatine. This point should not be over-exaggerated, however. None of them is especially high (although no doubt they would have been more impressive before they were covered by the city). For example, the height of the Palatine (the most central of the hills) above its surroundings is only around forty metres, around half that of Castle Rock in Edinburgh.

northern Italy, and Rome was strongly influenced by them. Elsewhere in Italy, other groups were to be found. Perhaps the most notable of these were the Greek colonies of southern Italy.[8] During the Monarchy, Rome became the dominant force in Latium, but was never more than a regional power during this period, and even beyond, into the early Republic. At this time:

> The wars between Rome and her neighbours were little more than scuffles between armed raiding bands of a few hundred men at most. It is salutary to recall that Fidenae (Fidene), against which the Romans were fighting in 499, lies now within the motorway circuit round modern Rome, and is all but swallowed up in its northern suburbs. Veii, the Etruscan city that was Rome's chief rival for supremacy in the Tiber plain, is a mere 10 miles to the north-west.[9]

(2) The Nature of the Monarchy and the Role of the King

During this period, Rome was ruled by a series of kings. The first thing to be aware of here is that this was not a hereditary monarchy. There was no succession from father to son, or anything like it. Indeed, there was a tendency if anything to choose kings from outside. Of the seven kings in the list accepted by later Roman writers, the majority of them are said to have been of non-Roman origin. This includes the final three, who were all said to be of Etruscan origin.[10]

Details of how the king was appointed are uncertain. According to Roman historians, writing centuries later, Romulus had established a council of advisors, called the Senate.[11] When the king died, his power devolved to the Senate, which appointed an *interrex*[12] to identify a successor. Once a suitable successor had been found, and had been approved by the Senate, the new king's appointment would be ratified by an assembly of adult, male citizens, called the *comitia curiata*. The precise scope of the king's powers is impossible now to determine. It is likely, though, that they were fairly broad, including administrative, military and religious matters.

One aspect of early Roman society[13] that is difficult for us to grasp from our modern standpoint is the nature of Roman religion and its role in public life. In the modern world, we take for granted the idea of members of the clergy as a distinct profession, and we are used to the concept of a separation of Church and state. We are also accustomed to religion having a great concern for questions of proper moral and ethical conduct. None of these things is true of early Roman religion. As far as we can tell, Roman religion was much less concerned

---

[8] The best known of these is Neapolis, modern Naples.
[9] L Keppie, *The Making of the Roman Army: From Republic to Empire* (B T Batsford 1984) 14.
[10] This most likely reflects Rome having had some form of subordinate relationship to the Etruscans at this time. That, unsurprisingly, is not the story that the Romans themselves told.
[11] This is related to the Latin *senex*, meaning 'old man'. In effect, a senate is a council of elders.
[12] Hence the modern word 'interregnum', for a period between two kings. *Rex* is Latin for 'king'. *Regnum* means 'kingdom'.
[13] And, indeed, this continued through much of Roman history.

with moral precepts and much more concerned with appeasement of the gods through ritual. Equally, there was no separation between religion and the state, and religious observance was a fundamental part of governance. This does not mean that early Rome was a theocracy; rather, the distinction between secular and sacred simply did not exist.[14] If it was the job of rulers to protect the well-being of the community, then appeasing the gods and determining their will through augury, haruspicy,[15] and the interpretation of omens and prodigies[16] were no less a part of this than military defence and the food supply. Rather than religion being a distinct sphere of activity, which was the concern of a class of professional priests, priesthoods were special responsibilities undertaken by prominent men as part of their public role.

Those outside the aristocracy were not entirely excluded from public life under this system, though any such role was limited. As explained above, each new king was confirmed in office by an assembly of adult, male citizens, called the *comitia curiata*. For these purposes, the Roman people were divided into three tribes,[17] and each of these was further divided into ten *curiae*. These thirty *curiae* were the voting units in the assembly.[18] While, however, the confirmation of the *comitia curiata* was a necessary part of the process of selecting a new king, it is unclear whether they had any real, practical role in choosing the king. It is also unclear whether the *comitia* played an important role in the political process at other times. Probably this depended on political factors as much as anything else: at times it would suit the king to put proposals before the assembly for approval; at other times, the king would feel himself to be in a secure enough position to do without this. Certainly, though, the scope for independent action by the assemblies was limited by two factors: the assembly could only meet when summoned, and could only vote to accept or reject the proposal put before it. The assembly could not amend the proposal or put forward proposals of its own. Even if the assembly nominally had a significant role, therefore, practical power of political initiative was retained by elite citizens and, particularly, the king.

By the late Monarchy, the *comitia curiata* had been superseded for practical purposes by a different assembly, called the *comitia centuriata*. As a citizen assembly, it had the same membership as the *comitia curiata*, and retained the characteristics of only being able to meet when summoned and only being able to accept or reject the proposal put before it. It was, however, organised differently. In the *comitia centuriata*, the people were divided into five classes, based on wealth. Each class was further divided into voting units called *centuriae*, with the number of these disproportionately high in the wealthier classes and disproportionately low

---

[14] C Smith, 'The Religion of Archaic Rome' in J Rüpke ed, *A Companion to Roman Religion* (Blackwell 2011) 35.
[15] Haruspicy is the process of inspecting the entrails of sacrificial animals in order to determine the will of the gods.
[16] Prodigies in this context are events that depart from the natural order of things, thought to be signs of the gods' anger.
[17] These tribes were called the Ramnes, the Tities and the Luceres.
[18] Throughout Rome's history, voting in the citizen assemblies was by group rather than by individual.

in the poorer classes. As in the *comitia curiata*, voting was by group rather than by individual. Votes were taken in order of class, so it would often be unnecessary to take the votes of the lower wealth classes.[19] As a result of these factors, the voting system was heavily weighted in favour of the wealthy.

(3) The Seven Kings

Between the founding of Rome in 753 BC, and the fall of the Monarchy in 509 BC, there were said to have been seven kings. This is almost certainly incorrect, as can be inferred even just by looking at the average length of reign (a little under thirty-five years).[20] Historical scepticism about the first four kings (Romulus, Numa Pompilius, Tullus Hostilius and Ancus Marcius) is particularly justified. Romulus is very likely entirely mythical. Of the other three, the most that can be said is that there may have been kings by those names. Certainly, no reliance can be placed on stories of their particular actions and achievements. What we have in the sources is archetypes, rather than real people. Names, in particular, can be a convenient peg to hang character traits on. Thus, for example, Tullus Hostilius was said to be warlike (hostile, in other words). Numa Pompilius was said to have a particular interest in religious reforms (Numa is similar to the Latin word *numen*, which means 'a divinity' and gives us the word 'numinous'). In reality, the history of the early kings as we have it consists of half-remembered scraps, handed down over many generations and then stitched together to form a narrative.

The historicity of the final three kings (Tarquinius Priscus, Servius Tullius and Tarquinius Superbus) is somewhat more reliable, though there is still much we can never know. There is an interesting change here: while none of the earliest kings had been related to each other, the final three were all related to each other by birth or marriage. Tarquinius Priscus was the father-in-law of Servius Tullius and the father or grandfather of Tarquinius Superbus. Tarquinius Superbus was also the son-in-law of Servius Tullius. This apparent shift to some form of dynastic succession may be a clue to the reasons for the ultimate downfall of the Monarchy, but this is speculation.

(4) The End of the Monarchy

According to the traditional dating, the Monarchy ended in or around 509 BC. According to the Roman historians, this was brought about by the rape by one of the king's sons of Lucretia, the wife of a Roman noble, followed by her suicide. Outrage at this prompted the expulsion of the king and his family. The rule of kings was replaced with shared rule, by two annually elected magistrates, called consuls. Rome therefore became a republic.

---

[19] For an overview of the early history of the assemblies, see Jolowicz and Nicholas, *Historical Introduction* 17–20; T G Watkin, *An Historical Introduction to Modern Civil Law* (Ashgate 1999) 14–20.

[20] By way of comparison, from the accession of Kenneth MacAlpin as first King of Scots in AD 843, Scotland had twenty-one kings over the same period. In England, from the accession of Alfred the Great in AD 886, there were also twenty-one kings over the same period. In both cases, some had very short reigns, and few reached the supposed average length of reign of Roman kings.

Once more, how much truth there is in this story is hard to say. The view could well be taken that there is more going on here than simply dissatisfaction at the misbehaviour of an individual king and his family. After all, there is no reason why the expulsion of one king should lead to the establishment of a republic, rather than the appointment of another king. However, we have already seen that most of the kings were non-Roman, and so this development could plausibly be linked to anti-foreigner sentiment. Equally, there could be hints here of feeling amongst elite members of the community against the concentration of power in the hands of a single family and the abuse of that power.

D. The Earlier Republic (509–264 BC)

(1) Constitutional Change: Kings to Consuls

The move from monarchy to republic meant the removal of the kingship, of course. It was less clear what would replace that role. It is likely that there was a period of uncertainty and experimentation before the new constitutional position was settled. Fundamental to the new constitutional settlement was the dispersal of the king's power, or *imperium*. On the view that the best way of avoiding tyranny was to avoid the concentration of too much power in a single pair of hands, the king's powers were transferred to a pair of magistrates, elected by the *comitia centuriata*, called consuls. The power of the consuls was limited in two ways. First, there were two consuls, so they had to share power, and each could veto the other's acts. Second, the consuls were elected only for a term of one year, so no individual would be in power for too long.

In practice, and especially as Rome's influence grew through the Republic, it was found that the business of running Rome was too big a job for the consuls to manage on their own. Over time, therefore, it became necessary to establish lesser magistracies to take over some of the consuls' functions.

One of these was the censorship, introduced in 443 BC. Two censors were elected at four- or five-year intervals, for periods of up to eighteen months, in order to conduct the census. This role included the supervision of morals, because they could place a mark (*nota*) against someone's name to show that they disapproved of his conduct. This could exclude that person from voting, and excluded him from becoming a senator.

Another was the quaestorship. The quaestors (originally two, increased to four in 421 BC) were originally assistants to the consuls. Their most important functions were related to state finances, and in particular to the management of the public treasury.

The aedileship was created in 367 BC.[21] The aediles had various responsibilities, such as the food and water supplies, the repair of roads, and the public

---

[21] There were, though, officials called aediles before this. These earlier aediles were assistants to the tribunes, considered below.

marketplace. In the last mentioned of these, they had a major impact on the development of the contract of sale.[22]

Of the greatest interest for the study of Roman law, though, was the praetorship, also created in 367 BC. The praetor was responsible for the administration of civil justice. In that capacity, he[23] had a major influence on the development of Roman law, as we shall see in Chapters 2 and 3.[24]

In addition to these, there were various minor magistracies, and also an individual could be given special powers to deal with some situations. The most important of these was the dictatorship. In emergencies, the consuls could name a dictator to take sole command of the state, with a term limited to six months.

(2) The Struggle of the Orders: Patricians and Plebeians

One important feature of Roman society in the earlier Republic is the division of the citizen body into two classes, or 'Orders': the patricians and the plebeians. The origin of the distinction is unknown: according the Roman sources, it emerged during the Monarchy, but it is likely that in fact it only crystallised during the early Republic. The patricians were a hereditary aristocracy; the plebeians, making up the great majority of citizens, were subject to a number of legal and political disadvantages. For example, the magistracies were only open to patricians, as were the priesthoods and the political influence that went with them. Resolutions (*plebiscita*) of the plebeian assembly, the *concilium plebis*, were denied legal validity over the whole community, even though the plebeians were the great majority. The patricians' superior legal position allowed them to monopolise knowledge of the law and access to public land. This is not to say that all of the plebeians were poor, though debt was a major problem. It would be a mistake to think of the plebeians as an impoverished underclass: many were, but also some were wealthy. It would be the wealthy plebeians who would benefit most from political reform, and any attempt by them at making common cause with the poor must be understood as involving a certain amount of self-interest.

Agitation for reform, as part of the so-called 'Struggle of the Orders', included actual or threatened secession to form a new state, the first of these secessions supposedly happening as early as 494 BC. Over time, reforms did improve the position of the plebeians. In the early Republic, new plebeian magistrates, called tribunes, were recognised with the purpose of protecting the interests of the plebeians. They were given the power to convene the *concilium plebis*; the right to veto any act of another magistrate; and the right to protect plebeians, especially against unjust punishment. Another major concession, which we will see in greater detail in Chapter 3,[25] was the publication of the law in the Twelve

---

[22] See p. 361.
[23] It is convenient to talk about 'the praetor' as having influenced Roman law in particular ways, as if it was always the same man. This was not, of course, the case: there would be a new praetor every year.
[24] See pp. 38–40, 50–2.
[25] See pp. 47–9.

Tables in 451–450 BC. From 367 BC, as part of a package of laws called the *leges Liciniae Sextiae* after the tribunes who proposed them, one of the consuls elected each year had to be a plebeian. From 300 BC, plebeians could be *pontifices*, in other words members of the most politically important of the priestly colleges. Finally, by an enactment of 287 BC called the *lex Hortensia*, *plebiscita* of the *concilium plebis* were made binding on the whole people. By these steps, the patrician/plebeian distinction was largely eliminated, but this did little to give greater political power to the masses. What actually happened was merely that political power was opened up to wealthier plebeians. There then emerged a new aristocracy, based on the holding of political office, and by the late Republic it was rare for someone to be elected to a magistracy who did not have any ancestors who had been magistrates.[26]

(3) Constitutional Continuity: Senate and Assemblies
(a) The Senate

Formal responsibility for the management of the Roman state lay with the magistrates, between whom the various responsibilities of state were divided. It would be a mistake to think of the magistrates as in any sense a government, as we understand that term today. In the modern world, public roles of the kind occupied by the Roman magistrates are carried out by ministers and other appointees. Government ministers in the modern world are all appointees of the head of state or the head of government, and typically share a party affiliation with the head of government.[27] The Romans, by contrast, did not have political parties.[28] The magistrates were all directly elected, and they were separately elected. Of course, two or more men standing for or elected to office might form an alliance, but the magistrates as a whole could not be expected always to work effectively together and certainly could not be expected to co-ordinate their activities according to a common programme of government. Indeed, even if the magistrates of a particular year were able to do this, they of course had only single-year terms, at the end of which they would be replaced.

It was in part because of this that, in practice, the Senate played the leading role in Republican politics. This was the case even though the Senate, just as had been the case under the Monarchy, had very little formal power. After all, the Senate was the only permanent body in the Republican constitution, and

---

[26] Although this was not unknown. A person who did manage to achieve this was known as a *novus homo* ('new man'). Cicero, elected consul in 63 BC, was a *novus homo*.

[27] Or, where there is a coalition government, they are members of parties which have entered into a coalition arrangement in order to form a government.

[28] In the late Republic, it is common to identify two broad groupings of politicians, the *Optimates* and the *Populares*. The *Optimates* were conservative traditionalists, who supported the Senate and aristocracy's leading role in the state. The *Populares*, by contrast, sought the people's support through reforms in their favour. These were not, however, political parties in any sense. They had no party organisation, for example. Even to call them loose associations of like-minded people is probably too strong. It is better to think of these labels simply as descriptive of an individual's general political outlook.

so provided the only forum in which longer term policy could be developed.[29] Moreover, the Senate was made up of the leading men in the Roman state. Its membership was chosen originally by the consuls, and from 312 BC by the censors, and in practice it came to be the convention that someone who had held a senior magistracy would be appointed to the Senate unless he had committed some serious misconduct. The senators, then, were very influential men, exercising considerable powers of patronage, and with immense collective political authority. As a result, although the Senate was in theory only a consultative body, in practice it expected to be consulted by the magistrates before they exercised their powers.

(b) The Assemblies
Legislation and the election of magistrates fell within the remit of the whole body of adult, male citizens, meeting as an assembly. We have already seen the nature of these assemblies, and we have met one of them, namely the *comitia centuriata*. The *comitia centuriata* elected consuls, praetors and dictators, and could be summoned only by a consul. There was another assembly, the *comitia tributa*. This had the same membership as the *comitia centuriata*, though organised differently, and was responsible for electing lesser magistrates. We have seen as well that the *concilium plebis*, from which patricians were excluded, acquired in the mid-Republic the power to pass legislation binding on the whole community. In fact, the *concilium plebis* became after this the dominant legislative organ.

(4) The External Situation
During this period, from Rome's beginnings as simply one of many city states, Roman power spread to dominate the whole of Latium and, eventually, the whole of Italy. This was not without setbacks, of course. Most notably, the city of Rome itself was captured and sacked by Gauls from the north of Italy in around 390 BC. From every setback, though, Rome managed to recover, and by the end of the period its dominance was undisputed. The process of establishing dominance over Italy was completed during the first half of the third century BC.

This does not always mean, though, that Rome was exercising direct rule over all of the communities over which it held sway. Sometimes it was, but the political picture in Italy was much more complicated, and Rome's relationship with another community would depend on the political and military considerations in play at any given time. In addition to conquest and direct rule, there were two further, very important means of spreading Roman influence and control. One of these was colonisation. Often, a settlement of Roman citizens would

---

[29] There is a quote, attributed (possibly apocryphally) to the former US diplomat Henry Kissinger: 'Who do I call if I want to call Europe?' The point is that Europe, being made up of numerous individual states, is not capable of developing a single, coherent foreign policy. If the same question had been asked of ancient Rome during the Republic, the answer would be: 'The Senate'.

be planted on new territory.[30] The other method was through making treaties of friendship with other communities. These treaties would leave the existing local authorities in direct control of their communities, but subject to duties to provide support to the Romans – especially military support – when called upon to do so. These treaties would often be very unequal, in favour of the Romans. For example, only particularly favoured allies would be given Roman citizenship rights, although with such allies Rome was relatively generous. The less favoured would be excluded from this.[31]

E. The Later Republic (264–27 BC)

(1) The Political and Economic Situation of the Later Republic

From the third century BC we see another shift. For this period, we have a much stronger evidence base. Rome was now a significant power, with a developing economy: it was during the third century BC that coinage was introduced.[32] As we shall see in Chapter 3,[33] it was also during this period that Roman law began to develop into a more sophisticated form.

The Republican constitution survived in the same general form as before, and it was only towards the end of this period that it was strained to breaking point. The government of Rome continued to be formally in the hands of the magistrates, with the consuls at the head, all of this *de facto* under the supervision of the Senate. There were some changes, however. For example, in 267 BC, four additional quaestorships were created to assist the consuls with the governance of Italy. More important for legal history, though was the division of the praetorship into two in 242 BC.[34] Administration of the law was henceforth divided between the urban praetor (*praetor urbanus*), who was responsible for disputes between Roman citizens, and the peregrine praetor (*praetor peregrinus*), who oversaw disputes involving non-citizens.[35]

There were major changes in Rome's external relations, however. Although Rome was dominant in Italy, it was only one power of many in the Mediterranean world. In the western Mediterranean, the major power was Carthage, in modern Tunisia. In the eastern Mediterranean, numerous powerful states had emerged from the break-up of Alexander the Great's continent-spanning

---

[30] This is a practice that continued through the Republic and into the Empire, and well beyond Italy. Many modern towns and cities find their origins in this practice. For example, the name of the German city of Cologne (in German, *Köln*) is simply a corruption of the Latin word *colonia* ('colony'). It was established in as a colony in AD 50, on a previously existing town, as Colonia Claudia Ara Agrippinensium.

[31] We shall see at p. 96 that the question of citizenship had much greater importance for private law in the ancient world than it does today.

[32] See S von Reden, 'Money and Finance' in W Scheidel ed, *The Cambridge Companion to the Roman Economy* (Cambridge University Press 2012) 267.

[33] See p. 54.

[34] Further praetorships were created during this period to govern new provinces acquired as a result of the Punic Wars (see below). These, though, were provincial governorships rather than having any responsibility for administration of the law at Rome.

[35] The Latin word *peregrinus* means 'foreigner'.

empire, following his death in 323 BC.[36] Rome's rise to Italian dominance brought it into this wider world.

(2) The Growth of Empire

It is during this period that Rome acquired the beginnings of its empire. Care is needed here, because in this chapter we will be using the term 'empire' in two senses. In one sense, an empire is a state ruling over multiple national groups.[37] In another, an empire is a state ruled by an emperor. Rome was an empire in the first sense long before it was an empire in the second sense, and it is the first sense that is meant here.

Rome's first imperial possession beyond Italy came to it when it fought the first of three Punic Wars against Carthage (264–241 BC) over control of Sicily.[38] In that war, Rome came very close to defeat, but eventually emerged victorious. Sicily now came under Roman rule. The Second Punic War (218–201 BC) was triggered by events in Spain, where the Carthaginians had extensive possessions. Rome declared war in defence of the city of Saguntum (modern Sagunto, a little to the north of Valencia). Once again Rome was seriously threatened. The Carthaginian general Hannibal unexpectedly invaded Italy from the north, crossing the Alps with his army (including, famously, a number of elephants), and inflicted heavy defeats on the Romans. Eventually, though, the Romans were able to turn the tide, and brought the war to a successful end by invading Africa itself. This war made Rome dominant in the western Mediterranean. Carthage was finally destroyed in the Third Punic War (149–146 BC). It must be said that this war was entirely provoked by the Romans, whose fear of their traditional enemy was greatly in excess of the latter's ability to harm them. Carthage, at this point, was no longer a threat.

In the east, Rome became involved with the Greek world through a series of wars with Macedonia (now restored to broadly similar borders to those inherited by Alexander the Great). The first of these was fought from 214 to 205 BC to guard against the risk of Macedonian intervention in the Second Punic War. Certain Greek states having sought Roman support to protect them against Macedonian aggression, three further wars were fought against the Macedonians. The last of these ended in 148 BC, and Macedonia and the rest of the Greek peninsula became Roman provinces.[39]

---

[36] Alexander the Great was king of Macedonia from 336 to 323 BC. From this base, he conquered a vast swathe of territory, including the whole of Greece, Egypt to the south, and in the east stretching as far as the Indus valley in modern Pakistan.

[37] Indeed, in this sense, the Romans could be said to have had an empire as soon as its power extended beyond Latium.

[38] The name of these wars comes from the Latin *Punicus*, meaning 'Carthaginian', a reference to the Carthaginians' supposed origins in Phoenicia. Dido, the legendary founder of Carthage, was supposed to have come from the Phoenician city of Tyre, in modern Lebanon.

[39] As we have seen earlier, though, this did not necessarily mean a replacement of local authorities with direct Roman rule in all matters. Often, existing governance structures would be left intact, although it might be necessary to install a pro-Roman regime from among local elites. For an overview of Roman provincial administration, see J Richardson, *Roman Provincial Administration, 227 BC to AD 117* (Macmillan 1976).

(3) Problems with the Republican Constitution

The Republican constitution was finely balanced in its design and in its operation, with power deliberately diffused among a number of different bodies and office-holders. As the second century BC entered its second half, this system had worked successfully for more than 350 years. Such a system, however, required a high level of co-operation and consensus-building among its participants, and so was vulnerable when that co-operation broke down.[40]

The first major sign of trouble in the system came with the election of Tiberius Gracchus as tribune in 133 BC. Tiberius Gracchus put forward a plan of land reform, by which public land (the *ager publicus*) was to be redistributed from the wealthy landowners who had unlawfully occupied it.[41] This scheme was opposed by the Senate, whose natural sympathies lay with the wealthier parts of Roman society, and who prevailed upon another tribune to veto the plan. Tiberius responded to this by appealing to the people to remove that tribune. With neither side willing to back down on the matter, and amid accusations that Tiberius wanted to make himself a king, Tiberius and a number of his followers were murdered in the Forum in Rome by a mob led by vengeful senators. Attempts to revive the land reform project by Tiberius' brother, Gaius, who was tribune in 123 BC, were also unsuccessful. Gaius appears to have lost public support because he proposed to extend Roman citizenship to Rome's Italian allies. He committed suicide in 121 BC, facing assassination.

The citizenship issue was also a matter of contention at this time. While Rome had in earlier times been relatively generous with grants of citizenship to its most faithful allies, it became less so in the second century BC. Resenting the shift to a relationship that was more openly one of superior and subordinate, a significant number of the allies attempted to break away. This led to the Social War of 91–88 BC (so called because it was fought between Rome and its erstwhile allies, or *socii*). While Rome was nominally victorious in this war, it was only able to gain this victory by granting the very citizenship that it had fought the war over.

A further issue with the Republican system was the organisation of the army. Originally, the Roman army was a citizen militia, made up of those citizens with the resources to equip themselves for war. As long as Rome was fighting only local wars, this meant only relatively short absences during the summer campaigning season. As Roman power expanded, though, soldiers would be expected to be absent for longer periods, at greater distances from home. This was particularly difficult for those without slaves to keep the farm going in their absence. Although the army would not become fully professional until the Principate, by around 200 BC an increasing proportion of the army was made up of individuals motivated by adventure and the possibility of booty, rather than by a sense of duty as a

---

[40] See generally on this J von Ungern Sternberg (H I Flower trans), 'The Crisis of the Republic' in H I Flower ed, *The Cambridge Companion to the Roman Republic* (Cambridge University Press 2004).

[41] On *ager publicus* and the issues it created, see D J Gargola, *Lands, Laws & Gods: Magistrates & Ceremony in the Regulation of Public Lands in Republican Rome* (University of North Carolina Press 1995).

citizen, and so they owed their primary loyalty to individual generals who could provide them with these things.[42]

Because of this, Republican politics were dominated in the final century BC by a serious of military strongmen, each seeking to make himself the leading man in Rome. The best known of these is Julius Caesar.[43] Caesar was elected consul in 60 BC, and made an alliance with two other prominent figures, Pompey[44] and Crassus.[45] This alliance is known as the First Triumvirate. The Roman historian Suetonius tells us that the three men agreed that 'nothing should be done in public affairs that is displeasing to any of the three'. This was a significant development, because it envisaged a complete change in the way the politics of the Republic operated. Political questions were to be determined on the basis of these men's private agreement, rather than on the basis of wider consensus among political actors. Opposition from the Senate was predictable, but in the end counter-productive.

After his consulship, Caesar was put in charge of the provinces of Illyricum,[46] Cisalpine Gaul[47] and Transalpine Gaul.[48] He used this as a platform to launch a conquest of the rest of Gaul,[49] which had not yet been subjected to Roman rule. Of this, the following has been said:

> The Gallic war was a gigantic plundering raid designed to provide Caesar with a powerful army and with the financial means he needed to fulfill his political ambitions in Rome. He destroyed Celtic civilization and deprived hundreds of thousands of their lives or their freedom. The cool elegance of his writings (*commentarii*), which were designed to inform the Roman public about his deeds, cannot disguise these facts.[50]

---

[42] L Keppie, *The Making of the Roman Army: From Republic to Empire* (B T Batsford 1984) 51–5.

[43] Full name Gaius Iulius Caesar, born 100 BC. He was not the only one, however. Before Caesar, there was the rivalry between the prominent figures Marius (Gaius Marius, 157–86 BC) and Sulla (Lucius Cornelius Sulla Felix, 138–78 BC). In 88 BC, as consul, Sulla was allocated the command of a war against King Mithridates VI of Pontus. Marius, himself a successful general, under whom Sulla had previously served, engineered the passing of legislation transferring the command to him. This led to civil war between factions led by Marius and Sulla, with Sulla marching on Rome itself. This war ended in victory for Sulla, with Marius being forced into exile. Although he subsequently returned, and was elected as consul for an unprecedented seventh time, he died shortly afterwards. Following a further civil war, Sulla was appointed dictator in late 82 or early 81 BC. Unusually, there was no time limit on this appointment, which gave him complete power over the state. Using this position, he launched a campaign of 'proscriptions', by which large numbers of people were outlawed as public enemies and killed, with their property confiscated. Julius Caesar was Marius' nephew, and narrowly escaped falling victim to the proscriptions. Sulla himself resigned the dictatorship in late 81 BC and successfully stood for election as consul for the following year. After this consulship, he retired to his estates.

[44] Gnaeus Pompeius Magnus (106–48 BC).

[45] Marcus Licinius Crassus (c. 115/112–53 BC).

[46] This is roughly co-extensive with modern Albania, Montenegro, Bosnia and Herzegovina and parts of Croatia.

[47] This is the north of what is now Italy. Its Latin name, *Gallia Cisalpina*, means 'Gaul on this side of the Alps'.

[48] This is the south of what is now France. Its Latin name, *Gallia Transalpina*, means 'Gaul across the Alps'. It is also known as *Gallia Narbonensis* after the city of Narbonne.

[49] This covered what is now France, Luxembourg and Belgium, as well as parts of the Netherlands, Germany and Switzerland.

[50] J von Ungern Sternberg (H I Flower trans), 'The Crisis of the Republic' in H I Flower ed, *The Cambridge Companion to the Roman Republic* (Cambridge University Press 2004) 103.

An alliance between men as ambitious as Caesar, Pompey and Crassus could not last forever, and indeed Caesar and Pompey eventually fell out (Crassus having died in 53 BC). This break between the two led to the Civil War, which began when, in January 49 BC, Caesar and his army illegally crossed the Rubicon, the river separating Italy from Cisalpine Gaul. Caesar defeated Pompey at Pharsalus, in Greece, in August of the following year. He was made dictator for a term of ten years in 46 BC. By 45 BC, Caesar was the undisputed leader of the Roman state, and in February of the following year his dictatorship was extended to a life term. That life was not to continue for much longer, however: on the Ides of March (15 March), 44 BC, Caesar was assassinated.

F. The Principate (27 BC–AD 284)

(1) The Emergence of Augustus

One of the most important figures of all Roman history is Caesar's great-nephew and heir, born Gaius Octavius Thurinus, but better known as Octavian (Octavianus, in Latin) or Augustus. He was eighteen at Caesar's death, and was named as Caesar's heir. At this point, he adopted his great-uncle's name with Octavianus added in recognition of his original name. In addition to being heir of Caesar's own, personal wealth, however, he asserted the right also to succeed to Caesar's political position.

To strengthen his position, Octavian formed a pact with two allies of Caesar, Marcus Antonius and Marcus Aemilius Lepidus (the Second Triumvirate). Over time, however, tensions grew between Octavian and Marcus Antonius,[51] which ended in another civil war. Octavian's victory over Marcus Antonius at Actium, in Greece, in 31 BC, left Octavian as the dominant figure in Roman politics. Here we move to a new phase in Roman history. From this point, the Roman state no longer operates as a republic. Instead, there is rule by a single man, an emperor. In 27 BC, the Senate awarded Octavian a new name, Augustus ('Venerable'), and he will be referred to by this name from here on.

(2) The Nature and Operation of the Principate

The nature of Augustus' rule is ambiguous, because it was never openly proclaimed. This is understandable, given what happened when Julius Caesar made too obvious a grab for personal power. Evidently, for the change Augustus represented to work at all, it had to be dressed up in republican forms. All of Augustus' formal powers[52] existed within the Republican constitutional framework – as we

---

[51] Lepidus tends to be overlooked here, and is seen as the least influential of the three. At least part of the cause of these tensions was Marcus Antonius' affair with Cleopatra, Queen of Egypt, while married to Octavian's sister, Octavia. Marcus Antonius' personal and political relationship with Cleopatra allowed Octavian to present him as having abandoned Roman virtues, helping Octavian undermine Marcus Antonius' support at Rome.

[52] These were wide-ranging. For example, his title of *imperator* ('general', and origin of the word 'emperor') gave him supreme command of the army. In 23 BC, he was granted the powers of a tribune for life. In the same year, he was given direct authority over a number of provinces. He was also granted the authority of a censor. For an overview, see G Mousourakis, *The Historical and Institutional Context of Roman Law* (Ashgate 2003) 237–9.

have seen, it was possible to grant special legal powers to an individual – although it was unprecedented for such broad powers to be gathered together in one pair of hands, or to be lifelong. In form, the Republic continued. Even the name used for the emperor in this period, *princeps* – the origin of the term 'Principate' – means nothing grander than 'first man'.[53] In terms of both official powers and personal, political authority, though, it was clear where ultimate power lay. In substance, Augustus had established a monarchy. This ambiguity is seen in the Romans' own writings:

> The first narrative tradition, which appealed to Republican traditionalism, depicted Augustus as merely a Roman magistrate who proposed laws that were then approved by the people, while the second viewed Augustus as a quasi-divine monarch with sovereign powers over the law.[54]

The first of these traditions is more characteristic of Augustus himself. In his own account of his reign, the *Res Gestae*, he boasted that, when offered the status of overseer of laws and morals, with full power and without any colleague, he rejected this as contrary to ancestral custom. His characteristic approach was to govern through established Republican institutions.

One consequence of the central role of the emperor was a shift of political power away from the traditional aristocratic elites. Now a 'court culture' developed, in which political influence depended on proximity to the emperor and the ability to get his ear. While the political connections of members of traditional elites would no doubt help with this, it would be no guarantee. Many emperors relied heavily on non-elite advisers, including even freedmen (former slaves).

In this situation, it might have been expected that the traditional institutions of Republican government would simply wither away. However, the need to preserve the appearance of continuity with the Republic complicated matters. As we have seen, Augustus sought to preserve the outward appearance of Republican government, however much the reality was that ultimate power was in his hands, and his successors continued this policy.[55] Accordingly, there continued to be annual elections to the traditional magistracies, but only candidates approved by the emperor would have any chance of being elected, and the political influence of office-holders arose from the emperor's patronage. The Assemblies still met to pass legislation, but only proposals approved by the emperor would be put before them. Thus, while these institutions did diminish in practical importance, their formal role continued much longer. Nonetheless, by the end of the first

---

[53] This was actually an older title. The original title is *princeps senatus*, used for the leading man in the Senate, carrying the privilege of speaking first in debates. Augustus was *princeps senatus* from 28 BC. However, from Augustus until the end of the Principate in AD 284, the title of *princeps* was used to refer to the emperor.

[54] K Tuori, 'Augustus, Legislative Power, and the Power of Appearances' (2014) 20 Fundamina 938, 939.

[55] There was perhaps an element of 'doublethink' here. This, in George Orwell's novel *Nineteen Eighty-Four* (Secker & Warburg 1949), is '[t]he power of holding two contradictory beliefs in one's mind simultaneously, and accepting both of them'. Romans had to accept the emperor's effectively monarchical authority, while also believing that the Roman state was still a republic, even though those two things were inconsistent with each other.

century AD, the Assemblies no longer had a significant role in law-making. The most interesting case is that of the Senate. In the Republic it had had no formal legislative role, being in theory no more than a consultative body, and its resolutions (*senatusconsulta*) being in principle no more than advice. In the Principate, however, the Senate came to be seen as having law-making powers. Initially, these were in the form of binding directives to magistrates, which would then be given effect through the magistrate's exercise of his own power. By around AD 130, however, *senatusconsulta* were seen as being capable of having direct effect. In all of this, though, the Senate was simply the organ through which the emperor had chosen to express his will rather than being an independent legislative body, and by the end of the second century the Senate had effectively ceased to function as a law-making body.

The major weakness of the imperial system was the absence of clear rules governing succession to the position of emperor. This was a legacy of the way the Principate arose: while the principle of one-man rule was generally accepted by the end of Augustus' reign, it was politically impossible to formalise the position of emperor in such a way as to allow this. Who, then, succeeded to this role when an emperor died? Nominally, the Senate would make the appointment, but the political reality was somewhat different. It helped to be a relative of the previous emperor: all things being equal, a member of the emperor's family had a better chance of succeeding him than did someone outside the family. Thus, for example, the first five emperors were all related through birth or marriage.[56] It helped even more to be the emperor's nominated successor, and this became common practice. What was most important, however, was to have the backing of the army. Even that, though, gave no certainty of success in becoming or remaining emperor. Often there would be rival claimants, proclaimed by different parts of the army, or an emperor would reign for only a short time before being overthrown. Indeed, in each of the years AD 69, 193 and 238 there were four or more different emperors. The last of those was part of the Crisis of the Third Century, considered below, during which the Roman Empire came close to falling.

(3) Territorial Expansion

Despite these problems, though, for a time the Empire continued to thrive. It was during this period that the Empire reached its maximum territorial extent, stretching from the Middle East to the island of Great Britain. Roman presence in Great Britain began with an invasion in AD 43, under the emperor Claudius. The southern two-thirds (*i.e.* largely modern England and Wales) became subject to Roman authority fairly quickly and, despite some early resistance,[57] remained

---

[56] Augustus was succeeded by his stepson, Tiberius (reigned AD 14–37). He was succeeded by his great-nephew, Caligula (reigned 37–41), who was succeeded by his uncle, Claudius (reigned 41–54). Claudius was succeeded by his great-nephew, Nero (reigned 54–68).

[57] Most notably the revolt in AD 60–1 of Boudicca, widow of the king of the Iceni, a tribe in East Anglia.

that way until the early 400s. In the north, though, what is now Scotland, matters were different. Although the Romans inflicted a heavy defeat on the Caledonians in AD 83 or 84, at Mons Graupius,[58] they failed to consolidate this. The boundary of the Roman Empire came to be fixed at the line of Hadrian's Wall, begun in AD 122 in the reign of Hadrian.[59] Under Antoninus Pius,[60] the boundary moved north to Antonine's Wall, which was begun in AD 142 and stretched[61] between the Firths of Forth and Clyde. However, this was abandoned only twenty years later, and the boundary reverted to Hadrian's Wall. Thus, aside from this short period, no part of what is now Scotland ever formed part of the Roman Empire.[62]

(4) Emergence of Christianity

During the Principate an event occurred, which was later to lead to fundamental social and religious change in the Roman world and beyond, but which would not at the time have been widely seen as being of any great significance. Nonetheless, it will be mentioned here to preserve chronology. In the early AD 30s, at Jerusalem in the Roman province of Judea, an itinerant preacher was crucified as a disturber of the peace.[63] This happened around the Jewish Passover festival. The preacher's name was Jesus, and he was believed by his followers to be the Messiah of the Jews, foretold by prophecy.[64] After Jesus' execution, though, his followers began saying that they had seen him, risen from the dead. His followers (calling themselves Christians from *Christos*, the Greek word used to translate *Messiah*) began to spread through the Empire, winning converts as they went.

During the whole period of the Principate, Christianity was very much a minority, although by AD 64 Christians were a big enough group in Rome to be scapegoated by the emperor, Nero, for a major fire that destroyed much of the city.[65] For the rest of the Principate, there were recurrent persecutions of Christians – sometimes with great savagery – though at other times legal prohibitions against Christianity were inconsistently applied.[66]

---

[58] The location of this battle is unknown. Various sites have been suggested, mostly in the north-east of Scotland. The supposed speech of the Caledonian leader, Calgacus (recounted by the Roman historian, Tacitus, in his *Agricola*), is stirring stuff. It may well, however, be complete invention. The same may be true of Calgacus himself.

[59] Reigned AD 117–38.

[60] Reigned AD 138–61.

[61] And still does stretch. Much of Antonine's Wall survives, and is worth visiting.

[62] Contrary to popular belief, Hadrian's Wall does not mark the boundary between Scotland and England. It is in fact entirely within England, though at its western end it is less than a mile from the border. At its eastern end, it is as far south as Wallsend, near Newcastle upon Tyne.

[63] This episode illustrates again the Roman tendency, already mentioned above, so far as possible to leave existing local power structures intact. Although Jesus' crucifixion was carried out under Roman authority, the initial arrest and trial were conducted by the local religious authorities in Jerusalem. We see throughout the Gospel accounts of Jesus' life a continuing interplay between Roman and local authorities.

[64] 'Messiah' is a Hebrew word, meaning 'Anointed One'.

[65] There is suspicion that Nero himself was in fact responsible for the fire.

[66] O F Robinson, 'The Repression of Christians in the Pre-Decian Period: A Legal Problem Still' (1990–2) 25–7 Irish Jurist (NS) 269.

(5) The Late Principate

The tendency has already been mentioned for the Romans to leave existing power structures in place when a territory was added to the Empire, although, as might be expected, this varied greatly from place to place. Even where Roman rule touched most lightly, however, there was a process of Romanisation, as Roman cultural practices became increasingly assimilated by provincials. In part, this was a tool of empire, but it was also something that provincials often actively sought. After all, Roman culture was the prestige culture, and its assimilation would readily have been seen as representing the acquisition of higher status. Writing at the end of the first century AD, the Roman historian Tacitus shows both of these aspects of the trend:

> our national dress came into favour and the toga was everywhere to be seen. And so they strayed into the enticements of vice – porticoes, baths and sumptuous banquets. In their innocence, they called this 'civilisation', when in fact it was a part of their enslavement.[67]

In the law, too, study of legal documents surviving from the provinces shows a readiness to adopt Roman forms.

A new phase in Roman–provincial relations began in the early third century, however. Until this time, the inhabitants of most communities in the Empire were citizens of their own community. Roman citizenship was held only by a minority outside Italy. In AD 212, though, an imperial pronouncement (the *Constitutio Antoniniana*) extended Roman citizenship to almost all of the free inhabitants of the Empire. This naturally meant that more people now had their affairs governed by Roman law, although in practice the picture on the ground is likely to have involved some continuity with previous practice as well.[68]

The rationale for the *Constitutio Antoniniana* is debatable. It may, though, have been an attempt to make more people liable for Roman taxation. If the *Constitutio Antoniniana* was motivated by a desire to broaden the tax base, that would be understandable, because public finance was one of the major problems in the third century. In an effort to maintain the loyalty of the army, successive emperors had substantially increased army pay. As the army itself had increased significantly in size as well, this was difficult to sustain, and placed unsustainable demands on a corrupt and inefficient tax system. Nor was the situation helped by the occasional debasement of the coinage, which led to high inflation during the period.

Economic difficulties were, however, only part of the difficulties faced by the Roman state in the third century. It was also a period of major political instability, known as the Crisis of the Third Century, mentioned above.

---

[67] Tacitus, *Agricola* s. 21 in Tacitus, *Agricola and Germania* (H Mattingly trans, London 1948).
[68] For discussion, see C Humfress, ''Laws' Empire: Roman Universalism and Legal Practice' in du Plessis, *New Frontiers*.

The Crisis of the Third Century arose from longer-running trends, and in particular the role of the army in proclaiming emperors. However, the difficulties this brought became particularly acute in the third century. The beginning of the Crisis can be conveniently dated to AD 235 when, for the first time, a man was declared emperor who was not of senatorial or equestrian[69] background. Maximinus Thrax was a man of humble origins, who had entered the army and risen through the ranks to military command. When the previous emperor, Severus Alexander, was assassinated by his own troops, Maximinus Thrax was declared emperor by the Praetorian Guard.[70] This appointment was then confirmed by the Senate, but only reluctantly. It can have been no surprise, then, when in AD 238 (the Year of Six Emperors) the Senate endorsed a rival claimant. This was Gordian,[71] the governor of Africa, who was declared co-emperor along with his son, also Gordian. They are known as Gordian I and Gordian II respectively. The Gordians, however, lasted less than three weeks. Gordian II was killed in battle,[72] and Gordian I subsequently committed suicide. The Senate then proclaimed two elderly senators, Pupienus and Balbinus, as co-emperors, with the grandson of Gordian I their designated heir. They were not up to the challenge, being unable to co-operate with each other, and their reign was cut short when they were killed by the Praetorian Guard after only ninety-nine days. In the meantime, Maximinus Thrax himself had been murdered by his own troops. The deaths of these three men left the thirteen-year-old Gordian III as undisputed sole emperor.

Gordian III, however, only lasted six years until his own death, either in battle or at the hands of his troops. A succession of mostly incompetent and often short-lived emperors followed. Over the fifty or so years from the reign of Maximinus Thrax to the accession of Diocletian in AD 284, there were some twenty-six emperors (including co-emperors), and even more claimants. Around half lasted no more than a year, and at least ten of the twenty-six were killed by their own soldiers.

G. The Dominate and the Fall of the West (AD 284–476)

(1) Diocletian and the Dominate

Such events are not conducive to long-term peace and prosperity, and it is almost a miracle that the Empire survived the Crisis of the Third Century. It must have been clear at least that change was needed, and that is what was brought by

---

[69] The senatorial and equestrian classes together made up the Roman aristocracy. The equestrians (*equites*, sometimes translated as 'knights') originally included those outside the senatorial elite but whose wealth qualified them for military service as cavalry.

[70] The Praetorian Guard was a part of the army, with the main function of forming the emperor's bodyguard. This role gave them enormous political importance. The Praetorian Guard was disbanded in the fourth century by Constantine.

[71] This was not entirely voluntary on Gordian's part. He was prevailed upon to take this step by a group of upper-class provincials, who had killed an imperial official, and who hoped that Gordian would then protect them.

[72] This was not even in battle against Maximinus Thrax. Instead, it was against a personal enemy of Gordian I, whom Gordian I had attempted to remove from his post as governor of a neighbouring province.

Diocletian, who became emperor in AD 284. From Diocletian's reign, the Empire enters a new phase. We are no longer in the Principate, in which the emperor was presented as merely *princeps*, or first citizen. We now enter the Dominate, so called because the emperor was now openly identified as *dominus*, lord or master, of the Roman world. Of course, the idea that the emperor was simply first among equals had always been a fiction. As we saw when we looked at Augustus, however, it was important at the beginning of the Principate to maintain at least the appearance that the Republican constitution was continuing, however threadbare that appearance was to become. With the Dominate, though, even the pretence of Republicanism was dropped. The emperor had always been in reality a monarch, and now he was to be openly treated as one.

Diocletian reorganised imperial government at all levels. He restructured provincial administration and expanded the civil service. He was not successful in all of his schemes – a notable failure was his edict on prices in AD 301, which was unsuccessful in controlling prices and wages – but, particularly in contrast with the upheavals of the previous fifty years, he was astoundingly successful. A mark of his success was that he was able to abdicate at a time of his own choosing (in AD 305), living out his days peacefully growing cabbages and trying to avoid getting drawn back into politics.

Diocletian's most enduring reform was his division of the Empire into eastern and western parts. Realising that the Empire was too big for a single person to govern, he appointed a co-emperor (Maximian). Maximian governed the western part of the Empire, while Diocletian was to manage the east, although Diocletian was to remain in overall charge. Each then appointed a deputy, known as a Caesar, who was to be his designated heir. This system is known as the Tetrarchy (rule by four people). It is notable that the senior emperor took the east, which did not include Rome itself. It is even more notable that none of the four men in the Tetrarchy in fact made his base at Rome at all. This was part of a long-term trend. Rome itself was becoming less important, and the east more important. It is no surprise, then, that in the Dominate the Senate dwindled in importance to being little more than a city council for Rome.

The Tetrarchy system did not long survive Diocletian's abdication in points of detail. However, subject to some interruptions, when a single man managed to establish sole control over the whole Empire, this division into east and west became an established feature.

(2) Constantine and the Conversion to Christianity

One of these interruptions in fact came very soon after Diocletian's abdication, with the emperor Constantine. He was proclaimed western emperor in AD 306, and established himself as such by 312 by defeating his rivals. Following civil war, he established himself as sole emperor in 324.

Constantine is one of the major figures of the Dominate, and had clear ambition. He established a new capital at the ancient city of Byzantium, which he called Constantinople after himself. This is modern Istanbul, and is another sign of the eastward shift in the Empire's centre of gravity.

The most important development of Constantine's reign, however, was the adoption of Christianity. We have already seen the emergence of Christianity in the Principate, as a group prominent enough to attract periodic persecution but still very much a minority. Indeed, there was major state-sanctioned persecution as late as Diocletian's reign. This was all to change dramatically under Constantine. The first step was his Edict of Milan in 313, by which religious toleration was granted to Christians. Constantine attributed his victory in 324 to the favour of the Christian God, and ultimately he himself converted to Christianity.

The consequences of this were profound. From being a persecuted minority, although by now a substantial one, Christians were thrust into political prominence. This naturally made Christianity much more attractive to the politically ambitious. It is notable that only one emperor after Constantine was a pagan, Julian the Apostate (reigned AD 361–3). The political influence of Christianity in the fourth century was spectacularly demonstrated when Bishop Ambrose of Milan excommunicated the eastern emperor, Theodosius I,[73] for ordering a massacre of thousands of civilians in 390, only readmitting him after months of penance. The very idea of a repentant Roman emperor, on his knees before a Christian bishop, would have seemed absurd – indeed unimaginable – to earlier generations.

(3) The Fall of the Western Empire

Ultimately, the Empire was not able to withstand the challenges that faced it. Power sharing between eastern and western emperors rarely worked well. Theodosius I was the last man to be emperor of both halves of the Empire.[74] There was a tendency for the two halves to be run, *de facto*, as separate empires, and after Theodosius I each was regarded as supreme in his own half.

By this time, though, the Western Empire had entered its final decline. Much ink has been spilled over the reasons for the fall of the Western Empire, more than can be satisfactorily explored here.[75] Whatever the underlying reasons, though, the brute fact is that in the fifth century AD the Western Empire could no longer rely on its ability to defend its borders or exert authority over its territory. Germanic tribes outside the Empire's borders sought to move into the Empire, hoping to share in its benefits. The Empire was unable to exclude them, or to control them once they entered. Piece by piece, the Western Empire crumbled. In AD 410, Rome itself was sacked by the Visigoths. In the same year, the inhabitants of the Roman provinces of Britannia were told that they would need to look to their own defence for the time being. The withdrawn Roman troops never

---

[73] Eastern emperor 379–95, western emperor 392–5.
[74] It is notable that he made his western capital at Milan rather than Rome, another sign of Rome's political eclipse.
[75] For discussion of the fall of the Western Empire and its effects, see B Ward-Perkins, *The Fall of Rome and the End of Civilization* (Oxford University Press 2005).

returned, and from the middle of the century onwards what is now England was largely overrun by invading Germanic tribes, the Anglo-Saxons (who give England its name). Throughout the century, Roman control retreated. The final step came in AD 476, when the final western emperor, Romulus Augustulus, was deposed by the barbarian leader Odoacer and not replaced.

H. Continuation in the East (AD 476–1453)

(1) The Eastern Empire

Although the Western Empire had fallen, the Eastern Empire continued. From this time onwards the Eastern Empire is often referred to as the Byzantine Empire, and indeed this was a very different place from what the Western Empire had been. For one thing, the dominant language was Greek rather than Latin. For another, it was wealthier and more economically developed than the West, facts which probably help to explain the East's survival when the West fell. Nonetheless, the eastern emperors themselves claimed continuity with Rome.

(2) Justinian

For legal history, by far the most important of the eastern emperors was Justinian I, in whose reign and on whose instructions the great compilation of legal materials known as the *Corpus Iuris Civilis* ('Body of the Civil Law') was produced. The *Corpus Iuris Civilis* will be considered in detail in Chapter 3,[76] but something must be said about Justinian now.

Justinian was born at Tauresium (now Taor, a village in North Macedonia) in approximately AD 482. His was a provincial background, not connected to the elites of the society into which he was born. Unlike them, he was a native speaker of Latin rather than of Greek. His uncle, however, rose from the army to become emperor in 518, as Justin I. Justin adopted his nephew,[77] and declared him co-emperor in 527. When Justin died later that year, Justinian became sole emperor, and remained so until his death in 565.

Justinian was a man of enormous ambition for *renovatio imperii* ('renewal of the Empire'), with the activity to match. As a religious reformer, he attempted to reconcile different factions in the Church. He also ordered the construction of the great cathedral of Constantinople, the Hagia Sophia. In the military sphere, his generals, Narses and Belisarius foremost among them, led his armies in reconquering much of the Western Empire, including Rome itself. In Chapter 3,[78] we will meet Justinian's great administrator, Tribonian, who was responsible for managing the creation of the *Corpus Iuris Civilis*.

One thing that clearly emerges from Justinian's life is that he had a great talent for surrounding himself with able people, who could be trusted to carry out the

---

[76] See pp. 63–70.
[77] Hence the name. Justinian was born Flavius Petrus Sabbatius. He added the name Iustinianus to indicate his adoption by Justin (Iustinus, in Latin).
[78] See p. 65.

tasks he gave them. Foremost among his circle, though, was his wife, Theodora. A former actress, she was his support during times of weakness. When major riots broke out in Constantinople in 532 (the Nika riots), it was Theodora who persuaded Justinian to stay in the city and be resolute in dealing with the situation, rather than fleeing as he had initially been minded to do. A great deal of the credit for Justinian's achievements is due to her.

(3) Later History and Fall

The Eastern Empire was a major power for many centuries, but the overall story was one of decline, as it was gradually forced back on all sides. Justinian's achievements turned out on the whole to be simply a temporary respite. By the middle of the seventh century, Byzantine power had been pushed back in the Balkans by Slavic settlement, and in the south by the Arabs. Although much was recovered between the ninth and eleventh centuries, this was only temporary. In 1204, Constantinople itself was sacked by crusaders, although it was later recovered. By the middle of the fifteenth century, the Empire consisted of little more than Constantinople itself. It finally fell to the Ottomans in 1453.

Chapter Summary

Roman history is divided into three periods, named according to the system of government in use during each. These are the Monarchy, the Republic and the Empire. The Monarchy lasted from the traditional date of Rome's founding (753 BC) until around 509 BC. During this period, Rome was ruled by a series of kings, supported by a council of advisers called the Senate.

With the transition to the Republic (509–27 BC), the kings were overthrown and their powers transferred to magistrates called consuls, of whom two were elected each year. Further magistracies were subsequently created to take on specific functions. Of these, the magistrate of greatest interest to legal history is the urban praetor, who was responsible for administration of the civil law. The Senate, however, was the dominant political force in the Republic. Also during this period, Rome's power and influence expanded, first throughout Italy and then beyond. By the end of the Republic, Rome ruled territory stretching from the English Channel to the Middle East.

During the last century or so BC, civil wars brought about the end of the Republic and the transition to the Empire in 27 BC. Although the institutions and magistracies of the Republic continued, this was under the supervision of an emperor, and the importance of the Republican institutions and magistracies declined.

> The Empire is itself divided into two periods. In the first, the Principate (27 BC–AD 284), attempts were made to preserve the appearance of Republican government, and the political dominance of the emperor was partially disguised by constitutional forms. Weaknesses in this system, and in particular with the issue of succession to the role of emperor, came to a head during the third century and brought about the transition to the Dominate in AD 284. During this period, the Republican forms were dispensed with, and the emperor was openly proclaimed as master (*dominus*) of the Roman world. The Dominate continued until the fall of the Western Empire in AD 476. The Eastern Empire continued until 1453.

Further Reading

Reading on Roman history is not difficult to come by. A very good general guide, with references to further reading, is L and R A Adkins, *Handbook to Life in Ancient Rome* (Oxford University Press 1994). Particularly recommended for their legal perspective are H F Jolowicz and B Nicholas, *Historical Introduction to the Study of Roman Law* 3rd edn (Cambridge University Press 1972), T G Watkin, *An Historical Introduction to Modern Civil Law* (Ashgate 1999) chapters 1–3, and G Mousourakis, *The Historical and Institutional Context of Roman Law* (Ashgate 2003).

An excellent way of learning more about Roman history is to listen to some of the many podcast series that are available in this area. As a sample of what is available, two very informative, accessible and entertaining podcast series on Roman history are the Partial Historians (https://partialhistorians.com/) and Totalus Rankium (https://totalusrankium.podbean.com/). The BBC Radio programme *In Our Time* also features Roman topics from time to time.

CHAPTER TWO

The Legal Process

A. The Context of Roman Litigation

Having considered in Chapter 1 the Roman constitution more generally, we now turn to the administration of justice within that constitutional context. It may be supposed that this is an area of less interest in modern law, but that would not be entirely accurate. On occasion, Roman texts in this area are still found to be of relevance to modern discussions.[1]

(1) The Parties Involved

Before going further, a preliminary point must be made about terminology. The Romans did not have specific, set terms for the parties to litigation. For the party bringing the action, we see various terms. Examples are *qui vindicat* ('one who vindicates'),[2] *qui agit* ('one who pursues an action'),[3] *eum qui acturus est* ('he who is to bring the action')[4] and *actor* ('pursuer').[5] We see something similar with the other party, who is sometimes referred to simply as the *adversarius* ('opponent')[6] or *reus* ('accused'),[7] or direct reference is avoided altogether.[8] The tendency in modern accounts of Roman law is to call these parties, respectively, 'plaintiff' and 'defendant'. These, though, are not general terms of the English language. Rather, they are technical terms belonging to the English legal tradition. Their use is, therefore, potentially confusing and misleading for those of other legal traditions. For this reason, in this book the Scottish terms 'pursuer' and 'defender' are preferred and will be used. In addition, 'pursuer' has the benefit of being a more literal translation of the Latin *actor*.

---

[1] See *e.g. Shields v Donnelly* 2000 JC 46; *Gibbs v Ruxton* 2000 JC 258.
[2] G.4.16.
[3] G.4.17a.
[4] D.2.13.1pr.
[5] G.4.17b.
[6] G.4.16; G.4.17a; G.4.17b.
[7] D.2.13.1pr.
[8] G.4.42.

(2) The Conduct of Litigation

Roman law developed over a very long period of time, and it is only to be expected that procedure developed along with it. The Romans in fact used, at different times, three distinct forms of procedure, namely the *legis actiones*, the formulary procedure and the *cognitio* procedure. The main formative period of Roman law occurred under the formulary procedure.[9] However, as the history of Roman law begins long before it was introduced, and continues long after it was superseded, it is necessary to consider all three. Moreover, if we are interested in the post-Roman influence of Roman law, the *cognitio* procedure is of particular interest. The canon law courts of the Roman Catholic Church (which, as we shall see in Chapter 4,[10] had jurisdiction over a wide range of subject matter) drew heavily on the *cognitio* in developing their own procedure. This 'Romano-Canonical procedure' has been described as the 'principal legacy of the *cognitio* procedure'.[11] This legacy spread beyond the Church courts and, for example, was influential in the development of Scots civil procedure.[12]

Before getting into the detail of each of these procedural systems, however, some general comments on Roman litigation seem appropriate.

(a) The Stages of Litigation

The first thing to note is a distinctive feature of the *legis actiones* and the formulary procedure. This is the division of litigation into two stages, each presided over by a different person and for different purposes.

We saw in Chapter 1 that the administration of civil justice was the responsibility of a magistrate called the praetor. Although the praetorship was one of the highest offices of state, the praetor's role was not simply one of oversight of the courts. Instead, the praetor had a direct role in individual cases.

The first stage of litigation took place before the praetor. This is known as the *in iure* stage,[13] and it had two main purposes. The first of these was to determine the legal question that was to be considered. The second was to appoint the judge who was to preside over the second stage of the litigation, the stage *apud iudicem* ('before the judge'). It was only when the matter moved to this separate, second stage that questions of fact would be considered.

As we shall see below, this two-stage process was superseded in the Empire, when the *cognitio* procedure was introduced.

(b) The Role of Lawyers

Another distinctive feature of the *legis actiones* and formulary procedures, surprising to modern eyes, is the comparatively limited role for the legally trained. Certainly, legal experts had an important role in *advising* those involved in the

---

[9] Indeed, as we shall see at p. 51, the formulary procedure was one of the things that allowed for these developments.
[10] See pp. 76–8.
[11] E Metzger, 'An Outline of Roman Civil Procedure' (2013) 9 Roman Legal Tradition 1, 29.
[12] *Stair Memorial Encyclopaedia* Civil Procedure (Reissue) para 5.
[13] *In iure* is sometimes translated as 'at law'.

legal process. We shall meet in Chapter 3[14] a special group of legal experts called the jurists, mostly high-status Romans whose writings largely form the basis of our knowledge of Roman law. There were also others engaged in legal practice at a humbler level, making a living giving legal advice, drafting documents and recording transactions.[15] However, the actual conduct of litigation largely took place in the absence of lawyers.

Take first the parties' advocates. Even once it was recognised that a litigant ought to be able to have someone more skilled act as a representative to plead the case,[16] legal expertise was not necessarily seen as a high priority for those acting as advocates in this way. It is traditional to draw a clear distinction between jurists and advocates. While the divide was by no means uncrossable,[17] it was nonetheless true that the parties' advocates were not normally lawyers as we would understand it. They were employed for their skill in oral argument rather than their legal expertise.

This does not mean to say that advocates were ignorant of the law. On the contrary, an experienced advocate could hardly avoid picking up a fair degree of knowledge of the law that he was arguing about. An orator who did not understand the law he was arguing about could attract justifiable criticism. For example, the jurist Pomponius tells us about the advocate Servius Sulpicius, who sought advice from the jurist Quintus Mucius on a point of law. Having twice failed to understand that advice, and having asked for further clarification, he was 'rebuked by Quintus Mucius. For he told him that it was disgraceful for a patrician of noble family to be ignorant of the law on which his cases turned.'[18] So stung by this was Servius Sulpicius that he turned his attention to serious study of the law, and became in the end a prominent jurist himself.[19] Cicero, the most famous of all the advocates, also studied the law in his youth.[20] Nonetheless, advocates as a group relied to a great extent on others to advise them on the law.

The same was true of judges. While an individual judge might happen to have legal knowledge, that is not what he was chosen for. The judge was not a professional or a trained lawyer, rather he was a respectable citizen, performing this role out of public duty rather than as a profession. If the judge needed to consider a point of law, he would be likely to consult those with expertise in that area rather than attempting to decide it himself.[21]

---

[14] See pp. 54–60.
[15] J C Brown, 'The Origin and Early History of the Office of Notary' (1935) 47 JR 201 and 355; W So, 'Access to Roman Civil Justice' (2014) 33 Civil Justice Quarterly 462.
[16] This became normal practice under the formulary system. See generally Buckland, *Textbook* 700–4.
[17] See generally on this the essays in P J du Plessis ed, *Cicero's Law: Rethinking Roman Law of the Late Republic* (Edinburgh University Press 2016).
[18] D.1.2.2.43.
[19] On these two jurists, see Stein, *Regulae Iuris* 41–4.
[20] See p. 57.
[21] At least, this is what he would be well advised to do. See pp. 437–9 for the liability of an erring judge. See though O E Tellegen-Couperus, 'The Role of the Judge in the Formulary Procedure' (2001) 22(2) J Leg Hist 1, where it is suggested that the normal view of judges' expertise and the importance of their decisions may be an underestimate.

(c) Conduct of the Proceedings before the Judge

It is not surprising that proceedings before the judge were very different from modern litigation. In modern litigation, the judge is an official of the state. The only public official involved in the *legis actiones* and formulary procedures was the praetor. Once the case had moved on to the next stage, the state took no real direct interest in proceedings. By contrast with the *in iure* stage, which was much more strictly regulated, there was very little formal regulation of proceedings *apud iudicem* in contrast with modern litigation. There were, for example, few developed rules of evidence. Nor were advocates expected to confine their arguments to matters that we would consider relevant. Adverse reference to a party's family origin, physical appearance and fashion sense was almost standard, whenever it could be used to influence a judge or jury's impression of the party's character. That party's own advocate, of course, would be doing his best to create a contrary, positive impression.[22]

Doubtless this process of public shaming acted as a disincentive to litigation. No doubt socio-economic factors often had the same effect. It would be a bold pursuer who brought a case against a defender of higher social standing, when political considerations would often lead the judge to favour the latter.

B. Earlier Procedure: *The Legis Actiones*

The earliest form of procedure was the *legis actiones* ('statutory actions'). These were noteworthy for their inflexibility. The second-century jurist Gaius explains:

> The actions in use among the ancient lawyers were called statutory actions [*legis actiones*], either because they were set out in statutes, since at that time the edicts of the praetor, in which numerous actions were introduced, were not yet in use, or else because they were adjusted to the very words of a statute and so had to be observed as immutably as statutes. This is why the opinion was given, that one who raised an action about the cutting of vines, using in the action the word 'vines', lost his case, because he should have called them trees, since the law of the Twelve Tables, on which the action for cutting down vines was available, spoke generally about cutting down trees.[23]

Great care was therefore needed, to avoid the case being lost on technical grounds rather than being decided on its substantive merits.[24]

---

[22] C Craig, 'Audience Expectations, Invective, and Proof' in J Powell and J Paterson eds, *Cicero the Advocate* (Oxford University Press 2004).

[23] G.4.11.

[24] It is often said that early law is a law of procedure, and that substantive law is 'secreted in the interstices of procedure', only to emerge as the meaning and scope of the procedural forms is worked out over time. See though A Watson, 'The Law of Actions and the Development of Substantive Law in the Early Roman Republic' (1973) 89 LQR 387, arguing that this view is exaggerated.

(1) Initiating the Action

Litigation began by the pursuer issuing a formal oral summons to the defender. This process was called *in ius vocatio*, which may be translated as 'calling to law'. What if the defender refused to comply with the summons? In modern law, the solution here is just to continue with the litigation. Normally, if a modern defender makes no attempt to defend the claim, decree in absence will be granted against the defender, and the pursuer will win by default. This was not the case in early Roman litigation. In principle – and this remained the case throughout the Republic and into the early Empire – litigation depended on the consent and participation of both parties, rather like modern arbitration. The pursuer's action could not proceed in the absence of the defender.

It was permitted for the pursuer to use force to compel the defender's appearance, although as an alternative the defender could find someone to act as a *vindex*, a guarantor for future appearance, instead of appearing immediately.[25] Compelling appearance must often have been difficult or impossible, especially where the defender was physically stronger or had support from others.[26]

(2) The Preliminary Hearing

There were five *legis actiones*.[27] Three of these (*sacramentum*, *postulatio* and *condictio*) were used for initiating an action. The other two were used for enforcement of judgments, and are considered below.

(a) Sacramentum

Sacramentum was used where no other form of action was provided for.[28] The term *sacramentum* relates to a form of wager entered into by the parties. This was a promise to pay on the event of failure in the action, the money to be paid to the state rather than to the other party.[29] The amount of the *sacramentum* varied depending on the value of the action. If the subject matter of the action was worth at least 1,000 *asses* (a Roman coin), then the *sacramentum* was 500 *asses*; otherwise, or if the matter in dispute was the free or slave status of a person, the *sacramentum* was 50 *asses*.[30]

How matters proceeded depended on the nature of the claim, and more precisely whether it was a claim to property or a claim against a particular person.[31] If the pursuer claimed to own the property in dispute or to have another right in the property, then the property had to be brought before the praetor. If it could

---

[25] E Metzger, 'An Outline of Roman Civil Procedure' (2013) 9 Roman Legal Tradition 1, 19.
[26] On the problem, see J M Kelly, *Roman Litigation* (Oxford University Press 1966) 4–11.
[27] G.4.12.
[28] G.4.13.
[29] G.4.13.
[30] G.4.14.
[31] This is the distinction between real actions and personal actions, considered at pp. 161–3. The following outline of the *sacramentum* procedure is taken from G.4.16–17.

not be brought to the hearing (*e.g* because it was not portable, as with land) then a part could be brought, for example a clod of earth. The pursuer would hold a rod and take hold of the property and then assert his or her claim. For example, if the property in dispute was a slave, the pursuer said: 'I declare that this man is mine according to his proper title. As I have said, look you, I have laid my staff.' The pursuer then laid the staff on the property. The defender then did the same things. The praetor then said: 'Let the man go, both of you', and they did so. The pursuer then addressed the defender, and said: 'I ask whether you will say on what title you have made a claim.' Then the defender said: 'I have asserted my right by laying of a staff.' The pursuer said: 'As you have claimed wrongfully, I challenge you to a *sacramentum* of 500 *asses*.' The defender said: 'And I you.' Then the praetor awarded interim possession to one of the parties, and ordered that party to give security for the property and its profits. A judge would be appointed after a delay of thirty days.[32]

(b) *Iudicis Postulatio*

The *iudicis postulatio* was used when specially authorised by statute.[33] In this procedure, the pursuer would begin by saying: 'I state under *sponsio* that you ought to give me 10,000 sesterces', or whatever the subject matter of the action might have been. 'I ask whether you affirm or deny this.' The defender then denied the claim. The pursuer then said: 'As you deny, I ask you, Praetor, to give a judge or arbiter.' The judge would normally then be appointed immediately.[34]

(c) *Condictio*

The third of the *legis actiones* was the *condictio*. The term *condictio* has had a surprisingly long life, particularly in the law of unjustified enrichment, in which context it is still used today. Its use there is considered in Chapter 25.[35] The term *condictio*, though, as used in modern law, has long since lost any connection with the procedural form named after it. Even in classical law, its use is anachronistic: *condictio* is an archaic Latin word referring to the formal giving of notice initiating the action, and in classical law such notice was no longer given. In classical law, the word referred to a particular kind of action, by which an obligation to convey a specific piece of property or a specific sum of money was asserted. The jurist Gaius explains the use of the *condictio* in earlier law.[36]

---

[32] G.4.15.
[33] G.4.17a. For example, the Twelve Tables (see pp. 47–9) authorised its use for enforcing the contract of *stipulatio* (see Chapter 18). It was also used for the division of an inheritance (see p. 172) or the division of common property (see pp. 171–2).
[34] G.4.17a.
[35] See pp. 429–30.
[36] G.4.17–20. Its introduction apparently rested on two statutes, a *lex Silia* for claims of specific sums of money, and a *lex Calpurnia* for claims to specific items of property. For discussion of the history of the *condictio*, see D Liebs, 'The History of the Roman *Condictio* up to Justinian' in N MacCormick and P Birks eds, *The Legal Mind: Essays for Tony Honoré* (Oxford University Press 1986); C St Tomulescu, 'Origin of the *Legis Actio per Condictionem*' (1969) 4 Irish Jurist (NS) 180.

Under the *condictio*, proceedings before the praetor began with the pursuer asserting the claim, like this: 'I state that you ought to give me 10,000 sesterces. I ask whether you affirm or deny this.' If the defender denied the claim, the pursuer would then say: 'As you deny, I give you notice to appear on the thirtieth day to take a judge.' As with the *sacramentum* procedure, but not the *postulatio*, there was then a delay of thirty days at the end of which, failing settlement by the parties, the proceedings before the judge would begin.

Nothing in the *condictio* prevented use of one of the other *legis actiones* as an alternative.[37]

(d) Litis Contestatio

Whichever of the *legis actiones* was used, once the formal exchange of words that is described above had happened, there occurred what is known as *litis contestatio*. This was the point of no return for the pursuer's claim: once matters had reached this stage, the cause of the pursuer's action was said to be 'consumed'. If the action was abandoned after this point, it would not be possible to bring another action on the same facts.

(e) Selection of Judge

All that then remained to be done was the selection of the judge. For this figure, both *iudex* and *arbiter* are used. It is not clear whether there is a distinction between these terms, though it may be that an *arbiter* sat in cases where the judge had a wider discretion to exercise.[38] The normal approach was for a single judge to sit, but there were exceptions: some cases fell within the jurisdiction of the *centumviri* or *decemviri*, or were judged by a panel of *recuperatores*.[39]

In principle, the parties could choose their own judge, whether by mutual agreement or by one party suggesting names until the other accepted one. If they could not agree, as would no doubt often be the case, the selection might be made by drawing lots. In later times, the selection would be from an official list (the *album iudicum*), compiled from men of the wealthier classes, although it seems that it was always possible for the parties themselves to agree a name that was not on the list. It is not clear exactly when the *album iudicum* was first introduced.[40]

(3) The Hearing before the Judge

As has been noted already, the hearing before the judge was much less formal than that before the praetor. There was no special place, such as a courtroom, for this hearing to take place, and it was often held in the open air. The Forum, in the centre of Rome, was often chosen.

---

[37] G.4.20.
[38] Buckland, *Textbook* 631.
[39] Buckland, *Textbook* 610–11.
[40] For an account of the process of selection, see P Birks, 'New Light on the Roman Legal System: The Appointment of Judges' (1988) 47 Cam LJ 36.

The parties normally had to appear personally, although a *procurator* could be appointed to act on a party's behalf in case of need, such as illness.[41] There were few formal rules of evidence. In principle, the burden of proof was seen as being on the pursuer, but in the absence of formal rules for relevance and admissibility of evidence, and with no system of appeals, it is hard to see how this could be relied upon.

(4) Enforcement of Judgments

A successful pursuer might be faced with a defender who was unwilling or unable to comply with the judge's decision. The next question to consider would be how the judgment could be enforced. Unlike the more normal situation in the modern world, though, there was no direct state involvement in the enforcement of judgments. Instead, if compliance could not be obtained by any other means, it was necessary for the pursuer to raise a further action on the judgment. There were two *legis actiones* for this, namely *manus iniectio* and *pignoris capio*.

(a) Manus Iniectio

Manus iniectio can be translated as 'laying on of hands', and was a procedure laid down by the Twelve Tables[42] for judgment debts.[43] After thirty days from the date of judgment,[44] the creditor once more brought the debtor before the praetor. The creditor would then speak in the following format, laying hold of the debtor at the same time: 'Whereas you have been adjudged liable [or condemned] to pay me 10,000 sesterces, as you have not paid, on that basis I lay my hand on you for the adjudged 10,000 sesterces.'[45] If the defender wished to dispute the validity of this procedure, for example by denying the existence of the debt, this could not be done personally. Instead, the defender had to find a third party, known as a *vindex*, to act instead.[46] If the defender failed to find a *vindex*, the defender was taken away and put in chains.[47] There then followed a period of sixty days' imprisonment, during which the parties could attempt to come to terms. If the parties did not come to terms during this period, the defender could be sold into slavery or (possibly) put to death.[48] This was altered by the *lex Poetelia*, legislation of 326 BC, by which the debtor could only be compelled to work off the debt, not sold into slavery or killed.

---

[41] Buckland, *Textbook* 701.
[42] Dated around 450 BC. See pp. 47–9.
[43] G.4.21.
[44] Twelve Tables, III.1.
[45] G.4.21.
[46] G.4.21.
[47] G.4.21.
[48] See G MacCormack, 'The "Lex Poetelia"' (1973) 19 Labeo 306, doubting that there was a right to put the debtor to death.

(b) Pignoris Capio
Pignoris capio means 'taking of pledge'. By this procedure, a creditor was allowed to seize property belonging to the debtor to hold as security until the debtor performed whatever obligation it was that the debtor owed.[49] It is not clear what happened if the debtor did not perform, as there is no evidence of the creditor being allowed to sell the property.[50] *Pignoris capio* was not available in all cases, though it is unfortunately not completely clear in what circumstances it was available.[51]

C. The Formulary Procedure

(1) The Emergence of the Formulary Procedure
We have seen that the *legis actiones* suffered from excessive formality, with the result that it was all too easy to lose a case through a minor procedural error, without regard to the justice of the claim. Another difficulty with the *legis actiones* was that they were only available to Roman citizens. As Roman power extended beyond Italy from the third century BC onwards, however, it would inevitably be the case that more and more disputes arising at Rome would involve foreigners. In recognition of this, as we saw in Chapter 1,[52] in 242 BC a new magistracy was created to exercise jurisdiction over legal disputes involving non-citizens. This was the peregrine praetorship. Not being bound by the *legis actiones* procedure, the peregrine praetor was free to develop a more flexible system, which is known as the formulary system or the formulary procedure. The formulary procedure was so called because it depended on the use of standardised written forms of pleadings, called *formulae*. This new approach came to be adopted by the urban praetor as well, for disputes between Roman citizens,[53] and by the end of the Republic the *legis actiones* were obsolete.[54] They were finally abolished under Augustus.[55]

(2) Initiating the Action
The summons operated in much the same way under the formulary procedure as it had under the *legis actiones*. It was still an oral summons, in which notice was given of what was being claimed. This last was essential, because it allowed the defender to decide whether to defend the claim or try to settle it, and to have time to prepare any defence that was to be made.[56] Submission to litigation remained

---

[49] G.4.26–9.
[50] Buckland, *Textbook* 620–1.
[51] Buckland, *Textbook* 619–20.
[52] See p. 14.
[53] This was formally recognised around 150 BC by the *lex Aebutia*, though it had probably already become established practice.
[54] This at least is the standard account. See though P Birks, 'From *Legis Actio* to *Formula*' (1969) 4 Irish Jurist (NS) 356.
[55] Subject to two exceptions mentioned by Gaius: G.4.31.
[56] D.2.13.1pr.

in principle voluntary, although it was still the case that the defender could be brought to court by force. It was unlikely that this was often resorted to, however, because the praetor could authorise the pursuer to seize the defender's property (*missio in possessionem*) if the latter failed to appear.[57]

The defender could agree to go immediately before the praetor, but there were alternative options. As under the *legis actiones*, the defender could provide a *vindex* to guarantee future appearance. Another course of action was to give a *vadimonium*. This term was already in use under the *legis actiones*, as a promise to reappear before the magistrate or judge after an adjournment. Under the formulary procedure, the same term was used for a promise to appear for proceedings to be initiated. This, it appears, was not so much a replacement for *in ius vocatio* as a promise to appear at a particular place and time so that *in ius vocatio* could be made.[58]

(3) The Preliminary Hearing

(a) *The* Formula

It no doubt often happened that a dispute was settled before or at this stage.[59] If this did not happen, the main function of the hearing before the praetor was to establish what the issues were that the judge was to determine. These would then be embodied in a *formula*, which was the written instruction to the judge to try the case. The starting point would normally[60] be one of the many draft *formulae* laid out in an edict issued by the urban praetor at the beginning of his year in office. The draft *formula* could then be adapted to take account of the particular issues arising in an individual case. There were many of these draft *formulae*, each concerned with different situations. The simplest came in three parts: *nominatio*, *intentio* and either *condemnatio* or *adiudicatio*. Every *formula* had to contain at least these three.

The first part of the *formula* was the *nominatio*. This was the appointment of the judge, in the form: 'Let Titius be judge.' The rest of the *formula* was then in the form of an instruction to the judge to try the case.

The *intentio* stated what was claimed by the pursuer.[61] In the examples we are given in the Roman texts, stock names are used: the pursuer is called Aulus Agerius and the defender Numerius Negidius. The first of these names is derived

---

[57] G.3.78.
[58] E Metzger, 'The Current View of the Extra-Judicial Vadimonium' (2000) 117 ZSS (rA) 133; D Cloud, 'Some Thoughts on Vadimonium' (2002) 119 ZSS (rA) 143. Compare W de Villiers, 'An Investigation into the Origins and Development of the Principles of Bail under South African Law (Part 1)' (2001) 34 De Jure 247, 254.
[59] D.12.2.1.
[60] Sometimes the praetor could be persuaded to allow an action for which there was no existing form. This was one of the ways in which the praetor was able to influence the development of the law. We will see more at p. 51 on this point, so it is not necessary to say any more about it just now. In the great majority of cases, the procedure would be as described in the text.
[61] G.4.41.

from the verb *agere*, to pursue an action, and the second from the verb *negare*, to deny. The *intentio* was in the following form: 'If it appears that Numerius Negidius ought to pay to Aulus Agerius 10,000 sesterces . . .'

The *condemnatio* came at the end, and authorised the judge either to condemn or absolve the defender.[62] In the draft *formula*, it would follow on from the *intentio*, as in the following: 'you, judge, condemn Numerius Negidius to pay Aulus Agerius 10,000 sesterces. If it does not so appear, absolve him.' Unlike the position under the *legis actiones*, condemnation under the formulary procedure was always for a sum of money. This was the case even where something other than a money debt was at issue: in such a case, the judge would condemn according to his valuation.[63] The amount stated could be a definite or an indefinite sum.[64] Where the sum sued for was indefinite, a limitation on the amount to be awarded (called a *taxatio*) could be included.[65]

A simple *formula*, then, with just *nominatio*, *intentio* and *condemnatio*, would look something like this:

> Let Titius be judge. If it appears that Numerius Negidius ought to pay to Aulus Agerius 10,000 sesterces, then you, judge, condemn Numerius Negidius to pay to Aulus Agerius 10,000 sesterces. If it does not so appear, absolve him.

Instead of a *condemnatio*, an *adiudicatio* could be used in two circumstances, namely where the judge is being asked to assign property to one or other party or where the action is purely declaratory.[66] An example of the first of those two circumstances would be an action raised by a co-owner of property for division of that property. An example of the second would be where there is a dispute over ownership of an item of property, and the judge is being asked simply to adjudicate on which of the parties is owner.

Other clauses were possible, though not found in every case.[67] Where the pursuer was seeking damages of an amount to be set according to the judge's discretion,[68] a *demonstratio* would be inserted before the *intentio* to outline the subject matter of the action.[69] An example would be: 'Whereas Aulus Agerius sold the slave to Numerius Negidius . . .'

If the defender wanted simply to deny the factual or legal basis of the pursuer's claim, nothing more was needed: the *formula* directed the judge to find in the pursuer's favour only if the judge found to be due what was claimed to be due.

---

[62] G.4.43.
[63] G.4.48.
[64] G.4.49.
[65] G.4.50.
[66] G.4.42.
[67] G.4.44.
[68] *I.e.* unliquidated damages. This is to be distinguished from liquidated damages, where the loss alleged to be suffered is in principle capable of being determined.
[69] G.4.40.

Sometimes, though, the defender would want to rely on some specific defence (*exceptio*), for example that the pursuer had agreed not to sue. Appropriate wording would be added to the *formula*, after the *intentio*, to reflect this. The pursuer might then respond to this with a *replicatio*, for example that the agreement not to sue had been induced by fraud. A *formula* with *exceptio* and *replicatio* might look like this:

> Let Titius be judge. If it appears that Numerius Negidius ought to pay to Aulus Agerius 10,000 sesterces, and there was no agreement between Aulus Agerius and Numerius Negidius that the sum should not be sued for, or that agreement was induced by fraud, then you, judge, condemn Numerius Negidius to pay to Aulus Agerius 10,000 sesterces. If it does not so appear, absolve him.

The finalised *formula* then laid out the legal issues that the judge was to determine.

Under the formulary procedure, there was for the first time the general ability to act through a representative (*procurator*). The name of the *procurator* would be inserted into the *formula* in place of that of the party he was representing. The *procurator* therefore became party to the action, in place of the principal. The principal could, however, enforce the judgment.

When the *formula* was finalised, including the appointment of the judge, the defender formally accepted the *formula*. At this point there was *litis contestatio* which, as with the *legis actiones*, consumed the cause of action.[70] It was not possible to bring a further action against the same defender on the same grounds. For this reason, although the formulary system was more flexible and less formal than the *legis actiones*, it was still necessary to be precise. A mistake in identifying what was owed would cost the pursuer the whole case.[71]

(b) Praetorian Remedies

Under the formulary system, a number of remedies were developed that could be awarded by the praetor. For example, among the most important of these were the possessory interdicts. These are considered in detail in Chapter 10[72] but, in brief, an interdict was an order by the praetor that something should be done or not done, and the possessory interdicts worked to regulate interim possession of property that was in dispute. A possessory interdict did not formally determine the question of ownership, but was highly advantageous to the party in whose favour the interdict was granted. Other examples of praetorian remedies include *restitutio in integrum* (an order for matters to be restored to their original state, for example in cases of fraud or coercion), *missio in possessionem* (an order authorising the taking of possession of another person's property) and praetorian stipulations (formal promises made by parties to proceedings).

---

[70] For this reason, if only part of what was owed was claimed, an additional clause called a *praescriptio* might be inserted. The *praescriptio* limited the claim, with the result that *litis contestatio* only affected what had actually been claimed.

[71] G.4.53–53d.

[72] See 187–9.

(4) The Hearing before the Judge
In general terms, the hearing before the judge was much the same under the formulary procedure as it had been with the *legis actiones*. It was still relatively unregulated, with few rules of evidence, and there was no system of appeals.

(5) Execution of Judgments
If the pursuer was successful before the judge, the defender would of course be obliged to comply with whatever the judge had ordered. As under the *legis actiones*, though, the pursuer had to wait thirty days before any action could be taken to enforce the judge's order. If the defender did not comply within those thirty days, the next step was to raise a further action to enforce the judgment, called an *actio iudicati*. The defender could oppose the *actio iudicati*, but had to provide security before doing so. The only defence in an *actio iudicati* was that the judgment was in some way invalid. The judgment could not be attacked on its merits. For example, it was no defence in an *actio iudicati* that the judge had misinterpreted the evidence or misapplied the law. If a defence was attempted in an *actio iudicati*, and it was unsuccessful, the defender was liable for double damages.

The procedure of *manus iniectio* was still available. However, other options also became available.

(a) Bonorum Venditio
Bonorum venditio can be translated as 'sale of [the debtor's] property', and is a procedure that was introduced by the praetor in the late Republic. It began with a *missio in possessionem*, by which the creditor was authorised by the praetor to seize possession of the debtor's property. There would then follow a period of thirty days, during which the matter was to be advertised.[73] This allowed other creditors to come forward and make their own claims. No doubt it was also often used by the debtor to scrape together the money needed for the sale to be called off, whether from friends or family or other sources.

The next step was for the creditors to meet and appoint one of their number to act as a manager (*magister bonorum*) to organise the sale,[74] usually by auction. The debtor's property would be sold to the highest bidder.[75] The debtor, though, remained liable for any unpaid part of the debts owed, and in addition incurred *infamia*.

This was an intentionally harsh procedure, and reflected the stigma of bankruptcy. There was an alternative procedure for high-status individuals, not involving *infamia*, by which the praetor would appoint a curator to sell off sufficient property to cover the debts.[76]

---

[73] G.3.79.
[74] G.3.79.
[75] Gaius tells us (G.3.80) that the purchaser would acquire only bonitary ownership, rather than full ownership. On bonitary ownership, see pp. 201–2.
[76] D.27.10.5.

(b) Cessio Bonorum

The final possibility, introduced under the emperor Augustus, was unusual in that it was sought by the debtor rather than the creditor. This was the *cessio bonorum*, a voluntary surrender of the defender's assets. This was only available where the debtor had genuine assets and had become bankrupt through misfortune. It allowed the debtor to avoid incurring *infamia* and to avoid the harsher procedures for debt enforcement that we have seen above.

There is therefore a distinction being made here between blameworthy bankrupts and blameless bankrupts. The same distinction was adopted in Scots law, along with the name *cessio bonorum*, although neither has survived into the current law.[77]

D. The *Cognitio* Procedure

(1) The Emergence of the *Cognitio* Procedure

As we have seen, under the *legis actiones* and formulary procedures, the magistrate's role was simply to oversee the initial stage of the litigation. Actual enquiry into the facts and the reaching of a decision would be done by another man, the judge, who was (at least in principle) agreed by the parties. Sometimes, though, beginning in the early Empire, the magistrate, or the emperor himself, would carry out an enquiry (*cognitio*) into the matter, with the whole case being decided on the authority of the magistrate or the emperor.[78] This procedure, because it was originally an exceptional procedure, is known as the *cognitio extraordinaria*. The name, though, is somewhat paradoxical, as the *cognitio* came in time to be the normal procedure: by the time that the formulary procedure was formally abolished in AD 342, the *cognitio* had long since replaced it as the normal procedure.

The changed approach had a number of consequences. The most obvious of these was that litigation was no longer divided into two stages, one before the praetor and one before the judge. Instead, the whole process was carried on under the authority of the magistrate. The parties could be compelled to submit to this process, and there was no longer even the theoretical idea of litigation as a private arbitration. The magistrate could appoint another person to act as judge, but in that case he was a delegate of the magistrate rather than a private individual appointed with the parties' agreement, and the appointment could only be objected to on specific legal grounds. On the other hand, the fact that the whole litigation was now carried on under the authority of the state opened the way, for the first time, to appeal against judges' decisions.

---

[77] D W McKenzie Skene, 'Morally Bankrupt? Apportioning Blame in Bankruptcy' (2004) JBL 171, 181. The *cessio bonorum* was abolished in Scotland by the Bankruptcy (Scotland) Act 1913.

[78] M Kaser, 'The Changing Face of Roman Jurisdiction' (1967) 2 Irish Jurist (NS) 129, 137–43; W Turpin, '*Formula, cognitio*, and Proceedings *extra ordinem*' (1999) 46 Revue Internationale des Droits de l'Antiquité (3rd series) 499. Indeed, we could trace the development back even further: every time the praetor intervened personally in a dispute, by granting a praetorian remedy, he was acting in a '*cognitio*-like' way.

(2) Initiating the Action

This change in approach, to a process entirely under the control of the state, affected the whole process of litigation, from the raising of the action onwards.[79]

The pursuer initiated proceedings by lodging a written statement of claim with the magistrate. A copy would then be served on the defender, who would be required to appear at a specified date not less than ten days later (increased to twenty days by Justinian).[80] The defender could be compelled to provide security for appearance. Unlike the previous situation, though, this undertaking was to the court rather than to the other party. An additional encouragement for the defender to appear lay in the fact that, even in the case of non-appearance, the court could proceed to decide the case anyway.[81] As we have seen, this possibility did not exist in the formulary procedure.

(3) The Trial

The trial would then proceed, with advocates representing the parties. The conduct of the trial was under the control of the presiding magistrate, or of a deputy appointed by him to hear the dispute. There developed in this period fairly extensive rules governing how the trial should be conducted, covering for example such matters as adjournments and the treatment of evidence. One important development related to the form of the remedy that could be offered. Under the formulary and *legis actio* procedures, condemnation was always for the defender to pay some specified sum of money. This was the case even where the action was to enforce a right in property: the defender would be ordered to hand over the value of the property rather than the property itself.[82] In the *cognitio* procedure, however, it became possible for the court to order specific implement of obligations, where that was an obligation to hand over something specific.[83]

(4) Execution of Judgments

If the pursuer was successful, the defender could be given time to comply with whatever the court had ordered.[84] If the defender did so comply, all was well and good. If not, what happened next depended on the nature of the defender's obligation. If the defender had been ordered to hand over some specific item of property, that property could be seized by court officers and delivered to the pursuer.[85] In the case of money debts, court officers could seize the defender's

---

[79] For an overview, see W de Villiers, 'An Investigation into the Origins and Development of the Principles of Bail under South African Law (Part 1)' (2001) 34 De Jure 247, 254–7.
[80] Nov.53.3 (AD 537).
[81] The defender had to be summoned three times without appearing, however, before this could be done: E Metzger, 'An Outline of Roman Civil Procedure' (2013) 9 Roman Legal Tradition 1, 28.
[82] The defender could, however, discharge this obligation by handing over the property.
[83] J.4.6.32; D.6.1.68; Zimmermann, *Obligations* 770–3.
[84] D.42.1.31. Justinian fixed the period at four months: C.7.54.2–3 (AD 529, 531).
[85] D.6.1.68.

goods for sale by auction,[86] or as an alternative the pursuer could simply accept these goods in satisfaction of the debt.[87] Any surplus on the sale was returned to the defender.[88]

(5) Appeals

For the first time, under the *cognitio* system, a system of appeals developed. A litigant might even appeal to the emperor, or a judge at a lower level might request a ruling by the emperor. As we shall see in Chapter 3,[89] this had considerable importance in legal development, as decisions by the emperor on particular points were relied on as authorities for subsequent cases.

> **Chapter Summary**
>
> Through Roman history, there were three different forms of procedure for litigation, beginning with the *legis actiones*, which were highly formal and rigid. During the second half of the Republic, this form of procedure was replaced with the more flexible formulary procedure. These two systems had in common a distinctive characteristic. In both, litigation was divided into two stages. In the first stage, the parties came before the praetor to settle what the legal question was that was to be determined. It was only in the second stage, before the judge, that evidence would be heard and the case decided. During the Empire, the formulary procedure was superseded by a single-stage procedure, the *cognitio*.

Further Reading

G.4
J.4.6–17
D.2; 3; 5.1; 11.1–2; 22.3–6; 42.1–2; 43.1; 44; 46.7; 47.23; 49.1–13
C.2.1–17; 3.1–27; 4.19–21; 7.43–75
J A Crook, *Legal Advocacy in the Roman World* (Duckworth 1995)
A H J Greenidge, *The Legal Procedure of Cicero's Time* (Clarendon Press 1901)
J Harries, *Cicero and the Jurists: From Citizens' Law to the Lawful State* (Duckworth 2006)
M Kaser, 'The Changing Face of Roman Jurisdiction' (1967) 2 Irish Jurist (NS) 129
J M Kelly, *Roman Litigation* (Oxford University Press 1966)

---

[86] D.42.1.31; D.42.1.15.2.
[87] D.42.1.15.3.
[88] D.42.1.31.
[89] See 53–4.

D Liebs, 'The History of the Roman *Condictio* up to Justinian' in N MacCormick and P Birks eds, *The Legal Mind: Essays for Tony Honoré* (Oxford University Press 1986)

E Metzger ed, *A Companion to Justinian's Institutes* (Duckworth 1998) chapter 6

E Metzger, *Litigation in Roman Law* (Oxford 2005)

E Metzger, 'An Outline of Roman Civil Procedure' (2013) 9 Roman Legal Tradition 1

J Powell and J Paterson eds, *Cicero the Advocate* (Oxford University Press 2004)

W Turpin, '*Formula*, *cognitio*, and Proceedings *extra ordinem*' (1999) 46 Revue Internationale des Droits de l'Antiquité (3rd series) 499

CHAPTER THREE

Development of Roman Law

A. Introduction

In the first two chapters, we have seen the context in which the law operated and developed. In Chapter 1, we saw the roles and powers of the various institutions and office-holders that formed part of the Roman constitution. In Chapter 2, we saw the procedures by which legal rights and remedies were declared and enforced. In this chapter, we consider where that law came from and how it developed over the centuries.

We begin with the earliest period of Roman law (part B), before looking at how it developed through the Republic and Empire. Next we look at the state's role in creating law, through legislation of the citizen assemblies[1] (part C) and the actions of magistrates (part D), and finally how this changed in the Empire (part E). In part F, we consider the work of the jurists, legal writers whose ideas were a major source of legal development. Finally, we look at the post-classical period (part G), culminating in the work of the emperor Justinian (part H), to which we owe almost all of our knowledge of Roman law. In the next chapter, we will see how that work came to influence later law.

We are concerned here and in the rest of the book almost entirely with private law[2] rather than public law.[3] The reason for this is straightforward. The jurists had, broadly speaking, much greater interest in private law than in public law. As their writings form the bulk of the Roman law that has come down to us, it is in private law that Roman law has primarily influenced later law.

B. Early Roman Law

(1) General Nature of Early Roman Law

Unless it has a comprehensive legal code imposed on it from the beginning,[4] the first law of a community is simply the customary rules of that community,

---

[1] See p. 13.
[2] The law governing relations between individuals.
[3] The law governing relations between individuals and the state.
[4] This is not particularly common, although it is not uncommon for communities to preserve a myth of some founding lawgiver.

interpreted and enforced by those recognised by the community as having the authority to do so.

Early Roman law was no exception. It was rigid and formal, dominated by the need to comply with strict procedural forms, and was strongly status-based. As we shall see in Chapter 7, a person's rights and obligations depended to a large degree on his or her family relationships. This was carried to the extent that a person whose father or paternal grandfather was still alive could not normally own property and had limited personal liberty. Even where a person could hold rights, the creation and transfer of those rights was subject to onerous and formal procedures. For centuries, the main form of contract involved a formal question and answer, using specific, required words, and failure to comply would render the contract void. Compliance with form was all, and the law did not look behind the formalities to see whether there was genuine agreement.[5] Similarly, the transfer of ownership of the most important kinds of property required the performance of ceremonial acts in front of witnesses. The validity of the transfer was judged according to whether there had been strict compliance with the requirements of that ceremony of transfer rather than whether there had been genuine consent to the transfer.[6]

(2) The *Leges Regiae*

Later Roman historians attributed extensive legal reforms to the kings enacting *leges regiae* ('royal laws'), although there is debate as to how much of this is genuine.[7] It is not even certain how much later historians' accounts correctly represent Roman law during the Monarchy.[8] It is, of course, perfectly possible that the rules attributed to a particular king could have been genuine law without in fact having been introduced by that king.

(3) The Twelve Tables

We begin to get a bit more of a glimpse of Roman law once we move into the early Republic, in the form of the Twelve Tables[9] (or, at least, those fragments of it that come down to us), an early legal code traditionally dated to the mid-fifth century BC.

The story of the Twelve Tables is part of the longer story of the Struggle of the Orders, which we saw in Chapter 1.[10] It will be remembered that early Roman

---

[5] See p. 339.
[6] See p. 200. The intention here is not to decry early Romans for irrationality. There is merit in including formalities in the transfer of property, and particularly of land. The need to comply with the formalities removes any possibility of doubt as to the parties' intentions, and the presence of witnesses reduces the difficulties of proof if there is a dispute later. Similar requirements have been common in many countries. For Scots law, see K G C Reid ed, *The Law of Property in Scotland* (Law Society of Scotland 1996) para 89. Biblical examples may be found in Jeremiah 32:9–16 and Ruth 4:7.
[7] A Watson, 'Roman Private Law and the "*Leges Regiae*"' (1972) 62 JRS 100.
[8] As we saw at p. 6, the Monarchy, during which Rome was ruled by a series of kings, is traditionally dated to the period 753–509 BC. The Monarchy was then replaced by a republican form of government.
[9] This is sometimes written as 'XII Tables', XII being twelve in Roman numerals.
[10] See pp. 11–12.

society was divided into two parts: the patricians, who were politically dominant despite being a small minority, and the majority plebeians, who were excluded from political power. One of the plebeians' demands was for the publication of the law, knowledge of which was monopolised by patricians. In response to this, a commission of ten men was appointed to put together a codification of the law, taking inspiration from Greek codifications, which was published in 451 BC in ten 'tables' or tablets, to be displayed in the Forum in Rome for all to see. These were joined by a further two tables in the following year, to bring the total to twelve. Later Romans saw the Twelve Tables as the foundation of their law, and the first century BC orator and politician Cicero speaks of schoolboys being required to learn it by heart.[11]

It is difficult to speak with any certainty about the contents of the Twelve Tables.[12] None of it has survived directly, in its original form, so our whole knowledge is derived from fragments preserved in the writings of later authors. Of the actual words of the original, we have 'appallingly little, mostly in the form of a mutilated phrase or of some words'.[13] We also cannot be sure of exactly how the subject matter was distributed among the Twelve Tables. Within these limitations, however, the Twelve Tables can be reconstructed to some extent.[14] Tables I–III, for example, seem to have been mostly concerned with the conduct of litigation. Table IV contained various rules concerning paternal authority, and Table V was concerned with guardianship and succession. From Tables VI and VII it is clear that the regulation of property boundaries was a significant concern. Table VIII covered various wrongs, including the casting of spells and wrongful grazing. Particularly striking to modern eyes is Table X, which contained quite detailed rules on mourning and the conduct of funerals.[15]

From this, it is clear that the Twelve Tables were not a law code in the modern sense of the term. In the modern world, a law code is a comprehensive, systematic account of the whole of the law or of a part of it. The Twelve Tables did not have that character. Instead, they contained 'a series of specific solutions to narrow sets of circumstances; lacking are abstract norms, general principles or definitions'.[16] For example, one of these 'specific solutions to narrow sets of circumstances' is found in Table X.8, which prohibits the adding of gold to a funeral pyre; however, it is provided that there is no breach of this prohibition if the deceased happens to have gold fillings in his teeth. Again, Table V.6 lays down a rule for who is entitled to be appointed as a person's guardian, but tells us

---

[11] Cicero, *De Legibus* 2.59.
[12] For discussion of the law of the period, see A Watson, *Rome of the XII Tables: Persons and Property* (Princeton University Press 1975).
[13] B Sirks, 'The Edition of the Twelve Tables in *Roman Statutes*' (2017) 85 TvR 65.
[14] A reconstruction, with commentary, can be found in M H Crawford ed, *Roman Statutes* (Institute of Classical Studies 1996) 555–721. For criticism of certain departures from the traditional ordering, see B Sirks, 'The Edition of the Twelve Tables in *Roman Statutes*' (2017) 85 TvR 65.
[15] This included, in Table X.1, the important prohibition on burials and cremations within the city. As a result of this prohibition, the roads around Rome were crowded with tombs.
[16] R Westbrook, 'The Nature and Origins of the Twelve Tables' (1988) 105 ZSS (rA) 74, 75.

nothing about the guardian's role or powers. The Twelve Tables were therefore not a complete statement of the law, and much was left unsaid. Equally, although the Twelve Tables contained various provisions about the conduct of litigation, they did not detail the *legis actiones*, the forms of actions detailed in Chapter 2,[17] without which it was not possible even to begin the litigation. A co-existing customary law, continuing in force, is assumed. This, indeed, is only to be expected at this period. In early law, statutes tended to be seen as declaratory of the existing law, rather than being intended to change the law. In this they are similar to modern court decisions: even though a decision of the court may, in substance, change the law, the theory is maintained that the court is simply declaring what the law already was.[18] In reality, the Twelve Tables have the appearance less of a major reforming statute than of a collection of decisions on individual points of law, together with elaborations on them.[19]

Certainly, the Twelve Tables did not have enough information to allow the plebeians to do without expert legal assistance:

> The law was bound to be revealed to them by the precedents that they themselves experienced; only its subtleties could be hidden from them, and these would rely on a level of sophistication or a mass of detailed exceptions of which there is no trace in the published text. The most ignorant plebeian could hardly have been unaware that it was forbidden to bury or burn bodies in the city, if that rule had been enforced but once. And by the same token, if there were subtleties concealed from the plebeians, then the provisions of the extant text are singularly inapt for removing them.[20]

There is then, to say the least, reason to doubt the story that the Twelve Tables were intended to benefit the plebeians, and the specific provisions of the Twelve Tables do little to contradict this. The only direct mention of the plebeians and the patricians was a prohibition on inter-marriage between members of the two Orders[21] (later repealed), and there is little or no sign elsewhere of any provisions clearly intended to favour the plebeians.

C. Legislation as a Source of Law

(1) Republican Legislation

(a) Leges

In Chapter 1,[22] we met the Romans' citizen assemblies. In these there met the adult, male citizens of Rome. These assemblies had various functions, such as the election of magistrates. Another of their functions was the passing of laws known

---

[17] See pp. 32–7.
[18] Stein, *Regulae Iuris* 9–25.
[19] See R Westbrook, 'The Nature and Origins of the Twelve Tables' (1988) 105 ZSS (rA) 74, linking the Twelve Tables to Middle Eastern codes with just this purpose.
[20] R Westbrook, 'The Nature and Origins of the Twelve Tables' (1988) 105 ZSS (rA) 74, 77.
[21] Table XI.1.
[22] See p. 13.

as *leges* (singular *lex*). The citizen assemblies had a relatively minor role in the development of private law, however. In most of the areas covered in this book, few reforms were introduced in this way, though there are exceptions. In any case, the impression of popular involvement in law-making, through the assemblies, is somewhat misleading. As we saw in Chapter 1,[23] the assemblies could only meet when summoned by the presiding magistrate and could only vote to accept or reject the proposal put in front of them. They could not, for example, make or amend legislative proposals.

(b) Plebiscita
Plebiscita (singular *plebiscitum*) were legislation of the plebeian assembly, the *concilium plebis*.[24] Originally, they were binding only on plebeians.[25] However, after approximately 287 BC, they became generally binding, and in fact they became the normal means of legislating. As with legislation of the other assemblies, however, *plebiscita* affecting private law were rare.

(c) Senatusconsulta
Senatusconsulta (singular *senatusconsulta*) were resolutions of the Senate. Strictly speaking, they were not a form of legislation in the Republic, as they had no directly binding force. In practice, however, legislative proposals often originated in the Senate. Equally, the political dominance of the Senate was such that a magistrate intending to put a legislative proposal before one of the assemblies would normally be expected to seek the Senate's approval first. The Senate's authority was thus mostly political rather than legal. It did, though, have the right to declare laws invalid or to suspend their operation.

D. The *Ius Honorarium* (Praetorian Law)

We saw in Chapter 2[26] that, in the later Republic and into the Empire, litigation was governed by a system known as the formulary procedure. This system of procedure, as did the earlier *legis actiones*, had the distinctive feature of dividing the trial into two stages. The first stage fell under the jurisdiction of an official called the urban praetor, commonly referred to simply as the praetor. At this stage, the legal question to be answered would be identified and the judge appointed. Proceedings would then move on to the second stage, at which the judge appointed at the first stage would consider the evidence and the parties' arguments, before deciding between them. In this chapter it is the first stage, which took place before the praetor, that is of interest to us.

As we saw in Chapter 1,[27] the urban praetor was the magistrate who was responsible for the administration of civil justice. If the praetor had simply been

---

[23] See p. 8.
[24] See pp. 11–12.
[25] Or, to put it another way, patricians were exempted from their operation.
[26] See pp. 37–42.
[27] See pp. 11, 14.

an administrator in the manner this suggests, however, he would have been of less interest to us than he is. In fact, however, the praetor's activities were a source of legal development in themselves. As the jurist Papinian explains: 'Praetorian law is that which the praetors have introduced, for the public benefit, to aid, supplement or correct the civil law.'[28]

The main vehicle for the development of the *ius honorarium* was the edict which, as a magistrate, the praetor issued on taking office at the start of the year. An edict was a statement of how the magistrate intended to execute his functions, and in the case of the praetor the edict detailed all of the grounds on which he would allow an action to proceed. A person wishing to pursue an action would be expected to select one of the forms of action provided for by the edict. Only exceptionally would a litigant be permitted to seek a remedy not previously provided for, by means of an *actio utilis*[29] or *actio in factum*.[30] Precisely what the distinction was between these terms is unclear (the Roman texts are not entirely consistent), but with both of them the idea is that the situation calls for a remedy which is not provided for by existing law.

In principle, the edict issued by each praetor was valid only for his term of office.[31] In practice, though, the edict would largely be carried forward from one year to the next. Changes were made, however, and by the end of the Republic the praetor's edict had been used as the vehicle for quite substantial reform of the law. This was, though, undoubtedly the product of a lengthy period of development.[32] It is, to say the least, unlikely that the praetor's powers to reform the law sprang forth fully formed. In reality, praetorian innovation would not have initially involved major law reform. It is rare that we can be certain of the date of a particular reform, but the likely progress of the praetor's law-making can be sketched out. As the magistrate responsible for the administration of the judicial process, though, the praetor would have felt himself empowered from an early period to introduce measures designed to promote the efficiency and effectiveness of the process. Of this kind are measures penalising defenders who fail to appear when summoned.[33] Such reforms are broadly unobjectionable, as they do not interfere with parties' substantive rights. Indeed, they assist parties in enforcing those rights.

Similar in nature are those reforms 'which do not *merely* shore up a weak procedural norm, but go a little further'.[34] Reforms of this kind involve the praetor intervening more actively in how rights are enforced. Probably the most important reform of this kind is the introduction of the possessory interdicts. We shall see these in detail in Chapter 10[35] but, in broad terms, they allowed the praetor

---

[28] D.1.1.7.1. See him also at D.19.5.11.
[29] This is sometimes translated as 'policy action'.
[30] This may be translated as 'action on the facts' or 'action on the case'.
[31] This is used as an analogy when considering time limits in litigation in *Brogan v O'Rourke Ltd* 2005 SCLR 337, para [10].
[32] J M Kelly, 'The Growth-Pattern of the Praetor's Edict' (1966) 1 Irish Jurist (NS) 349; Watson, *Law Making* 31–62.
[33] See p. 38.
[34] J M Kelly, 'The Growth-Pattern of the Praetor's Edict' (1966) 1 Irish Jurist (NS) 349, 349–50.
[35] See pp. 187–9.

to regulate the interim possession of property that was in dispute. The ultimate question of ownership of the property was in principle unaffected – this was a procedural measure, only regulating possession until ownership was determined – but it gave the party awarded interim possession an enormous advantage.

From the last decades of the second century BC onwards, until the end of the Republic, the praetor seems to have largely superseded the assemblies as a source of new private law. The natural next step would have been to allow defences in favour of those sued using a claim that was valid under the civil law, but which the praetor considered to be improper. An example might be the praetor refusing to allow enforcement of a contract that the defender had been induced to enter into by the pursuer's fraud. In fact, though, in the first century BC, the praetor was going further than this, and granting new rights of enforcement. By the end of the Republic, there was hardly an area of private law that had not been touched by praetorian intervention. We see the praetor, then, progressing step by step towards being in substance a lawmaker.

E. Law-Making in the Empire

(1) Legislation in the Empire

(a) The Continuing Role of the Assemblies

As we saw in Chapter 1,[36] when Augustus, the first emperor, established his authority as leading man in the Roman state, he was keen for political reasons to emphasise continuity rather than change. His position depended on him being seen as the restorer and protector of the Republic. Accordingly, he worked so far as possible through existing, Republican institutions. During his reign, significant use was made of the assemblies in law-making. This was largely for show, though, and the use of the assemblies faded as the new political realities of the Empire became more firmly established. The last significant *lex* on a matter of private law was probably around AD 28.

(b) The *Ius Honorarium*

In a very similar way, and for much the same reasons, the importance of the praetor as a source of legal development also declined in the Empire. There were simply more straightforward ways for emperors to change the law, and no emperor would be likely to tolerate a praetor who presumed to act too independently in introducing his own innovations. In any case, as with other magistracies, appointment as praetor came to be seen as more of a mark of imperial favour than anything else. Acting on the instructions of the emperor Hadrian, in around AD 135, the jurist Julian compiled the *Edictum Perpetuum* ('Perpetual Edict'), which came to be seen as the final version of the praetor's edict. The praetor continued to issue the edict each year, but its role as a vehicle for significant legal innovation was by now long past.[37]

---

[36] See pp. 18–20.
[37] For different views on the nature and significance of the *Edictum Perpetuum*, see K Tuori, 'Hadrian's Perpetual Edict: Ancient Sources and Modern Ideals in the Making of a Historical Tradition' (2006) 27 J Leg Hist 219.

(c) Senatusconsulta

The position of the Senate makes an interesting contrast with the other Republican institutions. As we have seen, the Senate had during the Republic no formal authority over the legislative process. Such authority as it exercised was political in nature rather than legal. During the early Empire, however, it benefited from close association with the emperor. The Senate came to be seen as the primary legislative body, initially through instructions to magistrates that were to be incorporated into their edicts. It was probably around AD 130, under Hadrian, that a *senatusconsultum* was first directly effective. In any case, the Senate's role was rarely more than nominal, and by the end of the second century AD there was not even the pretence.

(d) Imperial Legislation

The political reality of the Empire was that the emperor was the sole source of authority, and in time practice came to reflect that underlying reality. For most of the Empire, the sole source of new law was pronouncements of the emperor, called *constitutiones* (singular *constitutio*). The doctrine was: that which has pleased the emperor has the force of law.[38] This must have been a gradual process, for all that Gaius, writing in the second century AD, tells us that the position had 'never been doubted'.[39] Certainly, before the end of the classical period it was well accepted that an imperial pronouncement made binding law. The only exception was where the pronouncement was intended to relate to a specific situation without creating a precedent, for example where the emperor wanted to apply exceptional indulgence or punishment to an individual.[40]

The scope of imperial pronouncements went beyond what we would consider to be legislation. In the modern world, we make a distinction between interpretation of the law and law-making. The former is the province of the courts, the latter of the legislator. This distinction does not apply to Roman emperors. A pronouncement of the emperor decided the law, even though it might be expressed as simply interpreting the law. Most pronouncements were responses to specific legal questions. The extent of the emperor's personal involvement varied – some were bound to be more interested than others – but typically emperors relied on expert legal advisers to formulate such responses.

Imperial pronouncements came in various forms. For example, as a magistrate, the emperor could issue edicts (though, unlike other magistrates' edicts, those of the emperor were unlimited in their potential scope). The emperor could also issue *mandata*, instructions to officials on how they should discharge their duties. His judicial decisions, called *decreta*, were an important source of law: while in form they were simply addressed to the parties, the fact that they had come from the emperor gave them special authority. Records were kept of

---

[38] D.1.4.1pr (Ulpian): *Quod principi placuit, legis habet vigorem*. This is said by Ulpian to be because the people have conferred on the emperor 'their whole authority'.
[39] G.1.5.
[40] D.1.4.2. The modern distinction between Public and Private Acts of Parliament is analogous.

the emperors' *decreta*, and they came to be seen as binding precedents. Finally, *rescripta* were answers to questions or petitions, either from officials (dealt with by the office *ab epistulis*) or private citizens (dealt with by the office *a libellis*). These offices were staffed by legal experts, and so were an important vehicle for the interpretation and development of the law.

F. The Jurists

(1) The Emergence of the Jurists

We have seen that early Roman law was rigid and formal, dominated by the need to comply with strict procedural forms. That began to change in the late Republic. The details of how this came to happen are unclear,[41] but from around the beginning of the first century BC, Roman law began to develop into something it had never been before, either at Rome or anywhere else: a science, meaning a body of knowledge based on reason. This did not happen overnight, and it was itself a development of earlier trends, but from about 100 BC to approximately AD 250, there developed a body of literature exploring and expounding Roman law as a body of principled rules. This is the period that we call the 'classical period' of Roman law, and the literature of that period was the work of a group of men we call the jurists.

To understand how this happened, we have to start at an earlier stage. In any community that is to have a system of law worthy of the name, where the exercise of authority is based on legal rules rather than on arbitrary decisions, the need will soon arise to have individuals develop expertise in understanding and advising on those rules. So, in the Roman system, who were the legal experts? To whom could one go for legal advice? On whose opinions were the decisions of judges and magistrates based? After all, as we saw in Chapter 2,[42] neither the judges nor the advocates pleading before them were seen as requiring any legal expertise of their own.[43] Equally, there was no requirement for the praetor to be knowledgeable in the law. He was a politician rather than a lawyer. Yet the Romans developed a sophisticated system of law, and this can hardly have happened without the existence of a class of people specialising in knowledge of that law.

In early times, this function was fulfilled by the priests. As we saw in Chapter 1,[44] in those days it was hardly possible to make a distinction between secular and religious affairs. Good governance meant keeping the peace with the divine forces controlling the world as much as it meant keeping the people safe from military threats. These priests were not full-time clergy, but men of the upper class, who might hold a priestly office alongside what we would consider to be more straightforwardly political roles. Pomponius tells us that one of these, a member

---

[41] K Tuori, 'The Myth of Quintus Mucius Scaevola: Founding Father of Legal Science?' (2004) 72 TvR 243.
[42] See p. 31.
[43] Although, as we saw at p. 31, it is possible to over-emphasise this lack of knowledge.
[44] See p. 8.

of the college of pontiffs, was appointed each year to take responsibility for private law matters.[45] As we saw earlier, the Twelve Tables was far from a complete statement of the law, so those who monopolised knowledge of the rest of the law had significant power. This monopoly was only broken when Appius Claudius[46] recorded the required forms[47] in writing, and his clerk, Gnaeus Flavius, copied them and made them available to the public.[48] Gnaeus Flavius was made aedile in 304 BC, in which capacity he published in the Forum a copy of the calendar that showed on which days an action could be brought.[49] Subsequently, Tiberius Coruncanius[50] was the first to make a 'public profession' of the law.[51] Quite what this means is not completely clear, but if we accept Pomponius' account then it suggests that there was a process going on by which awareness of the law and the ability to advise on it were becoming more widely distributed. It is from this process that the class of men we call jurists emerged.

The term 'jurist' should not be seen as synonymous with 'lawyer'. The classical period only lasted around 350 years, and during this period we know the names of under 100 jurists. This number cannot possibly have satisfied the demand for legal advice even in the city of Rome itself, a major commercial centre with more than a million inhabitants, so common sense alone should be enough to tell us that there must have been other people giving legal advice. However, as we have seen, we do in fact directly know this to be the case.[52]

Exactly how then we distinguish the jurists from these other lawyers is difficult. However, it is clear from the jurists' writings that they constantly cited one another, so we can suggest that it was a self-identified group, membership of which depended on recognition by other jurists. They were a group of mostly upper-class men, many of whom also held senior positions in government. For most of them, being a jurist was more of a hobby than a profession. Their influence came through their *interpretatio*. As is fairly obvious from its form, this word means 'interpretation', but the jurists' *interpretatio* was a broader, more active enterprise than we would nowadays expect or consider appropriate. It was:

> the use of the words of a statute as a peg upon which to hang the novel legal doctrine which was being framed. It was not, as one might think, statutory construction to determine the presumed intention of a legislator; it was rather a device by which living legal principles could be worked into the corpus of the Roman law.[53]

---

[45] D.1.2.2.6.
[46] Censor in 312 BC.
[47] The *legis actiones*, on which see pp. 32–7.
[48] D.1.2.2.7. This document was known as the *ius civile Flavianum* (Flavian civil law) after him.
[49] Jolowicz and Nicholas, *Historical Introduction* 91.
[50] Died 241 BC; first plebeian *pontifex maximus* around 253 BC.
[51] D.1.2.2.35.
[52] See pp. 30–1.
[53] A A Schiller, 'Jurists' Law' (1958) 58 Colum L Rev 1226, 1227.

It is true that, at least at first, this was not seen as a formal source of law. However, if their views were habitually acted on by judges, and came to be accepted as correctly representing the law, we may suggest that the question of whether juristic *interpretatio* was a formal source of law makes little practical difference.

(2) Schools of Jurists

In the reign of Augustus, says Pomponius,[54] the leading jurists were Ateius Capito and Antistius Labeo. They were the founders of two competing juristic traditions.[55] Pomponius calls them *sectae*, 'sects', but they are more commonly referred to as schools. Each attracted adherents and a tradition of school loyalty through generations of jurists. The schools are named, not after their founders, but by prominent successors. Members of Capito's school are known as Sabinians after his successor, Massurius Sabinus. Members of Labeo's school are known as Proculians, after a later head, Proculus. While jurists did pay attention to views expressed by those of the other school, there does appear to have been some tendency for a jurist to prefer to cite members of his own school.[56] Some differences of approach can be identified. According to Pomponius' account, Capito tended to follow the traditional view of the law, while Labeo was more prepared to innovate. There is some tendency for Proculians to base their views on general principles, with Sabinians more willing to take individual circumstances into account. We shall see many disputes between Sabinians and Proculians as we go through the book.[57]

The nature of these schools is unclear. Were they simply schools of thought, with views being passed down through successive generations of jurists, kept going through loyalty? Alternatively, were they more formal educational institutions? Various ideas have been put forward,[58] though the fact that Pomponius identifies successive heads of the schools suggests some level of formal organisation. Whatever may have been their nature, though, it is beyond doubt that the existence of these schools was a major influence on the law's development in the first and second centuries AD.

(3) The *Ius Respondendi*

In the first book of the *Digest*, the jurist Pomponius gives us an account of Roman legal history. In the course of this, Pomponius tells us that Sabinus was the 'first to give legal opinions publicly',[59] having been granted this right by the emperor Tiberius.[60] This right is known as the *ius respondendi* (the right of giving

---

[54] D.2.2.47.
[55] They seem to have differed in politics as well. Capito was made consul by Augustus, but Labeo refused this, instead devoting himself to teaching and writing. Pomponius tells us that Labeo divided the year into two, spending six months in Rome with his pupils, and six months in the country writing.
[56] P A Viton, 'On the Affiliations of the Severan Jurists' (1980) 46 SDHI 507.
[57] For examples, see pp. 198, 232, 308n, 355 and 373.
[58] See e.g J W Tellegen, 'Gaius Cassius and the Schola Cassiana in Pliny's Letter VII 24,8' (1988) 105 ZSS (rA) 263; G C J J van den Bergh, 'Seeing Roman Law as History?' (1989) 106 ZSS (rA) 573.
[59] D.1.2.2.48 (*publice primus respondit*). An alternative translation of *publice* might be 'under state authority'.
[60] Reigned AD 14–37.

legal opinions). One of the puzzles about this is that Pomponius goes on to say that this right began to be granted by Tiberius' predecessor, Augustus,[61] so it is not clear how Sabinus can have be the first. The biggest puzzle, however, is what the *ius respondendi* actually entailed. Indeed, it has been suggested that the *ius respondendi* did not actually exist.[62] If it did exist, one possibility is that only those who had it were permitted to issue legal opinions at all. This, though, seems implausible, unless the *ius respondendi* was given to a huge number of people. As we have seen, the jurists alone could not have serviced Rome's need for legal advice. Alternatively, perhaps the *ius respondendi* gave its holder the right to give binding opinions, which judges had to follow. Certainly, the jurist Gaius indicates that Hadrian[63] declared in a rescript that, where multiple holders of the *ius respondendi* were unanimous, their opinion had the force of statute. Only where they differed could the judge pick the opinion he thought best.[64] Earlier in the Empire, though, it seems unlikely that this was the case. As we saw in Chapter 1,[65] Augustus' policy as first emperor was to appear to be preserving and restoring the Republic, and the grant of unprecedented new powers of this kind would not be in keeping with that. Perhaps the most likely explanation is that the grant of the *ius respondendi* was a mark of imperial favour and an indicator of eminence and respect, which did not formally bind judges, but which would undoubtedly add a certain weight to the opinion. A comparable modern example might be an advocate or, in England, a barrister becoming a QC.

(4) The Jurists' Roles

(a) Teaching

Jurists certainly taught. It appears that, perhaps especially in the Republic, an aspiring jurist's education was based on observation rather than formal classes. Cicero tells us of his own early legal education:

> Now, I, upon assuming the *toga virilis*, had been introduced by my father to [Quintus Mucius] Scaevola [the augur] with the understanding that, so far as I could and he would permit, I should never leave the old man's side. And so it came to pass that, in my desire to gain greater profit from his legal skill, I made it a practice to commit to memory many of his learned opinions and many, too, of his brief and pointed sayings.[66]

---

[61] D.1.2.2.49. Augustus reigned from 27 BC to AD 14.
[62] See O F Robinson, 'Lawyers and Jurists' (2013) 41 GaJICL 711, 718, suggesting that, if Sabinus was granted some special status by Tiberius, it was 'more likely in connection with his work as head of one of the Schools'.
[63] Reigned AD 117–38.
[64] G.1.7. For discussion, see F de Zulueta, 'Reflections on Gaius 1.7' (1947–8) 22 Tulane LR 173.
[65] See pp. 18–20.
[66] Cicero, *De Amicitia* 1.1 (W A Falconer trans), in Cicero, *De Senectute, De Amicitia, De Divinatione* (Heinemann 1965). The *toga virilis* was the toga worn by adult men. Cicero probably assumed this in 90 BC, when he was 16. Scaevola the augur died in 88 BC.

Thus, the student would learn by observing the jurist at work and, no doubt, through discussion of cases with the jurist. Of more formal teaching, we hear little. If it is the case that the juristic schools were educational establishments, there was presumably some form of more structured teaching, but beyond that it is impossible to say with any degree of certainty what form it took.

(b) Advice

Jurists undertook the full range of legal advice work, including assisting with legal transactions (which might include the drafting of legal documents),[67] assisting with the conduct of litigation,[68] and advising on legal problems. This did not simply mean advising private parties, but might also include advising judges and magistrates. Many of the reforms embodied in the praetor's edict will have come from jurists.

(c) Writing

It is, however, to their writing that we owe our knowledge of the jurists' work. Some of the jurists were highly prolific. They wrote a range of types of literature, including commentaries on the praetor's edict and the *ius civile*, monographs on particular topics, student texts, practitioner texts, and epitomes of other jurists on which they provided their own comments. One striking characteristic of juristic literature is its casuistic approach, which means an approach focused on the discussion of specific cases rather than on general principles. There were exceptions to this, most notably Gaius, about whom we are about to hear, but by and large the jurists showed little interest in abstract theorising.[69] Of course, as we have seen, this is characteristic of the way that jurists learned the law in the first place: through observation and discussion of individual cases.

Of the different types of legal literature that we are used to in the modern world, however, one that was not prominent in Roman juristic literature was law reporting, that is the production of collections of court decisions.[70] This was understandable enough under the formulary system of procedure,[71] in which the judges were private citizens rather than legally trained professionals, and in which the judge did not have to give reasons for his decision. However, this continued even under the *cognitio* procedure,[72] in which written decisions became the norm, and appeals to the emperor were possible. Of course, advice given to a

---

[67] This kind of work is sometimes called cautelary jurisprudence.
[68] Although, as we have seen, they did not normally actually appear in court to plead the case.
[69] This is true both at the level of the whole book and at the level of the individual case. It has been mentioned that jurists wrote commentaries (separately) on both the *ius civile* and the *ius honorarium*. As the latter amended and supplemented the former, it makes no sense to consider them separately if one is interested in presenting a coherent picture of the law.
[70] W J Zwalve, 'Decreta Frontiana: Some Observations on D.29.2.99 and the "Law Reports" of Titius Aristo' (2015) 83 TvR 365.
[71] See pp. 37–42.
[72] See pp. 42–4.

judge, magistrate or litigant might find its way into a jurist's own writings, but then the authority of the jurist's opinion would come from the standing of the jurist rather than that of the recipient of the advice.

(5) Gaius and the Institutional Scheme

There is one other Roman writer who deserves special attention here, because he is something of an enigma. Little is known about him except that he lived during the second century AD (perhaps from approximately 110 to 180) and was a teacher of law. It is unlikely that the jurists of his time would have considered him to be one of them. In all of the preserved juristic writings, there is only one apparent reference to him by another jurist.[73] This is particularly striking given that the jurists cited each other constantly.

Gaius' special contribution to Roman law came through a book called the *Institutes*. To set the context for this, we need to remind ourselves of how Roman litigation worked. As we saw in Chapter 2,[74] the development of classical Roman law was strongly linked to the litigation system known as the formulary procedure. According to this system, before a case could be put before the judge, it first had to be brought before the praetor, where it would be expressed in terms of one of a number of set *formulae*. The permitted *formulae* were contained in the edict issued by the urban praetor at the start of his term of office.[75] We have seen in this chapter how this could be used by the praetor to introduce innovations in the law. A common form of juristic literature was the commentary on the edict, in which the jurist would take each form of action in turn, expounding its requirements and the meaning of individual terms within the relevant *formula*.

Much can be achieved by this method. What it does not readily allow for, though, is the development of general concepts or the exploration of links between different areas. The edict was not a systematically arranged document, having grown up organically over many years, and areas that we would now consider closely related might be widely separated in the edict. Take the law governing contracts, for example. As we shall see in Chapters 17 to 21, Roman law recognised a number of distinct contracts – sale, hire, different types of loan, and so forth – each with its own specific rules. As long as the different types of contract are considered separately, though, it is difficult to develop such general legal concepts as consensus which, in modern discussions of contract law, have a prominent place.

---

[73] D.45.3.39.
[74] See pp. 30, 37–42.
[75] 'The praetor's edict contained model formulae for every action. It is hardly an exaggeration to say that, before anything was known of the conceptual map of the law achieved by Gaius' *Institutes* in the second half of the second century AD, the law consisted almost wholly in the edictal list of formulae and in expert knowledge of the meaning of their words. If you knew the list of model pleadings and could say on what facts litigants would win and lose under each of them you knew all there was to know about the law' (P Birks, 'The Model Pleading of the Action for Wrongful Loss' (1990–2) 25–7 Irish Jurist (NS) 311, 311).

Gaius' achievement, arising from his practice as a teacher of law, was to provide a map of the law, allowing a beginner to see how different areas of the law related to each other. Gaius was in this way unusual among jurists, who generally showed little interest in this kind of systematisation. Most jurists' accounts of the law were based on the decidedly unsystematic order of the Twelve Tables or that of the praetor's edict.

At the heart of the institutional scheme lies the realisation that private law disputes can be analysed in three parts. First, we must consider the parties to the dispute. A person's status may affect their rights in various ways. For example, whether a person is male or female, married or unmarried, adult or child, free or slave affects that person's rights and obligations in various ways. Second, we must consider the subject matter of the dispute. Unless the parties are litigating purely over an issue of personal status, there will be some economic asset at the centre of the dispute, such as an item of property or a right under a contract. Third, we have to think about the procedures for enforcing the parties' rights and obligations. The institutional scheme divides the law accordingly. The first part is the law of persons, which is concerned with matters of personal status. The second part is called the law of things (*res*), which is a very broad category made up of 'whatever could be assessed in terms of money, have a cash value placed upon it . . . the objects and contents of a person's estate'.[76] It includes the law of property, obligations and succession. The third and final part is the law of actions, which is concerned with matters of evidence and procedure. Every private law dispute can be analysed in accordance with this scheme. This is obviously helpful to the student who is trying to build a mental picture of how the different parts of the law fit together and who is learning to navigate through the material covered in the law course.

It is difficult to over-estimate the importance of the *Institutes* and its scheme of organisation.[77] The merits of its organisational scheme gave it lasting importance after Gaius' own day. In the fifth century, Gaius was named as one of five classical jurists whose writings were to carry special authority.[78] In the sixth century, it was used as a model for the *Institutes* of the emperor Justinian, part of Justinian's legal compilation,[79] and through this Gaius' institutional scheme was carried into medieval and then modern law. It has been used, for example, by the Scots institutional writers for organising their own accounts of the law,[80] and is the basis for the organisation of the French *Code civil*. Gaius' *Institutes* themselves were lost until their rediscovery in 1816, so the book's influence was indirect, but it was nonetheless considerable. It is still important today, for another reason in addition to this. It is the only more or less complete classical legal text that we have, and there are numerous points of classical Roman law that we would know little about but for it.

---

[76] Thomas, *Textbook* 125.
[77] A Watson, 'The Importance of "Nutshells"' (1994) 42 Am J Comp L 1.
[78] Under the Law of Citations, on which see below.
[79] The *Corpus Iuris Civilis*, considered below.
[80] See pp. 84–7.

G. Law in the Post-Classical Period

(1) Characteristics

The classical period of Roman law came to an end in the first half of the third century AD. In the period that follows, known as the post-classical period, we see an almost complete disappearance of juristic literature. In the post-classical period, the major form of legal writing is the imperial pronouncement, and private efforts are to a great extent limited to elementary texts, including collections and summaries of classical texts. It is true that the significance of this shift can be overstated. Legal writing was still going on, albeit largely anonymously, and the imperial pronouncements were composed in the emperor's name by the same kind of men who, in an earlier age, formed the class of jurists. It has been said that imperial pronouncements:

> were functionally continuous with the answers of the private jurists in classical times. They are given in the same spirit, applying the law, not making it. In the transitional period at the end of the second century and the beginning of the third we can see that the same jurists whose names we know were, anonymously, the draftsmen of the imperial replies. The end of the classical period is, and perhaps is no more than, the withdrawal of the great names into the anonymity of the imperial chancery.[81]

Nonetheless, it is clear enough that there was a shift, and this is something that requires explanation.

There are various possible explanations. We might point to the growth of Christianity, and the resulting attractiveness of careers in the Church for young men who might otherwise have gone into the law. That cannot be the whole answer, though, because the adoption of Christianity as the state religion did not happen until the fourth century. At the end of the classical period, Christians were still an intermittently persecuted minority. Equally, while the absorption of jurists into imperial administration may have reduced their capacity to write freely about the law, this cannot be the whole answer either. After all, many leading classical jurists held senior positions in the imperial administration.

Another candidate is the effect of the *constitutio Antoniniana* of AD 212. As we saw in Chapter 1,[82] by this imperial pronouncement a general grant of Roman citizenship was made to the free inhabitants of the Empire. As a result, there was a major increase in the number of people who were expected to organise their affairs according to Roman law. This seems likely to have created a demand for more elementary legal literature.[83]

---

[81] P Birks and G McLeod, 'Introduction' in P Birks and G McLeod trans, *Justinian's Institutes* (Duckworth 1987) 11.
[82] See p. 22.
[83] Robinson, Fergus and Gordon, *European Legal History* para 1.3.2. In practice, though, it seems likely that the picture was more complex than this brief treatment suggests, with considerable continuity of previous local custom.

It has been suggested that the answer is simply that the jurists ran out of things to write about: 'The law of diminishing returns means that after a certain point there is little purpose in writing yet another commentary, especially because the basic law had not changed.'[84] While it is true that the post-classical period was not generally a period of major legislative innovation in private law, this view may not completely convince. After all, it is far from unknown for new questions to arise even from well-established legal principles.

Finally, it must surely be relevant that the third century AD was a time of severe political turmoil, the Crisis of the Third Century.[85] The environment this created was perhaps less conducive than that of earlier centuries to high-level legal scholarship. At the same time, though, the first century BC was also a time of major political turmoil, and it fell within the classical period of Roman law, so this point should not be overstated. Whatever the explanation, the undeniable fact is that after the first decades of the third century we see little original legal literature. Here we move into the post-classical period.

(2) **Problems of Access and Attempted Solutions**

One of the major problems in the ancient world, which became greater in the post-classical period, was the difficulty of knowing what the law actual was. As we have seen, the emperor had a major role in developing the law, and his pronouncements were seen as legally binding. It is easy enough to say that in principle, though, but considerably harder for the person in the street to know what the emperor had decided:

> The legal pronouncements of the emperors were of different types, and so was the degree of publicity given to each. *Edicta* were posted at the emperor's residence for a short time, and he might order that they be displayed, also for a short time, in a particular province or provinces. *Decreta*, statements of the law issued to an individual with a problem, would be known at once by that party, and they would be registered in the court office. *Epistulae*, replies to officials or public bodies who had asked for advice, would be sent to them, but no other publication was forthcoming unless the emperor requested it. Presumably, a copy was kept in the chancellery. *Subscriptiones*, the emperor's replies written at the bottom of petitions, were set up publicly for a few days only, and the petitioner and the chancellery would each receive a copy. Apart even from the difficulty of access to the chancellery, there is no evidence of an index system according to the subject matter of the rescripts. Thus, for all types of imperial legal pronouncements knowledge was hard to obtain.[86]

Mass circulation of imperial pronouncements was out of the question: in an age before printing, such an undertaking would have required a great expenditure of time and labour to make sufficient copies.

---

[84] A Watson, 'The End of Roman Juristic Writing' (1995) 29 Israel L Rev 228, 230.
[85] See pp. 22–3.
[86] A Watson, 'Prolegomena to Establishing Pre-Justinianic Texts' (1994) 62 TvR 113, 114–15.

The difficulty of access was partially mitigated in the classical period. Many jurists held senior positions in the imperial administration. As such, they would have had access to imperial pronouncements (some of which, indeed, the individual jurist might have drafted himself). They could therefore make reference to imperial pronouncements in their writing, and legal developments arising from them could be disseminated in that way.

One solution to this was to issue collections of imperial pronouncements, thus giving wider access to them. The *Codex Gregorianus* and *Codex Hermogenianus* were private collections from the reign of Diocletian (reigned AD 284–305), including pronouncements from 196 to 294. Later, in AD 438, Theodosius II issued an official collection, known as the *Codex Theodosianus*.[87]

Theodosius also attempted to make it easier to work with the great mass of juristic literature that existed in his time. In the Law of Citations, dated, AD 426, five jurists were identified as being of special authority. These were Papinian, Ulpian,[88] Paul, Modestinus and Gaius.[89] Where there was disagreement on the point between these five, including any passages quoted in another author, the majority view was to be followed. If there was no majority view, Papinian was to be followed. Only if there was no majority and Papinian had expressed no view was the judge free to make up his own mind. This rule may be criticised for being artificial, mechanical and not conducive to coherent legal development. It is all of those things. However, we should not be too harsh. After all, it is not very different from the system of binding precedent that is applied in Scottish and English courts.

H. Justinian

The great majority of the information on Roman law that we have available to us comes to us, not directly from the original writings, but indirectly through a compilation made in the sixth century under the authority of the emperor Justinian.[90] This compilation, the *Corpus Iuris Civilis*,[91] consists of an introductory textbook, a collection of (mostly classical) juristic writings, and a collection of imperial pronouncements, and is the focus of the final section of this chapter.

---

[87] Much of this is unfortunately lost. What we have 'is to be understood as a partial reconstruction rather than the actual Code as promulgated in 438' (J C Tate, 'Codification of Late Roman Inheritance Law: Fideicommissa and the Theodosian Code' (2008) 76 TvR 237, 238).

[88] Ulpian is of particular interest as the source of around a third of the juristic texts included in Justinian's *Digest*, discussed below, more than any other jurist. On Ulpian's life and work, see T Honoré, *Ulpian: Pioneer of Human Rights* 2nd edn (Oxford University Press 2002).

[89] The first four of these were all near contemporaries. Papinian, Ulpian and Paul all held the office of praetorian prefect, and as such were close advisers of the emperor. They visited Britain together with the emperor Septimius Severus in AD 208. They were all jurists of high reputation. Modestinus was not at their level, but is described by Ulpian as his pupil: D.47.2.52.20. He can be described as the last of the classical jurists. The odd one out is Gaius. As we have seen, he was not recognised as a jurist in his own time. The lucidity of his *Institutes*, however, gave him a prominent place in the post-classical period.

[90] Emperor of the East 527–65. See pp. 26–7.

[91] 'Body of the Civil Law'.

(1) Preliminary Work

On becoming emperor in 527, Justinian did not launch immediately into the *Corpus Iuris Civilis*. Instead, his initial aims seem to have been less ambitious than they were to become.

The fruits of these initial efforts were two collections, both unfortunately now lost to us (though much of what they contained undoubtedly found its way into the *Corpus Iuris Civilis*). The *First Codex* was a collection of imperial pronouncements prepared by a commission chaired by John of Cappadocia, issued in 529 to update the collection issued by Theodosius II almost a century before. The other work is the *Fifty Decisions*, in which a number of controversial legal questions were settled.

(2) The *Corpus Iuris Civilis*

At some point, Justinian conceived a more ambitious project, a collection that would give a comprehensive statement of the whole law. This is what would become the *Corpus Iuris Civilis*. It is sometimes described as a codification of Roman law. This term, though, is misleading: a code in the modern sense is a systematic statement of the whole law or a part of it. In only one of its parts is there any attempt at a systematic approach. This is the *Institutes*, whose structure is based on Gaius' textbook of the same name (considered above). Subject to this exception, the structure of the *Corpus Iuris Civilis* is not in the least systematic. To give one example of this, in a modern code an attempt would be made to include all provisions relating to the same topic together, so far as possible. In the *Corpus Iuris Civilis*, however, the major division is not by subject matter, but by type of source. Aside from the *Institutes*, two further parts were envisaged. One, called the *Digest*, is a collection of juristic texts covering all topics. The other, called the *Codex*, is a collection of imperial pronouncements on all topics. The *Codex* as we have it is in fact an updated version of the *First Codex*. As we shall see below, later imperial pronouncements are contained in a further compilation, the *Novels*. A comprehensive account of any area of Roman law, therefore, requires the use of texts scattered across these separate collections. This is especially the case given that the compilers were expressly told not to repeat anything in the *Digest* that was in the *First Codex*, where that could be avoided.[92]

It may not be out of place to note here that, in its own time, the awkwardness of this arrangement was increased by the part that the *Corpus Iuris Civilis* played in Justinian's reforms to legal education. In this reformed scheme, the student would start by spending most of first year studying the *Institutes*, to get a general overview. The student would then move on to the *Digest*, and only in his fifth and final year would he move on to look at the *Codex*. Given that almost everything in the *Digest* was more than 300 years old at the time the *Digest* was compiled, it

---

[92] A Watson, 'Justinian's *Corpus Iuris Civilis*: Oddities of Legal Development, and Human Civilisation' (2006) 1 Journal of Comparative Law 461, 463.

is hard to see how it could ever have been hoped that a student would acquire an accurate knowledge of the law as it stood. For comparison, imagine a five-year course in Scots law, in which almost everything until the fifth year was taken from Stair's *Institutions*[93] or earlier works, with some editing,[94] and later cases and statutes were not seen until that final year.

(3) The *Digest*

(a) Compilation

The compilation of the *Digest* was instructed by Justinian in a pronouncement called, for its opening words, *Deo auctore* ('By the authority of God'), dated 15 December 530. The task was entrusted to a commission headed by an official named Tribonian, the *quaestor sacri palatii* (Quaestor of the Sacred Palace), and containing also a government minister, four professors of law and eleven practitioners. The commissioners were instructed to compile a collection of extracts from juristic writings in fifty books. They were instructed to edit the texts for style and to correct errors,[95] and to remove anything obsolete.[96] As has been noted, unless unavoidable, nothing was to be included that was also in the *First Codex*.[97] No doubt the editing process sometimes involved deciding between alternative interpretations in the name of removing errors, but beyond that nothing in the instructions authorised making any changes of substance except to remove obsolete material.

From the work of a German scholar named Bluhme in the early nineteenth century, it appears that the commission managed its workload by dividing itself into three committees, each dealing with a particular collection, or 'mass', of material.[98] These committees and masses of material have been given the names Sabinian, Edictal and Papinian,[99] and are normally found in each title[100] of the *Digest* in that order. There was also a fourth mass, called the Appendix, normally found at the end of the title, perhaps made up of texts that were only found after the three masses had already been allocated.[101]

---

[93] This is the most important of the institutional writings of Scots law, on which see pp. 84–7. The second edition, on which modern editions are based, was published in 1693.
[94] As we shall see below, the extent to which the extracts in the *Digest* were edited by the compilers is a matter of debate.
[95] *Deo auctore* 7.
[96] *Deo auctore* 10.
[97] *Deo auctore* 9.
[98] We may note in passing that the fact that it was possible for Bluhme to identify these masses is another reason to suspect that the compilers were not engaged in large-scale rewriting of texts. If they had been, there would likely have been much more active reordering of the texts as part of that process.
[99] The reason for the names is this. The Sabinian mass contained commentaries on the *ius civile* according to a system originating with Sabinus. The Edictal mass consisted of commentaries on the praetor's edict. The Papinian mass consisted of problematic literature, a form characteristic of Papinian.
[100] For the arrangement of books and titles in the *Digest*, see below.
[101] T Honoré, 'Late Arrivals: The Appendix in Justinian's Digest Reconsidered' in Burrows and Rodger, *Mapping the Law*.

The completed *Digest* was issued almost three years to the day after *Deo auctore*, on 16 December 533.[102]

(b) Interpolations

It is not to be expected, then, that all of the texts in the *Digest* are in the form that their original writers gave them, and it is undoubtedly the case that alterations were made. These alterations – whether by substituting, deleting or adding words, or in any other way giving something other than the jurist's own words – are known as 'interpolations'. Some of these are more significant than others. Some are purely cosmetic, edited for presentation. Indeed, a text may have been altered quite substantially without alteration to its substance. On the other hand, an alteration may be more serious, and a jurist may be made to appear to have said something quite different from what he actually said. To this, a further point may be added, bearing in mind the point that the texts as we have them are divorced from their original context. Even without changing the jurist's words, the compilers may have given a misleading impression by the context in which they have placed those words.

So much is certain. What is more difficult, though, is determining to what extent the *Digest* is interpolated. There are fashions and trends in this, as in all things. At times, scholars of Roman law have been very prepared to consider a text to be interpolated. Indeed, at one point, in the early twentieth century, this enthusiasm was such as to attract the name 'interpolation hunt'. It would be an exaggeration to say that there is scarcely a single text in the *Digest* that has not been said at some point, on some grounds, to be interpolated. It would not, however, be a gross exaggeration. There is no doubt that some scholars have allowed their support for a particular position on a point of Roman law to colour their view, and have failed to resist the temptation to dismiss any text not fitting that view as interpolated. Often these views depended on dubious linguistic arguments to the effect that a particular word or phrase could not have been used by a classical jurist, or that what a jurist is presented in the *Digest* as saying is not consistent with his alleged style.[103]

Nowadays, a more restrained view prevails, possibly even to the extent of overreaction to the interpolation hunt.[104] It has been pointed out that Justinian's instructions to the compilers did not authorise them to innovate.[105] The compilers' conscientiousness in attributing even very short fragments to the correct jurist

---

[102] Its completion was announced in a pronouncement of that date, called *Constitutio omnem* from its first word (*omnem*, meaning 'all' or 'whole'). It was confirmed as law by a pronouncement of the same date, *Constitutio tanta* (*tanta* means 'so great').

[103] See criticisms in W W Buckland, 'Interpolations in the Digest' (1924) 33 Yale LJ 343, 354–64.

[104] D Johnston, 'Justinian's *Digest*: The Interpretation of Interpolation' (1989) 9 OJLS 149.

[105] A Watson, 'Prolegomena to Establishing Pre-Justinianic Texts' (1994) 62 TvR 113; J H A Lokin, 'The End of an Epoch: Epilegomena to a Century of Interpolation Criticism' in R Feenstra *et al* eds, *Collatio Iuris Romani: Études Dédiées à Hans Ankum à l'Occasion de son 65e Anniversaire*, vol 1 (J C Gieben 1995); Robinson, *Sources* 105–15.

also weighs against the idea of widespread interpolation of substance.[106] Again, the lack of significant Christianisation of the texts is a strong argument that the compilers were not engaging in large-scale law reform, given that the jurists were all pagans and Justinian was a man of strongly Christian convictions.[107] Add to this the fact that the whole job was completed in three years, a tall enough order even without the compilers taking on the added burden of law reform.[108]

In detecting those interpolations that do exist, linguistic arguments are rarely seen as conclusive without more: it would be rash to assume that classical jurists were incapable of writing bad Latin. Every writer slips up on occasion, and this is true even though the compilers, coming from the Greek-speaking Eastern Empire, were perhaps more likely to make linguistic mistakes in the Latin than were the jurists. Moreover, even where a linguistic error[109] suggests that part of a passage is interpolated, it is not always easy to tell which part is original and which part is interpolated.[110] Equally, faulty reasoning is not conclusive of interpolation: no legal writer is immune from making bad arguments.[111] Again, disagreement between individual texts is not conclusive evidence of interpolation: this may simply reflect a disagreement on the point among classical jurists, or it may be that the contradiction in the texts reflects different stages of the development of the law. It is also important to note a further point, which is that not all of the alterations in the texts will have been made by the compilers of the *Digest*: it must be remembered that this was an age long before the invention of printing, in which copying of texts had to be done by hand. In such circumstances, copying errors will inevitably have crept into the texts over the 300 and more years separating the compilers from even the latest classical jurists.

So how are interpolations to be detected? Something has already been said of linguistic arguments, but there are other tools available. The clearest test is where a text has survived independently. Obviously, if an independently surviving text differs from how it is presented in the *Digest*, one or both of the versions that we have must have been altered at some point. Where there has been no such independent survival, the most reliable sign of interpolation is where the text states something as law which is known from other sources not to have been the position at the time the jurist was writing.[112] Cases where a text has been presented by the compilers in a misleading context can sometimes be identified by considering the inscription showing the original source of the text. If enough of the original source is preserved in the *Digest*, it may be possible to determine the original context of the words used. Even where none of these signs is present, though, the possibility cannot necessarily be excluded of the compilers misreporting a jurist's

---

[106] A Watson, 'Prolegomena to Establishing Pre-Justinianic Texts' (1994) 62 TvR 113.
[107] A Watson, 'Law Out of Context' (2000) 4 Edin LR 147, 149.
[108] W W Buckland, 'Interpolations in the Digest' (1924) 33 Yale LJ 343, 344.
[109] For example, a switch between first and third persons part of the way through the text.
[110] W W Buckland, 'Interpolations in the Digest' (1924) 33 Yale LJ 343, 346–7.
[111] W W Buckland, 'Interpolations in the Digest' (1924) 33 Yale LJ 343, 347.
[112] For examples, see A Watson, 'Prolegomena to Establishing Pre-Justinianic Texts' (1994) 62 TvR 113, 120–2.

original words or meaning, whether through error in their own understanding or because errors had crept into the manuscripts they were working from.

(c) Contents

The contents of the *Digest* are divided into fifty books, most of which are subdivided into titles. It is not in any way systematically organised.[113] The order of books and titles is based on that of the praetor's edict, which, having grown up over centuries, was rather haphazardly organised. As a result, related subject-matter is often scattered through the whole compilation, and the *Digest* is extremely difficult to manage without guidance.

Each title is made up of extracts from the writings of a number of jurists. In all, extracts from the writings of thirty-eight jurists are included, although many more are referred to by the jurists who are included. Some jurists are featured much more prominently than others: around a third of the total content of the *Digest* comes from Ulpian, and around a sixth from Paul. A considerable amount is taken from Gaius as well. Each text has an inscription at the beginning, showing the author and source. There is a tendency to take a single jurist's treatment as the basis for coverage of a topic, with linking words (called *catenae*) taken from another jurist when the first does not deal with a particular point. The following is an example taken from D.41.1 (*Digest*, book 41, title 1):

> 5 Gaius, *Common Matters or Golden Things, book 2*: . . . 7. Again, under the law of nations, that which is taken from enemies immediately becomes the property of the taker,
>
> 6 Florentinus, *Institutes, book 6*: so also under the same law are the young of animals which we own,
>
> 7 Gaius, *Common Matters or Golden Things, book 2*: so indeed freemen are taken into slavery . . .

Here the compilers have made Gaius the basis of their account.[114] Presumably Gaius' own words, in the original, went straight from telling us that according to the 'law of nations' (*ius gentium*) one can acquire ownership of things taken from an enemy, to telling us that on the same basis prisoners of war become slaves of their captors. The compilers decided to add in a few words from Florentinus, in which we are told something else about the *ius gentium*, namely that it also is the basis on which we own the offspring of animals we own.[115]

Justinian boasted that there was no apparent conflict in the texts that could not be reconciled by a sufficiently agile mind.[116] This claim has not, however,

---

[113] Despite the impression given by *Constitutio tanta* 1–8c.

[114] D.41.1 is entitled 'Acquisition of Ownership of Things'. D.41.1.1, 3, 5, 7 and 9 are all substantial passages taken from Gaius' *Common Matters or Golden Things*. The intervening passages are all brief extracts from other jurists (Florentinus, except in one case).

[115] It must be said that this passage from Florentinus does not fit particularly well here, a sign of the haste with which the compilers completed their task.

[116] *Constitutio tanta* 15.

been borne out by experience. There are many conflicts in the texts that almost a millennium and a half of debate has been unable to resolve.

(4) The *Institutes*

The *Institutes* were intended as an introductory textbook to be studied, as we have seen, as part of the first year of the five-year law course. It must be said that it is an unusual student textbook, as Justinian enacted it as law, and so it had a somewhat greater authoritativeness than is usual for such books.[117] It was issued almost a month before the *Digest*, on 21 November 533, although it was apparently commissioned only after the *Digest* was completed, in March 533.

Justinian's *Institutes* followed the structure of Gaius' work of the same name – the institutional scheme – and included much of its content, though other sources were used too. Justinian's version was compiled by Tribonian and two of the professors in the *Digest* commission, namely Theophilus and Dorotheus. It must be said that it is a flawed work, containing errors:

> They seem to have had in front of them when they worked only the writings of the old – pre-235 – writers of elementary works . . . When these works were insufficient, the draftsmen relied upon their memories, with disastrous results.[118]

Nonetheless, it was a highly important part of the *Corpus Iuris Civilis* and of Justinian's reforms of legal education. In his foreword to the *Institutes*, Justinian calls it a *legum cunabula*, a 'cradle of the law'. It is intended to provide the beginner with an overview of private law, with the intention that more advanced material will be more easily absorbed once this firm foundation is laid down. Without this, he goes on to say, the student would either give up or would in the end 'with great toil reach the same level that they would have reached earlier without great effort and self-doubt if they could have been taken along an easier road'.[119]

Through this, the influence of the institutional scheme has been profound, to the extent indeed that it distracts us from the shortcomings of the jurists' more usual approach to organising their material. The institutional scheme is commonly used to organise textbooks covering private law (including this one). As we saw earlier, though, its influence has gone well beyond introductory textbooks.

(5) The *Codex*

The *Codex* is, as has been said above, a collection of imperial pronouncements.[120] By and large, the contents of the *Codex* are later than the texts included in the

---

[117] P van Warmelo, 'The Institutes of Justinian as Students' Manual' in Stein and Lewis, *Studies in Justinian's Institutes* 164.
[118] A Watson, 'Law Out of Context' (2000) 4 Edin LR 147, 151. For some examples of errors in Justinian's *Institutes*, see pages 151–3 of that article.
[119] J.1.1.2.
[120] The name is often anglicised as 'Code', but this is misleading. The name means 'book', and it is not a code in the modern sense.

Digest, although there are some overlaps. As has already been said, it updates the *First Codex* to take account of subsequent developments (and in particular the *Fifty Decisions*), and for this reason it is sometimes called the *Second Codex*. It was compiled by a sub-committee of the *Digest* commission, chaired by Tribonian, and was issued on 16 November 534.

(6) The *Novels*

Legislative activity did not cease with the *Codex*, of course, and many major reforms postdate the promulgation of the *Codex* in AD 534. As we shall see in Chapter 16,[121] for example, Justinian substantially overhauled the law of succession after 534. Later pronouncements were collected in a compilation called the *Novels* (in Latin, *Novellae Constitutiones*, or 'New Pronouncements'). Unlike the rest of the *Corpus Iuris Civilis*, however, this is not an official compilation. Instead, the *Novels* as we have them are based on unofficial collections.

Chapter Summary

The earliest Roman law we have reasonably reliable knowledge of is the Twelve Tables, compiled in the mid-fifth century BC by a special commission charged with that task. Other than that, while legislation (of the citizen assemblies) was a valid source of private law (and in theory the only source of new law in the Republican constitution), there were few statutes of major significance in private law. In the Republic, the major source of legal development was not formal legislation, but rather innovations by the urban praetor. The praetor used his control over litigation to develop the law by introducing new remedies or qualifying existing ones. Law developed in this way was called the *ius honorarium*, by contrast with the *ius civile* (civil law).

During the Empire, the *ius honorarium* became less important as power became centralised in the emperor's hands. Initially acting through existing institutions, especially the Senate (whose resolutions became formally binding in this period), and then legislating directly through imperial pronouncements, the emperor became the major source of legal development in the Empire.

Underlying both the *ius honorarium* and imperial pronouncements, however, was the work of the jurists. It was these men who developed the law into a sophisticated system, and whose ideas were the major source of the developments embodied in the *ius honorarium* and the pronouncements of the emperors.

---

[121] See pp. 290, 300n, 302–3.

Further Reading

R A Bauman, *Lawyers and Politics in the Early Roman Empire: A Study of Relations between the Roman Jurists and the Emperors from Augustus to Hadrian* (Beck 1989)

S W Bell and P J du Plessis, *Roman Law before the Twelve Tables: An Interdisciplinary Approach* (Edinburgh University Press 2020)

P Birks and G McLeod, 'Introduction' in P Birks and G McLeod trans, *Justinian's Institutes* (Duckworth 1987)

B W Frier, *The Rise of the Roman Jurists: Studies in Cicero's pro Caecina* (Princeton University Press 1985)

T Honoré, *Justinian's Digest: Character and Compilation* (Oxford University Press 2010)

T Honoré, *Tribonian* (Duckworth 1978)

H F Jolowicz and B Nicholas, *Historical Introduction to the Study of Roman Law* 3rd edn (Cambridge University Press 1972) chapters 5–7

J M Kelly, 'The Growth-Pattern of the Praetor's Edict' (1966) 1 Irish Jurist (NS) 349

D J Osler, 'The Compilation of Justinian's Digest' (1985) 102 ZSS (rA) 129

D Pugsley, *Justinian's Digest and the Compilers* (University of Exeter 1995)

O F Robinson, *The Sources of Roman Law: Problems and Methods for Ancient Historians* (Routledge 1997)

A Watson, 'The Birth of the Legal Profession' (1986–7) 85 Mich L Rev 1071

A Watson, 'Justinian's *Corpus Iuris Civilis*: Oddities of Legal Development, and Human Civilisation' (2006) 1 Journal of Comparative Law 461

A Watson, *Law Making in the Later Roman Republic* (Oxford University Press 1974)

R Westbrook, 'The Nature and Origins of the Twelve Tables' (1988) 105 ZSS (rA) 74

CHAPTER FOUR

Reception of Roman Law

Most of the major legal systems in the world are divided by scholars of comparative law into two great 'families' of legal systems. One of these, the Common Law family, will be considered briefly below. It is derived ultimately from medieval English law. The other major family is the Civil Law family, which has its roots in Roman law.[1] The process by which Roman law was received into medieval and later legal systems is called the Reception of Roman law (or just the Reception), and is the subject matter of this chapter.

A. Roman Law after Justinian

(1) The East

As we saw in Chapter 1,[2] the decline of the Western Empire culminated in the deposition of the final western emperor, Romulus Augustulus, in AD 476. In the east, though, the situation was different, and it was in the east that the *Corpus Iuris Civilis* was created. As may be expected, there is greater continuity in the east between Justinian's compilation and the present day. Eastern developments had, however, very little direct impact on the Reception of Roman law in Western Europe,[3] so only a brief summary is given here.

Justinian forbade commentaries on the *Corpus Iuris Civilis*, although he allowed brief summaries and translations into Greek. This prohibition was not strictly applied even in Justinian's own time, however. Even though new law schools were founded during Justinian's reign, lawyers of the time found the *Corpus Iuris Civilis* difficult to use without further help. After Justinian's time, in fact, the *Corpus Iuris Civilis* itself largely went out of use in the Eastern Empire.

Instead of the *Corpus Iuris Civilis* being used, what tended to happen is that lawyers would rely on unofficial (and, sometimes, official)[4] summaries, commentaries

---

[1] It is called the Civil Law from the Latin term *ius civile*, which translates in this way.
[2] See p. 26.
[3] When Constantinople fell in 1453, however, this did make significant quantities of literature available in the West, which had been previously thought lost, and which were of great use to the Legal Humanists, discussed below.
[4] For example, the *Basilica*, started by Basil I and completed in around AD 890 by his son, Leo, was a Greek paraphrase of the *Corpus Iuris Civilis*.

and epitomes of the *Corpus Iuris*. The most influential of these was the *Hexabiblos*, a compilation by a judge named Harmenopoulos made in 1345. The *Hexabiblos* formed the basis for Greek law until the twentieth century.

(2) The West

There is a certain amount of artificiality and hindsight in talking about the end of the Roman Empire in Western Europe. There was no single, catastrophic event that could have been identified at the time as the end. For example, when in AD 410 the Romans' British subjects were told to look to their own defence rather than expecting Roman assistance, this was expected to be a temporary state of affairs. It is only with hindsight that this can be identified as the end of Roman rule in Britain. Indeed, as late as the end of the sixth century AD, 'it was not clearly apparent to contemporaries that the ancient world, the Roman world, had ended in the West'.[5] Although the Western Empire was as a matter of fact carved up into a number of independent kingdoms, these remained for a time at least nominally subject to Roman authority. Even those Germanic tribes whose migrations into Roman territory (and Rome's inability to resist or control them) brought about the end of the Western Empire did not intend to destroy Roman rule. Rather, they sought to share in its benefits. Widespread use was made by the new rulers of existing governance structures. It must be remembered that the Romanised inhabitants of Western Europe were generally not displaced in this process,[6] and this included legally educated individuals. This fact allowed the new rulers of the West to draw on Roman texts and Roman legal expertise in their own law-making activities. There are numerous examples of this, of which the best known is the *Lex Romana Visigothorum* of AD 506, intended mainly for the use of Roman subjects of the Visigoths.[7] This consisted largely of abridged versions of the *Codex Theodosianus* and Gaius' *Institutes*, as well as some later enactments and other juristic texts. There was thus considerable survival of Roman law, albeit in debased form.

B. Revival and Reception

There was, then, some continuity in legal practice after the fall of the Western Empire, although its extent is not always clear. Certainly it varied from place to place in Western Europe, but everywhere it was patchy and partial. What was used was abridgements and adaptations of the Roman materials, mixed together

---

[5] Robinson, Fergus and Gordon, *European Legal History* para 1.7.1.
[6] This is testified to by the fact that, with one exception, all of the main languages of what was the Western Empire are derived from Latin. The exception is English, which is classed as a Germanic language and was brought by the Anglo-Saxons. These were Germanic incomers who, over the centuries following the Romans' departure, carved up what is now England into a series of kingdoms, and indeed gave England its name. Although a large part of the vocabulary of modern English is Latin-derived, this is largely not a survival of Roman rule, but is rather almost entirely a result of the Norman Conquest of England in 1066.
[7] The Visigoths were a Germanic people who carved out a kingdom in what is now Spain and southern France. For an account, see R Collins, *Visigothic Spain: 409–711* (Blackwell 2004).

with non-Roman sources. The *Corpus Iuris Civilis* was not in use in Western Europe. The next part of our story is the process by which Roman law, as depicted in the *Corpus Iuris Civilis*, came to be rediscovered by Western Europeans as a source of legal rules and principles.

(1) Glossators

Compared with what had come before, the centuries following the fall of the Western Empire had been a Dark Age. Where there had been (relative) order, there was political instability. Economic activity declined, so people were poorer, and literacy levels were lower. An additional point that must be made, because it is contrary to modern assumptions, and that is the general absence at this time of national legal systems. In the modern world, we tend to assume that each nation or state will have its own unified legal system. This assumption is not fully justified even in the modern world, but certainly in the Middle Ages such a thing as a national legal system is not generally to be looked for. Instead, there was a greater role to be played by the customary rules of a locality than we would nowadays expect. A national legal system takes time to develop, and that could only happen once the political situation began to stabilise. This began to happen after the turn of the first millennium, and there can be identified an eleventh-century renaissance.

It was in this setting that the study of Roman law was revived in Bologna, in the late eleventh and early twelfth centuries. Credit for this is traditionally given to a grammarian called Irnerius, who turned to the *Corpus Iuris Civilis* in search of material for his linguistic studies.

This was only made possible by the rediscovery in the eleventh century of the full text of the *Corpus Iuris Civilis*, which had previously been lost. Earlier medieval lawyers, as we have seen, only had access to abridgements and summaries of Roman legal materials. There were, however, other factors that were friendly to this revival of the study of Roman law. One was the disputes of the day between the Church and secular authorities over the right to appoint bishops and abbots (the 'Investiture Contest'), which led to people on both sides searching the Roman sources – authoritative because of their antiquity – for texts to support their respective positions. More generally, there was in this period an increase in commerce, which is always likely to give rise to legal disputes. Most important, however, was the simple fact that the contents of the *Corpus Iuris Civilis* were superior to anything else that was available. The *Corpus Iuris Civilis* was a treasury of texts that could be used – or adapted to use – in almost any legal dispute that could be imagined, and it had simply fallen into the hands of lawyers. It was inevitable that they would make use of such a gift.

The first task was to make the texts usable. The *Corpus Iuris Civilis*, and especially the *Digest*, is a very large, ill-arranged collection, which was very difficult to use even at the time of its compilation. This was the work of the first major group of medieval scholars of Roman law. They were known as the Glossators, because their characteristic form of literature was the gloss, a marginal or interlinear note explaining a word, phrase or longer passage, including cross-references to other texts dealing with the same or similar issues. This was rather like a modern annotated statute. The term 'gloss' can also be used for a collection (*apparatus*) of individual glosses, and the most famous of these was a mid-thirteenth-century collection compiled by Accursius, and known variously as the *Great Gloss*, *Glossa Ordinaria* or *Accursian Gloss*. It did not take long for this to be accepted in Italy as the standard commentary on the *Corpus Iuris Civilis*, to the extent that copies of the *Accursian Gloss* were sometimes produced without the texts that it was commenting on, and there was a tendency for lawyers to consult the *Gloss* rather than the Roman texts themselves.

The Glossators did produce other forms of literature as well, though. For example, the *Summa Codicis* of Azo (died 1220) was a comprehensive commentary in the order of the *Codex*. This was so widely used by practitioners that it was said 'nobody can go to court without Azo'. In addition, the Glossators taught, first at Bologna but later also at the other law schools that were founded in this period, especially in Italy. Their typical approach to teaching reflected their typical approach to writing. They would go through the texts in order, explaining each in turn and referring to other passages dealing with the same issue, and resolving apparent conflicts in the texts.

It should not be thought, though, that the Glossators were simply academics, isolated from practical issues. On the contrary, many prominent Glossators were active in legal practice and administration, and they undoubtedly used the new legal learning in those activities. Their great contribution was to make the Roman texts manageable. At the same time, however, the Glossators were guilty of believing Justinian when he said that his compilation contained no contradictory material.[8] The harmony that the Glossators sought in the texts had to be imposed. It is important to understand that the law that the Glossators and later writers presented, although based on the Roman texts, was not in fact the Roman law of Justinian's time. Still less was it classical Roman law. We shall see examples of this throughout this book.[9] For now, though, one will suffice. In a text in the *Codex*, Justinian pronounces that *quod omnes tangit ab omnibus comprobetur* ('what touches all must be approved by all').[10] In its original context, it is nothing more than the justification for the rule that, where a child has more than one guardian, any act dissolving the guardianship must be approved by all if it is to be valid. In that context, it is a very limited rule. In fact, it is expressly stated not to apply to any other kind of decision, the consent of a single guardian normally being enough to make a valid decision. Divorced from that context, however, the principle is clearly capable of much broader application, and so, indeed, it was used. Indeed, with its fine, democratic overtones, it is apt to be used as a political slogan, notwithstanding that an absolutist monarch like Justinian would hardly have used it with that intention.[11]

---

[8] See pp. 68–9.
[9] See *e.g.* the discussion of *aemulatio vicini* at p. 167.
[10] C.5.59.5.2 (AD 531).
[11] H F Jolowicz, 'The Stone that the Builders Rejected: Adventures of Some Civil Law Texts' (1954) 12 Seminar (Jurist) 34, 40.

(2) Commentators

The next major tradition to develop was that of the Commentators, from the fourteenth century onwards, by which time there were other law schools with a prominence to rival Bologna, beyond Italy as well as inside it. For example, the law school at Orléans is known to have existed in the thirteenth century.[12] There was, though, no clear break between the Commentators and earlier writers. They worked with essentially the same material as the Glossators did, they had similar teaching methods, and they wrote many of the same kinds of literature. The difference is more one of emphasis: 'To distinguish, perhaps over-simply, the former school laid a foundation for the study of Roman law; the latter developed the application of Roman law in practical affairs.'[13] At this period, basic mastery of the texts had been achieved through the work of the Glossators, so more focused literature was possible, discussing and developing specific topics. In the writings of the Commentators, there is greater emphasis on adaptation of the texts to the needs of legal practice. For this reason, it has been said that the period during which the Commentators were working 'saw the true beginning of the reception of Roman law'.[14]

The best known of the Commentators is Bartolus of Sassoferrato (1314–57). He produced a massive *Commentary* on the whole *Corpus Iuris Civilis*. This became so much the standard reference work that it came to be said *nemo iurista nisi Bartolista* ('nobody is a jurist except a Bartolist'). Bartolus' pupil, Baldus de Ubaldis, was a prolific writer of *consilia* (opinions), which were the other main type of literature. These opinions might be given to one of the parties or to the court itself. Because these were intended for application in practice, they could not be simply discussions of Roman law. Instead, they had to take account of the particular law of the place concerned. Local statutes or customary law took precedence, with Roman law being used as a subsidiary source to interpret the local law or fill gaps in it. As with the Glossators, interpretations of Roman law were often quite free. For example, they might take a principle from one context and apply it to another, the important thing being to find a practical answer to the problem.

(3) Canon Law

We saw in Chapter 1 that, in the early fourth century, under Constantine, Christianity became the official religion of the Roman Empire.[15] From this point onwards, the Church played a key political role. Even after the fall of the Western Empire, the Western (Roman Catholic)[16] Church survived as a major political player.

---

[12] Scholars here are sometimes classed as a group of their own, the *Ultramontani* ('Those beyond the mountains', *i.e.* those across the Alps from Italy).
[13] Robinson, Fergus and Gordon, *European Legal History* para 4.1.2.
[14] T Wallinga, 'The Common History of European Legal Scholarship' (2011–12) 4 Erasmus Law Review 3, 9.
[15] See p. 25.
[16] This is slightly anachronistic. The primacy of Rome in the Western Church was asserted early, but was not conclusively accepted until well into the medieval period. Moreover, the division of the Church into Eastern Orthodoxy and Western Catholicism was not finally accepted until the eleventh century. Nonetheless, the usage is convenient.

Canon law is the law of the Church. Medieval canon law, however, was more than just the internal rules and doctrine of the Church as an organisation. The medieval Church was powerful enough to assert authority in its own right, separate from the secular authorities:

> from the twelfth to the sixteenth century there was throughout western Europe a relatively uniform structure of ecclesiastical courts, administering a fairly regular system, and staffed by men who had undertaken a reasonably common education in canon, and frequently in civil, law. There were local variations . . . Nevertheless, there was one international system.[17]

These courts had direct jurisdiction and, where this jurisdiction extended, it excluded that of the secular courts. Thus, for example, a dispute over the validity of a marriage would be determined, not by the secular courts applying local or national law, but by the courts of the Church applying universal canon law. The jurisdiction of the canon law courts was fairly broad. Matters such as marriage had clear religious significance, so it is unsurprising that that fell within Church jurisdiction, but less obvious matters, such as wills and succession, were covered too. Moreover, parties would often prefer to submit their dispute to the canon law courts where possible, as they often offered a higher standard of justice than the secular courts. At any rate, at a time when the secular courts were using such methods as ordeal[18] or trial by battle as truth-finding techniques, the canon law courts offered at least a more rational procedure.[19] The procedure used by the canon law courts is known as Romano-Canonical procedure, because it was based on the *cognitio* system of procedure in the Roman Empire.[20]

The starting point of developed canon law is the *Decretum* or *Concordia Discordantium Canonum* ('Harmonisation of Discordant Texts'), a collection of canon law materials, with discussion, made around 1140. The compiler of the *Decretum* was an individual named Gratian, about whom little is known except that he worked at Bologna and was possibly a monk. In origin, the *Decretum* was an unofficial collection, but its value was such that it was quickly accepted in practice as authoritative. Together with three later official collections of papal decisions (decretals) from 1234,[21] 1298[22] and 1317,[23] it formed the *Corpus Iuris Canonici* ('Body of the Canon Law'), a canon law counterpart to the *Corpus Iuris Civilis*.

The importance of all of this for our purposes here is in the heavy use made of Roman law by the canon lawyers. Roman influence on canon law procedure has already been mentioned, but there was extensive use of Roman texts on

---

[17] Robinson, Fergus and Gordon, *European Legal History* para 5.1.2.
[18] Common ordeals included an accused person plunging the hand into boiling water or carrying red-hot iron. Lack of injury from the ordeal was taken to be a divine declaration of innocence.
[19] On the rationality of trial by ordeal, however, see P T Leeson, 'Ordeals' (2012) 55 Journal of Law and Economics 691.
[20] On the *cognitio*, see pp. 40–4.
[21] The *Liber Extra* of Pope Gregory IX.
[22] The *Liber Sextus* of Pope Boniface VIII.
[23] The *Clementinae* of Pope Clement V.

substantive law. Indeed, so much was canon law permeated by Roman law, that it was said that one could not be understood without the other. Moreover, where the canon law adopted a Roman rule, the status of canon law meant that that rule was then directly effective, binding law. Canon lawyers' use of Roman legal ideas was, however, never simply slavish copying. Canon lawyers' emphasis on conscience, for example, was the major impetus behind the law's adoption of the general principle that any seriously intended agreement should be considered binding.[24] As we shall see in Chapter 17,[25] this allowed the law to break out of the Romans' rigid categories of binding contract. Equally, where a Roman rule conflicted with Church doctrine, the canon lawyers felt quite free to reject it. A major example of this will be seen in Chapter 8: canon law adopted Roman principles on the formation of marriage; the Roman position on divorce, by contrast, was not acceptable to the Church, and so canon law rejected it.[26]

(4) The *Ius Commune*

It is common among legal historians to talk of the Reception of Roman law (meaning, as we have seen, Roman law as interpreted by the medieval jurists rather than the Roman law of Justinian's time). This is the process which has been described, by which there developed a European 'common law', a phrase which is usually given in Latin as *ius commune*.[27]

Why did the *ius commune* develop? The main reason, really, was the inadequacy of the other legal resources that were available. We have already seen that, following the Dark Ages, factors such as economic growth resulted in greater demands being placed on lawyers to find solutions to legal problems. Lawyers turned to the Roman sources, if for no other reason than that there was no adequate alternative. Local law was fragmentary and underdeveloped. It could hardly be otherwise: it is hard to see how a national legal system can develop to a high level of sophistication without a national system of courts or advanced legal education in the national law. Generally speaking, state authority in this period was too weak to be able readily to establish national systems of justice, and university legal education meant education in Roman law. At the same time, state authorities were often themselves keen to support Roman law, as it could be used to support the state's claims of authority. Finally, in those areas falling within the jurisdiction of the canon law courts, there really was a common European legal system, and we have seen that that was strongly influenced by Roman law.

Talk of a *ius commune*, common law, of Europe is, however, potentially misleading. To speak in this way is perhaps to imply that there was a single system of law applying across all of those countries that experienced Reception. *Ius commune*

---

[24] Or, according to the Latin maxim, *pacta sunt servanda* ('agreements ought to be kept').
[25] See p. 140.
[26] See pp. 144–5.
[27] The two parts of the *ius commune* that are of interest to us are Roman law and canon law. Joining these was a third part, feudal law, which was not Roman in origin. A treatise on feudal law, the *Libri Feudorum* ('Books of the Feus') was often included with the *Corpus Iuris Civilis*.

should not, though, be understood in this way. It should be seen rather as a common stock of legal ideas, a shared resource, that could be drawn on to fill gaps in local law and using which local law could be interpreted and developed. *Ius commune* is a common legal culture rather than a common legal system.

(5) The Exception: England

Something must be said at this point about England. Although medieval English law was not completely unaffected by developments on the Continent, England never experienced a full Reception of Roman law. The main reason for this is that, at much the same time that the Glossators were carrying out their work, the comparative strength and stability of the English state allowed it to establish a nationwide system of royal justice. From the work of these royal courts, there emerged a single, national legal system, known for this reason as a common law. By the time that the *ius commune* emerged, English lawyers had a relatively highly developed system of law of their own. They also had developed their own, non-university based, system of legal education. For these reasons, medieval English lawyers by and large saw little use for the *ius commune* learning, which in any case most of them did not have the educational background necessary to make the most of. English law tended (and still tends, to some extent) to be developed on a case by case basis, rather than by application of general principles. As part of Western Christendom, of course, England was subject to the jurisdiction of the canon law courts, but there was resistance even to this influence. For example, in the Statute of Merton 1235, a different rule on legitimacy of children was applied from that in the canon law.[28]

These developments are the source of the second major family of legal systems in the world today, the Common Law family. The British Empire carried English law around the world,[29] and it provides the basis of the legal systems of the United States (except for Louisiana), Canada (except for Quebec), Australia, New Zealand and more.

C. The Development of National Legal Systems

(1) Why Did National Legal Systems Develop?

The picture we have seen is of a transnational legal culture, with lawyers trained to think first in terms of a *ius commune* transcending national borders, and only

---

[28] The specific point at issue was the status of a child born to parents who were unmarried at the time of birth, but who subsequently married. As we shall see at p. 126, the canon law adopted a rule that such a child was born illegitimate, but was legitimated by the parents' subsequent marriage. The Statute of Merton rejected legitimation by subsequent marriage. As a result, the same person could be legitimate for some purposes but illegitimate for others.

[29] One may ask why it should be English law that was spread through the British Empire, given that England is only part of the UK. Regrettably, the assumption exists in some quarters that English law is the default. Thus, terms such as 'British law' and 'the British legal system' are sometimes heard, regardless of the fact that neither exists.

then in terms of particular laws of particular places. In medieval Europe, the concept of a national legal system barely existed. Let us take France as an example. Until the introduction of the French *Code civil* under Napoleon in 1804, there was really no such thing as French law. Instead, the country was broadly divided between the south, where there had been some survival of Roman law (the *pays de droit écrit*, or 'country of written law'), and the north, where non-Roman customary law prevailed and Roman influence was much more limited (the *pays de droit coutumier*, or 'country of customary law'). Even within this, there was regional variation. France was not atypical in this. Nowadays, by contrast, we take it for granted that different countries will have their own legal systems. How did this situation come to pass?

In part, the change was a result of factors ceasing to apply, which had promoted Reception. Where political fragmentation and weak central authority had encouraged Reception, strengthening of central authorities allowed the development of national court systems. Similarly, insofar as canon law was a vehicle for Reception, its unifying potential was reduced when the authority of the Roman Catholic Church was ended in those countries that embraced the Protestant Reformation.[30] When authority over areas falling within Church jurisdiction passed to national authorities, it was inevitable that the law would come to develop on national lines.

At the same time, though, there were intellectual trends that ran counter to universalising ideas. One such was the school of thought known as Legal Humanism, active particularly in the sixteenth and early seventeenth centuries. Humanism in this sense[31] was concerned with the study of what is often called the humanities, and particularly with the classics, and they were especially interested in the history, literature and philology of the ancient world. It was with the Legal Humanists that there began attempts to recover the 'pure' classical law hidden behind the 'distortions' of Justinian in the *Corpus Iuris Civilis*. Legal Humanism was particularly prominent in French universities, and so was known as the *mos gallicus* (French way). It was severely critical of the *mos italicus* (Italian way) of the Glossators and Commentators, which it accused of misrepresenting the Roman law. This is somewhat unfair: the major concern of the Glossators and Commentators was to make the Roman sources useful for practical purposes, and so it is questionable whether they are really open to criticism according to the standards of quite a different intellectual endeavour. Nonetheless, though, the Humanists' idea of the law as a product of the historical development of a society weighed against the idea of Roman law as universally applicable, regardless of time and place.

It must be said that Legal Humanism had limited immediate impact on legal practice, albeit it perhaps had greater impact in legal education. Even in the

---

[30] In Scotland, this happened in 1560.
[31] It has really very little, if anything, to do with the secular humanism that the term is often used to refer to nowadays.

universities, though, it did not have the field to itself. For example, the German *usus modernus Pandectarum* ('modern usage of the *Pandects*')[32] of the seventeenth and early eighteenth centuries was focused on the application of the sources to practical problems. Still, it was indicative of intellectual trends of the period. There is, it has been said:

> no difficulty in finding in the work of the legal humanists the seeds of much that later changed the face of legal science. As so often in the history of legal thought, it took centuries for their ideas to bear fruit, but when they did so, legal science was reborn.[33]

Another important school of thought was that of Natural Law. This was particularly prominent in Germany, although perhaps its most influential exponent was the seventeenth-century Dutch jurist Grotius. The idea behind this school of thought was that it should be possible to deduce true, universal principles of law by rational consideration. The implication of this was that Roman law should only be seen as authoritative insofar as it was consistent with those rational principles.

The Natural Law jurists' emphasis on rationality also lent itself to thoughts of codification, the idea that it was desirable to present the law in the form of a rationally ordered code. Bavaria and Prussia, for example, both introduced codes of private law in the eighteenth century. The French *Code civil* of 1804 has already been mentioned. The German *Bürgerliches Gesetzbuch* (BGB) came into force in 1900. German codification was delayed by the fact that Germany was not unified until 1871, but also by debates on the form that codification should take, between Germanists and Romanists of the German Historical school. The former emphasised the role of Germanic tradition, the latter the *ius commune* element. In our time, though, the great majority of countries that experienced Reception now have their own codes of private law.

The intellectual unity of the *ius commune* was thus broken. This should not be taken to mean, however, that its influence has come to an end. Even though modern lawyers now think primarily in national terms, the national legal systems in which they work are still rooted in the *ius commune*. The national codes of the eighteenth and nineteenth centuries were not a clean break with the past, but were based on existing law. For this reason, a lawyer from one of these legal systems will find much that is familiar in other such systems and still has much to gain from study of the Roman legal tradition.[34] This is why scholars of comparative law are able to group these legal systems together as a single legal family, the 'Civil Law' family.

---

[32] The *Pandects* is an alternative name for the *Digest*.
[33] P Stein, 'Legal Humanism and Legal Science' (1986) 54 TvR 297, 306.
[34] U Babusiaux, 'The Future of Legal History: Roman Law' (2016) 56 Am J Leg Hist 6. Beware, though, the unfortunate conflation at page 7 of 'English-speaking areas' and 'common law systems'.

(2) The Mixed Systems: Civil Law and Common Law

In some places where the *ius commune* had been received, or to which it had spread through European colonisation, a further development occurred that is of considerable interest from the Scots lawyer's point of view, for reasons we shall see below. This was the emergence of the mixed legal systems, in which elements of both Civil Law and Common Law appear.

Let us consider one of the main examples of this, the law of South Africa. European occupation here began in 1652, when the Dutch East India Company established a permanent settlement at the Cape of Good Hope, as a stopping-off point between Europe and East Asia. As such, the law of the developing colony was the amalgam of *ius commune* and local law that developed in the Netherlands, and which is known as Roman-Dutch law.[35] However, the colony was seized by the British in 1795 and, although the Dutch managed to recover and hold it from 1803 to 1805, British rule was formally recognised at the Congress of Vienna in 1815. South Africa was granted Dominion status within the British Empire in 1910, but has been a *de facto* independent state since then. During the period of British rule, however, South Africa's *ius commune*-derived legal system experienced considerable English influence.[36]

This process has left the legal system of South Africa as what comparative lawyers call a 'mixed legal system'. The same is true of the law of Sri Lanka,[37] Louisiana[38] and Quebec,[39] which experienced a similar historical process. As we shall see below, Scots law is another example. In these places, a system of law with a historical Roman foundation has subsequently received English rules and concepts. The process tends to pan out in strikingly similar ways in the different mixed systems. Some areas are very little affected by the mixing process. Property law, for example, tends to remain very strongly based on fundamentally Roman principles. Other areas are more strongly influenced by English law, such as commercial law.

D. Roman Law in Scotland

(1) Early Scots Law

We have seen that, across Europe, there was great legal diversity through the earlier Middle Ages. Despite the partial survival of Roman law, the laws governing

---

[35] This term was invented by the Dutch jurist Simon van Leeuwen, whose treatise *Het Roomsch-Hollandsch Recht* was published in 1664. Other prominent Dutch writers include Voet and, perhaps especially, Grotius, whose *Inleydinge tot de Hollandsche Rechtsgeleertheyt* ('Introduction to the Jurisprudence of Holland') was completed in 1621 and published in 1631. For an account of the Reception of Roman law in the Netherlands, see B Beinart, 'Roman Law in South African Practice' (1952) 69 **SALJ** 145.

[36] R W Lee, 'The Roman Law and Common Law Elements in Law of South Africa and Ceylon' 1959 AJ 114; B Beinart, 'Roman Law in a Modern Uncodified Romanistic System' 1971 AJ 131.

[37] The Dutch arrived in Sri Lanka in the seventeenth century, under a treaty made in 1638 with a native king, to eject its Portuguese occupiers. By 1660, the Dutch controlled almost the whole island. The British occupied the island in 1796 to deny it to Napoleon. The Dutch-controlled areas were formally ceded to the British in 1802 under the Treaty of Amiens. The remaining native-controlled areas were conquered by the British in 1815. The island gained Dominion status in 1948, followed by full independence.

[38] Louisiana was a colony of France and then Spain before its acquisition by the United States in 1803.

[39] Quebec was a French colony before its acquisition by the British in 1763.

people's lives were to a great extent matters of local custom, and disputes were determined by men with expertise in local law. In Scotland, the development of a 'common law', in the sense of a single system, can be traced to the twelfth and early thirteenth centuries. The process was not complete for a long time after that. Indeed, arguably the process can still not be held entirely complete, as the possibility remains that some local customary rule might be held to apply to a dispute.[40] During this period, though, there began to develop '[c]ommon mechanisms and broad rules governing conflict resolution'[41] as the Crown began to exert its authority in matters of justice, and it is from here that it becomes possible to talk about something called Scots law.

Scots law in this period was strongly influenced by the developing English Common Law. This can readily be seen by comparing the Scots law treatise *Regiam Majestatem*, probably composed in the first half of the fourteenth century, with the English law book known as *Glanvill*, probably dating from the late 1180s. While it would be wrong to see *Regiam Majestatem* as *simply* a Scottish edition of *Glanvill*, nonetheless large parts of the former are directly lifted from the latter. After the early fourteenth century, though, English influence lessened for political reasons: this was the period of the Wars of Independence. The English king, Edward I, had taken the opportunity of being asked to act as arbiter of a succession dispute[42] to place John Balliol on the Scottish throne in 1292 as, in effect, a puppet king. Balliol having proved insufficiently reliable, Edward invaded and imposed direct rule in 1296, in the face of strong resistance. The most notable resister was the patriotic hero William Wallace, whose greatest success was at Stirling Bridge in September 1297, but whose resistance was effectively brought to an end at Falkirk in the following year. Wallace was captured and killed in 1305, after a show trial. King Robert I (The Bruce), however, seized the throne in 1306, and succeeded in expelling the English over long years of campaigning. As is well known, the decisive battle of this process was the outnumbered Scots' crushing victory over Edward I's less effectual son, Edward II,[43] at Bannockburn in June 1314. It was not until 1328, though, that the English king (by this time Edward II's son, Edward III) formally recognised Scottish independence, in the Treaty of Edinburgh–Northampton.

---

[40] For example, a small number of fragments of Norse law survive in Orkney and Shetland, which only became part of Scotland in 1468 and 1469 respectively. On this, see K Anderson, 'The Influence of Scots and Norse Law on Law and Governance in Orkney and Shetland 1450–1650' (unpublished PhD thesis, University of Aberdeen 2016). On customary law generally, see *Stair Memorial Encyclopaedia*, vol 22 paras 355–93.

[41] Simpson and Wilson, *Scottish Legal History*, vol 1 3.

[42] This had arisen after Alexander III died in 1286, falling from his horse while riding in the dark and in bad weather from Edinburgh to Kinghorn, Fife, to visit his new, young queen on her birthday. The queen was pregnant at the time, but this pregnancy miscarried. This left as Alexander's sole heir his granddaughter, Margaret, the daughter of the King of Norway. She herself died in Orkney in 1290, aged only seven, on her way to Scotland but without ever entering her kingdom (Orkney not becoming part of Scotland until 1468). It was then unclear who should succeed.

[43] The 1995 film *Braveheart*, which tells the story of William Wallace's career, is notorious for its historical errors. In its depiction of the relative abilities of Edward I and his son, however, it was all too accurate. Unfortunately for future relations between the two kingdoms, the latter's son, Edward III, was much closer in character to his grandfather than to his father.

From this, it might be thought obvious that English influence on the law would dwindle. This is not quite as obvious as it appears, though. Accepted legal rules and institutions will often survive even when the political factors that allowed them to arise in the first place cease to exist. As we shall see below, for example, canon law continued to be applied in Scotland even after the Reformation in 1560. More to the point, *Regiam Majestatem*, with all its English-derived content, was almost certainly compiled after Bannockburn, when receptiveness to English ideas might be thought likely to be at its lowest. There is little doubt that some English legal ideas persisted after the Wars of Independence, though the extent of this is a matter of debate.[44] In the longer term, though, divergence between the two was inevitable. In the case of later medieval Scots law, however, there was an additional factor promoting divergence, in the form of the *ius commune*. What is not denied by anyone involved in debates about the Scottish legal history of the period is that Scotland experienced a Reception of Roman law.

(2) Reception in Scotland

In a way very similar to the situation on the Continent, until the eighteenth century there was no university education in Scots law. Indeed, for much of this period, there was no university legal education in Scotland at all. Although three universities existed in Scotland before the Reformation, provision of legal education there was patchy, and came to an end altogether by the early 1600s, for reasons that are not altogether clear.[45] Instead, the practice was to study law at a foreign university (often in France before the Reformation, the Netherlands afterwards). Significant numbers of Scots students continued to do this even after legal education became re-established in Scotland in the eighteenth century,[46] though no doubt the growth of these Scottish law schools contributed to a tailing off of numbers in the second half of that century.[47]

Those seeking a career pleading before the Scottish courts, then, had their whole way of thinking about legal problems shaped at the basic level by the *ius commune*. Scots law could be learned later through observation or private tuition, but it is inevitable that it would be viewed through a Romanistic prism, and interpreted according to Roman assumptions.[48] Indeed, until 1750 there was no requirement for aspiring advocates to be examined in Scots law at all. Before that

---

[44] W D H Sellar, 'Scots Law: Mixed from the Very Beginning? A Tale of Two Receptions' (2000) 4 Edin LR 3. Part of the difficulty with this debate is that, very often, sources are open to suspicion of being motivated by a political position to over- or under-emphasise the continuity.

[45] J W Cairns, 'Academic Feud, Bloodfeud, and William Welwood: Legal Education in St Andrews, 1560–1611' (1998) 2 Edin LR 158 and 255.

[46] Glasgow's Regius Chair was founded in 1713. Edinburgh's oldest chair in law is that of Public Law and the Law of Nature and Nations, established in 1707. Chairs in Civil Law (1710) and Scots Law (1722) followed.

[47] S D Girvin, 'Nineteenth-Century Reforms in Scottish Legal Education: The Universities and the Bar' (1993) 14 J Leg Hist 127 gives a useful review of the situation.

[48] See *e.g.* the Leases Act 1449, which has been interpreted as giving a tenant a real right (see pp. 163–5), despite making no mention of any such thing. What the Act does is make leases binding on acquirers of the land from the original landlord. In Roman law terms, this can only mean that the tenant has a real right, with all of the consequences of that.

time, the normal way of gaining admission to the bar was by examination in civil law, meaning Roman law. An alternative way, through examination in Scots law, was available, but seems to have been seen as less honourable and involved payment of double entry money.[49]

In addition, the courts themselves would look to the *ius commune* for solutions. The modern Court of Session, the highest civil court in Scotland, has its origins in the practice that developed in the fifteenth century of circumventing the jurisdiction of the lower courts by taking a dispute directly to the king and his advisors. The judicial 'sessions' of the king's council that dealt with these matters were often staffed by men with expertise in Roman and canon law. This continued after the session was put on a formal, institutional basis in 1532 as the College of Justice.[50]

From the beginning, then, the Court of Session was staffed by judges who were learned in Roman and canon law, and the cases before it were pled by advocates whose first learning in the law was in the *ius commune*-based law schools of the Continent and who made free use of Roman-based learning in their arguments. Although this is not always obvious from the most important native legal literature of the time, the practicks,[51] it is clear that Scots law at the end of the 1500s had extensively absorbed the learning of the *ius commune*.[52]

This continued into the following century, despite an attempt to impose English law in the Interregnum of the 1650s,[53] during which Scotland was subject to military occupation by English forces. A picture of Scots law as it stood at the end of the seventeenth century, shortly before the Union of 1707, can be obtained from Viscount Stair's *Institutions of the Law of Scotland*, the first edition of which was published in 1681. The second edition, on which modern editions are based, was published in 1693. This is one of a number of works published between the late seventeenth and early nineteenth centuries which are collectively called institutional writings, and which are considered to be a formal source of Scots law. As we have seen, similar works existed in Europe.[54]

---

[49] For a general account of the requirements and procedures for admission as an advocate, see J W Cairns, 'Advocates' Hats, Roman Law and Admission to the Scots Bar, 1580–1812' (1999) 20(2) J Leg Hist 24.

[50] Thus, judges of the Court of Session each bear the title of Senator of the College of Justice. The year 1532 is often seen as the foundation date of the modern Court of Session, though that underemphasises the degree of continuity.

[51] The practicks were collections of court decisions and other legal materials. For a brief overview, see Simpson and Wilson, *Scottish Legal History*, vol 1 282–4. Even if the focus of the practicks is on native Scots materials, however, this does not mean that practitioners did not make regular reference to *ius commune* sources. As has been observed, the practicks 'seem almost to presuppose the existence of a literature somewhere else' (K Reid, 'Property Law: Sources and Doctrine' in *History of Private Law in Scotland*, vol I 199). This literature 'somewhere else' was the learning of the *ius commune*. As Simpson and Wilson observe (at page 172 of their book, and talking of the situation in the 1540s), there was a belief among the Scottish judiciary that 'the learning of Roman law and canon law constituted a more reliable guide to justice and legal "truth" than the local laws of the Scottish realm'. If this attitude subsequently came under challenge, that did not displace the *ius commune* as a fundamental part of Scottish legal thinking.

[52] J W Cairns, 'Ius Civile in Scotland, ca 1600' (2004) 2 Roman Legal Tradition 136.

[53] This followed the execution of Charles I (of Scotland and England) in London in 1649, on charges of treason, and the abolition of the English monarchy. His son, Charles II, was crowned King of Scots, but was deposed in 1651 by English forces.

[54] For Stair's place in this tradition, see P Birks and G McLeod, 'Introduction' in P Birks and G McLeod trans, *Justinian's Institutes* (Duckworth 1987) 16.

Stair is quite clear that Roman law is not formally authoritative in Scotland. He says of Roman law: 'though it be not acknowledged as a law binding for its authority, yet being, as a rule, followed for its equity . . .'.[55] It would be easy to take from this that Roman law was a relatively minor, subsidiary source. That impression would, however, be greatly mistaken, as even a cursory examination of the *Institutions* shows.

First, let us consider the structure of Stair's work. We saw in Chapter 3[56] that the second-century Roman jurist, Gaius, wrote an introductory text (the *Institutes*), in which private law was divided into three parts: persons, things and actions. The law of persons covers matters of personal status; the law of things is concerned with a person's assets, both physical and non-physical, and so including property, succession and obligations; and the law of actions is the law of procedure, the rules by which rights and duties arising from the other parts of the law are enforced. Neither Stair nor any of his predecessors could have been directly influenced by Gaius, as his *Institutes* was lost until the nineteenth century. However, Gaius' scheme survived through its use in Justinian's *Institutes*. Stair does not follow this scheme slavishly,[57] but it is clearly the model from which he began. Property, succession and procedure find the same place in Stair's scheme as in Gaius'.

We find Roman influence when we look at the substance of what Stair writes. Let us take, for example, Stair's general account of possession.[58] As we shall see in Chapter 10,[59] the distinction between ownership and possession is strongly characteristic of a Roman-based system of property law. It is no exaggeration to say that most of Stair's account could almost have been written by a Roman jurist, writing about Roman law. His sources, too, are predominantly Roman here: five Roman texts are cited as authority, whereas only two Scots sources are cited. These are cases concerned with points for which there was no Roman analogue, but even they are viewed through a Roman lens. This is followed by an account of the right of a possessor of property in good faith to the fruits of the property.[60] Here the general principle and justification for the rule is drawn from a number of Roman sources. Only then does Stair resort to reference to Scots case law, to explain the detailed application of the rule. Later, when he is talking about *occupatio*[61] (the acquisition of ownerless property, principally wild animals),[62] seven Roman passages are cited. Only one Scots source is referred to, a case from 1677, for a point on which Scots law has adopted a different rule, and even that is presented as arising from the Roman principles. Beyond property law, in his account of the scope of the law of delict (civil wrongs),[63] almost the only sources cited are seven Roman passages and

---

[55] Stair, *Institutions* 1.1.12.
[56] See pp. 59–60.
[57] Stair's great innovation is to classify obligations as 'conventional' and 'obediential', the latter being 'such as we are bound to perform solely by our obedience to God' (*Institutions* 1.3.2), and to include the subject matter of the law of persons as obediential obligations.
[58] Stair, *Institutions* 2.1.8–22.
[59] See p. 173.
[60] Stair, *Institutions* 2.1.22–4.
[61] Stair, *Institutions* 2.1.33. See pp. 217–21.
[62] See pp. 218–19.
[63] Stair, *Institutions* 1.9.3–4. See Chapters 22–4.

one from a *ius commune* writer, Jacques Cujas. The only Scots source cited is a case from 1669, depending on a point of Scots procedure.

The picture that emerges is of a strong tendency on Stair's part to prefer citation of Roman and, to a lesser extent, *ius commune* sources,[64] especially to explain the general principles of an area of law. There is a matching tendency to cite Scots authority only where the Scots position differs from that of Roman law, or to explain the detailed application of a legal principle.[65]

(3) Scots Law since the Union of Parliaments
(a) *The Influence of English Law*

Scotland and England had shared a monarch since James VI became King of England in 1603 (as James I). This is known as the Union of the Crowns. Despite James's desire for a closer union, however, the two countries remained separate. It was not until the Union of the Parliaments in 1707 that, against strong public opposition, the individual parliaments of Scotland and England were replaced by a new parliament for both countries.[66] The jurisdiction of the Court of Session was expressly preserved.[67] No provision was made for any kind of merger of the law of the two kingdoms, or the replacement of the law of one with that of the other. Quite the contrary: it was expressly enacted that 'no alteration be made in Laws that concern private Right except for evident utility of the subjects within Scotland'.[68] It must be said that the UK Parliament has never felt in any way restrained in legislating on such matters. Moreover, despite the absence of any justification for this in the Treaty of Union, or in the Union with England Act 1707 which implemented it,[69] the House of

---

[64] On Stair's use of *ius commune* sources, see A L M Wilson, 'Stair and the *Inleydinge* of Grotius' (2010) 14 Edin LR 259. It has recently been said judicially that 'modern Scots law, through jurists such as Stair, is derived from the Roman Dutch law of the 17th century' (*Dean v Lord Advocate* [2019] HCJAC 31, para 84 (Lord Drummond Young)). The word 'derived' puts it much too strongly as a general proposition, though it is truer in the particular area considered in that case. Nonetheless, it shows the continuing awareness of the connection.

[65] For a view somewhat contrary to this, see K Luig, 'The Institutions of National Law in the Seventeenth and Eighteenth Centuries' 1972 JR 193, 220–3.

[66] At least that is, or ought to be, the position in theory. In practice, the new parliament looked very much like a continuation of the old English Parliament.

[67] Union with England Act 1707, s. XIX.

[68] Union with England Act 1707, s. XVIII.

[69] Union with England Act 1707, s. XIX provided that, following the Union, no Scottish case was to be 'cognoscible by the Courts of Chancery, Queens-Bench, Common-Pleas or any other Court in Westminsterhall'. The House of Lords did not sit in Westminster Hall, and through this loophole it was allowed to slip. The argument would be that, because it was not expressly excluded, the House of Lords was entitled to claim the authority to hear appeals. This argument is lent some superficial plausibility by the fact that it was possible before the Union to complain to the Scottish Parliament against a decision of the Court of Session, by means of a 'protestation for remeid of law' (Simpson and Wilson, *Scottish Legal History*, vol 1 371–4). However, this procedure was limited in scope, and did not allow the Parliament to review the substantive merits of the decision. It was therefore quite different from an appeal in the normal sense. It is not unlikely that the commissioners responsible for negotiating the terms of the Union envisaged some form of appeal to the House of Lords. If that was the case, however, it is unclear why no express provision was made on the matter. On the whole issue, see A J MacLean, 'The 1707 Union: Scots Law and the House of Lords' (1983) 4(3) J Leg Hist 50; J D Ford, 'The Legal Provisions in the Acts of Union' (2007) 66 Cam LJ 106, 122–8; Simpson and Wilson, *Scottish Legal History*, vol 1 378–80.

Lords[70] had little hesitation in declaring itself to have the right to hear appeals from the Court of Session.

For very similar reasons to those we see in, for example, South Africa, Scots law has gone from being a civil law system to being a mixed system. Significant areas of Scots law have been strongly affected by English law, and in very similar ways. The result is that 'the private lawyer of Scotland and of South Africa have a great deal in common, and a lawyer from the one jurisdiction feels immediately at home with the law books of the other'.[71] This is the case even though there has been very little influence by one system on the other, or even very much contact between lawyers working in each system.

This mixing process was not, however, an immediate result of Union. For example, the *Institute of the Law of Scotland* of another institutional writer, John Erskine, which appeared in 1773, has much the same approach as we have seen in Stair's *Institutions*. The education of advocates was still rooted in the *ius commune*, and during the 1700s Scots law students were still travelling in significant numbers to continental universities for their studies. Moreover, the most obvious vehicle for the imposition of English legal ideas – the House of Lords – heard relatively few Scots appeals during the eighteenth century. The reasons for this are not completely clear, but may have something to do with the expense and inconvenience of appealing to London. In the eighteenth century, it might take two weeks or more to travel from Edinburgh to London by stagecoach. With the development of the railways in the nineteenth century, the journey could be completed within a single day.

Whatever may be the reason for the delay, English influence on the development of Scots law accelerated in the nineteenth century. More appeals went to the House of Lords, where the absence of Scottish judges at that time tended to result in English law being applied.[72] Contact with continental Europe became much more difficult with the Napoleonic Wars.[73] By the time that the Dutch universities that had been most popular with Scots students became accessible once more, Roman-Dutch law no longer applied.[74] In any case, the language factor meant that English books and cases were more accessible than was continental literature, increasingly written in the vernacular rather than in Latin. It was easier, therefore, to turn to English sources, especially in areas then in rapid development such as commercial law. For example, in the nineteenth-century *Principles*[75] and *Commentaries*[76] of the last

---

[70] In 2009, this role of hearing appeals was transferred to a new Supreme Court.
[71] Zimmermann, Visser and Reid, *Mixed Legal Systems*, preface.
[72] For a particularly egregious example, see the discussion of *Bartonshill Coal Co v Reid* (1858) 3 Macq 266 below at pp. 400–1.
[73] 1803–15.
[74] T B Smith, 'Scots Law and Roman-Dutch Law: A Shared Tradition' 1959 AJ 36. After the French conquest of the Netherlands in 1806, under Napoleon, the law was codified along the lines of the French *Code civil*. This tradition continues into the Dutch Civil Code as it is today, the *Burgerlijk Wetboek*.
[75] G J Bell, *Principles of the Law of Scotland* (1st edn published 1829).
[76] G J Bell, *Commentaries on the Municipal and Mercantile Law of Scotland, Considered in Relation to the Subject of Bankruptcy*. The first of two volumes of this work appeared in 1800 as *Treatise on the Laws of Bankruptcy in Scotland*. However, in 1804, when the second volume was published and the first reissued, the name was changed to the more familiar *Commentaries*.

institutional writer, George Joseph Bell, we see considerable use of English sources, although *ius commune* materials continue to be prominent as well. Finally, it must be remembered that, from 1707 until the re-establishment of the Scottish Parliament in 1999, Scotland had no legislature of its own, despite largely being governed as a separate entity. The UK Parliament rarely showed much interest in Scottish legislation but, when it did, it had a strong tendency to be lazily insensitive to the specific needs of the system. Often legislation designed for England would simply be transplanted with little attempt made to adapt it to Scots law.

(b) The Current Position
So what, then, is the current position? Does the study of Roman law retain its relevance to Scots lawyers and law students? In 1969, the following was written of the (then) new Department of Law at the University of Strathclyde:

> its attitude is modern and forward-looking . . . The study of the ancient Roman, Babylonian and other systems of law of the early periods of civilisation must be left to those of the ancient universities which feel that it is part of their task to do this. However interesting and academically sound such studies may be, they have no place in Strathclyde . . .[77]

No doubt it is easy to speak with the benefit of hindsight, but this view has more recently been described (justly) as 'very quaint'.[78] Indeed, it is almost embarrassingly so, given how out of step it is with subsequent developments. This is the case even if we disregard the bizarre ranking of Roman law alongside ancient Babylonian law. Whatever one may think about the proper role of Roman law in modern law schools, it is clearly in a different position from Babylonian law. At the time of writing (2020), a pass in Roman law is still required for admission to the Faculty of Advocates, and the late twentieth century saw a flowering of historically conscious writing on Scots law greater than at any time since that of the institutional writers. The fact that speaks most eloquently, however, is perhaps that undergraduate law students at the University of Strathclyde do, now, have the opportunity to study Roman law. So much, one may say, for being 'modern and forward-looking'.

Let us look at how Roman sources are actually used in the courts. It is helpful first to look at trends over time in the courts' use of these sources. While, of course, it is only to be expected that sometimes the courts will use principles derived from Roman law without making direct reference to any Roman source or mentioning that origin, it is interesting to consider how often such reference is made. Figure 4.1 shows, by decade, the number of references made to certain terms[79] in cases decided by the Scottish courts between 1830 and 2019, found

---

[77] I P Miller, 'Teaching Law in Britain's First Technological University' 1969 SLT (News) 83, 84.
[78] J W Cairns and P du Plessis, 'Ten Years of Roman Law in Scottish Courts' 2008 SLT (News) 191, 191.
[79] The terms used were 'Roman law' itself, as well as the names of three prominent Roman jurists (Ulpian, Papinian and Modestinus), and Justinian.

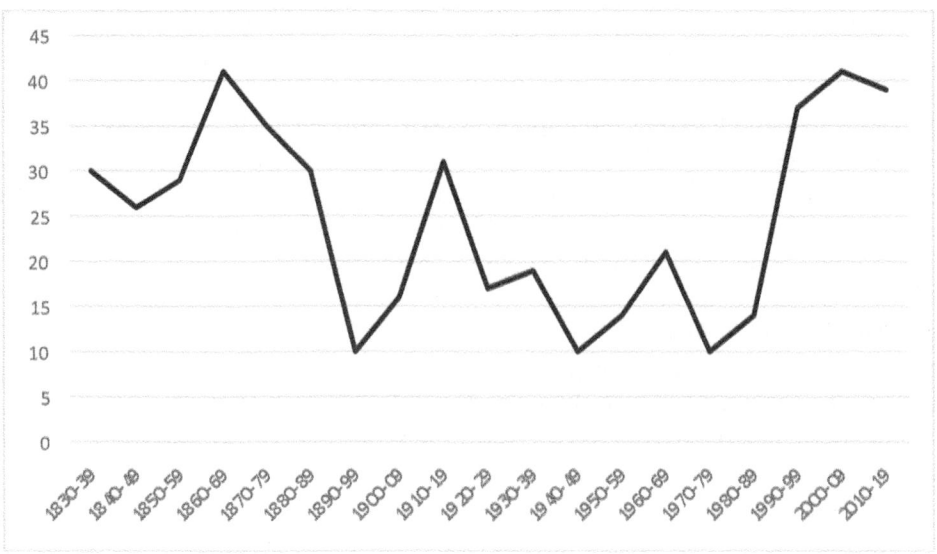

Figure 4.1 Trends in references to Roman law

by searching the Westlaw database. It is not entirely scientific. It does not take into account, for example, the total number of cases decided in each decade. Nonetheless, there does seem to be long spell from the 1920s to the 1980s when less reference was made to the search terms and, so the assumption would be, less reference to Roman law itself. This has been followed by a substantial increase in direct reference since then, to a level not reached since the 1860s.

When the data is broken down a little more, a further interesting fact emerges. All things being equal, it seems that a reference to a specific Roman jurist is more likely to form part of a detailed consideration of the Roman sources than is a simple use of the phrase 'Roman law'. From that point of view, it is interesting to note that there has been a distinct increase in references by name to the specific jurists referred to since around the year 2000 (see Figure 4.2). It seems likely that the same is true of other jurists, not searched for. Fourteen cases were found since 2000 that referred to at least one of these jurists by name. That is just one short of the number found from the previous 140 years before that. That is suggestive, not just of an increase in awareness and use of the Roman sources, but also of an increasing sophistication in the handling of these sources.

Of course, even where reference is made to Roman law, it does not follow that that reference was decisive. It may not even have been very important. Sometimes a reference to Roman law will be little more than ornamental, perhaps simply illustrating the historical origins of a rule without the Roman sources actually playing any part in the court's reasoning. Sometimes the courts will go a little further than this, and use the Roman sources to give additional support

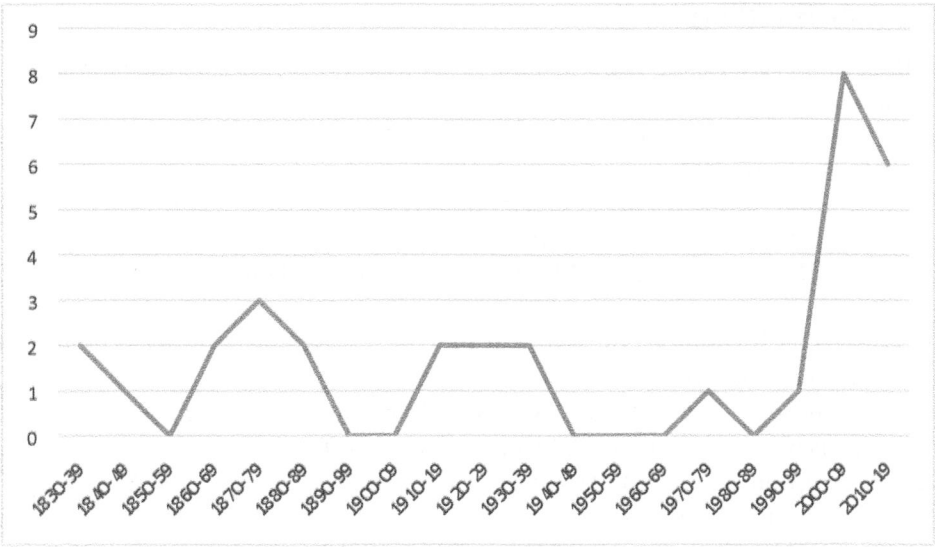

Figure 4.2 References to Ulpian, Papinian and Modestinus

to a decision that could, nonetheless, have been reached without them. It does sometimes still happen, though, that Roman and *ius commune* sources are used to fill in gaps in the law. Justly it has been said that 'Roman law is still a living source of Scots common law'.[80]

Chapter Summary

Roman law's survival in Western Europe was patchy at best after Rome fell in AD 476. However, the study of Roman legal texts was revived in the Middle Ages, and came to form the basis of a general European *ius commune* ('common law'). This was not a single legal order, but instead a shared resource that could be drawn on to interpret and fill gaps in local laws. Although the unity this created began to break up from the sixteenth century onwards, threads of continuity can be traced into modern legal systems. Indeed, in some countries, including Scotland, Roman and *ius commune* literature continues to be used in the present day.

---

[80] J W Cairns and P du Plessis, 'Ten Years of Roman Law in Scottish Courts' 2008 SLT (News) 191, 193. See also K Reid, 'Property Law: Sources and Doctrine' in *History of Private Law in Scotland, vol I* 192–3.

Further Reading

P Birks and G McLeod, 'Introduction' in P Birks and G McLeod trans, *Justinian's Institutes* (Duckworth 1987)

H Coing, 'The Sources and Characteristics of the *ius commune*' (1986) 19 Comp & Int LJ S Afr 483

W M Gordon, 'Roman Law in Scotland' in R Evans-Jones ed, *The Civil Law Tradition in Scotland* (Stair Society 1995)

A Lewis, 'Roman Law in the Middle of Its Third Millennium' (1997) 50 CLP 397

K Luig, 'The Institutions of National Law in the Seventeenth and Eighteenth Centuries' 1972 JR 193

O F Robinson, T D Fergus and W M Gordon, *European Legal History: Sources and Institutions* 3rd edn (Oxford University Press 2000)

A R C Simpson and A L M Wilson, *Scottish Legal History, Volume One: 1000–1707* (Edinburgh University Press 2017)

A Watson, 'The Importance of "Nutshells"' (1994) 42 Am J Comp L 1

PART TWO

The Law of Persons

In Part One of this book, we considered the wider context in which the study of Roman law is set. This included, in Chapter 4, the influence of Roman law on later law, up to the present day. The rest of the book focuses on the part of Roman law that has been most influential on later law, and which is most often studied, namely Roman private law. Private law is the law governing relations between persons, whereas public law is the law governing relations between persons and the state. Private law can itself be divided into a number of parts. As we saw in Chapter 3,[1] the jurist Gaius divided private law into three parts: the law of persons, the law of things and the law of actions. This is known as the 'institutional scheme', and is the scheme on which Gaius' introductory textbook, the *Institutes*, is organised. The law of actions is the law governing the enforcement of rights, and was considered in Chapter 2.[2] It remains, therefore, to consider the law of persons and the law of things.

Part Two of the book is concerned then with the law of persons. It considers the different ways in which a person's legal status may affect their rights and obligations. This part of Roman law was very influential in the formative period of Scots law, particularly through its influence on the canon law of the Roman Catholic Church. Its continuing influence is rather less, as much of the ground covered in the law of persons is now governed by modern statutes. Nonetheless, there are certain points in which Roman sources are of continuing importance.

Part Two begins in Chapter 5 by considering the meaning of the term 'person' in a legal context. Chapters 6 to 8 focus on, respectively, the legal institutions of slavery, parenthood and marriage. Finally, Chapter 9 considers the issues that arise when one person acts on another's behalf.

---

[1] See pp. 58–60.
[2] See pp. 29–45.

CHAPTER FIVE

Categories of Person

A. Legal Personality and Legal Status

(1) Natural and Juristic Persons

It is as well to begin with a definition of what we mean by a person, because the category of legal person goes beyond human beings. In law, a person is an entity capable of holding rights and being subject to obligations. Most persons are, indeed, human beings. However, in modern law, we make a distinction between natural and juristic persons. The former are human beings and the latter are other entities recognised by the law as capable of holding rights and being subject to obligations. For example, in modern law, companies and partnerships are juristic persons. There was some recognition of this in Roman law, and various types of corporate body were recognised as being capable of owning property, being beneficiaries under wills and suing or being sued in their own name, all separately from the individual human beings that were members of them.[1] Examples include private members' associations (*collegia*), self-governing communities (*municipia*), the state and, after the conversion to Christianity, churches.[2] In this chapter, however, the focus will be on natural persons.

(2) The Elements of Legal Status

The Romans identified three elements to a person's legal status: liberty, citizenship and family.[3]

(a) Liberty

This first element, liberty, is concerned with what Gaius calls the 'great distinction in the law of persons . . . that all men are either free or slaves'.[4] As we shall see in Chapter 6, Roman society depended very greatly on slave labour, and slaves were incapable of acquiring rights or incurring obligations. Instead, they were considered to be property themselves, to be owned by others.

---

[1] See *e.g.* D.3.4.1pr; D.3.4.7.1.
[2] For a fuller account, see Buckland, *Textbook* 174–81.
[3] D.4.5.11.

(b) Citizenship

The second element of personal status is citizenship. This carried with it various public law consequences, such as the right to vote and liability to taxation. Unlike the situation in modern law, however, in which we consider citizenship to be almost entirely a matter for public law, with few private law consequences, in the ancient world the situation was quite different. The Romans made a distinction between the *ius gentium* ('law of nations'), which applied to everyone, and the *ius civile* ('civil law'), which was special to those with Roman citizenship rights.

The Romans identified three private law citizenship rights. The first, *commercium*, was the right to enter into transactions falling into the *ius civile*. For example, certain methods of acquiring ownership fell within the *ius civile*, and so only those with the right of *commercium* could acquire in this way. Next, *testamenti factio* was the right to participate in the making of a will under Roman law. Finally, *conubium* was the right to enter into a Roman marriage. These rights were common to citizens, but sometimes they were granted to non-citizen communities or individuals as well.[5]

The most common way of acquiring citizenship, however, was birth as a citizen. The rule of the *ius gentium* was that a child followed its mother's status, and so the child of a citizen mother would itself be a citizen. Where, though, the parents were married in a Roman marriage,[6] the *ius civile* rule was that the child followed the father's status. Normally this would make little difference, as it was for the most part only Roman citizens who could enter a Roman marriage anyway. However, it could be that a Roman woman married a non-citizen who had *conubium*. This had the anomalous result that, where a Roman woman married a non-citizen who had *conubium*, the child would be a non-citizen (because it would follow the father's status, the marriage being a Roman one). Where, however, a Roman woman married a non-citizen **without** *conubium*, the child **would** be a citizen (because, the marriage not being a valid Roman one, the child would follow the mother's status). This anomaly was removed by a *lex Minicia*, as a result of which all such children were to follow the father's status.[7]

Another important way of becoming a citizen related to freed slaves. Where a person was freed from slavery, he or she became a Roman citizen. We shall see more on this in Chapter 6.[8]

(c) Family

The third part of status was membership of a Roman family. We must make a distinction between two categories of people here. Some were *sui iuris* ('of their own right') and some were *alieni iuris* ('of another's right'). The Roman family

---

[4] G.1.9; D.1.5.3.
[5] Foremost among such communities were those with Latin rights, modelled on those enjoyed by the communities of Latium with which early Rome was allied (see pp. 6–7). Citizens of such communities had none of the public law rights of Roman citizenship and lacked *conubium*, but had *commercium*.
[6] On marriage, see Chapter 8.
[7] G.1.77–8. In the converse case, where a male Roman citizen married a non-citizen with *conubium*, the child of the marriage would be a citizen (G.1.76).
[8] See pp. 112–3.

structure was highly patriarchal, in that the oldest man in the male line had legal authority (called *patria potestas*) over all of his descendants in the male line.[9] This person was called the *paterfamilias* ('father of the family'), and in principle his authority lasted for his lifetime.[10] The legal capacity of *alieni iuris* persons was severely restricted and, for example, such a person could not own property.[11] In legal terms, the position of an *alieni iuris* person was therefore not altogether different from that of a slave, although of course such a person's *social* status was very different.

(d) *Capitis Deminutio* (Status Loss)

Loss of any of these three parts of a person's status was called *capitis deminutio* ('status loss'). Reflecting the three parts of status, there were three forms of *capitis deminutio*, each different in degree.[12] The greatest of them was *capitis deminutio maxima*, which occurred when a person became a slave, and which necessarily extinguished that person's citizenship and family relationships. This was laid down as a punishment in various situations.[13] Next comes *capitis deminutio media*, also sometimes imposed as a punishment,[14] which was loss of citizenship. Such a person was not made a slave. However, a non-citizen could neither be subject to nor exercise *patria potestas*, and so lost membership of his or her family. Finally, *capitis deminutio minima* involved a person remaining a free citizen, but losing family status. In practice, this was the most common form of *capitis deminutio*, and occurred whenever a person was adopted into a family or was emancipated (*i.e.* released from *patria potestas*).

B. *Sui Iuris* Persons with Limited Capacity

Both slaves and those subject to a *paterfamilias* were *alieni iuris*, that is subject to the legal authority (*potestas*) of another. By contrast, those who were *sui iuris* were not subject to this kind of authority. Nonetheless, some categories of *sui iuris* persons were subject to various kinds of restriction on their legal capacity.

(1) Women

The jurist Papinian tells us that 'in many points of our law the position of females is worse than that of males'.[15] This was certainly true in public law, women being barred from holding any public office[16] and being unable to vote. In private law,

---

[9] So, for example, his authority extended to all of his children, and to his sons' children, but not to his daughters' children.
[10] As we shall see at p. 127, it could be brought to an end in various circumstances, and came to be qualified in certain respects.
[11] Although, as we shall see at p. 121, certain exceptions to this principle were developed.
[12] D.4.5.11.
[13] G.1.160.
[14] G.1.161.
[15] D.1.5.9.
[16] D.50.17.2.

too, women were subject to a range of restrictions. In parenthood, as we shall see in Chapter 7,[17] a mother could not have the same legal authority over her children that was held by their *paterfamilias*, who was usually their father. Again, until the procedure was abolished by Hadrian,[18] a woman could not make a will without first going through *coemptio*, a kind of fictional self-sale,[19] with the apparent purpose of terminating her relationship with family members who would otherwise have a claim on her property on her death.[20]

Often these restrictions were justified by 'the weakness of the sex',[21] or on the idea that men had a responsibility to protect women.[22] At the same time, though, the limitations imposed on women's capacity were less than in many legal systems, and not just in the ancient world. Even up to fairly modern times, women had restricted legal capacity. Moreover, there were changes over time. For example, while in early law marriage involved the wife passing into the *potestas* of her husband (or of his *paterfamilias*), by the early Empire this form of marriage was almost obsolete.[23] Again, while most women were required to have a guardian, or *tutor*, for life,[24] in the second century AD Gaius is finding the traditional explanation implausible:

> For that which is commonly accepted, that by weakness of mind many are deceived, and it is fair that they should be governed by the authority of tutors, seems more specious than true. For women of full age manage their own affairs, and in certain cases the interposition of the tutor's authority is a mere formality. Indeed, often a tutor is compelled by the praetor to give his authority against his will.[25]

An alternative explanation for the rule is that it is intended to protect the woman's property in the interests of those entitled to succeed on her intestacy.[26]

A restriction of particular interest is that imposed in AD 46 by a *senatusconsultum*, the *SC Velleianum*.[27] This provided that, where a woman agreed to guarantee another person's debts,[28] that agreement was not enforceable against her. The purpose of this was, Ulpian tells us, to protect women, who could be misled on account of the 'weakness of the sex'.[29]

---

[17] See p. 116.
[18] Reigned AD 117–38.
[19] G.1.115a.
[20] S Dixon, 'Infirmitas Sexus: Womanly Weakness in Roman Law' (1984) 52 TvR 343, 354.
[21] D.16.1.2.2 (Ulpian). The specific reference is to the *SC Velleianum*, considered below.
[22] J.4.4.2; D.47.10.1.9. The specific reference is to the husband's right to take action where his wife is a victim of the delict of *iniuria*. See Chapter 23.
[23] See p. 142.
[24] See pp. 131–2.
[25] G.1.190. Compare G.1.144.
[26] J Dodds, 'The Impact of the Roman Law of Succession and Marriage on Women's Property and Independence' (1992) 18 MULR 899, 909.
[27] D.16.1. Ulpian gives the wording of the *senatusconsultum* at D.16.1.2.1.
[28] On such guarantees, see pp. 277–8.
[29] D.16.1.2.2. For discussion of the policy behind the *senatusconsultum*, see R van den Bergh, 'Roman Women: Sometimes Equal and Sometimes Not' (2006) 12 Fundamina 113. As van den Bergh points out at page 116 of that article, there were exceptions to its operation, it being aimed specifically at situations when 'she had been deceived and the family property was prejudiced'.

The restriction imposed by the *SC Velleianum* is one that has had continuing significance in medieval and later law. It survived, under the Roman name, until 1971 in South Africa.[30] A similar rule found its way into the law of Quebec, even though the *SC Velleianum* had been abolished in France (from which the law of Quebec is derived) in 1606.[31] It was not received in Scots law, although women were subject to a number of other restrictions in Scots law that persisted to some extent until the nineteenth century.[32]

Nonetheless, the issue never entirely goes away, because it will always be the case that there will be people prepared to guarantee the debts of friends or relations when they would be better advised not to do so. In the 1990s, the House of Lords moved, in both Scotland[33] and England,[34] to limit the capacity[35] of presumptively vulnerable groups of people[36] to guarantee the debts of close relations.[37] Similar developments occurred in Germany.[38] Although these modern developments are in gender neutral terms, women were clearly a major group intended to fall within their scope.

(2) Children

A person with a living *paterfamilias* had limited legal capacity. This state of affairs only ended when the *paterfamilias* died and his children became *sui iuris*, or when an individual *alieni iuris* person was emancipated. Indeed, a person who died

---

[30] B A Hepple, 'Women Sureties' (1959) 76 SALJ 322; I D, 'The Senatusconsultum Velleianum and the Authentica Si Qua Mulier' (1969) 86 SALJ 239; E Kahn, 'Farewell Senatusconsultum Velleianum and Authentica Si Qua Mulier' (1971) 88 SALJ 364; S Evans, 'Senatusconsultum Velleianum' (1971) 88 SALJ 533. The *authentica si qua mulier*, referred to in the title of two of these articles, was derived from legislation of Justinian (Nov.134.8 (AD 556)), making specific provision for the case where a woman consents to a document burdening herself or her property with her husband's debts. It is provided that this consent will be void unless it is proved that the money was used for her benefit.

[31] H Newman, 'An Historical and Juridical Analysis of Article 1301 of the Quebec Civil Code' (1951) 29 Can Bar Rev 345.

[32] W M Gordon, 'Property and Succession Rights' in *Roman Law, Scots Law and Legal History* (Edinburgh University Press 2007).

[33] *Smith v Bank of Scotland* 1997 SC (HL) 111.

[34] *Barclays Bank v O'Brien* [1994] 1 AC 180.

[35] No doubt both the House of Lords in the 1990s and the Senate in AD 46 believed that they were protecting women from the consequences of their actions rather than limiting their capacity, but both of those things can be true. If a person cannot enter into a binding transaction on his or her own judgement, but must first seek some kind of third party verification, that person's legal capacity has been restricted to that extent. This is what the courts in England have done (*Royal Bank of Scotland plc v Etridge (No 2)* [2002] 2 AC 773), though the Scottish courts have not gone this far (*Clydesdale Bank plc v Black* 2002 SC 555). Nor is this necessarily in the affected person's own interests. If women are protected from enforcement of their guarantees, lenders will be less likely to enter into such arrangements with them, even in the case of a woman who perfectly well understands what she is agreeing to, who is subject to no unfair pressure and who is perfectly capable of meeting the obligation she has entered into.

[36] By this phrase is meant, not people who can be shown by their own individual characteristics to be vulnerable, but people who are presumed from their membership of a category of people to be vulnerable, such as wives guaranteeing the debts of their husbands or adult children doing the same for their parents.

[37] For discussion, see *e.g.* G L Gretton, 'Sexually Transmitted Debt' 1997 SLT (News) 195; C Anderson, 'Cautionary Wives Again: *Cooper v Bank of Scotland*' 2014 SLT (News) 185.

[38] M Habersack and R Zimmermann, 'Legal Change in a Codified System: Recent Developments in Germany Suretyship Law' (1999) 3 Edin LR 272.

young or who had a long-lived *paterfamilias* might go through his or her whole life without ever becoming *sui iuris*. Equally, it could easily happen that a person could acquire full capacity while still very young and in need of protection. A child who became *sui iuris* under the age of puberty,[39] therefore, would need to have a guardian (*tutor*).[40] In addition, even after this age, legislation in the Republic provided additional protections against the taking advantage of a young person's inexperience, up to the age of twenty-five. We shall see these issues in greater detail in Chapter 7.[41]

(3) Freedmen

Although a freed slave acquired Roman citizenship, the newly created citizen's rights were subject to certain limitations. The law made a distinction between the freeborn (*ingenui*), on the one hand, and freedmen and freedwomen (*libertini*), on the other.[42] As we shall see in more detail in Chapter 6, a freedman or freedwoman was subject to certain public law restrictions, and continued to owe various duties to the former master or mistress.

(4) Others

There were other groups whose capacity was limited. As early as the Twelve Tables, it was recognised that the insane (*furiosi*) could not simply be left to their own devices. *Furiosi* had no legal capacity to enter into transactions, except during lucid intervals. A magistrate could appoint a *curator* to take care of the property and affairs of the *furiosus*. This role included taking care of the health and well-being of the *furiosus*.[43] Later, by analogy with this, the praetor acquired the power also to appoint a *curator* to manage the property of spendthrifts (*prodigi*),[44] who by this procedure were deprived of the capacity to transact with their property.[45]

Infames were those who had incurred a form of legal disgrace called *infamia*, which imposed upon them various legal disabilities, such as the inability to act in litigation or to hold public office.[46] The jurist Julian gives a lengthy, non-exhaustive,

---

[39] This was considered to be fourteen for boys and twelve for girls.
[40] For women, this normally continued for life.
[41] See pp. 130–1.
[42] Commonly, the term 'freedmen' is used to cover both men and women who had been freed from slavery.
[43] D.27.10.7pr.
[44] D.27.10.1pr. The term 'prodigals' is sometimes used, reflecting the Latin *prodigi*. The best-known prodigal is undoubtedly the title character of the Parable of the Prodigal Son, found in Luke 15:11–32, who claims his inheritance while his father is still alive, leaves home and squanders it, only then returning and gaining forgiveness. From this, many people have understood a prodigal to be someone who leaves home and then later returns. This is not so. The prodigal son is so called because he squandered his inheritance, not because he left home to do so.
[45] D.27.10.10pr.
[46] Compare the censors' power to impose legal disgrace, noted above at p. 10. Sometimes *infamia* was automatic, and sometimes it arose only where a person had been found liable in one of a limited range of actions. On the distinction, see A Watson, 'Some Cases of Distortion by the Past in Classical Roman Law' (1963) 31 TvR 69, 76–85. For a more detailed account of the consequences of *infamia*, see A H J Greenidge, *Infamia: Its Place in Roman Public and Private Law* (Oxford University Press 1894).

list of cases in which *infamia* is incurred, all cases in which the individual in question has engaged in some form of discreditable conduct.[47] Included on the list are dishonourably discharged soldiers; brothel-keepers; vexatious litigants; thieves, robbers, fraudsters and those held liable for *iniuria*; anyone found liable in a case of partnership, tutelage, mandate or deposit; and anyone who gives or receives a widowed daughter in marriage during her proper time of mourning.

Similar to *infames* were *intestabiles*, who were barred from acting as witnesses in litigation or in formal transactions, such as the making of a will.[48] There seems to have been some doubt as to whether it was permissible for anyone to witness a transaction by an *intestabilis* either.[49] If that was not permissible, then the effect would be that an *intestabilis* could not make a will or make a formal conveyance of property.[50] This status was in principle separate from *infamia*, although the same conduct might incur both consequences.

Chapter Summary

The main elements of a Roman's status were liberty (the status of being free rather than slave), citizenship (the status of being a Roman citizen) and family (membership of a Roman family). All of these had implications for a person's legal capacity, and liberty and family are the subject matter of Chapters 6 and 7. There were, however, other ways in which a person's legal capacity could be affected. The most important of these was marriage (considered in Chapter 8), but there were others. We have seen some of these in this chapter.

Further Reading

J.1.16

D.1.5

M L Colish, 'The Roman Law of Persons and Roman History: A Case for an Interdisciplinary Approach' (1974) 19 Am J Juris 112

J Evans Grubbs, *Women and the Law in the Roman Empire: A Sourcebook on Marriage, Divorce and Widowhood* (Routledge 2002)

B W Frier and T A J McGinn, *A Casebook on Roman Family Law* (Oxford University Press 2004) chapter I

J F Gardner, *Women in Roman Law & Society* (Croom Helm 1986)

---

[47] D.3.2.1.
[48] See pp. 294–300.
[49] Compare D.28.1.26 (Gaius) and D.28.1.18.1 (Ulpian).
[50] Not all property required a formal conveyance, however. See pp. 198–9.

O F Robinson, 'The Status of Women in Roman Private Law' 1987 JR 143

A Watson, *The Law of Persons in the Later Roman Republic* (Oxford University Press 1967) chapters 12 and 13

M M Wethmar-Lemmer, 'The Legal Position of Roman Women: A Dissenting Perspective' (2006) 12 Fundamina 174

L Winkel, 'Forms of Imposed Protection in Legal History, Especially in Roman Law' (2010) 16 Fundamina 578

CHAPTER SIX

Slavery

A. Slavery and Society

(1) The Nature of Slavery

We are told in the *Corpus Iuris Civilis* that slavery is a status that is 'contrary to the law of nature'.[1] This should not mislead us into thinking that the Romans were very concerned with slaves' welfare or with the humanity that they had in common with their masters. Quite the contrary: the Roman jurists asked few moral questions about slavery,[2] and certainly never questioned its legitimacy. Slavery was a universally accepted fact of the *ius gentium*, the law of nations, and the idea of slavery as being contrary to nature should be understood simply as being based on an observation that human beings are by nature free, and can only be made slaves through positive law.

From this, it might be thought that there would be little in this topic for the modern lawyer, given that Scots law has never recognised slavery, whether by the imposition of slavery on someone within Scotland[3] or even by recognising as a slave someone enslaved outside Scotland and then brought into the country.[4] Even here, though, there has been some influence. It is now a statutory offence to hold a person 'in slavery or servitude'.[5] In a decision of the High Court of Justiciary on this offence, it is observed that this was also a crime under the common law, and implies that this offence was derived from Roman law.[6] Still, all told, this is not an area of Roman law that has influenced Scots law particularly strongly.[7] However,

---

[1] J.1.2.2; D.1.5.4.1.
[2] A Watson, 'Morality, Slavery and the Jurists in the Later Roman Republic' (1968) 42 Tulane LR 289. For discussion of the issue that Watson considers at pages 291–5 (ownership of a slave child born of a mother held on usufruct), see pp. 261–2.
[3] *Reid v Scott of Harden* (1687) Mor 9505. For background on this case, see <http://www.tumblinglassie.com/about-the-tumbling-lassie> (last accessed 14 September 2020).
[4] *Knight v Wedderburn* (1778) Mor 14545.
[5] Human Trafficking and Exploitation (Scotland) Act 2015, section 4(1)(a).
[6] *Miller v HM Advocate* [2019] HCJAC 7, para [12], citing D.48.15.6.2.
[7] That does not mean to say that there have not been classes subject to restricted civil status. For example, formerly in Scots law colliers and salters were bound for life to their place of work and could be forced to return to it (see Erskine, *Institute* 1.7.61). In a similar way, medieval law had its serfs and post-classical Roman law had an analogous class, *colonii adscriptii*, who were bound to the land. On the differences between Roman *adscriptii* and Scots colliers and salters, see 'Serfdom in Scotland' (1878) 22 Journal of Jurisprudence 393, 399–400.

in countries (such as the United States) that have recognised slavery into modern times, Roman slave law has been very influential.[8]

In total contrast with the modern world, slavery was completely accepted in the ancient world, as indeed it has been in probably most societies through history. Rome was certainly no exception, and for the Romans slavery had fundamental social and economic importance. What, then, is slavery? In simple terms, a slave is a human being who is subject to another person's ownership.[9] A slave, then, is an item of property, able in principle to be used (or abused) according to the whim of the slave's owner. As property, slaves themselves had and could have no rights of their own of any kind, any more than household pets or livestock were capable of holding rights.

(2) The Role of Slaves

There is a paradox here, however. While the law said that slaves were things rather than persons, the Romans could hardly have avoided being aware that slaves were nonetheless human beings with the full range of abilities possessed by human beings. Among the Romans, slaves filled a wide range of functions. We should not think of slaves simply as being unskilled or semi-skilled agricultural labourers or household servants. While very many slaves did fill such roles, others had functions requiring a high level of skill and carrying considerable responsibility, such as medicine, teaching and business management. It may be supposed that such skilled slaves could expect better treatment from their owners. We shall see more on the treatment of slaves below.

B. Becoming a Slave

(1) Birth as a Slave

A person could be born a slave, and this would happen where a child was born of slave parents. What if only one of the parents was a slave? For example, it must often have happened that a slave woman's child was the biological child of the master. In these cases, the rule of the *ius gentium* was followed, that the child followed the status of its mother. Thus, the child of a slave mother would be a slave, even if the father was free.[10] Where the status of the mother changed during pregnancy, the child would be born free if the mother was free at any time between conception and birth,[11] a rule that appears to have emerged under Hadrian.[12]

In principle, the same rule was applied where the father was a slave and the mother free. The child would follow the mother's status and be free.[13] However,

---

[8] R B Robinson and J D Hardy, 'An *Actio de Peculio* in Ante-Bellum Alabama' (1990) 11 J Leg Hist 364.
[9] There was an exception to this in public slaves (*servi publici*), who were owned by no specific person except, perhaps, the state.
[10] For an example, see D.19.5.5pr.
[11] J.1.4pr.
[12] D.1.5.18.
[13] J.1.4pr.

the situation was complicated by a resolution of the Senate in AD 52, the *SC Claudianum*.[14] This applied where a free woman cohabited with a slave.[15] Where this was done without the consent of the slave's owner then, after notice (*denuntiatio*) had been given to the woman three times,[16] both she and any children of the union were enslaved. Originally, if the slave's owner agreed to the cohabitation, the woman remained free, but the children of the union were enslaved. That latter rule, however, was abolished by Hadrian, with the result that in the case of a cohabitation with the owner's consent both the woman and her children remained free.[17] Hadrian's reform did not, though, affect the position of a woman who cohabited with the slave without the consent of the slave's owner. She continued to be subject to enslavement. This continued to be the case until the *SC Claudianum* was repealed by Justinian,[18] with the result that, thereafter, the child of a free woman would always be free.

(2) Imposition of Slavery on a Free Person

Other than the rules under the *SC Claudianum*, considered above, there were other ways in which a free person could become a slave. For example, enslavement could be imposed as a punishment for wrongdoing of various kinds.[19] A particularly striking example of enslavement as a punishment is the case where a free person fraudulently arranged to be sold as a slave, with the intention of having an accomplice then assert his freedom. Such a person was to be enslaved.[20] Otherwise, a free person could not voluntarily submit to slavery. Equally, a *paterfamilias* could not sell his children into slavery.[21] An exception, however, appears to have developed in post-classical law: a *paterfamilias* under pressure from severe poverty could sell a newborn child, subject to a right to reclaim the child later on paying the child's value or providing a substitute slave.[22]

The most important way in which a free person could become a slave, however, was capture in war. The rule was that anyone (not just soldiers) captured in wartime became the slave of the captors. This applied both to Romans captured by enemies and also to enemies captured by Romans. A captive who returned, however, might regain freedom. This was known as *postliminium*. The general idea was fairly straightforward, though its detailed application was often complicated and much is unclear from the texts.[23] Essentially, if a Roman citizen was captured

---

[14] For a full account, see W W Buckland, *The Roman Law of Slavery: The Condition of the Slave in Private Law from Augustus to Justinian* (Cambridge University Press 1908) 412–18.
[15] It did not apply in the converse case, in which a free man cohabited with a female slave: C.7.16.3 (AD 225).
[16] C.Th.4.12.2 (AD 317). On the third occasion, the notice had to be given in the presence of seven witnesses who were Roman citizens.
[17] G.1.84.
[18] C.7.24; J.3.12.1.
[19] *E.g* following a process of *manus iniectio*. See p. 36.
[20] A Watson, *Roman Slave Law* (Johns Hopkins University Press 1987) 9.
[21] C.4.43.1 (AD 294); C.7.16.1. The rule may have been different in early law.
[22] C.4.43.2 (AD 329). For Scots law, compare *Reid v Scott of Harden* (1687) Mor 9505.
[23] For a detailed account, see W W Buckland, *The Roman Law of Slavery: The Condition of the Slave in Private Law from Augustus to Justinian* (Cambridge University Press 1908) 291–311.

by enemy forces, his or her status was considered to be in suspense. If the captive died while in captivity, he or she was treated as having died at the moment of capture.[24] If the captive returned, however, he or she was normally entitled to resume his or her previous status. If the captive had been a *paterfamilias*, for example, the *patria potestas* he had previously had was restored. There were exceptions to this, however, most notably with marriage. There is a fairly obvious difficulty that the non-captive spouse might have remarried during the period of captivity. The rule in classical law therefore was that the marriage did not survive,[25] and was only reconstituted on the captive's return by renewed consent.[26] According to a pronouncement of Justinian, however, the rule was that the marriage survived as long as it was clear that the captive survived. If it was not known whether the captive had survived, the non-captive spouse would have to wait for five years before being able to remarry.[27]

C. Relations Between Slave and Master

(1) The Slave's Capacity

The basic position was that, as far as private law was concerned,[28] the slave had no legal capacity whatsoever. A slave could not marry, although favoured slaves might as a privilege be allowed by their masters to cohabit as if married.[29] A slave could neither sue nor be sued, although they were competent witnesses in legal proceedings.[30] They could not own property, and anything they acquired became the property of the master, not of the slave. Equally, they could not make contracts in their own name, and any contract that a slave made on the master's behalf could be enforced by the master but could not be enforced against him. The basic idea was that, while the slave could improve the master's position, the slave could not worsen it.

In practice, though, it must always have been common for a slave to be put in a position of managing the master's money or property, even if only in a minor way, such as being sent to market to buy goods for use in the household. Indeed, from early times, it was common for a slave to be given a fund of money or property (possibly even including other slaves) to manage. This might, for example, be money for the slave's personal use, or a business intended to make a profit to benefit the master. Such a fund was called a *peculium*, and to a great extent it was treated socially as if it belonged to the slave. Indeed, so much was this the case

---

[24] See *e.g.* D.28.1.12.
[25] D.49.15.12.4.
[26] D.49.15.14.1. As we shall see at pp. 140–1, marriage was based on consent by the parties.
[27] Nov.22.7 (AD 536). There are also references to this five-year period in the *Digest* (see *e.g.* D.49.15.8), but these are widely seen as interpolated. See A Watson, 'Captivitas and Matrimonium' (1961) 29 TvR 243.
[28] Matters were not quite the same in public law. A slave could be held liable for a crime.
[29] See *e.g.* D.23.3.39pr.
[30] Often with torture having been applied to ensure that the slave revealed all. Indeed, when the master was murdered, it was compulsory under the *SC Silianum* of AD 10 for all of the slaves living in the household to be tortured and then executed: D.29.5.1.

that it was common for the slave to be allowed to buy freedom with the *peculium*. The master accepted payment from the *peculium* even though, in law, it already belonged to the master.

Clearly, slave-owners saw it as being in their interests to allow slaves a *peculium*. A slave who was successful in business would obviously benefit the master. However, it is fairly obvious that a slave who cannot make enforceable contracts and who cannot transact with property is unlikely to have much success in business. This problem must have become apparent as soon as slaves began to manage substantial *peculia* (the plural of *peculium*). In the late Republic, therefore, the praetor intervened to allow the master to be sued, in certain circumstances, over matters arising from transactions entered into by the slave. The same issue arose with those of the free population who were subject to the authority of a *paterfamilias*, who had similar restrictions on their capacity, so fuller details of how this worked will be left until Chapter 9. However, in simple terms, the position from the classical period onwards was that the master could be held liable under transactions entered into by the slave up to the value of the *peculium*, and beyond the value of the *peculium* for transactions authorised by the master.[31]

(2) Treatment of the Slave

In principle, as a slave was property, he or she was completely subject to the will of his or her owner. The basic position was that the owner had the power of life and death over the slave.[32] That does not mean that slaves were often killed by their owners. After all, even a slave with no special skills, used only for unskilled manual labour, was a valuable piece of property. Even without humanitarian concerns, which were rare in early times anyway, it would be a waste of resources to kill a slave without cause. The more valuable the slave, the more this was the case, and as we have seen, many slaves had highly sought-after skills and could only be purchased at a high price. A skilled and trusted slave in a wealthy owner's household could well enjoy a more comfortable life than much of the free population, especially if furnished with an extensive *peculium*. There is, though, no getting away from the fact that some slave-owners treated their slaves brutally, and even if death was not the intention, either it or the maiming of the slave could easily be the consequence of excessive punishment.

So was there any protection for a slave against mistreatment? Originally, no, except for the possibility that the mistreatment might incur the disapproval of the censor, with resulting legal disgrace.[33] It seems unlikely, though, that this was much of an impediment to maltreatment of slaves. For one thing, the censors were not permanently in office. For another, even when the censors were in office, there is no reason to think that they were taking any particular care to monitor

---

[31] This authorisation could be general (*e.g.* where the slave had been given a business to run) or specific (*e.g.* where the slave had been ordered to enter into a particular transaction).
[32] G.1.52.
[33] See p. 10 on the role of the censors.

owners' treatment of their slaves. Furthermore, both the existence of slavery and the physical punishment of slaves were taken for granted by the Romans, so only truly exceptional abuses would be likely to occasion much adverse comment.

As time went on, limitations on the master's powers were introduced. For example, in the first century AD, masters were prohibited by a *lex Petronia* from sending their slaves to fight wild animals in the arena, unless a magistrate had first given consent. Under Domitian,[34] castration of slaves was prohibited. Hadrian,[35] in fact, provided that the penalty for murder was to apply to those who made a eunuch.[36] Hadrian also prohibited the killing of one's own slave without the approval of a magistrate.

Under Antoninus Pius,[37] it was considered to be homicide to kill one's own slave just as much as it was to kill someone else's slave.[38] In addition, under this emperor, for the first time slaves could initiate a procedure to protect themselves. He provided that, where a slave sought refuge from the master's treatment at a temple or a statue of the emperor, the matter was to be investigated. If the owner was found to be excessively harsh in his or her treatment of the slave, there was to be a forced sale of the slave.[39]

Given that, in the early days of the Church, St Paul had said that among Christians there was 'neither slave nor free',[40] the conversion to Christianity might have been expected to have a significant impact on the law of slavery. There was, though, no radical change, and certainly no obvious push for the abolition of slavery. There was, however, continuation of the existing trend, and by the time of Justinian the master was restricted to reasonable chastisement of slaves only.

Even so, though, the humanitarian aspect of these developments should not be overstated. All in all, they perhaps should make us think more of modern animal protection legislation than of any kind of real questioning of the idea that human beings could properly be considered capable of being owned.

D. The End of Slavery

(1) Manumission

The act of freeing a slave is called 'manumission' (*manumissio* in Latin). This could happen in various ways. One of these was manumission by inclusion in the census. The census was a list of all citizens, so if a slave was entered in that list with the owner's consent, the slave became a free citizen. The census, however, ceased to be taken during the early Empire. After the conversion to Christianity,

---

[34] Reigned AD 81–96.
[35] Reigned AD 117–38.
[36] D.48.8.4.2.
[37] Reigned AD 138–61.
[38] G.1.52.
[39] D.1.6.2; G.1.52.
[40] Galatians 3:28; Colossians 3:11.

it became possible to free a slave by making a formal declaration in church.[41] During the classical period, however, there were two main ways of manumitting a slave. The first of these was *manumissio vindicta*, by which the owner freed the slave before a magistrate while the owner was still alive. The other involved the owner freeing slaves in a will. These formal methods of manumitting slaves all had in common the remarkable effect that the slave was not simply freed from slavery, but actually became a Roman citizen.

(a) Manumissio Vindicta
Manumissio vindicta was in origin a form of a collusive litigation,[42] modelled on the procedure that would be used where it was asserted that a person held as a slave was in fact free. It required the involvement of a third party called the *adsertor libertatis* ('assertor of freedom'), who would play the part of the pursuer. The parties would appear before the magistrate as if it was a genuine litigation, and the *adsertor libertatis* would assert that the slave was in fact free, to which the slave's owner would either assent or offer no objection. The magistrate would then declare the slave to be free. However, even though the procedure was based on the fiction that the slave was already free, this was not the legal effect. Instead, the slave was treated as only becoming free as a result of the procedure. This result is not entirely logical, but does show an 'ability not to extend conclusions to the point of absurdity [which] is typical of Roman law'.[43]

There were limitations on a slave-owner's power to manumit slaves in classical law. In AD 4, under Augustus, a statute called the *lex Aelia Sentia* was passed which prohibited manumission in fraud of creditors.[44] This prohibition was breached if the slave-owner was insolvent at the time of the manumission, or the manumission made him or her insolvent.[45] Justinian required an actual intention to defraud on the part of the manumitting owner.[46]

The *lex Aelia Sentia* also imposed age limits on manumission, both for the master and for the slave. If the owner of the slave was under twenty years old,[47] or the slave was under thirty,[48] manumission was prohibited unless good cause for it was established before a council (*consilium*). Gaius tells us that the *consilium* would be made up of five senators and five *equites* if in Rome, or twenty *recuperatores* if in the provinces.[49] There was no fixed list of what counted as good cause. However, grounds that were considered acceptable included blood relationship

---

[41] J.1.5.1.
[42] Despite this origin, the process came over time to be much more informal. While retaining the essentials of the original procedure, in the classical period it was no longer necessary to carry out the manumission in a formal sitting of the magistrate. See *e.g.* J.1.5.2.
[43] A Watson, *Roman Slave Law* (Johns Hopkins University Press 1987) 25.
[44] G.1.37; J.1.6pr, 3.
[45] D.40.9.10.
[46] J.1.6.3.
[47] G.1.38; J.1.6.4–6.
[48] G.1.17–19.
[49] G.1.20.

between slave and owner or the slave having been the owner's tutor or minder.[50] Alternatively, the slave might have performed exceptional services for the owner, sufficient to justify a display of gratitude to the slave, such as helping the owner in battle or uncovering a plot against him or her.[51] A manumission of a slave under thirty was not void, but the freed slave did not become a Roman citizen in such a case.[52] Where there was a breach of the requirement for the owner to be at least twenty, the manumission was by contrast void and ineffective.[53]

(b) Manumission by Will

It was possible to manumit slaves by will. There were some doubts about how specific the identification of the slave had to be, but the developed position was that it was enough to give a clear description, even if the slave's actual name was not mentioned. For example, a reference to 'my steward' or 'my cook' in a will was enough, as long as that individual could be identified.[54] If the slave was named as heir, although the position seems to have been doubted at an earlier time, that implied a grant of freedom.[55] After all, the slave could only validly be heir if freed. The grant of freedom could be conditional, in which case the conditionally freed slave was known as a *statuliber*. The idea was that the slave would only become free when the condition was fulfilled, although the outcome would be the same if the heir prevented the fulfilment of the condition.[56]

The restrictions imposed by the *lex Aelia Sentia*, outlined above, also applied to manumissions by will, although the minimum age for unrestricted manumission was changed by Justinian from twenty to seventeen.[57] In addition, even a slave aged under thirty could be freed by will if made the heir of an insolvent master.[58]

Another restriction was imposed by the *lex Fufia Caninia*. Between its introduction under Augustus in 2 BC and its repeal by Justinian,[59] the *lex Fufia Caninia* imposed restrictions on manumissions by will. According to this statute, a slaveowner who owned more than two slaves could only manumit certain proportions of the slaves by will. Those who only owned one or two slaves were subject to no restrictions.[60] Those who owned between three and ten slaves could manumit only half by will. Those who owned between eleven and thirty could manumit up to a third by will. Those who owned between thirty-one and 100 could manumit up to a quarter, while those who owned more than 100 could manumit up

---

[50] J.1.6.4–6.
[51] D.40.2.15.1.
[52] G.1.17–18.
[53] G.1.38–40; C.2.30.3pr (AD 260).
[54] D.40.4.24.
[55] J.1.6.2.
[56] D.40.7.3.16.
[57] J.1.6.4–6. See though Nov.119.2 (AD 544), equalising this with the age at which other property could be disposed of by will.
[58] G.1.21.
[59] J.1.7.
[60] G.1.42–3.

to a fifth, with an absolute limit of 100 (*i.e.* for those who owned more than 500 slaves). To avoid the anomaly that, according to these rules, the owner of ten slaves could manumit five (*i.e.* a half), but the owner of twelve slaves could only manumit four (*i.e.* a third), anyone could manumit by will at least as many slaves as anyone who owned fewer.[61] Table 6.1 should make the rules clearer.

Where too many slaves were named, they would be manumitted in order until the maximum was reached. Attempts to circumvent the restrictions, for example by writing the names in a circle so that none of them could be said to be first, resulted in none of the slaves being freed.[62]

(c) Informal Manumission

Sometimes an attempt would be made to manumit a slave informally, without following one of the formal methods. Examples were manumission *per epistulam* ('by letter') and manumission *inter amicos* ('among friends', *i.e.* by declaration in front of friends of the master). According to the *ius civile*, these methods were ineffective, and the slave remained a slave. However, in the second half of the Republic, the praetor intervened on behalf of informally freed slaves. An informally freed slave could not be a citizen. However, we saw in Chapter 5[63] that some communities were granted 'Latin rights' by Rome, which gave citizens of those communities some but not all of the rights of Roman citizenship. This gave such individuals an intermediate position between that of citizens and *peregrini* (foreigners). The effect of the praetorian intervention was to put an informally freed slave in a position analogous to that of a Latin. The position was put on a formal footing, probably in the reign of Augustus, by a statute called the *lex Iunia*. Informally freed slaves were called Junian Latins after the name of the statute.

Table 6.1 The rules on manumissions by will under the *lex Fufia Caninia*

Number of slaves owned	Maximum number of slaves who can be manumitted by will
1 or 2	No restriction
3–10	Up to half
11–14	5
15–30	Up to a third
31–40	10
41–100	Up to a quarter
101–125	25
126–500	Up to a fifth
More than 500	100

[61] G.1.45.
[62] G.1.46.
[63] See p. 96n.

Slaves freed under the age of thirty, in contravention of the *lex Aelia Sentia*, fell into this category as well. The emperor Claudius provided that, where a slave-owner abandoned a slave while the latter was ill, the slave would become free with the status of Junian Latin. The position of a Junian Latin was essentially that he or she was free during life, but on the Junian Latin's death the former master would succeed to his or her property, unless the Junian Latin was able to attain citizenship first.[64]

Justinian made substantial reforms to the law here by providing for more methods of manumission to be fully effective. These were the following:

- manumission *per epistulam* ('by letter'), with the letter signed by five witnesses;[65]
- manumission by declaration *inter amicos* ('among friends'), in writing with five witnesses;[66]
- abandonment of slave on account of illness;[67]
- allowing a slave to march in the master's funeral procession, wearing a freedman's cap (*pileatus*), according to the intention of the deceased or the deceased's heir;[68]
- in the presence of five witnesses, giving to the slave documents evidencing his or her slavery, or destroying them;[69]
- giving a slave woman in marriage to a freeman, and providing a dowry for that marriage;[70]
- naming the slave in an official document as the master's own child.[71]

In the Justinianic law, all of these were effective in making a slave a free Roman citizen.

(2) Freedmen

(a) The Freedman Status

As we have already seen, a slave that was formally freed not only ceased to be a slave, but also became a Roman citizen. That does not mean, though, that the ex-slave (now called a freedman or freedwoman, though the former is often used as a general term) had the full rights of a freeborn citizen. The freedman (though not any child of the freedman)[72] was subject to certain restrictions. For example, the freedman could not become a senator or hold certain public offices. In practical terms, though, the most important restrictions arose from the continuing relationship with

---

[64] J.3.7.4.
[65] C.7.6.1c (AD 531).
[66] C.7.6.2.
[67] C.7.6.3–3a.
[68] C.7.6.5.
[69] C.7.6.11–11a.
[70] C.7.6.9.
[71] J.1.11.12. This did not, however, actually *make* the freedman legally the former master's child.
[72] J.1.4pr.

the former owner. These will be considered below. First, though, something must be said about the different classes of freedman that existed.

In classical law, distinctions were made between three different classes of freedmen: citizens, Junian Latins and *dediticii*.[73] Only those who were freed using one of the formal methods of manumission, and whose manumission was subject to no restriction (such as those under the *lex Aelia Sentia*), would become a Roman citizen.

The second class was Junian Latins. We have seen already who fell into this class.

Freedmen of the final class were called *dediticii*, which was originally the name given to citizens of states which had fought against the Romans and then had surrendered unconditionally. In terms of the *lex Aelia Sentia*, they are those slaves who have been branded or put in chains by the master, who have been convicted of wrongdoing after being questioned under torture, who have been sent to fight in the arena, or who have been sent to gladiator school or prison, and so have imposed on them the status of *dediticii*.[74] This barred them from ever becoming Roman citizens, and they were not permitted to live within 100 miles of Rome. If they breached this prohibition, they would be re-enslaved and sold subject to a condition of being kept outside this distance from Rome.[75]

These distinctions were abolished by Justinian.[76] In the Justinianic law, all slaves who were freed according to a recognised method became citizens.

(b) The Continuing Relationship with the Former Owner
While the freed slave was now a citizen, he or she continued to have a relationship with the former owner, who was now the freed slave's *patronus* ('patron'). To a great extent, this was a matter of social expectations about proper behaviour towards the former owner, beyond legal obligation. There were, however, legal aspects to this ongoing relationship.

First, the freedman owed respect (*obsequium*) to the patron, and was restricted in what he or she could do if it could reflect badly on the patron. For example, the freedman could not sue the patron without the praetor's consent, and could not do so at all if the action would impose on the patron the kind of legal disgrace, which we saw in Chapter 5, called *infamia*.[77] In severe cases of disrespect towards the patron, the freedman could be punished with re-enslavement for ingratitude.[78]

Second, the freedman would normally be expected to perform services for the patron, although, unlike the other obligations considered here, services could only be demanded if agreed upon at the time of manumission.[79] Typically, the services

---

[73] G.1.12.
[74] G.1.13–15.
[75] G.1.27.
[76] J.1.5.3.
[77] C.6.6.1 (AD 223). See pp. 100–1.
[78] See *e.g.* D.25.3.6.1.
[79] D.38.1.31.

to be rendered would relate to the freedman's trade or profession, and the services could be required to be provided to the patron's friends. As the jurist Julian observes, the patron of a freedman who is a dancer or doctor 'does not have to be forever giving entertainments or being ill in order to use his freedman's services'.[80] For the obligation to be enforceable, the services would have to be reasonable, judged according to the parties' age, status, health, need, way of life and 'other such considerations'.[81] In particular, services could not be required that endangered the freedman's life or reputation. For example, a manumitted prostitute or gladiator could not be required to perform those professions for the patron's benefit (even if the former slave did otherwise perform those professions).[82]

Third, the patron had a claim on the freedman's estate if the freedman died. Under the Twelve Tables, we are told, the patron only had a claim if the freedman died intestate and childless.[83] However, the praetor intervened to give the patron a right to half of the freedman's estate even if the freedman left a will, although any children of the freedman could still exclude the patron's claim.[84]

Chapter Summary

Slavery was an institution by which a human being was subjected to the ownership of another, either by being born into slavery or by being subjected to it later. As a piece of property, and even though the master's absolute power over the slave was restricted over time, the slave was not capable of owning property or of holding rights. Slaves, however, fulfilled a wide range of functions, including business activities, and might be entrusted with a fund of money or property called a *peculium*. Moreover, a slave might be freed by the master. In the process, the ex-slave became a Roman citizen, albeit one with continuing obligations towards the former master.

Further Reading

G.1.9–47
J.1.3–1.8
D.1.6; 37.14–15; 38.1–5; 40
C.1.13; 2.30; 7.1–23

---

[80] D.38.1.27.
[81] D.38.1.15pr (Paul).
[82] D.38.1.38pr.
[83] G.3.40. More specifically, this would be the outcome if the freedman died without a *suus heres*, which is anyone to whom the freedman is *paterfamilias*. See pp. 284–5.
[84] G.3.41.

W W Buckland, *The Roman Law of Slavery: The Condition of the Slave in Private Law from Augustus to Justinian* (Cambridge University Press 1908)

D Johnston, *Roman Law in Context* (Cambridge University Press 1999) 42–4

A J B Sirks, 'Informal Manumission and the *Lex Junia*' (1981) 28 Revue Internationale des Droits de l'Antiquité (3rd series) 247

A J B Sirks, 'The *Lex Junia* and the Effects of Informal Manumission and Iteration' (1983) 30 Revue Internationale des Droits de l'Antiquité (3rd series) 211.

A Watson, *The Law of Persons in the Later Roman Republic* (Oxford University Press 1967) chapters 14–20

A Watson, 'Morality, Slavery and the Jurists in the Later Roman Republic' (1968) 42 Tulane LR 289

A Watson, *Roman Slave Law* (Johns Hopkins University Press 1987)

CHAPTER SEVEN

Parents and Guardians

A. The Concept of *Potestas*

(1) The Nature of *Potestas*

The core concept of the Roman law of parent and child is the *potestas* ('power')[1] held by the senior male in the family over his descendants. More specifically, this was power exercised over all descendants in the male line,[2] the term for which is 'agnatic descendants', as agnates are those related through the male line. In addition, *potestas* only arose in relation to the offspring of a valid Roman marriage.[3] Subject to this, a person was in the *potestas* of his or her oldest living male, agnatic, direct ascendant. The person exercising this *potestas* was known as the *paterfamilias* ('father of the family'). A person subject to this *potestas* is generically known as a *filiusfamilias* ('son of the family'), though the feminine form for a daughter would be *filiafamilias*. We saw in Chapter 5 the distinction between those who were legally dependent (*alieni iuris*) and those who were legally independent (*sui iuris*).[4] The *paterfamilias* was *sui iuris* and those subject to his *potestas* were *alieni iuris*. When a person had no agnatic male ascendants, for example because of the death of the *paterfamilias*, that person was *sui iuris* and, if male, he was considered to be a *paterfamilias*.[5]

It is important to understand that only a man could hold *potestas* over a descendant. A woman could not be a *paterfamilias*,[6] though she could certainly be *sui iuris* just as much as a man could.[7] This does not, of course, mean that the mother

---

[1] More fully, this is often called *patria potestas*, 'paternal power'.
[2] J.1.9.3.
[3] J.1.9pr. As a consequence, the children of an invalid marriage were not in their father's *potestas*: J.1.10.12. The canon law rule, received into Scots law, was different. Under the canon law rule, it was enough for the child to be legitimate that at least one of the parents was ignorant of the facts making the marriage void (Erskine, *Institute* 1.6.51).
[4] See pp. 96–7.
[5] This was the case even if he had no children: D.50.16.195.2.
[6] The female equivalent would be *materfamilias*. This is a term that is used occasionally (*e.g.* in D.25.7.1pr), but without the same kind of legal significance as *paterfamilias*.
[7] See below, though, on guardianship of women.

was not an important authority figure in a child's upbringing. They clearly were.[8] Only the *paterfamilias*, though, exercised this special legal authority.

An example may illustrate how this worked. Suppose a man, whose parents and grandparents are all dead, and who was therefore a *paterfamilias*, had a son and a daughter.[9] The son and daughter each had a son. The *paterfamilias* would have *potestas* over both his son and his daughter.[10] He would also have *potestas* over the son's child, but not over the daughter's child, because the latter is not an agnatic descendant. Instead, the daughter's child would be in the *potestas* of his or her father (or of the father's own *paterfamilias*). When the *paterfamilias* died, both of his children would become *sui iuris*. The *potestas* over the daughter, for example, did not in any sense pass down to anyone else, such as her brother. The son would now be his own son's *paterfamilias*.

We shall see in this chapter what exactly the scope of this *potestas* was. One important limitation should be mentioned now, though, which is that it was only relevant for private law matters. The fact of being a *filiusfamilias* did not limit a person's capacity to act in public law matters, and such a person could for example hold a magistracy.[11]

It is unlikely that there has ever been a society in which the law did not give parents some degree of legal authority over their children. To us, the extent of the preference for fathers seems unusual, but such paternal preference was hardly uncommon in earlier societies. Where the Roman approach was unusual was in two of its features. The first was its scope. As Justinian said: 'there are no other people who have such rights over their children'.[12] Second, it was unusual in that it was in principle lifelong.

(2) Rights over the Person

The *paterfamilias* had extensive rights over the persons of those in his *potestas*. Indeed, in early times, these rights were so extensive that the *paterfamilias* could almost be characterised as the owner of those in his *potestas*. Thus, for example, until the end of the classical period he could sell his children into a status analogous to that of a slave.[13] Such a child was said to be *in mancipio* (in bondage). The idea was revived in the post-classical period by Constantine: parents under pressure of poverty were permitted to sell their children.[14] Something very similar was permitted in classical law in the case

---

[8] Thus we see references in Roman literature to mothers exercising *potestas* over their children. These refer, though, to social rather than legal authority. See M E Roccia, '"*In fabrorum potestate*": Plautus and the Mother's Power in Ancient Rome' (2018) 39 J Leg Hist 1.
[9] This example assumes that all of the offspring mentioned were born of a valid Roman marriage.
[10] This must be slightly qualified. As we shall see at p. 142, there was a form of marriage that brought a wife into the *potestas* of her husband (or of her husband's *paterfamilias*). By the classical period, though, the usual form of marriage had no such effect.
[11] D.1.6.9; D.36.1.14.
[12] J.1.9.2. See also G.1.55.
[13] G.1.117. For an overview of the institution, see Buckland, *Textbook* 133–4.
[14] C.4.43.2 (AD 329). Before rushing too quickly to judgement of Constantine here for allowing this, we should bear in mind that the probable alternative would be the abandonment (and likely death) of the child.

where a son had committed a wrong: his *paterfamilias* could choose to surrender him to his victim in bondage instead of paying damages. This process was called noxal surrender, and will be considered in Chapter 9.[15] Other than this, the *paterfamilias* had extensive rights, considered here. He had the power of life and death over those in his *potestas*; he could inflict punishments; he was in principle entitled to physical custody of his children, or to regulate their residence; he was entitled to support from them (as were they from him); and he had rights over their marriages.

(a) Power of Life and Death
From the earliest period, part of the authority of the *paterfamilias* was the power of life and death over those in his *potestas*. The general view seems to be that this power was originally unfettered.[16] However, in the classical period this does not appear to have been the case, and a *paterfamilias* who abused this power could expect punishment if this came to the attention of the authorities:

> It is said that, when in the course of a hunt a certain man killed his son, who had been committing adultery with his stepmother, Emperor Hadrian[17] deported him to an island, because he acted more like a robber in killing him than this being based on a father's right. For paternal authority should consist in duty, not cruelty.[18]

Later, but still within the classical period, Ulpian tells us that a *paterfamilias* cannot kill someone in his power without first obtaining the approval of a magistrate.[19] Finally, in AD 318, Constantine provided that the killing of one's own child, or of any other close relative, was to be criminally punished as parricide.[20]

A special case of the power of life and death applied to adulterous daughters. In terms of the *lex Iulia de adulteriis coercendis*, legislation passed in 17 BC under Augustus,[21] a *paterfamilias* could kill any married woman in his *potestas* who committed adultery.[22] The adulterous pair had to be caught in the act of intercourse, and had to be killed without delay.[23]

---

[15] See pp. 155–6.
[16] See though R Yaron, 'Vitae Necisque Potestas' (1962) 30 TvR 243.
[17] Reigned AD 117–38.
[18] D.48.9.5 (Marcian). The word translated here as 'duty' is *pietas*. The word is the root of our word 'piety', but the Latin word is broader in its connotations. It goes beyond religious duties, to respect for all one's duties. The point is that the power of life and death should be exercised to inflict just punishment for wrongdoing, rather than being motivated by personal feelings. The *paterfamilias* can be seen as a kind of quasi-magistrate, with authority over those subject to his *potestas*, and should act accordingly. In the specific case mentioned in this passage, it may be that the son's wrongdoing justified his death. However, the proper approach for the *paterfamilias* to take would have been to summon a *consilium* (council of advisers), taking their advice and allowing the son to speak in his own defence, before deciding whether the son should die.
[19] D.48.8.2.
[20] C.9.17.1. The prescribed punishment is to be sealed in a sack filled with serpents and drowned.
[21] Reigned 27 BC–AD 14.
[22] D.48.5.21–2. The existence of this *lex* suggests that, by Augustus' time, the power of life and death was already restricted. If things were otherwise, why would the *paterfamilias* need this express power to kill his daughter? It is true that legislation sometimes has the function of expressing a political or moral principle, rather than being intended to change the law, but the provisions of the *lex* seem too specific for that to be the case here.
[23] D.48.5.24. If one escaped, and was only caught and killed some hours later, that still counted as happening without delay.

The final case of the power of life and death to be considered is the right of the *paterfamilias* to expose newborn children. While this is often considered separately, it seems appropriate to consider it here, as the child's death would be the result of this unless the child was found and rescued. Such a child would often be raised and treated as a slave, though he or she technically remained free. This right of infant exposure persisted through the classical period and beyond, but was declared unlawful in AD 374.[24]

(b) Punishment

If the *paterfamilias* was entitled to kill those in his *potestas*, so much the more did he have the right to inflict punishments on them. This too, however, could attract adverse consequences if abused. Trajan,[25] for example, compelled a father who was maltreating his son to emancipate him.[26] After the son's death, the father was denied the normal rights of succession of an emancipating father.[27] In later law, the right of punishment was restricted to reasonable chastisement.[28]

(c) Custody

In principle, the *paterfamilias* was entitled to regulate the residence of those in his *potestas*. A child in *potestas* was considered capable of being stolen, and could be recovered as stolen property.[29] In addition, the praetor would provide interdicts to compel the production of a *filiusfamilias* or *filiafamilias* who was in another's keeping,[30] or to prohibit anyone from preventing the *paterfamilias* recovering him or her.[31]

Actually, though, there was more control over the father's rights here than would at first appear. Where a *paterfamilias* sought to recover a prepubescent child, the judge could decide to defer a decision until the child reached puberty. The relative characters of the parties would be relevant here. If both parties were of bad character, it might even be considered appropriate to appoint a third party to take responsibility for the child's upbringing until puberty.[32] Similarly, the mother might be preferred to the father where the father was of poor moral character.[33]

(d) Support

Parents and children had mutual obligations of support.[34] This included children born outside marriage[35] and those who had been released from *potestas*

---

[24] C.8.51.2.
[25] Reigned AD 98–117.
[26] As we shall see below, to emancipate a child is to free him or her from *patria potestas*.
[27] D.37.12.5.
[28] C.9.15.1 (AD 365). If a more severe punishment was considered necessary, this could be imposed by a judge.
[29] G.3.199. The position is similar in modern law, for children under the age of puberty, influenced on this point by Roman law. See J Brown, 'Plagium: An Archaic and Anomalous Crime' 2016 JR 129.
[30] D.43.30.1pr. This interdict did not apply if the child was voluntarily in another's keeping: D.43.30.5.
[31] D.43.30.3pr.
[32] D.43.40.3.4.
[33] D.43.30.1.3; D.43.30.3.4; C.5.24.1 (AD 294).
[34] D.25.3.5pr. Indeed, this went beyond parents and children, and extended to all ascendants and descendants: D.25.3.5.2.
[35] D.25.3.5.4.

by emancipation.[36] An impoverished parent might, therefore, be able to obtain financial support from an emancipated son who had greater means. The same would be true if the positions were reversed: the son could seek financial support from the parents.

This obligation of support only existed to the extent it was necessary, however, so nobody was entitled to support who had sufficient means of his or her own.[37] Support could be refused on other grounds as well. For example, a father could refuse to support a son who had informed against him.[38]

(e) Rights over Children's Marriages
The *paterfamilias* also had powers over the marriages of those within his *potestas*. Where the party to a marriage was *alieni iuris*, the consent of his or her *paterfamilias* was necessary to the validity of the marriage.[39] The *paterfamilias* could also compel those in his *potestas* to divorce.[40]

Legislation under Augustus had the effect of limiting the ability of the *paterfamilias* to abuse these powers. Those who wrongfully prevented those in their *potestas* marrying could be compelled by a magistrate to arrange a marriage.[41]

(3) Rights over Property
(a) The Legal Capacity of Those Subject to Patria Potestas
As far as legal capacity is concerned, the basic position of a *filiusfamilias* was not all that different from that of a slave. Though we shall see certain limited exceptions below, the position in principle was that nobody subject to another's *potestas* could own any property at all. Anything acquired by the *filiusfamilias* was acquired not for himself, but for the *paterfamilias*. Where the *filiusfamilias* acted on behalf of the *paterfamilias*, he could benefit him[42] but not bind him. Further, while the *filiusfamilias* (unlike a slave) could incur liabilities and be sued in his own name,[43] this was unlikely to be found particularly useful until the *filiusfamilias* became *sui iuris* and could have property of his own with which he could satisfy any judgment against him.

(b) Peculium
We saw in Chapter 6[44] that, although slaves could not own property, they could be allowed to manage a fund of money or property called a *peculium*. This *peculium* remained the property of the master, but was for practical, day-to-day purposes treated as belonging to the slave. Much the same situation applied with free persons

---

[36] D.25.3.5.1. On emancipation, see below.
[37] D.25.3.5.7.
[38] D.25.3.5.11.
[39] D.23.2.2.
[40] On divorce, see pp. 142–3 and 144–5.
[41] D.23.2.19. It is doubtful whether this extended to sons as well as daughters, however.
[42] For example, by acquiring property on his behalf.
[43] D.44.7.39. Probably, however, a *filiafamilias* did not have even this level of capacity: G.3.104.
[44] See pp. 106–7.

who were subject to *patria potestas*. A *filiusfamilias* could also hold a *peculium*, which the *paterfamilias* still owned but which the *filiusfamilias* was allowed to treat as his own.

Still, the inability of those subject to *potestas* to own property or to transact in their own right must have proved inconvenient. We shall see below that means were developed to hold the *paterfamilias* liable to a certain extent for the actions of the *filiusfamilias*. That was beneficial to third parties dealing with a *filiusfamilias*. From the point of view of a *filiusfamilias* who wanted to transact or to sue in his own name, however, it was still unsatisfactory.

An exception to the proprietary non-capacity of the *filiusfamilias* was introduced in the early Empire, by Augustus. This was the *peculium castrense*, and it was made up of property acquired by a *filiusfamilias* while on military service. This was owned by the *filiusfamilias*, who could transact freely with it and who could be held liable to its extent.[45] Under Constantine, this was extended to any earnings in public service (the *peculium quasi castrense*).[46]

The *peculium adventitium* was another exception, also introduced by Constantine. This was made up of property acquired by a *filiusfamilias* on the death of the mother. Although the *paterfamilias* could use this property and retain any profits, he did not own it and could not diminish the capital.[47] This category was progressively extended, and under Justinian it included anything not acquired from the *paterfamilias* or forming part of a *peculium castrense* or *quasi castrense*.[48]

In the developed law, therefore, the position could be quite complex. There were now four types of *peculium*, with the original *peculium* owned by the *paterfamilias* now confined to property and money derived from him, and called *peculium profecticium* to distinguish it from the other types. An individual might have any or all of these types of *peculium*.[49]

(c) The Liability of the *Paterfamilias*

The introduction of the *peculia*[50] *castrense* and *quasi castrense* cannot, however, have solved the problem completely. In particular, it hardly seems fair on third parties dealing with a person for matters to depend so much on whether they were dealing with someone *sui iuris* or *alieni iuris*. After all, they could hardly have always known whether the person they were dealing with was subject to *potestas*.

Despite the inconvenience of the system, the Romans never got rid of it. Instead, in an example of the Romans' strange mixture of conservatism and inventiveness, they kept the system but devised ways of circumventing its consequences. In simple terms, the *paterfamilias* could be held liable for the actings of those in his *potestas* up to the level of the *peculium*, or for anything he had authorised

---

[45] D.14.6.2; D.49.17.10–11.
[46] C.12.30.1 (AD 326).
[47] C.6.60.1 (AD 319). In other words, he had usufructuary rights, on which see Chapter 14.
[48] C.6.61.8 (AD 531).
[49] For an overview, including an account of the impact of the Roman law on South African law, see E Spiro, 'The Law of Peculium in South Africa' (1954) 17 THRHR 256.
[50] This is the plural form of *peculium*.

the *filiusfamilias* to do. In addition, a special form of liability (called noxal liability) could be imposed on the *paterfamilias* for the wrongdoing of those in his *potestas*. We have seen in Chapter 6 that much the same approach was taken with slaves. The issues will be considered in Chapter 9, in more detail, for both categories of *alieni iuris* persons.

B. Creation of *Potestas*

(1) Birth

As already stated, a child born of a valid Roman marriage would be subject to the *potestas* of its father (or of the father's *paterfamilias*, if there was one), this being judged according to whether the parents were married at the moment of conception.[51] This was the case even if the *paterfamilias* exercised his right to expose the child at birth: the texts seem to indicate that the abandoned child nonetheless remained in his *potestas*,[52] at least until Justinian provided that such a child was free and could not be recovered by the *paterfamilias* or held by anyone as a slave.[53]

It is one thing to state the rule. It is, however, another matter to prove who the father is when the matter is disputed. Maternity disputes are rare (though not completely unknown).[54] Certainly, the Romans did not have to contend with modern techniques whereby an embryo may be created using fertilised egg from one woman and carried to term by another woman. Therefore, to the Romans, there could be no doubt that the woman who gave birth to the child was that child's mother.

Paternity, however, is much more difficult to demonstrate, and it must have been the case that, at any period of human history, some people have been raised by men they believed to be their biological fathers, but who were not. The rule adopted by the Romans, and received also by Scots law through the canon law, was *pater est quem nuptiae demonstrant*: he is the father whom the marriage demonstrates.[55] In other words, the mother's husband was presumed to be the father, and would be considered to be so until the contrary was proved.

In part, this is a simple reflection of the fact that the mother's husband is likely to be the man who most obviously had sexual access to her. He can therefore be presumed to have done so, and to be the child's father, unless contrary evidence is produced. There is more to it than this, though. In systems following this rule, there is a tendency to make this presumption a particularly strong one, not rebuttable without the strongest evidence. There is a reluctance to disturb an established[56]

---

[51] D.1.5.12; D.22.3.29.1.
[52] D.22.6.1.2; D.40.4.29; C.5.4.16. See though O Tellegen-Couperus, 'Father and Foundling in Classical Roman Law' (2013) 34 J Leg Hist 129, arguing for the contrary position.
[53] C.8.51.3 (AD 529).
[54] One of the very few examples is *Douglas v Duke of Hamilton* (1769) 2 Pat 143. Probably the most famous case is a biblical one, at 1 Kings 3:16–28.
[55] D.2.4.5.
[56] Possibly long-established. In *Baronetcy of Pringle of Stichill* [2016] UKPC 16, 2016 SC (PC) 1, for example, a man's parentage was questioned more than a century after his birth and long after his own death.

family situation and to deprive the child of the family relations that he or she was believed to have.[57] To avoid this, a legal system might for example restrict the possibility of challenge to the husband's paternity by making the presumption conclusive,[58] or by excluding anyone other than the mother or the presumed father from raising the question.[59]

Quite how far Roman law went with this is unclear. Certainly, the presumption could be rebutted by proof that the mother's husband was absent at the time of conception. Even then, though, Roman law was very flexible with the determination of when conception happened. Gestation periods of as long as ten months[60] or as short as 182 days[61] were accepted. Elsewhere, a period of seven months was accepted.[62] There seems to have been some dispute as to whether a husband who had lived with the child's mother at any possible time of conception could deny paternity. Ulpian tells us that this is permissible where it can be proved that no intercourse occurred at the relevant time.[63] He gives two examples of reasons why this might have happened (infirmity and impotence) but it is not clear whether these are intended to be exhaustive.

A special case was provided for by a *senatusconsultum* where, following a divorce, a woman claimed to be pregnant by her ex-husband. Either she or, if she was *alieni iuris*, her *paterfamilias* could give notice of this to the ex-husband within thirty days of the divorce. The ex-husband had a choice of either sending observers (to prevent substitution of another child) or giving notice that he denied paternity. If he did neither, he would be obliged to accept the child as his own.[64] The praetor provided a similar procedure for the case where a woman claimed to be pregnant after her husband's death.[65]

(2) **Adoption**

Potestas could also be created by adoption. There were two forms of adoption. *Adrogatio* was the adoption of a *sui iuris* person, and required the use of special procedures, because it meant the extinction of a Roman family. The other form, *adoptio*, was used for the adoption of a person who was already *alieni iuris*.

---

[57] See B Häcker, 'Honour Runs in the Blood' (2017) 133 LQR 36; G Black, 'Identifying the Legal Parent/Child Relationship and the Biological Prerogative: Who then is My Parent?' 2018 JR 22.
[58] J Bocobo, 'The Conclusive Presumption of Legitimacy of Child' (1933) 12 Philip LJ 301.
[59] P J Thomas, 'F v L 1987 4 525 (W)' (1988) 21 De Jure 161. For example, in the case discussed in this article, a third party was denied the right to claim that he was the child's true father, even though the mother admitted to having had intercourse with him around nine months before the child's birth. For a general account of the reception of the presumption in Roman-Dutch law, and thereafter South African law, see P J Thomas, 'Paternity: Legal or Biological Concept?' (1988) 105 SALJ 239.
[60] D.38.16.3.11.
[61] D.38.16.3.12.
[62] D.1.5.12.
[63] D.1.6.6.
[64] D.25.3.1.
[65] D.25.4.10. For discussion of this procedure, see D H van Zyl, 'Custodia Ventris and Custodia Partus' (1969) 32 THRHR 43.

Although these two forms of adoption were distinct, they did have some common features. For example, adoption was taken to imitate nature, so the adopter had to be old enough to be the adoptee's biological father.[66] This was taken to mean that the adopter had to be at least eighteen years older.[67] Most importantly, both forms of adoption had the effect of subjecting the adoptee to the adopter's *potestas*.[68] For this reason, only a man could adopt, as a woman did not hold *potestas* over even her biological children.[69] In post-classical law, it is true, a woman whose children had died was allowed to enter into an *adoptio*, but this did not create *potestas*. Instead, the legal effect was simply to give the adoptee rights to succeed to the adopter's estate on the latter's intestacy.[70]

(a) Adrogatio
As stated above, *adrogatio* was the adoption of a *sui iuris* person. As it involved the extinction of a Roman family (at least, as was more usual, if the adoptee was male, as he would be a *paterfamilias*), it was a serious matter. It involved the parties appearing before the *comitia calata*,[71] presided over by the *pontifex maximus*,[72] who would investigate whether the proposed adoption should be allowed. If he was satisfied, he would then ask the parties and the *comitia calata* whether they agreed to the adoption. This procedure came in the post-classical period to be superseded by a new procedure of adoption by imperial rescript.[73]

Whereas the aim of modern adoption is to provide for the welfare of the adoptee, who will always be a child and usually a young one, Roman adoptions had a different purpose. Their primary function was to secure the succession to the adopter's estate. This was reflected in the restrictions imposed on *adrogatio*. Thus, the adopter had to be childless himself and likely to remain so, and at least sixty years of age. Normally he could only adopt one person in this way. Originally, there could be no *adrogatio* of women or of boys under puberty. These groups were excluded anyway, as they could not appear before the *comitia calata*, but there were also practical reasons to exclude them. Women could not have *potestas* over anyone, so adopting a woman would only extend the adopter's family by one generation. As for boys, childhood mortality rates were high enough that it would make sense to prefer to adopt an adult man. The position varied over

---

[66] D.1.7.15.3; D.1.7.16. It was, however, no obstacle that the adopter was physically incapable of procreation: G.1.103.
[67] D.1.7.40.1.
[68] Although, as we shall see, Justinian limited this effect in the case of *adoptio*.
[69] G.1.104.
[70] J.1.11.10.
[71] This was the name used for the *comitia curiata* when meeting for certain purposes with religious implications: Jolowicz and Nicholas, *Historical Introduction* 127. As we shall see at p. 297, it had an important role in the early law of wills.
[72] The *pontifex maximus* was the head of the most politically important priestly colleges, on which see p. 12.
[73] On this procedure, see J A C Thomas, 'Some Notes on *adrogatio per rescriptum principis*' (1967) 14 Revue Internationale des Droits de l'Antiquité (3rd series) 413.

time, however. Diocletian[74] allowed *adrogatio* of women. In the second century, Gaius tells us that *adrogatio* of boys under puberty had been both allowed and disallowed. He goes on to tell us, though, that in the law of his day it was allowed if sufficient cause was shown.

The effect of *adrogatio* was to subject the adoptee to the adopter's *potestas*, with all that that implies.[75] For example, any property owned by the adoptee would pass to the adopter.[76] This was also true of anyone who had been in the adoptee's *potestas*. Suppose, for example, A adopted B, who had a son (C) in his *potestas*, by *adrogatio*. After the *adrogatio* had taken place, B would be in the *potestas* of A, in the position of A's son. C would likewise be in A's *potestas*, in the position of A's grandson.

(b) Adoptio
Adoptio was, as already noted, the adoption of an *alieni iuris* person. This was carried out under the authority of a magistrate, and took advantage of a provision in the Twelve Tables that allowed a *paterfamilias* to sell his son into bondage up to three times.[77] After the third time, the child was permanently freed from the *potestas* of the original *paterfamilias*. Because the Twelve Tables only mentioned sons, it was decided that one sale would do for daughters or grandchildren. This then was the procedure followed for *adoptio*, although in this case the sales were of course fictitious. Once the final sale had been carried out, the intended adopter would then claim the child as his own in front of the magistrate.[78] Unlike the position with *adrogatio*, any children of the adoptee were unaffected. They stayed in their original family.[79]

The procedure for *adoptio* was simplified by Justinian, who required simply a declaration before a magistrate by the three parties involved.[80] Unlike the position with *adrogatio*, it seems always to have been accepted that a woman[81] or a boy under puberty[82] could be adopted by *adoptio*. Justinian also provided that *adoptio* did not subject the adoptee to the adopter's *potestas*, instead acquiring only rights on succession to the adopter. The exception to this was where the adopter was an ascendant of the adoptee, such as the adoptee's maternal grandfather. In such a case, *adoptio* affected *potestas* as it had in earlier law.[83]

---

[74] Reigned AD 284–305.
[75] G.1.107; D.1.7.15pr.
[76] Although this was subject to the same limitations as applied to the *peculium* of a biological child of the adopter. In Justinianic law, any such property would be *peculium adventitium*, over which the adopter would have only usufructuary rights.
[77] This, at least, is the general view. For discussion and an alternative suggestion for the origins of this procedure, see B Stoop, 'The Sins of Their Fathers: *Si pater filium ter venum duit*' (1995) 42 Revue Internationale des Droits de l'Antiquité (3rd series) 331.
[78] G.1.134.
[79] D.1.7.40pr.
[80] J.1.12.8; C.8.47.11 (AD 530).
[81] G.1.101.
[82] G.1.102.
[83] J.1.11.2.

(3) Legitimation

In classical law, legitimacy of a child was judged as at the date of conception (although, as we have seen, the Romans were prepared to stretch biological plausibility in determining when that happened). A child conceived when his or her parents were unmarried was not in the *potestas* of the father (or of his *paterfamilias*). The only possibility of changing this would lie in the father adopting his own child. As the child would be *sui iuris*, this would be by *adrogatio*.

An alternative option became available under Constantine,[84] namely legitimation by subsequent marriage.[85] The precise rules varied over time. However, the essential idea was that, where a man had children by a concubine,[86] and they subsequently married, the children became legitimate and subject to the father's *potestas*. The parents had to have been legally able to marry at the time of conception.[87] Because the child would lose the status of *sui iuris*, the child's consent was necessary. Justinian required that the marriage be evidenced by a written marriage settlement.[88] Abolishing an earlier rule to the contrary, Justinian allowed legitimation even where the father had existing legitimate children.[89] Justinian also abolished the previous rule that legitimation could not operate when the mother was a freedwoman.[90] If the children had been born in slavery, the marriage freed them without need for any special manumission.[91]

The possibility of legitimation by subsequent marriage was adopted by the canon law, in a more expansive form. In the canon law, when an unmarried couple had a child, and they subsequently married, the child would then be legitimated by this marriage. *Kerr v Martin*[92] is a case that illustrates both the reception of this idea in Scots law, by way of canon law, and also the importance of being able to approach a difficult case from first principles, by examining the historical development of a rule or principle. In *Kerr*, an unmarried couple had had a child. The mother then married a different man and only later, after his death, did she marry the child's father. The question was whether this intervening marriage to a third party prevented the legitimation of the child by the parents' marriage. After lengthy discussion of a wide range of writers on civil and canon law, a bench of thirteen judges held (by a majority of seven to six) that the child was legitimated.

---

[84] Reigned AD 306–37.
[85] Two other methods of legitimation appeared, but these did not affect later law. These were legitimation by imperial rescript, on request to the emperor; and *oblatio curiae* ('offering to the council'), by which an illegitimate son given to be a *decurio* (town councillor), or an illegitimate daughter married to a *decurio*, was allowed to be treated as legitimate. The reason for the introduction of *oblatio curiae* was the widespread reluctance to serve as a *decurio*, due to the expense and lack of profit involved.
[86] See p. 136.
[87] J.1.10.13.
[88] C.5.27.10 (AD 529). This should be read alongside C.5.27.11 (AD 530).
[89] Nov.12.3 (AD 535).
[90] Nov.18.11 (AD 536).
[91] Nov.78.4 (AD 539).
[92] (1840) 2 D 752.

C. Termination of *Potestas*

(1) Death of the *Paterfamilias*

The death of the *paterfamilias* terminated his *potestas* over his agnatic descendants. The effect of this differed, though, depending on the situation of the surviving descendants. Anyone with no surviving agnatic ascendants would now become *sui iuris*. This meant primarily the deceased's children, but also included for example any agnatic grandchild whose father had predeceased the *paterfamilias* or whose father had been emancipated by the *paterfamilias*. Anyone who did have such an ascendant would remain *alieni iuris*, but would now have a new *paterfamilias*. For example, suppose that the family consists of a grandfather, his son, and the son's children. The son and his children have the grandfather as their *paterfamilias*. If the grandfather dies, their father becomes their *paterfamilias*. It is only when their father dies that they become *sui iuris*.

(2) Emancipation

The *paterfamilias* could release a person from his *potestas* through a process known as emancipation. Until Justinian introduced a simplified procedure, involving the parties appearing before a magistrate,[93] the emancipation process was very similar to that for *adoptio*. As we have seen above, this involved a triple conveyance of the *filiusfamilias* (or a single conveyance for a *filiafamilias*). In emancipation, though, the child would be released at the end of the process, and would thereafter be *sui iuris*. The consent (or at least acquiescence) of the child was necessary, certainly in later law, and possibly earlier.[94] Unless the *paterfamilias* was emancipating the child as a punishment, usually the child took any *peculium* that had been accrued, and this would be implied unless expressly withheld.[95]

What if an emancipated son had children of his own? Were they emancipated as well? The answer is that this was up to the *paterfamilias*. He could choose, for example, to emancipate his son, but to keep that son's own children in his *potestas*.[96]

D. The *Sui Iuris* Child

We have focused so far on the concept of *potestas*, and what this meant for the relationship between the *paterfamilias* and those in his power. Among free citizens, the fundamental distinction was between those who were *alieni iuris* and those who were *sui iuris*. The former were legally dependent, and the latter were legally independent. That could not be the end of the story, however. A young child, for example, would be legally independent in this way if he or she had no *paterfamilias*, yet such a child could hardly be expected to manage his or her own affairs. The law, therefore, had to provide ways of dealing with this. One of these was the

---

[93] J.1.12.6.
[94] C.8.48.5 (AD 502).
[95] D.39.5.31.2.
[96] D.1.7.28.

institution of guardianship (*tutela*), by which a guardian (*tutor*) could be appointed to safeguard the interests of a person deemed incapable of properly managing his or her own affairs.[97] We saw certain examples of this in Chapter 5. The most important examples, however, are guardians of those under the age of puberty and guardians of women. These will both be considered in this section. Also to be considered is the situation of those who had reached puberty, but whose youth meant that they were still seen as being in need of protection.

(1) Guardianship *(Tutela)*

A *sui iuris* child who was under the age of puberty (which was set at twelve for girls and fourteen for boys) had to have a guardian (*tutor*) to manage his or her affairs. Guardians were of different types. A testamentary guardian was one appointed by the *paterfamilias* in his will for those becoming *sui iuris* on his death.[98] Failing this, a person could be appointed as a statutory guardian under rules derived from the Twelve Tables. For most cases, this was the nearest agnate,[99] but there were two special cases. The first was that a father who had emancipated his son was the son's statutory guardian.[100] If the father died before the son reached puberty, any other son he might have, who had reached full age, would be fiduciary guardian.[101] In the case of a manumitted slave, the former master was the ex-slave's statutory guardian.[102] Failing a testamentary, fiduciary or statutory guardian, a magistrate could appoint someone to act.[103] The appropriate person could be compelled to act if necessary,[104] with only limited excuses accepted as absolving him from taking on the role.[105] In principle, acting as a guardian was considered a 'masculine duty', inconsistent with 'feminine weakness', and so women were not permitted to take on the role.[106] In post-classical law, however, a woman would occasionally be allowed to be guardian of her own children, on condition that she not marry.[107]

The guardian had two main duties: he was to administer the child's property, and where appropriate he was to give his authorisation (*auctoritas*) to the child's transactions. This was necessary because the child had no legal capacity to enter into any transactions that had the potential to worsen his or her position. Thus, the child could not be made liable under a contract or alienate property without the guardian's authorisation,[108] nor could the child free a slave without authorisation,[109]

---

[97] D.26.1.1pr.
[98] G.1.144–6.
[99] G.1.155.
[100] G.1.166.
[101] J.1.19.
[102] G.1.165.
[103] G.1.185.
[104] D.26.7.1pr.
[105] An extensive list of excuses is found at J.1.25. See also D.27.1.
[106] C.5.35.1 (AD 224).
[107] C.5.32.2 (AD 390); C.5.32.3 (AD 530); Nov.118.5 (AD 543).
[108] D.26.8.9pr.
[109] D.26.8.9.1.

or accept an inheritance, even a profitable one.[110] They could not even validly receive payment of a debt owed to them.[111] The child could, however, acquire property, for example through a gift.[112] Children aged under seven, however, did not even have this degree of legal capacity. Such children were known as *infantes*.[113]

The focus here was the preservation of the child's property rather than the child's welfare, which explains why the child's agnates were statutory guardians: as we shall see in Chapter 16,[114] they had rights in the child's intestacy. The guardian was not specifically responsible for the personal care of the child, who would usually be left with his or her mother if possible. However, the guardian was required to spend money on the child's upkeep in accordance with the child's social status and resources.[115]

On taking office, the guardian was required to take an inventory of the child's property, and manage it with proper care.[116] Failure in this would render the guardian liable for the child's losses.[117] Except for testamentary guardians or those appointed by a magistrate, a guardian had to give security on taking office.[118] A negligent or dishonest guardian could be removed by court action.[119] Otherwise, the guardianship would normally continue until the child reached puberty,[120] or the guardian stood down on giving sufficient reason.[121]

Later law was strongly influenced by the Roman law on this point. For Scots law, Stair says: 'The Romans have in this matter kept clearly and closely by the law of nature; and therefore our customs have kept as near by them; and so have the customs of other nations.'[122] In his account,[123] Stair draws extensively on Roman sources, and there is substantial similarity between his account and the Roman law. For example, the age at which the guardianship comes to an end is the same (fourteen for boys, twelve for girls) and the same terminology is used as in Roman law ('tutor' for the guardian; 'pupil', from *pupillus*, for the child subject to it). The term 'guardian' has been used instead of 'tutor' here, however, because it is the modern terminology and to avoid confusion with pupils and tutors in an educational context.[124]

---

[110] D.26.8.9.3. The reason for this is that it might involve liabilities as well.
[111] J.2.8.2.
[112] D.26.8.9pr.
[113] C.6.30.18 (AD 426). The term *infans*, however, literally means 'one who cannot speak', so presumably at an earlier time a person could cease to be *infans* at an earlier age.
[114] See p. 289.
[115] D.26.7.12.3.
[116] D.26.7.7.
[117] On the guardian's liability, see G MacCormack, 'The Liability of the Tutor in Classical Roman Law' (1970) 5 Irish Jurist (NS) 369.
[118] J.1.24pr.
[119] In the case of actual dishonesty, *infamia* would result: D.26.10.3.18.
[120] J.1.22pr.
[121] J.1.22.6.
[122] Stair, *Institutions* 1.6.4. See also Erskine, *Institute* 1.7.1.
[123] Stair, *Institutions* 1.6.1–38.
[124] This area is now regulated by the Children (Scotland) Act 1995, in terms of which a guardian may be appointed for a child by his or her parents (s. 7) or by the court (s. 11(2)(h)).

(2) Cura Minorum

In principle, a *sui iuris* person acquired full legal capacity on reaching puberty. Still, though, it is fairly obvious that an inexperienced person may make unwise decisions, and the need came to be seen to protect them from the consequences of those decisions. Around 200 BC, a statute called either the *lex Plaetoria* or the *lex Laetoria* was passed, which penalised those who took unfair advantage of those aged under twenty-five (known as 'minors'). Furthermore, the praetor introduced a defence against anyone who tried to enforce against a minor a contract that was disadvantageous to the minor.[125]

In one sense, this was in the interests of the minor, and limited the extent to which unfair advantage could be taken of the minor's lack of experience. However, it had the severe disadvantage that the existence of this protection would make people reluctant to make contracts with minors, even where the terms of the contract were reasonable and the minor had not been circumvented in any way. For this reason, the practice arose of minors appointing a curator to assist them with their transactions. The involvement of a curator was not strictly required. If the minor had sufficient capacity to enter into the transaction, the curator added nothing. Equally, if the transaction was challengeable, the presence of the curator did not in principle save it. After all, except for the special case of a curator *ad litem* (a curator who could be appointed by a judge to look after the minor's interests in legal proceedings),[126] the curator was appointed by the minor personally.[127] The curator had no special legal power to authorise transactions. He did, however, provide a check on the reasonableness of transactions. The presence of a curator would have been strong evidence that the transaction was a reasonable one and was not challengeable.

For this reason, the appointment of a curator became standard practice. From the time of Marcus Aurelius,[128] it became possible for the minor to apply to a magistrate to have a curator appointed. This curator would then act until the minor reached the age of twenty-five. Often, though, the person who had been the minor's guardian would simply continue as curator. In time, the distinction between the two offices of guardian and curator came to be blurred, and by Justinian's time the two had virtually merged.

Much as was the case with guardianship, the Roman law on curatorship strongly influenced later law.[129] For Scots law, again, Stair's account makes extensive use of Roman sources.[130] Thus, following Roman law,[131] Stair makes a distinction between the curator *ad litem*, who is appointed by the court, and other curators,[132] who are

---

[125] D.4.4.1.
[126] C.5.31.1 (AD 214).
[127] C.5.31.6 (AD 224).
[128] Reigned AD 161–80.
[129] For example, for its influence on the law of France, Spain and Louisiana, see R A Pascal, 'Contracts of the Minor or His Representative under the Louisiana Civil Code' (1947) 8 Louisiana LR 383.
[130] Stair, *Institutions* 1.6.29–37, 44.
[131] J.1.23.2.
[132] Called by Stair curators *ad negotia*. The singular would be curator *ad negotium*.

appointed with the minor's consent.[133] The same terminology (curator and minor) is used. One difference, though, is that in the Scots common law minority ends at the age of twenty-one, rather than twenty-five as in Roman law.[134]

Modern law, however, has no room for curatorship in this sense, because in the current Scots law a child has no legal capacity to enter into any transaction at all up to the age of sixteen[135] (subject to certain limited exceptions),[136] and on reaching sixteen has in principle full legal capacity.[137] There is a remnant of the older idea of the minor as having in principle full capacity subject to certain protections, in the rule that a person who enters into a 'prejudicial transaction' while aged sixteen or seventeen may apply to the court to have the transaction set aside before reaching the age of twenty-one.[138] There is, however, no provision for a curator to act as in Roman law.[139] It is, though, still possible for a court to appoint a curator *ad litem* to protect the interests of a child involved in litigation[140] or a curator *bonis* to manage some transaction of the child's.[141]

(3) Guardianship of Women *(Tutela Mulierum)*

While a boy ceased to require a guardian at puberty, the same was not true of girls. Instead, as we saw in Chapter 5,[142] *sui iuris* girls and women were subject to lifelong guardianship. This was true even of married women, whose fathers were free to appoint guardians for them in their (the fathers') wills.[143]

Women's guardians were appointed in the same ways as children's guardians. Appointment by will has already been mentioned. Failing this, a statutory guardian would be appointed. Emperor Claudius[144] abolished the statutory guardianship of

---

[133] Stair, *Institutions* 1.6.31–2. However, while a minor need not appoint a curator in Stair's account, if one is appointed then Scots common law goes further than Roman law by making any act without the curator's consent void, without any need to show loss (Stair, *Institutions* 1.6.33).
[134] Stair, *Institutions* 1.6.37.
[135] Age of Legal Capacity (Scotland) Act 1991, s. 1(1)(a).
[136] The exceptions are found in s. 2 of the 1991 Act.
[137] Age of Legal Capacity (Scotland) Act 1991, s. 1(1)(b).
[138] Age of Legal Capacity (Scotland) Act 1991, s. 3(1).
[139] The transaction may, however, be ratified by the court (s. 4(1)), or by the young person on reaching the age of eighteen (s. 3(3)(h)).
[140] This person is a curator rather than a tutor, even when appointed to a younger child. For the justification for this terminology, see A B Wilkinson and K McK Norrie, *The Law Relating to Parent and Child in Scotland* 3rd edn by K McK Norrie (W Green 2013) para 5.58: 'At one time the expression "tutor *ad litem*" was often employed and can be found in at least one statute, but "curator" is the modern, and always was the better, usage. There is no personal connection with the child, nor an overall protective function such as the title "tutor" previously suggested.'
[141] This would be unusual, however, as such matters would usually be the responsibility of the child's parent or guardian. Nonetheless, 'it may exceptionally be considered more appropriate to appoint a curator *bonis* because his or her role is purely administrative and representational while the guardian's role involves the exercise and fulfilment of all the parental responsibilities and parental rights' (A B Wilkinson and K McK Norrie, *The Law Relating to Parent and Child in Scotland* 3rd edn by K McK Norrie (W Green 2013) para 5.62).
[142] See pp. 131–2.
[143] G.1.144.
[144] Reigned AD 41–54.

a woman's agnates, however, so the only statutory guardians of women after this were the father of an emancipated woman and the patron of a freedwoman.[145]

A woman's guardian had a more limited role than a child's guardian, having only the responsibility for authorising her transactions. A woman's guardian did not manage her property. Even so, many women must have found it inconvenient to have to get their guardian's approval for their transactions. As part of his marriage legislation,[146] Augustus excused women the need to have a guardian if they had three children (four for freedwomen), which must have been welcome to those benefiting. It seems clear, though, that in the classical period the guardianship of women was hollowed out of practical consequences. By Gaius' time, only statutory guardians could not be readily replaced at the woman's instance.[147] Moreover, a guardian could be compelled to give authority against his will.[148] For this reason, a woman's guardian was not liable for his conduct: there was nothing he could do to incur any liability. Women's guardianship is not mentioned by Justinian, and may have disappeared by the end of the third century AD.[149]

Chapter Summary

The central figure in the Roman family was the *paterfamilias*. A person's *paterfamilias* was his or her oldest agnatic ascendant (*i.e.* ascendant in the male line). The power (*potestas*) of a *paterfamilias* over the persons and property of agnatic descendants (including adoptive descendants) was initially absolute, and remained extensive through the whole Roman period. For example, although certain exceptions to this principle were created, the rule was that a person subject to *potestas* (a *filiusfamilias*) was incapable of owning property. In much the same way as with a slave, though, a *filiusfamilias* could hold a *peculium*, a fund of money or property that was treated as the *filiusfamilias*' own.

The law also had to deal with the issue of persons with no *paterfamilias*, but who were nonetheless in need of protection. A person below puberty who did not have a *paterfamilias* (*i.e.* who was *sui iuris*) would have a guardian (*tutor*) to manage his or her property and approve transactions. This arrangement normally continued for life with women, though with a diminished role for the guardian. Finally, for *sui iuris* individuals up to the age of twenty-five, protections were introduced for their inexperience, and it became normal for such a person to appoint a curator to act as an external check on the reasonableness of transactions.

---

[145] G.1.157.
[146] Specifically the *lex Iulia de maritandis ordinibus* (18 BC) and the *lex Papia Poppaea* (AD 9). The right thereby given is known as the *ius liberorum*.
[147] G.1.173–4.
[148] G.1.190–1.
[149] See generally S Dixon, 'Infirmitas Sexus: Womanly Weakness in Roman Law' (1984) 52 TvR 343.

Further Reading

G.1.55–107; 1.142–200
J.1.8–9; 1.11–15; 1.17–26
D.1.6, 7; 26–7; 37.12, 15
C.5.25, 27–74

D Daube, 'Actions between *Paterfamilias* and *Filiusfamilias* with *Peculium Castrense*' in *Studi in Memoria di Emilio Albertario*, vol 1 (Giuffrè 1953)

B W Frier and T A J McGinn, *A Casebook on Roman Family Law* (Oxford University Press 2004) chapters III and V

H Kruger, 'The Legal Nature and Development of Parental Authority in Roman, Germanic and Roman-Dutch Law – A Historical Overview' (2004) 10 Fundamina 84

J Mackintosh, 'Curatory of Minors in the Civil Law' (1906–7) 18 JR 18

D Nörr, 'The Matrimonial Legislation of Augustus: An Early Instance of Social Engineering' (1981) 16 Irish Jurist (NS) 350

A Watson, *The Law of Persons in the Later Roman Republic* (Oxford University Press 1967) chapters 8–11

CHAPTER EIGHT

Husband and Wife

A. Introduction

It is obvious that, for a society to continue, it must produce children to carry it into the next generation. Where the birth rate drops below the level required to replace the adult population, this becomes a matter of public concern.[1] In the classical period, in fact, the decline in birth rate was such, especially among the upper classes, that there was state intervention to encourage reproduction. The facts of human biology are such, however, that this requires a great deal of the women who are to bear those children. This is especially the case in a society with a high rate of infant mortality, such as ancient Rome and, indeed, every pre-modern society. In such a society, a woman may spend much of her adult life either pregnant or recovering from childbirth.[2] Unless she has independent means, she will have difficulty in supporting herself in that situation. Equally, in a society (like ancient Rome) where much of a child's social status and life chances depend on the identity of his or her father, and in which a father is expected to support his children, then there must be some way of identifying that father.

These factors point in the direction of giving legal recognition to a permanent relationship formed between parents or between people who are at least capable of becoming parents. A woman with a husband can expect to be supported by him, and we saw in Chapter 7[3] that Roman law presumed him to be the father of her children. This is the primary function of marriage in Roman law. It is true that marriage had and still has other functions, such as companionship between the spouses, and so for example we see Justinian defining marriage as 'the union of a man and a woman, committing them to joint habits of life'.[4] The primary reason for recognising marriage as a legal institution, however, is the centrality of its role in reproduction. Many of the fundamental features of marriage are explicable on

---

[1] In Roman history, we see this particularly with the marriage legislation of Augustus (emperor 27 BC–AD 14). Along with a desire to reverse a perceived moral decline, one of the motivations of this legislation was the raising of the birth rate. See generally on Augustus' motivations, D Nörr, 'The Matrimonial Legislation of Augustus: An Early Instance of Social Engineering' (1981) 16 Irish Jurist (NS) 350.
[2] This assumes that she survives. Death of women in childbirth was also prevalent.
[3] See pp. 122–3.
[4] J.1.9.1.

this basis, such as the minimum ages for marriage and the prohibitions on marriage between close relations. By contrast, the relationship between the spouses themselves received what to us must seem a surprising lack of attention from the law. As we shall see below, the form of marriage that was normal in the classical period had strikingly little effect on the spouses' rights and obligations with regard to each other.

This did not mean that the Romans did not engage in extra-marital relations. They did, of course. It is unlikely that there has ever been a society without such conduct. Where it is considered important to identify a child's father, however, that gives reason for there to be at least social disapproval for sexual relations outside marriage, if not legal penalties.[5]

Social disapproval there certainly was of *stuprum*, as sexual activity other than between husband and wife was called,[6] as well as legal penalties. The *lex Iulia de adulteriis coercendis* (the Julian law on suppressing adultery), passed under Augustus, established a special court for cases of *stuprum*.[7] Within marriage, the *lex Iulia de adulteriis coercendis* also penalised wives who strayed (though not directly husbands who did the same, unless their conduct amounted to *stuprum*).[8] After all, a wife's adultery potentially led to her husband having to raise a child who was not his. A wife who committed adultery was criminally liable under this legislation. Her husband was under an obligation to prosecute her for this, and was obliged to divorce her as well. If he failed to do so, he himself risked being held liable for *lenocinium* (pimping).[9]

The wife's lover did not necessarily get off scot-free. If the husband caught the wife and her lover in the act in his own house, he was permitted to kill the lover, as long as the lover was a pimp, had performed on stage, was a convicted criminal who had not yet been restored to his former status, was a freedman of either spouse or of a parent or child of either spouse, or was a slave.[10] Unlike the wife's *paterfamilias*, who did have this right in certain circumstances,[11] he was not permitted to kill her. If he did kill her in the heat of the moment, however, he would be treated more leniently, and excused the usual penalty for murder.[12]

---

[5] It must be said that there is at least a tendency for this stigma to affect women disproportionately. See *e.g.* A Jacobs, '*Maritus v Mulier*: The Double Picture in Adultery Laws from Romulus to Augustus' (2015) 21 Fundamina 276; N L Nguyen, 'Roman Rape: An Overview of Roman Rape Laws from the Republican Period to Justinian's Reign' (2006) 13 Michigan Journal of Gender & Law 75.

[6] Papinian complains (D.48.5.6.1) that the terms *stuprum* and 'adultery' are often used indiscriminately, including in the *lex Iulia de adulteriis coercendis*. He explains, however, that adultery strictly only occurs where one of the parties involved is married (to someone else). *Stuprum* covers other cases (including homosexual relations).

[7] See generally J F Gardner, *Women in Roman Law & Society* (Croom Helm 1986) 121–5.

[8] Heterosexual intercourse only counted as *stuprum* for a man if the woman involved was marriageable. Accordingly, intercourse with a prostitute (for example), or with the man's female slave, would not be considered to be *stuprum*.

[9] D.48.5.2.2; D.48.5.30pr.

[10] D.48.5.25pr–1.

[11] See p. 118.

[12] D.48.5.39.8. This is not to say that he would be let off. His punishment would be serious, but he would not be put to death. The punishment would vary depending on his status. If he was of low status, he would be subjected to perpetual labour. If of high status, he would be banished to an island.

To this disapproval of sexual relations outside marriage there was a curious exception in the form of concubinage. A concubine is a woman with whom a man lives in a permanent or quasi-permanent relationship, as if married but without actually being married. There were certain points of similarity between concubinage and marriage. For example, at least in the post-classical period, a man could only have one wife or one concubine, not both or more than one of either.[13] Again, intercourse between a man and his concubine did not count as *stuprum*.[14] In the final analysis, however, concubinage was not marriage, and children of the union would not fall into their father's *potestas*. Only the children of a valid Roman marriage could have a *paterfamilias* and be subject to *potestas*. By later standards, however, it is noteworthy that there seems to have been little or no stigma against a man keeping a concubine, as long as she was of a lower social status than his.[15] Indeed, concubinage could even be seen as preferable to marriage, even for the concubine. Ulpian presents the case of a freedwoman living as her patron's concubine. She leaves without his consent and seeks to marry another. This, he said, should not be permitted, 'because it is more honourable for a freedwoman to be her patron's concubine than to be the mother of a family (*matrem familias*)'.[16]

This chapter is concerned with marriage. There is a complication, however, in that the Romans recognised two forms of marriage, and which was chosen had a profound impact on the legal position of the spouses. Of these two forms, the more common one in earlier times was the marriage *cum manu*. The phrase *cum manu* is not easy to translate. Literally, it means 'with the hand', but the hand is metaphorical here. *Manus*, or 'hand',[17] refers to the husband's power over his wife, analogous to the *potestas* held by a *paterfamilias* over the descendants he has in his power. In effect, in the *manus* marriage, the wife became subject to the *potestas* of her husband (or of his *paterfamilias*, if he had one). Here this form of marriage is simply called '*manus* marriage'. The other form, the marriage *sine manu* or free marriage, by contrast had no such effect.[18] By the classical period, the free marriage was the more common form. These two forms of marriage must, therefore, be considered separately. First, though, we shall look at some general issues in the formation of marriage, applying to both types.

B. Formation of Marriage

(1) Betrothal

A marriage would often be preceded by a betrothal, although this was not a formal requirement. The betrothal could be agreed fairly informally, and the

---

[13] C.5.26.1 (AD 326); A Jacobs, 'The Ghost of the Roman *Concubinatus*' (2004) 10 Fundamina 59, 61.
[14] D.25.7.3.1. Compare, though, D.25.7.1.1 and D.25.7.3pr on who can properly be a concubine.
[15] D.25.7.3pr.
[16] D.25.7.1pr.
[17] For those without Latin, *manu* in the phrase *cum manu* is a form of the word *manus*. The grammatical term for this form is the ablative case, and it is used when the word follows certain prepositions, such as *cum* ('with').
[18] Literally, the words *sine manu* mean 'without the hand'.

parties themselves did not need to be present.[19] If the parties were not present, however, it was necessary for them to know it was happening or to ratify the betrothal afterwards.[20] Although the actual negotiations for the marriage might be carried out by each party's *paterfamilias* (arranged marriages being common, at least among the elite), the parties' own consent was still needed.[21] It seems, though, that it was enough for each party to acquiesce in the choice of marriage partner made by his or her *paterfamilias*. The jurist Julian tells us, moreover, that the prospective bride may only refuse consent if her *paterfamilias* has chosen someone to marry who was actually unfit for this.[22] Betrothals might be contracted years in advance of the marriage taking place, and they were not subject to the same minimum ages as marriage. As long as the parties were aged at least seven, they could be betrothed, even though they could not yet marry for several years.[23]

Betrothal did have some legal consequences. For example, a man could recover damages if the delict of *iniuria* was committed against his fiancée, just as a husband could if his wife was the victim.[24] Again, a man was barred from marrying the fiancée of his father or of his son.[25] A betrothal, however, was not a marriage, and either party (or that party's *paterfamilias*) could break off the engagement at will, without penalty.[26] Even where there was an express agreement for the payment of penalties if the marriage did not happen, this agreement would be unenforceable.[27] This differs from many later legal systems, in which it has been considered an actionable wrong to break off an engagement without good cause.[28]

(2) Formal Requirements for Marriage

There were various requirements for the validity of a marriage. If any of them was not met, the purported marriage was void and of no effect. As a result, any children of the relationship would not be considered legitimate and would not fall into their father's *potestas*.[29]

---

[19] D.23.1.4; D.23.1.18.
[20] D.23.1.5.
[21] D.23.1.11.
[22] D.23.1.12.
[23] D.23.1.14.
[24] D.47.10.15.24. On *iniuria*, see Chapter 23.
[25] D.23.2.12.1–2.
[26] C.5.1.1 (AD 293); D.23.1.10.
[27] D.45.1.134pr.
[28] This was at one time true of Scots law. Though Erskine (*Institute* 1.6.3) only allows damages for 'anything done in consequence of the promise, whereby damage arises to any of the parties from the non-performance', in *Hogg v Gow* 27 May 1812, FC, the contrary was held and seems to have been accepted as settled law. An oddity of the case is that the majority in the Court of Session relies on no authority beyond a change in 'the manners of mankind' and the need for the law to adapt to 'the present state of morals and society' (Lord Bannatyne). The previous position is denounced as 'barbarism' by Lord Meadowbank. Such an action is, however, no longer competent: Law Reform (Husband and Wife) (Scotland) Act 1984, s. 1(1).
[29] J.1.10.12. Exceptions could be made, however: see *e.g.* D.23.2.57a.

(a) Conubium

Both of the parties to a valid Roman marriage had to have *conubium*. As we saw in Chapter 5,[30] this was a right of marriage, that formed part of the rights of Roman citizens. It was, therefore, mostly confined to Roman citizens, although non-citizen individuals and communities sometimes had *conubium* as well. Non-Romans did, of course, marry, but they did so according to the laws of their own community, and so the marriage did not have the consequences of a Roman marriage. Thus, for example, if a Roman man married a woman without *conubium*, the children of the marriage would not fall within his *potestas*.

(b) Parties of Different Sexes

Marriage in Roman law was between male and female, unsurprisingly given the association between marriage and procreation. Homosexuality existed in the ancient world, of course, but it never seems to have been suggested that homosexual unions should be recognised as capable of being valid marriages.[31]

(c) No Subsisting Marriage

A person could only have one spouse at a time.[32] If the parties purported to marry while either of them was married to someone else, not only would this second marriage be void, but knowingly to do this would incur *infamia*[33] and liability for *stuprum*.[34]

(d) Age

The parties to the marriage had to have reached puberty.[35] There was debate among jurists as to how this was to be determined.[36] The Sabinian school of jurists favoured a determination according to whether the individuals in question had reached sexual maturity. As is well known, this is reached by different people at different ages, so the result would be that different people would acquire the capacity to marry at different times. The view finally followed, however, was that fixed ages should be adopted.[37] Girls could marry at twelve, boys at fourteen, though they might (especially the latter) not marry until much later than that.[38]

---

[30] See p. 96.
[31] At least two emperors (Nero, emperor AD 54–68, and Elagabalus, emperor AD 218–22) are said to have gone through marriage ceremonies with other men. However, it is one thing to go through a marriage ceremony with someone; it is another thing to marry that person. There is no reason to think that a same-sex marriage was ever seen as being capable of being legally effective.
[32] G.1.64.
[33] See pp. 100–1.
[34] C.9.9.18 (AD 258).
[35] J.1.10pr.
[36] G.1.196.
[37] C.5.4.24 (AD 530).
[38] The reason for the difference is, of course, that on average girls reach sexual maturity earlier than boys.

(e) Prohibited Degrees

There was a prohibition on marriage between parties who were closely related. The general rule was that two people could not marry unless they were both at least two degrees of descent from their nearest common ancestor. Thus, for example, first cousins could marry, as they were both two degrees removed from the common ancestor.[39] As might be expected, marriage between siblings was prohibited.[40] Siblings are, after all, only one degree from the common ancestor. Marriages between ascendants and descendants were also absolutely prohibited[41] There could be no marriage between a man and his great-niece or a woman and her great-nephew, the great-uncle or great-aunt being only one degree removed from the common ancestor.[42] Variations on the rules might also be introduced from time to time. The emperor Claudius[43] introduced a rule that a man could marry his brother's daughter, to allow himself to marry his niece, Agrippina.[44] Such marriages were expressly prohibited by Justinian.[45]

All of these prohibitions were based on blood relationship rather than legal relationship. Persons who were biologically related within the forbidden degrees were barred from marrying, even if they had no legal relationship. For example, a freedman could not marry his biological mother or sister.[46] Another example would be a purported marriage between two biological siblings, one or both of whom had been emancipated by their *paterfamilias*. Even though the emancipation would have destroyed their legal relationship, they would still be unable to form a valid marriage.

In addition to these rules, there were also prohibitions based on relationship by affinity (*i.e.* relationship through marriage) and relationship by adoption.

To take adoption first, similar rules applied as with blood relationships, at least as long as the adoptive relationship lasted. Where adoption created a relationship of ascendant and descendant, marriage was prohibited, and in this case the prohibition continued even if the adoptive relationship came to an end.[47] Equally, adoptive siblings could not marry. In this case, however, the prohibition lasted only as long as the adoptive relationship lasted. If, for example, one of the adoptive siblings was emancipated, the pair would cease to be related to each other and would be permitted to marry.[48]

---

[39] J.1.10.4.
[40] G.1.61; J.1.10.2. Such prohibitions are common in history, though not universal. Marriage between siblings was common among Egyptian pharaohs. One such was Cleopatra (reigned 51–30 BC, and famous for her affairs with two prominent Romans, Julius Caesar and Mark Antony), who was married to her brother.
[41] G.1.59; J.1.10.1.
[42] J.1.10.3; D.23.2.17.2.
[43] Reigned AD 41–54.
[44] G.1.62. A man could not, however, marry his sister's daughter.
[45] J.1.10.3.
[46] J.1.10.10; D.23.2.8.
[47] G.1.59; J.1.10.1.
[48] G.1.61; J.1.10.2; D.23.2.17pr–1.

In the case of more distant adoptive relationships, the position seems to have been that marriage was only barred if the adoption created an agnatic relationship (*i.e.* a relationship through the male line). Thus, for example, a man could marry his adopted sister's daughter,[49] but not his adopted brother's daughter.

Finally, certain pairings who were related by affinity (*i.e.* through marriage) were prohibited from marrying, even if the marriage that created the relationship ceased. It was not permitted to marry an ascendant or descendant of a former spouse, such as a step-child or parent-in-law.[50] Step-siblings were, however, permitted to marry.[51]

(f) Consent

For a valid marriage, the parties had to consent. If either was *alieni iuris*, his or her *paterfamilias* had to consent as well.[52] A sham marriage, where the parties had exchanged apparent consent but without any genuine intention to marry, would be of no effect.[53]

As might be expected, it was normal to have a wedding ceremony at which the consents would be given.[54] What is less certain is the extent to which this ceremony was necessary. Some flexibility was apparently possible, because it was possible for the marriage to be constituted in the absence of the groom, with his consent being given by letter or messenger.[55] The question is whether the ceremony could be dispensed with altogether.

Pomponius tells us that 'consent, not sleeping together, makes a marriage'.[56] This seems to imply that the consent to be married (known as *affectio maritalis*) was the sole determinant of whether the parties were married. That was certainly how the medieval canon law took these texts, considering a marriage to be formed by simple exchange of words of consent, without any need for formal ceremony.[57] Following canon law, that was also the law of Scotland until such 'irregular marriages' were abolished by the Marriage (Scotland) Act 1939.[58] It is unlikely that classical Roman law would have taken such a generous view of

---

[49] J.1.10.3; D.23.2.12.4.
[50] G.1.63; J.1.10.6–7.
[51] J.1.10.8.
[52] J.1.10pr.
[53] D.23.2.30.
[54] S Treggiari, *Roman Marriage: Iusti Coniuges from the Time of Cicero to the Time of Ulpian* (Oxford University Press 1991) 161–70.
[55] D.23.2.5. The bride, however, could not be absent, as she had to be led to her new husband's house after the wedding.
[56] D.35.1.15. See also Ulpian's very similar formulation at D.24.1.32.13.
[57] See *e.g. Petrie v Petrie* 1911 SC 360. Indeed, the canon law went further, and deemed this consent to exist when sexual intercourse had taken place in reliance on a promise of marriage (marriage *per verba de futuro, subsequente copula*). On this latter form of marriage in Scots law, see *e.g. Maloy v McCosh* (1885) 12 R 431; *Mackie v Mackie* 1917 SC 276; *X v Y* 1921 1 SLT 79. For a general overview of the medieval canon law of marriage, including the influence of Roman law on it, see O F Robinson, 'Canon Law and Marriage' 1984 JR 22.
[58] There is one exception to this statement, to be mentioned below. The survival of irregular marriages much longer in Scotland than in England made communities just on the Scottish side of the border (most famously Gretna, but not exclusively) popular destinations for generations of eloping English couples.

consents unaccompanied by formalities. Pomponius is probably simply making the point that the marriage is constituted by the parties' agreement, even before it is consummated.

All the same, there does appear to have been some scope for the existence of a marriage to be established even in the absence of a formal wedding. For example, the late classical jurist Modestinus tells us that, where a man and a woman cohabit, this 'is to be understood not as concubinage, but as marriage, as long as she is not a prostitute'.[59] Similarly, an imperial pronouncement of the late third century held that a marriage could be demonstrated by the parties openly living together and having a child, even in the absence of the documentation that would normally accompany a marriage.[60] It is not difficult to draw an analogy between this and the modern marriage by cohabitation with habit and repute, which existed in Scots law[61] until its abolition by the Family Law (Scotland) Act 2006,[62] and which also allowed the outward appearance of marriage to stand as evidence of consent to marriage.[63]

(g) Prohibited Marriages

Various other restrictions existed on what was considered to be a suitable marriage. For example, there could be no valid marriage between a woman and her guardian or his son.[64] It was also prohibited for a senator, or an agnatic descendant of a senator down to his great-grandchildren,[65] and a former slave or anyone who had either been an actor or was the child of actors.[66] Justinian's predecessor Justin, however, abolished all previous prohibitions on marriage between freeborn persons of different social class.[67]

---

[59] D.23.2.24.
[60] C.5.4.9 (undated, but under Probus, emperor 276–82). See also C.5.4.22 (AD 428).
[61] See *e.g. Campbell v Campbell* (1866) 4 M 867; *S v S* 2006 SLT 471.
[62] Specifically section 3 of that Act. This does not affect any marriage already constituted in this way before that section came into force. Accordingly, the possibility will exist for some time yet that the concept of marriage by cohabitation with habit and repute will have to be pressed into service.
[63] This allowed a marriage to be constituted by the parties living openly as if married for a long enough period to create a repute of marriage. This cohabitation was supposed to demonstrate the intention to marry. It may be wondered how marriage by cohabitation with habit and repute can have survived until 2006, when marriage by agreement alone was abolished in 1939. The answer is that this does not make sense in principle. It seems, however, that it was forgotten that cohabitation with habit and repute of marriage was simply evidence of the consent to marry that was the true ground of the parties being held to be husband and wife. Somewhere along the way, marriage by cohabitation with habit and repute came to be treated as a free-standing means of constituting marriage (and so was not abolished by the 1939 Act, not being mentioned by it) rather than being simply an evidential device.
[64] D.23.1.15.
[65] That is, a descendant in the male line. Thus, the restriction extended to the child of a son, or the child of a son's son, but not to the child of a daughter, or to the child of a son's daughter.
[66] D.23.2.44pr; D.23.2.23. Special permission for such a marriage could, however, be given by the emperor: D.23.2.31.
[67] C.5.4.23.7 (AD 520–3, precise date uncertain). No such restriction has ever existed in Scots law either, although there might be *social* stigma against a marriage between two persons of widely diverging social positions. This is no doubt the reason why so many of the reported cases on irregular marriages involve a man who has married his servant in secret. See *e.g. Mackenzie v Mackenzie's Trs* 1916 1 SLT 349.

C. *Manus* Marriage

(1) Prevalence and Constitution

In early law, it is generally assumed, *manus* marriage was the normal form of marriage, and there were three recognised ways of constituting such a marriage. The first was *coemptio*, which took the form of a fictitious sale, before witnesses, of the bride to the groom.[68] Secondly, this form of marriage could be brought about by *confarreatio*, which was a religious ceremony involving a sacrifice to the god Jupiter, a special cake made with spelt (a type of wheat), and formal acts and words in the presence of ten witnesses. This seems to have survived at least until Gaius' day because certain priesthoods could only be held by those married in this way and born of parents married in this way.[69] Thirdly, where the parties had entered into a free marriage, it would be converted to a *manus* marriage by continuous cohabitation for a year. This was called *usus*. A provision in the Twelve Tables provided that this consequence could be avoided if the wife absented herself for three nights in the year. By Gaius' time, however, *usus* had fallen out of use, 'partly abolished by statutes, partly obliterated by desuetude'.[70] In his day, the parties could cohabit continuously without their marriage being converted to a *manus* one.

(2) Legal Consequences

The marriage had consequences for both the spouses and their children. As far as the children are concerned, by virtue of having been produced within marriage they were legitimate children of their father, and would fall into his *potestas* (or that of his *paterfamilias*). For the wife, there were also significant consequences. On entering into a *manus* marriage, the wife fell into the *potestas* of her husband (or of his *paterfamilias*). She was therefore in much the same position as her husband's daughter, unable to own property and with the succession rights of a daughter.[71]

(3) Divorce

A marriage could be brought to an end by divorce. The position of divorce in early law is not particularly clear. However, it was certainly the case that only the husband could initiate it. According to rules attributed by later Roman writers to Romulus, the first king, there were three grounds on which a man could divorce his wife. These were adultery, 'substitution of keys' and 'poisoning of children'. The meaning of adultery is clear enough, but the other two grounds are unfortunately less so. Poisoning of children may refer to abortion. The idea of substitution of keys is, however, mysterious.[72] At any rate, a man who divorced his wife without

---

[68] G.1.113. The fictitious sale was effected by *mancipatio*, on which see pp. 199–200.
[69] G.1.112.
[70] G.1.111.
[71] C F Amunátegui Perelló and P-I Carvajal Ramírez, 'Some Considerations on the Expression "*Loco Filiae*" in Gaius' *Institutes*' (2016) 22 Fundamina 1.
[72] It may relate in some way to a wife's role as custodian of the household keys. For brief discussion, see A Watson, *Rome of the XII Tables: Persons and Property* (Princeton University Press 1975) 33–4.

one of these justifications had to give the wife half of his property. The other half was forfeited to the goddess Ceres.

Divorce seems to have become more readily available from around 230 BC, when an upper-class Roman named Carvilius Ruga was allowed to divorce his wife without suffering the prescribed penalty. This was the case even though none of the prescribed grounds of divorce was present. Despite this, he was not seen as being at fault.[73]

In the case of a marriage constituted by *confarreatio*, the divorce was effected by a ceremony called *diffareatio*.[74] In other cases, the procedure was for the husband to emancipate his wife, as if she were his daughter.[75] This then was a procedure initiated and carried out by the husband, and it is likely that in early law the wife had no power to initiate a divorce at all. In the classical period, however, it seems that a wife in a *manus* marriage could compel her husband to emancipate her on sending him a notice of repudiation.[76]

D. Free Marriage

(1) Prevalence and Constitution

In the classical law, the normal form of marriage was the free marriage. There is, however, much about the process by which this came to be the case that we do not know.[77] We do not know when and how free marriage developed. We do not know whether free marriage was always possible, or whether it only became possible at some point during the Republic. It is true that the existence of *usus* as a way of constituting a *manus* marriage suggests that free marriage existed already by the time of the Twelve Tables in around 450 BC, for it assumes that the parties are already married before the year of *usus* expires. However, the suggestion has also been made that *usus* originally existed to cure defects in the marriage ceremony or to regularise informal cohabitation as marriage. We cannot be sure when or why free marriage became the dominant form, though there is a widespread scholarly view that the decisive moment was around the end of the third or beginning of the second century BC.[78] We do not even know how the distinction between free and

---

[73] For discussion, see A Watson, 'The Divorce of Carvilius Ruga' (1965) 33 TvR 38; A Jacobs, '*Carvilius Ruga v Uxor*: A Famous Roman Divorce' (2009) 15 Fundamina 92. In simple terms, what is said to have happened is this. Carvilius Ruga, as a married man, was compelled by the censors to make an oath that he had married for the purposes of procreation. (This is reflective of the state's concern with the birth rate, mentioned above.) His wife, however, turned out to be infertile. Carvilius Ruga, therefore, considered that his oath required him to divorce her, despite his great love for her. Thus, neither spouse was at fault, she because she obviously could not help being infertile, and he because he was bound by an oath that was inconsistent with the continuation of the marriage. Accordingly, the established penalty was not appropriate to the situation.

[74] For a description of this ceremony, see F de Coulanges, 'Marriage in Greece and Rome' in A Kocourek and J H Wigmore eds, *Evolution of Law: Select Readings on the Origin and Development of Legal Institutions, Volume II: Primitive and Ancient Legal Institutions* (Little, Brown & Co 1915) 290.

[75] G.1.137. On emancipation of children, see p. 127.

[76] G.1.137a.

[77] For discussion of the issues raised in this paragraph, see S E Looper-Friedman, 'The Decline of Manus-Marriage in Rome' (1987) 55 TvR 281.

[78] Whether coincidentally or not, this is fairly soon after the divorce of Carvilius Ruga, mentioned above.

manus marriage is best characterised. Are these to be viewed as two distinct forms of marriage, or are marriage and *manus* two separate, though related, institutions? On the latter view, the marriage relationship as such is the same in both forms, and the difference is that in a *manus* marriage the wife has submitted to an additional legal relationship in the form of *manus*.[79] What we do know is that, by the end of the Republic, *manus* marriage was uncommon, and free marriage was the norm. This was constituted simply by consent, as described above.

(2) Legal Consequences

The main legal consequence of a free marriage, as with a *manus* marriage, was that the children of the marriage were the legitimate children of their father. As far as the spouses' relationship was concerned, however, there were surprisingly few legal consequences to the free marriage. Neither husband nor wife changed family. The wife remained in the *potestas* of her own *paterfamilias* or, if she was *sui iuris*, she remained so.[80]

One striking consequence of the marriage, however, was that gifts between the spouses were generally void. Ulpian tells us that this arose 'from custom', in order to prevent couples' mutual affection causing them to impoverish themselves.[81] There were, though, some exceptions to this rule. For example, conventional gifts (such as birthday presents) were permitted, as long as they were not excessively valuable,[82] as were payments to the wife for household expenses.[83]

(3) Divorce

As a free marriage was based on the parties' consent (and on the consent of each party's *paterfamilias*, if he existed),[84] likewise was it brought to an end by the withdrawal of that consent.[85] When either party intended permanently to bring the marriage to an end, the marriage ceased.[86] It was not necessary to establish any

---

[79] The distinction perhaps makes little practical difference. However, if the latter view is correct, the co-existence of free and *manus* marriage is easier to understand. It is not easy to understand why there would be two distinct forms of marriage. It is easier to conceive a choice of marriage and 'marriage-plus', where the latter has additional consequences. In effect, the parties to a *manus* marriage are entering into two legal relationships: a marriage relationship and a *potestas*-type relationship. On this view, the purpose of *confarreatio* and *coemptio* was not to create the marriage as such – that was created simply by the parties' consent – but to impose *manus* on the wife.

[80] Thus, it was quite possible for a wife to be *sui iuris* but for her husband to be *alieni iuris*.

[81] D.24.1.1. See, however, D Cherry, 'Gifts between Husband and Wife: The Social Origins of Roman Law' in J-J Aubert and B Sirks, *Speculum Iuris: Roman Law as a Reflection of Social and Economic Life in Antiquity* (University of Michigan Press 2002), where quite a different explanation is suggested.

[82] D.24.1.31.8.

[83] D.24.1.31.9. This exception could be pushed fairly far: the examples given include banquets and perfume.

[84] Emperor Marcus Aurelius (reigned AD 161–80), however, provided that a *paterfamilias* should not be allowed to separate spouses who were content with each other. See C.5.17.5 (AD 294); D.43.30.1.5.

[85] Roman law then differs here from the position later taken by canon law. While, as we have seen, canon law took and developed the rule basing marriage on the parties' consent, for scriptural reasons it rejected the Roman position on divorce.

[86] This is very different from even those modern systems where divorce is permitted with the agreement of the spouses. Even in those systems, the divorce is an act of the court, not of the parties, and does not occur until the court has made the appropriate order.

ground justifying the divorce. The emphasis here is on the word 'permanently', however. Thus, things said or done in anger did not end the marriage unless persisted in. Accordingly, if one spouse purported to repudiate the marriage and left, but returned shortly afterwards, the marriage was considered to have continued.[87]

Divorce in classical law was notable for its ease and informality, although the rule emerged in the Empire that notice of the divorce had to be given in the presence of seven witnesses.[88] In principle, though, it was enough simply that one or both of the spouses withdrew the intention to be married (*affectio maritalis*).[89]

It might be expected that this would change after the conversion to Christianity.[90] However, while there were attempts to reduce divorce numbers by penalising those divorcing without good cause,[91] there was no attempt to make the divorce itself ineffective. The one exception to this is Justinian, who abolished divorce by mutual consent in most circumstances. This provision was, however, repealed shortly after his death.[92]

E. Dowry

(1) Nature and Role of Dowry

Marriage did not impose any legal duty on the husband to maintain the wife (or *vice versa*). A husband was, however, subject to a social duty to maintain his wife. He was seen as bearing the financial burden of marriage.[93] It was common, therefore, for the wife to come to the marriage with money or property provided by her or by her *paterfamilias* as her contribution to household expenses. This is known as a dowry. So ingrained was this custom that, under Augustus' marriage legislation, a woman's *paterfamilias* could be compelled to provide her with a suitable dowry.[94]

(2) Rights in the Dowry

The original concept of a dowry was that it was transferred outright to the husband, and the wife or her *paterfamilias* had no rights in it either during or after the marriage. No attempt seems to have been made in earlier times to regulate what happened with the dowry following a divorce. The reason for this may be that the wife's interests were seen as sufficiently protected by the penalty imposed for divorces that were not justified by one of the prescribed grounds. After the

---

[87] D.24.2.3.
[88] D.24.2.9.
[89] It was not enough, however, simply to enter into a new marriage with someone else, as Messalina, third wife of Emperor Claudius, found out in AD 48. In her husband's absence, she went through a ceremony of marriage with her latest lover, a senator called Gaius Silius. She was considered to be a bigamist, and was executed for her trouble. It was necessary to give objective sign of the intention to end the marriage before a new marriage could validly be entered into.
[90] As it certainly did in canon law. While canon law took marriage by consent from Roman law, the Roman law on divorce was rather less congenial to the Church's viewpoint.
[91] See *e.g.* C.5.17.8 (AD 449).
[92] Nov. 140 (AD 566).
[93] D.23.3.7pr.
[94] D.23.2.19.

divorce of Carvilius Ruga, discussed above, it might be expected that steps would begin to be taken to protect wives' interests in their dowries, as it created the possibility of a wife being divorced without fault and without compensation. Whether or not this development is indeed connected with that divorce, we do see developments of this kind. The practice emerged of expressly contracting for either the dowry itself[95] or its value[96] to be returnable.

In time, the wife's right to have the dowry restored came to be implied. The wife could bring an action called the *actio rei uxoriae* to reclaim a share of the dowry on termination of the marriage, subject to certain deductions by the husband, for example for any necessary expenses he had incurred in maintaining the property. He was, moreover, permitted to retain any profits arising from the dowry, on the basis that he bore the financial burdens of the marriage.[97] Furthermore, if the divorce was due to the fault of the wife or her *paterfamilias* (*e.g.* if she had committed adultery),[98] the husband could retain a sixth of the dowry for every child of the marriage, up to three. Augustus formalised these rules, and also provided that, if the marriage was terminated by the wife's death, the husband had to restore such of the dowry that had been provided by a still-living donor to that person. He was, though, entitled to retain a fifth of the dowry for every child of the marriage. The husband was also prohibited from selling any Italic land[99] forming part of the dowry without the wife's consent or from securing debt of the land even with the wife's consent.[100] The position of classical law, therefore, was that the husband was considered more of a steward of the dowry than an owner, and he was obliged to exercise the same care in managing the dowry that he did in managing his own affairs.[101]

Justinian went even further. He extended the prohibition on alienation to all land, and made it apply even with the wife's consent.[102] The husband had no more right to make deductions from the dowry, except for necessary expenses, and the dowry reverted to the wife in all circumstances at the end of the marriage. The wife was even given an implied security over her husband's property for the dowry, with preference even over secured creditors.[103]

(3) Donatio Propter Nuptias

A *donatio propter nuptias* ('gift on account of marriage') was the reverse of a dowry. It was a gift by the prospective husband to his intended bride, typically to ensure

---

[95] Such a dowry was called *dos receptitia*.
[96] In this case, the dowry was called *dos aestimata*.
[97] D.23.3.7pr. This was the case even though, as we have seen, he had no actual obligation to support his wife.
[98] See *e.g.* D.48.5.12.13.
[99] See p. 198.
[100] J.2.8pr.
[101] D.23.3.17pr.
[102] J.2.8pr.
[103] C.5.13.1b (AD 530).

provision for her in the event of her husband predeceasing her. It was unknown to the classical law, but was introduced in the post-classical period. As an exception to the rule barring gifts between spouses, Justin[104] allowed the *donatio propter nuptias* to be increased after the marriage.[105] In addition, Justinian provided that, where a dowry was given, there had to be a *donatio propter nuptias* of the same amount.

One major concern in the law of marriage was the parties' respective interests in the dowry, made up of money or property brought into the marriage by the wife and provided either by her or by someone else (such as her *paterfamilias*). In early law, the husband acquired outright ownership of the dowry. However, over time his rights were restricted, until he was finally little more than a custodian of the dowry for the benefit of the wife.

Chapter Summary

Roman law recognised two forms of marriage, one of which was more common in early law and the other of which became the dominant form by the classical period. The older form, *manus* marriage, imposed *manus* on the wife, a *potestas*-like relationship by which she entered the power of her husband or of his *paterfamilias*. The alternative was a free marriage, without *manus*, in which the wife did not lose her previous family relationships and did not enter her husband's power. This form was notable for its minimal legal consequences as far as the relationship between the spouses was concerned. It had in common with *manus* marriage, however, that the children of the marriage were the legitimate children of their father, subject to his *potestas* or to that of his *paterfamilias*.

Further Reading

G.1.108–15b
J.1.10
D.23–5
C.5.1–24, 26
B W Frier and T A J McGinn, *A Casebook on Roman Family Law* (Oxford University Press 2004) chapter II
D Nörr, 'The Matrimonial Legislation of Augustus: An Early Instance of Social Engineering' (1981) 16 Irish Jurist (NS) 350

---

[104] Emperor AD 518–27.
[105] J.2.7.3. For this reason, Justinian changed the name from the original *donatio ante nuptias* ('gift before marriage').

S Treggiari, *Roman Marriage:* Iusti Coniuges *from the Time of Cicero to the Time of Ulpian* (Oxford University Press 1991)

A Watson, *The Law of Persons in the Later Roman Republic* (Oxford University Press 1967) chapters 1–7

CHAPTER NINE

Liability for Another

A. Introduction

In this book, most of the discussion assumes individuals acting on their own behalf, whether entering into contracts, acquiring property, incurring liability for wrongdoing, or anything else. The real world, however, is more complicated than that, and in the modern world individuals frequently act through others, such as employees or agents. For example, if there is a sale of a house between two people, they do not normally carry out the negotiations in person or manage the legal formalities without assistance. Instead, each will normally instruct solicitors, as having the required expertise, to act on his or her behalf. Again, if I own a business, a contract made by one of my employees may well bind me even though I was not directly involved in making it.

The same was true of the Romans. Although Roman law in this area had many differences from modern law, it was equally true that Romans would frequently act through others. We have seen already[1] that the Romans made extensive use of slaves in business, often allowing them a high level of responsibility and autonomy. Such a slave might act in such a way that, for a free person, rights would be acquired or liabilities incurred. The same is true of those subject to *patria potestas*. The law had to be able to square the position that someone who had a *paterfamilias* could not own property and had limited capacity to act on his or her own behalf, with the fact that such a person would often in fact act as if these things were possible. In the case of both the slave and the *filiusfamilias*, the only person who could be held liable would be the slave-owner or the *paterfamilias*.

In Chapter 5, legal personality was defined as the capacity to hold rights and be subject to obligations. In Chapters 5 to 8, we have seen how that capacity could be restricted or qualified by the different kinds of personal status that an individual could hold. In this chapter we see how an individual's legal personality, in the sense of the ability to become subject to obligations, could in effect be extended to the acts of others, whether slave, *filiusfamilius* or free employee. This chapter divides into two. First, we shall look at the imposition of contractual

---

[1] See p. 104.

liability by the acts of another. We have already seen that contractual *rights* could be acquired through the acts of a slave or *filiusfamilias*. After this, we shall consider delictual liability for the wrongdoing of another.

Before going further, however, there is a point of terminology to consider. Almost everything in this chapter about the position of a slave-owner applies equally to a *paterfamilias* and *vice versa*. The same is true of a slave and a *filiusfamilias*. To avoid unnecessary repetition, both slave-owner and *paterfamilias* will be referred to as 'master'. The slave or *filiusfamilias* will be referred to as 'dependant'.

B. Contractual Liability

In modern law, the way in which a person becomes contractually bound by another person's acts is through the law of agency. Although it is the agent who acts, the person who acquires rights and incurs obligations through those acts is not the agent but the principal, the person on whose behalf the agent acts. Roman law, however, did not develop a concept of agency in the way that it exists in modern law.[2] There was no general principle of liability for another's acts. While there was a form of contract (called mandate)[3] by which one person could be authorised to act on another's behalf, this was not true agency as the authorising party (the mandator) did not directly acquire any rights or incur any obligations from the transactions entered into by the other. Again, while a dependant could acquire rights for the master, he or she could not impose binding obligations.[4] The praetor did, however, intervene to create a range of actions by which a master could be held liable for acts carried out by those subject to his or her authority.[5] These actions came to be known as the *actiones adiecticiae qualitatis*.

The precise details of the development of these actions is unclear, including their dates and the order in which they were introduced.[6] A basic distinction can be made, however. Some of these actions are based on the authorisation by the master for the dependant (or, sometimes, someone else) to enter into binding transactions. We shall look at these first. The other actions, to be considered afterwards, are based on the holding of a *peculium* by the dependant, with the liability of the master being limited to the extent of the *peculium*.

(1) Actions Based on Authorisation

The first group of actions is based on the consent of the master to be bound. It was not enough just to be aware of the transactions in question.[7] Three actions fall into this category.

---

[2] In a modern agency arrangement, the agent acts entirely for another person (the principal), and is not a party to the contracts that he or she makes.
[3] See pp. 371–3.
[4] D.50.17.133.
[5] This was not unrestricted, however. See in particular the *senatusconsultum Macedonianum*, which made loans to those subject to *potestas* unenforceable. This is discussed at pp. 346–7.
[6] L De Ligt, 'Legal History and Economic History: The Case of the *Actiones Adiecticiae Qualitatis*' (1999) 67 TvR 205.
[7] D.14.1.1.20.

(a) Actio Quod Iussu

The *actio quod iussu* (the 'action for what has been ordered') was available to make the master liable in full under any transaction that he[8] has specifically authorised the dependant to enter into. This authorisation could be for a single transaction, or could be more general.[9] The justification for holding the slave or *paterfamilias* liable was that 'one who enters into such a transaction puts faith in the father or the master rather than the son or the slave'.[10] It was therefore reasonable to hold the master liable. The implication of this is that the third party had to be made aware of this authorisation. The master could, however, ratify the transaction after the fact.[11] This would have the effect of imposing liability on the master retrospectively.

(b) Actio Institoria and Actio Exercitoria

The *actio institoria* and the *actio exercitoria* were two very similar actions, and were the only ones of the *actiones adiecticiae qualitatis* that applied to the actions of persons other than a dependant. They were therefore the closest that Roman law came to agency in the modern sense.

The *actio exercitoria* was available when a slave, *filiusfamilias* or third party was put in charge of a ship, and the *actio institoria* applied when such a person was put in charge of a land-based business. In either case, the master or employer was liable in full for transactions entered into by the person put in charge,[12] as long as they were in the scope of the appointment.[13] The justification for this is much the same as with the *actio quod iussu*, although the authorisation here is general rather than there being specific authorisation for individual transactions. The reasoning behind this is obvious, however, especially for the *actio exercitoria*. If I put someone in charge of my ship for a trading voyage, they will not be able to seek my authorisation for transactions while they are away. Even with a land-based business, such as a shop, it is unlikely that I will find it convenient to have to authorise every transaction personally. That would take away most or all of the advantage in appointing someone to manage the business for me. The effect of these two *actiones* would be to make my general authorisation to manage the ship or the business sufficient.

(2) Actions Based on the *Peculium*

In circumstances where a dependant had authorisation to enter into a transaction, the master was liable without limit, as we have seen. Where no such authorisation could be identified, whether that authorisation was general or specific, there was, however, an alternative.

---

[8] Or potentially she, in the case of a slave-owner.
[9] D.15.4.1.1.
[10] G.4.70. This justification implies (as is indeed accepted as being the case) that the authorisation had to be communicated to the third party.
[11] D.15.4.1.6.
[12] G.4.71.
[13] D.14.3.5.11.

We have seen (in Chapters 6[14] and 7[15]) that a dependant might be entrusted with a fund of money or property, called a *peculium*. The dependant would be allowed to treat this as his or her own, even though a dependant could not own property and could not effectually contract on his or her own behalf.[16] The *peculium* remained the property of the master. The praetor introduced various actions that allowed the master to be held liable up to the extent of the *peculium*.

It might be difficult to prove the existence and extent of the *peculium*. Accordingly, as Gaius points out, it would be better to use the *actio quod iussu*, the *actio exercitoria* or the *actio institoria* where possible.[17] Where it was not possible to meet the requirements of any of those actions, the actions based on the *peculium* provided an alternative. First we need to consider how the content of the *peculium* was determined.

(a) The *Peculium*

The scope of a *peculium* was potentially very broad:[18]

> In a *peculium* there can be any kind of property, both moveables and land. It can also contain underslaves and the underslaves' *peculium*. Furthermore, it can contain debts.[19]

Thus, as we can see, a slave's *peculium* could include other slaves, with *peculia* of their own. It could also contain debts, including debts 'owed' by master to slave.[20] Even though such a debt was not legally possible,[21] it was treated as being possible for these purposes. In the same way, anything owed to the master could be considered as reducing the value of the *peculium*.[22]

All of the property in the *peculium* continued to belong to the master, and it could be difficult to tell whether a particular item was included in the *peculium*. The basic principle was that this question was determined by the intentions of the master, who could add or remove items at will.[23] It therefore did not include anything that the master was not aware of the dependant having.[24] The awareness of the master could be quite general, however:

---

[14] See pp. 106–7.
[15] See pp. 120–1.
[16] As we have seen at pp. 106–7, the slave had no contractual capacity at all. The situation was slightly different for a *filiusfamilias*. While a *filiusfamilias* could make a valid contract, without the ability on his part to own property there was no real way of enforcing it against him as long as he remained *alieni iuris*.
[17] G.4.74.
[18] For discussion of the issues arising in the determination of what was in a particular *peculium*, see D Johnston, 'Peculiar Questions' in P McKechnie ed, *Thinking Like a Lawyer: Essays on Legal History and General History for John Crook on His Eightieth Birthday* (Brill 2002); J-J Aubert, '*Dumtaxat de peculio*: What's in a Peculium, or Establishing the Extent of the Principal's Liability' in du Plessis, *New Frontiers*.
[19] D.15.1.7.4 (Ulpian).
[20] G.4.73; D.15.1.7.6.
[21] Except as a 'natural obligation'. See p. 322.
[22] D.15.1.5.4.
[23] D.15.1.4pr.
[24] For example, goods that a slave had stolen from the master would not form part of the slave's *peculium*: D.15.1.4.2.

The *peculium* cannot exist without the master's knowledge and agreement. He, however, may be unclear about its content and components, both in terms of nature (or quality) and quantity.[25]

Transfer of an item to the *peculium* required delivery of that item to the dependant.[26] The master could, however, remove anything from the *peculium* by mere intention.[27] If, though, the master removed anything from the *peculium* with the intention of defrauding creditors, that thing would be deemed still to form part of the *peculium*.[28]

(b) Actio de Peculio

The *actio de peculio* was an action used to impose liability on the master, for the actings of the dependant, up to the value of the *peculium*.[29] For these purposes, debts owed to the master were deducted from the value of the *peculium*.[30] As we have seen, the value of the *peculium* was deemed to include anything removed by the master with the intention of defrauding creditors.

A party who had made a contract with a dependant could pursue the master using the *actio de peculio*, and the result would be that the master would be held liable under that contract to the extent of the *peculium*. This was the case even if the master was unaware of the use to which the *peculium* was being put.[31] It was enough that the dependant had been allowed to have a *peculium*.

There was no time limit for the bringing of the *actio de peculio* as long as the dependant remained in the power of the master. However, if that power ended – whether through death, emancipation, manumission or alienation – any *actio de peculio* had to be brought within one year of that ending.[32]

(c) Actio de In Rem Verso

The next action to consider is the *actio de in rem verso*, the 'action for what has been turned to the master's account'. This could be combined with the *actio de peculio*: Gaius, for example, refers to a single *actio de peculio et de in rem verso*.[33] However, it does appear that they could be brought separately, and there were

---

[25] J-J Aubert, '*Dumtaxat de peculio*: What's in a Peculium, or Establishing the Extent of the Principal's Liability' in du Plessis, *New Frontiers* 195–6.
[26] D.15.1.8. On the requirements of delivery, see pp. 210–14.
[27] D.15.1.4.1.
[28] D.15.1.21pr; D.15.1.8.
[29] Calling this an action is slightly misleading, although it is described as such in the Roman texts themselves. Rather than being a freestanding action, it was an adaptation of existing contractual actions by the addition of a clause indicating that the transaction had been entered into by the slave or *filiusfamilias* of the defender rather than by the defender personally, and limiting the defender's liability to the extent of the *peculium*. See D Johnston, 'Suing the Paterfamilias: Theory and Practice' in Cairns and du Plessis, *Beyond Dogmatics* 174–5.
[30] D.15.1.5.4.
[31] G.4.72a; J.4.7.4.
[32] D.15.2.1pr–1.
[33] G.4.72a, 74a.

situations in which the *actio de in rem verso* could be brought even though the *actio de peculio* was unavailable.[34]

The *actio de in rem verso* was intended to deal with the situation where the holder of the *peculium* did something that benefited the master,[35] such as paying creditors of the master, repairing buildings or buying food.[36] As long as the expenditure was consistent with the habits of the master, the effect of the *actio de in rem verso* was that expenditure from the *peculium*, to the benefit of the master, could be treated as if it was still part of the *peculium*.[37]

Given that medieval and modern law has no place for the concept of *peculium*, it might have been expected that the *actio de in rem verso* would not have been received as part of the *ius commune*. However, in what has been called 'one of the more extravagant episodes within the history of the European ius commune',[38] the medieval jurists used the Roman texts on the *actio de in rem verso* as part of the basis of the law of unjustified enrichment.[39] This allowed the *ius commune* to deal with such situations where a benefit provided to one person ended up benefiting someone else.[40] By this means, Scots law received the *actio de in rem verso*, not at all as the Romans understood it, but as a basis on which (Stair says) 'whatsoever turneth to the behoof of any makes him thereby liable, though without any engagement of his own'.[41] This development is an excellent example of the tendency of the medieval jurists to use the Roman texts to build something that the Romans would not have recognised as their own.[42]

(d) Actio Tributoria

The final action we need to consider is the *actio tributoria*. Where the action against the master was based on the *peculium*, the *actio de peculio* was usually preferred over the *actio tributoria*. There were two reasons for this. First, the

---

[34] D.15.3.1.1. For example, the master or *paterfamilias* might have withdrawn the *peculium*, or the slave or *filiusfamilias* might have died and a creditor of the *peculium* then have failed to bring the *actio de peculio* within the required year. The *actio de peculio* would not be available in those circumstances, but the *actio de in rem verso* could still be brought.
[35] G.4.72a.
[36] J.4.7.4a.
[37] D.15.3.3.3–4 (Ulpian). Thus, for example, needless expenditure that had 'more to do with luxury than utility' would not be caught by the *actio de in rem verso*, unless the master or *paterfamilias* would have made that expenditure.
[38] Zimmermann, *Obligations* 878–9. On these developments, see also *e.g* B Nicholas, 'The Louisiana Law of Unjustified Enrichment through the Act of the Person Enriched' (1991–2) 6 Tulane European and Civil Law Forum 3; C A Verderame, 'Unjust Enrichment Remedy: *Actio de in rem verso*' (1975) 21 Loy L Rev 219.
[39] On unjustified enrichment, see pp. 429–34. In simple terms, the law of unjustified enrichment is concerned with situations in which one person has been enriched at another's expense, without proper justification, and compels the enriched person to give up that enrichment. An example would be where one person pays another a sum of money, in the mistaken belief that it is owed.
[40] As an example, suppose that a tenant farmer orders a quantity of fertiliser, which he uses on the land. Before he has paid, however, he becomes insolvent and his lease is terminated for non-payment of rent. The landlord now has the benefit of the fertiliser, but cannot be successfully sued under the contract of sale, not being a party to it. The medieval jurists might have allowed the *actio de in rem verso* to be used to compel the landlord to pay for the benefit he has received, even though this is well beyond the original scope of the action.
[41] Stair, *Institutions* 1.8.7.
[42] See pp. 75 and 76.

actio de peculio was available even if the master was unaware of the use to which the *peculium* was being put, whereas the *actio tributoria* required that knowledge.[43] Second, the *actio de peculio* was available in respect of the whole *peculium*, while the *actio tributoria* was only available in respect of that part of the *peculium* that had been used in business.[44] The *actio tributoria* did have one great advantage, however. Where the *actio tributoria* was brought, the master was not entitled to deduct from the *peculium* any debts owed to him.[45]

As a result, we can think of the *actio tributoria* being used as, in effect, an insolvency procedure. It would typically only be resorted to where the *peculium* was so burdened by debts to the master that third parties would be entirely or mostly excluded if the *actio de peculio* were used. The effect of the *actio tributoria* was to compel the master to divide up the *peculium*[46] proportionately among the creditors of the *peculium* (including the master himself).[47]

C. Delictual Liability

A slave-owner or *paterfamilias* might also be made liable for the wrongdoing of a dependant. In addition, there were limited circumstances in which a person might be held liable for losses caused by another person.

(1) Noxal Surrender

Where a dependant committed a delict, the master had a choice. He could either pay off the victim of this wrongdoing, or he could surrender the offending dependant to the victim.[48] This is known as noxal surrender. The offender would then pass into the victim's power, and could be made to work off the damage.[49]

A curiosity about noxal liability and noxal surrender is that it attached to the dependant, not to the master, even though it was the master who was liable either to compensate or to make noxal surrender.[50] Suppose, for example, that my slave stole from you. I then sold the slave to a third party. You would have to bring the noxal action against the new owner, not against me.[51] If the slave was subsequently emancipated, the master's noxal liability would be extinguished, and the slave would be personally liable for the wrongdoing.

In classical Roman law, noxal liability could attach either to a slave or to a *filiusfamilias*. By Justinian's time, however, it was limited to slaves. A *paterfamilias* could no longer noxally surrender his children.[52]

---

[43] D.14.1.6pr.
[44] G.4.74a; J.4.7.5a.
[45] D.14.4.1.2.
[46] Or, more strictly, the part of the *peculium* that had been used for business.
[47] G.4.72.
[48] G.4.75–6.
[49] Once the wrongdoer had brought in enough money to make good the loss, however, he or she could be emancipated by order of the praetor: J.4.8.3.
[50] G.4.77; J.4.8.5; D.9.4.7pr.
[51] The new owner might, however, have a remedy against me. See pp. 359–64.
[52] J.4.8.7.

Not having slaves, and no longer thinking noxal surrender of our children appropriate, this concept has of course no place in modern law. It is possible, however, that noxal surrender may make an unexpected return. It has been suggested that, if and when artificial intelligence develops to the point that autonomous devices can be held morally responsible for their actions, noxal surrender of a robot may be an appropriate response to its wrongdoing.[53]

(2) Quasi-Delictual Liability

Generally speaking, nobody was liable in Roman law for the delicts of any other person, except for the case of noxal liability. Unlike in modern law, there was no general principle of vicarious liability.[54] However, special provision was made for a limited number of cases, where a person was made liable as being in control of particular types of place in or from which loss or damage occurred. These special cases were classed as 'quasi-delictual', and are considered in Chapter 26.

Chapter Summary

Roman law had no general principle by which a person could be held liable for another person's acts. Unlike the position in modern law, a person was normally only liable for his or her own acts. However, there were certain special cases where this was not the case. A slave-owner or *paterfamilias* could be held liable under transactions entered into by a slave or *filiusfamilias* which the owner or *paterfamilias* had authorised (either specifically or generally). In the absence of such authorisation, the owner or *paterfamilias* could be held liable under transactions entered into by the slave or *filiusfamilias* up to the value of any *peculium* held by the latter. In addition, the slave-owner or *paterfamilias* could be 'noxally' liable for wrongs committed by the slave or *filiusfamilias*, and was faced with the choice of either paying appropriate damages for the wrongdoing or surrendering the slave or (until post-classical law) the *filiusfamilias* to the victim.

---

[53] Y Hu, 'Robot Criminals' (2019) 52 U Mich JL Reform 487, 531. The reference is not directly to Roman law, but to the medieval concept of deodand, by which an inanimate object that had caused harm might be required to be noxally surrendered. However, in the case of a thinking machine, the original, Roman concept seems somewhat more apt.

[54] This is the basis on which, in modern law, a person might be held liable for the wrongdoing of another. The main example is the liability of an employer for the wrongdoing of an employee.

Further Reading

G.4.69–81

J.4.7–8

D.9.4; 14.3–5; 15

C.3.41

J-J Aubert, '*Dumtaxat de peculio*: What's in a Peculium, or Establishing the Extent of the Principal's Liability' in P J du Plessis ed, *New Frontiers: Law and Society in the Roman World* (Edinburgh University Press 2013)

R van den Bergh, '"He's the One Who Minds the Boss's Business . . ."' (2015) 21 Fundamina 359

B W Frier and T A J McGinn, *A Casebook on Roman Family Law* (Oxford University Press 2004) 240–96

W M Gordon, 'Agency and Roman Law' in *Roman Law, Scots Law and Legal History: Selected Essays* (Edinburgh University Press 2007)

D Johnston, 'Peculiar Questions' in P McKechnie ed, *Thinking like a Lawyer: Essays on Legal History and General History for John Crook on His Eightieth Birthday* (Brill 2002)

D Johnston, 'Suing the Paterfamilias: Theory and Practice' in J W Cairns and P J du Plessis eds, *Beyond Dogmatics: Law and Society in the Roman World* (Edinburgh University Press 2007)

A Kirschenbaum, *Sons, Slaves and Freedmen in Roman Commerce* (Magnes Press, Hebrew University/Catholic University of America Press 1987)

G MacCormack, 'The Later History of the "Actio de in Rem Verso" (Proculus-Ulpian)' (1982) 48 **SDHI** 318

R Zimmermann, *The Law of Obligations: Roman Foundations of the Civilian Tradition* (Oxford University Press 1996) 51–3, 1118–20

PART THREE

The Law of Things: Property

In Part Two, we looked at the first part of Gaius' institutional scheme, the law of persons. It now remains to us to consider the law of things. We saw in Chapter 3[1] that, while the law of persons is concerned with matters of personal status, the law of things is concerned with economic assets. The law of things is by far the largest part of the institutional scheme, and can be further subdivided. In Part Three of this book, we look at the first part of the law of things, namely property law. Here we focus on physical assets and the different kinds of right that a person can have in relation to these assets. In Parts Four and Five, we will look at the remaining subdivisions of the law of things, namely the law of succession and the law of obligations respectively.

Part Three begins in Chapter 10 by examining some of the fundamental principles of property law, and in particular the distinct concepts of ownership and possession. In Chapters 11 and 12, we look at how ownership is acquired, and in Chapters 13 to 15 we consider the rights that a person can have in property other than ownership and possession.

It is in the law of things that Roman law undoubtedly has the greatest continuing influence on modern law. In the field of property law, for example, the distinction between ownership and possession can be seen as fundamental to legal systems that have received Roman legal ideas. The same is true of the distinction between real and personal rights that we shall meet in Chapter 10. Most of the ways of acquiring ownership that are considered in Chapters 11 and 12 are found in Scots law. Likewise, most of the specific rights in property that are considered in Chapters 13 to 15 have counterparts in Scots law. The rest of this book makes considerable reference to modern law, and there is considerable discussion of actual or possible application of Roman ideas to current legal issues. In addition to modern Scots law, there is also reference to other legal systems, such as that of South Africa, where the law has been similarly affected by Roman law. Those whose interest is only in the law as applied by the Romans, rather than its application in modern law, are of course free to skip these discussions.

---

[1] See p. 60.

CHAPTER TEN

Ownership and Possession

A. Introduction

In this chapter, we begin looking at the law of property, and more specifically at the concepts of ownership and possession. Property law is the area of modern Scots law in which the influence of Roman law is perhaps the most obvious, and the same is true in many other legal systems. This influence, though, mostly comes through in the general principles involved rather than in specific rules. Much of an account of Roman property law has to concern itself with the procedural rules for enforcing property rights, and these have had less influence on later law. For this reason, in this chapter we will look first at some of the general principles of property law, specifically the concepts of real and personal rights, ownership and possession, noting where appropriate the Roman influence on modern law. We will then look at the procedural mechanisms by which an owner or possessor could protect his or her position, an area that has had less direct influence on modern law. Finally, we will consider briefly certain rights that fulfilled a similar function to ownership, but which do not appear in modern Scots law.

In Chapters 11 and 12, we will continue looking at ownership, and in particular how ownership is acquired. Property could be classified in various ways, which was significant in the transfer of ownership. These classifications of property will, therefore, be considered in Chapter 11.

B. Real Rights and Personal Rights

(1) The Procedural Background: Real Actions and Personal Actions

The Roman jurists often said that, in such-and-such circumstances, one person 'had an action' against another, in other words that, in the circumstances of the case, the law gave the former a legal remedy against the latter. To put it another way, to say that a person has an action is to say that that person has a right that will be recognised by the court as enforceable. In terms of historical development, though, this puts things the wrong way round. As we saw in Chapter 3,[1] legal development begins with the procedures of the law and the remedies that they provide, with the rights underlying those procedures and remedies only being articulated later. We tend in modern law to talk about rights. In particular, we recognise a distinction between real rights and personal rights. These, though, developed from a procedural distinction. Accordingly, before talking about the rights, we need first to consider that procedural distinction.

We saw in Chapter 2[2] that, in classical law and earlier, litigation proceeded on the basis of more or less set forms of action, by which the judge was directed to try the issue between the parties. The law laid down a number of these, into which the claim had to be fitted. One way of classifying these was into real actions and personal actions. An example of a real action (from the Latin *res*, meaning a thing),[3] under the formulary system, is the following:

> If it appears that the property this action concerns belongs to Aulus Agerius by Quiritary law, and that property is not restored, then let the judge condemn Numerius Negidius to Aulus Agerius for whatever that property is worth. If it does not so appear, let him be absolved.

This is the form of action known as the *rei vindicatio*, the claim for recovery of an item of property by a person claiming to own it. Aulus Agerius is the stock name for the party making the claim (in modern terms, the pursuer), Numerius Negidius for the party against whom the claim is made (the defender). In a real case, the names of the actual parties would be substituted. The words 'by Quiritary law' reflect the fact that the *rei vindicatio* was only available to those with *commercium*,[4] which mostly meant Roman citizens.[5] It will be noticed here that what is alleged by Aulus Agerius is that the property belongs to him. In other words, he is alleging a relationship between himself and the property. Numerius Negidius is only involved because he is the person who happens to have the property. The point then is that the *rei vindicatio*, and other real actions, could be successfully brought against anyone denying a person's right in the property.

By contrast, personal actions asserted a relationship with some specific person. For example:

> If it appears that Numerius Negidius ought to pay Aulus Agerius 100, then let the judge condemn Numerius Negidius to Aulus Agerius for 100. Otherwise, let him be absolved.

Here a direct relationship is asserted between Aulus Agerius and Numerius Negidius. It is claimed that Numerius Negidius, personally, is subject to a specific

---

[1] See pp. 59–60.
[2] See pp. 32–42.
[3] As we saw at p. 60, property law is part of a wider 'law of things', including also the law of succession and the law of obligations. The word *res* is therefore a very broad term.
[4] See p. 96. The term 'Quiritary' comes from the Latin *Quirites*, which denotes the Roman people.
[5] A modified form was available for non-citizens.

obligation to pay the stated sum. A personal action arises from the law of obligations, in which it is claimed that the party against whom the action is raised, and that party specifically, 'ought to give or do something'.[6] A personal action is therefore more restricted in its scope. It is only available against someone who, it is claimed, owes some specific obligation to the claimant.

(2) Real Rights and Personal Rights

From this distinction arises a distinction between two kinds of right: real rights and personal rights. A claimant who has a personal action is said to have a personal right, which may be defined as 'a legal tie, by which we are bound to the necessity of making some performance'.[7] A personal right is a right to enforce a duty owed by some other person, and is enforceable only against that other person. Thus, for example, a right arising from a contract can only be enforced against the other party to that contract. The following gives an example of how this idea works:

> Appius owns a house. He enters into a contract to sell it to Marcus. As we shall see in Chapter 11,[8] certain further acts are necessary before Marcus actually becomes owner of the house. Until those acts are carried out, Appius remains owner, even though Marcus is entitled under the contract of sale to become owner. Suppose that, before ownership is transferred to Marcus, Appius gets a better offer from Cornelia, and transfers the house to her instead. Where does this leave Marcus? His contractual right to become owner is only a personal right, enforceable against Appius but not against Cornelia. Accordingly, Marcus has no claim to the house itself, and no remedy against Cornelia. Marcus is limited to a claim against Appius for a breach of their contract.

This principle was applied in *Burnett's Trustee v Grainger*,[9] in which the court made express reference to it as being derived from Roman law. In that case, the Graingers agreed to buy a house from Burnett. They paid the price and took possession. However, they (or rather their solicitors) failed to register the transfer of ownership in the appropriate register, which in Scots law is an essential step in the transfer of land. They therefore had a personal right against Burnett, but not yet any real right in the property. Burnett then became insolvent, and (in accordance with the relevant procedure) a trustee was appointed to realise the value of her assets and use that value to make payment towards her debts. The relevant legislation allowed the trustee to take ownership of property belonging to Burnett, so the trustee registered as owner of the house. The House of Lords held that, as the Graingers had not yet registered, they were not owners. Their right being only personal, it could not be enforced against the trustee.

---

[6] J.4.6.1.
[7] J.3.13pr.
[8] See pp. 199–214.
[9] 2004 SC (HL) 19.

Most rights that the law recognises are personal rights, enforceable against some specific person or persons. Thus, if I enter into a contract with you, I can enforce that contract against you but not against some other person. If you injure me or my property by your wrongful acts, my remedy is against you personally rather than against someone else. This makes sense, as you are the one who injured me. In any case, though, this limitation arises from the nature of the procedure used, as the procedural form asserts a relationship between us personally. Likewise, if I claim that you have breached our contract by giving to someone else some item of property that you were supposed to give to me, the procedural form that is used asserts a relationship with you rather than with the property. From this characteristic of the procedure used there arises what we now know as personal rights, and this characteristic persists even after the formulary system of procedure has been abandoned.[10]

As we saw above, though, certain rights were protected by actions known as real actions. Instead of asserting a relationship with another person, a real action asserts a relationship with a particular item of property. These rights are known as real rights. This category includes most importantly ownership, but also certain other rights such as praedial servitude[11] and usufruct.[12] If I claim to be owner of an item of property, I am asserting a relationship between myself and the property itself, rather than simply between me and the person who took it from me.

It follows from this that an owner of property can normally recover it from anyone into whose hands it comes, regardless of how that person acquired it. Suppose that Flavia is owner of a necklace. She lends it to Aurelia, who then dies with the necklace in her custody. Quintus, Aurelia's heir, finds the necklace in Aurelia's house and assumes that it was hers. Quintus takes possession of the necklace and sells it to Tullia. As owner, Flavia can recover the necklace from Tullia without having to refund her the price that she paid, regardless of Tullia's genuine and reasonable belief that Quintus was entitled to sell the necklace to her. Tullia is left with only a contractual claim against Quintus.[13]

Normally the holder of a real right cannot lose that right through the actions of a third party without his or her consent. To lose the right in those circumstances would be inconsistent with the idea that a real right is enforceable against anybody. Those exceptions to this principle that exist tend to involve the holder of the real right having given prior authority to the third party,[14] or else the authority of the court or some other public authority.[15]

---

[10] On procedure, see Chapter 2.
[11] See Chapter 13.
[12] See Chapter 14.
[13] On the nature of this claim, see pp. 359–60.
[14] See *e.g.* J.2.8.1 on sale by a creditor holding goods on pledge, on non-payment by the debtor; J.2.1.43 on transfer of ownership by a slave given management powers.
[15] See *e.g.* G.2.64 on the appointment of a curator to manage the affairs of an insane person, with power to alienate property.

This distinction between real and personal rights has been highly influential, and is one of the most distinctive characteristics of systems of property law that are based on Roman law.[16] This is certainly true in Scots law, in which the examples given in this section would have the same outcome.[17]

C. Ownership

(1) The Nature of Ownership

Ownership, or *dominium*, is generally seen as being difficult to define.[18] The Roman jurists themselves said little about it – not surprisingly, given their characteristic focus on practical working out of legal consequences rather than legal theory – although attempts do exist in the later civil law tradition. One such attempt defines ownership as the *ius utendi, fruendi, abutendi*: the right of using, enjoying and abusing (including alienating the property).[19] This definition does suffer from the weakness that the owner may not presently have these rights. For example, a tenant occupying the property will have the present right to use the property. It is true that, in that case, the owner will at least benefit from collecting rent payments, but if the property is subject to a usufruct[20] then the owner does not even have that. However, by and large, while the owner's rights may be postponed to another person's rights, this is only postponement. If the other person's right falls away, the owner's right will be left. Ownership is the ultimate, residual right, from which all other real rights are derived. In principle, there can only be one right of ownership in a given thing,[21] and no right to use the property will be valid unless it is derived from the owner. Thus, no lease or usufruct or other right of use will be valid if it is granted by someone other than the owner.[22] Only the owner has the right to damage or destroy the property without having to acquire that right from someone else.[23] In the same way, risk of damage to the property ultimately lies

---

[16] K Reid, 'Property Law: Sources and Doctrine' in *History of Private Law in Scotland, vol I* 192–3.

[17] Scots law does not, however, make any distinction between personal and real *actions*. In Scots law, for example, the same procedural form would be used for an action for delivery of the property, regardless of whether the claim was based on a real right or a personal right. See B Holligan, 'Ownership and Obligation: Restitution, Vindication and the Recovery of Moveables in Stair's Institutions' (2017) 21 Edin LR 169.

[18] For interesting discussion of the nature of ownership in Roman law, see P Birks, 'The Roman Concept of Dominium and the Idea of Absolute Ownership' 1985 AJ 1; H Scott, 'Absolute Ownership and Legal Pluralism in Roman Law: Two Arguments' 2011 AJ 23.

[19] R Zimmermann, D Visser and K Reid, 'Property Law: Some Themes and Variations' in Zimmermann, Visser and Reid, *Mixed Legal Systems* 659–60.

[20] See Chapter 14. In simple terms, a usufruct is a right to use and enjoy property belonging to someone else, without payment of rent.

[21] In the next chapter (at pp. 201–2) we will see a partial exception to this, in the form of bonitary ownership. See also the functional equivalents to ownership, outlined below at pp. 191–200. Modern Scots law, however, is entirely consistent with the statement in the text.

[22] The lease will be valid as a *contract*, and so the grantor will be liable for breach of contract if the owner of the land appears and excludes the tenant. However, it will give no right to occupy the land at all.

[23] Of course, the owner will normally have acquired that right from a previous owner, but that is not invariably so. In Chapter 12 we shall see that there are certain ways of acquiring ownership, collectively known as 'original acquisition', in which ownership is acquired otherwise than by transfer from a previous owner.

with the owner. It is true that that risk may be transferred to another by contract,[24] but then it will manifest itself as an obligation to compensate the owner.[25]

None of this is to say, however, that the owner's rights are unlimited, even where nobody else has any right to use the property. As we shall see below, the owner's rights are restricted in various ways where the owner's actions may cause loss or injury to neighbouring properties.

(2) Rights Arising from Ownership

Various rights arose from ownership. In principle, unless someone else could show an immediate right to possession, enforceable against the owner, the owner was entitled to possession of the property. This included the right to use the legal process to recover the property from anyone who was in possession of it without right. An owner was also entitled to things attached to the property and produce derived from the property.

(a) Right to Non-Interference and Recovery

Much as in modern law,[26] an owner who was not in possession had the right to recover the property from whoever was in possession. This was the case even if the current possessor acquired the property in good faith.[27] The right to recover the property was, however, subject to limitations. It is fairly obvious that, if I give you a lease of my land, I am bound by my contract to allow the occupation of that land for as long as the lease lasts, and that I cannot recover the land from you during that time. Equally, if you have a usufruct over the land,[28] I cannot recover the land from you as long as the usufruct lasts. The recovery of property by the owner is considered in more detail below.

Various other remedies were available to an owner to protect his or her interest in the property. Some of these are discussed below, as restrictions on the neighbour's rights.

(b) Fruits, Accessories and Pertinents

Ownership of land included anything attached to it, such as buildings and plants.[29] Unlike the situation in modern law, there was no exception for individual flats in tenement buildings.[30] The whole building belonged to the owner

---

[24] For example, a purchaser of property normally bears the risk of damage from the moment the contract of sale is concluded, even though the purchaser will not usually have become owner yet. See pp. 356–7.
[25] Alternatively, in the case of a sale contract, the passing of the risk to the purchaser will mean the purchaser having to pay the price despite the damage to or destruction of the goods.
[26] Although the actual procedure for recovering the property differs.
[27] As a general principle, this is the case in modern Scots law as well, although modern law has introduced some limited protections for good faith acquirers. See *e.g.* Sale of Goods Act 1979, ss. 24 and 25; Land Registration etc (Scotland) Act 2012, s. 86. Where no relevant exception applies, the Roman rule will govern the situation. Some legal systems have a more general protection for acquirers in good faith. See *e.g.* the French *Code civil*, art. 2276.
[28] See Chapter 14.
[29] J.2.1.29–32.
[30] For the modern Scots law on flat ownership, see the Tenements (Scotland) Act 2004. This is an issue that has caused difficulties in other legal systems.

of the ground underneath, and so the individual flats could not be separately owned. They could certainly be leased, but in Roman law a lease of land was no more than a contract, and could not give the tenant a real right in the property.[31]

An owner also had the right to the 'fruits' of the property, meaning the produce of the property. Of course, the right to take the fruits could be given by the owner to another: an obvious example is a tenant of a farm, who will clearly need to have the right to harvest his crop; another example is the holder of a usufruct, who had the right to the fruits of the property.[32] The category of natural fruits included the produce of plants grown on land – apples grown in an orchard, for example – and also plants to be removed from the land on being harvested, such as cereal crops.[33] In the case of animals, their offspring are fruits,[34] as are milk, hair and wool produced by them.[35] There is also a category known as civil fruits, which essentially means rent paid by tenants of land. If I own land, and I lease it to you, the rent you pay me can be seen as a fruit of the land. In this case, though, my right to the rent arises, not from my ownership of the land, but from our contract.

A purchaser of land might be entitled to additional things as pertinents to the land, meaning simply things the right to which is carried along with the land. One example of this is the right to enforce a praedial servitude.[36] For instance, if I have a right of way over your land to get to mine, and I sell my land, the benefit of the right of way will pass to the purchaser.

(3) Restrictions on the Rights of an Owner
(a) Interference with Neighbours
In modern law, a general principle has developed that an owner or occupier of land is not to use the land in such a way as to cause an intolerable disturbance to a neighbour.[37] In a very similar way, the *ius commune* lawyers of the Middle Ages and later[38] developed a concept called *aemulatio vicini* (often called 'abuse of rights').[39] The idea of this was that a person was not to be permitted to use his or her property with the intention of harming a neighbour. This principle was received into Scots law, but its scope in modern law is limited.[40]

---

[31] This was also the position in Scots law until the Leases Act 1449.
[32] See also, below, the right to fruits given to a person possessing the property in good faith.
[33] Trees, by contrast, are not considered to be fruits. They do, though, belong to the owner of the land, as they are attached to the land on taking root.
[34] With the result that, if my bull impregnates your cow, a calf that results will belong to you.
[35] J.2.1.37.
[36] See Chapter 13.
[37] See *e.g. Watt v Jamieson* 1954 SC 56.
[38] See Chapter 4.
[39] For an overview of the basis of the doctrine and its development, see J E Scholtens, 'Abuse of Rights' (1958) 75 SALJ 39.
[40] See E Reid, 'Abuse of Rights in Scots Law' (1998) 2 Edin LR 129; E Reid, 'Strange Gods in the Twenty-First Century: The Doctrine of *Aemulatio Vicini*' in E Reid and D L Carey Miller eds, *A Mixed Legal System in Transition: T B Smith and the Progress of Scots Law* (Edinburgh University Press 2005). For an example of the application of the doctrine in modern law, see *More v Boyle* 1967 SLT (Sh Ct) 38.

However, although *aemulatio vicini* was developed from Roman foundations, it was not of itself Roman.[41] Instead, it is an example of the ingenuity of the *ius commune* lawyers in adapting the Roman texts to meet their needs. The Roman law itself had no such general principle. In certain circumstances, for example where a person harmed a neighbour's property through fault, one of the normal delictual remedies might be available.[42] Beyond this, though, the law regulating neighbourhood relations developed in a piecemeal fashion, often through the intervention of the praetor. The result was a range of specific remedies dealing with specific situations, rather than a general principle of not harming or disturbing neighbours.

One such remedy was the *cautio damni infecti*. This was concerned with *damnum infectum*, or 'anticipated injury', which is 'injury that has not yet happened, but which we fear may happen in the future'.[43] The aim of this was to provide protection to a person concerned about damage resulting from the dangerous state of neighbouring property. The individual who feared that damage would occur could apply to the praetor, who would order the neighbour to give a *cautio*,[44] or undertaking, against damage to the property. The advantage of this was that it was available even where there would otherwise have been no remedy for the damage to the property: in the event of damage, liability would be contractual, based on breach of the undertaking. By the same token, though, there was no liability unless the undertaking had been sought and obtained before the damage happened.[45] If the neighbour refused to give the undertaking, the praetor would issue a decree authorising the complainer to enter upon the neighbouring land to take preventive measures.[46]

If the undertaking was given, the neighbour only counted as being in breach if damage happened because of a weakness or defect in the neighbour's building. For example, if tiles were blown off by the wind and caused damage after an undertaking had been given, the owner of the building would not be liable if this had happened because of an exceptionally strong wind.[47]

Where it was feared that harm would result from construction work being carried out on neighbouring property, protection could be sought by means of the *operis novi nuntiatio*, which can be translated as 'denunciation of new work'. This procedure was initiated by service of a notice on the neighbour carrying out the work, and the praetor could then order the neighbour to give an undertaking[48] that harm would not result. If work continued after the notice was served, the praetor could order the demolition of the work carried out.[49] The wording of the undertaking was such that there would be no liability if the work was lawful.

---

[41] D Johnston, 'Owners and Neighbours: From Rome to Scotland' in Evans-Jones, *Civil Law Tradition* 182–4.
[42] See Chapters 22 and 23.
[43] D.39.2.2. The roots of the protection against *damnum infectum* are very old, and Gaius tells us (G.4.31) that in his day it was, exceptionally, still possible to use the *legis actiones* procedure for this (see pp. 32–7). The procedure described here was the normal one in the classical period.
[44] This was in the form of the contract known as *stipulatio*. See Chapter 18.
[45] D.39.2.6.
[46] D.39.2.4.1. Ultimately, the complainer might be able to acquire ownership of the property by *usucapio*, or possession for a period of time: D.39.2.5pr. On *usucapio*, see pp. 239–43.
[47] D.39.2.43pr.
[48] This was in the form of the contract known as *stipulatio*. See Chapter 18.
[49] By means of the *interdictum ex operis novi nuntuatione*: D.39.1.20pr.

The *operis novi nuntiatio* was only available where the work complained of was not completed. Where the work had been completed, the interdict *quod vi aut clam* ('because of force or stealth') might be available. The interdict instructed anything done by force or stealth, if damaging to the land, to be undone. These terms were interpreted broadly: to do something by force in this context meant simply to do it contrary to a prohibition;[50] to do something by stealth was to do it without giving notice to a person one suspected might object.[51] The requirement for force or stealth meant that, if the work was done openly, it would be necessary to object before the work was complete.

The *actio aquae pluviae arcendae* ('action for warding off rainwater')[52] was a very old remedy, existing already at the time of the Twelve Tables.[53] Where the management of land increased the risk of rainwater running onto neighbouring land and causing damage, the neighbour could sue using this action for the restoration of the previous position and for compensation for any damage caused. An example given by the jurist Neratius is of a person making a construction to keep out water normally overflowing from a neighbouring marsh. If rainwater then increased the size of the marsh and damaged a neighbour's field, the person making the construction that caused this would be liable under this action to remove it.[54] Liability could also arise from a failure to maintain an existing construction, such as a failure to keep a drainage ditch clear.[55] Not all constructions gave rise to liability, though. There was a partial exception for work carried out for agricultural purposes, such as ploughing and the digging of drainage ditches. There is some doubt about the precise scope of this exception, though, as various views are reported in the *Digest*.[56]

We shall see in Chapter 13 a category of rights called praedial servitudes, which are rights held by the owner of one area of land over neighbouring land. An example is the right to cross neighbouring land to get to your own land. Where a neighbour was doing something that could only be done if the neighbour had a servitude, and the neighbour did not have a servitude, protection could be obtained using the *actio negatoria*, the action for denying that a servitude exists.[57] For example, it appears that the owner of a house had a right to such light as was necessary for 'reasonable daily use',[58] although a servitude could be acquired to allow a building to block out a neighbour's light. In the absence of such a servitude, the blocking of light could be restrained using the *actio negatoria*.

---

[50] D.50.17.73.2.
[51] D.43.24.4.
[52] For a detailed account of this, see Watson, *Property* chapter 7.
[53] See pp. 47–9.
[54] D.39.3.1.2 (Ulpian).
[55] D.39.3.2.1.
[56] D.39.3.1.3–7; D.39.3.24pr.
[57] D.8.5.8.5.
[58] D.8.2.10. For discussion of this right, see A Rodger, *Owners and Neighbours in Roman Law* (Clarendon Press 1972).

(b) Boundary Issues

From early times, the management of the boundaries between adjacent properties was subject to detailed regulation. For example, rules existed prohibiting building close to boundaries.[59] If your tree overhung my house, I was entitled to cut it down; if it overhung my field, I was entitled to cut it back up to a height of fifteen feet. This right appears to have existed already in the time of the Twelve Tables, but the praetor later provided an interdict against you using force to prevent me doing this if you did not take care of the matter.[60] The jurist Pomponius said, though, that I did not have the right to cut back encroaching roots,[61] perhaps because this would be more likely to damage the tree. If acorns – later interpreted to mean any fruits – fell from your tree onto my land, you were entitled to come onto my land to gather them.[62]

Where land was bounded by a river, there seems to have been doubt about the ownership of the river. Certain rivers were considered to be public, meaning at least that the public had use of them.[63] The position in the Justinianic law seems to have been that the river was owned to the midpoint by the owners on either side of the river. This, at any rate, is implied by the rules allocating ownership of dried-up river beds and of islands arising in a river on this basis.[64] On this view, the public would have only the right to use the river, ownership remaining private.[65] However, there are also texts suggesting that the public had not only the right of use, but also ownership, of public rivers.[66] In any case, where a river changed its course through gradual erosion and build-up of the banks, the boundary between the properties on either side changed with it.[67] The same was not true of sudden changes, caused for example by a flood. In circumstances of that kind, ownership of the affected land remained unchanged.[68]

Where there was a dispute over the boundaries between two areas of land, the matter could be resolved using the *actio finium regundorum* (the action for regulating boundaries). This action gave broad powers to the judge to resolve the dispute. Notably, the judge had the power to adjust the boundary where he thought it appropriate, with any party losing land being entitled to compensation from the party gaining land.[69]

(c) Restrictions Arising from Third Party Rights

In addition to restrictions arising from the nature of ownership itself, an owner's rights may also be restricted by rights held by third parties. For example, if I own

---

[59] See *e.g.* D.10.1.13.
[60] D.43.27.1.8–9.
[61] D.47.7.6.2.
[62] D.43.28.1.
[63] See p. 226.
[64] J.2.1.22–3.
[65] D.41.1.30.1.
[66] See *e.g.* D.10.1.5–6, applying the same rule also to public roads.
[67] J.2.1.20.
[68] J.2.1.21–4; D.10.1.8pr.
[69] J.4.17.6; D.10.1.2.1; D.10.1.3.

an area of land, and lease it to you, our contract obviously restricts my right to use the land as long as the lease lasts.[70] Again, there are various real rights that an individual may have in another person's property, such as a right of way over a neighbour's land.[71]

(4) Co-ownership

It was possible for two or more people to share ownership of property, whether because of joint purchase or some other reason. It may be supposed that it was particularly common where an owner died, given that a man's[72] children had equal rights to succeed on intestacy to their father's estate. This contrasts with modern Scots law where, until the Succession (Scotland) Act 1964, there was a preference for the eldest son.[73] This preference no longer applies in the modern law.

Common property is dependent on co-operation between the co-owners to make it work. While a co-owner was an owner, and as such was entitled to use the property, this right had to be balanced with the right of other co-owners to do the same. Thus, any co-owner had an absolute right of veto over any building work on the land, as long as the veto was exercised before the building was complete.[74] Equally, no one co-owner could create or discharge a real right affecting another co-owner's share.[75] This restriction arises from the principle discussed above that, generally, nobody can grant a real right in property except for the owner of that property. It follows from that principle that, as owner of only a share of the property rather than the whole property, a co-owner can only create or discharge real rights insofar as they affect his or her own share. In addition, the manner in which the property was managed might also give rise to an obligation to compensate another co-owner when the relationship of co-ownership came to an end.

Roman law gave co-owners an absolute entitlement to end the relationship of co-ownership.[76] For the situation where one of the co-owners wanted to do this, Roman law provided the *actio communi dividundo* ('action for dividing common property'). The starting point was physical division of the property.[77] Where this was not possible, for example with a slave or mule, the judge would award the property to one co-owner subject to an obligation to compensate the others. The judge had discretion in how to divide the property. He could divide it as seemed fair and reasonable, with compensation due by anyone getting more than his or her fair share.[78] Alternatively, if any of the co-owners could not afford this,

---

[70] Although, unlike in modern Scots law, a tenant's right under a Roman contract of lease cannot be made a real right. See pp. 367–8.
[71] See Chapter 13.
[72] For reasons that we shall see at p. 309n, a woman's children had (at least originally) no rights on intestacy in her estate.
[73] This practice of male primogeniture was common in other countries as well.
[74] D.10.3.28.
[75] D.8.1.2; D.8.3.34pr. The specific example in these texts is the creation and discharge of a praedial servitude.
[76] C.3.37.5 (AD 294). The same right exists in modern law. However, unlike the position in modern law, in Roman law it was not possible to exclude this right permanently by contract: D.10.3.14.2.
[77] J.4.17.5.
[78] J.4.6.20.

the property might be sold off to an outside bidder and the proceeds of the sale divided.[79] A similar procedure existed for dividing inheritances among co-heirs, the *actio familiae erciscundae*.[80] These actions have been influential on Scots law in this area. In *Brock v Hamilton*,[81] the Lord Ordinary said:

> It cannot, indeed, be disputed, in the face of clear authorities, that we have borrowed from the Roman law, and introduced into our common law actions of the same nature and import with those of the Roman law *familiae erciscundae* and *de communi dividundo*.

Thus, in *Scrimgeour v Scrimgeour*,[82] the pursuer sought the transfer to her of her former husband's share of the matrimonial home, in exchange for the discharge of a debt owed to her by him. The amount of this debt was roughly equivalent to the value of the defender's share in the house. Counsel for the pursuer argued that 'the Scots law on the matter is in fact not just derived from the Roman law but is taken in its entirety from the Roman law'. While not expressly adopting this statement, the Lord Ordinary gave the pursuer the remedy she had asked for. However, some subsequent cases have been more doubtful of whether the court does have any discretion over the form of the remedy given,[83] and so the current position is uncertain.

In its developed form, the *actio communi dividundo* and the *actio familiae erciscundae* could also be used to consider questions about the rights and duties of co-owners. For example, one co-owner might be found liable to the other for excessive consumption of fruits, or might be judged liable to contribute to necessary expenditure incurred by the other.[84] The accounting between the co-owners could also take into account gains taken by a co-owner or damage done to the property.[85]

D. Possession

(1) Nature of Possession

We have seen already that the distinction between real and personal rights has been very influential in the later civil law tradition. The same is also true of possession, and the distinction between it and ownership. A prominent characteristic of systems of property law that are based on Roman law is the strong distinction made between ownership and possession.

---

[79] C.3.37.3.1 (AD 224).
[80] D.10.2.
[81] (1852) 19 D 701, 702. For discussion of the reception of this remedy in Scots law, see G MacCormack, 'The *actio communi dividundo* in Roman and Scots Law' in Lewis and Ibbetson, *Roman Law Tradition*. For developments since *Scrimgeour*, see A Eccles, 'Division and Sale: Smash in Case of Emergency' 2014 SLT (News) 87.
[82] 1988 SLT 590.
[83] See *e.g. Berry v Berry (No 2)* 1989 SLT 292.
[84] J.3.27.3.
[85] D.10.2.17; D.10.3.3pr.

(a) Ownership and Possession
In general usage, the word 'possession' is one with a fairly imprecise meaning, very much dependent on context. On the one hand, if I refer to my 'possessions', it is likely that I mean by that the things that I own. On the other hand, a person might be referred to as being in possession of stolen goods. We have already seen above that an acquirer of stolen goods gets no right to them. Accordingly, clearly the person who is in possession of stolen goods is not owner of them. There is, though, no contradiction in saying that that person possesses the stolen goods, for possession in this context denotes simply physically having the goods. Roman law is closer to this second meaning of possession, though it is rather more precise even than this, as we shall see below.

Roman law thus made a very strong distinction between having a right to an item of property on the one hand and, on the other, simply having the item. Unlike the position in, for example, English law,[86] in Roman law nobody acquired ownership rights in a thing by simply having it. Equally, whether a person possessed an item of property was not determined by whether that person had any right to the thing. Ownership and possession are two separate things and, indeed, the jurist Ulpian went so far as to say that ownership 'has nothing in common with possession'.[87] This is not to say that possession was without legal consequences. On the contrary, a possessor was normally entitled at least to interim protection of that state of possession, and possession has a number of other important consequences. However, in the final analysis, an individual who could demonstrate ownership would succeed in recovering the property, unless the other party could show some other real right, derived from the owner's right.

Scots law has been particularly strongly influenced by the Roman law in this area. Scots law, too, makes a clear distinction between possession and ownership, along Roman lines.[88] As in Roman law, possession is 'a distinct lesser right than property',[89] with important legal consequences but not in itself implying any entitlement to the property.

(b) Elements of Possession
Possession is dependent on acquiring physical control of the property, but this is not the end of the story. Not everyone with physical control of property is in possession of it. It was also necessary to hold the property with the right state of mind. The jurist Paul said: 'we acquire possession by body and mind, not by mind alone or by body alone'.[90] From this, it is often said that there are two elements to possession, one physical (often called *corpus*, which means 'body') and one mental (*animus*, or 'mind'). It is doubtful whether the Romans themselves

---

[86] See *e.g. Costello v Chief Constable of Derbyshire Constabulary* [2001] EWCA Civ 381, [2001] 1 WLR 1437.
[87] D.41.2.12.1.
[88] C Anderson, *Possession of Corporeal Moveables* (Edinburgh Legal Education Trust 2015) paras 1-02–1-08; Reid, 'Property Law: Sources and Doctrine' in *History of Private Law in Scotland, vol I* 210–16.
[89] Stair, *Institutions* 2.1.8.
[90] D.41.2.3.1.

thought of it this way: in all of the surviving juristic writings, only Paul attempts to give a general account of possession with such a theoretical basis. Instead, the jurists tend to proceed on a case by case basis, considering on the specific set of facts whether a person does or does not possess. Nonetheless, the *corpus/animus* scheme has been influential and is generally followed in accounts of the Roman law of possession and in later systems influenced by it, including Scots law.

(2) Physical Element

The physical element of possession was based, as already noted, on control of the property. For this reason, it was said, two people could not separately possess the same thing. To hold otherwise would be 'contrary to nature', said the jurist Paul.[91] As you and I cannot both stand on the same spot at the same time, if you take control of the property then I necessarily lose control and, with it, possession.

This principle, though, became problematic when it was accepted that one person could possess through another's acts, as we shall see below. An example of this is a landlord retaining possession through a tenant. Normally, in such a case, the person with actual custody of the property was not considered to possess. In the example of a landlord and tenant, the tenant did not possess the property; instead, the landlord alone possessed. However, there were exceptions to this. For example, suppose that I give you a diamond ring as security for a loan of money that you give me.[92] I still possess here, as you hold partly on my behalf. However, Roman law also gave possessory protection to you in this situation. The solution was to say that you possessed for the purposes of possessory protection,[93] while I possessed for all other purposes.[94]

(a) Land

To possess land, it was necessary to have control of it. Thus, for example, there was no possession of land permanently covered by a river or the sea.[95] A particular problem that arises with possession of land, though, is knowing the extent of that possession. After all, I can only stand on one spot at a time. The rule was that possession of a part of an area of land counted as possession of the whole, up to the boundaries of the land. It was not necessary to go around the whole of the land.[96] The same approach is taken in Scots law.[97] For example, in *Bain v Carrick*,[98] it was held that a farmer possessed up to the fence surrounding his land. In the same way, he did not possess a disputed strip of ground that was outside the fence of his land.

---

[91] D.41.2.3.5.
[92] This is known as a pledge. See pp. 271–4.
[93] D.41.3.16; D.41.2.1.15.
[94] For criticism of this compromise, see Watson, *Roman Law & Comparative Law* 119.
[95] D.41.2.3.17. The Roman position on this must be read bearing in mind the special status of river beds and the sea bed as *res publica*, on which see pp. 195–7. Scots law differs in this regard. It would in any case be difficult to establish possession of land permanently covered with water. See *Safeway Stores plc v Tesco Stores Ltd* 2004 SC 29.
[96] D.41.2.3.1.
[97] Stair, *Institutions* 2.1.13.
[98] 1983 SLT 675.

(b) Moveables

As with land, the physical element of possession of moveable things was satisfied when control was gained.[99] This was most easily shown by having the thing on one's person or in some secure place. However, Roman law did not require such a high degree of control. Exactly how much control was needed would depend on the circumstances: money placed on a table at my instruction and in my presence would be readily seen as possessed by me if this happened in private, as there would be less chance of interference in that case.[100] If the money was placed on a table in a busy public place, it would not be so clear that I was attempting to possess it, unless it was placed right in front of me. Part of the point here also seems to be my awareness of the presence of the item: I will possess things in my house if they have been placed there at my instructions,[101] but not if I am unaware that they are there.[102]

(c) Possession through Another

In modern law, it is quite possible to acquire possession through someone else. If an agent acting on my behalf acquires goods for me, it is clear in modern law that I immediately acquire possession of the goods through the agent's acts. The situation was different in Roman law, to some extent because Roman law never developed a law of agency in the modern sense.[103] In modern law, as a general rule, the acts of my agent are considered in law to be my acts, and are treated as if I had carried out those acts personally. This is not so in Roman law. The closest equivalent in Roman law to an agency arrangement in the modern sense is the contract of mandate,[104] in which one person (the mandatary) agrees to act on behalf of another person (the mandator). Where something was purchased by a mandatary on behalf of the mandator, the mandator did not acquire possession until it was actually delivered to him or her.[105] This was the general position in classical law,[106] although by imperial pronouncement an exception was made for acquisition of possession through someone acting as an agent with general authority.[107] This exception was, however, interpreted narrowly. For example, because it was not possible for obligations to be imposed on the principal by the agent's acts, a pledge could not be constituted by delivery to the agent.[108]

Only in limited circumstances, then, was it possible to acquire possession through someone else's acts. The clearest cases arose from those in a person's

---

[99] For discussion, see C Anderson, *Possession of Corporeal Moveables* (Edinburgh Legal Education Trust 2015) paras 2-02–2-05.
[100] For the example, see D.46.3.79.
[101] D.41.2.18.2.
[102] D.41.2.30pr.
[103] See Chapter 9 for further discussion.
[104] See pp. 371–3.
[105] D.41.1.59.
[106] G.2.95. Compare, though, D.41.1.13 and D.41.3.41, both taken from the writings of the jurist Neratius.
[107] C.7.32.1 (AD 196).
[108] D.13.7.11.6.

potestas,[109] such as slaves. The owner of a slave could acquire possession through the acts of the slave.[110]

However, despite the difficulties of *acquiring* possession through another person's acts, it was possible to *maintain* possession through another. For example, where the possessor of property leased it out or lent it to someone, possession would be retained even while the property was in the hands of the tenant or borrower.[111] The point here seems to be that control is retained when someone else is holding on one's behalf. Consistency would suggest the same should apply to the acquisition of possession, as it does in modern law, but this final step was never taken.

(d) Possession of Incorporeals
So far, we have been talking about possession in terms of physical control of the property. It may be thought, therefore, that possession is restricted to corporeal things, and indeed the jurist Paul is quite specific that only 'those things that are corporeal can be possessed'.[112] The general view among scholars of Roman law is to the same effect, and the same view is common in modern legal systems.[113] All the same, the apparent exercise of certain rights was protected in much the same way as was possession of corporeal property. For example, we shall see in Chapter 13 that Roman law recognised a type of right, called a servitude, which allowed the owner of one area of land to make some limited, specified use of neighbouring land. A right of way over the neighbour's land is an example of this. In certain circumstances, a person using land as if authorised by a servitude could obtain protection from the praetor in much the same way as someone possessing the land itself.

In these situations, the party entitled to protection from the praetor is often said to have had 'quasi-possession',[114] a name reflecting both the similarities in the nature of the protection given and also the reluctance to recognise this as involving possession. These cases will be considered in more detail later.[115]

(3) Mental Element
(a) General Account
Not everyone who was in control of a given item of property possessed it. As well as the physical element of control, possession also had a mental element. It was

---

[109] See Chapters 5–7.
[110] J.2.9pr. The same rule applied to those possessed in good faith as slaves, whether or not they were in fact free. For discussion of the question of whether authorisation by the master was needed, see W M Gordon, 'Acquisition of Ownership by Traditio and Acquisition of Possession' in *Roman Law, Scots Law and Legal History: Selected Essays* (Edinburgh University Press 2007).
[111] J.4.15.4; G.4.153.
[112] D.41.2.3pr (Paul).
[113] For discussion, see T Rüfner, 'Possession of Incorporeals' and D Kleyn, 'The Protection of Quasi-Possession in South African Law' in E Descheemaeker ed, *The Consequences of Possession* (Edinburgh University Press 2014).
[114] Another term that is used is *possessio iuris*, meaning possession of a right.
[115] See Chapter 13 (praedial servitudes) and Chapter 14 (usufruct).

necessary to have the intention to possess the property. Thus, if I am on a friend's land 'by right of friendship', I do not intend to possess and do not possess.[116] Similarly, the insane and young children cannot take possession, as they are not capable of forming the necessary intention.[117]

Even then, though, not all of those with intentional control of the property were held to possess, even if they held on their own behalf. The point here is that not every kind of holder qualified for protection by means of the possessory remedies (considered below). From this point of view, the mental element of possession can be defined as the intention to hold on a basis justifying possessory protection.

Someone holding in the manner of an owner certainly had possessory protection. Furthermore, because possession was distinct from ownership, and depended on a factual relationship with the property rather than having any kind of right to the property, such a person possessed even if not actually owner. Indeed, even a thief would have possession as long as he or she had the property. The reason for this is that the thief is treating the property as if it is his or her own.

Those holding on a different basis normally did not possess, whether they held by arrangement with a possessor (such as a tenant or hirer of property) or otherwise (such as a finder of lost property who was keeping it safe until the owner appeared).

We have seen already that a pledge creditor (i.e. a creditor holding a debtor's property as security for a debt) had possession, and so was protected against dispossession, whether by the debtor or anyone else. The same was true of one purportedly exercising a right of *emphyteusis* (see below).

Another example of a possessor is the precarist. This was the grantee of a *precarium*, or licence to use property until permission is withdrawn.[118] It could be revoked at will, and the praetor allowed an interdict (the interdict *de precario*) for restoration of the property.[119] The precarist was considered to possess the property as long as the *precarium* lasted,[120] and so had possessory protection.[121]

Another possessor was the *sequester*,[122] one who held property on the basis of *sequestratio*.[123] This was a form of contract of deposit,[124] in which the parties to a dispute over an item of property deposited it with the *sequester*. The *sequester* was then to hand it over to the appropriate person when the dispute was resolved.

In all of these cases, it is important to bear in mind that it was not relevant for the purposes of possession whether the holder actually had a valid right in the property. For example, if I take an item in pledge from a non-owner, I will have

---

[116] D.41.2.41.
[117] D.41.2.1.3.
[118] D.43.26.1pr.
[119] D.43.26.2pr–2.
[120] D.41.2.3.5.
[121] As we shall see below, however, the precarist normally only had possessory protection against third parties, not against the granter of the *precarium*.
[122] D.16.3.17.1.
[123] D.16.3.5–6; D.50.16.110.
[124] See pp. 349–50.

no valid right of pledge. However, because actual right to the property is not considered in possessory proceedings, I will nonetheless have possession.

We see then that some with physical control of property were not considered in law to possess it. We need, therefore, to distinguish between those holders who possess and those who do not. Unfortunately, though, the Romans did not develop consistent terminology to express this distinction. Sometimes, the term 'civil possession' (*civilis possessio*) is used for possession in the sense meant here, of a holding of property that is protected by the possessory remedies outlined below. The holder who does not have that protection is said to have 'natural possession' (*naturalis possessio*). This has the disadvantage, though, of calling someone a possessor who does not have the protection of the possessory remedies.[125] It is also confusing to Scots lawyers, for whom natural and civil possession mean something different.[126] Here, instead, the term 'possession' will be used for the cases where a person meets the requirements for possessory protection, in other words where the person fulfils both mental and physical requirements for possession. A person who holds property without the necessary state of mind for possession will be referred to simply as having detention. A person who has detention only does not qualify for possessory protection.

(b) Theories of *Animus*

The meaning of the mental element of possession in Roman law is a subject of long-standing debate.[127] It is not easy to explain in theoretical terms why one particular type of holder is said to be a possessor and another is not. The two leading attempts at theoretical explanation were developed in the nineteenth century by the German scholars Savigny[128] and Jhering.[129]

Savigny, relying primarily on texts taken from the writings of the jurist Paul, argued that possession depended on the holder of the property having *animus domini*, the intention to hold as owner. The person primarily entitled to be called possessor is the person who is holding the property as if owner. Those cases where someone else is called a possessor are examples of 'derivative possession'.

Jhering criticised Savigny's reliance on Paul.[130] For Jhering, there was no separate, free-standing mental element in possession, beyond the simple awareness of

---

[125] On occasion, the jurists also distinguish between 'possessing' and 'being in possession', only the former giving an entitlement to possessory protection. See *e.g* D.41.2.10.1. This is worse than useless, and should be avoided.

[126] In Scots law, natural possession is possession held personally, and civil possession is possession held through another person. The two are both possession in the fullest sense, and have identical consequences (or very nearly so).

[127] For a detailed review of the relevant texts, see G McCormack, 'The Role of Animus in the Classical Law of Possession' (1969) 86 ZSS (rA) 105.

[128] F K von Savigny, *Das Recht des Besitzes* (1837), available in English translation by E Perry (1848).

[129] R von Jhering, *Über den Grund des Besitzesschutzes* (1869) and *Der Besitzwille* (1889). Unfortunately, neither is available in English translation.

[130] Although, given that most of the *Digest* title on possession (D.41.2) comes from Paul's writings, Savigny could hardly have avoided at least some reliance on them.

having control of the property. Instead, for him, any conscious holder of property was considered in principle to be a possessor. Those holders who were not considered to be possessors were excluded for policy reasons. Rather than paying attention to the holder's subjective state of mind, then, for Jhering it was more important to know the objective basis on which the property was held.

Both approaches have had their supporters, but it is unlikely that very many people would give either their unqualified support. The major difficulty with Savigny's approach is that it cannot explain satisfactorily those cases where someone holding otherwise than as owner (*e.g.* as pledgee) is held to have possession. On the other hand, Jhering's theory cannot explain why, for instance, a usufructuary was not said to possess.[131]

It seems most likely that the fundamental problem with both approaches is that they were looking for something that was not there to be found. Arguably, there is no grand unifying theory that can explain why some holders are possessors and others are not. On this view, to be a possessor is simply to be someone who has the protection of the possessory interdicts, and it is not possible to go further than that in terms of principle.

Matters are more straightforward in modern Scots law. As Stair says, possession is based on the coming together of an 'act of the body' and an 'act of the mind'.[132] Thus far, Scots law follows Paul and anticipates Savigny.[133] However, the existence of anomalous cases that then have to be accounted for is avoided by stating the mental element in general terms: 'the inclination or affection to make use of the thing detained'.[134] Thus, in modern Scots law, anyone holding on his or her own behalf is a possessor, and is entitled to possessory protection. This includes holders recognised in Roman law as possessors, such as pledgees. It also, though, includes many holders not recognised by the Romans as possessors, such as tenants.

(c) Changing *Animus*

As a general principle, the view was taken from an early period[135] that, having begun to possess on one basis, a person could not change to possessing on a different, more beneficial, basis.[136] This rule, the purpose of which is not entirely clear, was however interpreted narrowly. For example, Paul gives the example of a person lending an item to someone, and then gifting or selling the item to the borrower. In those circumstances, the recipient could begin possessing as owner, even though

---

[131] Although, as we shall see at pp. 266–7, a usufructuary was given protection equivalent to that provided by the possessory interdicts.

[132] Stair, *Institutions* 2.1.17.

[133] See though R Caterina, 'Concepts and Remedies in the Law of Possession' (2004) 8 Edin LR 267.

[134] Stair, *Institutions* 2.1.17. See also the somewhat earlier formulation in Roman-Dutch law of 'the intention to hold for ourselves' (Grotius 2.2.2).

[135] D.41.2.3.19.

[136] A similar rule is found in Scots law. See Stair, *Institutions* 2.1.27; C Anderson, *Property: A Guide to Scots Law* (W Green 2016) para 3–17; C Anderson, 'Unilateral Permission and Prescriptive Acquisition: A Scottish Perspective' (2020) 40 *Legal Studies* 477.

he or she already had physical custody.[137] Likewise, the jurist Marcellus gives the example of a person possessing land as if owner, then taking a lease from the actual owner. As a tenant was not held to possess, possession was lost when the lease was granted.[138] It seems, then, that a holder of property could change the basis of his or her holding in a way that caused either the loss of possession altogether, or the acquisition of possession where it had not existed before, even if it was not possible to change from one basis of possession to another.

(4) Loss of Possession

We saw above that possession was acquired through physical control coupled with the necessary state of mind. The jurist Paul said that 'Just as no possession can be acquired except by mind and body, in the same way none is lost until both elements are lost.'[139] This, though, does not seem to reflect the actual approach taken. In fact, possession could be lost where only one element was lost. For example, suppose that an owner of land sells that land on condition that the buyer will lease it back to him.[140] The seller remains in occupation throughout. However, because a tenant does not have the necessary mental state for possession, the seller loses possession.[141] This is the case even though, here, physical control is retained.[142]

It seems, therefore, that possession was lost if either the physical or the mental element of possession was lost. Physical control did not, though, have to be exercised constantly. An example given by the jurist Paul is of summer and winter pastures, which are still possessed even though they are not used at certain times of year.[143] The key points are the intention and the ability to return. A moveable item that has been mislaid is still possessed, as long as it can be found through a diligent search. If, however, the item is lost beyond reasonable hope of recovery, possession is lost.[144] An example would be a purse dropped in a busy street, the absence of the purse not being discovered until later.

Because two people could not separately possess the same property, possession would be lost if someone else took possession of the property. An example would be squatters entering a house and taking up occupation during the owner's absence. Somewhat inconsistently,[145] though, the position reached was that the owner in this case would not lose possession until he or she was excluded from

---

[137] D.41.2.3.20.
[138] D.41.2.19pr.
[139] D.41.2.8. For detailed discussion, see C Anderson, *Possession of Corporeal Moveables* (Edinburgh Legal Education Trust 2015) paras 2-35–2-36.
[140] See D.41.2.18pr.
[141] D.41.2.3.6.
[142] This particular form of transfer of possession is known as *constitutum possessorium*. See pp. 212–13.
[143] D.41.2.3.11. See also, more generally, J.4.15.4; G.4.153.
[144] D.41.2.3.13.
[145] Scots law takes a more consistent position on this, with possession being lost immediately on someone else taking possession, although the law on loss of possession is otherwise very similar.

the property on his or her return,[146] or else the owner heard what had happened and decided not to return to the land out of fear.[147]

It is important to understand that, just as possession does not in and of itself give any right to the property, equally the loss of possession does not directly affect anyone's rights. An example given by the jurist Pomponius is of stones lost in the River Tiber[148] in a shipwreck.[149] Possession of the stones is lost, as the ability to resume control at will has been lost. However, ownership is not lost. Accordingly, if the stones are subsequently recovered from the river, the owner who lost them is entitled to get them back.[150] Equally, where an owner of land is excluded from that land by someone else, ownership of the land is unaffected even though possession is lost.

(5) Protection of Possession

The jurist Paul described possession as 'a matter of fact, not of right'.[151] In one sense, this is true (and from context this appears to be the sense that Paul is intending): possession arises from a factual situation, rather than being dependent on having any right to the property. If, though, Paul's words were taken to mean that possession did not have legal consequences or that it was not protected, that would be false. Although possession did not give of itself any right to the property, a possessor was nonetheless protected against dispossession. This possessory protection will be discussed in more detail below. However, to state the principle in general terms, a possessor was normally entitled to keep possession of the property until anyone disputing the possessor's claim established a better right to the property through the proper legal process. A person claiming to have a right to the property was not entitled simply to take the property from the current possessor. *Matheson v Stewart*[152] gives an example from Scots law, which also accepts this principle, although in a different procedural form. In *Matheson*, there had been a sale of an area of land from a larger area. There was a dispute between the buyer and seller over the question of whether a particular piece of land was included in the sale. Without the agreement of the seller, the buyer simply moved into this area. The court ordered that possession be restored to the seller. It is important to understand here that the court made no decision on who was right on the question of entitlement to the disputed piece of land. That was irrelevant in proceedings on possession. If the buyer thought that this piece of land was included in the sale, the appropriate course was for him to go to court to demonstrate that. The seller was entitled to be undisturbed in his possession until that question was determined.

---

[146] D.41.2.6.1.
[147] D.41.2.7; D.41.2.3.8.
[148] This river runs through Rome.
[149] D.41.2.13pr (Ulpian).
[150] The position will be different if the owner has treated the stones as abandoned. In that case, they will become ownerless. See pp. 217–18.
[151] D.41.2.1.3.
[152] (1872) 10 M 704.

Given that even a thief qualified as a possessor of the property he or she had stolen, this may seem surprising. However, it is a consequence of the separation between possession and ownership that is characteristic of Roman property law and the systems based on it, and the principle that possession is protected apart from ownership has been received into Scots law and other modern systems.[153] So, suppose that Quintus has stolen a vase from Publius. Subsequently, Marcus breaks into Quintus' house and removes the vase. Even though Quintus is himself a thief, his possession is nonetheless protected against Marcus, and Quintus will be entitled to have the vase restored to him. It is important to bear in mind, though, that possession gives no ultimate right to the property. In the end, assuming that he can prove ownership to the satisfaction of the judge, Publius will be entitled to the return of the vase.

As to the justification for this possessory protection, one approach is that taken by Justinian in the *Institutes*.[154] Here, the settling of the question of possession is presented as simply the initial stage of the enquiry into ownership. Before asking questions about ownership, it must be decided which party is to raise the action and which defend it.

That, though, does not explain why a thief is protected. Nor does the explanation, favoured by Jhering, that the current possessor is most likely to be owner. As one writer puts it, 'the person who has possession usually has good title to the thing, so protection of possession is protection of the right to the thing'.[155] No doubt this is true in general, but we are concerned here with the special circumstance that the right to the thing is disputed. There is less reason to make assumptions in favour of the possessor here.

An alternative view, espoused among others by Savigny, is that the purpose of possessory protection is to discourage self-help. If I believe that the property you have in your possession is actually mine, the proper way to recover it is to seek your consent, failing which I should go to court to have you ordered to hand the property over. I should not simply take it from you against your will. As Cicero, an advocate of the late Republic, said:

> The collecting of men together because of a disputed ownership is not right: the arming of a mob in order to maintain a right is inexpedient: nothing is so inimical to private rights as force, nor anything so hostile to public justice as that men should be collected together and armed.[156]

In other words, the public interest in the preservation of peace trumps my right simply to retake possession. This view of the matter has been influential in Scotland. As Stair said:

---

[153] Y Emerich, 'Possession' in M Graziadei and L Smith, *Comparative Property Law: Global Perspectives* (Edward Elgar 2017) 183–8.
[154] J.4.15.4.
[155] Watson, *Roman Law & Comparative Law* 48.
[156] *Pro Caecina* 11.33 (in H G Hodge trans, *Cicero, The Speeches* (Heinemann 1927)). See also D.43.3.1.1.

by equity, every man might at any time recover the possession of that which is his own, by force . . . but civil society and magistracy being erected, it is the main foundation of the peace, and preservation thereof, that possession may not be recovered by violence, but by order of law . . .'[157]

(6) Additional Rights of a Good Faith Possessor

In addition to being protected against dispossession by improper means, a possessor who is in good faith has certain further rights. We shall consider first what is meant by good faith, before looking at what these further rights are.

(a) What Is Good Faith?

In its essentials, good faith (in Latin, *bona fides*) means simply lack of knowledge of another person's right.[158] A person possesses in good faith if that person possesses in the honest belief that he or she is entitled to the property. The Roman texts contain little analysis of the concept, however, and so there is room for debate as to whether good faith is judged by an objective or a subjective standard.[159] An objective standard would require that the holder have objective grounds for the belief, or in other words that the belief be reasonable. Modern Scots law applies an objective standard, as we see in Erskine's statement that the good faith possessor is one who 'believes himself proprietor **upon probable grounds**, and with a good conscience'.[160] A subjective standard, by contrast, would judge someone to be in good faith if the belief was honestly held, even if unreasonably so.[161]

The jurist Ulpian tells us that good faith is lost when the possessor becomes aware of a contrary right.[162] In real life, though, things will not always be so clear-cut. For example, suppose that I am in possession of an area of land in the genuine and reasonable belief that I am owner. You turn up and claim that you in fact own the land. Assuming that you are right, do I lose my good faith simply because I am aware of your potential claim? Or do I cease to be in good faith at some later point, perhaps when I have had time to consider the situation, or when you have begun proceedings to prove ownership, or at *litis contestatio*[163] in those proceedings? Alternatively, do I only cease to be in good faith when the issue of ownership is finally determined by the court? Depending on the circumstances, and in particular the relative strengths of our cases, justification could be given for any of those possibilities. In modern Scots law, the matter is

---

[157] Stair, *Institutions* 2.1.22.
[158] J.2.1.30.
[159] For an overview, see A Földi, 'Remarks on the Notion of "Bona Fides"' (2007) 48 Annales U Sci Budapestinensis Rolando Eotvos 53.
[160] Erskine, *Institute* 2.1.25 (emphasis added). For an example of the application of this principle, see *Faulds v Townsend* (1861) 23 D 437.
[161] In practice, of course, it will often make little difference whether the test adopted is objective or subjective, as it will be difficult to persuade a judge that an unreasonable belief was in fact genuinely held.
[162] D.6.1.37.
[163] *Litis contestatio* is the point in court proceedings when it has been agreed what the points to be decided are, and (in the *legis actiones* and formulary procedures) the matter is ready to go before the judge. See pp. 35, 40.

subject to the discretion of the court, depending on the circumstances of the particular case.[164]

(b) Fruits

We have already seen the notion of 'fruits', meaning the produce of property. Although these normally belonged to the owner of the property,[165] there was an exception for good faith possessors. One who possessed property in good faith had, as we have seen, no right to keep the property itself. However, the good faith possessor acquired a right to the fruits.[166] This right was given, says Justinian, 'by natural reason',[167] on account of the work involved in cultivating the fruits. It was not, though,[168] restricted to fruits that the possessor had in fact expended effort on.

An alternative justification is the one adopted in Scots law:

> they who enjoy that which they think their own, do consume the fruits thereof, without expectation of repetition[169] or account . . . and if it were otherwise, there would be no quiet or security to men's minds, who could call nothing securely their own, if the event of a dubious right might make them restore what they had consumed *bona fide*; and as this is in favour of the innocent possessor, so it is in hatred of the negligence of the other party not pursuing his right.[170]

In other words, where the true owner has stood by and allowed the possessor to treat the property as his or her own, it would be unfair to make the possessor account for the benefits received from the property. This is especially so given that, had the possessor considered the position doubtful, he 'would probably have lived more sparingly' and now, by having to compensate the owner, 'might, without the least blame imputable to him, be at once reduced to indigence'.[171]

In the Justinianic law, the good faith possessor's right was limited to the fruits that had been consumed, and unconsumed fruits had to be restored to the owner of the property.[172] In other words, in the Justinianic law, the good faith possessor was not given ownership of the fruits, but instead simply had a defence to a claim for consumption of fruits. In the classical law, though, it seems that the good faith possessor acquired ownership of the fruits as soon as they were separated from

---

[164] Stair, *Institutions* 2.1.24.
[165] This is by the doctrine of accession, on which see pp. 221–31.
[166] We are not concerned here with 'civil fruits', in the form of rent derived from renting out the property. The possessor's right to these derives from the contract entered into with the tenant, and so does not depend on good faith.
[167] J.2.1.35.
[168] Despite D.22.1.45. See D.41.1.48pr.
[169] *I.e.* repayment.
[170] Stair, *Institutions* 2.1.23.
[171] Erskine, *Institute* 2.1.25.
[172] J.2.1.35.

the property, and did not have to restore unconsumed fruits.[173] Scots law follows the classical position.[174]

(c) Improvements

In Scots law, where a possessor in good faith of another's property builds on or otherwise improves the property, the improvement is considered to be part of the property and so belongs to the owner of the property. However, the good faith possessor is entitled to be compensated for the value of the improvement, and is entitled to retain the property until that compensation is paid.[175] The Roman position is similar, but not quite the same. In Roman law, the good faith improver did, if in possession, have a right to retain the property until the owner paid the cost of the labour and materials, and had a defence[176] against any attempt by the owner to recover the property without paying up.[177] However, it does not appear from the material available to us that the good faith improver could directly sustain an action for compensation. If the owner did not want to pay compensation, and was willing to forgo the property, there was no way of making the owner pay up.

Alternatively, the good faith improver could remove any improvements made, as long as this was done without harming the property, and it was done reasonably and without malice.[178]

(d) Actio Publiciana

A further form of protection was available to possessors in good faith, in the form of the *actio Publiciana*.[179] There is no equivalent to this in Scots law, so it is only considered briefly here.

As we have seen, if I buy property from you, I only become owner if you were owner. This is the case even if I am in good faith. However, we shall see in Chapter 12 that it was possible in certain circumstances for an acquirer in good faith to become owner after possessing for a period of time. This form of acquisition was known as *usucapio*.[180] The praetor introduced the *actio Publiciana* to protect good faith possessors in the course of acquiring by *usucapio*. The *actio Publiciana* was similar to the *rei vindicatio*, the standard action for a claim of ownership, but included a fiction that the possessor had had the property for

---

[173] See D.41.1.48. There are other indications that this was the classical rule. For example, there is no discussion in the classical jurists of what is meant by 'consumption' of the fruits: for example, whether it includes sale of the fruits.
[174] Erskine, *Institute* 2.1.25, noting the dispute on the position in Roman law.
[175] Bankton, *Institutes* 1.9.42; *Binning v Brotherstones* (1676) Mor 13401.
[176] The *exceptio doli*, or 'defence of fraud'.
[177] J.2.1.30, 32. See also D.6.1.27.5.
[178] D.6.1.38. The example given here of spiteful removal is the possessor who removes plaster from the walls and defaces pictures.
[179] This is normally said to date from 67 BC. For discussion of doubts as to this date, see Watson, *Property* 104–7.
[180] See pp. 239–43.

the required period for *usucapio*.[181] The *actio Publiciana* was available to the good faith possessor against anyone except the actual owner.[182]

E. Recovery of Property

(1) The Choice: Recovery Based on Ownership or Recovery Based on Possession

In, probably, 69 BC, the orator Cicero appeared as an advocate in a case on behalf of a client named Caecina.[183] The background to this case was a dispute over a farm. The farm had been held on usufruct by a lady named Caesennia.[184] On the death of the owner (Caesennia's son), the farm had been acquired at auction by Caesennia's friend Aebutius. Caesennia then died. Caecina was Caesennia's husband. He claimed that Aebutius had acquired the farm on her behalf, and that therefore it belonged to Caecina as her heir. By contrast, Aebutius took the position that he had acquired the farm for himself. Aebutius excluded Caecina from possession of the land, whereupon Caecina initiated proceedings for its recovery.

The ultimate dispute was over ownership of the land. Caecina, however, chose to proceed on the basis of possession only (by means of the interdict *de vi armata*). Why might he have done this? After all, he could have proceeded straight to raising an action based on ownership. Proof of ownership would have the benefit of conclusively settling the dispute, whereas the possessory remedies gave interim protection only. It is impossible to say why this route was chosen in a particular case. However, the possessory remedies did have two major advantages. First, it was easier to satisfy their requirements: the remedy was based simply on proof of possession, without having to establish any kind of right in the property. This would be particularly attractive where, as in Caecina's case, the question of ownership raised difficult issues and was genuinely open to dispute. Second, even though it did not give a final resolution to the issue, it was advantageous to be the party in possession, as that put the burden on the other party to prove ownership. In addition, in the particular circumstances of a case, it might be advantageous at least to get interim possession. For example, a farmer engaged in a dispute might value at least having possession long enough to complete the harvest, even if he ultimately lost on the question of ownership. Much the same is true in Scots law and other systems of property law based on Roman law, where the same principle applies, although not the specific procedural form of possessory protection. In Scots law, the remedies of spuilzie (for moveables) and ejection and intrusion

---

[181] G.4.36; J.4.6.3–5.
[182] D.6.2.16–17. In fact, as we shall see at p. 201, there was one situation in which the *actio Publiciana* was available even against the owner of the property.
[183] The published version of his speech is thus known as *pro Caecina* ('for Caecina'). For full discussion of the case and its context, see B W Frier, *The Rise of the Roman Jurists: Studies in Cicero's Pro Caecina* (Princeton University Press 1985).
[184] On usufruct, see Chapter 14. This is essentially a right to occupy property belonging to someone else for life (or some shorter period).

(for land)[185] were developed. These were influenced by Roman law: the institutional writer Bankton says that they 'come in place of' the Roman remedies,[186] and the institutional writers make regular reference to Roman sources in discussing them.[187] They also have native antecedents, however,[188] and canon law influence has also been suggested.[189]

(2) Recovery Based on Possession

Justinian presents the possessory remedies as the preliminary stage in a dispute over ownership, determining who should have interim possession until that dispute is resolved. As he says, 'both law and reason require that one possess and the other seek possession'.[190] However, it was not in fact necessary to go through this stage, and it would be pointless to seek possessory protection if it was clear that you would lose.

Possessory protection was given by means of interdicts, which were in origin orders by the praetor that something should be done or not done. In the classical law, once the praetor had issued the interdict, a judge[191] would consider whether either party was in breach of the requirements of the interdict.[192]

The interdicts were classified as being for obtaining, for retaining or for recovering possession.[193] The first of those classes, though, is not really possessory in the sense used here, as it is not concerned with protecting an existing or recently disturbed possession. Instead, interdicts falling into this class are concerned with the acquisition of possession for the first time.[194] Even leaving these aside, though, the classification is not perfect: as we shall see, interdicts classed as being for retaining possession could sometimes be used to recover possession.[195]

(a) Uti Possidetis

For the protection of possession of land, the interdict *uti possidetis* was used. By this interdict, interim possession was awarded to the current possessor, unless he or she acquired possession from the other party by force, stealth or licence,[196] in

---

[185] Ejection means the dispossession of someone who is in present occupation of the land. Intrusion is the same carried out in the possessor's temporary absence. Spuilzie is often used as a collective term for all three. See C Anderson, *Property: A Guide to Scots Law* (W Green 2016) para 3–25 onwards.
[186] Bankton, *Institutes* 2.1.31.
[187] See *e.g.* Stair, *Institutions* 1.9.25; Erskine, *Institute* 2.1.23. There is an additional possessory remedy in Scots law, the possessory judgment, which does not appear to have any Roman basis, even though it has sometimes been equated with the interdict *uti possidetis*, considered below. See C Anderson, 'The Protection of Possession in Scots Law' in E Descheemaeker ed, *The Consequences of Possession* (Edinburgh University Press 2014).
[188] Simpson and Wilson, *Scottish Legal History*, vol I 83.
[189] K Reid, 'Property Law: Sources and Doctrine' in *History of Private Law in Scotland, vol I* 212–13.
[190] J.4.15.4.
[191] Or sometimes a panel, known as *recuperatores*.
[192] G.4.141. In later procedure, no distinction was made between interdicts and ordinary actions, and a possessory question would be tried using the same procedure as an ownership dispute.
[193] G.4.143; J.4.15.2.
[194] The use of these in the context of succession is considered at p. 293.
[195] They are therefore known as double interdicts (G.4.160), meaning that they are addressed to both parties.
[196] J.4.15.4a. Force could, however, be used to defend *existing* possession: D.43.16.1.27.

Latin *vi, clam aut precario*. The final word, usually translated 'licence', is a reference to the arrangement known as *precarium*, described above.

For example, suppose that Decimus is in possession of a farm. Publius forcibly drives Decimus out of the farm and takes up possession himself. Decimus can recover possession using the interdict *uti possidetis*, even though Publius is the one in possession, as Publius took possession from him by force. This is the case even if Publius is in fact owner of the farm: possessory proceedings are not concerned with the ultimate question of who owns the property, but only with the issue of who should have possession in the meantime.

The interdict could only be used against the immediate dispossessor, and so possession obtained by force, stealth or licence from a third party could still be protected by it.[197] For example, in the situation given in the previous paragraph, suppose that Publius is himself forcibly dispossessed by Servius. Decimus will not be able to use the interdict against Servius. An action based on ownership will be his only option.

(b) Utrubi

The interdict *utrubi* was used for the protection of possession of moveable property. In classical law, possession would be awarded to the party who had had possession for longer in the previous year. You could add to your period of possession the possession of anyone from whom you acquired the property by voluntary transfer or as their heir.[198] For example, if Tullia had possession for three months, then sold to Septimus, who possessed for a further four months, Septimus would be counted as having possessed for the full seven months that they possessed between them. Possession before the previous year did not count.[199] Therefore, where Lucius possessed for eight months and then Titus possessed for the following seven months, Titus would be successful in *utrubi* as the first three months of Titus' possession were more than a year previously

Possession acquired by force, stealth or licence from the other party did not count.[200] Thus, for example, suppose that Quintus has had possession of a horse for five months. Claudia sneaks into its stable in the night and removes it. She then possesses it for the next seven months. In proceedings for the interdict *utrubi*, Quintus will be successful. Even though Claudia has had possession for longer, her possession does not count as she acquired possession from Quintus by stealth.

This position changed, and in the law stated by Justinian *utrubi* worked in the same way as *uti possidetis*.[201] In other words, the winner in the interdict proceedings would be the current possessor, unless that party got possession from the other by force, stealth or licence.

---

[197] D.43.16.1.30.
[198] G.4.151.
[199] G.4.152.
[200] J.4.15.4a.
[201] J.4.15.4a.

(c) De Vi/De Vi Armata

Another option for a person dispossessed of land was one of the interdicts *de vi*,[202] which were concerned with dispossession by force. In classical law, there were two forms of these: the simple interdict *de vi*, sometimes called the interdict *de vi cottidiana* ('concerning everyday force'); and the interdict *de vi armata*, which was concerned with armed force.

The interdict *de vi cottidiana* allowed a possessor, who had been ejected by force, to be restored to possession, as long as proceedings were begun within a year. The interdict was not available to a person who held by force, stealth or licence from the ejector.[203] In post-classical law, it was provided that, in addition to restoring possession, the ejector forfeited ownership (if owner) or had to pay the value (if not owner).[204]

The interdict *de vi armata* was available where armed force had been used. 'Armed force' included not just the case where actual weapons were used, but also sticks and stones.[205] The interdict *de vi armata* was available even when the dispossessed party had held by force, stealth or licence from the ejector, and did not have the one-year time limit.

The interdicts *de vi cottidiana* and *de vi armata* seem later to have undergone a merger, and Justinian presents a single interdict for restoration of possession taken by force, regardless of whether possession was acquired by the dispossessed person by force, stealth or licence.[206] This was in addition to the forfeiture of ownership or payment of value mentioned above.

(3) Recovery Based on Ownership

(a) Vindication and Other Remedies

The standard remedy for recovery of property by an owner was the *rei vindicatio*, or 'vindication'. Where the party claiming the property was successful in proving ownership, the possessor would be ordered to yield up the property as well as any fruits obtained from it,[207] unless there was some defence available.[208] Good faith was not a defence (except with respect to fruits), as we have seen. However, if, for example, the party in occupation was able to show that he or she had some other

---

[202] Or *unde vi*. Both terms are used.
[203] G.4.154.
[204] C.8.4.7 (AD 389). This kind of forfeiture was not unprecedented, though it went further than earlier such enactments. For example, Marcus Aurelius (emperor AD 161–80) provided that seizure of money or property belonging to a debtor without a court order resulted in forfeiture of the claim: D.4.2.13; D.48.7.7. In addition, violent conduct of the kind affected by these interdicts might also attract criminal sanctions, for example under the *lex Iulia de vi privata aut publica* ('Julian law on private or public force'). On this *lex*, see D.48.6–7.
[205] G.4.155; D.43.16.3.2–4.
[206] J.4.15.6.
[207] J.4.17.2.
[208] D.6.1.9.

real right in the property, that would be a defence. For instance, if the occupier had a usufruct in the property, that would entitle the occupier to carry on in occupation of the property. The obligation to hand over the fruits of the property included any fruits that might have been acquired through proper management of the property.[209] If the possessor had given up the property, obviously he or she could not be compelled to hand it over. If the property had been disposed of in good faith, there would be no liability. However, if the possessor had disposed of the property fraudulently, he or she would be liable as if still in possession,[210] essentially meaning liability to pay the value of the property.[211]

Another action that was available was the *actio ad exhibendum*, the 'action for production'. This was an action to have someone compelled to produce something in court, and was mainly introduced as a preliminary step to an action for vindication.[212] However, it could be used for other actions as well, so it was not necessary in the *actio ad exhibendum* to claim or prove ownership.[213] It was only necessary to have a relevant interest in the property to be produced, although where the line was drawn between relevant and irrelevant interests was not entirely clear.[214]

One further point should be mentioned here for completeness when considering an owner's options in recovering his or her property. Where the property was moveable and had been stolen,[215] the owner could sue the thief for theft, as an alternative or in addition to vindication. The action for theft was a personal action based on the thief's own wrongdoing, and so in principle it was only available against the thief personally.[216]

(b) Proof of Ownership

When the case came to trial, the judge would hear the evidence and the speeches on either side, and then reach a decision on the question of ownership.[217] In practice, because simply being in possession gave of itself no right to the property (beyond the interim protection given by the possessory interdicts), that would mean that the judge would have to be satisfied that the person asserting ownership had acquired ownership in one of the recognised ways.[218]

In contrast with modern law, though, in which there are detailed rules of evidence governing the process of truth-finding, Roman law had a relatively

---

[209] D.6.1.33.
[210] D.6.1.27.3.
[211] The position in Scots law on the points covered in this paragraph is very similar. See C Anderson, *Property: A Guide to Scots Law* (W Green 2016) paras 2-21–2-23.
[212] D.10.4.1–2. For an example, see D.19.1.17.6.
[213] Ulpian (D.10.4.3.7) gives the example of a person claiming to have been wronged by another's slave. If he did not know which slave it was, he could use the *actio ad exhibendum* to have the whole household produced so that the correct slave could be identified.
[214] See *e.g* D.10.4.19.
[215] Land could not be stolen, although this point seems to have been disputed in earlier law.
[216] For theft and the remedies available against a thief, see pp. 417–22.
[217] For a general account of civil procedure, see Chapter 2.
[218] On these, see Chapters 11 and 12.

undeveloped law of evidence. The judge had a comparatively free hand in this matter. It was, though, accepted that it was up to the person asserting a fact to prove it.[219] The effect of this was that the party raising the action would bear the overall burden of proof, while any specific defence raised by the other party would be for him or her to prove.[220] What we do not see much of is discussion of how much evidence must be brought to satisfy that burden of proof. This raises a genuine difficulty, because, as we shall see in Chapter 11, normally it was not possible to acquire ownership without getting it from a previous owner.[221] Thus, if I buy property from you, I can only become owner if you were owner. But you were only owner if you yourself got the property from a previous owner. The same is true of that previous owner, and so on, right back to when the property first came into existence or was ownerless property acquired for the first time. In practice, therefore, it is likely that a similar approach would be taken to that of modern law, and that the challenger would normally need to show that he or she had once had the property, or at least some kind of entitlement to it, and that the property had come to the current possessor in a manner inconsistent with the acquisition of ownership.[222] An example would be the property having been stolen from me, regardless of whether you were aware of the theft when you subsequently acquired the property.

F. Functional Equivalents to Ownership

Above we saw the principle that, in relation to any item of property, there could only be one right of ownership in any given item of property. Although this principle was always observed in theory, in practice there were certain rights that were so extensive that they put the holder in a position indistinguishable from that of an owner, or very nearly so. For this reason, these rights can be described as functionally equivalent to ownership.[223]

(1) Superficies

We have seen that the owner of an area of land also owned any buildings on the land. As a general principle, it was not possible to have a real right in a building or any part of it separately from the land itself.[224] To this general principle, *superficies* was an exception. This right, which had its origin in building leases, was a real right in the building itself rather than the land on which it sat. The owner of the

---

[219] D.22.3.2.
[220] D.22.3.19pr.
[221] See pp. 202–3.
[222] For the modern position in Scots law, see *e.g. Chief Constable, Strathclyde Police v Sharp* 2002 SLT (Sh Ct) 95.
[223] These are considered only briefly here, as they have no direct equivalent in Scots law, although they do in some other systems. For example, on emphyteusis, see the French *Code civil*, art. 2521.
[224] For this reason, it was not possible to have separate ownership of a flat in a tenement building. It seems, however, that *superficies* provided a functional equivalent. For discussion, see B C Stoop, 'Roman Law Antecedents of the Horizontal Division of Ownership' (1999) 5 Fundamina 107.

land retained in theory ownership of the building itself, but in functional terms the grantee of the *superficies* was in a position very similar to that of an owner as long as the rent was paid and as long as the term (which could be perpetual) lasted.

(2) Emphyteusis

Emphyteusis was originally a long-term or perpetual lease of public land for an annual rent, later being used for private land as well.[225] Unlike in a normal lease of land,[226] the right of *emphyteusis* could be inherited or alienated. Also unlike in a normal lease of land, the holder of the *emphyteusis* was a possessor and, in its developed form, *emphyteusis* was a real right.

(3) Bonitary Ownership

A final example of functional equivalence to ownership is the case of bonitary ownership. The status of bonitary owner was created by praetorian intervention, and gave protection to those who had acquired an item of property in a way other than that required by the law. As this topic is very strongly related to the requirements for transfer of ownership, it is considered more fully in Chapter 11.[227]

Chapter Summary

This chapter has mostly focused on two conceptual distinctions, both of which are characteristic of systems of property law drawing on Roman law, and both of which have been adopted in Scots law.

The first of these is the distinction between real rights and personal rights. This is the distinction 'between owning and being owed something'.[228] Ownership is a real right, and to say that I own something is to say that it is mine; to say that it is mine is to say that I have a right enforceable against the whole world. I can therefore recover the property from any person into whose hands it comes, even if that person is in the most complete good faith. By contrast, if I enter into a contract to sell the thing to you then, until ownership is transferred to you, you have a personal right, enforceable against me but nobody else. As a result, if I sell the thing to someone else, I may be liable to you for breaching our contract, but you will not normally have any remedy against the acquirer of the property.

---

[225] *Emphyteusis* has some similarity to the right of a vassal in land held on feudal tenure, but does not seem to be its historical source: see *Stair Memorial Encyclopaedia*, vol 18 para 43 n 3. *Emphyteusis* also has some similarity to modern ultra-long leases (now limited by statute to 175 years: Abolition of Feudal Tenure etc (Scotland) Act 2000, s. 67), but in Scots law there is no theoretical distinction between leases of different lengths (although of course the practical differences may be substantial).
[226] See pp. 367–9.
[227] See pp. 201–2.
[228] Nicholas, *Introduction* 99. As we shall see in later chapters, though, there are other real rights than ownership.

> The other distinction is that between ownership and possession. To own something is to have a right to it; to possess it is, in simple terms, merely to have it. A person can only become owner in one of a limited number of ways, mostly by acquiring the property from a previous owner. A person can become a possessor simply by taking control of the property with the appropriate state of mind, regardless of entitlement. In the owner there resides the ultimate right to the property. The possessor may be protected against dispossession, but normally only against the immediate dispossessor and only as an interim remedy until the question of ownership is considered. This fundamental distinction exists also in modern Scots law, although the procedural details differ substantially.

Further Reading

G.4.139–70
J.4.6, 15
D.41.1–2; 43.16–18, 31
C.3.32, 37–9, 42; 4.52; 7.32; 8.4, 6
W W Buckland, *A Text-Book of Roman Law from Augustus to Justinian* 3rd edn, revd P Stein (Cambridge University Press 1963) 180–204
H Hausmaninger and R Gamauf, *A Casebook on Roman Property Law* (G A Sheets trans, Oxford University Press 2012) chapters I–IV
D Johnston, *Roman Law in Context* (Cambridge University Press 1999) chapter 4
E Metzger ed, *A Companion to Justinian's Institutes* (Duckworth 1998) 42–9
J A C Thomas, *Textbook of Roman Law* (North-Holland 1976) chapters X and XI
A Watson, *The Law of Property in the Later Roman Republic* (Oxford University Press 1968) chapters 1, 3–7 and 10

CHAPTER ELEVEN

Acquisition of Ownership: Derivative Acquisition

A. Introduction

In this and the following chapter, we are concerned with how a person acquired ownership of property. This could happen in various ways. We make a distinction here between two broad situations: derivative acquisition, which is the focus of this chapter; and original acquisition, which is considered in Chapter 12. Derivative acquisition is the more common situation, in which ownership is acquired from a previous owner. Original acquisition, by contrast, is the umbrella term for those limited situations in which the law allows a person to acquire ownership without getting it from a previous owner.

The derivative/original distinction is the main one used here, as it is most appropriate to the purposes of this book. After all, it is a standard way of classifying modes of acquisition of ownership that is used in modern law. It is not, however, the only one. The Romans also distinguished between civil law modes of acquisition, on the one hand, and natural law modes, on the other. The natural law modes were part of the *ius gentium* ('law of nations'), and were thought of as being universal principles, open to all. Civil law modes of acquisition, by contrast, were only open to those with Roman citizenship rights.[1] As we shall see below, the civil law modes tended to involve a certain degree of formality.

The appropriate method for acquiring ownership thus depended on various factors. A further factor was that property itself was classified in various ways, and this affected the question of the appropriate mode of acquisition. The first matter to consider, therefore, is the classification of property.

B. Types of Property

(1) Property Excluded from Private Ownership

Not all property was capable of private ownership. Gaius' main distinction between types of property is that between those subject to divine right (*divini iuris*)

---

[1] Specifically, the right of *commercium*. See p. 96.

and those subject to human right (*humani iuris*).² Only things *humani iuris* could be privately owned. Things *divini iuris* were of three kinds. *Res sacrae* were things consecrated 'by the authority of the Roman people',³ such as temples, shrines or, after the conversion to Christianity, churches.⁴ *Res religiosae* were burial places,⁵ made either on a person's own land or on a third party's land with that person's permission.⁶ The third category, *res sanctae*, included the walls and gates of a city.⁷

Things *divini iuris* could not be owned,⁸ and so any attempt to transfer ownership of such a thing would be invalid and ineffective. We are therefore concerned only with things *humani iuris*. These were also subject to a distinction. Some were public and some were private. Public things were 'regarded as belonging to nobody', and were excluded from private ownership.⁹ The precise status of public rights was often unclear. For example, as we shall see below, the public had certain rights of use of riverbanks, even though the banks themselves were privately owned. More important, though, was the content of the rights held by the public over this land.

A major example of public property was provincial land, that is land outside Italy. This was regarded as belonging either to the Roman people or to the emperor. The significance of this was, however, rather more theoretical than practical,¹⁰ especially after the categorisation of property as *res mancipi* and *res nec mancipi* (see below) became less important. Of rather more practical significance were public rights to use roads¹¹ and streets,¹² the position with respect to which has had some influence on modern law.¹³

Members of the public had rights over those rivers which were defined as public.¹⁴ Public rivers were those which were perennial rather than seasonal,¹⁵ and everyone had the right of fishing¹⁶ and navigation¹⁷ in them. This right of

---

² G.2.2.
³ *E.g.* by a statute or *senatusconsultum*. On types of legislation, see pp. 49–50, 52–4. It could not be done by a private person with his or her own property: J.2.1.8.
⁴ In the last case, this was done by a priest consecrating the building: J.2.1.8.
⁵ G.2.6.
⁶ J.2.1.9.
⁷ G.2.8. As we shall see below, a similar category exists in modern law. However, owing to the influence of feudal concepts, there is a tendency to see these rights as being held by the Crown on behalf of the public. See Erskine, *Institute* 2.1.6.
⁸ G.2.9. On this category in Scots law, see Erskine, *Institute* 2.1.8.
⁹ G.2.11.
¹⁰ See *e.g.* G.2.7–7a.
¹¹ On the definition of public road, see D.43.8.2.21–4; D.43.7.3pr; D.43.11.2.
¹² On management of urban streets, see D.43.10.
¹³ See *Innes v Magistrates of Edinburgh* (1798) Mor 13189, in which, on the authority of D.43.8.2.24 and D.9.2.29.7, the defenders were held liable when the pursuer was injured falling into a pit that had been dug in a city street. See also *Macdonald v Aberdeenshire Council* [2013] CSIH 83, 2014 SC 114, in which *Innes* was discussed.
¹⁴ For a comprehensive account of the regulation of water rights in Roman law, see C Bannon, 'Fresh Water in Roman Law: Rights and Policy' (2017) 107 JRS 60. For detailed discussion of the reception in Scots law of the ideas in this and the succeeding paragraphs, see N Whitty, 'Water Law Regimes' in *History of Private Law in Scotland, vol 1*; J Robbie, *Private Water Rights* (Edinburgh Legal Education Trust 2015) chapter 2.
¹⁵ D.43.12.1.3. A river is perennial even if, on occasion, it dries up, as long as it normally does not: D.43.12.1.3.
¹⁶ J.2.1.2.
¹⁷ J.2.1.4.

navigation extended, according to a passage adopted by Erskine as representing Scots law,[18] to use of the riverbanks for purposes incidental to navigation.[19] Examples given are using the banks to moor boats and unload cargo. Otherwise, however, the rights of the owner of the bank are unaffected.[20] Where a question arises in modern law as to the meaning of navigation and what incidental uses are permissible, the Roman sources may usefully be consulted. As to other uses, however, the law has developed significantly. In modern law, there is no public right to fish in non-tidal rivers.[21] As far as navigation is concerned, the leading case is *Wills' Trustees v Cairngorm Canoeing and Sailing School Ltd*,[22] in which there was some discussion of Roman law.[23] Although Roman law was accepted as forming the historical basis for Scots law in this area, there are some clear differences. In modern law, the rivers in which the right of navigation can arise are those which are navigable rather than simply those which are perennial.[24] Moreover, in Scots law, the right of navigation does not arise automatically, but instead must be acquired through use. The only exception to this is in tidal parts of a river, where (in common with other tidal waters) there is an automatic right of navigation.

Members of the public also had rights over the sea, the seabed and the foreshore.[25] This included a right of fishing, so anyone who prevented me fishing would potentially be delictually liable.[26] The public right also extended to using the foreshore for drying nets, erecting a hut for shelter or beaching a boat.[27] For Scots law, Stair (using J.2.1.5 as his basis) adds the casting of anchors and the taking on of ballast or water.[28] However, as far as the erection of shelters is concerned, Stair envisages something very much temporary such as a tent. It is clear that Roman law was much more liberal than modern Scots law on public rights to make more permanent alterations to the foreshore and seabed. The jurist Neratius tells us that, not only may a member of the public build on the foreshore, but in addition the builder has ownership of the building.[29] The only apparent restriction on such work is that it should not inconvenience others exercising their rights.[30] It is true that Pomponius says that a decree of the

---

[18] Erskine, *Institute* 2.1.5, relying on J.2.1.4. See also *Scammell v Scottish Sports Council* 1983 SLT 462.
[19] J.2.1.4.
[20] J.2.1.4.
[21] *Grant v Henry* (1894) 21 R 358.
[22] 1976 SC (HL) 30.
[23] See especially Lord Wilberforce (116–17) and Lord Hailsham (140–2).
[24] As Lord Hailsham points out (141), for those living in 'moister climates' such as Scotland, the question of a river being perennial would hardly ever arise.
[25] The foreshore is the area of the seashore below the high tide mark, defined in Roman law as meaning the level of the highest winter tide: J.2.1.3. The modern position is slightly different: in modern Scots law, the foreshore is defined by the ordinary spring tides. See J Robbie, *Private Water Rights* (Edinburgh Legal Education Trust 2015) para 3–40.
[26] D.47.10.13.7. Liability is for *iniuria*, on which see Chapter 23.
[27] J.2.1.5.
[28] Stair, *Institutions* 2.1.5.
[29] D.41.1.14pr. Elsewhere (D.43.8.3.1) the same is said of the sinking of piles into the seabed.
[30] D.41.1.50; D.43.8.3.1.

praetor should be obtained before building work begins,[31] but it is not clear what the consequences would be of failure to follow this procedure. Nor is it entirely clear what is the nature of the builder's right in the land built on, as Neratius says that, on removal of the building, the land reverts to its previous state rather than remaining the property of the builder.[32] At any rate, it is clear that in Scots law the public right does not allow such alterations to the foreshore or seabed.[33]

The right to use public land could be asserted by anyone,[34] and an interdict was available to prevent building on public land that damaged anyone else.[35]

(2) Corporeal and Incorporeal Property

We saw in Chapter 3[36] that Gaius included as the second part in his institutional scheme the 'law of things'. This embraced the law of property in the narrower sense of physical assets, the law of obligations and the law of succession. All of these areas were bound together in that the rights arising from them all can be considered economic assets. Gaius thus proposes a law of property in a wider sense, to include all economic assets. These assets can be classified as either corporeal or incorporeal. Corporeal things are those things 'which can be touched' (the word 'corporeal' means 'having a physical body').[37] Examples given by Gaius are land, a slave, an item of clothing, gold and silver.[38] Incorporeal things cannot be touched. They have no physical existence, and instead 'exist only in the law'.[39] In other words, incorporeal things are legal rights. Examples given are an inheritance, a usufruct,[40] 'obligations however contracted' and a praedial servitude.[41] A right is incorporeal property even if it relates to corporeal property.[42] This distinction between corporeal and incorporeal property is familiar in modern law. However, in Roman law, the implications of classing rights arising from the law of obligations and the law of succession as incorporeal property were not fully worked out, and these rights were not fully incorporated into property law. In particular, the idea that rights arising from the law of obligations could be transferred emerged only slowly and with difficulty, and was never fully accepted.[43]

---

[31] D.41.1.50.
[32] D.41.1.14.1.
[33] See *Crown Estate Commissioners v Fairlie Yacht Slip Ltd* 1979 SC 156.
[34] D.43.7.1.
[35] D.43.8.2pr.
[36] See p. 60.
[37] G.2.13; J.2.2.1.
[38] G.2.13. The same list is found at J.2.2.1.
[39] G.2.14. See also J.2.2.2.
[40] A usufruct is a type of right to occupy and enjoy property belonging to someone else, usually for life. See Chapter 14.
[41] G.2.14; J.2.2.2. A praedial servitude is a right to make some specified use of a neighbour's property (such as a right of way over it) or a right to restrict a neighbour's use of that property (such as a building restriction). See Chapter 13.
[42] G.2.14; J.2.2.2.
[43] On this, see pp. 323–4.

(3) Moveable and Immoveable Property

It is usual for legal systems to make a distinction between land and other types of property. Such a distinction is made in Roman law. The category of immoveable property includes land and things attached to it, such as buildings and plants.[44] Moveable property is everything else. This is broadly in line with the modern Scots distinction between heritable and moveable property, although it is not identical with it.[45] Where there is a clear difference between Roman and modern law, though, is in the relative importance of the distinction. While there were certain legal differences between moveable and immoveable property,[46] on the whole the distinction between moveable and immoveable property was far less important than it tends to be in modern law. Far more important was the Roman classification of property as *res mancipi* or *res nec mancipi*, which cuts across the moveable/immoveable distinction.

(4) *Res Mancipi* and *Res Nec Mancipi*

A distinction was made between property which could only be transferred using certain formal procedures (*mancipatio* and *in iure cessio*, considered below) and property which did not require these procedures. Things requiring formal transfer were known as *res mancipi*, and those that did not require this were known as *res nec mancipi*. The category of *res mancipi* included the following items:[47]

- Italic land, meaning land in Italy. Provincial land was not included.[48]
- Slaves.
- Animals 'commonly broken to draught or burden', oxen, horses, mules and asses being the animals identified as falling into this category. There was a dispute between the Sabinians and Proculians[49] as to when individual animals became *res mancipi*. The Sabinians held them to be *res mancipi* at birth. The Proculians held them to become *res mancipi* only when they were broken in or, if the individual animal was too wild to be broken in, when they reached the usual age for breaking in.[50] Wild animals – Gaius gives bears and lions as examples – were not *res mancipi*. The same was true of animals such as elephants and camels, which were often used as beasts of draught or burden, but which were not known to the Romans when the list of *res mancipi* was fixed.[51]
- Rustic praedial servitudes.[52]

---

[44] On the degree of attachment needed, see the discussion of accession at pp. 221–31.
[45] On this distinction, see C Anderson, *Property: A Guide to Scots Law* (W Green 2016) paras 1-35 – 1-38.
[46] For example, in the required periods for *usucapio*. On this, see pp. 239–43.
[47] G.2.14a.
[48] G.2.21.
[49] On these juristic schools, see p. 56.
[50] G.2.15.
[51] G.2.16.
[52] These were rights of use of neighbouring land, such as rights of way. See Chapter 13. The other form of praedial servitudes, urban praedial servitudes, were *res nec mancipi*.

The basis of the list is unclear. It is not simply a question of value,[53] as many items not on the list would have been more valuable than many that were included. It is common for legal systems to require particular publicity and formality in the transfer of land,[54] but that does not explain the other items included. The list does suggest a connection with agriculture, an indication perhaps that it dates from a period when agriculture was an activity of particular economic importance for the Romans.[55] At any rate, for reasons outlined below, the special methods for transfer of *res mancipi* fell out of use in the classical period. The classification of property as *res mancipi* or *res nec mancipi* was finally abolished by Justinian,[56] and it is not found in later law.

(5) Fungible and Non-Fungible Property

A final distinction to be made is that between fungible and non-fungible property. Fungible things are those that are identical or sufficiently similar to others of the same type that they are interchangeable. The term is most often used in relation to things that are consumed by use,[57] but mass-produced items may also fall into this category.[58] The distinction has significance in various contexts.[59]

C. Transfer of *Res Mancipi*

As already mentioned, the legal significance of the classification of certain types of property as *res mancipi* was the use of certain special methods for transfer of ownership. These special methods, *mancipatio* and *in iure cessio*, were civil law modes of transfer, meaning (as we saw above) that they were only available for use by those with a Roman citizen's right of *commercium*. As they were abolished by Justinian, they were not discussed in the *Corpus Iuris Civilis*, and so did not influence later law. They will therefore be considered only briefly here.

(1) Mancipatio

The first of the methods available for the transfer of *res mancipi* was called *mancipatio*. This, says Gaius, was in the form of a 'sort of imaginary sale'.[60] It involved the parties coming together with five witnesses, plus a sixth person to hold a

---

[53] See Johnston, *Roman Law in Context* 54.
[54] In modern Scots law, for example, registration in the Land Register is required. The Land Register is regulated by the Land Registration etc (Scotland) Act 2012.
[55] C F Amunátegui Perelló, 'Problems Concerning *Mancipatio*' (2012) 80 TvR 329 argues that it was fixed by the end of the Monarchy period. See also this article for discussion of the origins of the classification, including a summary of the various theories that have been put forward.
[56] C.7.31.1.5 (AD 531).
[57] Examples would include money, oil or grain.
[58] Nicholas, *Introduction* 167 n 4.
[59] See in particular the law of usufruct (Chapter 14) and the contract of loan for consumption, called *mutuum* pp. 344–7).
[60] G.1.119.

bronze scale.[61] All had to be Roman citizens of full age.[62] The transferee would hold a bronze ingot, and then say: 'I declare that this slave[63] is mine by Quiritary right,[64] and he is purchased by me with this bronze ingot.'[65] Finally, the transferee would strike the scale with the ingot and give it to the transferor as a symbolic price.[66] With the exception of land, the transfer of which did not have to take place on the land, the property being transferred had to be present during the ceremony and be grasped by the transferee.[67] As a result, *mancipatio* could not be used for incorporeal things. Gaius explains that the bronze and scales are used because the ceremony pre-dates the introduction of coined money.[68] At that period, bronze ingots, valued by weight, were used.[69]

This procedure is characteristic of the formalism typical of early law,[70] and it seems that compliance with the formal procedure was all (or almost all). While the transferor did have to have the right to transfer the property,[71] the validity of the transfer was not affected by (for example) fraud on the part of the transferor. The procedure was also cumbersome and inconvenient.[72] In practice it seems that, in the classical period, it became common to rely on documents narrating that a *mancipatio* had taken place, with this very likely standing in for the actual performance of the procedure.

(2) In Iure Cessio

An alternative – available in fact for *res nec mancipi* as well – was the procedure known as *in iure cessio*. It was carried out in the presence of a magistrate,[73] and took the form of a collusive litigation.[74] In its essentials, the procedure involved the intended transferee asserting ownership of the property, and the transferor acquiescing in that assertion. The magistrate would then give formal confirmation (*addictio*) of the property as belonging to the intended transferee.[75] As with

---

[61] This last person was known as the *libripens*, or 'scale-holder'.
[62] G.1.119.
[63] Or whatever else the property concerned was.
[64] *I.e.* by the law of Rome. *Quirites* was a term used for the Roman people.
[65] G.1.119.
[66] G.1.119.
[67] G.1.121.
[68] G.1.122.
[69] Roman coinage did not develop until the third century BC. See S von Reden, 'Money and Finance' in W Scheidel ed, *The Cambridge Companion to the Roman Economy* (Cambridge University Press 2012) 267.
[70] See pp. 46–7.
[71] This is confirmed by the fact that there was implied into a transfer by *mancipatio* a warranty against eviction of the transferee by a person with a better right. This warranty, on which see Watson, *Property* 16, would be redundant if compliance with the formal requirements was enough.
[72] This is not to say that there are no advantages to formal procedures for transfer. Formality has the benefit of confirming the intentions of the parties and, particularly where witnesses or public registration are involved, helps avoid disputes. For these reasons, many modern systems have particular formal requirements for transfer, especially with land. For example, in Scots law, transfers of ownership of land must be effected in writing and must be registered in a public register, the Land Register.
[73] Or, in the provinces, the provincial governor.
[74] In accordance with the *legis actiones* procedure. See pp. 32–7.
[75] G.2.24.

mancipatio, the validity of the transfer was unaffected by such things as fraud or coercion. We are not directly told that the transferor actually had to have a right to the property. However, if the procedure was viewed as being in substance a collusive litigation as well as being one in form, that would suggest that such a right would be needed. The true owner not being a party to the litigation, there would be nothing here that could prevent the true owner coming forward and asserting his or her own right in subsequent proceedings.

The need for the presence of a magistrate meant that this procedure was even more cumbersome than *mancipatio*. In practice, this meant that it tended to be used for the most part for the creation of servitudes, these being incorporeal and *mancipatio* thus being excluded.[76]

(3) Informal Transfer and Bonitary Ownership

Both *mancipatio* and *in iure cessio* were cumbersome procedures, unsuited to commercial needs. It is hardly to be supposed that whenever, say, there was to be a sale of a horse, the buyer and seller went to find the nearest magistrate or gathered together the six additional people needed for *mancipatio*. In practice, many transfers of *res mancipi* would be effected informally. This would avoid undue formality, but had the severe disadvantage that the transferee did not become owner.[77] It is true that the transferee might become owner by *usucapio*, by possessing for a period of time.[78] However, that would take either one or two years, depending on the type of property, and in the meantime the transferee would be vulnerable to challenge. Intervention by the praetor helped in two ways. First, if the transferee was in possession, the praetor gave him or her a defence if the transferor attempted to recover the property on the basis of ownership. Second, the *actio Publiciana*[79] allowed the transferee, if out of possession, to recover the property from whoever was in possession. This included the transferor, and was achieved by allowing the transferee to plead based on a fiction that the required period for *usucapio* had already run. To a very great extent, this put the transferee in the practical position of owner, even though strictly the transferor was still owner (and could enforce his or her right against anyone other than the transferee). For Gaius, the result of this was that ownership was divided.[80] The transferor was owner according to civil law, while the transferee was owner according to praetorian law. A transferee in this position is known as a 'bonitary owner', so called because in the words of Gaius the property was *in bonis* of the transferee (*i.e.* among his or her goods).[81] As a result, either could defend their position against the rest of the world, while the bonitary owner would take precedence

---

[76] Watson, *Property* 21.
[77] G.2.41.
[78] By *usucapio*, a possessor of property could acquire ownership by possessing it in good faith for a certain period of time. See pp. 239–43.
[79] See pp. 185–6.
[80] G.2.40.
[81] G.2.41.

in a dispute between the two. With the abolition of the *res mancipi/res nec mancipi* distinction, the idea of bonitary ownership became redundant, and has not been received in Scots law.[82]

D. Transfer by Delivery *(Traditio)*

The appropriate mode of transfer for *res nec mancipi* (and, in the Justinianic law, for all property) was delivery, or *traditio*. This was a natural law mode of transfer, and so was open to non-citizens. As we have seen, delivery was also commonly used for *res mancipi* before Justinian's time, even though this only gave the transferee bonitary ownership. In simple terms, delivery was a transfer of possession by the transferor to the transferee. Before looking at the act of delivery, however, we must first consider some general requirements for a valid transfer of ownership.

(1) General Requirements for Transfer

(a) Title

Suppose that you buy a book from a dealer in second-hand books. You have every reason to believe that the dealer is the owner of the book, and no reason to suspect otherwise. In other words, you are in good faith. It then turns out that, some time ago, the book was stolen from me. I claim the return of the book from you. The law has to choose here between two innocent parties, you and me. We neither of us deserve to lose out. However, there is only one book so, unless we are to share it, one of us must lose out. Which of us is it to be? There is no obviously decisive reason to favour either of us.[83]

In Roman law, the decision was taken to favour the original owner.[84] The transferee cannot get any greater right than the transferor has. If the transferor has no right to the property, the transferee will equally acquire no right. Good faith is irrelevant to this question. This rule arises from the nature of real rights, considered in the previous chapter.[85] In the example given above, I was owner of the book. Ownership is a real right. It is in the nature of real rights that they are enforceable against anyone. As my ownership is a real right, I can enforce it against you just as much as I could have done against the thief. You are therefore obliged to let me have the book back, and must look to the bookseller for a remedy under your contract.[86] This rule is often expressed using the maxim: *nemo plus*

---

[82] For a decisive rejection of the idea that a transferee can have ownership rights despite failing to complete the necessary steps to become owner, see *Burnett's Trustee v Grainger* 2004 SC (HL) 19.

[83] Although justifications could be suggested for either view. On my side, it could be said that you chose to trust to the right of the bookseller, and must stand by that choice in a question with me. In addition, you have more chance of finding the person who sold to you and claiming your money back than I have of finding the thief and getting compensation. On your side, it could be said that the interests of justice are better served by letting the loss lie where it falls, as neither of us is at fault. It could also be said that the interests of commerce favour allowing good faith acquirers to rely on the right of sellers to sell the goods they offer. In any event, the point was clearly settled in Roman law.

[84] G.2.20; D.41.1.20pr.

[85] See pp. 163–5.

[86] See pp. 358–64 for remedies under a contract of sale.

iuris ad alium transferre potest quam ipse haberet ('nobody can transfer a greater right to another than he himself has').[87] Sometimes a shorter version, *nemo dat quod non habet* ('nobody gives what he does not have'), is used. The rule is often referred to as the *nemo dat* rule or the *nemo plus* rule, and remains the law in Scotland.[88]

The right to transfer ownership is often known as 'title', and normally arises from ownership. Sometimes, however, someone other than the owner has title, and so can validly transfer ownership.[89] Justinian gives the example of a pledgee.[90] Suppose I hand over some item of my property to you as security for a debt. I retain ownership. However, if I fail to repay, in most cases you will have the power to sell the item to pay off the debt, and can give ownership to the person you sell it to. As Justinian observes, though, this is only a partial exception to the rule, as you have this power because I have given it to you in our contract. A clearer exception existed for currency. While stolen coins continued to belong to the person from whom they were stolen, ownership was lost if they were given to someone else who was in good faith, and the coins became so mixed with the recipient's own money that they could not be identified. The original owner was left with a claim against the person who gave the coins to the recipient.[91] This is a practical rule, arising because the nature of currency justifies special treatment, and is commonly found in modern legal systems.[92]

(b) Capacity and Excluded Transfers

It sometimes also happened that the owner of property, although having title in the sense in which that word is used here, was nonetheless unable to transfer ownership.[93]

This inability might be a result of restricted capacity. As we saw in Chapters 5 to 8, a person might be subject to various legal incapacities because of their civil status. Examples include the prohibition on gifts between spouses. Another is the inability of children subject to guardianship to alienate property without the guardian's consent.

There could also be a general restriction on particular forms of transaction. A statute might prohibit transactions of a particular kind. The effect these had on transfer depended on the terms of the statute, which might either expressly state the consequences of breach or else leave this as a matter of interpretation. A distinction is made between three broad situations.[94] A *lex* (statute) might be *perfecta* (perfect), *minus quam perfecta* (less than perfect) or *imperfecta* (imperfect). The distinction between these does not lie in the consequences of entering into a prohibited agreement. Any such agreement would be unenforceable, whichever category

---

[87] D.50.17.54. Where the property was co-owned by the transferor, the transfer would be effective only with respect to the transferor's share, not with respect to the rest of it: D.18.1.18pr.
[88] Although there are some exceptions. See *e.g.* Sale of Goods Act 1979, ss. 24 and 25; Land Registration etc (Scotland) Act 2012, s. 86.
[89] J.2.8pr.
[90] J.2.8.1. On pledge, see pp. 271–4.
[91] D.46.3.78.
[92] See *e.g.* Stair, *Institutions* 2.1.34, citing D.46.3.78 as authority.
[93] J.2.8pr.
[94] On these, see Zimmermann, *Obligations* 697–702; J M J Chorus, 'Illegal Alienations in Classical Roman Law' in Birks, *New Perspectives*.

it fell into.⁹⁵ Rather, the distinction lay in the consequences of carrying out the prohibited agreement. After all, merely to say that people may not do something tells us nothing about the consequences if they proceed anyway.⁹⁶ A statutory prohibition could have the consequence that a transfer in breach is void, but there are other possibilities. For example, suppose that there is a statute imposing additional requirements on the sale of livestock in the public marketplace. I buy a cow from you in breach of this prohibition, and pay you the agreed price. If the purpose of the prohibition is to protect purchasers, it makes no sense to deny effect to the transfer of ownership. If that was the consequence, you would still own the cow and also have the money, which would hardly be consistent with protecting the purchaser. On the other hand, it might make sense to allow me to keep the cow and also reclaim the price. Again, if the purpose is the protection of public health, it might make more sense to have the state confiscate both the cow and the purchase price. In that case, the validity of the transfer of ownership is neither here nor there, because neither of us is getting to keep the cow anyway. It may not always have been clear into which category a particular statute fell, any more than it is in the modern world. It is not unknown for a legislature to lay down that some activity is unlawful, but to fail to specify in full the consequences that are to ensue if someone carries out the forbidden activity anyway. The first thing to consider would be the actual terms of the legislation. There is not enough surviving material, however, for us to be completely certain how the Romans would have approached cases of doubt.

Of the three categories, however, the *lex perfecta* seems to have been more common over time. A *lex perfecta* was a statute that provided that any attempted transfer in breach of the *lex* was void and ineffective. The transferor remained owner. A transfer in contravention of a *lex minus quam perfecta* would be effective, in the sense that the transferee became owner, but the *lex* imposed some other penalty on one or both of the parties.⁹⁷ For example, some punishment might be imposed on the parties, while leaving the validity of the transfer itself unimpaired. Finally, a transfer in contravention of a *lex imperfecta* was effective and did not incur any penalty, but the money or property transferred could not be recovered.⁹⁸ An example of a *lex imperfecta* is an early statute, the *lex Cincia*,⁹⁹ which prohibited gifts above a certain limit. This rendered a promise to give such a gift unenforceable. If the gift was given anyway, though, the donor could not recover it.¹⁰⁰

---

⁹⁵ See p. 334.
⁹⁶ For Scots law to the same effect, see Erskine, *Institute* 1.1.59.
⁹⁷ For an example, see G.4.23.
⁹⁸ As would normally be the case when a transfer was made that was not due. See p. 430.
⁹⁹ A date of 204 BC has been suggested for this statute. See L Winkel, 'Forms of Imposed Protection in Legal History, Especially in Roman Law' (2010) 16 Fundamina 578, 582.
¹⁰⁰ It may be wondered what the point is of prohibiting conduct, but not imposing consequences on breaches of that prohibition. Part of the answer is that a breach is not completely without consequences: as has already been noted, an agreement to do something in breach of the prohibition would be void and so unenforceable. Another part of the answer may be that even a *lex imperfecta* may make use of the 'expressive function' of law in changing or reinforcing a community's behavioural norms. See on this T A J McGinn, 'The Expressive Function of Law and the *Lex Imperfecta*' (2015) 11 Roman Legal Tradition 1. The idea would be to discourage particular conduct by giving official disapproval to it.

(c) Consent

There could be no valid transfer of ownership without the mutual consent of the parties.[101] The transferor had to intend to transfer ownership to the transferee, and the transferee had to intend to receive ownership from the transferor. Suppose that Marcus is owner of a particular item of property. Intending that Titius should receive it as a gift, Marcus gives the item to Quintus to hand over to Titius in Marcus' name. In fact, Quintus hands the item to Titius in his (Quintus') own name. In this situation, the jurist Javolenus tells us, Titius does not become owner.[102] This is presumably because the intention of Titius was to receive ownership from Quintus rather than from Marcus, and the intention of Quintus was to transfer the property himself rather than simply acting on behalf of Marcus.

This requirement for consent allowed the parties to make the transfer conditional on some event. This condition might be suspensive or resolutive. We shall see more in Chapter 17 on suspensive and resolutive conditions, including how to identify into which category a condition falls.[103] However, in simple terms, a suspensive condition in a transfer would provide that the transferee would only become owner on the occurrence of the stated event. If the transfer was subject to a resolutive condition, by contrast, the transferee would become owner immediately, subject to a right of the transferor to reclaim the property or the transferee to restore it on the occurrence of some event. Unless and until that happened, the transferee would be owner, and so the transferor would not have any remedies based on ownership with respect to the property.[104] If the transfer was subject to a suspensive condition, though, the transferee would remain owner. An important example of this was that parties to a sale could agree that the seller would remain owner until the buyer had paid the price in full.[105] This agreement might take the form of the buyer agreeing to hold as lessee until the price was paid, essentially as in a modern hire purchase contract.[106]

Consent to transfer ownership could be vitiated by deceit or coercion. These are discussed more fully in Chapter 24.[107] However, because they have property law consequences, it is appropriate to say something about them here. In brief, coercion (*metus*, also translated as duress) involves the use of either force or serious threats to overcome a person's resistance.[108] Deceit (*dolus*) refers to the activities of 'shifty and deceitful persons'.[109] *Dolus* is often translated as fraud, but it is broader than that term would imply.[110] It included situations where a person was denied

---

[101] D.44.7.54.
[102] D.39.5.25. For a similar situation in Scots law, see *Morrisson v Robertson* 1908 SC 332.
[103] See pp. 335–7.
[104] D.6.1.41pr.
[105] D.43.26.20. Compare *Armour v Thyssen Edelstahlwerke AG* 1990 SLT 891.
[106] D.19.2.21; D Daube, 'Tenancy of Purchaser (*Digest* 19.2.21)' (1948–50) 10 Cam LJ 77; D Daube, '*Si* . . . *tunc* in D.19.2.22pr: Tenancy of Purchaser and *Lex Commissoria*' (1958) 5 Revue Internationale des Droits de l'Antiquité (3rd series) 427; J A C Thomas, 'Tenancy by Purchaser' (1959) 10 Iura 103.
[107] Chapter 24 pp. 423–5). considers these in their delictual aspect. For contractual issues arising from deceit and coercion, see pp. 333–4.
[108] D.4.2.1.
[109] D.4.3.1pr.
[110] Though see *e.g.* Bankton, *Institutes* 1.10.62 on the definition of fraud in Scots law in his time.

enforcement of a right as having acted in bad faith, or where it would be unfair to allow that to enforce a right. For example, in the example (in the previous paragraph but one) of the gift to Titius, even though Titius strictly does not become owner, nonetheless Titius has a defence based on *dolus* (the *exceptio doli*) if Marcus attempts to recover the property from him. As Marcus did intend Titius to get the property, it would be inappropriate to allow Marcus to recover the property from him. Ulpian gives a similar case where one person gives another money as a gift, but the recipient believes it to be a loan, with the same outcome.[111]

The distinction between coercion and deceit in property law becomes particularly important when third parties become involved. Consider the following two situations:

- Aulus owns a particular item of property. By deceiving Aulus about the value of the property, Numerius prevails upon Aulus to sell it to him. Shortly afterwards, Numerius sells the property to Tertius at its true value, which is much higher than Numerius paid Aulus.
- Aulus owns a particular item of property. Numerius turns up with an armed gang and, using threats of serious violence, prevails upon Aulus to hand over the property. Shortly afterwards, Numerius sells the property to Tertius.

In both cases, Aulus would have a remedy against Numerius. Numerius may have disappeared or be insolvent, though, and at any rate is in no position to return the property to Aulus. Could then Aulus recover the property from Tertius? Here the answer differs between cases of coercion and deceit. Recovery of property on the basis of deceit was only normally possible against the actual perpetrator of the deceit.[112] Third parties acquiring from the perpetrator would only be liable to hand over the property to the victim of the deceit if they were in bad faith or had taken the property without giving value for it.[113] As to coercion, Ulpian indicates that the point was debated.[114] However, he tells us that the conclusion reached was that, in cases of transfer resulting from coercion, a third party acquirer was liable even if in good faith. This was the case even if the coercion was applied by someone other than the transferee.[115]

The position of third party acquirers was thus very different in cases of coercion and of deceit. Ulpian points to a procedural difference: the *actio metus* is a real action, meaning that it can be brought against anyone having the property.[116] This explanation, however, is not open to the modern lawyer, even though the law on this point is the same in Scotland.[117] A more theoretical explanation would

---

[111] D.12.1.18pr.
[112] D.44.4.4.33.
[113] D.44.4.4.31.
[114] D.4.2.14.5.
[115] D.4.2.14.3.
[116] D.4.2.9.8.
[117] See the accounts in Stair, *Institutions* 1.9.8 and 1.9.10, citing heavily from the Roman sources.

be the following. In cases of coercion, the transferor has not truly consented to the transfer at all. There is therefore a necessary element in the transfer that is missing, with the result that the ostensible transferee does not become owner. As a non-owner, the transferee is therefore unable to transfer ownership to the third party. By contrast, where a person is persuaded through deceit to agree to transfer ownership, he or she has nonetheless given that agreement. As a result, the deceitful transferee does become owner. The deceit justifies the transferor having a personal remedy against the transferee, but that remedy (being personal to the original transferor and transferee) cannot affect a third party acquirer.[118]

(d) Identification

A valid transfer also required that the property be identified.[119] As Pomponius tells us, an 'uncertain part' of property cannot be transferred.[120] As a result, I would not be able to transfer to you 'whatever right I have in the land'. Equally, I would not be able to transfer to you ten bottles of wine from my wine cellar, without identifying which specific bottles you were to get. Again, suppose that I was to decide to build a number of houses and sell them off. Some open ground will remain once the houses are built, and I intend that the purchasers of each house are to have co-ownership of the open ground. When I build the first house, I sell it to you, stating that you are getting it together with co-ownership of the open ground, along with the purchasers of the other houses to be built.[121] In fact, in this situation you would acquire no right at all in the open ground.[122] The reason for this is that, until the other houses are built, it is not possible to say what the extent of the open ground is (because it will be whatever is left over once building is complete) or what your share is (because that depends on how many other houses are built, and so how many other purchasers you have to share the open ground with). If, however, the only problem is that the wrong name has been used for the property, it still counts as identified if the parties are in fact agreed about what it is that is being transferred.[123]

(e) Just Cause *(Iusta Causa)*

Even where an undoubted owner, voluntarily and with full capacity, delivers clearly identifiable property to another, the fact of that delivery does not of itself necessarily mean that ownership is being transferred. After all, there are many reasons why someone might hand over property to another without any intention to transfer ownership. The transaction may be one of loan,[124] for example,

---

[118] In modern terminology, a coerced transfer is void but a transfer induced by deceit is voidable. For discussion of the distinction between void and voidable transfers, see T B Smith, 'Error and Transfer of Title' (1967) 12 JLSS 206, discussing *Macleod v Kerr* 1965 SC 253 and *Morrisson v Robertson* 1908 SC 332.
[119] Identification also raises contractual issues, on which see pp. 328–33.
[120] D.41.2.26.
[121] These are essentially the facts of *PMP Plus Ltd v Keeper of the Registers of Scotland* 2009 SLT (Lands Tr) 2.
[122] D.41.2.26.
[123] D.41.2.24pr.
[124] Specifically, the form of loan contract called *commodatum*. See pp. 347–9.

or hire. While we have seen that consent to a transfer is necessary for the validity of that transfer, that consent does not exist in isolation from the transaction or purpose that has led to it. If I transfer ownership to you, there will be some reason for it, such as a contract of sale, an intention to make a gift, or whatever it may be. Whenever one person delivers an item of property to another, it will be necessary to establish the reason for this delivery, because there will only be a valid transfer of ownership where that underlying reason justifies the conclusion that a transfer of ownership was what the parties intended. It is possible to go further, though. According to the jurist Paul, such an underlying transaction, justifying the transfer of ownership, was necessary to the validity of a transfer in Roman law.[125] Thus, for Paul, it was necessary for a valid transfer of ownership that there be some valid underlying transaction such as a sale or a gift, justifying the transfer of ownership. This underlying transaction is known as the *iusta causa*, or just cause for the transfer.

It is one thing to identify certain transactions as justifying a transfer of ownership and others as not justifying this. A more difficult situation arises, though, where the underlying transaction is invalid for some reason. We have already seen one possibility, that the underlying transaction is illegal under some statute. Another possibility could be the parties having different understandings of the nature of the transaction. Suppose, for example, that I intend to give the property to you as a gift, while you believe that it is a sale. Here there is neither a contract of sale nor a valid gift, because there is no consensus between us.[126] Nonetheless, we both intend that you should become owner. What, then, is the outcome? We have seen Paul's opinion, which would seem to suggest that there would be no transfer of ownership here. On the other hand, the jurist Julian appears to take a different view: 'When indeed we agree on the thing being delivered, but disagree on the basis for delivery, I see no reason why the delivery should not be effective.'[127] He gives the examples of the transferor believing himself bound to transfer under a will, but the transferee believing that the transfer is due under contract, and the transferor giving money as a gift, but the transferee taking it as a loan.[128] On this view, the requirement for *iusta causa* is simply a requirement for some objective evidence of an intention to transfer.

There is then an apparent conflict in the texts here, as to whether a genuine underlying transaction is required for the validity of the transfer of ownership. It is impossible to speak with complete certainty about what the Roman law actually was.[129] The view taken depends on the extent to which contract and

---

[125] D.41.1.31pr. See also D.12.1.18pr (Ulpian).

[126] D.12.1.18.1. This is known as *error in negotio*, or error as to the nature of the transaction, on which see p. 329.

[127] D.41.1.36. See also C.2.19.2 (AD 226), which (in a very different context) appears to hold that there can sometimes be a valid transfer even where the underlying contract is void.

[128] This is a reference to a particular form of loan called *mutuum*, in which the borrower becomes owner of the property but must restore an equivalent. See pp. 344–7.

[129] For discussion, see R Evans-Jones and G D MacCormack, '*Iusta Causa Traditionis*' and W M Gordon, 'The Importance of the *Iusta Causa* of *Traditio*' in Birks, *New Perspectives*.

conveyance (transfer) can be considered separately. This divergence in the texts has given rise to a major division in the legal systems drawing on Roman law. On one side, there are the systems that are said to have a causal theory of transfer, so called because they require a genuine *iusta causa* to exist. In causal systems, if the underlying transaction is void, the transfer will also be void. On the other side, there are countries adhering to an abstract theory of transfer. In an abstract system of transfer, the validity of the transfer is viewed in the abstract, separate from consideration of the underlying transaction. In an abstract system, ownership may therefore pass to the transferee even where the underlying transaction is void. Where this leaves ownership in the 'wrong' place, the imbalance may be corrected by other means, such as the law of unjustified enrichment.[130] France is the most prominent example of the causal theory of transfer, Germany of the abstract theory. Scotland probably, though not certainly, has an abstract system of transfer.[131]

In favour of the causal view, the following may be said: 'The principle of abstraction makes an artificial segregation between two legal acts which economically and in the mind of the parties are part of one and the same transaction.'[132] All the same, there is much to be said for the abstract view of transfer. After all, contract and transfer are two separate things. They involve different sorts of relationship, created in different ways. Take a sale as an example. When we enter into a contract of sale, we create rights and obligations as between ourselves, but rights under a contract only bind the parties to that contract. The act that makes the buyer owner, thus binding third parties as well, is in principle a separate act. It is one thing to agree to make someone owner, another actually to carry that out.

Moreover, we have already seen above with the *lex Cincia* that a transfer can be valid even where an underlying agreement is invalid. The same is true of the converse situation. Suppose that I agree to sell you goods that are in fact stolen. The transfer to you will be invalid and ineffective, for reasons we have already seen. The contract of sale, however, is undoubtedly valid,[133] or else you would have no contractual remedy against me for failing to make you owner.[134]

Finally, for all its intuitive attractions, it is not clear that a causal system gives a more just outcome between the parties, and an abstract system gives better protection to third parties acquiring in good faith. Suppose that we attempt to make

---

[130] On the development of the abstract and causal theories of transfer, see L P W van Vliet, 'Iusta Causa Traditionis and Its History in European Private Law' (2003) 11 Eur Rev Priv L 342.

[131] *Stair Memorial Encyclopaedia*, vol 18 paras 608–12; D L Carey Miller with D Irvine, *Corporeal Moveables in Scots Law* 2nd edn (W Green 2005) paras 8.06–10; L P W van Vliet, 'The Transfer of Moveables in Scotland and England' (2008) 12 Edin LR 173.

[132] L P W van Vliet, 'Iusta Causa Traditionis and Its History in European Private Law' (2003) 11 Eur Rev Priv L 342, 376.

[133] That is to say, the fact that the goods are stolen does not make the contract invalid. It may of course be invalid for some other reason, unrelated to the theft.

[134] The law governing your remedy in this situation is in fact a little more complicated than this, but it is not necessary to go into that here. It does not affect the argument. On the remedies of a buyer of stolen goods, see pp. 359–60.

a contract involving the sale of an item of property. However, for some technical reason or other, the contract is not validly constituted. Nonetheless, we proceed to carry out the agreement. I give you the property, and you pay me the agreed price. In a causal system, the invalidity of the contract will mean that you do not become owner. I remain owner, yet since I have been paid it would not appear just to allow me to recover the property from you. Still less would it appear just to allow me to recover the property from a third party acquiring from you in good faith.[135] An abstract system of transfer avoids the difficulty by giving ownership to you, and so in turn to the third party acquirer, leaving me with a remedy in unjustified enrichment against you where that is appropriate.[136]

(2) Operation of *Traditio*

Even if all of the above requirements were met, a further step was necessary for the transfer of ownership. This was *traditio*, the delivery of the goods to the transferee: 'Ownership of property is transferred, not by bare agreement, but by delivery and *usucapio*.'[137] *Usucapio*, the acquisition of ownership through a period of possession, is considered in Chapter 12.[138] Here we are concerned with delivery.

(a) General Nature of Traditio

Delivery, in simple terms, means the giving of possession by the transferor to the transferee.[139] There was a general discussion of possession in Chapter 10.[140] Here we will consider the specific application of the idea of possession to the transfer of ownership. In brief, then, delivery requires the transferee to take physical control of the property, with the consent of the transferor, and with the necessary intention to hold as owner.[141] In the early classical period, there appear to have been suggestions that less was required, for example that it was enough for the transferee to attach his or her seal to goods being transferred.[142] However, this view was ultimately rejected, the position being instead that the purpose of the seal was to identify the goods being transferred rather than to effect delivery.[143] There is evidence that, in the case of gifts, a weaker delivery requirement was imposed, recognising delivery of documents as a symbolic equivalent of delivery of the property itself.[144]

---

[135] It appears likely in Roman law that any attempt by me to recover the property would be met by an *exceptio doli*, considered above. Nonetheless, in a causal system that leaves the awkward situation that I remain owner but cannot recover the property, and leaves the third party acquirer in an uncertain position.
[136] On unjustified enrichment, see pp. 429–34.
[137] C.2.3.20 (AD 290).
[138] See pp. 239–43.
[139] See *e.g.* D.41.1.20.2.
[140] See pp. 172–86.
[141] Although, as we saw at pp. 176–8, it was possible to possess on a different basis from that of ownership, holding with this intention is required when it is intended to acquire ownership. For a general discussion of the relationship between delivery and possession, see C Anderson, *Possession of Corporeal Moveables* (Edinburgh Legal Education Trust 2015) paras 1-45 – 1-57.
[142] D.18.6.15.1; D.18.6.1.2.
[143] D.18.6.1.2.
[144] C.8.53.1 (AD 210).

(b) Direct Delivery

The simplest method of making delivery of property is simply by physically handing the property over to the transferee. When the transferee takes possession, he or she will become owner (assuming that there is no other difficulty, such as a lack of title on the transferor's part). Delivery should not be understood so narrowly as to require a direct physical handing over, however. As mentioned already, delivery means a transfer of possession, and the essence of possession is physical control coupled with the requisite intention. Assuming that the mental element of possession is present, what delivery requires is that the transferee be given control of the property. This can be done, for example, by the transferor placing the thing in the transferee's presence,[145] the transferor leaving the thing at the transferee's house,[146] or the transferee placing a guard on the thing.[147]

Another way in which control can be given is by handing over the key to the place where goods are kept. This is known as *traditio clavium* (delivery of keys).[148] The jurist Papinian tells us that the key had to be handed over at the store itself.[149] It is sometimes said that the reason for this is that the delivery of a key elsewhere than at the store itself would be a merely symbolic act. However, Gordon gives a more nuanced view, which seems more consistent with the idea of delivery as a transfer of control:

> If the handing over of the keys took place in such circumstances that there was no real control it would still be possible to deny it efficacy. On the other hand, if the principle of acquisition of possession is control of the thing it is probably too narrow to limit the efficacy of a transfer of keys to the case where the delivery takes place at the store.[150]

(c) Traditio Longa Manu

Traditio longa manu (long hand delivery, or delivery by pointing out) was used particularly for large, heavy items, which could not easily be carried off.[151] This was done, in effect, by declaring in the presence of the thing that the transferor was giving up possession to the transferee. More difficult to justify, but nonetheless accepted, was the idea of a transfer of possession of land by pointing out its boundaries from a tower on neighbouring land, without the transferee even setting foot on the land.[152]

(d) Delivery by Permission to Take Possession

Although to talk of property being delivered implies an active handing over of possession to the transferee, this was not quite the position. More accurately, what was required was that the transferee take possession with the consent of

---

[145] D.46.3.79. This could also be classed as *traditio longa manu*, on which see below.
[146] D.41.2.18.2.
[147] D.41.2.51.
[148] J.2.1.45; D.41.1.9.6; D.41.2.1.21.
[149] D.18.1.74.
[150] W M Gordon, *Studies in the Transfer of Property by Traditio* (University of Aberdeen 1970) 81.
[151] D.41.2.1.21.
[152] D.41.2.18.2.

the transferor. For example, a politician throwing coins to a crowd of voters[153] does not know who is going to pick up each coin. He intends ownership to go to the first to pick each up, and this is what happens.[154] This situation is known as *traditio incertae personae* (delivery to an uncertain person). Another example, given by Ulpian, is a case where one person is given permission to take stone from another's ground. Here, too, the transferee becomes owner by his or her own act, with the transferor's permission.[155]

(d) Traditio Brevi Manu
Suppose that the property to be transferred is already in the physical custody of the transferee. Perhaps the owner of land has agreed to sell it to the tenant, or the owner of goods on hire has agreed to sell them to the hirer. It would seem unreasonable to require the tenant or hirer in these cases to hand the property back so that it can be delivered to them, and that was not in fact required. Delivery would instead be deemed to occur when the parties agreed on that. Gaius and Justinian both present this as a case of transfer by intention.[156] For Scots law, too, Erskine considers this to be a purely fictional delivery.[157] However, given that delivery is a giving of possession, perhaps the better view is to say that this is a case where the mental element of possession is acquired later than the physical element. The physical element is already satisfied when (in the case of a hire) the property is taken on hire. The mental element comes into existence later, when the sale takes place. Mental and physical elements then coinciding, the transferee acquires possession and delivery takes place.

(e) Constitutum Possessorium
Suppose that I am owner of an item of property, say a carriage. To raise some money, I enter into an agreement with you whereby I will sell the carriage to you, and you will then hire it back to me. I will remain in physical custody of the carriage throughout.[158] Is there effective delivery here? On one hand, it would seem just as unreasonable here as in *traditio brevi manu* (above) for the property to be handed over to you only then to be immediately handed back. As we saw in Chapter 10,[159] it is possible to possess through another, so you can possess the carriage even though it remains in my hands. On the other hand, though, if this becomes effectively transfer by agreement, that threatens to undermine the delivery requirement altogether. Indeed, the name given to this form of delivery (*constitutum possessorium*), translates as 'possessory agreement'.[160]

---

[153] A common enough occurrence in Roman politics; less so nowadays. A modern example might be a pantomime performer throwing sweets into the audience.
[154] J.2.1.46; D.41.1.9.7.
[155] D.39.5.6.
[156] J.2.1.44; D.41.1.9.5.
[157] Erskine, *Institute* 2.1.19.
[158] These are, in their essentials, the facts of *Eadie v Young* (1815) Hume 705.
[159] See pp. 175–6.
[160] Modern systems requiring delivery have also been faced with this difficulty. One solution, found in Germany, is to accept that delivery may be made by simple agreement by the transferor to hold for the transferee. See *Bürgerliches Gesetzbuch*, s. 930. See also DCFR 4475–90.

There are also theoretical arguments against its recognition. While it is quite possible to possess property through someone else, as we saw in Chapter 10 the idea of *acquiring* possession through another's acts is more problematic.[161] The jurist Celsus points to another objection, if only to reject it: 'What I possess in my own name, I can possess in the name of another: nor do I thereby change the basis of my possession, but rather I cease to possess and make the other possessor through my agency.'[162] The reference to 'the basis of my possession' relates to the rule that a person possessing on one basis cannot change to possessing on another basis.[163] Because of these concerns, there is some doubt as to whether *constitutum possessorium* was accepted in classical law.[164] It was, though, certainly accepted in post-classical law.[165] This often involved the transferor reserving a purely fictitious, short-term usufruct,[166] as a means of circumventing the delivery requirement.[167]

(f) Traditio in Scots Law

Scots law has been greatly influenced by Roman law in this area,[168] at least as far as moveable property is concerned. The development of the law regarding transfer of ownership of land was strongly influenced from the Middle Ages onwards by the (non-Roman) feudal law, which has tended to make the relationship with Roman law more complex.[169] Even in moveables, the Roman-influenced rules are now largely restricted to transfers other than by sale.[170] In other transfers of corporeal moveable property, however, the delivery requirement applies.[171] Indeed, if anything, the requirement for the giving of control to the transferee has been more strictly applied in Scotland. For instance, there is little trace of any acceptance of delivery by purely symbolical means,[172] and there is no sign in Scots law a person could be given possession of land simply by having its boundaries pointed out from a distance.

Greatest difficulty has perhaps been caused by *constitutum possessorium* as a method of making delivery. On one view, the acceptance of *constitutum possessorium* should

---

[161] See pp. 175–6.
[162] D.41.2.18pr.
[163] See pp. 179–80.
[164] Indeed, the name *constitutum possessorium* is itself medieval rather than Roman. For discussion of this form of delivery, see W M Gordon, *Studies in the Transfer of Property by Traditio* (University of Aberdeen 1970) chapter 2.
[165] C.8.53.28 (AD 417); C.8.53.35.5 (AD 530).
[166] On usufruct, see Chapter 14.
[167] W M Gordon, *Studies in the Transfer of Property by Traditio* (University of Aberdeen 1970) 76–8.
[168] D L Carey Miller, 'Derivative Acquisition of Moveables' in Evans-Jones, *Civil Law Tradition*; D L Carey Miller, 'Systems of Property: Grotius and Stair' in D L Carey Miller and D W Meyers eds, *Comparative and Historical Essays in Scots Law: A Tribute to Professor Sir Thomas Smith QC* (Butterworth 1992).
[169] D L Carey Miller, 'Transfer of Ownership' in *History of Private Law in Scotland, vol I*. However, insofar as transfer of ownership is governed by general principles, these apply equally to land. Thus, for example, the *nemo dat* rule, discussed above, applies both to moveables and to land.
[170] Sale of Goods Act 1893, now Sale of Goods Act 1979.
[171] See C Anderson, *Property: A Guide to Scots Law* (W Green 2016) paras 5-08 – 5-16.
[172] C Anderson, *Possession of Corporeal Moveables* (Edinburgh Legal Education Trust 2015) chapter 6.

have been easier in Scots law, which has no difficulty with the idea of acquiring possession through another's acts. There is indeed authority justifying the position that *constitutum possessorium* has been received in Scots law, at least where the transferor's continued holding is on some proper, new legal basis. In *Orr's Trustee v Tullis*,[173] the tenant of a printing office entered into an agreement whereby he sold his printing machinery to his landlord. The landlord then granted a new lease to him, including hire of the machinery. The tenant retained physical custody of the machinery throughout. It was held that the machinery had been validly delivered to the landlord. Referring to Roman law and to *ius commune*[174] writers, the Lord Justice-Clerk said:[175]

> it is not correct to say . . . that some ostensible corporeal act – some change in the actual local situation or custody of moveables sold, is necessary to pass the property. That is only true when possession has not been attained by the purchaser. It is manifestly not true when possession has been attained. The simplest illustration of this is the case in which the thing sold is at the time of the sale in the possession of the purchaser. If a man hire a horse or carriage, and purchase it while his contract of hire is current, the property has passed; for no delivery could make the possession more complete than it was before. But as possession may be acquired and held through another just as effectually as by the owner himself, so, when the subject of the sale is in the hands of a third party who holds for the buyer, the property is as effectually transferred as if the buyer personally had possession.

The same rule has been followed more recently in *Milligan v Ross*.[176] On the other hand, where questions of delivery have been raised in cases in which the Sale of Goods Acts have been engaged, *constitutum possessorium* has been overlooked.[177]

Scots law does recognise one other form of delivery. This applies where goods to be delivered are in the hands of an independent third party. Delivery is made by giving notice of the transfer to the third party with custody of the goods.[178] By contrast with other forms of delivery, this does not appear to be derived from Roman law.

---

[173] (1870) 8 M 936. See also *Eadie v Young* (1815) Hume 705; D Hume, *Baron David Hume's Lectures, 1786–1822*, vol III (G C H Paton ed, Stair Society vol 15, 1952) 251–2. These all date to before the Sale of Goods Act 1893, so delivery was required even in a sale.

[174] See Chapter 4. The *ius commune* was the common legal tradition of Europe, to a great extent based on Roman law, that arose in the medieval period.

[175] (1870) 8 M 936, 945–6.

[176] 1994 SCLR 430.

[177] See *e.g Scottish Transit Trust Ltd v Scottish Land Cultivators Ltd* 1955 SC 254.

[178] For a full account of this form of delivery, see C Anderson, 'Delivery of Goods in the Custody of a Third Party: Operation and Basis' (2015) 19 Edin LR 165; C Anderson, 'Delivery of Goods in the Custody of a Third Party: The Role of the Custodier' (2017) 21 Edin LR 143.

Chapter Summary

We have seen, then, that ownership could be acquired in Roman law in various ways, depending on the circumstances. Our focus in this chapter has been on the acquisition of ownership from a previous owner, this being known as derivative acquisition. We saw that, until Justinian, for property falling into the category of *res mancipi* (which included Italic land, slaves and certain animals) special, formal modes of transfer were required. The consequences of this were avoided, however, by the development of the concept of bonitary ownership, in which an acquirer was protected as if owner.

For other kinds of property, transfer was by delivery, meaning a transfer of possession from transferor to transferee. When Justinian abolished the category of *res mancipi*, this became the mode of transfer for all property.

Further Reading

G.2.1–64

J.2.1.40–8

D.41.1–2

C.7.25

W W Buckland, *A Text-Book of Roman Law from Augustus to Justinian* 3rd edn, revd P Stein (Cambridge University Press 1963) 228–41

H Hausmaninger and R Gamauf, *A Casebook on Roman Property Law* (G A Sheets trans, Oxford University Press 2012) 111–23

E Metzger ed, *A Companion to Justinian's Institutes* (Duckworth 1998) 42–5, 49–55

J A C Thomas, *Textbook of Roman Law* (North-Holland 1976) 151–7, 179–83

A Watson, *The Law of Property in the Later Roman Republic* (Oxford University Press 1968) 1–21, 61–2

CHAPTER TWELVE

Acquisition of Ownership: Original Acquisition

A. Introduction

Original acquisition is the acquisition of ownership without acquiring it from a previous owner. The acquirer acquires a new right in the property, rather than acquiring any previous owner's right.[1] Normally it is carried out by the acquirer's own act. Most of the original modes of acquisition were natural law modes,[2] and so were open to non-citizens. Much of the law here has been accepted in Scots law, although with modifications. There was also one important civil law mode of original acquisition, *usucapio*, which was not received in Scots law.

It should be said at the outset that the natural law modes of original acquisition are all closely related to each other, and the texts do not always clearly distinguish between them. Indeed, the very terminology used to identify them is largely non-Roman, being instead medieval. Four modes in particular cause difficulty:

- accession, the attachment of two things in circumstances where one can be described as accessory to the other;
- *specificatio*, where materials are used to create a new thing;
- *commixtio*, where two or more things are mixed together, in circumstances where they can be separated;
- *confusio*, where two or more things are mixed together, in circumstances where they cannot be separated.

This chapter will distinguish between these, but the reader should be aware that a Roman lawyer would be unlikely to recognise such a clear-cut distinction.[3]

---

[1] For interesting discussion of the effect of original acquisition on subordinate real rights (*i.e.* real rights other than ownership), see G Pienaar, 'The Effect of the Original Acquisition of Ownership of Immovable Property on Existing Limited Real Rights' (2015) 18 Potchefstroom Electronic LJ 1480. This article focuses on South African law, but draws on Roman and *ius commune* ideas.

[2] As we saw at p. 194, natural law modes of acquisition were those open to all, while civil law modes of acquisition were only open to Roman citizens.

[3] For example, A Plisecka, '*Accessio* and *Specificatio* Reconsidered' (2006) 74 TvR 45 argues that accession and *specificatio* were not in Roman law autonomous modes of acquisition of ownership. The difficulty has also had some effect on Scots treatments of the area. For example, the Scots institutional writer Erskine says (at *Institute* 2.1.16) that *specificatio* can be considered to be a form of accession. Similarly, at *Institute* 2.1.17 he says that *commixtio* and *confusio* 'frequently fall under the description of' *specificatio*.

We will begin, though, by considering *occupatio*, the acquisition of ownerless things by taking possession of them.

B. Occupatio

(1) Scope

Occupatio is a natural law mode of acquisition, and involves a person acquiring ownership of a thing by taking possession of it. It was only available in limited circumstances. In general terms, *occupatio* was concerned with the acquisition of property that was ownerless. The clearest case of this would be property that had never been owned. This category consisted mostly of wild animals in their natural state, although the acquisition of stones and gems found on the seashore is also given as an example.[4] Furthermore, it was possible for ownership to be lost, and for property to become ownerless again. In addition, as an exception to the general position that *occupatio* was restricted to ownerless property, enemy property was open to acquisition by *occupatio*. Before looking in more detail at how *occupatio* worked, it is necessary to say a bit more about three categories of property to which it applied: abandoned property, enemy property and wild animals.

(a) Abandoned Property

Ownership of property could be given up by abandonment, the property then being open to acquisition by another person. It appears that there was some debate as to whether the property became ownerless immediately on abandonment, or whether the person abandoning only lost ownership when the property was found and acquired by someone else. The jurists of the Sabinian school favoured the former view, those of the Proculian school the latter, and Paul tells us that the Sabinian view prevailed in this case.[5]

Acquisition was not possible unless the property was actually abandoned with an intention of giving up ownership. Accordingly, property salvaged from the sea was not acquired by the finder unless and until it was treated as abandoned by the owner.[6] Equally, the acquirer had to believe the property to be abandoned. Accordingly, a finder of abandoned property who believed it to be merely lost did not acquire ownership.[7]

We saw in Chapter 11 that, in classical law, there was a special category of property called *res mancipi*.[8] This category included land, slaves and certain animals, and for these things special, formal methods of transfer were required. There is

---

[4] J.2.1.18.
[5] D.41.7.2.1. The Proculian view essentially assimilates this case to *traditio incertae personae*, considered at p. 212. See though D Daube, 'Derelictio, Occupatio and Traditio: Romans and Rabbis' (1961) 77 LQR 382. He criticises here the *traditio incertae personae* view as 'artificial'. For Roman law, the difference may not matter very much, as the finder acquires either way. For Scots law, the distinction is essential for, as we shall see, abandoned property in Scots law does not become ownerless but instead falls to the Crown. A person in Scotland 'abandoning' a thing to be acquired by the first taker must therefore intend a *traditio incertae personae*.
[6] D.41.1.58.
[7] D.41.7.2pr.
[8] See pp. 198–9.

some doubt as to whether *occupatio* could be used to acquire ownership of an abandoned *res mancipi*.[9] On the one hand, to deny such acquisition would potentially lead to *res mancipi* not falling into ownership again, which would not be a welcome consequence.[10] On the other hand, natural law modes of acquisition were not normally available for acquisition of *res mancipi*. Moreover, to allow it in this case would allow the requirement for special methods of transfer for *res mancipi* to be circumvented by having the transferor simply abandon the property, with the transferee then stepping in to acquire by *occupatio*.[11] The better view may therefore be that an acquirer of abandoned *res mancipi* got only bonitary ownership[12] until he or she had possessed long enough to fulfil the requirements of acquisition by *usucapio*.[13]

(b) Enemy Property

Property of an enemy of Rome, which was on Roman territory, could be treated as ownerless and acquired accordingly.[14] This, says Justinian, is the basis for the enslavement of war captives.[15] However, booty captured through military action would be acquired for the state rather than individual soldiers, and so would fall under the control of the general concerned.

(c) Wild Animals

The final category to consider here is that of wild animals. A wild animal might be ownerless either because it has never been owned or, as we shall see below, because it was once owned but has escaped. In both cases, the animal was treated in the same way for the purposes of *occupatio*.

We are concerned here specifically with wild animals. A distinction was made between wild animals (*ferae naturae*) and domestic animals (*mansuetae naturae*). This distinction was crucial, as only wild animals were normally ownerless, domestic animals being treated in the same way as other property.[16] The nature of the distinction, though, is not entirely clear. It is normally assumed that animals were classed as wild or domestic according to species[17] rather than according to the disposition of the individual animal.[18] Accordingly, a dog would be considered

---

[9] See pp. 198–9.
[10] Borkowski, *Textbook* para 7.2.2.3. On the other hand, the argument made there that there were other natural law ways in which *res mancipi* could be acquired is not necessarily convincing. The example given is one of accession, which operates because the accessory ceases to have any separate existence at all (see below). The case here is quite different.
[11] D.42.8.5 appears to treat such a manoeuvre as effective, albeit that it is penalised in the circumstances with which that text is concerned (collusive disposal by an insolvent person of his or her assets to defraud creditors).
[12] See pp. 201–2.
[13] *Usucapio* was a way of acquiring ownership by possessing the property for a period of time. See below.
[14] D.41.1.51.1.
[15] J.2.1.17. On this, see pp. 105–6.
[16] Although a domestic animal could be abandoned, and would be treated in the same way as other abandoned property.
[17] This does not necessarily correspond to species as a technical term of modern zoological classification.
[18] See though G McLeod, 'Wild and Tame Animals and Birds in Roman Law' in Birks, *New Perspectives*. See also T G Watkin, '*Occupatio* and the *Pastio Villatica*' (1990) 11 J Leg Hist 5 for discussion of the basis for the distinction.

domestic however fierce, and a bear would be considered wild however placid an individual was. Household animals and farm animals, such as dogs, horses, cattle and sheep, would certainly be considered domestic. Bees,[19] deer, peacocks and pigeons[20] were considered wild. Ducks and geese were considered to exist in both wild and domestic species.[21] It is not clear how hybrid offspring of wild and domestic parents were classified,[22] nor how domestic animals that had become feral were treated.

(2) Acquisition

Acquisition by *occupatio* was based on taking possession of the property.[23] Although this was a rule of general application in *occupatio*, it raises particular issues in the acquisition of wild animals, which will therefore be the focus of the rest of this section.

The owner of land could exclude anyone from hunting or fishing on his or her land, and potentially had a delictual remedy against anyone who did so.[24] However, this did not imply that the owner of the land had any right in the wild animals that happened to be on the land, and even someone hunting or fishing unlawfully became owner of what he or she caught.[25] This was true even if there was a fence around the land so that the animals could not escape, or in the case of fish in a lake, if there was insufficient restraint to deprive the animals or fish of their 'natural liberty'.[26] On the other hand, animals in a pen or fish in a pond were possessed.

There was some discussion of what level of control was required for acquisition of ownership of a wild animal by a hunter. A lengthy text giving an opinion of the jurist Proculus is of interest here:

> A wild boar fell into a trap which you had set for the purpose of hunting. When he was caught in it, I released him. I ask: am I to be seen as having stolen your boar? And supposing him to be yours, would he cease to be or remain your property, if having released him I set him free in a wood? And if he ceased to be yours, what action would you have against me? The answer was: let us consider whether the trap was set on a public or private place and, if it was set in a private place, whether the land was mine or another's and, if another's, whether it was with the permission of the person whose land it was or not that the trap was set. Moreover, let us consider whether the boar was so caught in the trap, that it could not escape or could only do so through a long struggle. Still I think that if the boar has come into my power, he becomes mine.[27]

[19] J.2.1.14.
[20] J.2.1.15.
[21] J.2.1.16.
[22] This often happens when closely related wild and domestic groups interact. The ability of Scottish wildcats to interbreed with domestic cats is a major current conservation concern.
[23] J.2.1.12.
[24] D.47.10.13.7. Of course, matters would be different if the person hunting or fishing could show some right to do so, such as a right under contract.
[25] J.2.1.12, 14.
[26] D.41.2.3.14.
[27] D.41.1.55.

The point here seems to be that the fundamental question is this: has the person who set the trap acquired control over the animal? The other factors mentioned are part of the background, and will assist in answering that question, but are not of themselves decisive. Thus, if I am a trespasser, it will be more difficult for me to show sufficient control over the animal caught in my trap, because I am likely to have to be more discreet in my movements in setting the trap and returning to check it. If, though, on the facts, I have in fact obtained control over the animal, it will be mine. In the same way, even if the animal might ultimately be able to escape the trap, if in fact it is currently caught, it is my property.

Suppose that I was in pursuit of a wild animal. Before I was able to catch it, you came onto the scene and were in fact first to lay hands upon the animal. Who became owner in this situation? This appears to have been the subject of some dispute. Some jurists, such as Trebatius,[28] thought that the first to pursue should acquire ownership. The view that prevailed, however, was that the first to make an actual capture of the animal acquired it, because when you are merely engaged in pursuit 'many things can happen to stop you capturing it'.[29]

(3) Maintenance and Loss of Ownership

The normal rule was that a person who lost property did not cease to be owner unless and until, as we have seen, he or she came to treat it as abandoned. There was, though, a special rule for wild animals.[30] Ownership of a wild animal was dependent on continued possession, so ownership was lost if the animal returned to its state of 'natural liberty'.[31] This did not necessarily mean that the animal had to be kept confined. Animals that had a 'habit of returning' were possessed as long as they retained that habit.[32] That was true both of creatures with a natural homing instinct (such as bees and pigeons) and of those that had been tamed sufficiently to have such a habit. Ownership was only lost when that habit was lost, as with swarming bees.[33] Even then, though, ownership of an escaping animal (whether or not one that had lost the habit of returning) was retained if the owner pursued, as long as the animal was in sight and was not difficult to pursue.[34]

(4) *Occupatio* in Modern Law

Occupatio in Scots law is of narrower scope than in Roman law: in Scots law, there is no rule allowing acquisition of enemy property. Abandoned property falls to the Crown rather than becoming ownerless,[35] and land cannot be ownerless

---

[28] D.41.1.5.1. We are not told the names of any of the others.
[29] J.2.1.13.
[30] Domestic animals, however, were subject to the normal rule.
[31] D.41.1.3.2.
[32] D.41.1.4.
[33] J.2.1.15.
[34] J.2.1.12, 14; D.41.1.5pr.
[35] See *e.g. Mackenzie v Maclean* 1981 SLT (Sh Ct) 40. See Scottish Law Commission, *Discussion Paper on Prescription and Title to Moveable Property* (SLC DP No 144, 2010) Part 9 for discussion of the rule and suggestions for reform.

at all.[36] In Scots law, therefore, *occupatio* is restricted to wild animals, and to other things that have never been owned.

However, within this more confined scope, much of the Roman law has been adopted in the Scots law of *occupatio*.[37] Directly relying on Roman authorities, Stair gives as correct for Scots law the position that even one who takes a wild animal unlawfully on another's land nonetheless acquires ownership of it.[38] The owner of the land has no right to a wild animal just because it happens to be on his or her land,[39] and so is restricted to (at most) a delictual remedy for the trespass.[40] Equally, and anomalously for Scots law, ownership of a wild animal is lost when it escapes beyond reasonable chance of recovery.[41]

The law of possession of wild animals more generally has also been strongly influenced by Roman law, and may for example be of considerable use if an issue arises concerning possession of an animal kept in a larger enclosure[42] or escape of a wild animal from captivity. One area where Scots law has departed from the Roman position, however, is where ownership is sought to be acquired by pursuit. Some modern systems follow the Roman position of requiring actual capture.[43] Scots law, by contrast, adheres in effect to the position we are told was taken by Trebatius, and holds that ownership may be acquired by the first to pursue with a reasonable chance of success.[44]

C. Accession

(1) Nature and Scope

Suppose that I buy some bricks to build a house. It turns out that the bricks actually belong to you. As we have seen,[45] I acquire no ownership of property that

---

[36] *Joint Liquidators of Scottish Coal v Scottish Environmental Protection Agency* 2014 SC 372, paras [97]–[109].
[37] For a general account, including historical and comparative discussion, see C Anderson, *Possession of Corporeal Moveables* (Edinburgh Legal Education Trust 2015) chapter 7.
[38] Stair, *Institutions* 2.1.33. For application of the principle, see *e.g. Scott v Everitt* (1853) 15 D 288; *Wilson v Dykes* (1872) 10 M 444.
[39] *Assessor for Argyll v Broadland Properties Ltd* 1973 SC 152.
[40] Stair, *Institutions* 2.1.33.
[41] Stair, *Institutions* 2.1.33.
[42] These issues were overlooked by the sheriff in *Valentine v Kennedy* 1985 SCCR 89. For discussion, see Rt Hon Lord Rodger of Earlsferry, 'Stealing Fish' in R F Hunter ed, *Justice and Crime: Essays in Honour of The Right Honourable The Lord Emslie, MBE, PC, LLD, FRSE* (T & T Clark 1993); C G van der Merwe and D Bain, 'The Fish that Got Away: Some Reflections on Valentine v Kennedy' (2008) 12 Edin LR 418; C Anderson, 'Ownership of Fish' 2020 SLT (News) 229.
[43] As an example, for the position in South Africa see *R v Mafohla* 1958 (2) SA 373, relying on J.2.1.13–14, D.41.1.5 and the Roman-Dutch writers Voet and Grotius.
[44] *Sutter v Aberdeen Arctic Co* (1861) 23 D 465. Scots law in this area has been complicated by the development, under English influence, of the 'fast and loose' rule for acquisition of whales. On this rule, by which the whale was only owned as long as it had a harpoon in it that was attached by cable to a whaling boat, see R C Deal, 'Fast-Fish, Loose-Fish: How Whalemen, Lawyers, and Judges Created the British Property Law of Whaling' (2010) 37 Ecology LQ 199, though this article should be read alongside a specifically Scots account for points of detail and terminology. The reference in the title to 'British' law is a warning sign. *Sutter* was reversed in the House of Lords ((1862) 4 Macq 355) on the ground that, in the circumstances, the fast and loose rule applied. For criticism of the House of Lords decision, see C Anderson, *Possession of Corporeal Moveables* (Edinburgh Legal Education Trust 2015) paras 7-116 – 7-119, and see also *Stove v Colvin* (1831) 9 S 633, in which the traditional Scots rule was applied.
[45] See pp. 202–3.

I buy from a non-owner. However, what if I have already built the house before you appear to reclaim the bricks? We are now no longer concerned simply with a question of ownership of the bricks. They are now attached to my land, and cannot readily be separated. Similar issues arise if you build on land that belongs to me. Again, suppose that a jeweller attaches a diamond to a ring. It turns out that the diamond is stolen property. It may be that the diamond cannot readily be separated from the ring.

In these situations, the law must take account of the attachment between the two items. This is especially so when the two are attached such that they cannot be readily separated, or cannot be separated without causing damage to one or other item. The doctrine of accession is relevant here. According to this doctrine, when two items of property are joined together such that they cease to have separate identities, and one can be said to be an accessory of the other, the identity of one is subsumed into the other. One of these is known as the principal and the other as the accessory. The accessory is said to 'accede' to the principal, and in this process the identity of the accessory is lost within that of the principal. The two become a single item of property. There are two main consequences to this. First, the owner of the accessory loses ownership. The person who owned the principal before the attachment took place acquires ownership of the accessory as well. Second, anyone who enters into a contract to acquire the principal is entitled to get the accessory as well.[46] As the accessory is considered in law to be part of the principal,[47] someone who contracts to get the principal contracts to get the accessory as well.[48]

Accession can operate between land and moveables, between land and land, or between moveables and moveables. As each raises special issues, they will be considered separately.

(2) Moveables to Land
(a) Requirements
It is clear that things constructed on the land acceded to the land and became part of it. The principle was *superficies solo cedit* (a structure becomes part of the land).[49] If the structure was made from materials belonging to someone else, the building nonetheless became the property of the landowner:[50] the land was always the principal, the structure the accessory. The same was true of plants, such as trees,

---

[46] In modern law, this is where issues with accession probably most often arise. A person buys a house or an area of land and, on taking possession, finds that the seller has removed things that were there when the contract was concluded. If no specific provision is made in the contract, the buyer's entitlement to get these things depends on whether they were part of the land or building by accession when the contract was agreed. See *e.g. Cochrane v Stevenson* (1891) 18 R 1208; *Christie v Smith's Executrix* 1949 SC 572.

[47] Although, in fact, the category of 'accessories' that a buyer is entitled to is somewhat broader. See p. 359.

[48] Unless, of course, the contract expressly excludes the accessory. In that case, the transferor would be quite entitled to remove the accessory before the sale was completed.

[49] G.2.73; Stair, *Institutions* 2.1.40.

[50] See though J.2.1.29.

grass or crops.⁵¹ This is the case even if the attachment of the structure or plant is carried out in bad faith,⁵² and regardless of the intentions of the parties: accession operated automatically.

Plants acceded when they took root in the land, and so belonged to the owner of the land in which they took root.⁵³ For this reason, ownership of a plant on the boundary between two properties was determined by the location of the roots.⁵⁴ When it comes to structures, however, the texts have little to say about how much attachment was required. It would be reasonable to think it relevant to consider whether the structure could be removed without too much effort or without damage, but the existence in certain circumstances of a *ius tollendi* (a right to remove the accessory) suggests that that cannot have been conclusive. Suppose that I was the tenant of your property, and I built on it. It is one thing to say that a permanent structure, such as a house, accedes and becomes yours. After all, it must be anticipated that the house will outlast the lease, and so there is no great injustice in it becoming yours. However, what if I build a temporary wooden shelter, resting on its own weight rather than with proper foundations? Different modern legal systems approach the problem in different ways.⁵⁵ Scots law takes into account, not just the degree of physical attachment, but also the degree of 'functional subordination' and permanence.⁵⁶ Where the degree of attachment is less than total, an item that is functionally subordinate to the land⁵⁷ and/or which shows a degree of permanence⁵⁸ may nonetheless have acceded.⁵⁹

As accession occurred automatically, without reference to the parties' intentions, it was not relevant what the parties' state of mind was or whether the owner of either accessory or principal agreed to the attachment. A person who lost ownership, however, might have a remedy. The precise situation depended on whether the owner of the principal or of the accessory was in possession, and also on whether the possessor was in good faith.

---

[51] G.2.74–5; J.2.1.31–2. On development of law regarding accession of plants, see D Daube, 'Implantatio and Satio' 1958 AJ 181. In Scots law, the same rules are applied, except in the case of 'industrial growing crops'. These are crops, such as corn, requiring annual seed and labour. They do not accede in Scots law, and remain moveable (Stair, *Institutions* 2.1.34; *Boskabelle v Laird* 2006 SLT 1079). Accordingly, if the land is sold, ownership of the crops is not automatically acquired with it.

[52] See *e.g.* D.41.1.7.13. The example given here involves a tree, but the point is a general one. See also Stair, *Institutions* 2.1.38, where Roman law is used as authority for this rule.

[53] G.2.74–5; J.2.1.31–2; D.41.1.7.13.

[54] Scots law follows a different rule in the case of trees, ownership of which is determined by the location of the trunk: *Hetherington v Galt* (1905) 7 F 706.

[55] For a comparative overview of accession in several countries, including Scotland, see L P W van Vliet, 'Accession of Movables to Land' (2002) 6 Edin LR 67 and 199.

[56] *Stair Memorial Encyclopaedia*, vol 18 paras 571 and 578–84.

[57] An item will be functionally subordinate to the land if it is attached for the better enjoyment of the land or of a structure that has acceded to it. See *e.g. Fife Assessor v Hodgson* 1966 SC 30.

[58] See *e.g. Howie's Trs v McLay* (1902) 5 F 214; *Dowall v Milne* (1874) 1 R 1180.

[59] See *e.g. Christie v Smith's Executrix* 1949 SC 572.

(b) Remedies

If a person possessing someone else's land in good faith built on it,[60] the owner could not recover the land without compensating the possessor.[61] Any attempt to vindicate[62] the land could be defeated by the *exceptio doli*, the defence of deceit.[63] The same was true also where a possessor had sown crops in good faith on another's land.[64] This defence barred recovery of the property by the owner until the good faith possessor was compensated for the improvements.[65] As an alternative, the good faith possessor was given the right to remove any improvements made, as long as the land was not thereby made worse than it would have been if there had been no building in the first place.[66] Malicious removal was not allowed, such as the removal of plaster from walls or the defacement of pictures. This implied *ius tollendi*, or right of removal, does not exist in Scots law, on the basis that the accessory is the property of the owner of the principal,[67] although it does exist in some other systems that have been influenced by Roman law in this area.[68]

Where the owner of land built on the land in good faith with another's materials, he or she became owner of the building. Oddly, however, the view was taken that the owner of the materials making up the building continued to own them, even though the owner of the land owned the building as a whole.[69] The ownership of the building materials was in a sense, however, in suspense as long as the building remained standing. As long as the building stood, the owner of the materials could not vindicate them, and the *actio ad exhibendum*[70] was not

---

[60] It was not enough that possession was taken in good faith, if the possessor was in bad faith by the time the building work was carried out: D.6.1.37.

[61] This included payment for the costs of workers' wages as well as the value of building materials: D.41.1.7.12. Celsus indicates that the amount to be paid was calculated as being the increased value of the land, capped at the cost of building: D.6.1.38.

[62] Vindication was the standard procedure for recovering property on the basis of ownership.

[63] G.2.76; J.2.1.30. On the *exceptio doli*, see p. 423.

[64] J.2.1.32; D.41.1.9pr.

[65] D.6.1.48. The position is similar in modern law, though in modern law the good faith possessor is conceived of as having a freestanding right to compensation, rather than simply a defence to a claim for recovery of the property. See C Anderson, *Property: A Guide to Scots Law* (W Green 2016) para 3–49. This is the case even though Erskine *Institute* 3.1.11 expressly founds the right to recompense for improvements on D.41.1.7.12. It does appear though that the good faith improver still has the right to retain the property until paid for the value of the improvement: *Binning v Brotherstones* (1676) Mor 13401. By contrast, in *Beattie v Lord Napier* (1831) 9 S 639, the possessor was not allowed to retain the property until payment was made. Not having taken the necessary steps to complete title, the possessor could not be held to be in good faith.

[66] D.6.1.38. Celsus tells us here that this decision was made in the interests of the owner rather than of the good faith improver, so that the owner would not be impoverished by paying for unwanted improvements.

[67] See *Stair Memorial Encyclopaedia*, vol 18 para 596, although the question was viewed as an open one in *Barbour v Halliday* (1840) 2 D 1279, 1284 and *Duke of Hamilton v Johnston* (1877) 14 SLR 298, 299. A tenant has an implied right to remove trade fixtures, a category of uncertain scope: *Brand's Trs v Brand's Trs* (1876) 3 R (HL) 16. For discussion of that decision, see K G C Reid, 'The Lord Chancellor's Fixtures: Brand's Trs v Brand's Trs Re-examined' (1983) 28 JLSS 49. A person may also have a right under contract to remove accessories and acquire ownership on doing so. An example would be a tenant of an orchard.

[68] See *e.g*, on South African law, D L Carey Miller, 'A Mala Fide Possessor's Improvements: Are the Rights to Compensation and Retention Coextensive?' (1982) 102 SALJ 697; D P Visser, 'The Rights of Possessors and Occupiers to Remove Improvements' 1994 Annual Survey of South African Law 223.

[69] J.2.1.29.

[70] This was a procedure for compelling property to be produced for the purposes of litigation. See p. 190.

available.[71] Instead, the owner of the materials had an action for twice their value, the *actio de tigno iniuncto*.[72] If the building subsequently collapsed or was demolished, and the owner of the materials had not already claimed under the *actio de tigno iniuncto*, the ownership of the materials revived.[73] The owner of the materials could recover them at that point.[74]

If a person in bad faith built on someone else's land, he or she was treated as making a gift to the owner of the land, and so could not recover the building materials even if the building collapsed.[75]

If the owner of land knowingly built on it with someone else's materials, he or she would be liable for theft.[76] In addition, Ulpian implies that the *actio ad exhibendum* could be brought to compel the wrongfully used building materials to be produced.[77]

(3) **Land to Land**

A form of accession also operated by means of the natural action of rivers. It is in the nature of rivers that their course does not stay constant. Instead, the course of a river tends to shift over time, as one bank is worn away and the other is built up as the river deposits material on it. A river's course may also change more quickly, for example when flooding occurs.

Roman law made a distinction between two processes. The gradual process of a bank being built up by the deposit of material, or diminished by material being washed away, was known as alluvion. The case where material is torn away from one bank by force and deposited elsewhere was known as avulsion.

Alluvion affected ownership. The owner of the bank that was built up acquired ownership of the increase. The owner of the bank that was worn away ceased to be owner of what was lost. This was justified on the basis that it was not possible to distinguish what had been gradually added from what was there before.[78] This approach has been adopted in Scots law. Says Erskine: 'what is added to a field by an imperceptible accretion cannot be distinguished from the ground itself to which it was joined, in order to its being restored to the former proprietor'.[79]

---

[71] D.6.1.23.6.
[72] We are told that this was created by the Twelve Tables. Although the wording of the action referred to beams specifically, it was extended to apply to building materials generally: J.2.1.29; D.41.1.7.10.
[73] Paul tells us (D.41.1.26.1) that the same did not apply where a tree belonging to one person took root in another's land, on the basis that the tree might have been altered by taking nourishment from another's soil. In modern law, consistently with the general exclusion of the *ius tollendi*, the rights of the former owner of the accessory do not as a matter of principle revive on separation.
[74] D.6.1.23.6–7; D.41.1.7.10–11, even if the possessor of the land had completed the period for *usucapio*. On *usucapio*, see below.
[75] J.2.1.30; D.41.1.7.12. Equally in Scots law the bad faith improver has no right to be compensated for the improvements: *Barbour v Halliday* (1840) 2 D 1279.
[76] See pp. 417–22.
[77] D.6.1.23.6.
[78] D.41.1.7.1. For discussion of the meaning of alluvion, see A D E Lewis, 'Alluvio: The Meaning of Institutes II.1.20' in Stein and Lewis, *Studies in Justinian's Institutes*.
[79] Erskine, *Institute* 2.1.14. See also Stair, *Institutions* 2.1.35. It is possible for the owners to contract out of the operation of alluvion by registering an agreement to that effect in the Land Register: Land Registration etc (Scotland) Act 2012, s. 66.

This gradualness and difficulty of identification may, though, be better seen as a justification for the rule rather than a requirement for its operation: some of the Roman texts appear to allow more rapid change to affect ownership.[80] Oddly, the rules on alluvion only applied to rivers. They did not apply to other bodies of water, such as lakes.[81] This was the case even though the shores of lakes are subject to the same physical process.[82] It does not appear that Scots law makes any such distinction between rivers and other bodies of water.[83]

The same idea applied when a new island appeared in a river. This belonged in common to the owners of either bank if it appeared in the middle of the river; if to one side, it belonged to the owner on that side.[84] This is to be contrasted with the 'rare occurrence'[85] of a new island arising in the sea: this was ownerless and so open to acquisition by the first taker.[86]

By contrast, if through avulsion a part of your land was forcibly detached by a river, and came to rest on a bank belonging to me, I did not immediately acquire ownership. This only happened if, over time, the addition became incorporated into my land, as where trees on the additional land put roots into my land.[87] In the same way, flooding did not affect ownership. When the flood receded, the boundaries were the same as before.[88] This does not explain what happened if, when the flood receded, it was found to have altered the layout of the land. The answer perhaps lies in Justinian's observation that when the flood recedes, it will be found not to change the geography of the land.[89] It may then be that, if the geography is permanently altered by the flood, the legal boundaries are altered accordingly. Certainly, we see something very similar happening if a river abandons its original course and takes on a new one.[90] The position was that the new course became public[91] and ownership of the original river bed was divided between the owners of the former banks. A similar approach was taken in the modern Scots case of *Stirling v Bartlett*,[92] in which a serious flood deposited large amounts of material,

---

[80] See *e.g.* D.41.1.30.3.
[81] D.41.1.12pr.
[82] For an example, see D.18.1.69.
[83] See *Stair Memorial Encyclopaedia*, vol 18 para 594, where this is assumed.
[84] J.2.1.22; D.41.1.7.3.
[85] It is not, though, completely unknown. The best known modern example is the volcanic island of Surtsey, which appeared to the south of Iceland in 1963.
[86] D.41.1.7.3. The same would not be true in Scotland, where a new island would belong to the Crown. The case of Rockall provides an analogous example. Although this was not a new island, it was added to Scotland by the Island of Rockall Act 1972.
[87] D.41.1.7.2. For avulsion in Scots law, see Erskine, *Institute* 2.1.14 who does not, however, address the issue of whether land carried away by avulsion can over time become incorporated in the land to which it has become attached.
[88] J.2.1.24; D.41.1.7.6.
[89] J.2.1.24.
[90] J.2.1.23. If a river split, however, ownership was unaffected.
[91] On public property, see p. 195.
[92] 1993 SLT 763, relying among other sources on J.2.1.20. For discussion, see D L Carey Miller, 'Alluvio, Avulsio and Fluvial Boundaries' 1994 SLT (News) 75.

causing a river to divide into a number of channels. With the agreement of the owners on both sides, a new channel was dug within the area across which the river had moved over the twentieth century. Appealing to common sense and to the practical concern that it would be difficult otherwise to determine the boundary, the court held that this was a case of alluvion rather than avulsion. There seems to be a suggestion here that alluvion does not need to be a very slow process, and it is certainly held that it can result from human action.

There could be no question of compensation for what was, after all, a natural process. Equally, given that it would not normally be possible to determine whose property the deposited material came from in a case of alluvion, there could be no right of severance. Alluvion or avulsion could, however, result from human acts. In that case, a delictual remedy[93] or the *actio aquae pluviae arcendae*[94] might be available in appropriate circumstances.

(4) Moveables to Moveables

(a) Requirements

Accession could also happen between two or more moveable things. The texts identify various situations, such as *textura* (the weaving of thread into a garment), *ferruminatio* (welding), *plumbatura* (soldering), *scriptura* (writing) and *pictura* (painting). Accession by fruits, such as the young of animals, was a special case. These are all examples, though, of a general concept. Accession was certainly not restricted to these cases. It must be said before continuing, however, that these are default rules, applying where the attachment happens without any agreement between the parties. If the parties agreed to the attachment, the terms of their agreement would govern the outcome. An example might be if I commissioned an artist to decorate an item belonging to me or I engaged a jeweller to attach my diamond to a ring. Clearly, in both cases, the intention would be for me to become owner of the final product, even though the general rules on accession might imply a different result.

As with accession between moveables and land, it is unclear what degree of attachment was required. Ulpian makes a distinction between welding and soldering based on the degree of attachment, but he appears to be thinking more of the appropriate remedies than he is of the question of whether accession has operated in the first place.[95] For Scots law, Bell speaks of accession as operating 'where there can be no separation' between the two things.[96] This, though, goes well beyond what is required in Roman law. For example, thread can easily enough be picked out from the garment into which it has been sewn, but there is

---

[93] See Chapters 22–4.
[94] See p. 169.
[95] D.6.1.23.5.
[96] Bell, *Principles* s. 1298.

no doubt that the thread acceded to the garment.[97] It is not clear that Bell is even quite correct for Scots law, for it is almost always *possible*, even if it may be difficult, to separate two things that have been joined together. If Bell's formulation was to be read strictly, it would impose a severe limitation on the applicability of accession between moveable things. Perhaps it is to be taken to mean merely sufficient attachment to indicate permanence. Alternatively, it could mean that accession occurs when the two cannot readily be separated without damage to one or the other. This approach would be consistent with the South African case of *J L Cohen Motors SWA (Pty) Ltd v Alberts*,[98] in which tyres were held not to accede to the wheels of a truck.

(b) Identifying the Principal

More attention is given in the texts to the question of determining which of the objects is the principal and which is the accessory. This must be determined, because it was the owner of the principal who acquired ownership of the whole. Matters were most straightforward with accession of fruits. The fruit was always the accessory, and so the offspring of animals belonged to the owner of the mother.[99] The same was true of other produce of animals, such as honey produced by bees.[100] One consequence of this was that the fruits of ownerless animals could not be stolen.[101]

Matters were more difficult in other cases. No single, clear rule was applied. Sometimes it was said that the larger or more valuable item was the principal.[102] Neither was conclusive, however. For example, even gold thread, far exceeding the garment in value, acceded to the garment.[103] Another test involved considering which of the two items gave the whole its identity or its overall character.[104] Thus, for example, where an arm or leg belonging to one person was attached to another person's statue, or a base belonging to one person was attached to another person's bowl, the statue or the bowl was the principal.[105] We are also told that, in the case of a ship being built, the keel is the principal.[106]

A special rule existed for paintings. While writing acceded to the surface on which it was written,[107] the outcome was reversed where a picture was made with one person's paint and another's board.[108] Gaius criticises this rule as being based on reasoning that is 'hardly satisfactory'.[109] Ulpian denies that this is the

---

[97] J.2.1.26.
[98] 1985 (2) SA 427.
[99] D.41.1.2; D.6.1.5.2.
[100] D.41.1.5.3. Other examples would include milk or wool.
[101] For a modern application of this point, see the South African case *S v Mnomiya* 1970 (1) SA 66, relying on J.2.1.14.
[102] D.41.1.27.2.
[103] J.2.1.26.
[104] D.41.1.26pr.
[105] D.6.1.23.2.
[106] D.6.1.61. Compare *Simpson v Duncanson's Creditors* (1786) Mor 14204.
[107] G.2.77; J.2.1.33; D.10.4.3.14; D.41.1.9.1.
[108] D.41.1.9.2.
[109] G.2.78.

rule at all. He argues that the painting must be the accessory as it cannot exist on its own, separately from the surface it has been painted on.[110] Justinian, however, settled that the picture itself was the principal, on the basis that 'it would be ridiculous for a picture by Apelles or Parrhasius to accede to a board of very little value'.[111] This argument has often been seen as unconvincing. A picture by a lesser painter may well not be more valuable than the surface on which it has been painted. One possible explanation is that one copy of a piece of writing is largely interchangeable with another, in a way that a copy of a painting is not interchangeable with the original. Some manuscripts are themselves works of art, however, and the distinction is difficult to maintain in such cases. The Scots institutional writer Erskine suggests that the distinction 'appears rather to arise from the change which the board or canvas undergoes by the work and skill of the artist; for it becomes thereby a new species'.[112] On this approach, the case is rather one of *specificatio*, considered below.[113] This suggestion does not sit comfortably with the Roman texts, however, which consider the case of the painting alongside other cases that we would certainly classify as cases of accession. An alternative view is that the exception was originally concerned with the more limited category of painted images of deities and ancestors. On this view, the religious significance of these images justified special treatment, but the nature of the exception was forgotten by Gaius' time.[114]

For Scots law, Bell more sensibly takes the approach of ranking the different criteria for identification of the principal.[115] According to Bell, the matter is determined by first considering whether one of the items can exist separately: essentially Ulpian's view with regard to the position of paintings. The one that can exist separately is the principal, the one that cannot is the accessory. Failing that, the one that 'is taken to adorn or complete' the other is the accessory. On this basis, an arm or leg added to a statue or a base added to a bowl would be the accessory, and the statue or bowl the principal. A gem would accede to a ring to which it was attached. A similar approach was taken in the South African case of *Khan v Minister of Law and Order*,[116] in which a car was constructed using parts taken from different cars. It was held that the engine acceded to the body, most of which came from a stolen car. Accordingly, the owner of the engine lost ownership when it was attached to the car. The proper approach, said the court, was to consider which part 'gives the ultimate thing its character, form and function'.[117] This was the body of the car: the engine and other components had been added to it, not the other way around.

---

[110] D.6.1.23.3.
[111] J.2.1.34. Apelles and Parrhasius were great Greek painters of antiquity.
[112] Erskine, *Institute* 2.1.15.
[113] This is also suggested by S Wickenden, 'Graffiti Art: The Rights of Landlords, Tenants and Artists: Creative Foundation v Dreamland Leisure Ltd' (2016) 38 EIPR 119. This article contains an interesting discussion of the relationship between the traditional rules of accession and *specificatio* and modern rules on copyright. Roman law did not feature any notion of copyright.
[114] T G Watkin, '"Tabula Picta": Images and Icons' (1984) 50 SDHI 383.
[115] Bell, *Principles* s. 1298.
[116] 1991 (3) SA 439.
[117] 1991 (3) SA 439, 443.

If neither of these rules answers the question, then in Bell's account of Scots law 'bulk prevails; next value'. Unfortunately, there is no later authority confirming that Bell's statement of the law here is accurate. It will be noticed that there is no mention of any special rule for paintings. It is not thought that the Roman rule on paintings has been received in Scots law, even though Stair and Erskine both appear receptive to it.[118] Indeed, they are willing to extend the rule to writings, on the basis that:

> it were very unreasonable to think, that the evidents and securities of lands, or any manuscript, should be accessory to the paper or parchment whereon they were written, and which were only designed to bear and preserve the writ, and not to be carried therewith.[119]

This view has not, however, prevailed.

(c) Remedies

As with the accession of moveables to land, remedies varied according to who was in possession and according to whether the attachment was carried out in good faith or bad.

If the owner of the principal added an item in good faith that belonged to someone else, the accessory could not be vindicated[120] as long as the two objects remained stuck together. However, Ulpian tells us that the owner of the accessory could bring the *actio ad exhibendum*, the action for production,[121] to compel the owner of the principal to detach and produce the accessory. It would then be possible to vindicate it.[122] Ulpian goes on to tell us, though, that this does not apply where the accessory had been welded to the principal, as opposed to lesser methods of attachment such as soldering. In the case of welding, the accessory lost its separate identity altogether, and could not be vindicated even if it later broke off. Ulpian does tell us, though, that an *actio in factum* was available in these circumstances for compensation for the value of the accessory.[123]

Where a possessor of a principal belonging to someone else had in good faith added his own property, he or she of course lost ownership of the accessory. However, the owner could only recover the property on paying the value of the possessor's contribution.[124] As with the accession of moveables to land, this was a defence only (the *exceptio doli*). It gave no separate right to claim compensation. Accordingly, if the item ended up back in the owner's possession, the former possessor had no remedy.[125]

---

[118] Stair, *Institutions* 2.1.39; Erskine, *Institute* 2.1.15.
[119] Stair, *Institutions* 2.1.39.
[120] See pp. 189–90.
[121] See p. 190.
[122] D.6.1.23.5.
[123] It has been suggested that this may be a post-classical addition. See *e.g.* Book Review: *The Elements of Roman Law* (1945–7) 9 Cam LJ 128.
[124] G.2.77; J.2.1.33.
[125] Unless, in the circumstances, a possessory interdict was available. See pp. 187–9.

Where the union between the items was carried out in bad faith, the party doing so would be liable for theft.[126] The person who was responsible for taking the accessory would also be liable for theft and in addition under the form of action known as the *condictio*.[127]

In the case of a painting made with one person's paint on another person's board, it appears that whichever of the two was out of possession could recover the painting from the other on payment of the value of the other's contribution.[128]

(5) Accession in Modern Law

We have seen that there has been clear influence from Roman law on the Scots law of accession. This influence has, however, mostly been at the level of the basic principles involved rather than in issues of practical application, the Roman texts giving little attention to the types of issue that tend to arise in practice.[129] In addition, the rules on compensation in modern law are quite different. Issues of accession have arisen commonly enough in the courts that it is a fairly well-developed area in modern law.[130] Although, therefore, the modern Scots law is Roman in its ultimate derivation, it is perhaps not an area where there is likely to be major resort to the Roman sources (except, perhaps, with water-related issues, where there is otherwise a shortage of authority).[131] On the other hand, the common Roman roots may mean that comparison with the solutions found to novel problems in related legal systems is likely to be fruitful.

D. Specificatio

(1) Nature

Suppose I have grapes that in fact belong to you, and make them into wine. To which of us does 'natural reason' assign the end product?[132] After all, while you supplied the materials, I supplied skill, labour and time. This is the area with which *specificatio* (often anglicised as 'specification') is concerned. Who owns the new thing, or new *species*, the manufacturer or the one who supplied the materials?[133] We are concerned here only with the case where the manufacture happens without an agreement between the parties. Where the manufacturing process took place under an agreement between the parties, that agreement would determine the outcome.[134] For example, where

---

[126] G.2.78.
[127] J.2.1.26. For the *condictio*, see pp. 429–30.
[128] G.2.78; J.2.1.43; D.41.1.9.2. If the owner of the board claimed, the action would be an *actio utilis*. On *actiones utiles*, see p. 51.
[129] In modern practice, questions of accession of moveables to land arise far more often than questions of accession between moveables. The focus of the Roman texts is in the contrary direction. For example, the Roman texts give little guidance on the degree of attachment necessary for a moveable to accede to land.
[130] For a detailed account, see *Stair Memorial Encyclopaedia*, vol 18 paras 570–96.
[131] See though *Zahnrad Fabrik Passau GmbH v Terex* 1985 SC 364, in which reference was made to J.2.1.25–8.
[132] J.2.1.25.
[133] For an overview of the requirements for *specificatio*, see C van der Merwe, '*Nova Species*' (2004) 2 Roman Legal Tradition 96.
[134] For this point in modern law, see *Wylie & Lochhead v Mitchell* (1870) 8 M 552.

an employee manufactured something in the course of employment, the employer acquired ownership.[135] *Specificatio* is accepted in Scots law, though, as we shall see, with some uncertainties as to its precise application.[136]

(2) The Sabinian/Proculian Dispute

It is clear enough that, by *specificatio*, the form of the property is changed. What is not clear is what the property law consequence of that should be, if indeed there should be any consequences. It would be perfectly possible to say that the owner of the original materials would own the final product. On this view, if you take my grapes and turn them into wine, the wine belongs to me. This was the view adopted by one of the two classical schools of jurists,[137] the Sabinians. By contrast, the Proculians took the position that the manufacturer owned the product. It is thought that these two views were influenced by the theories of Greek philosophers on the relative significance of the substance and the form of property.[138] However, the Proculian view also addressed another, more practical consideration. As a matter of procedural law, if I wanted to recover property from you that I claimed to own, I had to identify that property.[139] In the case of wine made by you from my grapes, I would have to assert that the wine was mine. Yet, in that example, what I had owned was not the wine but the grapes. Thus, it has been said:

> The main reason why the Proculians awarded the final product to the maker was therefore the practical difficulty of the owner in identifying his or her materials.[140]

Again:

> In Roman law, change of identity was not simply a 'component of specification': it was the problem for which specification was the answer. If a person brought an action to recover an item of property, and the property had been substantially altered by some manufacturing process, the praetor would understandably hesitate to allow that person to prosecute the recovery of 'his' property ... [T]he Romans did not actively seek out identity problems to solve.[141]

A similar point has been made in a Scots case, *Oliver & Boyd v The Marr Typefounding Co Ltd*.[142] In this case, metal type had been stolen from the pursuers and was sold

---

[135] On the principle that a workman's employer acquired ownership of what the workman made, see B C Stoop, 'Non Solet Locatio Dominium Mutare: Some Remarks on *Specificatio* in Classical Roman Law' (1998) 66 TvR 3. The first words of the article's name mean 'hire does not usually change ownership'.
[136] On the reception of *specificatio* in Scotland, see D J Osler, '*Specificatio* in Scots Law' in Evans-Jones, *Civil Law Tradition*.
[137] On the schools of jurists, see p. 56.
[138] C van der Merwe, '*Nova Species*' (2004) 2 Roman Legal Tradition 96, 100–1.
[139] On the requirements for identification, see D.6.1.6.
[140] C van der Merwe, '*Nova Species*' (2004) 2 Roman Legal Tradition 96, 102.
[141] E Metzger, 'Acquisition of Living Things by Specification' (2004) 8 Edin LR 115, 117.
[142] (1901) 9 SLT 170.

to the defenders, who melted it down and made new type. The Lord Ordinary observed:

> Here the shape of the article was changed so much, and its identity so completely lost, that it is impossible to say what has now become of the metal which was stolen: some or all of it may have been sold; some or all of it may still be among the defenders' stock in the form of new type.[143]

(3) The Justinianic Law

There seems to have developed an intermediate view (*media sententia*) between the Sabinian and Proculian positions, depending on whether the new thing could be restored to its original materials.[144] If it could, then the owner of the materials owned the final product; otherwise, the manufacturer owned it. This position was modified where the manufacturer supplied part of the materials. In that case, the manufacturer owned the new thing regardless of whether it could be restored to its original materials.[145] This intermediate view was adopted by Justinian.[146]

The position in the Justinianic law was therefore that the manufacturer owned the new thing where either he or she had contributed to the materials or the new thing could not be restored to its original materials. This process destroyed the real right of the owner of the materials.[147] Thus, for example, if I made a pot from your ingot of metal, I did not become owner, as the pot could be turned back into an ingot.[148] By contrast, wine cannot be turned back into grapes, and olive oil cannot be put back into the olives. Mead[149] cannot be separated into wine and honey, nor can clothes made from another's wool be turned back into the wool. In all of these cases, the manufacturer became owner.[150] The same was true of a ship made from another's planks.[151]

There could sometimes be questions as to whether there had been sufficient change of form for *specificatio* to operate. If I dyed wool belonging to you, *specificatio* did not operate and I did not become owner, as 'there is no distinction between purple wool and wool that has fallen into the mud or mire and lost its original colour'.[152] The threshing of grain from ears of corn did not amount to *specificatio*

---

[143] (1901) 9 SLT 170, 171.
[144] D.41.1.7.7.
[145] J.2.1.25.
[146] J.2.1.24. It is not clear how this operated outside the question of ownership. For example, suppose that I left you a legacy of wool in a will, but then the wool was turned into clothes. Did this destroy the legacy, on the basis that the wool no longer existed? Both Ulpian (D.30.1.44.2) and Paul (D.32.1.88pr, 3) address this question. Unfortunately, though, they give different answers, although Ulpian does make the question ultimately depend on the testator's intentions.
[147] It also destroyed any other real right in the materials, such as a pledge: D.13.7.18.3. On pledge, see pp. 271–4.
[148] J.2.1.24. See also D.41.1.24.
[149] Actually a drink called *mulsum*, made from a mix of wine and honey. Mead in the modern sense is made using fermented honey.
[150] J.2.1.24.
[151] D.41.1.26pr.
[152] D.41.1.26.2.

either, as 'the grains have their perfect form while contained in the ears, so he who threshes the ears does not make something new, but only uncovers something that is already there'.[153] By the same argument, it would seem reasonable to suppose that *specificatio* did not operate in the squeezing of grapes to make grape juice. A text from Paul suggests the contrary, however.[154]

In Scots law, Stair laid out various alternatives, including the Roman rules, suggesting that the law could 'without injustice, follow any of these ways, reparation being always made to the party who loses his interest'.[155] There is no doubt, however, that Scots law has adopted Justinian's *media sententia*.[156] Thus, for instance, it has been held that *specificatio* operated when oil was used to make lard,[157] when wheat was turned into flour,[158] and when cloth was cut up and made into clothes.[159] On the other hand, *specificatio* was held not to operate when the front part of a stolen car was welded to the rear part of another car, as the two parts could be separated again.[160] Difficult questions can arise, as in Roman law. In *Armour v Thyssen Edelstahlwerke AG*,[161] it was suggested by the Lord Ordinary that *specificatio* might occur when coils of steel were flattened and cut into different lengths.[162] This suggestion was disapproved in the Inner House, however,[163] and the case was ultimately decided on different grounds.[164]

(4) The Role of Good Faith

Was the state of mind of the manufacturer relevant? What if the manufacturer knew that the materials belonged to someone else, or at least had reason to suspect that? In other words, was good faith a requirement for the operation of *specificatio*?

There is one text from Paul that suggests that good faith was required.[165] However, the dominant view is that good faith was not required. The reason for this is that, in allowing the manufacturer to acquire ownership, *specificatio* proceeded on the basis that the original materials no longer existed.[166] On this view, it could hardly make any difference that – say – the manufacturer of wine knew that the grapes it was made from belonged to someone else, as the grapes no

---

[153] D.41.1.7.7. This may seem to be inconsistent with the example of olive oil, which belongs to the manufacturer even though it already exists in the same form within the olives.
[154] D.10.4.12.3.
[155] Stair, *Institutions* 2.1.41.
[156] Erskine, *Institute* 2.1.16.
[157] *International Banking Corporation v Ferguson, Shaw & Sons* 1910 SC 182.
[158] *Black v Incorporation of Bakers, Glasgow* (1867) 6 M 136.
[159] *McLaren, Sons & Co Ltd v Mann, Byars & Co Ltd* (1935) 51 Sh Ct Rep 57.
[160] *McDonald v Provan (of Scotland Street) Limited* 1960 SLT 231.
[161] 1986 SLT 452 (Outer House).
[162] 1986 SLT 452, 458.
[163] 1989 SLT 182 (Inner House). In particular, the idea that industry practice might be a factor was disapproved.
[164] 1990 SLT 891 (House of Lords).
[165] D.10.4.12.3.
[166] G.2.79; D.41.1.7.7.

longer existed. In effect, therefore, the new thing was ownerless, and was acquired by the manufacturer by *occupatio*.

It is not clear whether Scots law follows Roman law on this point. The question is disputed,[167] and there is no direct Scots authority on the point.[168] It does seem counter-intuitive to reward with ownership a person manufacturing a thing in bad faith with someone else's materials. However, it must be borne in mind that the dispute is unlikely to be between the owner of the materials and a thief who has made a new thing with them. The dispute is much more likely to be with a third party acquirer from the thief. Moreover, it may be that to disregard bad faith is the more practical option. After all, the issues with identification, set out above, exist whether the manufacturer is in good faith or bad. The Draft Common Frame of Reference takes the approach of disallowing a manufacturer in bad faith from acquiring, 'unless the value of the labour is much higher than the value of the material'.[169] This, though, seems to introduce excessive uncertainty into the question, and moreover is a test whose applicability will depend on differing values of labour and materials over time and in different places,[170] rather than on anything intrinsic to the process of manufacture itself.

(5) Compensation

In Scots law, it is clear that the manufacturer is obliged to compensate the owner of the materials for their value.[171] The Roman rules were somewhat more complex, and depended on whether the manufacturer was in possession and whether he or she was in good faith or bad. The rules were similar to those applying to accession. Where the maker was in bad faith, he or she would be liable as having stolen the materials,[172] although, as owner, he or she would be able to recover the product from any other person in possession. A manufacturer in good faith was also owner, and so could recover the property from anyone in possession, paying the value of the materials if attempting to recover from the owner of the materials.[173] If a manufacturer in good faith was in possession, there is no direct evidence that the owner of the materials had any remedy at all. This seems so obviously unfair that it must give pause. However, in the absence of direct textual support for a remedy, it would be speculative to conclude positively that there was one.

---

[167] For discussion, see C Anderson, *Property: A Guide to Scots Law* (W Green 2016) para 8–11.
[168] In *Oliver & Boyd v The Marr Typefounding Co Ltd* (1901) 9 SLT 170, there was some basis for suggesting that the manufacturer was in bad faith, at least through negligence, but the Lord Ordinary expressly declined to reach this conclusion.
[169] DCFR VIII.-5:201(2).
[170] We may expect grapes, for example, to be more expensive in northern Europe, where they must be imported, rather than in southern Europe, where they can be grown.
[171] *International Banking Corporation v Ferguson, Shaw & Sons* 1910 SC 182. This is an additional reason why it is less problematic than it might at first appear to give ownership to a manufacturer who is in bad faith.
[172] G.2.79. On liability for theft, see pp. 417–22.
[173] On the basis that the *exceptio doli* would apply, as above.

(6) *Specificatio* in Modern Law

As we have seen, *specificatio* forms part of modern law. In more recent times, it has most often come up in cases on retention of title clauses in sales of goods. The situation is this. The owner of goods enters into a contract of sale with a purchaser, and delivers the goods to the purchaser. To protect the position of the seller, the contract of sale provides that the seller is to retain ownership until the goods are paid for in full. Suppose, though, that the purchaser performs work on the goods sufficient for *specificatio* to operate. Does this cause the purchaser to acquire ownership of the end product, defeating the retention of title clause?[174] Arguably it should not, at least where the parties' contract makes express provision dealing with the issue,[175] or the change was anticipated by the parties.[176] After all, when the manufacturing process happens in accordance with a contract between the parties, ownership is normally determined in accordance with that contract rather than according to the general rules of *specificatio*.[177]

One retention of title case has raised the interesting question of whether *specificatio* might apply to living things. In *Kinloch Damph Ltd v Nordvik Salmon Farms Ltd*,[178] a large number of salmon smolts (immature salmon) were sold, subject to a retention of title clause. The purchasers husbanded the smolts, which grew into mature salmon. The purchasers then went into receivership, without having paid in full. Ownership of the salmon was then disputed. The receivers claimed that the purchasers had acquired ownership on the basis of *specificatio*, as the adult salmon could not be restored to their original form.[179] This argument is not implausible, and a similar argument was successfully made in a Dutch case.[180] In *Kinloch Damph*, however, the argument was rejected. This seems correct, as the adult salmon were still clearly the same entities as the smolts. On the other hand, the Lord Ordinary may have gone too far in holding that *specificatio* had no application to living things at all. While it is reasonable to exclude the natural development of living things from *specificatio*, there is still scope for arguing for its application in cases where there has been some form of interference with that natural development. Examples might include the manipulation of a tree's

---

[174] For discussion, albeit with a focus on English law, see A Hicks, 'When Goods Sold Become a New Species' (1993) JBL 485; D Webb, 'Title and Transformation: Who Owns Manufactured Goods?' (2000) JBL 513.
[175] D L Carey Miller with D Irvine, *Corporeal Moveables in Scots Law* 2nd edn (W Green 2005) para 4.03.
[176] *Kinloch Damph Ltd v Nordvik Salmon Farms Ltd* 30 June 1999, OH, available at <http://www.scotcourts.gov.uk/search-judgments/judgment?id=7f2087a6-8980-69d2-b500-ff0000d74aa7> (last accessed 14 September 2020). For discussion, see E Metzger, 'Postscript on *Nova Species* and *Kinloch Damph Ltd v Nordvik Salmon Farms Ltd*' (2004) 2 Roman Legal Tradition 115; E Metzger, 'Acquisition of Living Things by Specification' (2004) 8 Edin LR 115.
[177] *Wylie & Lochhead v Mitchell* (1870) 8 M 552.
[178] 30 June 1999, OH, available at <http://www.scotcourts.gov.uk/search-judgments/judgment?id=7f2087a6-8980-69d2-b500-ff0000d74aa7> (last accessed 14 September 2020).
[179] Arguing from J.2.1.25 and Scots sources following this.
[180] *Stichting Crediteurenbelangen Hollander's v Coöperatieve Raiffeissenbank 'Domburg'* 24 March 1995, Hoge Raad, summarised in S van Erp and B Akkermans, *Cases, Materials and Text on National, Supranational and International Property Law* (Hart 2012) s. 7.40.

development to make a bonsai,[181] or the genetic manipulation and reproduction of living cells using modern scientific techniques.[182]

E. *Commixtio* and *Confusio*

Specificatio must be distinguished from *commixtio* and *confusio*. *Commixtio* and *confusio* involved the mixing together of goods belonging to two or more people without the creation of a new *species*. It appears that the Romans had difficulty determining quite which processes resulted in *specificatio* and which *commixtio* or *confusio*. For example, Justinian states both that the mixing together of wine and honey to make mead is an example of *specificatio*[183] and also that it is an example of *confusio*.[184] Ulpian argues that the former is correct, as the mixed ingredients in the case of mead do not retain their original character.[185] The mead is therefore a new *species*.[186] *Commixtio* and *confusio* must also be distinguished from accession. While all three involve a combination of two or more different things, *commixtio* and *confusio* do not require any physical attachment. In addition, the element of functional subordination is absent in *commixtio* and *confusio*.

The difference between *commixtio* and *confusio* appears to have been the following: 'the distinction is between mixing events by which the contributions to the mix become irreversibly joined or united (*confusio*), and mixing events where no such union occurs (*commixtio*)'.[187] Thus, if you mixed your wine with mine, or our bars of gold were melted down and combined, *confusio* would occur, the result of which was that the end product would be common property between us in proportion to our contributions.[188] This could also happen where things of different nature were combined, as long as separation was not possible, as with certain alloys.[189] The end product of *confusio* was common property, regardless of whether the parties consented.[190] Other mixes could be readily separated, however, and so in those *confusio* would not occur. For example, the jurist Callistratus tells us that an alloy of copper and silver belonging to different people will not become common property in this way, as they can usually be separated by craftsmen and reduced to the original materials.[191]

---

[181] C van der Merwe, '*Nova Species*' (2004) 2 Roman Legal Tradition 96, 113.
[182] E Metzger, 'Acquisition of Living Things by Specification' (2004) 8 Edin LR 115, 117–18. See also N R Whitty, 'Rights of Personality, Property Rights and the Human Body in Scots Law' (2005) 9 Edin LR 194, 223–9.
[183] J.2.1.24.
[184] J.2.1.27.
[185] D.6.1.5.1.
[186] Conceivably, it could also be considered as an example of accession, with the honey viewed as an accessory of the wine.
[187] R W J Hickey, 'Dazed and Confused: Accidental Mixtures of Goods and the Theory of Acquisition of Title' (2003) 66 MLR 368, 370.
[188] D.41.1.7.8.
[189] D.6.1.5.1. Compare though D.41.1.7.8–9.
[190] J.2.1.27.
[191] D.41.1.12.1.

Commixtio was the mixing of things that were capable of being separated. A distinction was made here depending on whether the parties consented to the mixing. If they both (or all) agreed, the resulting mix was common property in proportion to the parties' contributions. If the mix happened accidentally or without the consent of at least one of the parties, there was no effect on ownership.[192] This was the case even if the individual contributions could not be identified. The example Justinian gives is the mixing together of corn grains belonging to two people. Clearly, one grain looking very much like another, it is not possible to identify which grains came from which person.

It is difficult to see how this can possibly have been made to work, at least while retaining the distinction between *commixtio* and *confusio*. Accordingly, the case of grains being mixed together may be better seen as a case of *confusio* rather than one of *commixtio*. As the Scots institutional writer Stair points out, where a mixture is made of things belonging to two or more people, this will 'of necessity introduce a community' between the contributors, which can only be resolved by division in proportion to contributions.[193] It may be suspected, therefore, that the difference between *commixtio* and *confusio* was often more theoretical than real. Indeed, Justinian tells us that, in the case of the mixture of grain, each owner was entitled to recover a share of the total.[194] In Scots law, the terms *commixtio* and *confusio* are used. However, the meanings have altered. In Scots law, *commixtio* is a mixture of solids, *confusio* a mixture of liquids (or, it may be supposed, gases). The rules of the two are now essentially the same: where the contributions cannot be separated or separately identified, the mixture is common property. Otherwise, there is no effect on ownership.[195] Other solutions are possible.[196]

F. Treasure

Ownership could be acquired by a finder of treasure. This will only be considered briefly, as the Roman rules were not received in Scots law. This can be explained by the fact that, in Scots law, abandoned property falls to the Crown rather than becoming ownerless. Accordingly, even where buried valuables have been left so long that they can be deemed abandoned, in Scots law they are still owned and so cannot be appropriated by the finder.[197] Scots law therefore has no need of special rules for treasure, because the only person for whom there is any purpose in disputing whether the item is abandoned or not is the person who buried the item (or someone deriving right from that person).[198] Matters were

---

[192] J.2.1.28; D.6.1.5pr.
[193] Stair, *Institutions* 2.1.37.
[194] J.2.1.28.
[195] Stair, *Institutions* 2.1.37.
[196] See *e.g.* DCFR VIII.-5:202 and 203.
[197] *Lord Advocate v Aberdeen University* 1963 SC 533.
[198] At least currently. In its *Report on Prescription and Title to Moveable Property* (SLC No 228, 2012), the Scottish Law Commission has made certain recommendations for reform. See chapter 5 of that Report.

different in Roman law, in which in principle abandoned property was open to acquisition by a finder. It was therefore necessary to have special rules to deal with the situation where valuable items were found, which might or might not have been abandoned, but at any rate for which an owner could not be traced. In the absence of special rules to deal with this, there would be uncertainty as to whether the finder had any right in the items. We are concerned here with the law of treasure trove.

Paul tells us that treasure is 'an ancient deposit of money, of which memory does not survive, so that it no longer has an owner'.[199] Although Paul mentions only money, other valuables were certainly included. Something dropped by accident does not appear to have been considered treasure, and nor was money left behind by mistake when a house was sold.[200] As Paul's words suggest, if the deposited items had a traceable owner, they did not count as treasure for the purposes of acquisition.

Earlier doubts about ownership of treasure were resolved by the Emperor Hadrian (reigned AD 117–38).[201] According to the rules laid down by Hadrian, a finder on his or her own land, or on sacred or religious land,[202] got the whole of the treasure. Otherwise, as long as the treasure was found by chance rather than by a deliberate search, half went to the finder and half to the owner of the land. In the case of imperial land, this meant the emperor; on public land, half went to the finder and half to the exchequer or the local authorities.

G. Usucapio

(1) Nature and Scope

Usucapio was a civil law mode of acquisition, which allowed a non-owner to acquire ownership of property by possessing it for a prescribed length of time.[203] When *usucapio* had operated, the possessor became owner. Until that happened, the possessor would have the protection of the *actio Publiciana* against anyone but the owner of the property.[204] The claimed purpose of this is to reduce uncertainty over title to property:[205] if possession ripens into ownership after a period of time, then an acquirer ought to be safe from any challenge to his or her title if he or she has acquired the property from someone who has possessed for that period. In practice, however, the usefulness of *usucapio* would have been much reduced by certain limitations on its applicability.

---

[199] D.41.1.31.1.
[200] D.6.1.67.
[201] J.2.1.39.
[202] I.e. *res sacra* and *res religiosa* respectively. On these categories of property, see p. 195.
[203] For detailed discussion of some of the issues arising from *usucapio*, see R Yaron, 'Reflections on Usucapio' (1967) 35 TvR 191.
[204] See pp. 185–6.
[205] J.2.6pr.

We are told that *res sacrae*,[206] *res religiosae*[207] and runaway slaves were excluded from *usucapio*, and also that ownership of a free person could not be acquired in this way (in other words, a free person could not become a slave through *usucapio*).[208] Things belonging to the exchequer of the state were subject to a general exclusion.[209] The most important exclusion, though, was stolen property. Such property was excluded from acquisition by *usucapio*, a rule that Justinian attributes to both the Twelve Tables and a *lex Atinia* of the second century BC.[210] This rule did not simply prevent the thief acquiring by *usucapio*: the thief would not be in good faith anyway, which, as we shall see, was required. Instead, the fact of the property being stolen tainted it and prevented the operation of *usucapio* altogether, even when the property came into the hands of a third party in good faith. Stolen property could only become available again for acquisition by *usucapio* if it was first returned to the owner.[211] This exclusion of stolen property greatly restricted the scope of *usucapio* in respect of moveables. It could, however, still apply in those cases where goods came into the hands of a non-owner without any theft having occurred. An example would be the case where an item was found among a deceased person's effects, and was assumed to belong to the deceased, but which in fact had only been borrowed or hired. It does seem, though, that the error could be one of either fact[212] or of law.[213] Land could not be stolen, and so the acquisition of land by *usucapio* was not subject to this restriction. A limitation of similar, but narrower, scope did apply to land, however: where possession of land was taken by force, it could not be acquired by *usucapio*.[214] If the land was occupied by stealth, however, in the absence of the owner, it could be acquired by *usucapio*.[215]

The requirements for *usucapio* are considered in more detail below. However, in brief, the position was that the acquirer had to take possession in good faith, and in circumstances where there was a *iusta causa* (just cause) for that taking of possession, such as a sale to the acquirer. The acquirer then had to retain possession for a specified period of time, the relevant periods being different for land and

---

[206] See p. 195.
[207] See p. 195.
[208] J.2.6.1.
[209] J.2.6.9.
[210] J.2.6.2.
[211] D.41.3.4.6. D Pugsley, 'The Misinterpretation of the lex Atinia' (1970) 17 Revue Internationale des Droits de l'Antiquité (3rd series) 259, 268–71 argues that, originally, the *lex Atinia* was intended to provide that someone in the course of *usucapio* could not complete the acquisition if the property was wrongly taken from him or her, unless the property was returned. On this view, the need was therefore to restore the property to the victim of the theft, not to the actual owner. Compare though P Bělovský, '*Usucapio* of Stolen Things and Slave Children' (2002) 49 Revue Internationale des Droits de l'Antiquité (3rd series), 57; R Barber, 'Usucapion and Theft at the Time of the Twelve Tables' (1977) 8 Sydney LR 613; D Daube, '*Furtum Proprium* and *Furtum Improprium*' (1937) 6 Cam LJ 217.
[212] J.2.6.4.
[213] J.2.6.5. The example given is of one holding a usufruct of a slave, selling the slave's offspring in the belief that the usufruct gives a right to the slave's offspring. On ownership of the offspring of a slave held on usufruct, see pp. 261–2. Of course, if a statute expressly prohibited *usucapio* in the particular circumstances of the case, *usucapio* would not operate, good faith or not: D.41.3.24pr.
[214] J.2.6.2, in terms of the *lex Iulia et Plautia*.
[215] J.2.6.7. The initial occupier would not, however, acquire, as he or she would lack the essential element of *iusta causa*.

for moveables. Until the position was changed by Justinian, land could only be acquired by *usucapio* if it was Italic land, in other words land in Italy.[216] In the late classical period, there developed the *longi temporis praescriptio* ('long term prescription'), which allowed the acquisition of provincial land by possession for ten or twenty years, depending on whether the parties were domiciled in the same or different provinces. The possession had to be taken in good faith and on a *iusta causa*, as with *usucapio*.[217] There also developed in the post-classical period a *longissimi temporis praescriptio* ('very long term prescription'), where a possessor could acquire ownership after forty years' possession,[218] later reduced to thirty,[219] even without good faith or *iusta causa*.

(2) Good Faith

Only someone who was in good faith could acquire by *usucapio*.[220] Good faith, though, does not have quite its normal meaning here of belief in ownership of the property. Normally, it is true, a person who knew that he or she was not owner could not acquire through *usucapio*. However, in Chapter 11, we saw the special case of the bonitary owner, a person who had acquired a *res mancipi* by *traditio*.[221] Such a transfer was not valid, so the bonitary owner knew that he or she was not in fact owner, however much the law treated him or her as owner. Nonetheless, a bonitary owner was able to acquire by *usucapio*. A bonitary owner's possession was, however, at least honest, in that he or she did not believe that that possession wrongfully infringed anyone else's rights.[222]

In the normal case, it was only necessary to begin possession in good faith.[223] A person who took possession in good faith, but then subsequently discovered the property actually belonged to someone else, could nonetheless acquire by *usucapio*.

(3) Iusta Causa

As with the transfer of ownership by delivery (*traditio*),[224] *usucapio* could only operate if there was a *iusta causa* ('just cause') underlying the possession. This is some sufficient legal basis for a valid transfer, such as a sale or a gift. This requirement would prevent anyone who simply moved onto vacant land acquiring by *usucapio*

---

[216] J.2.6pr. On Italic land, see p. 198.
[217] D Nörr, 'Time and the Acquisition of Ownership in the Law of the Roman Empire' (1968) 3 Irish Jurist 352.
[218] The original legislation is not extant, but C.7.39.2 (AD 365) appears to refer to legislation of Constantine providing for this.
[219] C.7.39.3 (AD 424).
[220] J.2.6.7. There were in fact some exceptions to this. For example, Gaius explains (G.2.59–61) that someone who has conveyed property in security (see Chapter 15), and then has subsequently reacquired possession, can acquire by possession for the necessary period of time. This is known as *usureceptio*: where *usucapio* can be translated as 'taking by use', *usureceptio* means 'taking back by use'.
[221] See pp. 201–2.
[222] After all, the person from whom the bonitary owner had acquired had agreed to the transfer, and so had no good ground for complaining of it. The only problem was that the wrong method of transfer had been used.
[223] See e.g. J.2.6.12. In the case of a person acquiring by gift, it was necessary, however, to be in good faith throughout, until this rule was abolished by Justinian: C.7.31.1.3 (AD 531).
[224] See pp. 202–14. This was the normal method of transfer for most property and, in Justinianic law, for all property. It involved a transfer of possession from transferor to transferee.

(although someone acquiring the land from that person on the basis, for example, of sale could acquire). Unlike one view of delivery, however,[225] it seems that in *usucapio* the *iusta causa* had to be genuine.[226] So, if I believed that I was acquiring from you under a contract of sale, but you believed the transaction to be a gift, *usucapio* would not operate in my favour. It appears that acquisition by succession did not count as a *iusta causa* for *usucapio*.[227] Accordingly, even if the heir was in good faith, he or she did not acquire where the deceased had been in bad faith. If, however, the deceased was in good faith, *usucapio* would continue to run in favour of an heir in bad faith.

(4) Possession

To acquire by *usucapio*, it was necessary to possess the property for the required period. This had to be actual possession as if owner. Accordingly, for example, a tenant could not acquire the property by *usucapio*.[228] The periods of *usucapio* were laid down in the Twelve Tables, and continued to apply through the classical period and beyond. For moveables, the required period was one year; for Italic land, two years.[229] The period was extended by Justinian to three years for moveables; for land, the required period was extended to ten years if the parties lived in the same province, twenty years if different provinces.[230] This extended to Italic land the periods developed for provincial land under the *longi temporis praescriptio*.

The possession did not all have to be by the same person. If the possessor died in the course of acquiring by *usucapio*, the period for which the deceased had possessed could be added to that of the heir to make up the whole period required.[231] In the same way, a purchaser's period of possession could be added to the seller's to complete *usucapio*.

(5) Modern Law

Most legal systems have a system like *usucapio*, by which ownership of property can be acquired by possessing it for a period of time. Scots law is no exception, at least for land.[232] There is no such rule for corporeal moveable property.[233] The Scots rules, however, have their origin in legislation of 1617,[234] rather than in Roman law, and are quite different in a number of respects.[235] Scots law also has

---

[225] See pp. 207–10.
[226] J.2.6.11.
[227] J.2.6.12.
[228] C.7.30.1 (AD 226). For general discussion of possession, see pp. 172–86.
[229] J.2.6pr.
[230] J.2.6pr; C.7.31.1 (AD 531).
[231] J.2.6.12.
[232] The current law is found in the Prescription and Limitation (Scotland) Act 1973.
[233] At least currently. See though Scottish Law Commission, *Report on Prescription and Title to Moveable Property* (SLC No 228, 2012) chapters 2–4, where it is proposed that such a system should be introduced.
[234] Prescription Act 1617 (repealed).
[235] Most obviously, the Scots law of positive prescription requires the possession to be founded on a deed entered in the appropriate property register, and does not require good faith. There is also no need for a *iusta causa*, although the need for a deed narrating an apparent transfer fulfils a similar function.

nothing equivalent to the *actio Publiciana* to protect the possessor in the course of acquisition. However, the importance of possession in both the modern law and the Roman law means that the Roman texts may be found to have continuing relevance.

Chapter Summary

In this chapter, we have considered those cases in which a person could acquire ownership without acquiring it from a previous owner. Of most importance of these, from the point of view of the modern Scots lawyer, were *occupatio* (in which a person acquired ownership of ownerless property by taking possession of it), accession (in which a person acquired ownership of property that had been attached to his or her property), *specificatio* (in which the manufacturer of a new thing made from another's materials acquired ownership), and *commixtio* and *confusio* (which both involved the creation of a co-ownership relationship between the owners of things that had been mixed together). All of these have been received into modern law, although of course differing on point of detail. Two other modes of original acquisition existed, which have not been received into modern Scots law, namely the finding of treasure and *usucapio*. The latter of these, though, which allowed the acquisition of ownership through possession of the property, has its modern equivalent in the form of positive prescription.

Further Reading

G.2.65–79
J.2.1pr–39; 2.6
D.41.1–10
C.7.26–35
W W Buckland, *A Text-Book of Roman Law from Augustus to Justinian* 3rd edn, revd P Stein (Cambridge University Press 1963) 207–28, 242–52
H Hausmaninger and R Gamauf, *A Casebook on Roman Property Law* (G A Sheets trans, Oxford University Press 2012) 124–204
E Metzger ed, *A Companion to Justinian's Institutes* (Duckworth 1998) 55–65
J A C Thomas, *Textbook of Roman Law* (North-Holland 1976) 157–79
A Watson, *The Law of Property in the Later Roman Republic* (Oxford University Press 1968) 21–61, 62–77

CHAPTER THIRTEEN

Praedial Servitudes

A. Nature and Scope of Praedial Servitudes

(1) What Is a Servitude?

(a) Nature

It is sometimes necessary for the owner of one area of land to have a right to make some particular use of neighbouring land. For example, suppose that I buy an area of land that is landlocked, with no direct access to a road. You own the land all the way around what I have bought. If I am dependent on your goodwill to be able to take access to my land, I will have a problem if we ever fall out. We could of course make a contractual arrangement regulating my access, which will naturally bind you even if you change your mind. However, that will not help me if you sell your own land to someone else, because our contract cannot bind the acquirer. It only binds us, not anyone else.[1]

An alternative would be to create a particular type of real right called a servitude. Servitudes came in different varieties, of which the one used in this example, a right of access, would have been the most common. We shall see some other types below. In Roman law, a distinction developed though between two broad categories of rights which were called servitudes, praedial servitudes and personal servitudes.[2] The usage is confusing, because the two really have very little in common.[3] When a modern lawyer talks about a servitude, he or she will certainly be talking about a praedial servitude, and that is what this chapter is concerned with. Personal servitudes, the main example of which is usufruct, will be considered in the next chapter. Nothing more will be said about them in this chapter.

The law of servitudes is arguably among the most Roman parts of Scots law. Indeed, it has been said that 'Scots law has largely adopted the Roman law of

---

[1] See pp. 163–5.
[2] D.8.1.1.
[3] The usage may only have arisen in the late classical period. See W W Buckland, 'The Conception of Usufruct in Classical Law' (1927) 43 LQR 326; K Kagan, 'The Nature of Servitudes and the Association of Usufruct with Them' (1947–8) 22 Tulane LR 94.

servitudes'.[4] This Scots definition of praedial servitudes will do equally well for Roman law:

> Servitude is a burden on land or houses ... in favour of the owners of other tenements;[5] whereby the owner of the burdened or 'servient' tenement, and his heirs and singular successors in the subject, must submit to certain uses to be exercised by the owner of the other or 'dominant' tenement; or must suffer restraint in his own use and occupation of the property.[6]

An important point to take from this definition is that a praedial servitude is not a relationship between two people as individuals. Rather, it is a right held by the owner of one area of land, in the capacity of owner of that land, in another area of land belonging to a different person. This is why it is called praedial, from the Latin *praedium*, which means an estate of land. In a praedial servitude, there must be two properties, one known as the dominant property and one the servient property.[7] The owner for the time being of the dominant property has the right to enforce the servitude against the owner for the time being of the servient property. The servitude is attached to the land, and this is the case at both ends. If the dominant owner sold the dominant property, the right to enforce the servitude would transfer to the buyer along with the land. In the same way, if the servient owner sold the servient property, the buyer of the servient property would become subject to the obligation to comply with the servitude.[8]

(b) Restrictions on Creation

We have seen then that a praedial servitude was a right, held by the owner for the time being of one area of land, either to use some other land for some specified purpose or to restrict the use of that land in some specified way. There were, though, restrictions on the circumstances in which a praedial servitude could be created. For example, it was established that the two properties had to be in separate ownership, so it was not possible to impose a servitude on one's own land.[9] Two particularly important restrictions on the content of a praedial servitude were, first, that it could not impose positive obligations on the servient owner; and, second, that the benefit taken from the servitude had to relate to the land.

---

[4] W M Gordon, 'Servitudes: Scots Law and Roman Law' in *Roman Law, Scots Law and Legal History: Selected Essays* (Edinburgh University Press 2007) 141. As Gordon explains, though, this did not come about through a lack of comparable native institutions. Instead, existing, non-Roman institutions were developed in accordance with Romanist doctrines. For discussion of the reception of Roman principles in the Scots law of praedial servitudes, see also M J de Waal, 'Servitudes' in *History of Private Law in Scotland, vol I*; W M Gordon and M J de Waal, 'Servitudes and Real Burdens' in Zimmermann, Visser and Reid, *Mixed Legal Systems*.
[5] The term 'tenement' here means simply land or buildings.
[6] Bell, *Principles* s. 979. Indeed, this definition is now more accurate for Roman law than for Scots law for, as we shall see below, the final category referred to (known as negative servitudes) no longer exists in Scots law.
[7] D.8.4.1.1.
[8] D.8.4.12.
[9] D.8.6.1.

On the first of these, a servitude could either give the dominant owner some right to use the servient land, or else restrict the servient owner's rights to use that land in some way. The former of these was known as a positive servitude, the latter as a negative servitude.[10] In the case of a positive servitude, the servient owner was required simply to do nothing to interfere with the exercise of the servitude. Where a negative servitude was concerned, all that was required of the servient owner was to refrain from doing whatever thing it was that the servitude prohibited. In either case, it was not possible for the servient owner to be required actually to do anything.[11] For example, suppose that I had a servitude right of way along a road running across your land. While you would not be permitted actually to block the road, or positively to interfere with my use of the road, equally you would be quite at liberty to allow the road to fall into disrepair to the point that I could not use it.[12] To this principle there was one exception. It was possible to have a servitude requiring the owner of one building to provide structural support to a neighbouring building. In that case, the servient owner could be required to make such repairs to his or her own property as were necessary to maintain that support.[13]

The second important restriction on the content of a servitude was that the benefit had to be praedial rather than personal, which meant that it had to relate to the land. For example, there could be no servitude right to gather fruit, stroll or picnic on another's land:[14] the fact that the holder of the right held neighbouring land would be entirely incidental here, as the same benefit could be obtained by someone who did not own any land. For the same reason, the two properties had to be close neighbours.[15] While a right to use a road that is ten miles from my house may well be useful to me, the benefit I take can hardly be said to relate to my house in any meaningful way. Equally, a servitude right of access could only be used to

---

[10] Scots law formerly made the same distinction, but it is no longer possible to create a negative servitude: Title Conditions (Scotland) Act 2003, s. 79. Instead, a restriction on the use of the property may be constituted as a real burden, which is a different form of condition on land. Real burdens have some relationship with servitudes, but developed separately from the eighteenth century onwards, and regulate the use of the affected property (known as the 'burdened property') by either requiring the owner of that land to do something (such as make repairs to a required standard) or to refrain from doing something (such as using the land for business purposes). The law on real burdens is now codified in the Title Conditions (Scotland) Act 2003. On real burdens, see W M Gordon and S Wortley, *Scottish Land Law*, vol 2, 3rd edn (W Green 2020) chapter 24.

[11] D.8.1.15.1.

[12] This must have caused some inconvenience in practice. Of course, the servient owner could have been contractually bound to make repairs. However, a merely contractual obligation would not have bound anyone subsequently acquiring the servient property. See *Dorion v Les Ecclésiastiques du Séminaire de St Sulpice de Montréal* (1880) 5 App Cas 362, a case from Quebec, where it was found that the law of Quebec had modified the Roman principle to allow a repair obligation to be imposed as part of a servitude right of way along a road. Scots law appears broadly to follow the Roman position: D J Cusine & R R M Paisley, *Servitudes and Rights of Way* (W Green 1998) para 2.85. In Scots law, however, it is possible to constitute a repairing obligation separately, as a real burden. On the other hand, the dominant owner had in Roman law the right to make repairs (D.43.19.3.11), unless that right was excluded when the servitude was created (D.43.19.3.14).

[13] D.8.2.33; D.8.5.6.2.

[14] D.8.1.8pr.

[15] D.8.3.5.1. They did not, however, need to be absolutely adjacent: D.8.3.7.1; D.8.4.6pr. Paul says that the two properties must be visible from each other: D.8.2.38.

take access to the dominant land, not to other land that the dominant owner happened to have in the neighbourhood.[16] Similarly, where a negative servitude was imposed, the restriction had to protect or enhance the enjoyment of the dominant land in some way. The standard examples, considered below, involve restrictions on building on the servient land in order to protect the light and prospect of the dominant land. Another example would be a restriction on the servient owner's use of a water supply – perhaps a spring on the servient land or a river running across both properties – in order to protect the dominant owner's use of that supply.[17] Where a servitude allowed for the taking of the materials from the servient land, this could not be done beyond the needs of the dominant land.[18] For example, it would be possible for a servitude to allow the taking of stone from the servient land for use in building on the dominant land, but not to take stone for commercial sale.[19] A borderline case was given by Paul. While a servitude could not allow the taking of clay for the manufacture of containers for sale, a servitude could allow a farmer to take clay to make containers for the produce of the farm.[20] This would be the case even though the containers were included in the sale of that produce.

(2) Types of Servitude

A number of specific types of servitude are identified in the texts that have come down to us. The Romans classified these into two broad categories, rustic and urban. This distinction was not concerned with whether the dominant and servient properties were themselves urban or rural. Instead, it was concerned with whether the servitude related to the use of buildings. Urban servitudes were those 'connected with buildings'.[21] This was the case even if the building was in a rural area. For example, a servitude concerned with the use of a farmhouse would nonetheless be urban.[22] Other praedial servitudes were rustic, although it is not always certain into which category a particular servitude fell.

The primary significance of the distinction between urban and rustic servitudes arose from the fact that rustic servitudes fell into the category of *res mancipi*.[23] As a result, they were created by different means.[24] As we have already seen,

---

[16] For the same point in modern law, see *Irvine Knitters Ltd v North Ayrshire Co-operative Society Ltd* 1978 SC 109. For consideration of similar issues in South African law, see J R Harker, 'Unlawful Extension of a Servitude of a Right of Way' (1987) 104 SALJ 44.
[17] D.8.1.15pr.
[18] D.8.3.5.1. See also D.8.3.29, applying the same principle to a servitude right to drain water onto neighbouring land.
[19] See *McTaggart v Macdouall* (1867) 5 M 534, 547 (Lord Benholme), where it was observed that a servitude could allow the taking of seaweed for use as a fertiliser on the dominant land, but not for use to create products for sale.
[20] D.8.3.6pr.
[21] J.2.3.1.
[22] An example might be a right to have water run from the roof of the farmhouse onto neighbouring land belonging to someone else.
[23] G.2.17. On *res mancipi*, see pp. 199–202. It is possible that only the earliest four rustic servitudes considered below (the three types of access rights and the right of aqueduct) were *res mancipi*. The likely reason for their classification as *res mancipi* is that, in early law, the dominant owner was seen as having been in some sense given ownership of the ground affected by the servitude: Watson, *Property* 184.
[24] See pp. 200–1.

though, the categorisation of property as *res mancipi* and *res nec mancipi* was abolished by Justinian.[25] Without that distinction, it is of little value to make a systematic distinction between urban and rustic servitudes. Certainly, in Scots law, the distinction has been all but abandoned. A more useful distinction is that between positive servitudes and negative servitudes, depending on whether they allow the dominant owner to do something or prohibit the servient owner from doing something. The discussion here is therefore based on that distinction.

Most of the servitudes mentioned in the texts were positive in nature, which is to say that they allowed the owner of the dominant land to do something that could otherwise be objected to by the owner of the servient land. They can be divided into a number of groups of related servitudes:

- Probably the most important form of positive servitude was the right of access. Rights of access were of three kinds, all of them rustic servitudes: *iter*, *actus* and *via*.[26] *Iter* was a right of passage across the servient land by foot.[27] We are told by Paul that passage by foot included being carried in a sedan chair or litter.[28] *Actus* was a right of passage along with livestock or driving a vehicle. It included the right to go on foot. *Via* was a general right of access. It included the rights comprised in *iter* and *actus*, and also other acts not included in them, such as the right to drag rocks and timber.[29] These servitudes are very old: we are told, for example, of provision concerning them in the Twelve Tables.[30]
- There were several servitudes concerned with issues of water management. Aqueduct was a rustic servitude allowing the running of a water supply through neighbouring land.[31] A similar servitude, also rustic, was *aquaehaustus*, which allowed the drawing of water from neighbouring land.[32] There was an urban servitude requiring the servient owner to submit to the run-off of water from the dominant land or buildings on it.[33] There was also the *ius cloacae*, a right to run a drain through neighbouring land.[34]
- There were two rustic servitudes allowing the dominant owner to drive his or her livestock to take water from the servient land or to pasture on the servient land.[35]
- A servitude could allow the temporary deposit of material on the servient land, such as the use of buildings on the servient land for the storage of farm produce or the deposition of stones and other material from a quarry.[36]

[25] See p. 199.
[26] J.2.3.pr.
[27] This included the right to go on horseback: D.8.3.12.
[28] D.8.3.7pr. Compare *Aberdeenshire County Council v Lord Glentanar* 1999 SLT 1456.
[29] D.8.3.7pr.
[30] D.8.3.8, concerning the width of the way. On the Twelve Tables, see pp. 47–9.
[31] J.2.3pr.
[32] J.2.3.2.
[33] J.2.3.1.
[34] D.8.1.7. This is discussed in *Kerr v Brown* 1939 SC 140.
[35] J.2.3.2.
[36] D.8.3.3.1–2, the latter of which is cited by Lord Rodger as part of the justification for the recognition of a servitude of car parking in modern law: *Moncrieff v Jamieson* 2008 SC (HL) 1, para [76].

- There could be a rustic servitude allowing the dominant owner to burn lime on the servient land.[37]
- Two important urban servitudes involved the use of a building on the servient land to provide structural support to a building on the dominant land.[38] One involved the servient building bearing the weight of the dominant building. The other allowed the dominant building to be supported by means of a beam that had been put into the servient building.
- The servitude right of projection allowed a construction on the dominant land to overhang the servient land.[39] This was used as part of the justification for the acceptance of such a servitude in modern law, in *Compugraphics International Ltd v Nikolic*.[40] This case involved pipework on the side of a building and overhanging neighbouring land.
- It appears that an owner of land had a right to a certain amount of light.[41] There was a servitude allowing the dominant owner to raise a building even to the effect of shutting out this light.[42]
- Various other servitudes are mentioned in the texts. Examples are the right to discharge smoke onto neighbouring land[43] and the right to pile up dung against a neighbour's wall.[44]

The texts mention fewer negative servitudes. Two were recognised, both urban.[45] These were the right to light and the right of prospect.[46] They both restricted building on the servient land. The difference between them was that a right to light was a right to see the sky and obtain the light from it, while the right of prospect was the right to preserve a view. It is generally thought that the right to light arose earlier:

> Light is a necessary commodity especially in an ancient society, and it would be astonishing if the law did not step into this sphere at a fairly early date. Prospect is different, having more to do with gracious living than with the necessities of life.[47]

What kind of view might be protected is a difficult question. Rodger suggests that 'the view must be pleasing, beautiful in some degree'.[48] This suggests a high degree of subjectivity. On the other hand, there is nothing surprising in the idea that an owner might seek to preserve the open outlook from his or her property.[49]

---

[37] J.2.3.2.
[38] J.2.3.1.
[39] D.8.5.17pr; D.8.2.2.
[40] 2011 SLT 955.
[41] A Rodger, *Owners and Neighbours in Roman Law* (Clarendon Press 1972) 38–89.
[42] G.2.14.
[43] D.8.5.8.5.
[44] D.8.5.17.2. For discussion of these, see Johnston, *Roman Law in Context* 75–6, and compare Watson, *Property* 177–8.
[45] J.2.3.1.
[46] D.8.2.16.
[47] A Rodger, *Owners and Neighbours in Roman Law* (Clarendon Press 1972) 125.
[48] A Rodger, *Owners and Neighbours in Roman Law* (Clarendon Press 1972) 129.
[49] For two modern cases, see *Ord v Mashford* 2006 SLT (Lands Tr) 15; *Franklin v Lawson* 2013 SLT (Lands Tr) 81.

The view from the dominant property might be a significant factor in the property's value, and so its preservation is consistent with the requirement for praedial benefit.

Could other servitudes be recognised beyond the ones listed here? As a preliminary point it must be remembered that, just because a servitude is not mentioned in the Roman texts as being recognised in particular circumstances, it does not necessarily follow that such a servitude was not in fact recognised. The *Digest* is, after all, an edited collection. As Lord Rodger has said, the omission of a particular type of servitude 'may just be due to an accident of the compilers' work in reducing the jurists' writings for inclusion in the *Digest*'.[50] According to Watson:

> For a right to be accepted as a servitude it had to fall within a recognized type or kind of servitudes . . . But this is not to suggest that there was a closed list of servitudes. Rather, when a new situation came under discussion the jurists considered whether they were willing to recognize that a right of servitude could exist in such circumstances.[51]

On this view, while there was no bar to the recognition of new types of servitude, a new servitude was more likely to be recognised if it was analogous to an existing type. There exists an argument that, given that acquirers of the servient property are bound by servitudes affecting the property, they should not be at risk of being taken by surprise by the recognition of a previously unknown type of servitude affecting it.[52] In Scots law, after a long period of reluctance to recognise new types of servitude,[53] the courts now seem more open to this.[54] We have seen that the servitude of projection has now been accepted as part of Scots law. Another example is the recognition of a servitude right of car parking.[55]

B. Creation of Praedial Servitudes

(1) Voluntary Creation

Speaking in general terms, there are three situations in which a person might want to create a servitude over land.[56] The first is the simplest, where there is a freestanding grant of a servitude over one person's land, by the owner of that land, in favour of the owner of neighbouring land. Alternatively, the grant of the servitude may take place in the context of a subdivision of an area of land, where part is transferred to a new owner (including the case where the land is

---

[50] *Moncrieff v Jamieson* 2008 SC (HL) 1, para [73].
[51] Watson, *Property* 176.
[52] Bell, *Principles* s. 979.
[53] For discussion and recommendations for reform, see Scottish Law Commission, *Report on Real Burdens* (SLC No 181, 2000) paras 12.22–26. These recommendations were implemented by the Title Conditions (Scotland) Act 2003, ss. 76–7.
[54] See though W M Gordon, 'The Struggle for Recognition of New Servitudes' (2009) 13 Edin LR 139.
[55] *Moncrieff v Jamieson* 2008 SC (HL) 1; *Johnson, Thomas and Thomas (A Firm) v Smith* 2016 GWD 25-456.
[56] There is another possibility, not considered here. Where common property was divided, a servitude might be imposed. On the division of common property, see pp. 171–2.

divided in accordance with a will).[57] It may be sought (and this is the second situation) to reserve a servitude in favour of the transferor, or else (third) a servitude may be granted to the acquirer over the retained land. An example of the second situation is where I sell part of my land to you but, because the access road to my house runs through the ground I am selling, we agree that I should have a servitude right to continue to use the road after the sale. An example of the third situation is the converse case. I sell you part of my land but, because the ground I am selling you is landlocked, I give you also a servitude right of way over the land I am keeping so that you can get to your land.

How is this done? In classical law, the answer depended on whether the servitude to be created was urban or rustic.[58] An urban servitude could be created only by *in iure cessio*, this in effect involving the parties appearing before a magistrate to declare the existence of the servitude.[59] A rustic servitude could be created in this way or, alternatively, by *mancipatio*.[60] These methods were available for all three of the situations referred to in the previous paragraph.[61] As we have seen, however, *mancipatio* and *in iure cessio* were only available for Italic land.[62] Accordingly, for provincial land, a different method was used, namely pacts and stipulations.[63] This involved an informal agreement between the parties,[64] reinforced with a penalty for failure to comply with the agreement, constituted by the formal type of contract called *stipulatio*.[65] This arrangement was treated as creating a right that ran with the land, even though the *stipulatio* is in its terms a contract between two people only.[66]

Just as the inconvenience of *mancipatio* and *in iure cessio* in the transfer of ownership caused them to fall out of use in practice,[67] it would not be surprising if the same happened with their use for the creation of servitudes. In fact, it seems that the use by a person of a neighbour's property as if by servitude, with the permission and tolerance of the owner of that land, attracted the protection of the praetor.[68] In the Justinianic law, servitudes were created by pact and stipulation or by will.[69] It was not possible to create a servitude in favour of a third party, as where a servitude was reserved in favour of the transferor of land and also in favour of a neighbour,[70] or where the intended dominant and servient properties were both sold off at the same time.[71] This issue, however, seems easy

---

[57] On creation of a servitude in a will, see D.8.2.31.
[58] G.2.29.
[59] See pp. 200–1.
[60] See pp. 199–200.
[61] D.8.4.3; D.8.4.6.
[62] See p. 198.
[63] G.2.31.
[64] See pp. 381–2.
[65] See Chapter 18.
[66] D.8.3.36.
[67] See pp. 201–2.
[68] D.8.3.1.2, and see below on possessory protection of servitudes.
[69] J.2.3.4.
[70] D.8.4.5. In this case, the servitude would only be valid in favour of the transferor, not of the third party.
[71] D.8.4.6.

enough to work around in practice, by simply involving the third party in the transaction as a party or, in the latter case, by having a time interval between the two sales.[72]

(2) Scope of Grant

When the servitude was created, it was of course necessary to identify the type of servitude that was intended. It was not, however, necessary to define in advance precisely the manner in which the servitude was to be exercised. Instead, this could be defined by use.[73] For example, where a servitude right of access over neighbouring land was created without defining the specific route, the dominant owner had to stick to the route first chosen.[74] In the absence of agreement, it might be necessary for an arbitrator to be appointed to set the line of the servitude.[75]

Further rights might exist along with the servitude. For example, if there was a right to draw water from the servient land, a right of access (specifically *iter*) would be implied on the basis that it was necessary to allow the servitude to be exercised.[76] Again, the holder of a servitude to pasture or water cattle on the servient land could acquire a right to build a shelter on the servient land for use in bad weather.[77]

A grant of a servitude could include limitations on its use. For example, a right of *actus* or *via* might restrict use of the way to particular types of vehicle.[78] Again, there could be a servitude right of access limited to certain times of day or to alternate days.[79] Justinian refers to a case where a servitude right of access was to be used only on one day every five years.[80] This is presumably hypothetical, but it is interesting to note that no issue was raised about the validity of such a limitation.[81]

(3) Creation by Use

Suppose that, without any actual grant of a servitude right, I make some use of your land without objection for an extended period of time. In modern law, assuming that what I have done is something that can be constituted as a servitude, I will eventually acquire the right to continue the activity in question.[82] For example, suppose that I make a habit of crossing your land to get to mine.

---

[72] See D.8.4.6.3a; D.8.4.8.
[73] For discussion, in relation to servitude rights of access specifically, see J A Lovett, 'A New Way: Servitude Relocation in Scotland and Louisiana' (2005) 9 Edin LR 352, 363–6 and sources cited there.
[74] D.8.1.9. Celsus here gives this as an example of the principle that a servitude must be exercised in a reasonable manner, on which see below.
[75] D.8.3.13.1–3.
[76] D.18.1.40.1; D.8.3.3.3. It seems from D.8.6.17 that this would not be a separate, freestanding servitude. As a result, if the right to take water was lost, the right of access would be lost as well.
[77] D.8.3.6.1, cited by Lord Rodger in *Moncrieff v Jamieson* 2008 SC (HL) 1, para [75].
[78] D.8.6.11pr.
[79] D.8.1.5.1; D.8.4.14.
[80] C.3.34.14pr (AD 531).
[81] The question instead was about the loss of such a servitude by non-use, on which see below.
[82] Prescription and Limitation (Scotland) Act 1973, s. 3. The required period is twenty years.

If you do not object and you take no steps to stop me, in modern law you will eventually lose the right to stop me.

In early Roman law, the position was similar, and it was possible to acquire a servitude by *usucapio*,[83] in other words by use without challenge for a period of time.[84] However, a *lex Scribonia*, of the late Republic but whose precise date is unknown, changed the law. While it was still possible to acquire ownership by *usucapio*, it was no longer possible to acquire a servitude. The reason for this is unclear. It has been suggested[85] that the change was motivated by the fact that, normally, someone acquiring a servitude in this way would do so simply by the factual exercise of what the servitude would allow. For example, one might acquire a servitude right of access by taking access without objection for the required period. Such a person would therefore not normally be in good faith and there would not normally be any purported grant of a servitude underlying the use to serve as a *iusta causa* (just cause), both requirements of the acquisition of ownership by *usucapio*. Alternatively, the original position, that servitudes could be acquired by *usucapio*, may have arisen from the idea in early law that a servitude involved ownership of the land affected by it.[86] In time, though, servitudes came to be seen as incorporeal, as rights in another's land, and at that point it may have been thought that this was inconsistent with the idea that they could be acquired by possession. However, as has also been said, 'the whole story of the *lex Scribonia* and its effects is hopelessly obscure'.[87]

Evidently, and unsurprisingly, this proved inconvenient in practice, as it denied the person claiming to have the servitude the benefit of having exercised an apparent right without challenge for an extended period.[88] This was the case even though, as time went on, it would become more and more difficult to prove positively that the servitude had originally been properly created. However, the rule developed, on the same lines as the *longi temporis praescriptio* (long-term prescription)[89] applying to ownership of land, that the apparent exercise of a servitude for an extended period would 'obtain the force of a servitude'.[90] The required period was ten years, or twenty if the parties were resident in different provinces.[91] If an owner of land acted as if there was a servitude over neighbouring land for the required period, a servitude would be acquired in accordance with the use that had been made, as long as the use had not been objected to within that period[92] and as long as the use was not exercised by force, stealth or

---

[83] On acquisition of ownership by *usucapio*, see pp. 239–43.
[84] Paul's explanation at D.8.1.14pr for the non-applicability of *usucapio* to servitudes, on the basis that they are incorporeal and so cannot be possessed, or else that they are not capable of continuous use, must therefore be rejected.
[85] R Yaron, 'Reflections on Usucapio' (1967) 35 TvR 191, 228.
[86] This is generally thought to have been the case. Thus, in early law, the holder of a servitude right of way would be regarded as, in some sense, the owner of the path over which the right of way ran. See Watson, *Property* 184.
[87] W W Buckland, 'The Conception of Servitudes in Roman Law' (1928) 44 LQR 426, 434.
[88] Although the relevant possessory interdicts, considered below, would have been of use here.
[89] See p. 241.
[90] C.3.34.1 (AD 211).
[91] Buckland, *Textbook* 266.
[92] C.3.34.2 (AD 215).

licence.[93] It was not necessary to show any legal basis for the use, in the form of an original grant or reservation of a servitude.[94]

C. Exercise of Praedial Servitudes

A servitude could, as we have seen, give to the dominant owner fairly extensive rights over the servient land. However, it must not be forgotten that the servient owner was still owner of the servient land, and was entitled to full use of the land except insofar as that interfered with the exercise of the servitude. Celsus says that the servitude must be exercised *civiliter modo*, which means 'in a reasonable manner'.[95] He gives this as the basis of the rule, which we have already seen, that the dominant owner had to stick with the first route chosen for a right of access. The *civiliter modo* rule as stated by Celsus, however, seems to be broader than this. It would exclude, for instance, the choice of a route that would be inconvenient to the servient owner where another was available that was just as good for the dominant owner.

The dominant owner was entitled to make improvements and repairs, such as the repair of a road to which a right of access related[96] or alterations to a watercourse to improve the flow,[97] as long as these alterations did not adversely affect the servient owner. This right could be excluded or limited when the servitude was created.[98]

Suppose that the dominant land was divided, and ownership of part of it was transferred to someone else. Did that now mean that there were two dominant owners, both entitled to exercise the servitude? The answer varied. It could be that the servitude had only been created to benefit part of the dominant land, in which case that part alone would continue to be dominant.[99] Normally, however, each part of the dominant land would continue to be dominant, and their owners would all be entitled to continue to benefit from the servitude. The reasoning for this was that the servitude attached to the whole of the dominant land, and so to each part of the dominant land when it was divided.[100] This is straightforward enough when each part of the dominant land is, say, drawing water from the same pipe, as the burden on the servient land is no greater. Difficult practical issues would often arise, however, when the servitude was a right of access or a right to take materials from the servient land. This is an issue that continues to cause difficulty to the present day.[101]

---

[93] D.39.3.1.23.
[94] D.8.5.10pr.
[95] D.8.1.9.
[96] D.43.19.3.11.
[97] D.8.3.15.
[98] D.43.19.3.14; D.8.4.11.
[99] D.8.4.7.1. See also D.8.6.13.
[100] D.8.3.23.3; D.8.3.25.
[101] See *e.g.*, with reference to Scots and South African law, R R M Paisley and C G van der Merwe, 'From Here to Eternity: Does a Servitude Road Last Forever?' (2000) 11 Stellenbosch L Rev 452. See also *Keith v Texaco Ltd* 1977 SLT (Lands Tr) 16; *Alba Homes Ltd v Duell* 1993 SLT (Sh Ct) 49.

D. Protection of Praedial Servitudes

We have seen in Chapter 10 that a distinction may be made between remedies based on ownership and remedies based on possession.[102] The former assert the existence of a right of ownership held by some specific person, and success in obtaining the remedy sought is dependent on establishing ownership. By contrast, a possessory remedy is not concerned with the question of who is ultimately entitled to the property. Instead, possessory proceedings are brought to preserve an existing state of possession or restore a previous state of possession, as an interim measure until the question of right is determined. An equivalent distinction existed in the law of servitudes.

(1) Remedies for Establishing or Denying a Servitude

The two standard remedies relating to servitudes were known as the *actio confessoria* and the *actio negatoria*.[103] The *actio confessoria*, which was a modified form of the *vindicatio*[104] used to assert ownership, asserted the existence of a servitude, and was brought by a person claiming to be dominant owner in a servitude. The *actio negatoria* denied the existence of a servitude. For example, if I claimed that I had a servitude right of access over your land, which you were refusing to allow me to exercise, I would bring the *actio confessoria* against you. I could bring the same action to assert a right to repair, for example, the road over which I had the right of access.[105] If, instead, you were using my land in a manner which I wanted to allege that you did not have a right to, I would bring the *actio negatoria* against you. It does not appear that you actually had to be asserting that a servitude did exist. It was enough that you were doing something that would only be lawful if you did have a servitude. In both the *actio confessoria* and the *actio negatoria*, compensation could be claimed.[106] In the *actio confessoria*, this was measured by the dominant owner's interest in not being prevented from exercising the servitude. In the *actio negatoria*, compensation was measured by the pursuer's interest in not having the supposed servitude exercised.

In addition to these remedies, a person asserting or denying the existence of a servitude could protect his or her position indirectly, if the other party was acting in bad faith in an attempt to cause offence or affront. This was done using a delictual remedy under the *actio iniuriarum*, the action for insult.[107] This might occur if a person knowingly trespassed on land in a manner affronting the owner of that land, or maliciously prevented the lawful exercise of a servitude.

---

[102] See p. 173.
[103] For the distinction between these, see D.8.5.2pr. For discussion of the scope of these actions, see W W Buckland, 'The Protection of Servitudes in Roman Law' (1930) 46 LQR 447, concerned also with the application of the same actions to usufruct. An equivalent remedy, in the form of an *actio utilis*, could be sought by a creditor given possession of the dominant land as security: D.8.1.16.
[104] *Vindicatio* is the standard procedure for recovering property on the basis of ownership. See pp. 189–90.
[105] D.8.5.4.5.
[106] D.8.5.4.2.
[107] See Chapter 23.

(2) Possessory Remedies

We have seen already that a person claiming to own property was not supposed to take the law into his or her own hands by seizing the property from the current possessor.[108] The current possessor was normally entitled to be left in undisturbed possession until the question of ownership was determined by a judge. The praetor would normally protect the current possessor in the meantime by means of special remedies called interdicts.

To talk of possession, though, suggests a relationship with a corporeal thing. A servitude is a right, with no physical existence. Can it then be possessed, and its exercise receive protection in the same way as possession of corporeal property? The general view is that servitudes, as rights, could not be possessed.[109] As Paul says, only 'those things can be possessed that are corporeal'.[110]

At the same time, though, a person in peaceful exercise of an apparent servitude seems just as deserving of interim protection as someone in peaceful possession of corporeal property. This is especially so where, as in Roman law after the *lex Scribonia*, defects in the creation of the servitude could not be cured after the passage of time. In other words, as we have seen, a servitude could not be created by *usucapio*. Thus, between the *lex Scribonia* and the development of the creation of servitudes by *longi temporis praescriptio*, it would always be necessary to prove that the servitude had been validly created. This would be the case even if the person claiming to have the benefit of a servitude had been exercising it peacefully for many years, and even though it would be increasingly difficult as time went by to prove that it had been properly created. Indeed, even though ownership and servitude are in principle two very different things, in practice it would often be difficult to tell which one was being asserted. A Scots case, *Ferrier v Walker*,[111] illustrates the point. This case involved the disputed use of a close or passageway in a town, formed by the gap between two buildings, which had been there for more than 100 years. From the written titles to the properties on either side, it was unclear what the parties' respective rights in the close were. The point is that, whether the two owners on either side co-owned the close, or instead one owned and the other had a servitude right of access over the land, it would make very little difference to how the close was used. Either way, both parties would be able to make use of the close and could not lawfully interfere with the other's use. However, as the issue was raised as a possessory question, it was not necessary to settle the issue of the parties' respective rights. The court was able to dispose of the case on the basis of the existing use of the close.

---

[108] See pp. 181–3.

[109] See *e.g.* T Rüfner, 'Possession of Incorporeals' and D Kleyn, 'The Protection of Quasi-Possession in South African Law' in E Descheemaeker ed, *The Consequences of Possession* (Edinburgh University Press 2014). Possessory protection of servitudes similar to that described below is, however, found in modern law. In addition to *Ferrier v Walker*, considered below, see *e.g. Macdonald v Watson* (1830) 8 S 584; *Kirkpatrick v Murray* (1856) 19 D 91. The latter two cases are concerned with public rights of way rather than servitudes, but the principle is much the same.

[110] D.41.2.3pr. Compare though D.43.26.2.3 and D.43.19.7.

[111] (1832) 10 S 317.

Faced with the theoretical difficulty of possession of incorporeal things, and also with the practical need for possessory protection of servitudes, the compromise position was reached of saying that the person in apparent exercise of the servitude had 'quasi-possession'.[112] The apparent exercise of a servitude was protected by special interdicts, modelled on the interdict *uti possidetis* that was used to regulate possession of land.[113] For example, the apparent exercise of a servitude right of access was protected by the interdict *de itinere actuque privato*.[114] For protection by this interdict, it was necessary to have exercised the access for at least thirty days in the previous year, not by force, stealth or licence. It was not concerned with whether the servitude actually existed. However, it would have the result of placing the burden of proof on the party denying the existence of the servitude, if that question was subsequently raised. In effect, the possessory interdict could be used in place of the *actio confessoria*. Success with the interdict would mean that the party exercising the access could continue to do so unless and until the other party successfully brought the *actio negatoria*.

E. Extinction of Praedial Servitudes

A servitude could be extinguished by the agreement of the parties.[115] This consent could be implied, as where the dominant owner consented to the building of something on the route of a servitude right of access.[116] If the same person became owner of both properties, the servitude was extinguished by *confusio*.[117] The servitude did not revive if the properties were separated again, and had to be expressly reconstituted if it was required.[118]

A servitude could be lost by non-use. In classical law, the period for this was two years,[119] the same as the period for acquisition of ownership of land by *usucapio*.[120] Paul explains that the reason for this is that the *lex Scribonia*, discussed above, abolished only the acquisition of servitude by *usucapio*, not the acquisition of freedom in that way.[121] By possessing for two years without being subjected to the servitude, the servient owner acquired unfettered ownership by the operation of *usucapio*. Justinian applied the same periods as for *longi temporis praescriptio*,[122] namely ten years if the parties were resident in the same province, twenty years otherwise.[123]

---

[112] See *e.g.* D.8.5.10pr.
[113] See pp. 187–8.
[114] D.43.19. For other examples, see D.43.20 and D.43.22.
[115] D.8.6.6.1.
[116] D.8.6.8pr.
[117] D.8.6.1. *Confusio* in this sense means the same person becoming both creditor and debtor in the same obligation. It should not be confused with *confusio* in the sense of a mixture of substances belonging to two or more people, considered at pp. 237–8.
[118] D.8.2.30pr.
[119] Mentioned in C.3.34.14pr (AD 531).
[120] See pp. 239–43.
[121] D.41.3.4.28. See also D.8.2.6 (Gaius).
[122] See p. 241.
[123] C.3.34.13 (AD 531).

F. Praedial Servitudes in Modern Law

It has already been mentioned that the Scots law on servitudes has been strongly influenced by Roman law. We have seen in particular that Roman law has in recent times been a fertile source in the development of new forms of servitude. This may well continue, and Roman sources may continue to prove useful more generally wherever fundamental principles of servitudes are concerned, as opposed to cases raising technical issues in the law governing court procedure or conveyancing of land.

Chapter Summary

A praedial servitude (often called simply 'servitude') was a right held by the owner of one area of land (the dominant property) to make some specified use of neighbouring land or in some specific way to restrict the use of that neighbouring land (the servient property). Both the benefit and the burden of the servitude transmitted to new owners of these properties. For this reason, the benefit taken had to relate to the property, and to the owner only in the capacity of owner, rather than being a personal benefit to the dominant owner. The most common form of praedial servitude was a right of way over the servient property, for access to the dominant property, but there were other types. The modern Scots law of servitudes has been very much influenced by the Roman law, and is one of the most Roman parts of Scots law.

Further Reading

J.2.3
D.8.1–6; 43.19–23
C.3.34
W W Buckland, *A Text-Book of Roman Law from Augustus to Justinian* 3rd edn, revd P Stein (Cambridge University Press 1963) 258–67
H Hausmaninger and R Gamauf, *A Casebook on Roman Property Law* (G A Sheets trans, Oxford University Press 2012) 244–55
E Metzger ed, *A Companion to Justinian's Institutes* (Duckworth 1998) 67–70
J A C Thomas, *Textbook of Roman Law* (North-Holland 1976) 195–202
A Watson, *The Law of Property in the Later Roman Republic* (Oxford University Press 1968) chapter 8

CHAPTER FOURTEEN

Usufruct and Related Rights

A. Nature and Classification

Suppose that Marcus, the owner of a farm, is considering how to dispose of the farm on his death. He may decide that he wants the farm to go to his son. However, to provide for his wife, he decides that he wants to delay this so that his wife can stay on the farm until her own death. An arrangement of this kind would be very common, and could be achieved using a legal device called a usufruct. A usufruct was 'the right to the use and the fruits of another person's property, preserving the substance of the property'.[1] It involved ownership being given to one person, but making this subject to another real right (the usufruct) being given to another person, entitling the latter to use and enjoy the property as long as the usufruct lasted, which was usually for the holder's lifetime. The person holding the usufruct is known as the usufructuary. Usufruct is equivalent to the modern Scots proper liferent, which it has influenced.[2] Its use was almost invariably in family situations. For this reason, it was considered personal to the usufructuary, who could not transfer his or her right to another.[3]

As long as the usufruct lasted, the usufructuary was in a very similar position to that of an owner. The actual owner was all but excluded from the property, having no present rights to use and enjoy the property, and for this reason is often referred to as 'bare owner'. It is important to understand, though, that the usufructuary was not owner. The usufructuary was under an obligation to preserve the substance of the property[4] so that, when the usufruct came to an end, it could be turned over to the owner unimpaired. This has been described as the 'overriding principle' of

---

[1] J.2.4pr; D.7.1.1. More complex arrangements were possible. A testator could appoint his children as his heirs, but have them also share in the enjoyment of the usufruct. See D.7.2.8 and, for discussion of such a situation, J W Tellegen and O Tellegen-Couperus, 'Joint Usufruct in Cicero's *Pro Caecina*' in Birks, *New Perspectives*.
[2] It does not appear, however, that liferent is derived from usufruct: 'it appears that the equation of liferent with usufruct is a post-medieval Romanisation of an uncivilian institution' (*Stair Memorial Encyclopaedia*, vol 18 para 74). As well as the Roman influence, the development of liferent has been affected by feudal ideas.
[3] J.2.4.3.
[4] The Latin phrase *salva rerum substantia* expresses this idea.

usufruct, referring to the Scots and South African law,[5] but it equally well applies to Roman law.

Because of this obligation, it was in principle not possible to create a usufruct over anything that was used up through normal use, such as money or wine.[6] However, this proving inconvenient, a resolution of the Senate altered the position to allow for a usufruct in such things, subject to the heir being given security.[7] In these cases, the usufructuary was given ownership of the property, subject to a personal obligation to restore an equivalent. It was therefore not a true usufruct, and was known as a quasi-usufruct instead.

Certain other, similar rights also came to be recognised. *Usus* was the right to use the property, but not to take the fruits.[8] *Habitatio* was similar to *usus*, but related specifically to a house.[9] Finally, it was also possible to grant a right to the services of slaves and animals.[10] These rights are not recognised in Scots law, and so they are not considered in detail in this chapter. These rights together – usufruct, *usus*, *habitatio*, and services of slaves and animals – are sometimes called 'personal servitudes'. This categorisation as servitudes, though, may be post-classical, and may even be Justinianic. It is not clear why this category of personal servitudes was devised, as they have very little in common with the praedial servitudes that we saw in Chapter 13. Accordingly, the term 'personal servitude' is avoided in this chapter.

B. Creation of Usufruct

In most cases, a usufruct would be created in a will, with the usufruct being given to one person and ownership to another.[11] If it was desired to grant a usufruct during the lifetime of the granter, this could be done in the same way as praedial servitudes, by pact and stipulation.[12]

C. Exercise of Usufruct

The usufructuary was given two rights, the right of use and the right to take the fruits of the property. The usufructuary was also subject to certain obligations.

---

[5] W M Gordon and M J de Waal, 'Servitudes and Real Burdens' in Zimmermann, Visser and Reid, *Mixed Legal Systems* 755.
[6] Despite what follows in this paragraph, this is still the position in Scots law. The same effect can be achieved, however, by the creation of a trust, in which the property is held by trustees. See W J Dobie, *Manual of the Law of Liferent and Fee in Scotland* (W Green 1941) 77. More generally, the greater flexibility of trusts has led to 'trust liferents' of this kind being normally preferred in modern practice to liferents in the proper sense.
[7] J.2.4.2.
[8] J.2.5pr–1; D.7.8.2pr.
[9] J.2.5.2; D.8.10pr.
[10] J.2.5.3.
[11] J.2.4.1.
[12] See pp. 250–2.

(1) Use

As long as the usufruct lasted, the usufructuary had the sole right to use the property. The owner was excluded from use of the property. This right to the use of the property included the right to share that use, for example with family, slaves, guests and lodgers.[13] The usufructuary could sell the produce of the property or lease it out.[14] As we shall see below, though, this right of use was limited by the obligation to manage the property to the standard of the *bonus paterfamilias*, the prudent head of household. This obligation limited the right of use and limited the right to share that use, so that the usufructuary could not hire out property if the *bonus paterfamilias* would not do so.[15]

(2) Fruits

The usufructuary was entitled to the fruits of the property, such as crops produced from land, and also such things as the offspring of animals and milk, hair or wool produced by animals.[16] The usufructuary gained ownership of the fruits when they were separated from the principal, with the result that any fruits unharvested when the usufruct came to an end went to the owner of the property rather than to the heir of the usufructuary.[17]

Where a slave was held on usufruct, the right to fruits included the right to the slave's labour and any profits derived from it. A gift or legacy to a slave was not a fruit, however, and so was acquired by the owner of the slave unless it was given for the usufructuary's sake.[18]

One curious exception to the rule that offspring belonged to the usufructuary was that, where a slave was held on usufruct, any offspring of the slave belonged to the owner rather than the usufructuary.[19] Justinian tells us that this is because it would be 'absurd' for a human being to be considered a fruit, as nature provides fruits for human beings.[20] The true basis for the rule is uncertain. On one view, it was 'on the basis of the noble idea that a human being could not be treated as fruit for the benefit of other humans that this decision was reached', even though this would have the 'appalling' result that the mother and child could immediately be separated if the owner so chose.[21] A contrary view is that the child was too valuable to be allocated to the usufructuary.[22] There is also an intermediate view:

> The concession to humanity went no further than this, that the law would not countenance a rule which implied that slaves might be farmed . . . Offspring are

---

[13] See D.7.8.2.1–7.8.7 for discussion of the extent of this right.
[14] J.2.5.1; D.7.1.12.2.
[15] D.7.1.15.4. The example given here is clothes, which the *bonus paterfamilias* would not hire out as excessive use would lead to them wearing out.
[16] J.2.1.36.
[17] J.2.1.36.
[18] D.7.1.22.
[19] D.7.1.68pr.
[20] J.2.1.37.
[21] A Watson, 'Morality, Slavery and the Jurists in the Later Roman Republic' (1968) 42 Tulane LR 289, 292–3.
[22] Nicholas, *Introduction* 140; Borkowski, *Textbook* 169.

not *fructus*[23] because, different from livestock, the fertility of slaves is not callously managed in the interests of productivity.[24]

It is impossible to be certain of the reasoning behind the rule. For us, for whom slavery is outside our experience, it is difficult or impossible to follow fully a course of reasoning where slavery is taken for granted. All the same, it is difficult to believe that a culture that allowed a human being to be held in slavery would have very much regard to that individual's humanity. Indeed, in a scholarly article, the late Supreme Court judge Lord Rodger pointed out that slave women were indeed bought with regard to their fertility.[25] An alternative view of the question of why slave children did not count as fruits might consider the fact that human children are much more dependent on others for their support, requiring adult care for a much longer time and to a much greater degree than is normal for animals. An infant animal has an immediate economic value. By contrast, considered solely in economic terms, a child is more of a burden than an asset for many years after its birth.[26] It might easily happen that either the usufructuary or the slave would die before the slave was old enough to be productive. Particularly in a society where the chances of the child reaching adulthood may be estimated as being less than 50 per cent,[27] it may have been thought more appropriate for this burden to fall on the owner of the mother rather than on the usufructuary.

(3) Preserving the Substance of the Property

As has already been mentioned, the usufructuary was required to preserve the substance of the property. This was a limitation on the rights of the usufructuary. Except for the taking of fruits, the usufructuary was not entitled in principle to encroach on the substance of the property. The usufructuary could not, for example, demolish a building on the land that was subject to the usufruct.

Particular issues arise with timber, mines and quarries. Timber was not considered to be a fruit of the land, and so did not fall within the usufructuary's right to fruits.[28] Instead, it was considered to be part of the land, and so had to be maintained just as the rest of the property did. The usufructuary could, however, cut smaller trees for ordinary domestic use.[29]

It might be expected that any activity involving removal of material from the property would be prohibited, as an encroachment on the substance of the

---

[23] *I.e.* fruits.
[24] P Birks, 'An Unacceptable Face of Human Property' in Birks, *New Perspectives* 69.
[25] A Rodger, 'A Very Good Reason for Buying a Slave Woman?' (2007) 123 LQR 446, especially the text at footnote 40. See also below at p. 362.
[26] In one text (D.7.7.6.1) Ulpian envisages that a slave will be able to provide services of value from the age of five. It is clear from D.9.2.23.7, though, that an infant under one year of age was nonetheless capable of being assigned a market value.
[27] W Scheidel, 'Demography' in W Scheidel, I Morris and R Saller eds, *The Cambridge Economic History of the Greco-Roman World* (Cambridge University Press 2007) 38–41.
[28] Unless the land was a timber estate, where trees were, in effect, being grown as a crop.
[29] J.2.5.1; D.7.1.10.

property.[30] In Scots law, this is only permitted to a very limited extent. Other than taking minerals (such as coal or peat) for domestic use,[31] in Scots law the liferenter may only use existing mines and quarries, and even then only to the extent of the previous use and as long as there is no danger of exhaustion.[32] Roman law was much more permissive of mines and quarries. In Roman law, the usufructuary could use any existing mines and quarries, and open up new ones as long as that did not prejudice the agricultural use of the land or at least was more profitable than the land's existing use.[33] This was, however, subject to the *bonus vir* ('reasonable man') standard so, for example, the usufructuary could not make improvements that would not be sustainable by the owner of the property.[34]

(4) Remedies of the Owner

The usufructuary did not own the property, and the owner was entitled to get the property back at the end of the usufruct unimpaired in its substance. In addition to the procedure already mentioned for compelling the usufructuary to comply with the maintenance obligation, the usufructuary could also be delictually liable, in the same way as any other non-owner, for causing damage to the property.[35] The interdict against force and stealth could also be sought.[36]

To supplement these general remedies protecting the owner's interest in the property, the praetor could compel the usufructuary to give an enforceable undertaking[37] regarding his or her management of the property. This undertaking is known as the *cautio usufructuaria*. First, the usufructuary undertook to manage the property in the manner of the *bonus vir*, which here can be translated as 'reasonable man'.[38] This, Ulpian tells us, means that the usufructuary undertakes not to allow the value of the property to deteriorate and to manage the property with the same care as with his or her own property.[39] Second, the usufructuary undertakes to restore the property to the owner at the termination of the usufruct.[40] Third, the usufructuary undertakes not to act fraudulently with regard to the property.[41] In addition, the *cautio usufructuaria* was supplemented by an obligation for the usufructuary to give security that he or she would manage the property

---

[30] There are exceptions to this, such as the cutting of peat or the collection of salt from a salt pan, both of which will renew themselves over time.
[31] *Duke of Roxburghe v Duchess Dowager of Roxburghe* 19 Jan 1816, FC.
[32] *Wardlaw v Wardlaw's Trs* (1875) 2 R 368.
[33] D.7.1.13.5.
[34] D.7.1.13.6.
[35] D.7.1.13.2.
[36] D.7.1.13.2. On this interdict, see Watson, *Property* chapter 10.
[37] This was done using the form of contract known as *stipulatio*: D.7.9.5pr. On *stipulatio*, see Chapter 18. Ulpian appears at D.7.9.1pr to limit this rule to usufructs created by legacy, but at D.7.9.1.2 he makes it clear that the same rule applies to usufructs created in other situations.
[38] D.7.9.1pr.
[39] D.7.9.1.3.
[40] D.7.9.1pr.
[41] D.7.9.5pr.

in the manner of a *bonus vir*.[42] The level of security required was also measured by the standard of the *bonus vir*.[43] If the usufructuary failed to give security when required, the owner could bring an action to recover the property.[44] Equally, the usufructuary could not enforce the usufruct until security was given.[45] Where the usufruct was created by will, the obligation to give security could not be dispensed with by the testator.[46]

What if the usufructuary did not give the *cautio usufructuaria*? Could he or she still be held liable for the maintenance of the property? There is some doubt about this. However, it is generally thought that the owner could obtain an *actio in factum* to compel the usufructuary to carry out maintenance. There is some disagreement about when this possibility developed, but it has been suggested that it was most likely to have been in the late classical period.[47]

The usufructuary then was under an obligation to maintain the property, with this duty measured according to the standard of the *bonus vir*, and the usufructuary could be compelled to comply with the duty.[48] This duty extended to an obligation to keep up the numbers of a herd or flock of animals given in usufruct, from its young.[49] The duty of maintenance, however, only extended to ordinary repairs. Accordingly, if a house fell down due to old age, the usufructuary was not obliged to rebuild it.[50]

Where ordinary repairs were necessary, the usufructuary was obliged to carry them out. A distinction must be made between repairs and alterations.[51] A usufructuary had to make necessary repairs, but the position of alterations was less clear. In one text, Ulpian tells us that the usufructuary could make improvements, as long as the fundamental character of the property was not changed.[52] Accordingly, the usufructuary could redecorate the property or add decorative elements such as statuettes. The usufructuary could not, however, divide rooms, demolish walls between rooms or change the layout of the gardens. This is clear enough, although of course in practice there is plenty of room for disagreement about whether a particular operation changes the character of the property. Unfortunately from the point of view of clarity, though, a different text (from Neratius) gives a much stricter opinion. According to Neratius, the usufructuary is not permitted to make any alterations at all, even to the extent of not being permitted to replaster walls left

---

[42] D.7.1.13pr.
[43] C.3.33.4 (AD 226).
[44] D.7.9.7pr.
[45] D.7.1.13pr.
[46] C.6.54.7 (AD 225).
[47] P Hellwege, 'Enforcing the Liferenter's Obligation to Repair' (2014) 18 Edin LR 1, 6–8.
[48] D.7.1.9pr; C.3.33.7 (AD 243).
[49] J.2.1.38; D.7.1.68.2, 69. This was the case even though the young, as fruits, would initially belong to the usufructuary. They would cease to belong to the usufructuary when used to replace dead or worthless animals.
[50] D.7.1.7.2. Nor was the owner under any obligation to repair it. Compare *Scot v Forbes* (1755) Mor 8278.
[51] This distinction is not always easy to apply in practice for, after all, every repair necessarily involves an alteration to the existing state of the property, and it will not usually be possible to restore exactly the original state of the property.
[52] D.7.1.13.7.

in a rough condition. 'It is one thing', he says, 'to maintain what has been received, and another to make an alteration.'[53] It seems that Scots law, which also imposes this duty of maintenance,[54] is closer to Ulpian's position on this, and indeed will sometimes oblige the owner to pay compensation for improvements.[55]

(5) The Position in Modern Law

This issue has been considered relatively recently in Scots law, with the court making reference to Roman law, so it is appropriate to spend some time considering the position in modern law. The starting point for this is to consider the normal remedies that are available from a Scottish court. These are specific implement, to compel the defender to carry out some required act; interdict,[56] to forbid the carrying out of some prohibited act; and damages, to compensate the pursuer where the defender has breached a duty in a way that has caused the pursuer recoverable loss. It might be expected that specific implement would be available to compel the liferenter to make necessary repairs, interdict where it was feared that the liferenter would do something harmful to the property, and damages where the liferenter had already harmed the property. However, the position is a little more complicated than that, not to mention uncertain.

The Liferent Caution[57] Acts 1491 and 1535 imposed an obligation on the liferenter to give security that he or she would not waste or destroy the property, under penalty of deprivation of the fruits of the property. The question is whether this was intended to supplement or to replace the normal remedies. The institutional writer Erskine said that 'where waste is already committed, no action is competent to him who stands presently in the fee [*i.e.* the owner] for recovering damages'.[58] The reasoning for this is that, when the damage occurs, the liferent may still have many years left to run. The owner only suffers any actual loss when the liferent comes to an end, and by that time someone else may be owner. Erskine's reasoning has been criticised.[59] In any case, Erskine only mentions the non-availability of damages. For this reason, it has been suggested that interdict and specific implement should still be available, not being subject to the same objection as a claim for damages.[60]

The issue was considered in *Stronach's Executors v Robertson*.[61] In that case, the defender was the liferenter of a house. The pursuers were the owners ('fiars', in

---

[53] D.7.1.44.
[54] W J Dobie, *Manual of the Law of Liferent and Fee in Scotland* (W Green 1941) 204–8.
[55] W J Dobie, *Manual of the Law of Liferent and Fee in Scotland* (W Green 1941) 83–5.
[56] In Scots law, interdict is a much more restricted term than in Roman law. In Roman law, the term is used for orders of the praetor generally, including those ordering something to be done. In Scots law, an interdict is a prohibitory order of the court.
[57] Note that this word, meaning personal security (for which see pp. 277–8), is pronounced 'KAYshun' rather than 'KAWshun'.
[58] Erskine, *Institute* 2.9.59.
[59] *Stair Memorial Encyclopaedia*, vol 13 paras 1660–1.
[60] W J Dobie, *Manual of the Law of Liferent and Fee in Scotland* (W Green 1941) 243–7.
[61] 2002 SC 540.

Scots legal terminology). The pursuers alleged that the defender had allowed the house to fall into disrepair, and sought an order from the court compelling him to make necessary repairs, which failing the payment of damages. The pursuer was unsuccessful. The Inner House of the Court of Session held that the proper remedy was for the liferenter to be ordered to lodge a sum of money in the court as security for the damage. Other remedies were unavailable before the termination of the liferent, except perhaps in relation to timber, in respect of which the owner has an immediate right. In effect, then, the court decided that the Liferent Caution Acts replaced the normal remedies rather than supplementing them. The case is of particular interest for the court's discussion of the Roman sources and their place in modern law. It has, however, been criticised for misunderstanding the historical sources and for rendering Scots law out of step with related legal systems.[62]

D. Protection of Usufruct

A person who claimed to be the holder of a usufruct could assert this using the *actio confessoria* which we saw in Chapter 13 for the protection of praedial servitudes.[63] As this was a real action rather than a personal one,[64] it could be successfully brought against a third party, such as a person acquiring ownership of the land. In other words, usufruct was a real right, just as liferent is in modern law. In the same way, the *actio negatoria* could be used to deny the existence of a usufruct.[65]

In addition to these remedies, which asserted the existence or otherwise of rights in the property, we have seen also that there existed possessory interdicts to regulate interim possession of the property until the question of right could be determined.[66] In simple terms, a person in possession of property was entitled to remain in possession until the question of entitlement was determined and, if dispossessed, was entitled to be restored to possession in the meantime. In possessory proceedings, it was not permissible to assert ownership or any other kind of right to the property, as these proceedings were concerned only with regulating interim possession. Instead, a claim to a possessory interdict could only be defeated by demonstrating that the possession had been acquired by force, stealth or licence from the other party. The issue of a possessory interdict did not, however, prejudge the question of who was ultimately entitled to the property. Accordingly, the loser in the possessory proceedings was quite able then to raise an action based on a claim of ownership or some other right in the property.

In modern Scots law, there is no doubt that a liferenter (the Scots equivalent of a usufructuary) possesses the property, and so in Scots law a person claiming to have a liferent has access to the normal possessory remedies. However, the Roman jurists seem to have felt some discomfort about calling a usufructuary a

---

[62] P Hellwege, 'Enforcing the Liferenter's Obligation to Repair' (2014) 18 Edin LR 1.
[63] See p. 255.
[64] On real actions, see pp. 161–3.
[65] See W W Buckland, 'The Protection of Servitudes in Roman Law' (1930) 46 LQR 447.
[66] See pp. 187–9.

possessor. This is presumably because, as we have seen, the owner of the property continued to have possession while the usufruct lasted, and it was seen as problematic to give the name of possessor to both the owner and the usufructuary. We are told in numerous texts that usufructuary does not have possession of the property.[67] Elsewhere, the term 'quasi-possession' or something similar is often used,[68] to indicate that the usufructuary is 'almost a possessor' or 'a sort of possessor'. All the same, we are told that the usufructuary had access to the normal possessory interdicts.[69] It is only from a passage preserved in a collection of classical texts known as the *Vatican Fragments*[70] that we know that, in the case of a person claiming to hold the property as usufructuary, the interdicts were given in *utilis* form[71] rather than in standard form.[72]

E. Extinction of Usufruct

The normal purpose of a usufruct was to provide for a family member, especially a widow, for life. Accordingly, although a usufruct could be given for a limited term if desired, it could not in any circumstances last any longer than the lifetime of the usufructuary. When the usufructuary died, the usufruct came to an end.[73] The usufruct would also end if the property was destroyed,[74] or if the usufructuary became a slave or ceased to be a Roman citizen.[75] In addition, a usufruct could also be extinguished in the same ways as a praedial servitude,[76] such as non-use or the same person becoming both owner and usufructuary.[77]

Chapter Summary

Usufruct, which has influenced the development of the modern Scots law of liferent, was a right to use and enjoy the fruits of property for a period of time, usually the lifetime of the holder of the usufruct (known as the usufructuary). It was limited, though, by the obligation not to encroach on the substance of the property.

---

[67] See *e.g.* G.2.93; D.43.26.6.2.
[68] See *e.g.* D.39.5.27; D.43.16.3.17; D.43.17.4.
[69] D.43.16.3.13; D.43.17.4.
[70] This was a post-classical compilation of classical texts. What remains of it was rediscovered in the early nineteenth century. For an overview, see Robinson, *Sources* 64–5, 113.
[71] See p. 51.
[72] *Vatican Fragments* 90.
[73] D.7.4.3.3.
[74] J.2.4pr; D.7.4.5.2; D.7.4.10.1. Compare though *Scot v Forbes* (1755) Mor 8278 (Scotland); *Kidson v Jimspeed Enterprises CC* 2009 (5) SA 246 (South Africa).
[75] J.2.4.3.
[76] See p. 257.
[77] J.2.4.3.

Further Reading

J.2.4–5
D.7.1–9
C.3.33
W W Buckland, 'The Conception of Usufruct in Classical Law' (1927) 43 LQR 326
H Hausmaninger and R Gamauf, *A Casebook on Roman Property Law* (G A Sheets trans, Oxford University Press 2012) 256–65
P Hellwege, 'Enforcing the Liferenter's Obligation to Repair' (2014) 18 Edin LR 1
E Metzger ed, *A Companion to Justinian's Institutes* (Duckworth 1998) 66–7
G Pugliese, 'On Roman Usufruct' (1965–6) 40 Tulane LR 523
J A C Thomas, *Textbook of Roman Law* (North-Holland 1976) 202–8
A Watson, *The Law of Property in the Later Roman Republic* (Oxford University Press 1968) chapter 9

CHAPTER FIFTEEN

Rights in Security

A. The Nature and Function of Security

Suppose that I want you to lend me money. If you agree to do that, you are taking a risk. All may go well – I may repay you in accordance with our agreement – but it cannot be guaranteed. I may run off with the money. I may have some financial crisis that prevents me paying my debts. The longer the term of the loan is, the greater the risk. A right in security is a means of protecting your position. Equally, it is in my interest to be able to offer security, because it will mean that I am more likely to be able to persuade you to lend to me, and the reduced risk to you is likely to mean that I will be able to get better terms. Justinian says therefore that a right in security 'benefits both parties, the debtor because it helps him get credit more easily, and the creditor because it helps him give credit safely'.[1]

The basic idea of a right in security is that it gives the creditor an alternative source from which payment[2] can be obtained.[3] This alternative source can be one of two things. First, the debtor may agree that some item of his or her property can be used in security for the debt. This is known as a real security, because it gives the creditor a real right in an item of property. Second, the debtor may find a third party willing to guarantee payment of the debt. The idea here is that, if the debtor fails to pay, the creditor can look to the third party for payment. This is known as a personal security.[4]

Where a right in security exists, the creditor thus has two rights: the personal right against the debtor, entitling the creditor to payment; and the right in security, which gives the creditor an alternative means of getting payment. The right in security is ancillary to the main obligation. In other words, a right in security has

---

[1] J.3.14.4. This is referring specifically to the form of security called pledge, but the point is a general one.
[2] Strictly speaking, there is no reason why a right in security cannot secure a non-financial obligation, but in practice securing a loan of money is the purpose for which it is almost always used. It is therefore convenient to talk in these terms.
[3] This is a simplification. As we shall see below, it is possible for a right in security to consist simply in a right to retain property belonging to the debtor until payment is made.
[4] We saw at pp. 98–9 that, in the first century AD, the *SC Velleianum* introduced an important limitation on personal securities, by prohibiting women from agreeing to act in this capacity.

to secure *something*. It cannot exist on its own, as a freestanding right.[5] Its purpose is to secure performance of the main obligation, and if the main obligation is extinguished then the right in security is extinguished as well. For example, suppose that you lend me a sum of money, and to secure the loan I grant you a right in security. If I repay the loan, that extinguishes the debt, and the right in security falls as well.[6] The same is not true in reverse, however. While the security depends for its existence on the main obligation, the main obligation can survive without the security. If the security is extinguished for reasons unconnected with the main obligation, the main obligation will survive intact.[7] For example, suppose that the security that I grant you is a real security over some item of my property. If the property is destroyed, the security right will be extinguished. After all, if the essence of a security right is that it gives the creditor alternative recourse to get payment, the security cannot survive if the means of that alternative recourse is destroyed. The main obligation will survive, however, so I will still owe you the money.

B. Real Securities

As stated, a real security involves the creditor getting a real right in some item of property belonging to the debtor.[8] The creditor thus has two rights: a personal right against the debtor, entitling the creditor to be paid; and a real right in some item of the debtor's property. A real right in security will typically operate in one of two ways: either it allows the creditor to take and keep possession until the debt is paid, or else it allows the creditor to sell the property to pay off the debt if the debtor defaults. Sometimes both will be present.

One early arrangement fulfilling a security function in Roman law was called *nexum*, in which the debtor in effect used his own person as security. Failure to pay the debt resulted in enslavement. *Nexum* was greatly restricted by a *lex Poetelia* in the fourth century BC, and does not appear in accounts of classical law.[9] It will not be considered further here. Classical Roman law recognised three forms of real security: *fiducia*, pledge (*pignus*) and hypothec (*hypotheca*). Before going into these, a preliminary point must be made. In the Roman texts, the terms *pignus* and *hypotheca* are often used interchangeably,[10] or almost so, and there does seem to be a historical relationship between them. As a result, it is sometimes difficult to determine which is being talked about and whether the point being made applies

---

[5] The same principle is followed in modern law. See *e.g. Trotter v Trotter* 2001 SLT (Sh Ct) 42; *Nisbet's Creditors v Robertson* (1791) Mor 9554.
[6] At least in principle. It may be necessary in practice for the security to be formally discharged.
[7] C.4.24.6 (AD 225).
[8] Thus, for example, where goods held on security were sold as part of the debtor's insolvency, the secured creditor was entitled to be paid first: D.42.1.15.5.
[9] For discussion, see F de Zulueta, 'The Recent Controversy about Nexum' (1913) 29 LQR 137; Jolowicz and Nicholas, *Historical Introduction* 164–6; A Watson, *Rome of the XII Tables: Persons and Property* (Princeton University Press 1975) chapter 9.
[10] See *e.g.* D.13.7.1pr.

to one or both of them. The usage here is the one generally used in modern texts, and is the usage of modern Scots law. According to that usage, the distinction is as follows: a pledge requires possession of the property to be given to the creditor; in a hypothec, the debtor is allowed to retain possession.

(1) Fiducia

The earliest form of security involved an outright transfer of ownership by the debtor to the creditor,[11] coupled with an undertaking by the creditor to transfer the property back when the debt was repaid.[12] This agreement was known as a *fiducia*.[13] If the creditor failed to reconvey the property to the debtor when the debt was repaid, the debtor was given an action, the *actio fiduciae*, for recovery of the property. *Fiducia* had the great disadvantage from the debtor's point of view that the debtor lost ownership of the property, retaining only a personal right against the creditor. As a result, the debtor's right to the property would be defeated if the creditor sold the property to a third party. *Fiducia* declined in importance in the classical period, possibly because of the development of hypothec.[14]

(2) Pledge

(a) Nature

Pledge as a right in security was created by the giving of possession to the creditor of property belonging to the debtor. The advantage of this to the debtor was that it allowed the debtor to borrow money on security of the property without giving up ownership.[15] On the other hand, it had the disadvantage of requiring the debtor to give up possession. It therefore restricted, for example, the ability of those in business to raise finance on security of their stock or the tools of their trade.[16]

A security of this type exists in Scots law under the name of pledge, and there has been clear Roman influence on its development.[17] However, although

---

[11] This transfer was effected using the formal methods of transfer used for conveyance of property falling into the category of *res mancipi*. On these, see pp. 198–9. For discussion of the relationship between *fiducia* and pledge, considered below, see J W Tellegen and O Tellegen-Couperus, '*Fiducia Cum Creditore* and *Pignus*: Two of a Kind?' in J Sondel, J Reszczyński and P Ściślicki, *Roman Law as Formative of Modern Legal Systems: Studies in Honour of Wiesław Litewski*, vol 2 (Jagiellonian University Press 2003).

[12] Until 1970, this was a normal way of securing debts against land in Scotland, under the name of *ex facie* absolute disposition. There does not, however, appear to be any historical connection with the Roman *fiducia*. The *ex facie* absolute disposition is no longer competent: Conveyancing and Feudal Reform (Scotland) Act 1970, s. 9(3).

[13] Specifically a *fiducia cum creditore*, or *fiducia* with a creditor. There could also be a *fiducia cum amico*, or *fiducia* with a friend, which could fulfil similar functions to those of a modern trust. The term *fiducia* is related to the word for faith, *fides*, and has a connotation of the transferee (whether friend or creditor) being entrusted with the property, and the transferor relying on the transferee's proper conduct.

[14] R Barber, 'Fiducia and Hypothec' (1978) 13 Irish Jurist 192. On hypothec, see below.

[15] See though below, especially on the *lex commissoria*.

[16] For similar concerns in modern law, see Scottish Law Commission, *Report on Moveable Transactions* (SLC No 249, 2017) paras 17.25–8.

[17] A J M Steven, *Pledge and Lien* (Edinburgh Legal Education Trust 2008) paras 3-66 – 3-71.

the core idea of creation of security by delivery of possession is accepted, the Scots law on pledge has departed from the Roman law in a number of respects. Perhaps the most obvious is that, in Scots law, a pledge can only be created over moveable property. In Roman law, pledges were not subject to that restriction, and could be created over land.[18]

(b) Parties' Rights, Duties and Liabilities

In a pledge, the creditor's primary right was to retain possession of the property until the debt was paid.[19] The creditor was not entitled to use the property, and indeed a pledge creditor who used the property was liable for theft.[20] Scots law by contrast does not impose liability for theft in this way. However, on this point Scots law of pledge does otherwise follow Roman law, the Roman rule having been adopted in place of an earlier, more liberal rule on use of the property by the creditor.[21] The creditor was also entitled to be reimbursed for any necessary expenses.[22]

The debtor's primary duty was to pay the debt owed. This duty, though, arose from the debt itself rather than from the right in security.[23] It was possible for the parties to agree that the creditor could take the fruits of the property in place of interest on the debt, these being either natural produce of the property or rent obtained from letting it out.[24] Such an arrangement, known as *antichresis*, was an exception to the rule that the creditor could not use the property. On payment of the debt, the debtor was entitled to bring an action, the *actio pigneraticia*, for return of the property.[25]

What if the property was lost or damaged while in the creditor's possession? Because the pledge was partly in the interests of the creditor, he or she was held to the 'highest standard of care' (*exacta diligentia*).[26] This was not, however, a guarantee of the property's safety. If the property was damaged accidentally and without fault, or through the fault of a third party, the normal rule applied that property perished at the risk of the owner.[27] The debtor was owner of the property, and so bore the risk of damage through accident or the fault of a third party.[28] The loss or destruction of the property would destroy the real right in security, although the debt itself would continue in existence.

---

[18] See *e.g.* D.13.7.8pr; C.2.81.1 (AD 290).
[19] The question of whether the creditor could sell the property on the debtor's default is considered separately, below. The emperor Gordian extended the creditor's right to allow retention of the property until all debts owed by that debtor to that creditor were paid: C.8.26.1.2 (AD 239).
[20] D.47.2.55pr.
[21] A J M Steven, *Pledge and Lien* (Edinburgh Legal Education Trust 2008) paras 7-04–7-07.
[22] C.4.24.7.1 (AD 241).
[23] Confusion on this point is particularly likely in Roman law since, as we shall see at p. 350, the contract for the creation of the pledge is itself constituted by the delivery of the property.
[24] D.20.1.11.1. See also C.4.24.1 (AD 207).
[25] J.3.14.1; D.13.7.9.3.
[26] J.3.14.4. See also D.13.6.5.2; D.13.7.24.3.
[27] D.20.1.21.2; C.4.24.9 (AD 293).
[28] See also *e.g.* C.4.24.6 (AD 225), concerning pledged property lost or destroyed in an attack by brigands. Of course, the brigands themselves would be liable for the damage, although the practical difficulties in enforcing a remedy against them might be formidable.

(c) Enforcement and the Power of Sale

If the debtor fails to pay the debt, it is likely that the creditor will want to recover the money owed by selling the property. Originally, however, there was no power of sale in a pledge unless expressly agreed by the parties. Such express agreement became standard. This development has been linked to the adoption of coined money in the third century BC facilitating the liquidation of assets into money.[29] An express power of sale was often coupled with a clause known as the *pactum legis commissoriae*, which gave the creditor ownership of the property on the debtor's default.[30]

So much did it become standard to agree an express power of sale that, during the classical period, it came to be implied even where not mentioned.[31] Rules developed, however, to moderate the potential unfairness of an unrestricted power of sale. For example, the debtor had to be notified before the sale could take place,[32] and could redeem the pledge by paying the debt at any time up to sale.[33] Again, if the sale raised more than enough to repay the debt, the surplus had to be turned over to the debtor.[34]

The emperor Constantine abolished the *pactum legis commissoriae*.[35] As an alternative to this, however, it was possible to apply to the emperor for an award of the property if a purchaser could not be found.[36] This involved an official valuation of the property, followed by notice to the debtor. After a year's delay, the creditor was awarded bonitary ownership,[37] and could acquire full ownership by *usucapio*.[38] The debtor could redeem the pledge at any time before *usucapio* was complete. The creditor was taken to have acquired the property at the official valuation, and had to be content with that if it was less than the debt. If it was more, the excess had to be paid to the debtor.[39] This procedure for awarding ownership to the creditor in place of payment is known as foreclosure.

Justinian laid down a new set of rules for sale and foreclosure.[40] According to these rules, if the parties had made express provision for sale, that would be followed. Otherwise, the creditor had to initiate the process of sale by giving

---

[29] D E Phillipson, 'Development of the Roman Law of Debt Security' (1967–8) 20 Stanford L Rev 1230, 1241.
[30] D E Phillipson, 'Development of the Roman Law of Debt Security' (1967–8) 20 Stanford L Rev 1230, 1242.
[31] H L E Verhagen, 'The Evolution of *Pignus* in Classical Roman Law: *Ius Honorarium* and *Ius Novum*' (2013) 81 TvR 52; D E Phillipson, 'Development of the Roman Law of Debt Security' (1967–8) 20 Stanford L Rev 1230, 1242–3.
[32] C.8.27.4 (AD 225).
[33] C.8.27.8 (AD 239).
[34] H L E Verhagen, 'The Evolution of *Pignus* in Classical Roman Law: *Ius Honorarium* and *Ius Novum*' (2013) 81 TvR 52, 70–2; D E Phillipson, 'Development of the Roman Law of Debt Security' (1967–8) 20 Stanford L Rev 1230, 1243.
[35] C.8.34.3 (AD 326).
[36] C.8.33.1 (AD 229); C.8.33.2 (AD 238).
[37] The term 'bonitary ownership' arises from the situation where a person has acquired property using an informal method, where a formal method should have been used. The bonitary owner was ultimately protected as if owner, but was strictly speaking not owner. See pp. 201–2.
[38] This was a mode of acquisition of property by possessing it for a period of time. See pp. 239–43.
[39] Buckland, *Textbook* 474.
[40] C.8.33.3 (AD 530).

notice to the debtor or obtaining a judgment from the court. Two years from this, the creditor had to give a further notice to the debtor, if the debtor could be found. A judge would then consider the circumstances and set a time limit for the debtor to appear and redeem the debt. If the debtor did not do so, the creditor could seek a further order of the court awarding him or her the property, at the valuation set by the court. Thereafter, the debtor still had two years to redeem the pledge before the property became irrecoverable. The creditor was entitled still to recover any shortfall in value, and the debtor was entitled to any surplus.

Scots law has not followed Roman law in this respect. In Scotland, at common law, the pledge creditor has no power of sale without express agreement[41] or the authority of the court.[42] In modern practice, most pledges are regulated by the Consumer Credit Act 1974.[43] This does contain a power of sale,[44] but it is not derived from Roman law.

(3) Hypothec

A hypothec was a form of real right in security which, unlike a pledge, did not require the creditor to have possession of the property. The origin of hypothec lay in agricultural tenancies.[45] It developed initially to deal with the problem that a tenant could often not afford to pay the rent until the crop had been harvested and sold, so the landlord then ran the risk of the tenant running into financial difficulties and being unable to pay. The crop might fail, for example. Equally, the tenant's main assets were livestock, slave labourers and farming equipment. These could not be given in pledge without giving up control, which would make farming impossible. Accordingly, the landlord and tenant might enter into an agreement whereby, on failure of the tenant to pay the rent, the landlord could take possession of the crops and the tenant's moveable goods. By the classical period, it could be said to be customary to agree to this,[46] to the extent that a hypothec over the crop came to be implied as security for the rent.[47] A hypothec in favour of the landlord was also implied in the case of leases of urban property, over goods present on the property.[48] The goods to which this hypothec applied were known as the *invecta et illata*, a term also used in modern Scots law, which means not simply any goods brought onto the property but those intended to remain there.[49] This differed from rural leases. While a hypothec over *invecta et*

---

[41] Stair, *Institutions* 1.13.13.
[42] Bell, *Principles* s. 207.
[43] For the scope of the Consumer Credit Act 1974, see ss. 8 and 189 of that Act.
[44] Consumer Credit Act 1974, s. 121.
[45] R van den Bergh, 'The Development of the Landlord's Hypothec' (2009) 15 Fundamina 155, 157. On leases generally, see pp. 367–9.
[46] D.47.2.62.8.
[47] D.20.2.7pr.
[48] D.20.2.3; D.20.2.4pr. In this case, the hypothec gave security, not simply for arrears of rent, but also for deterioration of the property resulting from the tenant's fault: D.20.2.2.
[49] D.20.2.7.1.

illata could be *expressly* created in a rural lease, they (as opposed to crops) were not covered by the *implied* hypothec. It has been suggested that this is because 'the *invecta et illata* of a rural tenant was too important to be tacitly hypothecated: these were the things he needed to make a living. Without them he could not work or survive.'[50] If this is the case, it can be seen as an example of a wider principle, applying to hypothecs generally. Ulpian tells us:

> A general hypothec over present and future assets does not cover things that someone is unlikely to give specially as security. For example, there must be left to the debtor household articles, clothes and those of his slaves which are used in such a way that he would certainly not want to give them in pledge, for example one employed in services that were essential to him or who held his affection.[51]

A number of other implied hypothecs also developed. One example of this was a preference given to the state for payment of taxes.[52]

As the quote from Ulpian indicates, even outside the context of leases, it was possible to create a hypothec by agreement. This could extend to the debtor's property generally, and even be agreed to extend to property acquired by the debtor in the future.[53] An express hypothec was created simply by the agreement of the parties, without any necessary formalities.[54]

Hypothec had the major advantage for the debtor that, because the debtor kept possession of the property, he or she could continue to make use of it. Further, the fact that it was not necessary for the debtor to give up ownership or possession of the property meant that the same property could be used to secure debts owed to more than one creditor. Where multiple hypothecs were created over the same property, the rule was that an earlier hypothec took precedence over a later one.[55] We would say that the earlier security 'ranked' before the later. This meant that the holder of the earlier hypothec had a prior claim on the property, and was entitled to be paid first from the proceeds of its sale.

The praetor provided an interdict, the *interdictum Salvianum*, allowing the creditor to take possession of the property subject to the hypothec.[56] This, though, is consistent with the hypothec being simply a matter of personal agreement between the parties. The hypothec became a real right when an action enforceable against third parties, the *actio Serviana*, was introduced.[57] Given the lack of

---

[50] R van den Bergh, 'The Development of the Landlord's Hypothec' (2009) 15 Fundamina 155, 161.
[51] D.20.1.6. An example of the last might be a slave who was the mistress or natural child of the master: D.20.1.8.
[52] C.8.14.1 (AD 213). For other examples, see D E Phillipson, 'Development of the Roman Law of Debt Security' (1967–8) 20 Stanford L Rev 1230, 1246–7.
[53] Such a hypothec thus operates in a very similar way to a modern floating charge.
[54] D.20.1.4. Of course, the hypothec would often be recorded in writing but, as Gaius tells us here, this was for purposes of making the hypothec easier to prove rather than it being a requirement for constitution.
[55] D.20.4.11pr. This was the case even if the later hypothec was agreed earlier. The important point was when the hypothec was actually created.
[56] G.4.147.
[57] R van den Bergh, 'The Development of the Landlord's Hypothec' (2009) 15 Fundamina 155, 165. See also C.8.13.14 (AD 293).

formality and publicity in the creation of a hypothec, this would often have harsh consequences for third parties acquiring in good faith.

In Scots law, a hypothec, in the broad sense of a non-possessory security, may be constituted voluntarily, although the term 'hypothec' is not normally used in this case. However, this requires registration in the Land Register, which is a public register, thus giving notice of the security's existence to third party acquirers.[58] This security, called the 'standard security', is not derived from Roman law. As far as moveables are concerned, other than ships and aircraft, for which special provision is made, and floating charges, which can extend to a debtor's whole property but which are only available to limited classes of debtor, it is not possible to create a hypothec over moveables in Scots law by agreement. The only recognised implied hypothec over moveables in Scots law is the landlord's hypothec. This is similar to the landlord's hypothec in Roman law, by which it has been influenced,[59] but it is now restricted to leases of commercial property.[60] Protection is given to good faith acquirers of property subject to the landlord's hypothec.[61]

(4) Retention

A final point to mention is retention, the *ius retentionis*. This is a right that arises in certain circumstances, where one person has custody of property belonging to another, and the law refuses to allow the owner to recover the property. In certain circumstances, the person with custody of the property could defend an action for recovery of the property with the *exceptio doli* (the defence of deceit).[62] We have seen one example of this, the right of a good faith improver of property to retain possession until compensated for the improvements.[63] Another example was the right of the borrower of property (under a contract of *commodatum*)[64] to retain the property until compensated for necessary expenditure.[65] It is unclear whether the person retaining the property was given a real right, though certain texts make an analogy with pledge, which was certainly a real right.[66] The Roman law of retention forms the basis of the Scots law of lien,[67] which is indeed a real right.[68]

---

[58] See generally C Anderson, *Property: A Guide to Scots Law* (W Green 2016) chapter 15.
[59] A J M Steven, 'Rights in Security over Moveables' in *History of Private Law in Scotland, vol I* 347–9.
[60] Bankruptcy and Diligence etc (Scotland) Act 2007, s. 208(3).
[61] Bankruptcy and Diligence etc (Scotland) Act 2007, s. 208(5).
[62] See p. 423.
[63] See p. 224.
[64] See pp. 347–9.
[65] D.47.2.15.2.
[66] See *e.g.* D.47.2.15.2.
[67] See A J M Steven, *Pledge and Lien* (Edinburgh Legal Education Trust 2008) para 10–65, describing the law laid down in one early Scots case as 'pure Roman law'. See also M Wiese, 'Liens: A Closer Look at Some Conceptual Foundations' (2011) 44 Comparative and International Law Journal of South Africa 80, considering Scots law alongside Dutch and South African law. There has also been considerable English influence over the Scots law of lien. Indeed, the name 'lien' itself seems to have come to Scotland from England: A J M Steven, *Pledge and Lien* (Edinburgh Legal Education Trust 2008) paras 10–96 and 10–127.
[68] A J M Steven, *Pledge and Lien* (Edinburgh Legal Education Trust 2008) chapter 14.

C. Personal Securities

(1) Adpromissio

There is an alternative means of giving security. This does not involve the creation of a real right in the debtor's property. However, it is included here because it has a similar function to real security. We are concerned here with personal securities. A personal security involves a third party who undertakes to pay the debt or perform the obligation if the debtor cannot. This arrangement is often called guarantee or surety. The Scots term, which is used here,[69] is caution (pronounced not as written, but as 'KAYshun'). There are then three parties involved: the creditor, who is owed performance of the obligation; the principal debtor, the person who has undertaken to perform the obligation; and the cautioner (pronounced 'KAYshunner'), who undertook to pay if the principal debtor did not. This kind of arrangement was very common in Roman times: evidently much more so than in the modern world, where real security is more often sought.[70]

(a) Sponsio and Fidepromissio

The earliest form of cautionary obligation in Roman law was *sponsio*. This was constituted by the form of contract called *stipulatio*. Later, in Chapter 18, we will see this contract in some detail. In simple terms, though, it involved here the cautioner undertaking the obligation using formal words. *Sponsio* was only available to Roman citizens, but later another form of caution called *fidepromissio* was developed, which was open to non-citizens. *Sponsio* and *fidepromissio* were very similar, and were subject to various limitations. They could only be used to guarantee obligations also created by *stipulatio*. Following a *lex Furia* of around 200 BC, both lapsed two years after the debt fell due, did not bind the cautioner's heirs and, where there was more than one cautioner, each was only liable for a proportionate share of the debt.

(b) Fideiussio

A new form, *fideiussio*, developed from the late Republic to avoid these limitations, and became the most common method of creating a cautionary obligation. In *fideiussio*, there was no limitation period, the cautioner's heirs were bound and, if there was more than one cautioner, each could be pursued for the whole debt. Indeed, it was not necessary to pursue the principal debtor at all. Instead, the creditor could proceed immediately against the cautioner. This gave rise to a practical difficulty. We have seen[71] that, once an action had reached the stage of *litis contestatio*,[72] the action was said to be 'consumed'. This meant that no further

---

[69] It is also used by the institutional writers even when referring to the Roman law. See *e.g.* Erskine, *Institute* 3.3.63.
[70] See Zimmermann, *Obligations* 115–16 for discussion of the reasons for this.
[71] See pp. 35, 40.
[72] This is the point at which the issues for determination have been agreed, and the matter is ready to proceed to trial. Under the *legis actiones* and formulary procedures, *litis contestatio* was the conclusion of the proceedings before the praetor.

action could be brought on the same facts. This meant that the creditor had to make a once and for all decision on which person to sue, the principal debtor or the cautioner. If the creditor sued one and failed for whatever reason to recover what was owed, it would not then be possible to sue the other. There was another difficulty as well. In practice, the creditor would be expected to seek performance first from the principal debtor. To choose to sue the cautioner would be seen as casting doubt on the principal debtor's creditworthiness. If this doubt was not well founded, the creditor would be open to potential delictual liability for the insult.[73]

Various reforms were made to *fideiussio* over time. The emperor Hadrian introduced the 'benefit of division' (*beneficium divisionis*).[74] This applied when there was more than one cautioner, and limited each cautioner's liability to a proportionate share (excluding any cautioners who were insolvent when the debt fell due). Justinian disapplied the rule that bringing an action against one of cautioner and principal debtor barred further action against the other.[75] He also introduced the 'benefit of discussion' (*beneficium excussionis vel ordinis*), by which the creditor could be compelled to proceed first against the principal debtor.[76]

Fideiussio has been very influential in later law.[77] Scotland is no exception to this.[78] For example, the benefit of division and the benefit of discussion have been accepted in Scots law, albeit the latter has been abolished for money claims,[79] and in his discussion of them Stair draws on Roman sources.[80]

(2) Adstipulatio

A somewhat different arrangement, though still involving the introduction of a third party, was *adstipulatio*. This did not involve the third party guaranteeing the obligation, however. Instead, after the initial promise to pay or perform had been made to the creditor (by *stipulatio*), the debtor made an identical promise to the third party. Performance to either would extinguish the obligation. This arrangement allowed the third party to enforce the obligation on the creditor's behalf if the creditor was unable to act. The main use of *adstipulatio*, Gaius explains,[81] was for cases where the original promise was to be carried out after the promisee's death. In other words, it was primarily a device used to circumvent the rule that a *stipulatio* to take effect after the promisee's death was void. *Adstipulatio* was obsolete by the late Empire.

---

[73] D.47.10.19. This would be based on the delict of *iniuria*. For *iniuria* generally, see Chapter 23.
[74] G.3.121.
[75] C.8.40.28 (AD 531).
[76] Nov.4 (AD 535).
[77] See *e.g* M Habersack and R Zimmermann, 'Legal Change in a Codified System: Recent Developments in Germany Suretyship Law' (1999) 3 Edin LR 272, 273.
[78] For a general discussion of the historical development of the Scots law of caution, see *Stair Memorial Encyclopaedia*, vol 3 paras 805–15.
[79] Mercantile Law Amendment Act (Scotland) 1856, s. 8.
[80] Stair, *Institutions* 1.18.5 and 20.
[81] G.3.117. See A Watson, 'Illogicality and Roman Law' (1972) 7 Israel L Rev 14, 21.

Chapter Summary

A right in security is a right that is ancillary to the main obligation owed by the debtor to the creditor. Rights in security fall into two broad categories, real and personal. A real security is a real right held by the creditor in some item of the debtor's property, entitling the creditor either to retain possession of that property until payment or performance, or to sell it to recover what is due. A personal security is a personal right held by the creditor against a third party who has agreed to guarantee performance of the obligation, and from whom performance can be demanded if the principal debtor should default. Both real and personal securities fall if the main obligation falls.

Further Reading

J.3.14.4; 3.20
D.13.7; 20.1–6
C.2.28; 4.24; 8.13–34

R van den Bergh, 'The Development of the Landlord's Hypothec' (2009) 15 Fundamina 155

R J Goebel, 'Reconstructing the Roman Law of Real Security' (1961–2) Tulane LR 29

W M Gordon, 'Roman Influence on the Scots Law of Real Security' in R Evans-Jones ed, *The Civil Law Tradition in Scotland* (Stair Society 1995)

H Hausmaninger and R Gamauf, *A Casebook on Roman Property Law* (G A Sheets trans, Oxford University Press 2012) 266–319

E Metzger ed, *A Companion to Justinian's Institutes* (Duckworth 1998) 70–3

D E Phillipson, 'Development of the Roman Law of Debt Security' (1967–8) 20 Stanford L Rev 1230

A J M Steven, 'Rights in Security over Moveables' in R Zimmermann and K Reid eds, *A History of Private Law in Scotland, Volume I: Introduction and Property* (Oxford University Press 2000)

H L E Verhagen, 'The Evolution of *Pignus* in Classical Roman Law: *Ius Honorarium* and *Ius Novum*' (2013) 81 TvR 51

R Zimmermann, *The Law of Obligations: Roman Foundations of the Civilian Tradition* (Oxford University Press 1996) 114–36

PART FOUR

The Law of Things: Succession

The next part of the law of things is the law of succession, which governs what happens to a person's property and obligations when that person dies. The Roman law of succession has some important fundamental differences from the Scots law, and much of the Roman influence that there was has been superseded by modern legislation. However, as we shall see as we go along, there are some points of continuing Roman influence.

Part Four consists of a single chapter, namely Chapter 16. This chapter begins by considering some general concepts in the law of succession. It then considers in turn the cases of intestate succession (*i.e.* where there is no will) and testate succession (*i.e.* where there is a will).

The Law of Things: Succession

CHAPTER SIXTEEN

Succession

A. The Nature of the Roman Law of Succession

(1) Introduction

The one unavoidable thing in life is death. When the inevitable comes, one thing that has to be considered is how the assets of the deceased are to be distributed and, just as importantly (not least for the deceased's creditors), the deceased's liabilities have to be considered.

In modern legal systems, we can distinguish two main approaches to this. In one of these, the deceased's whole patrimony – both assets and liabilities – vests in a trustee, called the executor.[1] The executor is responsible for satisfying the liabilities and distributing the assets in accordance with any will left by the deceased or according to legal rules. An executor in modern law, however, does not act in a personal capacity. Instead, he or she acts as a trustee, holding the property on behalf of those entitled to benefit from the deceased person's estate. Accordingly, a modern executor is not personally liable for the deceased's debts, and nor are the deceased's assets available to the executor's personal creditors. Equally, the beneficiaries of the deceased are not personally liable for the deceased's debts. This is the approach taken in Scots law.

Roman law took an alternative approach, known as universal succession. In a system of universal succession,[2] both the assets and the liabilities of the deceased pass directly to the heir (or heirs), in the heir's personal capacity. The heir thus becomes personally liable for the deceased's debts[3] or other liabilities,[4] a situation

---

[1] See B Beinart, 'Heir and Executor' 1960 AJ 223, which finds the origin of the role of executor in the medieval canon law. Note that the 'anomaly' in Scots law referred to at p. 232 no longer exists. In modern law, the whole of the deceased's patrimony vests in the executor, not merely the moveable part of it.

[2] For a brief overview, see M J de Waal, 'A Comparative Overview' in K G C Reid, M J de Waal and R Zimmermann, *Exploring the Law of Succession: Studies National, Historical and Comparative* (Edinburgh University Press 2007) 22–5.

[3] D.29.2.37.

[4] For example, if the deceased was owner of land which had been let out to a tenant, the heir would be bound by the lease just as the deceased owner was: see *e.g.* D.19.2.24.5. The same would not be true of a purchaser of the land or someone who had been left the land as a legacy, as such a person would not have any contractual relationship with the tenant. On leases, see pp. 367–9.

that can lead to the so-called *damnosa hereditas*, or 'ruinous inheritance', when the deceased's debts exceed the assets available to pay them. This is particularly so given that the heir need not necessarily be the sole or even the main beneficiary under the will. The will may also include legacies to other people, which may have the effect of leaving the heir with nothing but debts. For these reasons, measures are often developed to protect the position of the heir. As we shall see, this was true in Roman law.

(2) The Position of the Heir and the Creditors of the Deceased

We see then that, in the Roman law of succession, the deceased's whole patrimony passed to the heir (or heirs), who therefore became in principle liable for the deceased's debts. In effect, the heir stepped into the shoes of the deceased, as if the heir and the deceased were the same legal person. This could have unfortunate consequences. How these consequences were resolved varied depending on circumstances. It is necessary at this point to distinguish between different types of heir, who were treated in different ways. It is also necessary to consider the position of the creditors of the deceased.

(a) Sui et Necessarii Heredes

We have seen[5] that, unless released from that authority by emancipation,[6] a Roman citizen who had been born of a valid Roman marriage was subject to the authority, or *patria potestas*, of his or her eldest male agnatic ascendant.[7] This person was called the *paterfamilias*. A woman in a *manus* marriage[8] was subject to the *patria potestas* of her husband or his *paterfamilias*, if he had one.

The *sui heredes*[9] were the people who became *sui iuris* (*i.e.* legally independent)[10] on the death of the *paterfamilias*.[11] These were the children of the *paterfamilias*[12] and, if married *cum manu*, his wife, and they could not refuse the inheritance.[13] Instead, they would 'immediately become heirs by force of law',[14] without any

---

[5] See p. 116.

[6] See p. 127.

[7] An agnate is a relation in the male line. A man is therefore agnatically related to his own children, and to his sons' children, but not to his daughters' children. A woman is not agnatically related to her own descendants, as she is not related to them in the male line. (This is leaving aside cases where a woman is agnatically related to her husband. She will then be agnatically related to the children of the marriage, but only indirectly, through the male relations connecting them.) However, she is agnatically related to her brother, as they share a father, and to his children.

[8] See pp. 142–3.

[9] The term can be translated along the lines of 'heirs to themselves', and is suggestive of conditions in early law, where the property was seen as family property, of which the *paterfamilias* was merely administrator rather than outright owner. See G.2.157; D.28.2.11.

[10] See p. 127.

[11] J.3.1.6.

[12] Including any posthumous children. On the position of children who had been abandoned at birth, see D.40.4.29 and, for discussion, O Tellegen-Couperus, 'Father and Foundling in Classical Roman Law' (2013) 34 J Leg Hist 129.

[13] G.2.157.

[14] D.38.16.14.

need for formal or informal acceptance of the inheritance, unless the deceased had left a will appointing someone else as heir. For this reason, they were said to be *necessarii heredes* (necessary heirs), hence the full title *sui et necessarii heredes*. Adopted children were included in the category,[15] but emancipated children were excluded. Children of a predeceasing or previously emancipated son were included.[16] A daughter's children would not, however, be included, as they would be in the *potestas* of their own father (or his *paterfamilias*). They did not, therefore, become *sui iuris* on the death of their mother's *paterfamilias*. A wife in a marriage *sine manu*[17] was excluded, as she was not in her husband's power.

The inability of *sui heredes* to refuse the position of heir could have harsh consequences if the *paterfamilias* was insolvent. As the heir was liable for the debts of the deceased, he or she could potentially end up being subjected to insolvency proceedings, with the stigma that went along with them, despite not being at fault. Accordingly, the praetor intervened to protect *sui heredes* in this position. The praetor allowed *sui heredes* the *beneficium abstinendi* ('the right of abstaining'), as long as they had done nothing to interfere with the deceased's property. This had two related consequences. First, if the deceased's property had to be sold on account of insolvency, this would be done in the name of the deceased rather than that of the heir.[18] As a result, the heir would avoid the stigma of insolvency. Second, the praetor would deny to creditors of the deceased any action against an heir exercising the *beneficium abstinendi* for the deceased's debts.[19] This was the case even though the heir was still liable according to the civil law: the *beneficium abstinendi* did not take away the status of heir.[20] Accordingly, if the estate turned out not to be insolvent after all, the heir remained entitled to the surplus.[21]

(b) Necessarii Heredes

A person who was doubtful of the solvency of his or her estate, and who had no *sui heredes* who had no choice about accepting the inheritance, had a problem. While someone else could be instituted as heir, as we shall see such a person did

---

[15] On these, see H Lindsay, 'Adoption and Succession in Roman Law' (1998) 3 Newcastle L Rev 57.
[16] J.3.1.2b. This assumes that the children of the emancipated son were born before the emancipation. If they were born afterwards, they would be in the *potestas* of their own father.
[17] See pp. 143–5.
[18] G.2.158.
[19] D.29.2.57pr.
[20] This, as we saw at pp. 50–2, is characteristic of the way that the praetor developed the law. Rather than outright changing the law, the praetor could use his position as gatekeeper to the litigation process to supplement, restrict or deny enforcement of rights given by the civil law. In theory, the civil law right remained. This could cause complications in practice. For example, at D.29.2.99, a case is reported in which two sisters were heirs to their father. One exercised the *beneficium abstinendi* but the other was willing to accept the estate, including the liabilities. Along with the liabilities, though, there were evidently debts owed to the deceased. Both sisters were heirs according to civil law, and so should strictly have been entitled to a half share each of these debts. However, it would obviously have been unfair to allow the abstaining sister to get her half share while she could not be made liable as heir. Accordingly, we are told, the praetor allowed the non-abstaining sister *actiones utiles* (see p. 51) to enforce rights held by the deceased, and denied any actions to the abstaining sister. On certain issues arising from this text, see W J Zwalve, 'Decreta Frontiana: Some Observations on D.29.2.99 and the "Law Reports" of Titius Aristo' (2015) 83 TvR 365.
[21] D.36.1.69.2.

not have to accept. In such a case, we are told, a common approach was to make a will appointing a slave as heir, who would be freed for this purpose. Slaves in this position could not refuse the inheritance, and were known as *necessarii heredes* for this reason. Institution of a *necessarius heres* had the advantage, therefore, of providing some assurance that the estate would not fall into intestacy.[22] Unlike the position with *sui heredes*, any sale of the deceased's property on the basis of insolvency would take place in the name of the freed slave, who would thus bear the stigma of insolvency.[23]

To give some protection to freed slaves in this position, the *separatio bonorum* ('separation of property') was introduced. By this, the ex-slave was entitled to have any property acquired after freedom excluded from liability for the debts of the deceased, excepting only things acquired in the capacity of heir.[24]

(c) Extranei

The third category of heirs was *extranei* ('outsiders'). Anyone who did not fall into the categories of *sui heredes* or *necessarii heredes* fell into the category of *extranei* instead. The main difference with *extranei* was that, unlike the other two categories of heir, they could refuse the inheritance.

It might be difficult for an *extraneus*[25] to decide whether to accept the inheritance. After all, as we have seen, acceptance (known as *aditio*) would make the heir liable for the debts of the deceased. Accordingly, the *extraneus* was allowed time for deliberation (*spatium deliberandi*) to consider whether to accept.[26] How this worked depended on the terms of the will, specifically whether the will contained a requirement for *cretio*.[27]

Where *cretio* was required, there was a period for consideration during which the heir could give formal acceptance of the inheritance. Failure to do so within the time allowed resulted in forfeiture of the inheritance. The term *cretio* could be used to refer both to the giving in the will of the period for consideration[28] and to the formal acceptance by the heir. Gaius gives a form of words for a will to provide for *cretio*.[29] As we shall see below, a will would begin with the appointment of the heir. The will would then continue with a direction to the heir to: 'make *cretio*

---

[22] Of course, this aim might still be frustrated, if for example the slave instituted as heir predeceased the testator.
[23] G.2.154.
[24] G.2.155. Gaius is a little misleading here. He presents this as automatic. However, Ulpian (D.42.6.1.18) makes it clear that the heir is only protected if he or she applies to the praetor for this. Compare M Rheinstein, 'European Methods for the Liquidation of the Debts of Deceased Persons' (1935) 20 Iowa L Rev 431, 466, commenting on provisions of the Austrian Civil Code on *separatio bonorum*: 'it is wise legislation to give such protection only where it is sought'. It is not inconceivable, for example, that a slave freed in such circumstances might wish to take on the debts of the deceased, out of gratitude to or personal regard for the late master or mistress.
[25] This is the singular form of *extranei*.
[26] C.6.30.22.13a (AD 531).
[27] On this, see H W Buckland, 'Cretio and Connected Topics' (1922) 3 TvR 239; Watson, *Succession* 188–93.
[28] G.2.164.
[29] G.2.165.

in the next hundred days in which you know and are able. If you do not make *cretio* in this way, be you disinherited'. The period given could vary. Gaius tells us[30] that a period of 100 days was considered reasonable but that, if a longer period was provided, the praetor might shorten it. The words 'in which you know and are able' (*quibus scies poterisque*) could be left out. If these words were included, the time for consideration was counted from the moment at which the heir became aware of the inheritance and was able to make *cretio*, and periods during which the heir was unable to make *cretio* did not count. Otherwise, the period given would run continuously from the death of the testator, regardless of the heir's knowledge of the inheritance or ability to make *cretio*. Acceptance had to be given in formal words. Gaius gives the form: 'Whereas Publius Mevius has by his will instituted me as heir, I enter upon and make *cretio* of that inheritance.'[31] Failure to make *cretio* within the prescribed period meant loss of the inheritance. This was the case even if the heir had informally accepted the inheritance, for example by behaving as heir. *Cretio* was abolished in AD 407.[32] Thereafter, any inheritance could be accepted informally.

Where there was no requirement for *cretio*, informal acceptance was enough.[33] This could even be implied by the heir's acts. Acts are ambiguous,[34] however, and so express words were always to be preferred. The civil law did not prescribe any maximum period for consideration. Lengthy delays no doubt sometimes caused anxiety to the creditors of the deceased, who after all wanted to know to what person they were to look for payment, and so creditors could petition the praetor to fix a time limit for the heir to accept the inheritance.[35]

When the person instituted as heir accepted the inheritance, he or she took the position of heir, including liability for the testator's debts. Unlike the position with *sui* and *necessarii heredes*, there was no protection in classical law for *extranei* if the deceased turned out to be insolvent. Indeed, it was not until AD 531 that any general protection for *extranei* was introduced, by Justinian.[36] This was the *beneficium inventarii*. If the instituted heir took an inventory of the deceased's estate, he or she would have no liability for the deceased's debts beyond the value of the estate, as long as the inventory was begun within thirty days of the opening of the will and was completed within another sixty days.[37] The civil law *spatium deliberandi* was retained as an alternative.

---

[30] G.2.170.
[31] G.2.166.
[32] C.6.30.17.
[33] G.2.167.
[34] For example, does arranging the testator's funeral count as implied acceptance of the position of heir? It is consistent with that, but also with the instituted heir acting from a sense of duty towards the deceased. See D.11.7.14.8.
[35] G.2.167.
[36] C.6.30.22 (AD 531); J.2.19.6. This is stated to have been based on earlier legislation protecting soldiers instituted as heirs.
[37] A year was allowed if the heirs were not in the place where the majority of the inheritance was.

(d) Protection of Creditors

It was not only the person instituted as heir who might be concerned with issues of solvency. What if it was the heir who was insolvent? As the deceased's patrimony merged with that of the heir, any creditors of the deceased might have unexpected difficulty in getting payment. This issue was resolved by allowing the creditors of the deceased to apply to the praetor for *separatio bonorum*, allowing them to enforce the rights they held against the deceased as if the two patrimonies remained separate.[38] This had to be done within five years from the heir's acceptance of the inheritance.[39]

B. Intestate Succession

In the law of succession, we must distinguish two broad situations. Either the deceased has left a valid will or has not. If there is a valid will, we are concerned with testate succession. The case where there is no valid will is known as intestate succession. We shall consider this first.

Intestacy arose when the deceased had left no valid will, either because there was no will at all or because a will the deceased had made had failed. In that case, the law distributed the deceased's assets according to rules laid down by the law rather than according to the deceased's intentions, even if they were known. Because of the principle of universal succession, and unlike modern law, there could be no partial intestacy. Either an heir had been validly appointed, in which case that person would take over the deceased's assets and liabilities except insofar as assets had been distributed by a will; or else no heir had been validly appointed, in which case the estate was intestate. The law of intestate succession is complex because of the way it developed over time. During both Republic and Empire, until replaced by Justinian, the basic civil law rules were those laid down by the Twelve Tables. However, these rules were qualified in their effect by subsequent developments, especially of the praetorian law.

(1) Succession under the Twelve Tables

The Twelve Tables laid down who should succeed on intestacy, prioritising potential heirs according to three classes. In the absence of an heir in one class, the next would be considered. First priority went to the class of people known as *sui heredes*. If there were no *sui heredes*, the nearest agnate had priority, followed by the deceased's *gens*. An heir could bring a *hereditatis petitio* (petition for an inheritance) to recover heirship property from anyone wrongly in possession.

(a) Sui Heredes

First in line were the *sui heredes* of the deceased, that is those becoming *sui iuris* on the death of the deceased. We have seen already who was in this category.

---

[38] D.42.6.1pr.
[39] D.42.6.1.13.

As a woman could not be a *paterfamilias*, she had no *sui heredes*. A woman's own children, therefore, did not inherit on her intestacy.

Where the *sui heredes* were all of the same degree (*e.g* all children or all grandchildren of the deceased, a wife in a marriage *cum manu* counting the same as her husband's children for these purposes), they took jointly, in equal shares. Where they were of different degrees, the *sui heredes* took *per stirpes*.[40] This term means 'by branch', in other words meaning that a man who would have been one of the *sui heredes* but who predeceased or had been emancipated was represented by his own children. For example, suppose that a *paterfamilias* died with one living son and one predeceasing son, who had himself two surviving sons. The living son would get half of the inheritance and the two grandsons would share the half their father would have got had he lived. Among the *sui heredes*, no distinction was made on the grounds of sex. Accordingly, a man's son and daughter would succeed equally on his intestacy.

(b) Nearest Agnate

In the absence of any *sui heredes*, the nearest agnate would inherit. If there was more than one agnate of the same degree, they would share equally. Originally, no distinction was made between male and female agnates. However, in the late Republic or early Empire, it came to be the case that women were excluded from this category, except for sisters of the deceased. Unlike *sui heredes*, the nearest agnate could refuse the inheritance.

(c) The *Gens*

If the nearest agnate refused the inheritance, it did not go to the next nearest agnate. Instead, the inheritance passed to the deceased's *gens* (clan). How this worked in practice is unclear.[41] At any rate, the rights of the *gens* became much less important in the classical period, by which time the *gens* barely existed beyond a shared name of its members.[42] These rights of the *gens* were largely superseded by the development by the praetor of rules greatly expanding the categories of people entitled to succeed on intestacy.

(2) Reforms

The stress that the civil law rules placed on the agnatic relationship, to the exclusion of other blood relationships, is clearly a relic of earlier times. This is particularly so for the succession of the *gens*. By the period for which we have evidence, other relationships were seen as more important than they had evidently been considered at an earlier time.

---

[40] J.3.1.6.

[41] For discussion, see Watson, *Succession* 180–2; R Yaron, 'Two Notes on Intestate Succession' (1957) 25 TvR 385, 385–9.

[42] This was the second part, or *nomen*, of the customary Roman naming system. For example, Gaius Julius Caesar was a member of the *gens Iulia*, the Julian clan. The other two names are the *praenomen*, or personal name (Gaius); and the *cognomen*, or family name (Caesar).

It is true that there were some changes over time. In particular, two *senatus-consulta* altered the order of succession in particular circumstances to recognise the relationship between mother and child. Under the emperor Hadrian, the *senatusconsultum Tertullianum* gave a mother with the *ius liberorum*[43] the right to succeed on her deceased child's intestacy, along with her daughters, as long as the deceased had no surviving father or brothers and no *sui heredes*.[44] In AD 178, the *senatusconsultum Orphitianum* gave children the right to succeed on their mother's intestacy.[45] These were limited reforms, however, and the primacy of the agnatic relationship was otherwise retained. This was the case all through the classical period, and the post-classical period. It appears in the *Digest* and *Institutes*, only being finally abolished ten years later by Justinian.[46] In the classical period, therefore, the agnatic principle dominated intestate succession, at least in principle. In practice, though, the position was moderated by praetorian intervention. The praetor modified the operation of the civil law rules by granting *bonorum possessio*, the award of possession of property, to persons in a different order of priority from that of the Twelve Tables.[47] Such persons may be referred to as praetorian heirs, as they are made heirs by the intervention of the praetor rather than by the civil law. We can distinguish them from civil law heirs, who are heirs under the Twelve Tables rules. Sometimes, but not always, a person would be both civil law and praetorian heir.

(a) The Praetorian Order of Succession
Under the praetorian order of succession, first priority was given to *liberi*. This term literally means 'children', but is in fact broader than that. It covered the *sui heredes* of the deceased (*i.e.* those becoming *sui iuris*, or legally independent, on the death of the deceased). It also included children who had been emancipated. This complicated things significantly. Unlike the *sui heredes*, an emancipated child might have acquired money or property from the former *paterfamilias*. As we have seen,[48] it was common for the emancipation to be accompanied by a gift to set the emancipated child up in life. By contrast, the other children could normally[49] own nothing. It would have been unfair not to take such gifts into account when dividing the estate

---

[43] The 'right of children'. This was held by freeborn women who had had at least three children, and freedwomen who had had at least four. The right given by the *SC Tertullianum* was extended by Justinian to all mothers: C.8.58.2 (AD 528). On the *ius liberorum*, see p. 132.

[44] J.3.3. If the deceased's father was still alive, even if the deceased had been emancipated, he would inherit before anyone except *sui heredes* of the deceased. If the father predeceased, there were no *sui heredes*, and the deceased had brothers and sisters, they would share equally, to the exclusion of the mother. If the deceased left a mother and sisters, the mother would take half and the sisters would share the other half. See discussion of R Yaron, 'Two Notes on Intestate Succession' (1957) 25 TvR 385, 389–97. Justinian extended this to all mothers, not just those with the *ius liberorum*.

[45] J.3.4.

[46] Nov.118 (AD 543), amended by Nov.127 (AD 548). This system gave priority to descendants, whether agnatic or not, with representation *per stirpes*; followed by ascendants and full siblings; half siblings; other collaterals, the nearer excluding the more distant; and, finally, the spouse of the deceased.

[47] J.3.1.13; D.38.15.1pr.

[48] See p. 127.

[49] See pp. 120–2. In the Empire, there were certain limited exceptions.

of the *paterfamilias*. Accordingly, lifetime advances to the emancipated child were subject to *collatio bonorum*, which means that they had to be counted as part of the deceased's estate for the purposes of calculating the shares to be given.[50] The same was true of any other property that the emancipated child had acquired up to the death of the former *paterfamilias*. Few things demonstrate more clearly the persistence of the influence of Roman law into the modern world, where circumstances are quite different and there is no such thing as emancipation of a child, than that the rules on collation of lifetime advances have been received into modern law.[51]

If there were no *liberi*, or no *liber*[52] validly claimed, the inheritance would fall next to the category known as *legitimi*. The *legitimi* were those persons, other than the *gens*, entitled to succeed under the Twelve Tables rules: *i.e.*, primarily, the nearest agnate.

Next came the cognatic relations of the deceased. This was limited to the sixth degree of relationship, or seventh in the case of a child of a second cousin.[53] Cognates in the same degree of relationship shared equally. If the closest cognates made no valid claim, the inheritance passed to the next closest cognate or cognates.

If no valid claim was made by anyone in any of the preceding classes, the spouse of the deceased would take.[54]

(b) Bonorum Possessio

The first step in enforcing an entitlement to an inheritance under the praetorian rules was to apply to the praetor for an award of *bonorum possessio*. The term *bonorum possessio* can be translated as 'possession of property', which is somewhat misleading as it did not actually give the claimant possession. Instead, it entitled the claimant to proceed to the next step in acquiring possession of the property.

There was a time limit for applying for *bonorum possessio*. This was 100 days, or a year for ascendants and descendants, following which the inheritance would pass to the person or persons next entitled. Any period during which a person entitled was unable to apply for *bonorum possessio* or was unaware of the entitlement did not count towards the time limit, and nor did any period of uncertainty about entitlement that subsequently arose.[55] Once the time limit had expired, the

---

[50] J.3.1.9.
[51] See *e.g. Douglas v Douglas* (1876) 4 R 105, where the court relied on the *ius commune* writers Domat and Voet in considering a question of collation of lifetime advances. In modern law, though, a child does not need to collate anything acquired otherwise than from the deceased.
[52] This is the singular form of *liberi*.
[53] D.38.8.1.3. The number of degrees of relationship is calculated by counting up from the deceased to the closest common ancestor, and then down to the claimant. The degree of relationship between ascendants and descendants is simply the number of generations from one to the other. Thus, a parent and child are related in the first degree. Siblings are related in the second degree (one step up to the parents and then one back down). Cousins are related in the fourth degree (two steps up to the common grandparents and then two back down).
[54] To modern eyes, this gives what appears to be a surprisingly low priority to the surviving spouse. Compare the Succession (Scotland) Act 1964, ss. 2, 8 and 9.
[55] D.38.15.2pr. This might mean, depending on the circumstances, that the time allowed would elapse on different dates for different people in the same class.

chance to claim as a member of that class was lost. Those next entitled would then have the same period to make a claim. Some people, however, would be members of both a higher and a lower class, and so could claim as part of the latter if the chance to claim as part of the former was missed. For example, every agnate was also a cognate,[56] and so could claim as such. Suppose, for instance, that a man died with only two living relations, the son of his brother and the son of his sister. The brother's son is the nearest agnate, and would be entitled to inherit on that basis. If he failed to do so, he could claim as a cognate, but his cousin would be entitled to share the inheritance as a cognate of the same degree of relationship. Although those related to the same degree in each class were entitled to inherit equally, the claim for *bonorum possessio* had to be made by each, with the result that anyone failing to claim would lose the share that he or she would otherwise have been entitled to.[57] An application by one did not count as an application by all. Suppose, say, two people were entitled to inherit equally. If one claimed within the time limit and the other did not, the latter's share would accrue to the former, who would get everything.

It will be obvious that, if the members of each class had to be given, in turn, the opportunity to refuse the inheritance, it might take a considerable time to work through them all. On the other hand, a person entitled could decline the inheritance, which would cut short their period for claiming, and it would often be obvious that there was nobody in a particular class. In addition:

> It must . . . be remembered that any *bonorum possessio* could in fact be given at any time. The praetor gave it on application, without serious enquiry, to anyone who set up a *prima facie* claim, on *ex parte* evidence. The praetor knew nothing about the facts. But such a grant would be a mere nullity, for all purposes, unless the person to whom it was made was the person or one of the persons entitled to it at that time.[58]

Still, even a *bonorum possessio* granted to someone not entitled to it would be of benefit to that person, as the true facts might well not come to light.

Bonorum possessio could be granted either *cum re* or *sine re*. These terms do not readily translate into English.[59] Essentially, though, *bonorum possessio cum re* gave a right that was enforceable against a person entitled to succeed under the Twelve Tables rules. By contrast, *bonorum possessio sine re* allowed the person granted it to seek possession of the property contained in the inheritance, but did not allow that person to prevail against the 'true heir', the civil law heir. Even then, though, ownership could be acquired by *usucapio* if nobody with a better right came forward in time.

---

[56] The reverse, of course, was not true. The exception to this was with adopted persons. Ulpian tells us that they retained all relationships in their original families, but in their adopted families only became cognates with those with whom they became agnates: D.38.8.1.4. On adoption, see pp. 123–5.
[57] D.37.1.3.9–37.1.5.
[58] Buckland, *Textbook* 384.
[59] A rough rendering might be, respectively, 'with a right to the property' and 'without a right to the property'.

It is not always clear when *bonorum possessio* was given *cum re* and when *sine re*. Indeed, it would not always be clear to the claimant whether the grant was *cum re* or *sine re*, as this would not always be stated. Moreover, whether a grant of *bonorum possessio* in particular circumstances was considered to be *cum re* or *sine re* changed over time. It would be reasonable to suppose that, originally, it was always *sine re*. This would be consistent with the way that the praetorian jurisdiction was conceived.[60] The category of *bonorum possessio cum re* would then be developed by the praetor allowing in particular cases a defence[61] against an attempt by the civil law heir to recover the property from the praetorian heir. By Justinian's time, *bonorum possessio* was normally granted *cum re*. In the classical period, we can certainly say that the emancipated child was entitled to *bonorum possessio cum re*. Otherwise, the rules on *collatio bonorum* would not make sense, as they assumed an emancipated child claiming alongside children who had not been emancipated. Other than this, there is most likely a general distinction to be made between those who were also civil law heirs, and those who were only praetorian heirs, with the latter getting *bonorum possessio sine re* only.

Once *bonorum possessio* had been granted, there were two main ways of actually recovering the property from whoever had it. One of these was the interdict *quorum bonorum*. This was a possessory interdict,[62] and so was concerned only with the question of interim possession. Because it did not settle the question of who actually had the final entitlement to the inheritance, it could be brought by the praetorian heir regardless of whether *bonorum possessio* had been given *cum re* or *sine re*. It also had the great advantage that, once the praetorian heir had acquired possession, anyone attempting to show a better right to the property would have the burden of bringing an action and proving that right. The interdict would likely therefore be particularly attractive when there was doubt about the parties' respective rights or whether there was uncertainty as to whether the *bonorum possessio* was *cum re* or *sine re*. *Quorum bonorum* was, however, subject to two important limitations. The first was that it could only be brought against a person possessing as heir (or who refused to state a basis for possession).[63] It could not, therefore, be successfully brought against someone claiming to possess as, for example, a purchaser. The second limitation was that it could not be used to recover debts owed to the inheritance.[64]

The alternative way to recover the inheritance was the *hereditatis petitio possessoria*, a variant of the standard *hereditatis petitio*. For this, it was necessary to show a valid grant of *bonorum possessio*. If this was *cum re*, it could be brought even against a civil law heir. If *sine re*, it would be effective against anyone other than the civil law heir. Either way, the *hereditatis petitio possessoria* was conclusive of the parties' rights.

---

[60] See pp. 50–2.
[61] This would be the *exceptio doli*. See p. 423.
[62] On the possessory interdicts generally, see pp. 187–9.
[63] D.43.2.1.
[64] D.43.2.2.

C. Testate Succession: Making a Will

As a person's last testament, a will can be about more than just disposal of property and dealing with the testator's financial affairs. Indeed, in Roman law, this was originally a secondary consideration. The main purpose of a will in Roman law was a religious one. The *paterfamilias* was seen as the religious head of the household, and was responsible for the *sacra*, the worship of the household gods. The original purpose of a will was to appoint an heir to take over the *sacra*. Even when this religious function fell away, though, a will had functions beyond distribution of property. A will could be used to memorialise one's achievements or to pass judgement on those left behind.[65] Indeed, it can still do these things: *McCaig v University of Glasgow*[66] and *McCaig's Trustees v Kirk Session of United Free Church of Lismore*[67] are concerned with an (unsuccessful) attempt to do the former.[68] *B's Executor v Keeper of the Registers and Records of Scotland*[69] gives a colourful example of the latter. However, setting aside the religious implications of early Roman wills, the most important purpose of a will, in Roman times as in the present day, was to deal with the testator's assets and debts. Will-making does seem to have been common among the Romans, at least among the better off, unsurprisingly given the unsatisfactory state of the rules on intestacy. However, the once common view, that the Romans had a 'horror' of intestacy, is now thought to be exaggerated.[70]

A will can be defined briefly as a written expression of how the testator's estate should be dealt with on his or her death. When writing is to be interpreted and applied, there is always the possibility of ambiguity and uncertainty as to the writer's actual intentions. In such cases, legal policy pulls in two directions. On the one hand, we want to ensure so far as possible that we are applying the writer's actual intentions, and this leads to an argument for allowing resort to extrinsic evidence (*i.e.* evidence from outside the document) to determine what was intended. On the other hand, if extrinsic evidence is given free rein in the interpretation of wills, the court comes 'perilously near to making a will for the testator', and risks relying 'too much on inference, conjecture, and supposition, which may have been right but may equally have been wrong'.[71] A further point may be added to this. The more that extrinsic evidence is allowed, the greater is

---

[65] For an interesting discussion of this aspect, from the perspective of US constitutional law, see D Horton, 'Testation and Speech' (2012) 101 Georgetown Law Journal 61.
[66] 1907 SC 231.
[67] 1915 SC 426.
[68] In the first of these cases, the testator (described by the court as 'possessed of an inordinate vanity as regards himself and his relatives, so extreme as to amount almost to a moral disease') directed that his estate be used to erect statues of himself and his family, to no benefit to anyone. The will was successfully challenged by his sister. In the second case, her own will, in much the same terms, was itself successfully challenged. In the second case, Lord Salvesen said (at p. 434): 'The prospect of Scotland being dotted with monuments to obscure persons who happened to have amassed a sufficiency of means, and cumbered with trusts for the purpose of maintaining these monuments in all time coming, appears to me to be little less than appalling.'
[69] 1935 SC 745.
[70] See D Daube, 'The Preponderance of Intestacy at Rome' (1964–5) 39 Tulane LR 253; D Cherry, 'Intestacy and the Roman Poor' (1996) 64 TvR 155.
[71] A L Cordiner, 'Interpretation of Wills' (1932) 44 JR 329, 356.

the uncertainty whether the document will be applied according to its terms, and the greater the risk to those responsible for acting on its terms.

The difficulty is particularly acute with wills as, by the time the will needs to be interpreted, the testator is no longer available to indicate what was intended. Two passages from the *Codex* may be given as illustration. In one, dated AD 223,[72] we are told of a case where a cavalryman named Alexander had named one Iulianus, his slave, as his heir, with one Vitalis as substitute if Iulianus was unable or unwilling to accept the inheritance. The idea was that Iulianus would be freed in order to be able to do this. It turned out that Iulianus was actually co-owned along with another person, called Zoilus. The inheritance was claimed by Vitalis and, presumably, Zoilus. The decision given was that the outcome depended on the deceased's intentions and whether he was aware that Iulianus was co-owned. How would these issues be decided? We are not told, but clearly there would have to be some form of enquiry into the deceased's intentions and his state of knowledge. This is not particularly helpful, but it is unavoidable if extrinsic evidence is allowed.

The second example – many others could be chosen – is a decision of Justinian from AD 531.[73] This was concerned with the situation where a man, not called Plotius, appoints an heir in the following terms: 'let Sempronius be the heir of Plotius'. What is the intention here? Various possibilities are discussed. For example, the testator may be the heir of someone called Plotius, and be wishing to transfer the benefit of this to Sempronius. Justinian dismisses the position of the classical jurists, that what we have here is a simple error of name, on the basis that 'such a man is not found who is so careless, or rather so stupid, that he does not know his own name'.[74] This may be over-optimistic, given the facts of the modern case *Williamson v Williamson*,[75] in which a witness named Wilson signed in error with the name Williamson.

(1) Capacity

The jurist Papinian tells us that the capacity to make a will was a matter of public rather than private law.[76] We have seen[77] that *testamenti factio* – the right to make a will according to Roman law – was one of the rights comprised in Roman citizenship. However, the issue is perhaps better seen as a mix of public and private law, for a person's ability to make a valid will depended on matters other than citizenship status.

First, only a *sui iuris*[78] person could make a valid will.[79] This makes sense, as only such a person could own any property anyway, other than *peculium castrense* and *quasi castrense*,[80] for which an exception was made. To make a valid will, the

---

[72] C.6.24.3.
[73] C.6.24.14.
[74] C.6.24.14.1.
[75] 1997 SC 94.
[76] D.28.1.3.
[77] See p. 96.
[78] See pp. 116–17.
[79] D.28.1.6pr.
[80] See p. 121.

testator had to be of sound mind. An insane person could not make a valid will. The same was true of a person who had been interdicted from managing his own property.[81] Soundness in body was not required, however.[82] This is hardly surprising, given that those most likely to be making wills are those faced with the approach of death. It is at first sight surprising, then, that those who were deaf or dumb were unable to make valid wills.[83] As neither deafness nor dumbness implies any mental deficiency, the most likely explanation for this restriction is that the standard procedure for making a will involved spoken words, which would pose obvious problems for those lacking the power of speech or hearing.[84] That this restriction was not based on any intrinsic lack of capacity is suggested by the fact that a soldier who had become deaf or dumb, but who had not yet been discharged from the army, could make a soldier's will, which (as we shall see below) did not involve the same formalities.[85] The same is suggested by the fact that a deaf or dumb person could seek imperial authorisation to make a valid will.[86] Finally, as we saw in Chapter 5, there was a particular restriction on women making wills.[87] Until this procedure was abolished by Hadrian,[88] a woman wishing to make a will had to go through *coemptio*, a kind of fictional self-sale, probably to terminate her agnatic relationships.[89]

Those capable of being witnesses to a will were, broadly speaking, the same as those capable of making a valid will, except that they had to be male.[90] The right to take under a will (the *ius capiendi*), however, was subject to various restrictions. A slave, of course, was not a citizen and could not own property, and so could not make a valid will, and nor could a slave take under a will unless first manumitted. A slave could be instituted as heir or named as a legatee, but took on behalf of the master unless freed. This restriction arose from the nature of slavery. Other than this, the various restrictions applying varied over time, especially as social views changed. For example, an early law, the *lex Voconia* of 168 BC, prohibited anyone in the first census class (made up of the wealthiest citizens) instituting a woman as heir.[91] This, though, was frequently circumvented in practice,[92] and became obsolete in the early Empire. During his reign as emperor, Augustus introduced significant changes to the law of marriage, some of which had an impact on the

---

[81] D.28.1.18pr. This could be done on the basis of a person being a spendthrift. See p. 100.
[82] D.28.1.2.
[83] D.28.1.6.1.
[84] See also G.3.105, where this is certainly the basis of Gaius' reasoning.
[85] D.29.1.4.
[86] D.28.1.7.
[87] See p. 98.
[88] Reigned AD 117–38.
[89] S Dixon, 'Infirmitas Sexus: Womanly Weakness in Roman Law' (1984) 52 TvR 343, 354.
[90] J.2.10.6.
[91] It did not, though, forbid legacies to women or prevent women becoming heirs on intestacy.
[92] This was frequently done by the use of a *fideicommissum* in favour of the woman who was intended to benefit, on which see below. For discussion, see S Dixon, 'Breaking the Law to Do the Right Thing: The Gradual Erosion of the Voconian Law in Ancient Rome' (1985) 9 Adelaide L Rev 519.

law of succession.[93] This was done through two pieces of legislation, the *lex Iulia de maritandis ordinibus* and the *lex Papia Poppaea*.[94] In line with Augustus' policy of restoring what he saw as traditional Roman virtues, and also of raising the birth rate, a requirement was introduced for men aged between twenty-five and sixty to marry. The same applied to women between twenty and fifty, with a requirement to remarry within prescribed periods if the marriage came to an end. No person in breach of this requirement could take under a will, unless they were within six degrees of relationship to the testator.[95] Childless couples could take only a tenth of each other's property under a will. *Caduca* (inheritances or legacies that a person could not take because of a rule of law excluding him or her) could pass to ascendants or *liberi* to the third degree, as long as that person was named in the will, even if childless. The stigma against celibacy lessened with the conversion to Christianity, however, and the penalties for failure to marry were repealed by Constantine.[96] The restrictions on succession between childless spouses were later also repealed.[97]

(2) Types of Will
(a) Early Wills
In early times, the common form of will was the comitial will. This was made before a citizen assembly, the *comitia calata*,[98] summoned twice annually for this purpose. This was obsolete before the classical period, and much of the detail of its workings is unclear. For example, it is unclear whether its function was merely to witness the will, or whether it was necessary for the *comitia* to approve its terms. The latter seems perhaps more probable: the involvement of the pontiffs suggests at least some assessment of the will's propriety.[99]

The requirements of the comitial will would obviously pose difficulty for soldiers on active service. For this reason, soldiers were permitted to make valid wills without the normal formalities. The soldier's will, known as the will *in procinctu* ('in readiness for battle'), was also obsolete before the classical period.[100]

(b) Wills in Classical Law
Although the will *in procinctu* fell out of use before the classical period, a new form of soldier's will, along the same lines, later arose. This too allowed soldiers[101] to make valid wills informally. Ulpian tells us that this was first allowed by Julius

---

[93] For discussion of the Augustan legislation on marriage, see S Treggiari, *Roman Marriage: Iusti Coniuges from the Time of Cicero to the Time of Ulpian* (Oxford University Press 1991) 60–80.
[94] On the effect of these, see G.2.111.
[95] This included also certain relationships by marriage. See Buckland, *Textbook* 291–2.
[96] C.Th.8.16.1 (AD 320).
[97] C.Th.8.17.2 (AD 410).
[98] This was the name used for the *comitia curiata* when meeting under the religious authority of, probably, the *pontifex maximus*: Jolowicz and Nicholas, *Historical Introduction* 127.
[99] See W W Buckland, 'The Comitial Will' (1916) 32 LQR 97, 114–15.
[100] G.2.103.
[101] And also sailors: D.37.13.1.1.

Caesar, in the first century BC, as a concession. In the Empire, it was allowed by the emperor Titus and by successive emperors thereafter.[102]

The soldier's will, though, was obviously of limited application. For those in civilian life, by the classical period a new form of will, more convenient than the comitial will, had developed. This new form was a development of the procedure called *mancipatio*, used for transferring certain types of property. As we have seen,[103] *mancipatio* involved transferor and transferee coming together with five witnesses, and also an additional person, called the *libripens* ('scale-holder'), who held a set of scales. The transfer would be formally declared by the parties, and then the scales would be struck with a piece of bronze, representing the weighing out of the price. This ceremony was adapted for the formation of wills. In such a will, known as a mancipatory will, the *mancipatio* would be made in favour of an individual, known as the *familiae emptor* ('purchaser of the household'), who was nominally transferee but who was obliged to follow the instructions given. Gaius tells us[104] that the *familiae emptor* was originally the person who was being appointed as heir. However, by the classical period, the involvement of the *familiae emptor* was purely a formality.

All wills suffer from the difficulty that, when they come to be applied, the person who made them is no longer available to clarify any doubts as to what was intended. This would inevitably be especially true of a will made orally. Understandably, therefore, it became normal practice to record the will in writing on wax tablets, signed and sealed by the witnesses, *libripens* and *familiae emptor* (though not by the testator, unlike the position in modern law). This was initially done simply to provide evidence of the making of the will and of its contents, the will itself being constituted by the *mancipatio* ceremony. However, it came to be the case that the praetor would recognise a will recorded on tablets as having been validly made, even without the accompanying *mancipatio*.[105] This was done by granting *bonorum possessio*[106] to the person or persons benefiting from the will, initially *sine re* but later *cum re*. This was the praetorian will.

A valid praetorian will had to be signed and sealed as a single continuous act. This does not necessary mean, though, that each step had to be taken immediately after the previous one. Instead, this requirement meant that the process should not be interrupted by any act unconnected to the making of the will: 'A will should be made by one continuous act. By one continuous act is meant that no act unrelated to the will should intervene.'[107] The reasoning is strikingly similar to that in the modern Scots case *Thomson v Clarkson's Trustees*.[108] This was concerned with the validity of the signatures of two witnesses to a will. Under the

---

[102] D.29.1.1pr.
[103] See pp. 199–200.
[104] G.2.103.
[105] G.2.119–21.
[106] In this case, it was known as *bonorum possessio secundum tabulas*, the last two words meaning 'according to the tablets'.
[107] D.28.1.21.3.
[108] (1892) 20 R 59.

law at that time, the witness had to sign 'at the time' that the testator acknowledged his or her signature.[109] The current law requires this to be done as 'one continuous process',[110] wording itself very similar to the Roman rule. In *Thomson*, the witnesses, who were two solicitors' clerks, visited the testator at home in Inverkeithing. They heard her acknowledge her signature. They then took the will back to their office in Dunfermline (a distance of a little over four miles), where they signed as witnesses between thirty and forty-five minutes after hearing the acknowledgement. The court held that this was sufficient in the circumstances to count as taking place 'at the time' of the acknowledgement. The Lord Justice-Clerk said:

> I hold that where a signature is acknowledged, and the deed is at once conveyed by the witnesses to the lawyer's office, and there signed by them within half-an-hour or so, and without the deed ever being out of their hands, or any other business being done by them in the interval, that such signature fulfils the statutory requirement of being 'at the time.' Such a case seems to me to be quite different from one in which there has been an interval in a true sense, where the piece of business has been set aside, other things done, and then the attestation of the witnesses taken up of new, and at a different time.[111]

No Roman authority is cited in the case, and so it cannot be conclusively shown that the position taken was inspired by Roman law (or indeed that a Roman jurist or court would take the same view on the facts of the case). However, it is at least plausible to suspect that the Lord Justice-Clerk had the Roman rule in mind at some level. After all, as with all Court of Session judges, the Lord Justice-Clerk was first an advocate, and so required to be educated in Roman law.[112]

There seems to have been some doubt among the Roman jurists as to whether a person asked to write the will on behalf of another person, perhaps someone unable to write or lacking the necessary expertise to write a valid will, could also act as a witness to the will, as shown in this passage:

> Domitius Labeo to his friend Celsus, greetings. I ask, whether someone may be added to the number of witnesses to a will, who has been asked to write the will. Iuventius Celsus to his friend Labeo, greetings. I do not understand what it is you are consulting me about, or else your consultation is very stupid. It is more than ridiculous to doubt whether someone may be a witness to a will because he has written the will.[113]

The obvious impatience here is fairly surprising, as the point is by no means self-evident.

---

[109] Subscription of Deeds Act 1681 (repealed). The need for the testator to sign is an obvious difference from Roman law.
[110] Requirements of Writing (Scotland) Act 1995, s. 3(4)(e).
[111] (1892) 20 R 59, 61.
[112] See p. 89.
[113] D.28.1.27.

(c) Wills in Post-Classical Law

There was considerable development of the law on wills in the post-classical period. We see oral wills being recognised, where the testamentary intentions of a person, expressed in front of seven witnesses, were given effect.[114] A will would also be considered valid if registered in the archives of the state or a court, without witnesses other than the public officials involved. This was the so-called public will.[115] In addition, from the time of Constantine, the holograph will (*i.e.* one made in the testator's own handwriting, without witnesses) was recognised as valid insofar as it benefited the testator's own children, though the precise details varied over time.[116]

However, the main form of will in the post-classical period came to be the so-called tripartite will (*testamentum tripertitum*), introduced in AD 439.[117] This name is somewhat misleading, as it was not the will itself that was in three parts. Instead, the reason for the name is that the rules for these wills were taken from three sources. From the civil law came the need for the execution of the will to take place as one continuous process; from the praetorian law came the need for seven witnesses to seal the will; and finally there was an element of imperial innovation, by which the testator had to sign the will.

(3) Institution of Heir

(a) Requirements for Institution of Heir

The main function of a will was to institute, or appoint, an heir. Indeed, the appointment of an heir was the only thing that was actually necessary, in terms of content, for a valid will. This was subject to the exception that any *sui heredes* that were not being appointed heir had to be disinherited expressly.[118] Otherwise, therefore, a will could thus be very short, and could even be three words, for example *Titius heres esto* ('Titius be heir').[119] The institution of the heir had to be expressed as an instruction, as for example 'Titius be heir' or 'I order that Titius be heir'. To say 'I want Titius to be heir' would not be sufficient. Gaius tells us that forms such as 'I appoint Titius as heir' or 'I make Titius heir' were considered to be of doubtful validity.[120] Such forms were therefore best avoided, until the emperor Constantine provided that any words would do as long as the intention was clear.[121] If there was further content, the appointment of the heir had to come first. Anything appearing before the appointment of the heir was disregarded,

---

[114] C.6.11.2 (AD 242); C.6.23.19 (AD 413); C.6.23.21.4 (AD 439).
[115] C.6.23.19 (AD 413).
[116] See Nov.107 (AD 541), in which Justinian lays down fairly precise rules for how this is to be done. In a pronouncement of AD 439 (C.6.23.21.3), Theodosius refers to this form of will as 'incomplete', suggesting that a common situation where there was cause to rely on a holograph will was the case where the testator died after writing the will but before it could be witnessed.
[117] C.6.23.21.
[118] G.2.123. This was the case even if the *suus heres* predeceased the testator.
[119] G.2.117; D.28.5.1pr.
[120] G.2.117.
[121] C.6.23.15 (AD 339).

although, as an exception to this, a rescript of the emperor Trajan allowed the disinheritance of someone by name to come before the appointment of the heir.[122]

It is important to understand that the heir was not necessarily the main beneficiary of the will. Indeed, legacies to others might exhaust the entire estate, which aside from any other consideration might make persons instituted as heirs reluctant to act. In the Republic, various statutes attempted to protect the position of the heir.[123] In the early second century BC, the *lex Furia testamentaria* restricted the size of individual legacies to non-family members. In 168 BC, the *lex Voconia* restricted legacies by testators in the first census class, that is the wealthiest citizens. Of more enduring importance was the *lex Falcidia* of 40 BC, which entitled the heir to at least a quarter of the net value of the testator's estate. Where necessary, legacies were reduced *pro rata* to achieve this. This did much to make the role of heir more attractive. However, the fundamental idea of universal succession was retained, and the *lex Falcidia* would be of no use if the testator was insolvent.

(b) Conditional Institutions

An heir could be instituted subject to conditions. For example, a person might be instituted as heir subject to a requirement to free a particular slave or to build a memorial to the testator. If the condition was not fulfilled, the institution of the heir failed. A condition that was illegal, immoral or impossible[124] was invalid.[125] Such a condition was simply ignored, and the institution treated as unconditional.[126] If the person instituted as heir was willing to fulfil the condition, but was prevented by a third party's refusal to co-operate, the condition was treated as having been fulfilled.[127]

(c) Substitution

The person instituted as heir might predecease the testator or might refuse the inheritance. To prevent the whole will failing as a result, it was common to institute someone as a substitute heir, to take if the principal heir did not.[128] This was

---

[122] D.28.5.1pr.
[123] On these, see Watson, *Succession* chapter 12.
[124] A condition was impossible only if objectively impossible in its nature. It was not enough that it was subjectively impossible for the intended heir. For example, a condition that the person instituted as heir be elected praetor at the youngest possible age would be valid, even if that person in fact had no realistic likelihood of fulfilling it. Impossibility was judged as at the date of the testator's death. Accordingly, if the condition only became impossible of fulfilment subsequently ('supervening impossibility'), the condition was simply treated as not having been fulfilled.
[125] Indeed, a condition that departed markedly from accepted standards of morality and propriety (standards which are of course variable by time and place) might raise questions about the testator's state of mind, and therefore the validity of the whole will. See *e.g.* D.28.7.27pr.
[126] J.2.14.10; D.28.7.1; D.28.7.14.
[127] See *e.g.* D.28.7.3 (condition of making payment to a person who then refuses to accept it); D.28.7.11 (condition of adopting a named individual, who refuses to be adopted); D.35.1.14 (condition of building statues in a particular town, but the authorities of the town refuse to allow this to be done). Compare D.9.2.23.2, which is concerned with where the fulfilment of the condition is frustrated by the positive acts of a third party, and appears to proceed on a different principle. Here the condition is that a named slave is to be freed. Before this can be done, the slave is killed by a third party's wrongful act. The effect is that the whole institution as heir fails (on the basis of supervening impossibility), rather than it falling to be treated as unconditional.
[128] See generally J.2.15.

known as vulgar substitution. Related to it was pupillary substitution.[129] Pupillary substitution was used when a *paterfamilias* instituted his own prepubescent child[130] as heir. The testator would be concerned (understandably, in an age of high child mortality) that the heir might then die before reaching the age of puberty. As the child could not have made a valid will, the result would be that the property would pass from the child according to the rules of intestacy. This result might not be welcome. Accordingly, the practice developed in such cases of appointing a substitute to take if the child inherited but then died before reaching puberty. This is different from vulgar substitution in that, with pupillary substitution, the intended heir does first inherit, and determines who should inherit from the child heir. In effect, therefore, a pupillary substitution amounts to making a will for the child as well as for the testator.[131] By analogy with pupillary substitution, Justinian allowed the same to be done if the testator had only insane descendants. The substitution would only operate if the heir never became sane.[132]

(4) Revocation of a Will

A testator could of course change his or her mind about the terms of the will. However, a will was not revoked simply by contrary intention on the part of the testator, and in principle this was true even if the testator destroyed the will.[133] Strictly speaking, the will was only revoked if the testator made a new will[134] or experienced *capitis deminutio* (status loss),[135] or else, for reasons that we shall see below, a child was born who was a *suus heres* of the testator. However, if there was a clear indication of a change of views, for example where the testator destroyed or defaced the will, the praetor would give *bonorum possessio*[136] to the person who would have been heir but for the will.[137]

In the post-classical period, further grounds of revocation developed. In the fifth century, a rule was introduced that a will was automatically revoked after ten years.[138] To avoid intestacy, the testator would then need to make a new will, even if his or her intentions had not changed. This rule was abolished by Justinian,

---

[129] See generally J.2.16. For discussion of some of the issues that could arise in a pupillary substitution, set in the wider context of the relationship between the roles of jurist and advocate, see F Wieacker, 'The *Causa Curiana* and Contemporary Roman Jurisprudence' (1967) 2 Irish Jurist (NS) 151.

[130] In other words, a boy under fourteen or a girl under twelve. Pupillary substitution is so called because such a child is known as a *pupillus*, or pupil, a term that was also formerly in use in Scotland. See Erskine, *Institute* 1.8.1.

[131] D.28.6.2pr.

[132] C.6.26.9 (AD 528).

[133] G.2.151.

[134] This had the effect of revoking the original will even if the new will failed, for example if the person instituted as heir declined the inheritance or a condition was not fulfilled: J.2.17.2.

[135] G.2.144–5. On *capitis deminutio*, see p. 97.

[136] In this case *bonorum possessio contra tabulas*, the final two words meaning 'against the will' or 'contrary to the will'.

[137] See e.g D.38.6.1.8, which refers to the possibility of the will being opened or cancelled. The significance of the will being opened was that, as a security measure against fraudulent alteration of the will, it was customary for the tablets on which the will was written to contain two identical copies. One of these was unsealed and the other was sealed, with the seals only being broken after the testator's death.

[138] C.Th.4.4.6 (AD 418).

who instead allowed revocation by making a new will or by making a declaration before three witnesses or recording such a declaration in a public record.[139]

D. Legacies and Disinheritance

Although the most important thing for a will to do was to institute an heir, the testator might not wish the heir to inherit all of his or her property. Part of the estate might be given over to others as legacies, the recipient of a legacy being known as a legatee. Part of the heir's duty was to allow the legatees to have what they were entitled to.[140] Indeed, once the legatees had had their legacies, there might be little or nothing left for the heir. At the same time, because a legatee was not an heir, a legatee was in no way liable for the debts of the deceased. This was the case even where the will directed the heir to share the estate with the legatee (a *legatum partitionis*, or 'legacy of a share').[141] Subject to the protections for heirs that were described above, the heir remained liable for the testator's debts. To that extent, therefore, a legatee was in a preferable position to that of the heir. In this section, we look at the position of a legatee, considering first the requirements for a valid legacy, and then the rules that developed to restrict the testator's freedom to dispose of his or her property in this way.

(1) Legacies

(a) Forms of Legacy

The precise effect of a legacy depended on the way in which it was expressed. In classical law, a legacy could be granted in four ways. Originally, the legacy had to be expressed in Latin, but later was allowed to be made in Greek.[142] The two main forms of legacy were the *legatum per damnationem* and the *legatum per vindicationem*.

The most common form of legacy was the *legatum per damnationem*. This was in the form *heres meus damnas esto dare* ('let my heir be under an obligation to give'). This was the most flexible form, as it could be used for any legacy of money or property. This was because the effect of a legacy in this form was to give the legatee a personal right against the heir, obliging the heir to deliver the property identified.[143] It could therefore be used for anything that a person might be put under an obligation to give. It could even be used for things owned by third parties, in which case the heir was obliged to attempt to acquire the thing.[144] It could also be used for a thing not yet in existence, such as an unborn slave-child or crops to be grown.[145]

---

[139] C.6.23.27.2 (AD 530).
[140] The heir's precise duties in this regard depended on the form in which the legacy was made, on which see below.
[141] See G.2.254.
[142] C.6.23.21.6 (AD 439).
[143] In effect, therefore, because of the vesting of the deceased's estate in the executor, in modern law all legacies are *per damnationem*.
[144] G.2.202. The position is the same under modern law: Erskine, *Institute* 3.9.10, under reference to Roman sources.
[145] G.2.204.

A *legatum per vindicationem* was made in the form *do lego* ('I give and bequeath').[146] With this, the legatee was given immediate ownership of the property.[147] The legatee therefore could bring a real action to recover the property from whichever person had it, rather than having simply a personal action against the heir. For this reason, though, there were restrictions on this form of legacy, arising from the general law on transfer of property. A person could not transfer property he or she did not own.[148] Accordingly, this form of legacy could not be used where the testator did not own the property. Nor, as general principles prevent the transfer of a thing that is not specifically identified,[149] could it be used to give a legacy of money without identifying the source or to give a legacy of a thing identified by a generic description (a *legatum generis*).[150]

Two other forms of legacy existed. The *legatum per praeceptionem* was in the form *Titius rem praecipito* ('let Titius take the thing first'), and directed the legatee to take the property so identified before the testator's estate was divided. A legacy in this form gave a real right to the legatee, as with the *legatum per vindicationem*. It could therefore only be used for things actually belonging to the testator, although if the legatee was also an heir then bonitary ownership[151] was enough.[152] The Sabinians in fact took the view that the wording of this form of legacy assumed that the legatee was also an heir, and accordingly denied its effectiveness in other cases.[153] The Proculian position to the contrary prevailed, however.[154]

Finally, and probably the least important in practice, was the *legatum sinendi modo*. This was in the form *heres meus damnas esto Titium sinere rem capere sibique habere* ('let my heir be under an obligation to allow Titius to take the thing to hold for himself'). This gave the legatee a personal right to take the thing.[155]

While, then, there was sometimes a free choice as to which form a legacy should take, in other cases the choice was constrained. This mattered because, at least in earlier law, use of an inappropriate form made the legacy void. This changed in time, however, consistently with a general trend of not allowing the testator's intentions to be frustrated by technicalities. Under the reign of Nero (reigned AD 54–68), a *senatusconsultum Neronianum* provided that inappropriate words were to be read in the most favourable way, that is as a *legatum per damnationem*.[156] Under

---

[146] G.2.193.
[147] On this and its reception in some modern systems, see L Salomon, 'The Acquisition of Possession in Legacies *per vindicationem* in Classical Roman Law and its Influence in the Modern Civil Codes' (2006) 3 Roman Legal Tradition 65.
[148] See pp. 202–3.
[149] See p. 207.
[150] On the *legatum generis*, see Buckland, *Textbook* 346.
[151] See pp. 201–2. Bonitary ownership was the protected state of a person who had acquired property by an informal transfer that required a formal mode of transfer.
[152] G.2.222.
[153] G.2.217. Even on this view, however, a legacy in this form to a non-heir would be saved, from the time of Nero, by the *Senatusconsultum Neronianum*, discussed below.
[154] G.2.221.
[155] G.2.209–14.
[156] G.2.197.

Constantine, it was provided that the specific words used were not of relevance.[157] Finally, under Justinian, the different types of legacy were abolished, and the legatee was given both a personal right and a real right to recover the legacy.[158]

A legacy could be revoked, either in the same will or in a codicil, by directly contrary words.[159] Thus, for example, a *legatum per vindicationem* (made in the form *do lego*, 'I give and bequeath') would be revoked with the words *non do non lego* ('I do not give and I do not bequeath'). This revocation was known as *ademptio* ('ademption').

(b) Identifying the Legatee

For a legacy to be effective, it was obviously necessary to identify who was to take. An error in the name of the legatee was not fatal, however, as long as the intention was clear.[160] This was true even where the legacy was motivated by a false belief on the part of the testator.[161] The law did not usually enquire into the testator's reasons for making the legacy. For example, suppose that the legacy was stated in the will to have been given on account of a service rendered by the legatee, such as managing the testator's affairs in the testator's absence. This would be a valid legacy, even if the legatee had not in fact managed the testator's affairs. The false belief would only undermine the validity of the legacy if it was expressed as a condition (*e.g* where the will gave a legacy to a particular person, 'if he was the one who managed my affairs in my absence').

There was a general prohibition on legacies to 'uncertain persons' (*incertae personae*).[162] Thus, for example, a legacy to 'whomsoever comes to my funeral' or to 'the person who gives his daughter in marriage to my son' would be void.[163] However, this rule was qualified when the uncertain person was a member of an identifiable group. For example, a legacy could not be validly given to 'the first person who comes to my funeral', but could be validly given to 'the first person among my relatives now living who comes to my funeral'.[164]

A special case of uncertain persons was the class of *postumi*, meaning those born alive after the making of the will.[165] The position of *postumi* of the testator himself was complicated by the rule that the birth of a *suus heres* invalidated previous wills. This rule, and the position of *postumi* of the testator himself, are

---

[157] C.6.37.21 (AD 339).
[158] C.6.43.1 (AD 529).
[159] J.2.21.
[160] J.2.20.29, 30.
[161] J.2.20.31. Erskine, *Institute* 3.9.8 cites J.2.20.29–31 as authority for the same rules in Scots law. Where there was doubt about which of two people was the intended legatee, however, it would be reasonable to use the statement of the testator's motivation as evidence of which person was intended.
[162] Although payments made by the heir, contrary to this rule, could not be recovered: J.2.20.25.
[163] G.2.238.
[164] G.2.238.
[165] G.2.130–1. Children delivered by Caesarean section were considered for these purposes to have been born, and so were included as *postumi*: D.28.2.12pr. Lest this be thought too obvious for argument, compare Shakespeare's play *Macbeth*, where a major plot point turns on it.

considered below. As far as *postumi* of someone other than the testator were concerned, the rule of the civil law was that no legacy at all could be made to such a person.[166] The praetor intervened, however, and allowed such a person a *bonorum possessio*.[167] This prohibition was abolished by Justinian, who allowed legacies to such persons.[168]

Sometimes a legacy might be made jointly to two or more people. The effect of this depended in part on the form the legacy took. In a legacy *per vindicationem* or *per praeceptionem* (in which the legatee got an immediate real right), the legatees were entitled jointly. If one did not take, that legatee's share went not to the heir but to the other joint legatee or joint legatees.[169] In the case of a legacy *per damnationem* or *sinendi modo*, in which the legatee got in the first instance only a personal right against the heir, a further distinction had to be made. The joint legacy could be made either conjunctively (*coniunctim*) or disjunctively (*disiunctim*). A joint legacy was *coniunctim* when it was stated to be to the legatees together (*e.g.* 'I give the property to Sextus and Lucius'). It was *disiunctim* when the same property was given separately to two or more people. Where the legacy was *coniunctim*, the legatees each took a share. Any share that was not taken fell to the heir. Where the legacy was *disiunctim*, each legatee was separately entitled to the whole property or its value. There was therefore no question of any legatee's share accruing to anyone else. The rules on joint legacies were, however, greatly affected by the rules on *caduca*.[170] Where these applied, and a legatee failed to take, that legatee's share went instead to those beneficiaries under the will who had children.[171] The original rules were restored by Justinian, with some modifications.[172]

A legatee who was considered to be unworthy could be made to forfeit the legacy to the imperial treasury. Examples given in the texts include a freedman who denounced his patron for committing unlawful acts. The freedman forfeited the legacy that the patron had made him, even though the freedman had earned a reward by making the denunciation.[173] This might also be the result if 'mortal enmity' arose between the legatee and the testator, such that the testator was unlikely to have wanted the legatee to have the legacy,[174] of if the legatee 'openly and publicly' insulted the testator.[175]

(c) Identifying the Legacy
It was of course also necessary to identify what was to be given as legacy. As with the identification of the legatee, an error in the description was not fatal if it was

---

[166] G.2.241.
[167] J.3.9pr.
[168] J.3.9pr; C.6.48.1.2 (AD 528/9).
[169] G.2.199.
[170] See above.
[171] G.2.206–8.
[172] C.6.51.1 (AD 534).
[173] D.34.9.1.
[174] D.34.9.9pr.
[175] D.34.9.9.1.

clear what the testator intended.[176] Problems could arise, though, particularly when the will contained merely a general description of the legacy. Pomponius gives a striking example:

> the intention of the testator causes difficulty, if he himself had been in the habit of using certain clothes which were also suitable for women. And so it must be said in the first place that the legacy is of what the testator intended, not what is in fact for women or for men. For Quintus Titius also says that he knows a certain senator who was in the habit of using women's dinner dress. If he were to make a legacy of women's clothes, he would not be regarded as having expressed an intention with respect to what he used as if it was suitable for men.[177]

Some special rules existed for particular situations. In a *legatum optionis* (legacy of an option), the legatee was given the right to select what he or she was to receive from an identified class of things. An example might be allowing the legatee to take whichever one of the slaves of a household the legatee preferred. In classical law, this was treated as a conditional legacy (see below), with the result that, if the legatee died without making the choice, the legacy was held to have failed.[178] This rule was changed by Justinian so that the right of choice passed to the legatee's heir.[179] Another special situation was the *legatum debiti* (legacy of a debt). Where a legacy was made of something already owed to the legatee, the legacy was void as it added nothing to what was already owed. The exception to this was where the legacy improved the legatee's position.[180] For example, suppose that I was under an obligation to deliver certain property to you on the Ides of March[181] next year. If I made a legacy to you of the same thing, that would be void. If, however, the legacy was to the effect that you should get the same thing immediately, that would be a valid legacy.

(d) Conditional Legacies
The normal rule was that the right to the legacy vested immediately in the legatee.[182] This, though, could be delayed by making the legacy conditional on the occurrence of a certain event or on the legatee doing or not doing a certain thing.

---

[176] J.2.20.29, 30.
[177] D.34.2.33. For brief discussion of this passage, see Watson, *Succession* 88 n 2; A Wacke, 'The *Potentiores*: Some Relations between Power and Law in the Roman Administration of Justice' (1978) 13 Irish Jurist (NS) 372, 372.
[178] J.2.20.23.
[179] C.6.43.3.1 (AD 531).
[180] D.34.3.11.
[181] The Roman dating system involved counting back from one of three named days in each month: the Kalends (1st of the month), Nones (5th or 7th, depending on the length of the month) and Ides (13th or 15th). Counting was inclusive of the named day itself, so (for example) the second-last day of the month was the called the third day before the Kalends rather than the second. The Ides of March is 15 March, which is famously the day on which Julius Caesar was assassinated in 44 BC.
[182] D.36.2.7pr. This was the case even though the legacy could not actually be demanded from the heir until the heir had accepted. As we have seen, of course, *sui* and *necessarii heredes* did not have to accept, and so where the heir fell into one of those categories the legacy could be demanded immediately.

Where a legacy was made conditionally, the legatee was only entitled to the legacy if the condition was satisfied. If it was not satisfied, the legacy failed. Where, however, the condition was illegal, immoral or impossible, it was simply ignored, and the legacy was treated as being unconditional.[183]

There was an obvious practical difficulty where the condition was that the legatee should not do some stated thing. What if the legatee took the legacy, consumed or otherwise disposed of it, and then did the forbidden thing? The answer was found in the *cautio Muciana*, named for the early jurist who devised it, Quintus Mucius Scaevola. The *cautio Muciana* was an undertaking that the legatee could be required to give to the person who would otherwise have taken the legacy under civil law.[184] If legatee took the legacy and then breached the condition, the legatee could be sued on the basis of this undertaking.

Gaius[185] deals with the situation where a legacy was intended to operate as a penalty against the heir doing or not doing something. An example might be a direction to the heir to pay money if he marries his daughter to a particular person. This money would obviously have to come out of funds otherwise falling to the heir. Such a condition was void, although this rule was abolished by Justinian.[186]

There was a general rule in the interpretation of legacies that, if a legacy would have been invalid if the testator had died immediately after making it, it could not be made valid by any subsequent event. This rule of interpretation was called the *regula Catoniana*.[187] An example of its operation might be to strike down a legacy to a person who did not have capacity to take at the time the will was made, but who later acquired capacity. The *regula Catoniana* did not, however, strike down conditional legacies where the condition was not met at the time of the will being made, but which was subsequently met. For instance, Paul gives the example of a legacy given on condition of the testator's daughter marrying a particular person.[188] It was no objection to this condition that the daughter was below marriageable age at the time the will was made. It was enough that she did subsequently go on to marry the person named.

(2) Disinheritance *(Exheredatio)*
In any legal system, the question arises: to what extent should the wishes of the deceased determine the distribution of his or her property after death? It would be possible for a legal system to deny the right to make wills at all, instead distributing

---

[183] D.28.7.14; D.35.1.3. It seems from G.3.98 that this was at one time a matter of disagreement between juristic schools. The Proculians thought that such a legacy was void altogether. The Sabinian position was the one that prevailed. Such a condition is also ignored in Scots law: *Stair Memorial Encyclopaedia*, vol 25 para 864. The question of which kinds of condition are immoral is, of course, one to which the answer is likely to vary a great deal with changing social conditions.

[184] D.35.1.7pr; D.35.1.18.

[185] G.2.235–7.

[186] J.2.20.36.

[187] D.34.7.1pr.

[188] D.34.7.2.

the deceased's property according to predetermined legal rules. Equally, a legal system could allow full testamentary freedom, including the power to exclude spouse and children from benefiting from the deceased's estate, and including the right to waste the estate on frivolous or immoral purposes. Arguments could be made for either position, or for any point in-between. This depends in part on the weight given to the respect owed to the wishes of the deceased, and in part on whether other considerations are recognised as overriding these wishes, especially family duties.[189]

In Roman law, some slight protection was given to the testator's own children by the rule that *sui heredes* had to be disinherited by express provision, this having to be by name in the case of sons.[190] Otherwise, though, the Roman testator's right to disinherit his[191] children was originally unrestricted. In time, however, restrictions on testamentary freedom did develop.

Before turning to these restrictions, though, there is a complication relating to *postumi*, who were children born after the will was made. The difficulty was that such children could neither be instituted as heirs (because they were *incertae personae*) nor be disinherited by name (since they had none). The result then was that the birth of a *suus heres* child to the testator, after the will was made, automatically revoked the will.[192] However, in the classical period both the requirement to disinherit by name and (as we have seen) the concept of *incertae personae* were interpreted in a fairly permissive way. The requirement of disinheriting by name was satisfied if a description was given by which the son was clearly identifiable, for example by the testator referring to 'my son' when he had only one.[193] Equally, potential *postumi* could be seen as a clearly enough defined class not to count as *incertae personae*. Thus, in classical law, it was enough to disinherit afterborn sons in the following terms: 'let any son that will be begotten by me be disinherited', while other *postumi* could be disinherited by general words.[194]

The Roman rules on *postumi* have influenced the development of Scots law, which operates a presumption (known as the *conditio si testator sine liberis decesserit*) that the testator would intend the will to be revoked in the event of a child subsequently being born. However, this is not a case of the Roman rules being directly transplanted. A direct transplantation would not make sense in this context, given that Scots law has not adopted the rule that children must be expressly

---

[189] For discussion of the arguments, from the point of view of the historical background to South African law, see K Lehmann, 'Testamentary Freedom versus Testamentary Duty: In Search of a Better Balance' 2014 AJ 9.
[190] G.2.129.
[191] The use of the masculine 'his' is intentional here: as we have seen, a Roman woman had no *sui heredes* as nobody was in her legal power.
[192] See D.28.3.12pr for the situation where a *postumus* was born after the will, but predeceased the testator. Ulpian tells us here that, strictly speaking, the will was nonetheless revoked by the birth of the *postumus*. However, the person instituted as heir could claim *bonorum possessio secundum tabulas*.
[193] D.28.2.2.
[194] See G.2.130–4. The law was changed by Justinian, so that all *sui heredes* and emancipated children had to be disinherited by name, irrespective of sex, or by express mention in the case of posthumous children: J.2.13.5; C.6.28.4 (AD 531).

disinherited. The development of the Scots position has also drawn, for example, on the *querela inofficiosi testamenti*, considered below, and 'the true position probably comprises a mixture of both unintentional and deliberate re-interpretation of Roman and Civilian sources'.[195]

(3) Protection against Disinheritance

In classical law, protection against disinheritance was provided by the *querela inofficiosi testamenti*, the 'complaint of the undutiful will'. Notionally, this claim was based on the idea that the testator must have been insane to make the will in the terms that he or she did. This was a fiction, however, as the logical conclusion of the testator being insane would be that the whole will was void, which was not the position that the law took.[196] Instead, the true basis of the *querela inofficiosi testamenti* was that the testator had excluded the complainer from the will, despite the complainer having good reason to expect to be included. It was failure of the testator's duty that was complained of, not a failure of the testator's wits. The duty referred to is a social or moral duty, rather than a legal duty.[197] Indeed, as the *querela inofficiosi testamenti* cast aspersions on the testator's character,[198] it was not available to anyone with any other remedy.[199] It could only be used as a last resort, where no other remedy was available.[200] For the same reason, a failed challenge on this ground resulted in loss of anything that had been given in the will.[201]

The duty that the testator was alleged to have breached was the duty owed to family. Non-family members therefore had no claim on this basis, no matter how apparently justified their expectations of taking something under the will. Only ascendants, descendants and siblings could claim.[202] There was no restriction to agnatic relations, so a son for example could claim on this basis in respect of his mother's will.[203] A sibling could only claim if a *turpis persona* ('disgraceful person') was instituted as heir.[204] What made someone a *turpis persona* is not entirely clear, however, beyond the term implying a poor moral character.[205]

To say that a will was undutiful was to say that the one should not have been passed over. It was not necessary that the failure of duty should have been intentional.

---

[195] R R M Paisley, 'The Roman and Civilian Origins of the *Conditio si Testator sine Liberis Decesserit* in Scots Law' (2015) 19 Edin LR 1, 8.
[196] D.5.2.2; J.2.18pr.
[197] The *querela inofficiosi testamenti*, of course, had the effect of erecting the social or moral duty into a legal duty. For discussion of the social context of the *querela*, see C G Paulus, 'Changes in the Power Structure within the Family in the Late Roman Republic' (1995) 70 Chi-Kent L Rev 1503.
[198] Even if this was only by claiming that the testator had been misled by others.
[199] For example, a son who had been overlooked entirely, not even being disinherited by name, would have to claim instead on the basis of the rules on *exheredatio*, considered above.
[200] The outcome of a successful claim would be a *bonorum possessio contra tabulas*. For a readable account of a case where the *querela* was used, see A D E Lewis, 'The Dutiful Legatee: Pliny, *Letters* V.1' in Cairns and du Plessis, *Beyond Dogmatics*.
[201] D.5.2.8.14. This went, not to the heir, but to the imperial treasury.
[202] D.5.2.1; J.2.18.1. On half siblings, see C.3.28.27 (AD 319).
[203] D.5.2.5.
[204] J.2.18.1.
[205] See C.Th.2.19.1; C.3.28.27 (AD 319).

It was enough that there was a failure of duty, even if it arose through a mistake or misunderstanding.[206] The traditional wicked stepmother makes her appearance here. Gaius says:

> For it is not to be allowed to parents that they do their children wrong in their wills. For they often do this, passing an adverse judgement on their own blood, when they have been led astray by the blandishments or incitements of stepmothers.[207]

This is unlikely to be altogether without justification, although the language used is probably over-dramatic in most cases.

The person bringing the complaint had to prove that he or she had been unjustly excluded from the will. A child claiming in respect of a parent's will had to show that he or she had continually shown proper obedience and respect (*obsequium*) to the parent.[208] If this had not been shown, the complaint would fail. Similarly, we are told that a mother challenging her son's will would lose if she had previously acted 'as an enemy rather than a mother', for example by befriending his enemies or committing dishonourable acts against him.[209] Later, Justinian enacted a list of acceptable grounds of disinheritance.[210] This included the case where a child committed a serious and dishonourable wrong against the parents or made plots against their lives. Also properly excluded from the will were a child who became a gladiator or mime against the parents' wishes, unless they were of the same profession, and a daughter who 'chooses to spend a life of self-indulgence' instead of being decently married in accordance with parental wishes.

Alongside the *querela inofficiosi testamenti* there developed the idea of the *portio legitima* or *pars legitima* ('legitimate share'), which a person was entitled to expect in normal circumstances. In classical law, this was a quarter of a person's share on intestacy. If less than this was given in the will, the *querela* could be brought to bring the complainer up to that share. Under Justinian, only those who had been excluded entirely could bring the *querela*. Those included in the will, but with a smaller share, were instead given an action for making up the deficit, the *actio ad supplendam legitimam portionem*.[211] Justinian also subsequently made new provision for the extent of the share that could be claimed by the testator's children. Where there were four or fewer children, they were entitled to share a third of the estate. Where there were five or more, they shared half of the estate.[212]

Could the testator avoid the consequences of the *querela inofficiosi testamenti* by making lifetime gifts, reducing the value of the estate in advance of death? To avoid this possibility, there developed the *querela inofficiosae donationis* ('complaint of the undutiful gift'). This allowed excessive gifts to be returned to make up the

---

[206] D.5.2.3.
[207] D.5.2.4.
[208] C.3.28.28pr (AD 321).
[209] C.3.28.28.2 (AD 321).
[210] Nov.115.3 (AD 542).
[211] J.2.18.2; C.3.28.30 (AD 528).
[212] Nov.18.1 (AD 536).

expected shares of the disappointed children.[213] What is unclear is whether the excessive gift had to be made with the intention of defeating the *querela inofficiosi testamenti*, or whether it was enough merely that it had that effect. Proof of intent was not required for the *querela inofficiosi testamenti* itself, so on one view it would be surprising if it was required for this, which is, after all, intended to prevent avoidance of the *querela inofficiosi testamenti*. On the other hand, some texts appear to imply that intent was required.[214]

The law in this area bears some resemblance to the modern law of legitim,[215] particularly the *portio legitima*. Indeed, Erskine says that that is the origin of the name 'legitim'.[216] However, it appears that the rule itself is a native Scots rule.[217] As one commentator has said of legitim and the equivalent rights given to widows and widowers: 'no institutions in our jurisprudence have more persistently and erroneously had their origins ascribed to the jurisprudence of Rome'.[218] This is a reminder, if one was needed, that not all rules of Scots law come from Roman law, even where they have a Roman name and a similar content to a Roman rule.

E. Similar Devices

Wills were not the only means by which a person could dispose of his or her property on death. In this final section of the chapter, we will consider three devices with a similar function.

(1) Donatio Mortis Causa

A person, contemplating death and wanting to dispose of property, could make a gift (*donatio*) instead of (or in addition to)[219] making a will. Gifts were of two kinds. They could either be *inter vivos* ('between living persons') or *mortis causa* ('on account of death'). In accounts of the law, these tend to be dealt with together.[220] However, they were in fact quite different. One of the main differences is that an *inter vivos* gift was irrevocable. In other words, it was a gift in the normal sense of the word, being an outright, gratuitous transfer. By contrast, a *mortis causa* gift could be freely revoked by the donor up until the donor's death.[221] We will focus here on *mortis causa* gifts. *Inter vivos* gifts are considered elsewhere.[222]

---

[213] See *e.g.* D.31.87.3; C.3.29.7 (AD 286); Nov.92.
[214] C.3.29.1 (AD 245); C.3.29.8 (AD 294).
[215] The rule is that part of the deceased's moveable property is designated as the 'bairns' part', and is reserved to the deceased's children. The surviving spouse, if any, has a right to a share of the same extent (the 'widow's part', although it is given to widowers as well). If there are both surviving children and a surviving spouse, the bairns' part and the widow's part are each a third of the moveables. If there are only surviving children or there is only a surviving spouse, the relevant part is a half of the moveables.
[216] Erskine, *Institute* 3.9.15.
[217] See the (probably) early fourteenth-century treatise *Regiam Majestatem*, 2.37, where the rule is stated in more or less its modern form.
[218] J C Gardner, 'The Origin and Nature of the Legal Rights of Spouses and Children in the Scottish Law of Succession' (1927) 39 JR 209, 209.
[219] D.39.6.25pr.
[220] See *e.g.* J.2.7.
[221] J.2.7.1.
[222] See pp. 382–3.

A *mortis causa* gift was a gift made by a person in contemplation of death. This might most commonly be done when death or danger of it was imminent, but this need not be so: the gift could simply be motivated by 'contemplation of mortality'.[223] The gift could be absolute or conditional and could be made in suspensive or resolutive terms. A gift made in suspensive terms would be one in which ownership only passed to the donee on the donor's death. In a gift in resolutive terms, ownership passed on delivery to the donee, subject to an obligation to restore the property if the gift failed, for example because a condition was not met. Where ownership had not passed to the donee, the gift could be recovered in the normal way by the donor, by *vindicatio*.[224] If ownership had passed, a *condictio* could be brought.[225] Under Justinianic law, ownership reverted automatically to the donor in such cases if the gift failed, and so presumably the property could be recovered by *vindicatio*.[226] The gift was made by delivery[227] or by whatever alternative means were appropriate to the property.[228] Justinian provided for gifts to be made in the presence of five witnesses, though without displacing previous methods, which therefore remained as alternatives.[229]

As a *mortis causa* gift took final effect only on the donor's death, it was not subject to the restrictions applying to *inter vivos* gifts. For example, it was not subject to the bar on gifts between spouses.[230] However, because *mortis causa* gifts operated in a very similar way to legacies, the limitations applying to legacies were progressively applied to *mortis causa* gifts as well. By the end of the classical period, the restrictions in the *lex Furia testamentaria*, the *lex Voconia* and the *lex Falcidia* applied to *mortis causa* gifts.[231] Ulpian gives a statement of general principle: 'It will be important to remember that, generally, *mortis causa* gifts are comparable to legacies. Accordingly, any rule that applies to legacies is to be accepted as applying to *mortis causa* gifts.'[232] Justinian, though, went too far in saying that *mortis causa* gifts were in his day 'completely assimilated to legacies'.[233] Some important differences remained. Unlike a legacy, a *mortis causa* gift did not depend on the valid making of a will or the valid institution of an heir. The gift was separate from any will made by the donor, and so did not fail simply because the will might happen to fail. Likewise, an unsuccessful challenge to a will based on the *querela inofficiosi testamenti* did not result in loss of the gift, as it was not contained in the will that was being challenged.

---

[223] D.39.6.2.
[224] *Vindicatio* was the standard procedure for recovering property on the basis of ownership. See pp. 189–91.
[225] D.39.6.35.3. On *condictio*, see pp. 429–30.
[226] C.6.37.26.1 (AD 532).
[227] On delivery, see pp. 210–14.
[228] On corporeal property not transferable by delivery, see pp. 198–9, though this distinction was itself abolished by Justinian. A gift could also be something other than corporeal property, such as discharge of a debt.
[229] C.8.56.4 (AD 530).
[230] See p. 144.
[231] G.2.225–6; D.39.6.35pr; C.8.56.2 (AD 239).
[232] D.39.6.37pr.
[233] J.2.7.1.

(2) Fideicommissa

In simple terms, a *fideicommissum*[234] involved property being vested in one person for the benefit of another. Originally it was purely a non-binding request to act in a particular way. The name of the institution indicates this: the property was entrusted (*commissum*) to the faith (*fides*) of the recipient. Most commonly, this would be done as a way of circumventing restrictions on a particular person taking under a will. Instead of directly instituting that person as heir or making a legacy to him or her, a request would be made to the heir or legatee to transfer the property to the intended beneficiary.

For example, suppose that the testator is Marcus. He wants to leave his farm to Lucius, who is for one reason or another barred from taking under the will. Marcus might then make a legacy of the farm to Quintus, followed by the words 'I, Marcus, ask you, Quintus, to transfer the farm to Lucius.' Originally Quintus could not have been compelled to comply with the request. This changed, however, in the reign of Augustus. The story[235] is that this began with a Roman politician called Lucius Lentulus, who died in AD 4 while attempting to supress a native uprising as governor of the province of Africa Proconsularis. While dying, he wrote some codicils[236] requesting that Augustus carry out certain acts. Augustus complied with the requests. Having given *fideicommissa* this recognition himself, he apparently regularly ordered the consuls to enforce compliance with *fideicommissa*, either because his own name had been invoked in the *fideicommissum* or because of 'outrageous breaches of trust'.[237] Litigation concerning *fideicommissa* became so common that a special praetorship, the *praetor fideicommissarius*, was created to deal with it.

Fideicommissa bear undeniable similarity to modern trusts. Both, after all, have the same basic form, with property being entrusted by one person to another for the benefit of a third. Indeed, the term *fideicommissum* is often translated as 'trust'.[238] That usage is avoided here as, despite the similarities, trusts do not seem to bear any historical relationship with *fideicommissa*. To call them trusts is therefore potentially misleading, by suggesting a relationship that does not exist.[239]

---

[234] *Fideicommissa* is the plural.
[235] See J.2.25pr.
[236] On codicils, see below.
[237] J.2.23.1.
[238] See *e.g.* D Johnston, *The Roman Law of Trusts* (Clarendon Press 1988).
[239] There is an idea also that modern trusts are unique to the English-based Common Law tradition (see p. 79), being based on a conceptual division between law and 'Equity' found only there. This involves ownership being divided between the trustee, who is owner 'at law', and the beneficiary, who is owner 'in Equity'. As the Scottish example shows, it is quite possible to have trusts without Equity (in the technical sense of the word that is used in English law), and so this idea is greatly overstated. For discussion, see G L Gretton, 'Trusts without Equity' (2000) 49 ICLQ 599. The dominant view in Scots law is that the trustee is owner in the fullest sense, with the beneficiary having a personal right only. The beneficiary is protected, however, by the fact that the trust assets and liabilities are held as a separate patrimony from the trustee's own personal patrimony. The South African law of trusts seems to be 'a *jus tripertitum* of Roman-Dutch, English, and indigenous South African rules' (B Beinart, 'Trusts in Roman and Roman-Dutch Law' (1980) 1 J Leg Hist 6, 44). The phrase *jus tripertitum* means 'tripartite law', and is an allusion to the tripartite will of Roman law, discussed above.

Further, there are important differences. Modern trusts can be (and often are) created by living persons. In that sense, their connection with the law of succession is incidental, arising because they are often created in wills. By contrast, *fideicommissa* developed entirely in the context of succession, and are intimately linked with it.

That being the case, it is no surprise that the rules of the general law of succession increasingly came to apply to *fideicommissa* as well. For example, *peregrini*[240] could originally take under a *fideicommissum* despite not being able to do so under a will, but this was changed under Hadrian. Instead, the property was forfeited to the imperial treasury.[241] The restrictions on succession by unmarried and childless persons also came to apply to *fideicommissa*.[242] Again, Hadrian extended to *fideicommissa* the rule barring legacies to uncertain persons.[243] This last is of particular interest because it prevented the use of *fideicommissa* to keep property in the family.[244] This device, called fideicommissary substitution, involved making a *fideicommissum* directing each successive heir in turn not to alienate the property and to bind his or her own heir in the same way. This was no longer possible after Hadrian. A liberalising enactment of Justinian allowed this once more,[245] until a particularly involved case caused him to limit fideicommissary substitution to four generations.[246]

The request made in a *fideicommissum* could be absolute or conditional and, where any such condition was not met, there was of course no need to comply with the request.[247] Where a *fideicommissum* was imposed on the heir, he or she remained heir, even after complying with it.[248] The heir therefore remained liable for the deceased's debts, even if all benefit had been transferred to the beneficiary of the *fideicommissum*. This understandably made heirs reluctant to agree to act in such cases. However, during the first century AD, two resolutions of the Senate improved the position of heirs taking subject to *fideicommissa*. Under Nero, the *SC Trebellianum* of AD 56/57 provided that, once the *fideicommissum* had been performed, the rights and obligations of the heir were divided with the beneficiary of the *fideicommissum* in proportion to what each ended up with.[249] Later, under Vespasian, the *SC Pegasianum* extended to *fideicommissa* the rule of the *lex Falcidia*, entitling the heir to take at least a quarter of the deceased's estate. If the heir was directed under the *fideicommissum* to make over

---

[240] *i.e.* non-citizens. See p. 96.
[241] G.2.285.
[242] G.2.285–6a.
[243] G.2.287.
[244] For an example, see D.31.88.15.
[245] C.6.48.1 (AD 528/9).
[246] Nov.159 (AD 555). This at least is the conventional interpretation. For a contrary view, see D Johnston, *The Roman Law of Trusts* (Clarendon Press 1988) 111–16.
[247] J.2.23.2.
[248] J.2.23.3.
[249] J.2.23.4; D.36.1.1.2.

more than three quarters of the estate, the heir could nonetheless retain a full quarter. It would then be necessary for heir and beneficiary to make stipulations between themselves dividing up the rights and liabilities.[250] Justinian later simplified the position by abolishing these stipulations, and otherwise merging these rules under the name of the *SC Trebellianum*.[251]

(3) Codicils

It was noted above that the *fideicommissa* of Lucius Lentulus were created in codicils. In modern practice, the term 'codicil' is used for a deed that amends an existing will, for example where it is intended to alter a legacy without having to redo the whole will. This is not the meaning of the term in Roman law.

A codicil in Roman law can be defined as a document that makes testamentary provision, but which does not meet the requirements for a will. They were not enforceable before Augustus. Their coming to be enforceable arises from the same story of Lucius Lentulus recounted above.[252] After he had performed the *fideicommissa*, Augustus consulted the leading jurists of the time, to ask whether codicils should be considered legally effective. Augustus accepted the view of Trebatius, that the ability to make a legally effective codicil would be useful to those on journeys, who might not be able to make a will. This accordingly became the law.

A codicil could be made even where no will was made.[253] A distinction was made between codicils confirmed by a will[254] and those not confirmed by a will. A codicil that was not confirmed by a will could only be used to create a *fideicommissum*. By contrast, a confirmed codicil could do anything a will could do except for instituting an heir.[255]

In classical law, there were no specific requirements of form for a valid codicil. It is no doubt this that led to the inclusion in wills of a clause called the *clausula codicillaris*, which Ulpian tells us was done in the majority of cases.[256] This clause provided that, if the will failed, it was to be treated as a codicil and its provisions as *fideicommissa*. In the post-classical period, though, the distinction between wills and codicils was reduced by the introduction of a witnessing requirement along the same lines as wills.[257] The final position was that five witnesses were needed for a valid codicil.[258]

---

[250] G.2.257.
[251] J.2.23.7.
[252] J.2.25pr.
[253] J.2.25.1.
[254] A codicil was considered confirmed thus if either a prior will authorised it or a subsequent will confirmed it.
[255] J.2.25.2.
[256] D.29.1.3.
[257] C.Th.4.4.1 (AD 326).
[258] C.6.36.8.3 (AD 424).

Chapter Summary

Of all the areas of Roman law considered in this book, the law of succession has perhaps the most complex history. The principal reason for this is that, while succession was a major focus of legislative and praetorian intervention, this tended to involve adding additional complexity to the existing system rather than replacing it. An example of this is the preference for agnatic relations in intestate succession. This was circumvented rather than abolished by praetorian intervention. Again, the fundamental principle of universal succession, by which the heir stepped entirely into the deceased's shoes for all purposes, including liability for debts, was preserved in theory but circumvented in practice by the introduction of protections for heirs and creditors.

Further Reading

G.2.97–289; 3.1–87
J.2.9.6–3.9
D.5.2–3; 28–38; 43.2–3
C.3.28; 6.9–62; 8.56–8
Nov.18; 92; 107; 115; 118; 127; 159

J C Gardner, 'The Origin and Nature of the Legal Rights of Spouses and Children in the Scottish Law of Succession' (1927) 39 JR 209 (Part 1) and 313 (Part 2)

D Johnston, *The Roman Law of Trusts* (Clarendon Press 1988)

H Lindsay, 'Adoption and Succession in Roman Law' (1998) 3 Newcastle L Rev 57

E Metzger ed, *A Companion to Justinian's Institutes* (Duckworth 1998) chapter 4

F du Toit, 'The Impact of Social and Economic Factors on Freedom of Testation in Roman and Roman-Dutch Law' (1999) 10 Stellenbosch L Rev 232

A Watson, *The Law of Succession in the Later Roman Republic* (Oxford University Press 1971)

PART FIVE

The Law of Things: Obligations

The final part of the law of things is the law of obligations. We shall see in Chapter 17 a more detailed discussion of what is meant by the term 'obligation', together with discussion of some basic ideas in the law of obligations. In simple terms, though, we are concerned with the situation where someone is personally bound to make some kind of performance to another. One example would be a debt, which is an obligation to pay money to another person.

Obligations can arise in various ways. Perhaps the most obvious is through a contract. The law of contracts is introduced in Chapter 17, and then different types of contract are considered in Chapters 18 to 21. Obligations may arise in other ways, however. The law of delicts is concerned with the obligation imposed on a wrongdoer to compensate the victim of his or her actions. The law of delicts is considered in Chapters 22 to 24. Finally, various further ways in which an obligation can be imposed are considered in Chapters 25 and 26.

It is sometimes quite a complex task to trace the influence of Roman law through to modern law in this area. Many of the ideas considered in this part of the book underwent quite extensive development and modification following the Reception of Roman law in the Middle Ages (see Chapter 4). As we shall see, though, there are numerous points on which Roman sources are of continuing relevance in modern law. The law of obligations is probably second only to property law in terms of how often the courts continue to make reference to Roman legal materials.

The Law of Things: Obligations

CHAPTER SEVENTEEN

Introduction to the Law of Obligations and the Law of Contracts

A. Nature and Structure of the Law of Obligations

We saw in Chapter 10 that Roman law made a distinction between real rights and personal rights,[1] a distinction that still exists in modern law. A real right can be considered as a right directly in an item of property, the right being therefore enforceable against anyone into whose hands the property comes. The main example of a real right is ownership, with the result that an owner of property that has been stolen, or otherwise gone astray, can always recover it from even a good faith acquirer.[2] As we saw in Chapters 13 to 15, however, other real rights were also recognised.

Not all rights, though, are real rights. Some rights are enforceable only against a particular person or against particular persons. These rights are called personal rights. A right under a contract is a personal right, for example, and so can only be enforced against the other party to the contract. A person who is not a party to a contract cannot have that contract enforced against him or her.[3] For example, suppose that I enter into a contract with you to sell you my house. At this point you acquire a personal right against me, by which you can compel me to transfer ownership to you. As we saw in Chapter 11, however, you do not actually become owner until a further act of transfer is carried out.[4] In the meantime, I am still owner. If I sell the property to someone else instead of you, I can validly transfer ownership to that someone else. I will certainly be in breach of my contract with you, and you will have a remedy against me for that. However, because our contract is enforceable only between us, you will not be able to get the house.

The corollary of the personal right is the obligation of the obliged party to comply with it. In the example in the previous paragraph, you had the right to

---

[1] See pp. 163–5.
[2] See pp. 202–3. The position is somewhat complicated by the possibility of acquisition of ownership by *usucapio*. As we saw at p. 240, though, *usucapio* did not apply to stolen property.
[3] For this proposition in Roman law, see D.45.1.83pr, but it is just as true for modern law.
[4] In earlier law, this was (normally) a ceremonial act of transfer called *mancipatio*. Later, a transfer of possession was enough.

have ownership transferred to you and I had the obligation to make the transfer. When we use the term 'obligation', we are normally referring specifically to the duty of compliance with the right. For the Romans, though, the term *obligatio* could refer to this whole relationship between the two parties. Thus, says Justinian, an obligation is 'a legal tie which binds us to the necessity of making some performance'.[5]

For this reason, we refer to the law of personal rights as the law of obligations. Obligations could arise in different ways and were classified in more than one way.

One important way in which obligations could be classified was according to whether they were part of the civil law (*ius civile*) or the praetorian law (*ius honorarium*).[6] Obligations that were part of the civil law were older, and had a tendency to involve a higher degree of formalism and rigidity. By contrast, obligations forming part of the *ius honorarium* were created by the praetor to supplement or correct the civil law, and often displayed a greater degree of flexibility.

There was also a category of obligations called natural obligations. These were seen as existing according to natural law, but were not legally enforceable. An example was an agreement made by a master to pay money to his slave. The slave could not enforce this, even after being freed from slavery. A natural obligation could, however, have certain legal consequences. If the master in fact paid the money after freeing the slave,[7] he would be unable to recover it.[8] This contrasts with the normal position: as we shall see in Chapter 25, normally when money is paid that is not due, that payment can be recovered by the person who made it.[9] Natural obligations are also known in modern law, although more rarely by that name.[10]

The most important classification of obligations, though, was according to the kind of conduct that gave rise to it. This way of classifying obligations took some time to develop. In his *Institutes*, Gaius said that obligations 'are divided into two main types: for every obligation arises either from contract or from delict'.[11] The law of delicts is considered in Chapters 22 to 24, and is concerned with wrongful acts. In other words, I incur an obligation towards you either by entering into an agreement with you or by committing some wrong against you. While, however, that covers the most important cases, it does not cover all of them. Other situations may give rise to an obligation. For example, suppose that

---

[5] J.3.13pr. See also D.44.7.3pr. These passages simplify the situation somewhat. As in modern law, a personal right could also impose an obligation not to do something.
[6] See pp. 50–2.
[7] If he paid the slave before the grant of freedom, the money would still belong to the master on account of the slave's inability to own money or property, although it would form part of the slave's *peculium*. On *peculium*, see pp. 106–7.
[8] D.12.6.64; D.4.5.2.2. For discussion, see Zimmermann, *Obligations* 7–10.
[9] See p. 430.
[10] An example is provided by the concept of limitation, by which, after a period of time, certain rights remain valid but cease to be enforceable. See Prescription and Limitation (Scotland) Act 1973, Part II.
[11] G.3.88.

I believe that I owe you a debt which, in fact, is not due. I pay you the money that I believe myself to owe. There is no contract here, and no wrongful act has been committed, but the law nonetheless allows me to reclaim the money.[12] Again, suppose that we are neighbours. While you are on holiday, a storm blows off the tiles from part of your roof. To avoid the rain getting in, I incur expense in carrying out temporary repairs to your roof. Once again, there is no contract between us and I have committed no wrong against you. Nonetheless, the law provides a ground on which I can recover my expenses from you.[13] Elsewhere, therefore, we find Gaius saying that obligations arise 'from contract, from wrongdoing or by some special right from various types of causes',[14] with the third category being a miscellaneous one to catch bases of obligation that are not included in either of the others. A further elaboration came in Justinian's *Institutes*, in which the miscellaneous category is divided into two, according to whether the basis of the obligation was closer to contract or to delict. Obligations arise, says Justinian, 'from contract, as though from a contract [*quasi ex contractu*], from wrongdoing or as though from wrongdoing [*quasi ex maleficio*]'.[15] This is the structure used in this book. Contracts are dealt with first, in Chapters 18 to 21. Delicts are considered, as has been said, in Chapters 22 to 24. Finally, quasi-contract and quasi-delict, as they are known, are addressed in Chapters 25 and 26 respectively.

B. Transfer, Enforcement and Extinction of Personal Rights

(1) Transfer of Personal Rights

In Gaius' institutional scheme,[16] the law of obligations was grouped together with property law and succession as the 'law of things'. The primary focus here is on the right itself, rather than on the way in which it arose. We are considering the right as an economic asset among other economic assets. The implication is that we should think of the personal right as itself a form of property.[17]

There is a long-standing debate on the question of whether rights can be considered property.[18] If they are, though, this raises the question of whether it ought not to be possible for the holder of the right to transfer it to someone else. This is certainly possible in modern law, by a process called assignation.[19] Assignation involves the right of enforcement being transferred from one person to another, with the result that the debtor, instead of owing performance to the original creditor (the assignor), now owes performance to a new creditor (the assignee).

---

[12] In modern terms, this is a case of unjustified enrichment. See pp. 429–34.
[13] This is a case of *negotiorum gestio*. See pp. 434–5.
[14] D.44.7.1pr.
[15] J.3.13.2.
[16] See pp. 59–60.
[17] See J.2.2.2.
[18] See e.g. G L Gretton, 'Owning Rights and Things' (1997) 8 Stell LR 176. See also, from a Common Law perspective, J Tarrant, 'Obligations as Property' (2011) 34 UNSWLJ 677.
[19] On this, see C Anderson, *Property: A Guide to Scots Law* (W Green 2016) chapter 6.

In Roman law, however, this was not possible. The 'legal tie' between the parties was seen as being strictly personal to them. This came to be seen as inconvenient, however. The right being an asset of economic value, it is to be expected that the creditor may wish to transfer the right to someone else. For example, where the creditor is entitled to payment of a sum of money in six months' time, he or she may wish to raise money now by selling the right to payment, doubtless at a discount. That way, the assignor at least gets partial payment now, and the assignee gets full payment in six months. Ways were developed of getting round the bar on assignment.[20]

One of these was *novatio* (novation),[21] which involved the original obligation being replaced by a new one. It was effected by the debtor making an undertaking, using the form of contract called *stipulatio*,[22] to make performance to the 'assignee'.[23] This, though, had the disadvantage of requiring the co-operation of the debtor, and it also extinguished any security rights that were accessory to the original obligation.[24] For these reasons, the more popular option was the *procuratio in rem suam*.[25]

How this worked was as follows. It was always possible to nominate another person to pursue a case on your behalf, as *cognitor* or *procurator*. If the *cognitor* or *procurator* was successful, of course, he would be expected to hand over his winnings to you. In *procuratio in rem suam*, however, the person authorised to pursue the case would only nominally be doing so on your behalf. In reality, he would be doing so on his own behalf.[26] Thus, something functionally equivalent to assignation was created. In the post-classical period, reforms allowed certain categories of 'assignee' to sue as creditor in their own right, a process completed by Justinian.[27] Even then, though, the 'assignor' was still technically creditor, and so payment to him or her would discharge the debt. For this reason, the rule was developed in the late classical period that, if notice (*denuntiatio*) was given to the debtor, the debtor could not discharge the debt by paying the original creditor.[28] In this way, the position in post-classical law became very similar to that in modern Scots law, in which an assignation is completed by notification (called intimation) to the debtor.[29]

(2) Extinction of Personal Rights

Personal rights could be extinguished in various ways. The most obvious way is by the debtor making performance (*solutio*) of the obligation.[30] A creditor could also accept a substitute performance or, indeed, excuse performance altogether.

---

[20] Generally on these, see Zimmermann, *Obligations* 58–67.
[21] On *novatio* as a way of discharging obligations, see below.
[22] See Chapter 18.
[23] G.2.38.
[24] See pp. 269–70.
[25] G.2.39.
[26] G.2.39; Birks, *Obligations* 127.
[27] C.8.53.33 (AD 528).
[28] C.8.16.4 (AD 225); C.8.41.3 (AD 239).
[29] C Anderson, *Property: A Guide to Scots Law* (W Green 2016) chapter 6.
[30] D.50.16.176.

This extinguished the obligation, and was called *acceptilatio* (acceptilation). In early law, it was held that this had to be done using a formal process, mirroring the procedure for the form of contract called *stipulatio*.[31] However, in classical law, it came to be accepted that even an informal agreement not to pursue a debt prevented enforcement of it.[32]

As has already been mentioned, an obligation could also be extinguished by *novatio* (novation), which happened when the original obligation was replaced with a new one with the parties' agreement.[33]

A special case of extinction happened in litigation, when the stage of *litis contestatio* was reached.[34] This discharged the original obligation, and replaced it with an equivalent one based on the *litis contestatio*. This was the basis of the doctrine of *res iudicata*, by which the same thing could not be sued for more than once.

An obligation was extinguished by *confusio* (confusion) when the same person became both creditor and debtor.[35] This might happen when the debtor was the creditor's heir, or *vice versa*.

As we shall see below, an obligation could be extinguished when its performance became impossible without either party being at fault.

Finally, when the parties were both creditor and debtor to each other, the debts could be held to cancel out except to the extent of any surplus.[36] This process was called *compensatio*. Thus, suppose that I owed you 100 and you owed me 200. With *compensatio*, this would simply resolve itself as you owing me 100. This was relatively straightforward with *bonae fidei* contracts, the *formula* for which allowed the judge discretion to take such matters into account.[37] With *stricti iuris* contracts, the *exceptio doli* (see below) had to be used.[38]

C. Introduction to the Law of Contracts

(1) Nature of the Law of Contracts

In modern law, we are used to thinking in terms of a general law of contract. What this means is that, while there will be special rules applying to some particular kinds of contract, most aspects of most contracts will be governed by the same general rules and principles. Typically, in an undergraduate course on the law of contract, this is how the law is approached. By and large, all contracts are formed, interpreted, enforced and extinguished in the same ways, with the idea of shared intention at its foundation.[39] Special rules applying to specific contracts

---

[31] G.3.169. If a right under another kind of contract was to be discharged, it had to be novated (see below) as a *stipulatio* first: G.3.170.
[32] See e.g. D.18.5.5.1.
[33] D.46.2.1pr.
[34] G.3.180. On *litis contestatio*, see pp. 35, 40.
[35] D.46.3.107.
[36] For the modern law, see *Stair Memorial Encyclopaedia*, vol 15 paras 877–9. The main difference is that, in modern law, compensatio must normally be specifically pled rather than applying automatically.
[37] G.4.61.
[38] See p. 423. For the practical difficulties of this, see Zimmermann, *Obligations* 762–4.
[39] G Black, 'Formation of Contract: The Role of Contractual Intention and Email Disclaimers' 2011 JR 97.

(*e.g.* sale, hire, partnership and so forth) are normally dealt with later, often in a separate course called commercial law or something of the sort.

In Roman law, the approach was quite different. Beyond a recognition that all contracts involved agreement,[40] there was altogether very little idea of general principles of contract. Instead, the focus was very much on specific contracts. In principle – though this principle was departed from in some respects, as we shall see – an agreement had to be fitted into one of the recognised contracts, or else it was not binding. This is not a problem that can arise in modern law.

The different types of contract could be classified in various ways. For example, most contracts were bilateral, but sometimes a unilateral contract could be made. The difference between these is that, in a unilateral contract, only one party was undertaking obligations. In a bilateral contract, both parties undertook obligations.

Another classification of contracts was into those that were *stricti iuris* (of strict law) and those that were *bonae fidei* (of good faith). The *stricti iuris* contracts were developed earlier, and arose from the civil law. Their validity depended on adherence to formal requirements rather than on the parties' underlying intentions. *Bonae fidei* contracts, by contrast, were less strict in form and had more scope to take into account issues such as error or coercion.

The method of classification of contracts used in the *Institutes* is a fourfold one, based on the way in which the different contracts were constituted: not all were constituted by consent.

Verbal contracts were constituted by the exchange of words in particular form. These are considered in Chapter 18.

Real contracts (contracts *re*) were constituted by the parties' conduct, specifically the delivery by one to the other of the property with which the contract was concerned. These contracts are considered in Chapter 19.

Consensual contracts were the only ones that were constituted by the parties' agreement alone. This category contained what can certainly be seen as the most important contract, the contract of sale, and is considered in Chapter 20.

Finally, literal contracts (contracts *litteris*) were constituted in writing. We are concerned here with writing as a necessary constitutive element, not simply for the purpose of evidencing the transaction. It has always been sensible to record important transactions in writing, but a contract of sale (say) is not in the category of literal contracts even if its terms are reduced to writing. Literal contracts are considered in Chapter 21, along with certain further forms of agreement that were given some legal effect.

In the rest of this chapter, we shall be looking at some general principles of contracts. This could be seen in one sense as anachronistic: as we have seen, the Romans themselves did not approach the material in this way. However, we are not Roman lawyers, and we are not altogether obliged to approach the issues in

---

[40] D.2.14.1.3.

the way they did. One of the main reasons for studying Roman law is for what it can teach us about modern law, and that justifies a different approach from that used by the Romans.

(2) The Role of *Causa*

As we have seen, the Romans had a law of specific contracts, rather than a general law of contract. They adhered to the maxim, *ex nudis pactis non oritur actio* (no action arises from bare agreements). Another way of expressing this is to say that there could be no obligation without a proper legal basis, or *causa*.[41] For the Romans, this seems to have meant simply that the agreement had to fall into one of the recognised types. In some systems, most notably French law, this has evolved into a more general principle that, to be binding, a contract must oblige both parties. This is very similar to the English doctrine of consideration, by which purely unilateral obligations are rendered non-binding.[42] Thus, for example, in English law a contract by which I agreed to do something I was already obliged to do would not be binding,[43] and the same would be true of a promise to do something in exchange for value already received.[44]

From a Scots law point of view, matters have moved on substantially, and here Scots law differs a great deal from English law (and indeed Roman law). The main source of this development was the medieval canon law which, as we have seen,[45] drew heavily on Roman law but did not follow it slavishly. The canon law, being concerned with matters of conscience and good faith, evolved the general rule that any seriously intended agreement was, in principle, enforceable. The maxim to follow was now *pacta sunt servanda* (agreements are to be kept). This meant a rejection of the idea that a contract was only valid if it could be fitted into a defined category. As Stair put it for Scots law, 'every paction produceth action'.[46]

This development has had three notable consequences for Scots law. The first is that an agreement may be a valid contract, even if it is of a novel type. The second is that a unilateral promise may be held binding:

> a promise is that which is simple and pure, and hath not implied as a condition, the acceptance of another ... Promises now are commonly held obligatory, the canon law having taken off the exception of the civil law, *de nudo pacto*.[47]

Thirdly, in much the same way as a binding promise may be made, a contract may in Scots law create an obligation enforceable by a person who is not a party

---

[41] D.2.14.7.4.
[42] See B S Markesinis, 'Cause and Consideration: A Study in Parallel' (1978) 37 Cam LJ 53.
[43] *Stilk v Meyrick* (1809) 170 ER 851.
[44] *Roscorla v Thomas* (1842) 3 QB 234.
[45] See pp. 76–8.
[46] Stair, Institutions 1.10.7. Indeed, in adopting this principle, Stair may even have gone further than the continental writers that inspired him: G Lubbe, 'Formation of Contract' in *History of Private Law in Scotland*, vol II 11–18.
[47] Stair, Institutions 1.10.4.

to the contract.[48] This third party right, traditionally called a *ius quaesitum tertio*,[49] could not have been created in Roman law.[50] This ability now also exists in English law. However, because the doctrine of consideration prevented parties gaining contractual rights for which they had not given value, this had to be introduced in England by statute.[51]

(3) Contract Formation and Intrinsic Grounds of Invalidity
(a) Consensus and Error

As we have seen, all of the Roman forms of contract depended at some level on agreement between the parties. What, though, if one or both of the parties suffered from an error as to some essential element of the transaction? With *stricti iuris* contracts, this could hardly be relevant:[52] in a *stricti iuris* contract, the parties' agreement was judged simply by externals, so an unexpressed error in understanding could not be founded on.[53]

The situation was different with *bonae fidei* contracts. With these, the contract's validity was dependent on genuine agreement between the parties.[54] There had to be *consensus in idem*: the parties' minds had to be at one on the essentials of the contract, or else the contract was void.[55] It does not appear to have mattered whether the error lay with one party or with both, if the latter whether the parties suffered from the same error or different ones, or even whether one party could have known of the other's error. It was enough to make the contract void that the error existed, as long as the error related to an essential element of the contract. This is referred to here as an *intrinsic* ground of invalidity of the contract, because it was a defect in the contract itself rather than being something from outside of it.

A number of different types of error were recognised as relevant. The starting point is a statement by Ulpian:

---

[48] Stair, Institutions 1.10.5. The law is now contained in the Contract (Third Party Rights) (Scotland) Act 2017. For the complex background to that Act, see Scottish Law Commission, *Review of Contract Law: Report on Third Party Rights* (SLC No 245, 2016).

[49] The Contract (Third Party Rights) (Scotland) Act 2017 uses the term 'third-party right'.

[50] D.45.1.38.17, although exceptions could be recognised where there was benefit to the stipulator. See e.g. D.45.1.38.20, which considers the situation where a guardian gives up his role to a new guardian, and stipulates with the new guardian for the safeguarding of the ward's property. This could be seen as valid, as the original guardian has potential liability for losses caused by mismanagement of this property. See also C.3.42.8 (AD 293) and, for discussion, Zimmermann, *Obligations* 34–40.

[51] Contracts (Rights of Third Parties) Act 1999. Probably as a result of the previous restriction on third party rights, as well as the doctrine of consideration, there has been a tendency in English law to find solutions in the law of delict (or, in English terminology, 'tort') for what are in reality contractual disputes. *Hedley Byrne & Co Ltd v Heller & Partners Ltd* [1964] AC 465 seems a clear example of this tendency, which is also found in Scots law, no doubt because of the English influence on the Scots law of delict that we will see at pp. 399–403. See W W McBryde, 'Contract Law – A Solution to Delictual Problems?' 2012 SLT (News) 45.

[52] Unless, perhaps, the error was such as to render the agreement genuinely undefined. For a modern example, see *Raffles v Wichelhaus* (1864) 159 ER 375.

[53] At least in early law. See below, however, on the situation where the error arises from the deceit of the other party.

[54] Everything that follows assumes that the parties have full legal capacity, which of course they may not, for various reasons. The most obvious of these is a lack of capacity on the basis of age, but there are others. See Chapters 5–8.

[55] Zimmermann, *Obligations* 588–9.

In contracts of sale, it is obvious that agreement must be present. The purchase is not valid if there is disagreement as to the contract itself, the price or some other element.[56]

The reference here is specifically to sale, but it is generally taken to be of wider application. Ulpian then identifies here two specific types of error as relevant, the nature of the contract and the price, as well as the miscellaneous category of 'some other element'.

The first type of error mentioned by Ulpian is known as *error in negotio*, which is an error as to the type of transaction that has been agreed:

> If I give to you as if by way of deposit, and you receive as if as a loan, there is neither deposit nor loan. It is the same if you give as if as a loan for consumption, and I receive as if as a loan for use.[57]

Many other examples could be given.

The second is *error in pretio*, which is an error as to the contractual price. Despite the term 'price', this is broader than sale:

> If I lease land out to you for ten, and you think that you are renting it for five, there is no contract.[58]

Beyond these two examples, others existed, but the error had to do with some fundamental element in the contract. It would not, for example, be enough that I believed the thing I was buying from you to be more valuable than it in fact was.[59] If, however, there was a mistake as to the identity of the actual subject matter of the contract (*error in corpore*), that would be sufficient reason to hold the contract to be void.[60] For example, if I thought I was buying the Cornelian farm, and you thought you were selling the Sempronian farm, there was no contract.[61] That assumes, though, that we are genuinely in disagreement about the plot of land to be sold. If we agree about what land is being sold, but differ as to its name, the contract is valid.[62] This kind of error is known as *error in nomine* (error as to name).

---

[56] D.18.1.9pr.
[57] D.12.1.18.1 (Ulpian).
[58] D.19.2.52 (Pomponius). Pomponius does go on to suggest that, if the reverse error is present, that is that the landlord thinks that the rent is lower than the tenant believes it to be, there may then be a valid contract at the lower price. This conclusion is perhaps more pragmatic than principled. (This is an observation, not a criticism.)
[59] As we shall see at pp. 360–4, though, certain remedies were developed for the case in which the goods were actually defective.
[60] For discussion of an interesting South African case which arguably falls into this category, but which also shows the difficulties of fitting every case into such clear categories, see J S McLennan, 'Justus Error, Snatching at Bargains, and Rectification' (1987) 104 SALJ 382. This article discusses a case in which the cause of the error was a typographical error in an offer to sell a plot of land, when the prospective purchaser knew that the plot number was not the one that he had expressed an interest in buying. The court held that he had snatched at a bargain, and was not entitled to rely on the error.
[61] D.18.1.9pr.
[62] D.18.1.9.1. See also D.35.1.17.1.

The identity of the other party to the contract might also be fundamental to the contract. An error as to identity was an *error in persona*. Celsus gives this example:

> If you asked both me and Titius for a loan of money, and I instructed my debtor to make a promise to you [*i.e.* by the *novatio* procedure outlined above, whereby my debtor agrees to pay you instead of me], and you took a *stipulatio* from him believing him to be Titius' debtor, are you under an obligation to me? I do not change my position, if it is the case that you have contracted no business with me. But it is closer to the truth to suppose that you are obliged to me, not because I lent you money (that cannot happen except between those who have agreed), but because my money has come to you, and it is right and proper that you should return it.[63]

The situation here is that you have asked to borrow money from me and also from another person, called Titius. The money has come (indirectly) from me, but you believe it to have come from Titius. You are liable to repay me, but not because of any contract. There can be no contract here, because of the error. Instead, your liability arises from your unjustified enrichment at my expense.[64] This appears to be a case, though, where both Titius and I are known to you. There will be many cases where the precise identity of the contracting parties is a matter of complete indifference to each of them. For example, suppose that a stallholder in a busy marketplace is agreeing a sale of apples with a customer, while also passing the time of day. While they chat, the customer mentions that his name is Paulus. The stallholder mishears this as Publius. It would be nonsensical to suppose that an error like this would render the contract void. All that the stallholder needs to know is that he is doing business with the man in front of him, not the name of that man. An error of this kind seems more like an *error in nomine* which, as we have seen, does not affect the validity of the contract.[65]

A final form of relevant error was *error in substantia*, error as to the substance of the property that was the subject matter of the contract. It is important to note here that we are not concerned with quality in the sense of the presence or absence of defects in the property. Rather, we are concerned with what kind of thing it is. Ulpian explains:

> Next it is asked whether, if there is no mistake in the identity of the property, but there is an error in the substance, there is a valid contract of sale, for example, if vinegar is sold as wine, copper as gold, or lead or something similar to silver as silver. In the sixth book of his *Digest*, Marcellus writes that there is a valid sale, because they are agreed about the identity of the property, even though there is a mistake about its substance. I agree in the case of the wine, because the substance is much the same, if the wine has gone sour. It is different if it is not wine that has gone off, but was vinegar from the start, as a condiment, then it appears that one thing has been sold as another.[66]

---

[63] D.12.1.32.
[64] See pp. 429–34.
[65] For the same distinction in modern law, compare *Morrisson v Robertson* 1908 SC 332 and *Macleod v Kerr* 1965 SC 253.
[66] D.18.1.9.2.

So, if there was an error as to the substance of the property, the contract would be void.[67] Unsurprisingly, there were often difficulties in determining whether an error was *in substantia* or not. For example, a sale purporting to be of a solid silver table, which was actually just silver-plated, would be void.[68] However, a sale of an alloy as a pure metal was not an *error in substantia*.[69] This last example makes reasonable enough sense if the unexpected ingredient is a trace amount only. The reasoning is rather more difficult to follow if the mix is such as to make something recognised as a different metal altogether, such as bronze or brass.

(b) Modern Developments
Modern Scots law has moved away from this subjective focus on the parties' *actual* intentions, and takes a more objective approach: the parties are taken to intend what an objective bystander would take them to intend. As this principle has been expressed: 'commercial contracts cannot be arranged by what people think in their inmost minds. Commercial contracts are made according to what people say . . .'[70]

A move to an objective understanding of intention was accompanied by a move to a more objective understanding of error. Under express reference to the Roman law on *error in substantia*,[71] Stair had said that those persons 'who err in the substantials of what is done, contract not'.[72] Modern law, however, has moved on substantially from this position, and the courts have developed an approach that more than simply unilateral error is required.[73] It has been said:

> What, however, the courts were doing, by increments, was evolving a philosophy that unilateral error was insufficient to affect consent. There had to be something more – misrepresentation, taking advantage of the error, error by both parties, or a gratuitous transaction. To affect consent there had to be 'error plus'.[74]

This, then, is quite different from the Roman position, where an uninduced, unilateral error would be enough for the contract to be void.

If a contract was not concluded, then in Roman law it followed that either party was free to walk away. The same is true in modern Scots law. Often that would give rise to no particular issues. Equally, though, there are situations in which that might seem unfair. For example, suppose there was an agreement for the sale of a quantity of goods. The buyer is in error as to some essential feature

---

[67] See also D.18.1.11.1.
[68] D.18.1.41.1.
[69] D.18.1.14.
[70] *Muirhead & Turnbull v Dickson* (1905) 7 F 686, 694 (Lord President Dunedin). Despite the wording, the point is not confined to commercial contracts. For an interesting discussion of lawyers' approaches to interpretation of language, see L Hoffmann, 'Language and Lawyers' (2018) 134 LQR 553. The specific focus is on English law, but many of the points are of wider application.
[71] Specifically to D.18.1.9.
[72] Stair, Institutions 1.10.13.
[73] *Stewart v Kennedy* (1890) 17 R (HL) 25.
[74] W W McBryde, 'Error' in *History of Private Law in Scotland*, vol II 78. In addition to that chapter, see P Stein, *Fault in the Formation of Contract in Roman Law and Scots Law* (Oliver and Boyd 1958) 171–208.

of the transaction. When the error emerges, the buyer withdraws from the transaction, but by this time the seller has, in reliance on the apparent agreement, incurred expense in transporting the goods or has rejected an alternative offer for the goods. Roman law gave the disappointed seller no remedy here. In the nineteenth century, however, the German jurist Jhering developed a doctrine called *culpa in contrahendo* (fault in contracting).[75] This was based on the idea that, by entering into negotiations, the parties undertook duties to each other even before the contract was concluded. Although this idea does not reflect the Roman law, it has been influential both in Germany and in other countries, where it has evidently met a perceived need. It has been observed that: 'the impact of Jhering's doctrine, both in Germany and abroad, shows the practical need for and legitimacy of (non-delictual) liability for culpa in contrahendo'.[76]

If such a doctrine as *culpa in contrahendo* is recognised, it is necessary to set clear limits to it in order to balance parties' legitimate expectations with the freedom to withdraw from negotiations. However, if this balance is properly achieved, the doctrine of *culpa in contrahendo* fulfils a useful function in cases where a negotiating party leads another on, causing that person to incur expense or pass up other opportunities, allows negotiations to proceed to an advanced stage and then withdraws from negotiations without good reason. Viewed in this way, *culpa in contrahendo* as a legal idea can be seen as part of a more general development of a duty of good faith owed between contracting parties.[77] When Jhering was developing his ideas on *culpa in contrahendo*, however, he was doing so at a time when the impact of continental legal scholarship on Scots thinking was relatively weak.[78] It is no doubt because of this that *culpa in contrahendo* has never been seen as forming part of Scots law.[79] Take, for example, *W S Karoulias SA v Drambuie Liqueur Co Ltd (No 2)*.[80]

In that case, the pursuers were wine and spirit distributors based in Greece. They had been the distributors of the defenders' products in Greece since at least 1977, on the basis of written agreements renewed every few years. In 2001, the defenders initiated negotiations for renewal of the agreement, which was due to expire in 2003. In January 2003, the defenders emailed the pursuers a final draft

---

[75] For a brief overview, see Zimmermann, *Obligations* 244–5. For more detailed discussion, the relevant literature is extensive, but for a representative sample see Y Ben-Dror, 'The Perennial Ambiguity of Culpa in Contrahendo' (1983) 27 Am J Leg Hist 142; F Kessler and E Fine, 'Culpa in Contrahendo, Bargaining in Good Faith, and Freedom of Contract: A Comparative Study' (1964) 77 Harv L Rev 401; S Colombo, 'The Present Differences between the Civil Law and Common Law Worlds with Regard to Culpa in Contrahendo' (1992) 2 Tilburg Foreign L Rev 341; M Tegethoff, 'Culpa in Contrahendo in German and Dutch Law – A Comparison of Precontractual Liability' (1998) 5 Maastricht J Eur & Comp L 341; J M Zieff, 'Culpa in Contrahendo – A Prescription for the Ills of the South African Law of Contract' (1989) 52 THRHR 348.
[76] Zimmermann, *Obligations* 245.
[77] On the role of good faith in Scots contract law, see *Smith v Bank of Scotland* 1997 SC (HL) 111 and, generally, the contributions in A D M Forte ed, *Good Faith in Contract and Property* (Hart 1999).
[78] See pp. 88–9.
[79] See though *Walker v Milne* (1823) 2 S 379. For discussion of some of the issues, see M Hogg and H MacQueen, 'Melville Monument Liability: Some Doubtful Dicta' (2010) 14 Edin LR 451.
[80] 2005 SLT 813.

agreement for their approval, indicating that, once the pursuers had approved it, the defenders would send them two copies for signing. The pursuers replied approving the terms of the draft agreement, and requested that the copies be sent for signing. The copies were not sent, and the defenders appear then to have begun dragging their feet on finalising the deal, failing to respond to communications and then eventually indicating that they wanted to alter some of the terms. As late as 2 June 2003, however, they were assuring the pursuers that their commitment to the pursuers as their distributors was 'absolute'.[81] They gave this assurance even though in fact they had been in discussions with a potential alternative distributor since at least April of that year. On 11 June 2003, the defenders gave notice terminating the current agreement, and moved their business to the alternative provider. The Lord Ordinary expressed sympathy:

> The defender, no doubt, strung the pursuer along from 5 February and relied on the fact that the agreement had not been executed to explore the possibility of replacing the pursuer . . . as the distributor in Greece. The defender could be seen to have exploited the longstanding, amicable and successful commercial relationship between the parties for its own ends. The terms of Mr Jeffray's email of 2 June 2003 to the effect that 'our commitment to Karoulias and more particularly to you is absolute' were somewhat cynical, if not downright misleading . . .[82]

Nonetheless, the pursuers were denied a remedy. No argument on *culpa in contrahendo* was made. In the current state of Scots law it would have been difficult – perhaps impossible – to make such an argument with any chance of success. Rather, the pursuers' argument was that a contract had been concluded in February 2003 even without the agreement being signed. Nonetheless, it is impossible to be very impressed with the defenders' conduct which, on the face of it, seems destructive of the trust that is essential to efficient commerce. It is perhaps unfortunate, therefore, that the pursuers were unable to get a remedy here.[83]

(4) Extrinsic Grounds of Challenge
A contract might also be challengeable for reasons *extrinsic* to the contract itself.

(a) Coercion *(Metus)*
If a person had been coerced by force or the threat of force into making a contract, that contract could not be enforced. For full detail of this matter, see Chapter 24.[84] For now, it is enough to note the difference in operation of this depending on whether the contract was *stricti iuris* or *bonae fidei*.[85] In a *bonae fidei*

---

[81] At para [13].
[82] At para [52].
[83] In many countries, there would be a potential remedy here. See DCFR II.-3:301 and the comparative discussion there.
[84] See pp. 424–5.
[85] For the operation of this as regards contracts, and especially for discussion of what kinds of threat constituted *metus*, see G Glover, 'Metus in the Roman Law of Obligations' (2004) 10 Fundamina 31.

contract, the good faith clause in the *formula* allowed the judge to take coercion into account. With *stricti iuris* contracts, however, a special defence (the *exceptio metus*) had to be pled.

(b) Deceit *(Dolus)*

As with coercion, deceit is dealt with in more detail in Chapter 24.[86] The essence of deceit as a defence to an action for enforcement of a contract is that the pursuer should not be allowed to enforce the contract, because he or she used trickery or dishonesty to induce the defender to enter into it. In the same way as with coercion, in the case of a *bonae fidei* contract the judge could take this into account on the basis of the good faith clause in the *formula*. In a *stricti iuris* contract, however, a special defence (the *exceptio doli*) was needed.

(c) Illegality and Immorality

Illegal and immoral agreements were invalid and unenforceable. It was considered to be the praetor's duty to refuse actions on such agreements.[87] What counts as immoral is, of course, to a significant extent culturally dependent: what we would consider immoral is not always going to be what the Romans would consider immoral, and *vice versa*.

(d) Impossibility

'There is no obligation to do the impossible', says Celsus.[88] Impossibility may be either factual, where what has been agreed is impossible as a matter of fact, or legal, where what has been agreed is something that is not possible in law. Take two examples given by Gaius.[89] A sale of property that is not subject to private ownership[90] is an example of legal impossibility.[91] By contrast, an agreement to sell a slave who, unknown to the parties, has died is an example of factual impossibility. Other examples of factual impossibility would include a contract for sale of a 'hippocentaur', as such an animal does not exist,[92] or a condition in a contract requiring a party to touch the sky.[93] The treatment of these differed somewhat. An obligation to do something that was factually impossible was simply void. Gaius says the same of obligations to do things that are legally impossible. However, the position seems to have been more precisely that that was the case only when the

---

[86] See pp. 423–4.
[87] D.45.1.26–7pr. This assumes the illegality or immorality is patent when the matter comes before the praetor, which might not be the case. How this worked depended somewhat on whether the supposed contract was bonae fidei or stricti iuris. If it was bonae fidei, any question of illegality or immorality could be dealt with by the judge without any adjustment needing to be made to the formula for the action. Matters were more difficult with stricti iuris contracts. For discussion, see Zimmermann, *Obligations* 710.
[88] D.50.17.185.
[89] G.3.97.
[90] See pp. 194–5.
[91] On this, see also D.45.1.103.
[92] G.3.97a.
[93] G.3.98.

parties were aware of the problem.[94] If, by contrast, I agreed to buy from you land that was, unbeknownst to me, in fact incapable of being owned, the agreement could of course not be implemented. However, it would be valid to the extent that I could claim damages from you for breach of contract when you failed to convey the land to me.[95]

The discussion in the previous paragraph is concerned with impossibility that exists at the time the contract is made. A contract may, however, be initially possible to perform and then become impossible because of some supervening event. As long as this happened without fault on the part of either party, this normally had the effect that the contract was discharged, with both parties freed of any further obligations under it.[96] In contracts of sale, though, a different rule was applied, based on the concept of risk.[97]

Impossibility was judged objectively. It was not a question of what was possible for the specific person subject to the obligation. Rather, it was a question of what was possible in principle. For example, a condition in a contract that depended on a party being elected consul was valid even if that person had no realistic prospect of achieving that office. Equally, it was not a case of impossibility where a person contracted to sell something he or she did not own.[98] For example, if I agreed to sell you my neighbour's house, it would be no objection to the validity of the contract that the house did not belong to me. Of course, unless I first acquired ownership from the neighbour, I could not transfer ownership to you. That, though, did not mean that the *contract* was void: after all, it is not the contract that makes the buyer owner, but rather the act of transfer itself. Quite the contrary: when I fail to give you ownership, you will expect to be able to sue me for breaching our contract, and that will only be possible if there is in fact a contract between us. You only have that remedy because there is a contract. There were, though, some borderline cases of impossibility. Take, for example, a promise by a dying man to build a tenement building. This was held by the classical jurists to be void on the grounds of impossibility, if the man did not have enough time to build it. Justinian, however, decided that the dying man actually intended to bind his heirs in those circumstances.[99]

(5) Suspensive and Resolutive Conditions

A contract could be made subject to a condition (*condicio*). This had the effect either that the obligation to perform under the contract did not come into existence until the occurrence of some later, uncertain event, or else that the contract

---

[94] D.18.1.4–6pr.
[95] For discussion of some of the issues, see R Evans-Jones and G MacCormack, 'The Sale of Res Extra Commercium in Roman Law' (1995) 112 ZSS (rA) 330.
[96] D.45.1.137.
[97] See pp. 356–7.
[98] As opposed to a contract for the sale of something not capable of being owned by anyone.
[99] C.8.37.15 (AD 532).

would lapse on that event. These kinds of condition are known, respectively, as suspensive and resolutive conditions.[100]

The difference between these was as follows. Where a contract was subject to a resolutive condition, the obligations under it came into existence immediately, but fell if the condition was not met. With a suspensive condition, by contrast, the rights and obligations under the contract were suspended and did not become due unless and until the condition was met. Care is needed here. This should not be understood as meaning that the contract itself did not come into existence until the condition was met. That is not the case: the contract itself came into existence immediately, and the parties were fully bound by it in the meantime. For example, suppose that I contracted to sell you my house, subject to a suspensive condition. The presence of that suspensive condition would not mean that I was free to sell to someone else. On the contrary, I would be in breach of our contract if I did.[101] What the suspensive condition means, rather, is that we are neither of us entitled to benefit under the contract until the condition is met. I am not entitled to payment; you are not entitled to get ownership of the house. It is only when the condition is met that we can enforce those entitlements against each other. At this point, the contract is said to have been 'perfected'. A contract subject to a suspensive condition was only perfected when that condition was met. By contrast, a contract subject to a resolutive condition was perfected immediately. Thus, someone who has bought land subject to a resolutive condition can begin *usucapio* immediately and is entitled to the fruits; equally, the purchaser bears the risk of accidental damage to the property.[102] With a suspensive condition, those consequences would not follow.

It was not always clear whether the condition was suspensive or resolutive. It depended on the intentions of the parties, and no doubt they would often fail to express themselves clearly on that point. Take, for example, the condition *in diem addictio*. This was an agreement to sell to the particular buyer, unless a better offer was received by a particular date.[103] Ulpian has this to say:

> When land is sold with a condition *in diem addictio*, there is a question whether the sale is perfect but subject to a resolutive condition, or whether it is subject to a suspensive condition. And really it seems to me to depend on what the parties intended. If it was intended that, on a better offer being received, the deal would be off, this is a sale subject to a resolutive condition. If, on the other hand, it was intended that the sale should become perfect unless a better offer was received, it is a sale subject to a suspensive condition.[104]

---

[100] A condition could also be positive or negative. If it was negative, for example that a party to the contract never does a stated thing, that was construed as being met when that party was on his or her deathbed: J.3.15.4.
[101] Birks, *Obligations* 76.
[102] D.18.2.2.1; D.18.3.5.
[103] D.18.2.1.
[104] D.18.2.2pr.

Fortunately, there were commonly used conditions where the position was rather clearer. A *lex commissoria*, for example, was a condition providing for forfeiture of a purchaser's rights if payment was not made in full by a specified date, at the option of the seller.[105] The presumption was that the *lex commissoria* was a resolutive condition. Again, a *pactum displicentiae* was a condition in a sale of goods making it conditional on the buyer's approval of the goods.[106] Ulpian tells us that it was 'settled' that this was a resolutive condition.[107] Ulpian's view on this has been referred to by the Scottish courts. In *Brown v Marr*,[108] the Lord Justice-Clerk accepted Ulpian's view as correct for Scots law, against the authority of Bell, although he ultimately held that a decision on the point was not necessary for that particular case.[109]

From conditions, we must distinguish contractual terms providing for performance on a particular date (*dies*).[110] In this case, the obligations arising under the contract were binding immediately and unconditionally, but could not be enforced until the specified date. Because of this, early performance was effective and, for instance, a payment made before the due date could not be recovered.[111]

(6) Implement of an Invalid Contract

If, for whatever reason, a contract was invalid, it would follow from that fact that the contract would not be enforceable. Suppose that I make an agreement with you that is illegal. If you attempt to compel me to comply with the agreement, you will be unsuccessful. That, however, does not answer the question of what happens if, regardless of the contract's invalidity, we carry out the agreement anyway. Perhaps I have transferred property to you in breach of some legal rule, for example. The issues raised here are considered in Chapters 11 (transfer of ownership)[112] and 25 (quasi-contract).[113]

---

[105] D.18.3.2. Any deposit paid, or other payment made, was also forfeited: D.18.3.6pr.
[106] Compare the innominate contract of *aestimatum*, considered at p. 381.
[107] D.18.1.3.
[108] (1880) 7 R 427, 434–5.
[109] See now, though, the Sale of Goods Act 1979, s. 18 rule 4, which takes a different approach.
[110] Special considerations applied when the obligation was linked to the date of one party's death. Gaius (G.3.100) tells us that an obligation to begin 'after I die' was invalid, as it would give a right to or impose a duty on a third party, namely the heir. An obligation to do something 'the day before I die' was also invalid, as that day cannot be known until the death takes place. An obligation to do something 'when I am dying', however, was considered valid, and was held to become due at the last moment of life. See A Watson, 'Illogicality and Roman Law' (1972) 7 Israel L Rev 14, 20–1. This restriction was abolished by Justinian: J.3.19.3.
[111] D.46.3.70. On the basis of the *condictio indebiti*, see p. 430.
[112] See pp. 203–4.
[113] See p. 430.

Chapter Summary

This chapter had two purposes. First, we saw the nature of the law of obligations, the area with which the remaining chapters of the book are concerned. In particular, we saw that the law of obligations can be defined as the law of personal rights, these being rights that are enforceable against some specific person or persons, and we saw how these rights are transferred or extinguished. These personal rights or obligations can be classified in various ways, but the most important is the distinction between the different kinds of conduct that give rise to obligations. A person may become subject to an obligation through agreement (*i.e.* through contract), through wrongdoing, 'as though from contract', or 'as though from wrongdoing'.

It is with the first of these categories – obligations arising from contract – that the remainder of this chapter was concerned. Unlike the usual approach to modern contract law, the Romans did not usually present the law in this area as depending on general principles. Instead, they viewed it as a law of multiple specific contracts, each with its own rules. Nonetheless, they are united by the idea of a contract being based on agreement. In medieval and modern law, this idea has been taken further, and there has been developed the idea that, in principle, any seriously intended agreement is legally binding, unless it is illegal, immoral or impossible, or that agreement is vitiated by some defect of consent.

Further Reading

G.3.88, 163–81
J.3.13; 3.29
D.4.2–3; 46.2–4
P Birks, *The Roman Law of Obligations* (E Descheemaeker ed, Oxford University Press 2014) chapters 1 and 2
E Metzger ed, *A Companion to Justinian's Institutes* (Duckworth 1998) 127–8, 172–4
A Watson, *The Law of Obligations in the Later Roman Republic* (Oxford University Press 1965) chapter 13
R Zimmermann, *The Law of Obligations: Roman Foundations of the Civilian Tradition* (Oxford University Press 1996) chapters 1, 2 and 17–25

CHAPTER EIGHTEEN

Verbal Contracts

A. Introduction

The verbal contracts were created through the use of spoken words. Only one of them requires detailed consideration, the *stipulatio*.[1]

B. Stipulatio

(1) Nature and Development

A *stipulatio* was a contract made by the exchange of formal words. It was 'a verbal expression, by which he who is asked to give or to do something answers that he will do what has been asked'.[2] A *stipulatio* was thus a unilateral contract: it consisted in one party, the promisor, agreeing to be bound to do or give something in favour of the other, known as the stipulator or promisee. If it was desired that both parties make some kind of performance, this could be done by having each party enter into a separate *stipulatio*, or else by making the *stipulatio* conditional on performance by the other party. A *stipulatio* was *stricti iuris*, and did not even have to state the basis of the obligation that was undertaken. It was enough, for example, for the *stipulatio* to state that the promisor was undertaking to pay a particular sum of money, without stating why he or she was doing so. As we have seen in Chapter 17,[3] the *stricti iuris* nature of *stipulatio* meant that, originally, it was no defence that the promisor had (for example) been fraudulently induced to enter into the *stipulatio*.

The *stipulatio* was unusual among Roman contracts, in not being defined by its subject matter. All of the other contracts, with one exception,[4] applied to specific types of transaction, such as sale, hire or loan. A *stipulatio*, by contrast, could be used for any kind of agreement that could lawfully be made. Indeed, the use of

---

[1] Gaius mentions two others. The first of these is the *dotis dictio*, by which a dowry was constituted by declaration (G.3.95a). The other is the *iusiurandum liberti*, in which a freedman undertook obligations to the former master on being freed (G.3.96). On dowry, see pp. 145–6. On freedmen, see pp. 112–4.
[2] D.45.1.5.1 (Pomponius).
[3] See p. 326.
[4] The contract created in writing, on which see Chapter 21.

the *stipulatio* went beyond voluntary agreements: Pomponius identifies the categories of judicial *stipulatio* and praetorian *stipulatio*, which were used in cases where a judge or magistrate could require a party to legal proceedings to give an undertaking in this form.[5]

If *stipulatio* was capable of such general use, the question may reasonably be asked why the other forms of contract were necessary. How is it that the Romans did not manage to develop a general law of contract, based on *stipulatio*? The answer seems to lie in the high level of formality of the *stipulatio*. Although this was mitigated to some extent in practice in later law, strictly speaking the *stipulatio* always had to comply with very formal requirements for its creation. Rather than simply relaxing the formalities of *stipulatio*, the Romans developed the other contracts to deal with cases where those formalities were inconvenient or were simply not used.

(2) Requirements for Formation

A *stipulatio* was constituted by question and answer. For example, if the obligation to be created was to pay a sum of money, the stipulator might say: 'Do you promise to pay me 1,000 sesterces?' The promisor would then reply: 'I promise.' This had to be done as one continuous process, with no other business intervening.[6] Both parties had to be physically present.[7] The *stipulatio* could be conditional or contain provision as to the date on which performance was due.[8]

Originally *stipulatio* was confined to Roman citizens, and for 'promise' the specific verb *spondere*, which had overtones of religious oath-making, had to be used. Even the verb *promittere*, which also meant 'to promise', would not be enough. However, in the later Republic, with the Romans falling away from traditional religious practices and with increasing contact with non-Romans, this strictness was relaxed.[9] Although *spondere* remained limited to use by Romans,[10] other formulations became available both to them and to others. Gaius mentions a number, such as: 'Will you give . . .?', 'I will give'; and 'Will you do . . .?', 'I will do.'[11] Greek could be used as long as it was understood by both parties.[12] Whether languages other than Latin or Greek could be used seems to have been disputed by the classical jurists,[13] but Justinian is clear that any language understood by both parties could be used.[14] The answer had to meet the question exactly. Therefore, if for

---

[5] D.45.1.5pr. We saw an example of this, the *cautio usufructuaria*, at p. 263.
[6] D.45.1.137pr. Compare the requirements for execution of wills, considered at pp. 298–9.
[7] J.3.19.12. There was an exception to this, that a slave or a child-in-power could stipulate on behalf of the master or *paterfamilias*: see *e.g.* D.45.1.38.17.
[8] For example: 'Do you promise to pay me 1,000 sesterces, if you are able to sell your estate in the next month?', or 'Do you promise to pay me 1,000 sesterces on the Ides of March?' For contractual terms of this kind, see pp. 335–7.
[9] Zimmermann, *Obligations* 70–1.
[10] G.3.93.
[11] G.3.92.
[12] D.45.1.1.6.
[13] D.45.1.1.6.
[14] J.3.15.1.

example a question was met with a conditional answer, no contract would be concluded.[15] It is doubtful, though, whether the question and answer had to use the same verb, or whether (for example) a question in the form 'Will you do . . .?' could be validly met with the reply 'I promise.' Ulpian's view that the question and answer could be in different languages appears to imply that the question and answer did not have to match to this extent.[16] A pronouncement of the emperor Leo, dated AD 472, could be interpreted as going further than this: 'All stipulations recognised by the law have their own force, even if not composed in solemn or direct words, from any words that express the parties' agreement.'[17] This could be seen as abolishing the requirement for formal question and answer. On that view, Justinian's account, which stresses the need for question and answer, would represent a conscious reversal of the position in Leo's pronouncement. That, however, is not the more common interpretation.[18] Probably Leo's pronouncement should be seen rather as essentially declaratory, simply confirming that there was no requirement to use one of a specific list of verbs and there was no need for the two parties to use the same verb.

(3) *Stipulatio* and Writing

As we have seen, *stipulatio* was constituted by spoken words. However, in the ancient world as in the modern, it was common to record important transactions in writing even when that was not a formal requirement. The purpose of recording a *stipulatio* in writing was simply to preserve evidence of its terms and of the fact it had been entered into. Strictly speaking, if the words were not spoken, there was no contract. In practice, though, a party who could produce a document purportedly recording a *stipulatio* would be in a strong position if the matter was disputed.[19] For example, in an imperial decision of AD 200 it was held that, where a document stated that a *stipulatio* had been made, it was to be assumed to have been made in the appropriate oral form.[20] Justinian went even further. Preserving the rule that the making of the *stipulatio* required the presence of the parties, he held that a statement that the parties were together created a presumption that could only be rebutted by proving that at least one of the parties was absent for the whole day that the document was made.[21]

Did the written document have any requirements of form? On one view, it was always necessary to state that the parties were present. In the classical law, according to this view, it was necessary to record also the exchange of a question

---

[15] G.3.102. See though D.45.1.13.
[16] D.45.1.1.6. The view attributed to Ulpian at D.45.1.1.2, however, that it was enough to answer 'Why not?' is viewed by Zimmermann, *Obligations* 74 as 'not credible at all' for classical law.
[17] C.8.37.10.
[18] See *e.g.* Metzger, *Companion* 135; G MacCormack, 'The Oral and Written Stipulation in the Institutes' in Stein and Lewis, *Studies in Justinian's Institutes* 99–100; B Nicholas, 'The Form of the Stipulation in Roman Law' (1953) 69 LQR 63 (part I).
[19] On the development of written *stipulationes*, see generally Zimmermann, *Obligations* 78–82.
[20] C.8.37.1.
[21] J.3.19.12.

and answer. In Justinian's law, this view goes on, it was enough just to state that a promise had been made, from which it was inferred that this had been made in response to a question in the appropriate form.[22] Arguing this way, though, risks losing sight of the fact that the document was strictly evidentiary in nature. Classical Roman law did not have a well-developed law of evidence, and what counted as evidence of a fact was simply whatever would help to persuade a judge of that fact. On this approach, any document that could be interpreted as supporting an argument that a *stipulatio* had been made could be seen as evidence of the *stipulatio*, even if there was no explicit statement that the parties were together and that the question and answer were given. The important thing was that the judge was satisfied of those matters, not that they were stated in the document. As the argument has been stated:

> If documentary evidence is admitted, as it obviously was, all that can be demanded is that the document should be clearly intended as evidence of a stipulation, and there should be no evidence inconsistent with there having been a stipulation.[23]

This area overlaps with Justinian's treatment of obligations created in writing, on which see Chapter 21.[24]

(4) Enforcement

The method of enforcement of a *stipulatio* varied depending on what had been promised.[25] If the promisor had promised to give a specific thing or a specific sum of money, the form of action called the *condictio*[26] was used. This had the advantage that it was not necessary for the pursuer to specify the basis on which the money or property was due; it was enough to state that it was due. In other cases, a specific action for enforcing a *stipulatio* would be used, the *actio ex stipulatu*.

Chapter Summary

The main verbal contract was *stipulatio*, which was one of the oldest forms of contract. Its requirements were very formal and, especially in earlier law, very strict: the contract was constituted by question and answer, using particular verbs. In time, though, the requirements came to be relaxed somewhat, especially where the agreement was reduced to written form.

---

[22] Metzger, *Companion* 137.
[23] B Nicholas, 'The Form of the Stipulation in Roman Law' (1953) 69 LQR 233 (part II), 239.
[24] Justinian's treatment of the matter under *stipulatio* assumes, though, that the basis of the document is that a promise has been made, rather than the existence of debt being acknowledged. See Metzger, *Companion* 136; G MacCormack, 'The Oral and Written Stipulation in the Institutes' in Stein and Lewis, *Studies in Justinian's Institutes* 106–9.
[25] J.3.15pr.
[26] For a fuller account of the *condictio*, see pp. 429–32.

Further Reading

G.3.92–127
J.3.15–19
D.45
C.8.37

P Birks, *The Roman Law of Obligations* (E Descheemaeker ed, Oxford University Press 2014) chapter 4

G MacCormack, 'The Oral and Written Stipulation in the Institutes' in P G Stein and A D E Lewis eds, *Studies in Justinian's Institutes in Memory of J A C Thomas* (Sweet and Maxwell 1983)

E Metzger ed, *A Companion to Justinian's Institutes* (Duckworth 1998) 134–48

B Nicholas, 'The Form of the Stipulation in Roman Law' (1953) 69 LQR 63 and 233

A Watson, *The Law of Obligations in the Later Roman Republic* (Oxford University Press 1965) chapter 1

R Zimmermann, *The Law of Obligations: Roman Foundations of the Civilian Tradition* (Oxford University Press 1996) chapter 3

CHAPTER NINETEEN
Real Contracts

A. Nature and Formation of Real Contracts

The category of real contracts is so called because these contracts all involved the delivery of a *res* (thing). It is important to understand with these contracts that, unlike modern law, in which these contracts are made by agreement just like any other, a contract falling into this category was not actually made until delivery took place. Until delivery took place, either party could withdraw from the agreement. A bare agreement to enter into one of these contracts would not be enforceable.[1]

Modern law has moved away from this approach. The equivalents of these contracts in modern law are (in common with modern contracts generally) created by the agreement of the parties. Thus, while in modern law these contracts all necessarily involve delivery (and in the case of pledge, this is still needed to constitute the real right in security), this is an obligation under a contract that has already been created by agreement rather than something that is constitutive of the contract.

Four real contracts were recognised: *mutuum* (loan for consumption), *commodatum* (loan for use), *depositum* (deposit) and *pignus* (pledge).[2]

B. *Mutuum* (Loan for Consumption)

(1) Nature and Development

There are two basic types of loan contract that can be imagined. If I lend you a sum of money, that money is only of use to you if you can spend it. I do not, therefore, expect to get the very same coins and notes back. By contrast, if I lend you my car, I expect to get back the very same car. The Romans had two different

---

[1] Unless the agreement was constituted by *stipulatio*. See Chapter 18.
[2] Actually, as we shall see at pp. 380–1, it is slightly misleading to suggest that these were the only situations in which a person became contractually bound on taking delivery of property for a particular purpose. A more general principle was developed, by which such an arrangement could be enforced following partial performance using the *actio praescriptis verbis*.

types of contract of loan, one for each of these situations. *Mutuum* was used for the former situation, where an equivalent was to be returned rather than the original. *Commodatum*, considered below, was for the case where the original thing was to be returned.

Mutuum was one of the oldest types of contract, having been known already at the time of the Twelve Tables.[3] It was used for loans of things that are reckoned by weighing, counting or measuring, which are consumed by use.[4] It was unilateral and *stricti iuris*: by the fact of receiving the property, the borrower undertook to restore an equivalent. The borrower indeed became owner of the thing lent,[5] and, once this had happened, the lender had no further duties. *Mutuum* was gratuitous: if payment was made, it would be a different sort of contract.

(2) The Borrower's Duties

The borrower was obliged to restore an equivalent to the thing lent. This had to be something of equivalent quality, not just something of the same kind:

> When something has been given on the basis of *mutuum*, even if there is no provision that something just as good should be returned, the debtor is not allowed to return something that, even though it is of the same kind, is of worse quality, such as new wine for old.[6]

What if the property was lost or damaged? If this happened before delivery to the borrower, there could be no liability on either party,[7] as the contract was not formed until delivery. After delivery, risk lay with the borrower as owner of the property.[8] The borrower became liable to repay on receipt of the thing lent, and it was no concern of the lender what happened to the thing lent thereafter. There were certain exceptions to this. The most important was the maritime loan, consisting of 'money carried overseas'.[9] In this case, the lender bore the risk from the date on which it was agreed that the ship should sail.[10]

If the borrower failed to make repayment, the lender could enforce the obligation, not by means of an ownership remedy[11] (because the lender was not owner any more), but by means of a *condictio*.[12]

---

[3] For discussion of its origins, see J M Kelly, 'A Hypothesis on the Origin of *Mutuum*' (1970) 5 Irish Jurist (NS) 156.
[4] G.3.90; J.3.14pr.
[5] D.12.1.2.2.
[6] D.12.1.3 (Pomponius).
[7] Unless, of course, the damage resulted from the fault of the borrower. In that case, the borrower would be liable on general delictual principles: see p. 386–404.
[8] J.3.14.2.
[9] D.22.2.1 (Modestinus).
[10] D.22.2.3. There were other examples, such as loans made to professional athletes to support them in their training. On this whole area, see Zimmermann, *Obligations* 181–7.
[11] On these, see pp. 189–91.
[12] On the *condictio*, see pp. 429–32.

(3) Moneylending

As the most common use for *mutuum* was in loans of money, it is appropriate to say something about moneylending here.[13]

First, as we have already seen, *mutuum* was gratuitous.[14] As a result, any provision for payment of interest had to be added on by way of *stipulatio*.[15] The exception to this was those loans, such as the maritime loan, where the lender undertook to accept the risk of loss or damage. In those cases, provision for interest could be made by agreement, without the parties needing to go to the formality of a *stipulatio*.[16]

There were limits on the interest rates permitted for loans already in the time of the Twelve Tables, though it is not clear precisely how the limits were intended to work.[17] Throughout the classical period and beyond, up to the time of Justinian, the maximum interest rate was 12 per cent annually, except for maritime loans, which had unlimited interest to reflect the different allocation of risk. A maximum of 6 per cent was introduced where the lender was a senator.[18] Justinian reduced the maximum rates to 4 per cent for lenders of high social status (*illustribus . . . personis*), 8 per cent for those running businesses, 12 per cent for maritime loans and 6 per cent for other cases.[19] If the maximum interest rate was exceeded, the contract itself was still valid, but the lender could not require payment of the excess interest. Only the maximum could be recovered.[20]

A more specific restriction was introduced in the first century AD by the *senatusconsultum Macedonianum*:

> Whereas Macedo, to whom nature gave the inclination to crime, had added indebtedness to this, and whereas those who lend money on terms which may be called doubtful often provide the means for evil men to do wrong; it has been decided that, in order to make an example of those who give money on the basis of *mutuum* to sons-in-power, so that they know that the debt cannot be made good on the death of the father, no action will be given, even after the death of the parent in whose power the son was.[21]

The background to this seems to have been that a young man by the name of Macedo had borrowed from moneylenders. Pressed for payment by the moneylenders and, being in *potestas*,[22] unable to pay them until his father's death, he murdered his father.[23] The purpose of the *senatusconsultum Macedonianum* was to remove

---

[13] On this whole area, see Zimmermann, *Obligations* 166–87.
[14] That does not necessarily mean that a *mutuum* was only ever entered into between friends. The lending of money without interest could also be a way of gaining influence through gratitude.
[15] See Chapter 18.
[16] D.22.2.5pr–1.
[17] Zimmermann, *Obligations* 166–7.
[18] C.Th.2.33.4 (AD 405).
[19] C.4.32.26.2 (AD 528).
[20] D.22.1.29.
[21] D.14.6.1pr (Ulpian).
[22] *Potestas*, here, means the authority of a *paterfamilias*. See pp. 116–27.
[23] For discussion of the background to the *SC Macedonianum*, see D Daube, 'Did Macedo Murder His Father?' (1947) 65 ZSS (rA) 268.

the incentive to patricide by providing that loans of money to sons-in-power were unenforceable, even after the death of the *paterfamilias*. The purpose here was to protect, not the son-in-power, but the *paterfamilias*. The *senatusconsultum* was, however, interpreted restrictively by the jurists. For example, it only applied to loans of money, not to other loans. Even though the debt was unenforceable, it nonetheless created a natural obligation,[24] so any payments made towards it were irrecoverable.[25] The *senatusconsultum* did not apply if the lender reasonably believed that the borrower was *sui iuris*.[26] If, notwithstanding the *senatusconsultum*, the *paterfamilias* made payments towards the debt, he was treated as having ratified it.[27] The same was true if the borrower began repayment after becoming *sui iuris*.[28]

C. *Commodatum* (Loan for Use)

(1) Nature and Development

Commodatum was a contract of loan where the original thing lent was to be returned to the lender. As with *mutuum*, it was gratuitous: if payment was made, the contract would be one of hire instead. Because the same thing had to be returned, this form of loan was not suitable for goods consumed by use, such as food, drink or money, unless the loan was for the purposes of 'ceremony or display'.[29] *Commodatum* was a good faith contract.[30] It was also bilateral, in that both parties undertook obligations.

(2) The Borrower's Duties

The borrower owed certain duties, enforced by means of the *actio commodati* (action on the loan for use).

The borrower's basic duty was to use the property only for the purposes for which it had been lent. Indeed, a borrower who used the property for any other purpose might well be held liable for theft.[31]

During the period of loan, the borrower owed a duty to take care of the property. Subject to contrary agreement, the standard of care required varied depending on who was intended to benefit from the loan. Most loans were intended to benefit the borrower, of course, and in that case the standard of care owed was 'that which the most careful *paterfamilias* shows in his own affairs'.[32] It was not enough for the borrower to apply his or her normal standard if others could do better. The borrower would therefore only be excused of liability for

---

[24] A natural obligation is one that is valid but unenforceable. See p. 332.
[25] D.12.6.19pr.
[26] D.14.6.3pr.
[27] D.14.6.7.15.
[28] D.14.6.7.16.
[29] D.13.6.3.6 (Ulpian). See also D.13.6.4 (Gaius), concerned with a *commodatum* of money lent to be counted out in compliance with some legal form, and then returned.
[30] D.13.6.3.2.
[31] On theft, see pp. 417–22.
[32] D.13.6.18pr (Gaius). See also J.3.14.2.

things that were completely outwith the borrower's control. The borrower would be strictly liable,[33] though, if the property was used for anything other than the agreed purpose (as well as potentially incurring liability for theft). The example Gaius gives is someone who borrows silverware for a dinner party, and who then takes the silverware abroad. Such a person is liable even if the silverware is lost to pirates or robbers or in a shipwreck.[34]

Some loans were thought of as being for the lender's benefit. For example, suppose that I want my wife or fiancée to cut an impressive figure, so I lend her expensive jewellery to wear. This would be seen as being for my benefit.[35] Another example would be a magistrate putting on a theatrical show, and lending costumes or props to the actors. In such a case, the borrower was liable only for intentional wrongdoing.

Finally, some loans were for the benefit of both borrower and lender. Gaius gives the example of one party lending silverware to another for a dinner party in which both are participating.[36] The position on this seems to have been disputed here, but it appears that the borrower would be required to exercise the same standard of care as in his or her own affairs.

The borrower was obliged to return the goods at the end of the loan period, in the proper condition. Any damage for which the borrower was liable as outlined in the previous two paragraphs, or which arose while the borrower was late in returning the property, had to be made good.[37]

(3) The Lender's Duties

The lender was obliged to allow the borrower to use the property for the agreed period. As Paul points out, the loan did not have to be given, but once it is given then decency requires the lender to carry through what has been agreed.[38]

Subject to the borrower's duty to take care, the lender was liable to pay any extraordinary expenses that arose with respect to the property, for example expenditure on treatment for a slave who has fallen ill or on tracking down a slave who has run off. Normal expenses, though, such as food for borrowed slaves or smaller repairs, fell on the borrower.[39] The lender was also liable where damage resulted from his or her fault, for example where someone knowingly lent defective containers from which wine or oil leaked and was lost.[40]

If any liability arose for the lender to compensate the borrower, the borrower could retain the property until this was paid. The lender, even though owner, would commit theft by taking the property back in such circumstances without

---

[33] *I.e.* liable without fault having to be shown.
[34] D.13.6.18pr.
[35] D.13.6.5.10.
[36] D.13.6.18pr.
[37] D.13.6.3.1.
[38] D.13.6.17.3.
[39] D.13.6.18.2.
[40] D.13.6.18.3.

the consent of the borrower.[41] If the amount due exceeded the value of the property, this could be claimed by means of the *actio commodati contraria* (counter-action on the loan for use).

D. *Depositum* (Deposit)

(1) Nature and Development

Depositum (deposit) was the handing over of a moveable thing for safe-keeping. It was again gratuitous: if the person with safe-keeping was paid, then the contract would be one of hire of that person's services. *Depositum* was distinct from *commodatum* as well, as a depositee had no right to use the property. This was a *bonae fidei* contract[42] and was bilateral: both parties undertook duties.

(2) The Depositee's Duties

The depositee was liable only for deliberate wrongdoing (*dolus*), not simply carelessness.[43] This could be altered by agreement, but could not exclude deliberate wrongdoing. Beyond this, the depositee was required to return the property on demand, along with any accretions.[44]

Enforcement of the depositee's duties was by an action called the *actio depositi* (action on the deposit). Because of the breach of trust involved, breach of the depositee's duties also incurred *infamia*.[45] The measure of damages depended on the situation in which the deposit was made. In ordinary circumstances, simple damages only would be due. If the deposit was made in an emergency, however, for example in a shipwreck or a riot, double damages were due.[46] Ulpian explains the distinction:

> This distinction is justified. Indeed, when someone has chosen to put his faith in another and the deposit is not returned, he must be happy with simple damages. However, when he deposits through necessity, the crime of perfidy increases and the welfare of the public must demand retribution in the public interest, for it is harmful to breach faith in matters of this kind.[47]

(3) The Depositor's Duties

The depositor was liable for any damage caused by his or her fault. The depositor was also liable for any necessary expenses incurred by the depositee.[48] Enforcement was by means of the *actio depositi contraria* (counter-action on the deposit).[49]

---

[41] D.47.2.15.2.
[42] D.16.3.1.23.
[43] D.16.3.1.8; J.3.14.3. Gross negligence, however, may have been considered equivalent to deliberate wrongdoing: D.16.3.32.
[44] For example, if the deposited property was a female animal, the depositee would be required to hand over any young to which the animal had given birth.
[45] On *infamia*, see pp. 100–1.
[46] D.16.3.1.1.
[47] D.16.3.1.4.
[48] D.16.3.12pr.
[49] See *e.g* D.16.3.23.

(4) Special Cases

Two special cases of deposit require some comment.

Depositum irregulare (irregular deposit) was a deposit of money, most likely with a banker.[50] When the depositee was a banker this was essentially a bank account, and was similar to *mutuum*, in that the depositee acquired ownership of the money and was permitted to make use of it. However, it differed from *mutuum* in that the deposit was made in the depositor's interest rather than the depositee's. This was an investment by the depositor, who would expect a return on that investment, and indeed it appears that provision could be made for payment of interest without a separate *stipulatio*.[51]

The second of the special cases is *sequestratio*.[52] This was a form of deposit[53] by which two or more people who were in dispute over an item of property would deposit the property with an individual known for these purposes as a *sequester*.[54] Unlike the situation with a normal deposit, the *sequester* was considered to have possession of the property rather than merely custody.[55] This had two significant consequences. First, as none of the parties to the dispute now had possession, *usucapio*[56] could not run in favour of any of them. Second, as the *sequester* had possession, the *sequester* therefore had the benefit of the possessory interdicts if dispossessed.[57]

E. *Pignus* (Pledge)

Pledge was a *bonae fidei*, bilateral contract, by which a creditor handed over property to a debtor as security for payment of a debt. As with the other real contracts, it was created by delivery of the property in question. However, in addition to the contractual aspects of pledge, there are also property issues to consider, because the creditor taking an item on a pledge acquired a real right over that item. For that reason, pledge is considered elsewhere, in Chapter 15,[58] as part of property law along with other rights in security.

---

[50] For discussion, see Zimmermann, *Obligations* 214–19; W M Gordon, 'Observations on "Depositum Irregulare"' in *Studi in onore di Arnaldo Biscardi* III (Istituto Editoriale Cisalpino-La Goliardica 1982). For a non-banking example, see A Watson, 'A Slave's Marriage: Dowry or Deposit' (1991) 12 J Leg Hist 132.

[51] D.16.3.26.1; D.16.3.28.

[52] For a general overview, see P J Schierse, 'Legislation on Sequestration in Roman Law and in the Decretals of Gregory IX' (1963) 23 Jurist 291, 291–305.

[53] D.16.3.5.1.

[54] For a definition of *sequester*, see D.50.16.110.

[55] See p. 177.

[56] Acquisition of ownership by possessing the property for a period of time. See pp. 239–43.

[57] See p. 177.

[58] See pp. 271–4.

Chapter Summary

The real contracts were among the oldest, and had in common with each other that they were all created by the delivery of the item of property with which they were concerned. Four contracts were recognised as falling into this category. These were *mutuum* (loan for consumption), *commodatum* (loan for use), *depositum* (deposit) and *pignus* (pledge), and each was quite distinct in its nature and consequences. *Mutuum*, *commodatum* and *depositum* were all gratuitous. If payment was made, the contract would fall into a different category. *Pignus* was different: the whole point was that the property was delivered in order to be held as security for a debt. Only in the two loan contracts was there a right of use of the property. Indeed, in *mutuum* the borrower became owner of the item delivered, and was simply subject to the obligation to restore to the lender an equivalent of the thing lent. For that reason, *mutuum* was the only one of these contracts that did not impose any particular obligations with regard to the care and use of the item delivered.

Further Reading

G.3.90–1
J.3.14
D.12.1; 13.6; 16.3
C.4.23, 24
P Birks, *The Roman Law of Obligations* (E Descheemaeker ed, Oxford University Press 2014) chapter 6
E Metzger ed, *A Companion to Justinian's Institutes* (Duckworth 1998) 128–34
A Watson, *The Law of Obligations in the Later Roman Republic* (Oxford University Press 1965) chapters 2, 8–10
R Zimmermann, *The Law of Obligations: Roman Foundations of the Civilian Tradition* (Oxford University Press 1996) chapters 6–7

CHAPTER TWENTY

Consensual Contracts

A. Nature and Development of Consensual Contracts

In modern law, we think of all contracts as being based on the parties' consent to be bound. In Roman law, however, the consensual contracts were a distinct group within the wider law of contracts. There were four types of consensual contract – sale, hire, mandate and partnership – and they were united by having no formal requirements for their constitution beyond the agreement of the parties (although, as we shall see, Justinian modified this principle in one case, sale contracts constituted in writing). Consensual contracts therefore had two great advantages: they could be made informally, and they could be made at a distance, by parties communicating by letter or messenger.[1] The consensual contracts were all bilateral, in that they imposed obligations on both parties.[2] All of them were also *bonae fidei* contracts, as the *formulae* for their enforcement directed the judge to take into account the requirements of good faith.

As with other categories of contract, the contents of this chapter should be considered alongside the general discussion of contracts in Chapter 17.

B. Sale *(Emptio Venditio)*

(1) Formation

A contract of sale was formed by agreement on the subject matter and price. There are therefore three elements to consider: agreement, subject matter and price.

(a) Agreement

As with all of the consensual contracts, the contract of sale was constituted by the parties' agreement. As we saw in Chapter 17,[3] if either party was in error as to an essential element of the agreement, the contract would be void. If payment was not to be made immediately, the buyer might give an *arra* (sometimes spelled

---

[1] G.3.136; D.18.1.1.2.
[2] G.3.137.
[3] See pp. 328–33.

arrha) or earnest to the seller. This could be in the form of money, as a deposit, or it could be something else. An *arra*, though, was in no sense necessary for the validity of the contract. Rather, it was merely evidence of the parties' intentions to enter into a sale transaction.[4] Nonetheless, Justinian provided that a buyer who wrongfully withdrew from the transaction forfeited the *arra*, while a seller who wrongfully withdrew had to pay double its value.[5]

In the classical period, there were no special formalities for a valid contract of sale. It was unsurprisingly common to record important sales in writing, but this was only as evidence of their terms. It was not a requirement. Justinian made a change here. He provided that, where the parties had agreed that the contract was to be recorded in writing, this was required for validity. Until the contract had been properly written in the correct form, either party could withdraw, unless an *arra* had been given.[6]

(b) Subject Matter

For a valid contract of sale, there had to be agreement on the property to be sold. Where a sale of a particular item of property had been agreed, the seller was bound also to transfer any accessories forming part of the property or anything produced by the property after the contract was made.[7] The question of whether some item was an accessory could cause difficulty in practice.[8]

One weakness of the Roman law of sale was that it made only limited provision for sales of generic goods. Parties wishing to contract for the sale of, say, 200 *amphorae* of wine without identifying the specific *amphorae* would have to use *stipulatio* instead. Parties wishing to use the consensual contract of sale would have to identify the specific *amphorae* to be sold or, at least, the specific source from which they were to be chosen (*e.g* '200 *amphorae* from my wine cellar').[9]

As we saw in Chapter 17, there could be no valid contract if the subject matter of the contract had, unbeknownst to the parties, been destroyed before the contract was made.[10] Such a contract was void for impossibility.[11] This could cause difficulties in practice where destruction was less than total, as Paul explains:

> I bought a house, when both the seller and I were unaware that it had burned down. Nerva, Sabinus and Cassius say that there is no sale, even though the site remains, and I can recover the money paid by *condictio*. But if part of the house remains, Neratius says that the question largely depends on how much of the

---

[4] G.3.139; J.3.23pr.
[5] C.4.21.17.2 (AD 528).
[6] J.3.23pr; C.4.21.17pr (AD 528).
[7] D.18.1.67. For an application of this principle in modern law, see *Christie v Smith's Executrix* 1949 SC 572.
[8] C J Bannon, 'Pipes and Property in the Sale of Real Estate (D.19.1.38.2)' in du Plessis, *New Frontiers*. As noted at p. 359, what counted as an accessory for the purposes of sale went beyond things physically attached to the property, and included for example keys.
[9] See *e.g.* D.18.1.35.7. For discussion, see Zimmermann, *Obligations* 236–9.
[10] See pp. 334–5.
[11] D.18.1.15pr.

house is left, so that if the greater part of the house has been destroyed, the buyer is not compelled to complete the sale and can recover whatever has been paid. However, if half of the property or less has been destroyed, then the buyer will be compelled to complete the sale, with an estimate being made, according to the standard of the reasonable man, of the extent to which the fire has reduced the value of the house, so that he can be relieved of the obligation to that extent.[12]

As we shall see below, when we consider the topic of risk, destruction that happened *after* the contract was made was treated quite differently.

In certain cases, the law was prepared to show some flexibility. There could be an *emptio rei speratae* (sale of an expected thing) or an *emptio spei* (sale of a chance). The sale of an expected thing was a minor concession to the practical needs of commerce: it was a sale of something that had not yet been brought into existence, but which could in principle be identified. A standard example is a farmer agreeing to sell this year's crop, before it has grown.[13] A farmer might be financially ruined by a poor crop, and so by selling the crop in advance he could assure himself a certain income even in bad years. Equally, a farmer selling in this way might be able to get payment up front, rather than having to bear all of the expense in advance in the hope of making enough from the sale of the crop at the other end.[14]

A sale of a chance is a more substantial departure from the principle that there had to be an identifiable piece of property. Pomponius explains:

> Sometimes indeed there is held to be a sale even without a thing, such as when, so to speak, a chance is bought. This is the case where there is sold a catch of fish or birds or largesse thrown, for a sale is contracted even if nothing results, because it is a sale of a chance . . .[15]

Here, the buyer was taking the risk that nothing at all might result.

As far as the validity of the contract was concerned, there was no requirement for the seller to be owner (assuming that the buyer was not aware that the seller was not owner).[16] Of course, a non-owning seller would not be able to make the buyer owner, but that is a separate issue.[17] The point here is that, when the true owner appears and demands the property, the buyer will need to have a contractual remedy against the seller, and there can only be a contractual remedy if there is a valid contract.

---

[12] D.18.1.57pr.
[13] D.18.1.8pr.
[14] D Paling, '*Emptio Spei* and *Emptio Rei Speratae*' (1973) 8 Irish Jurist (NS) 178.
[15] D.18.1.8.1. For another example, see D.18.4.11.
[16] D.18.1.34.3.
[17] Furthermore, there are situations in which it is appropriate for a person to agree to sell something which he or she does not own. The most obvious is if I agree to sell something that I do not yet own, but which I expect to acquire from a third party. This is not an unusual arrangement, and there is no good reason to have a rule that frustrates it. Another situation would be where my rights are unclear, and I agree to sell the property insofar as I own it.

(c) Price

There could no sale without a price,[18] which had to be *certum* (certain).[19] There was some doubt as to whether it was possible to provide for the price to be set by a third party,[20] but it was settled by Justinian that such a term was a valid condition in a sale.[21]

It was disputed between the two schools of jurists, the Sabinians and Proculians, whether the price had to be in money. On the view that sale was simply a development of bartering that took place in the pre-monetary economy, the Sabinians took the position that the price did not have to be in money, and that an exchange of one item of property for another was a sale. That position suffered from the difficulty of identifying who was buyer and who was the seller, which was important because buyer and seller had different obligations. The view that prevailed, therefore, was that of the Proculians, according to which sale and barter are two different transactions. The settled view, then, was that the price to be paid had to be in money.[22]

That did, though, leave the problem of transactions in which payment was to be made partly in money and partly in something else. A modern example would be a car being traded in as part payment for a new car. There is no text addressing part-payment in goods specifically. However, a passage in the *Digest* taken from Pomponius does say that part of the price may be made up of services to be rendered,[23] and the analogy with part-exchange seems clear. The same view has been taken in modern law.[24]

The price to be paid did not have to be a fair one: it could be either higher or lower than the true value of the property.[25] To this rule, though, there arose a major exception in the post-classical period.[26] According to this exception, if the price paid for land was less than half of the *iustum pretium* (fair price), the seller was said to have suffered from *laesio enormis*. The buyer could be required to

---

[18] D.18.1.2.1.
[19] This does not mean that the price necessarily had to be known at the point of the making of the contract. For example, a price of 'whatever is in my safe' would be valid: D.18.1.7.1. Such a price is certain, even though it is not known until the safe is opened and the money inside counted. For discussion of the issues arising here, see D Daube, 'Certainty of Price' in Daube, *Studies in Sale*.
[20] G.3.140.
[21] J.3.23.1; D.18.1.7.1.
[22] G.3.141; J.3.23.2; D.18.1.1.1.
[23] D.19.1.6.1.
[24] *Sneddon v Durant* 1982 SLT (Sh Ct) 39. Curiously, the sheriff here did not refer to Roman or *ius commune* sources, but to a textbook account relying on English cases. For discussion of the treatment of the matter in modern law, see T B Smith, 'Exchange or Sale?' (1973–4) 48 Tulane LR 1029.
[25] D.19.2.22.3. See also D.18.1.38, in which it is said that even if the price is set very low, with the intention of gifting the excess value, the transaction is nonetheless a sale. If, however, the price was entirely nominal, or was not intended to be exacted by the buyer, the transaction was treated as gift rather than sale (Metzger, *Companion* 155).
[26] Quite when this happened is uncertain. The authority for it is to be found in two pronouncements from the reign of Diocletian (C.4.44.2 (AD 285) and C.4.44.8 (AD 293)), but Zimmermann (*Obligations* 259–61) considers these to be Justinianic interpolations.

choose between returning the property in exchange for the price paid, or making the price up to the *iustum pretium*.[27]

(d) The Parties' Position after the Making of the Contract

Suppose that I agreed to sell you a certain quantity of wine. After the contract was made, but before the wine was handed over to you, the container in which I was keeping the wine cracked and the wine drained away. If this had happened through my fault, it would be reasonable enough for me to bear the loss, but let us suppose that the damage was entirely accidental or arose from the fault of a third party. Who should bear the loss then? In other words, are you still obliged to pay the price? Which of the two of us should suffer for a loss that is the fault of neither of us? We are concerned here with the concept of risk. Normally, the owner of an item of property bears the risk of damage to that property. However, at some point during the transfer of ownership, risk will pass to the transferee, and this need not necessarily happen at the same time as ownership passes to the transferee. The rule that is followed varies between different legal systems.[28] The consequence though is that, if the damage happens after risk has passed to the buyer, then the buyer will have to pay the agreed price, even if the buyer has not yet become owner.

In Chapter 17, we came across the concept of 'perfection' of contracts.[29] In Roman law, risk passed to the buyer of goods when the contract became 'perfected'. In most sales, this happened as soon as the contract was made. Sometimes, though, perfection of the contract was delayed. This happened in three cases: where property to be sold had still to be identified; where the price still had to be determined; and where the contract was subject to a suspensive condition.[30] Thus, for example, where the goods had been identified but had to be weighed to determine the price, the contract was not perfected until the goods had been weighed.[31] Similarly, if I sold you three *amphorae* of wine from my cellar, the contract was not perfected until the *amphorae* had been identified and set aside for you. Again, if the sale was subject to a suspensive condition, the contract was not perfected unless and until that condition was met.

As we shall see below, unless the property was handed over to the buyer immediately, the buyer would not yet be owner at this point. Nonetheless, the buyer

---

[27] From a modern point of view, the fundamental difficulty with *laesio enormis* is that it assumes that there is such a thing as an objectively ascertainable *iustum pretium* aside from the price set by the market. According to modern economic ideas, the value of property is whatever someone is willing to pay for it. By the same token, the fact that the seller has only been able to achieve a particular sale price is itself strong evidence that that price represents the true value of the property. If the owner of the property does not like that price, he or she is free to reject any offers, and acceptance of an offer implies that the owner considers the price fair. In modern as in classical law, though not as in Justinianic law, a sale price cannot be challenged on the ground of unfairness, unless the buyer has acted in some improper way, such as where the buyer has been guilty of fraud or coercion.

[28] See DCFR IV. A.-5:101.

[29] See p. 336.

[30] D.18.6.8pr. On suspensive conditions, see pp. 335–7. As we saw there, a resolutive condition would not prevent perfection of the contract.

[31] D.18.1.35.5.

would remain liable to pay the price if damage happened after perfection of the contract. This rule, which has been followed in Scots law in direct reliance on the Roman texts,[32] may seem surprising. Justinian explains a rationale for it:

> Thus if a slave dies or some part of his body is injured, or a building is wholly or partly destroyed by fire, or all or part of a piece of land is carried away by the force of the water, or also if it is made much smaller or worse by *alluvio*[33] or the blowing down of trees in a gale, the loss falls on the buyer, and he must pay the price even though he has not obtained the property. The seller is not liable for anything that happens without malice or fault on his part. But if anything is added to the land by *alluvio* after the sale, that goes to the buyer, for the benefit must go to the one who bears the risk.[34]

On this view, then, the buyer bears the risk because the buyer is also the one who is entitled to benefit from the property.[35] For example, the buyer will be entitled to any fruits of the property that emerge after the contract is made and, indeed, the seller will be liable for any steps taken to prevent such fruits emerging.[36] Still, the transfer of risk to the buyer before he or she has physical control of the property, and thus can take steps to safeguard it, and before he or she can sue as owner for damage to it, is not altogether easy to justify. This difficulty is not completely eliminated by the requirement for the seller of property, damaged after the passing of risk but before the passing of ownership, to assign to the buyer any rights the seller may have to be compensated for the loss.[37]

(e) The Transfer of Ownership

The making of the contract did not in and of itself transfer ownership from seller to buyer. We saw in Chapter 11 how ownership transferred: either by delivery to the transferee or, according to strict law with certain types of property, by one or other of the formal procedures known as *mancipatio* and *in iure cessio*.[38] In sale, unless it was intended to give the buyer credit, it was also necessary for the buyer

---

[32] *Sloans Dairies Ltd v Glasgow Corporation* 1977 SC 223. See A Rodger, 'Roman Law Comes to Partick' in Evans-Jones, *Civil Law Tradition*. That case was concerned with a sale of land. Different rules now apply to sales of moveable property: Sale of Goods Act 1979, s. 20; Consumer Rights Act 2015, s. 29. On the course of reception of the Roman rule, see W M Gordon, 'Risk in Sale – From Roman to Scots Law' in J Sondel, J Reszczyński and P Ściślicki eds, *Roman Law as Formative of Modern Legal Systems: Studies in Honour of Wiesław Litewski*, vol 1 (Jagiellonian University Press 2003).

[33] *Alluvio* (alluvion) is the gradual building up or wearing away of land by the action of watercourses bounding it. See pp. 225–7.

[34] J.3.23.3.

[35] Though whether this was in fact the original rationale is doubtful. See *e.g.* A Rodger, 'Roman Law Comes to Partick' in Evans-Jones, *Civil Law Tradition* 201.

[36] D.18.1.8pr.

[37] J.3.23.3a.

[38] See pp. 199–201. As we saw there, methods were devised in the classical period to circumvent the requirements of these procedures. Strictly speaking, however, they were required until Justinian for property falling into the category of *res mancipi*, which included slaves, certain animals and land in Italy. Most property was *res nec mancipi*, and was always transferred simply by delivery.

to pay the price or to find security for it.[39] Only once all of these things were done did ownership pass to the buyer. Until that point, the seller remained owner and could effectually sell to someone else instead. Of course, if that happened, the seller would be in breach of his or her obligations under the contract of sale, and would be liable to the buyer accordingly, but the buyer would have no right to recover the property from the third party who ended up with it.

(2) Seller's Duties

The law imposed various duties on the seller. The general remedy for enforcement of these was the *actio empti*, the *formula* for which ran (translated) as follows:

> Whereas Aulus Agerius bought from Numerius Negidius the slave Stichus, whatever Numerius Negidius ought to give or do for Aulus Agerius on the basis of good faith, let the judge condemn Numerius Negidius to Aulus Agerius. If it does not so appear, let him be absolved.

Liability could go beyond simply the agreed price. Instead, damages for breach of the seller's duties were based on the buyer's 'interest in having the thing'.[40] This could be greater than the value of the property or the price paid, but had to be closely related to the property. For example, the seller's liability might be increased where the value of the property had risen since the sale was agreed, but the seller would not be liable, for instance, for the death of a slave that resulted from the seller's failure to deliver agreed upon wheat.[41]

(a) Care of Property

The seller was under an obligation to take care of the property until delivery was made to the buyer.[42] The standard of care to be met, though, is unclear. Certainly, the seller would not be liable for loss caused by *damnum fatale*[43] or overwhelming force.[44] Was the seller liable for anything falling short of this?[45] This may have been the classical law,[46] but some texts suggest the slightly lower standard of the most careful *paterfamilias*.[47] In many cases, of course, the outcome would be the same either way, because in many cases it would be clear either that the seller was at fault

---

[39] J.2.1.41. Sometimes it was agreed that the buyer should have the property as a hirer, paying rent for it, until the price was paid. See D.19.2.21; D Daube, 'Tenancy of Purchaser (*Digest* 19.2.21)' (1948–50) 10 Cam LJ 77; D Daube, '*Si . . . tunc* in D.19.2.22pr: Tenancy of Purchaser and *Lex Commissoria*' (1958) 5 Revue Internationale des Droits de l'Antiquité (3rd series) 427; J A C Thomas, 'Tenancy by Purchaser' (1959) 10 Iura 103.
[40] D.19.1.1.1.
[41] D.19.1.21.3.
[42] D.19.1.36.
[43] This term is often translated as 'Act of God'. Essentially, it means an event that could not have been reasonably foreseen or guarded against, such as earthquake or extreme weather conditions.
[44] D.18.6.2.1; D.19.1.31pr.
[45] In other words, for safekeeping (*custodia*). For discussion of the meaning of this problematic term, see G C J J van den Bergh, '*Custodiam Praestare*: *Custodia*-Liability or Liability for Failing *Custodia*?' (1975) 43 TvR 59.
[46] Zimmermann, *Obligations* 287.
[47] See *e.g.* D.18.6.2, 3.

or that there was nothing that could have been done. There would be cases, however, in which the circumstances did not count as *damnum fatale*, but in which the seller was not clearly at fault. In those cases the precise rule would matter.

(b) Delivery with Vacant Possession

As already mentioned (and which is obvious in any case), the seller was obliged to give the buyer possession of the property. The buyer was also entitled to get possession of certain things that were considered to be pertinents of the land. For example, the buyer would also be entitled to any keys,[48] and to things dug or cut from the land, such as chalk or felled trees, unless they were expressly reserved in the sale.[49] If these were not produced, the *actio ad exhibendum* ('action for production') could be used to compel their production.[50]

The possession given had to be 'vacant possession', which is to say, without any encumbrances of which the buyer was unaware.[51] For example, if the land was burdened by a servitude[52] or creditors of the seller took possession of the property,[53] the seller would be liable to compensate the buyer. Similar obligations exist in modern law.[54]

(c) Guarantee against Eviction

The seller was certainly bound to transfer whatever right he or she had, but what if, in fact, the seller was not owner of the property? As we have seen,[55] a seller who was not owner could not make the buyer owner. Strictly speaking, though, the seller gave no guarantee that the buyer would become owner. However, the practice arose of the seller agreeing by *stipulatio* to compensate the buyer with double damages if a third party came forward and successfully challenged the buyer's right to the property. Such a challenge is known as 'eviction'. In the classical law, it came to be seen as a breach of the duty of good faith that was imposed by the form of the *actio empti* to refuse to do this.[56] The developed position, then, was that the seller did not guarantee ownership, but instead guaranteed to compensate the buyer if the latter should be evicted from the property.[57] It should be noted here that, while eviction may involve physical removal from the property, it need not necessarily do so. The essence of eviction is not physical removal, but the successful challenge by a third party. For example, suppose that I buy an area of land from you. It turns out that part of the land in fact belongs to a

---

[48] D.19.1.17pr. For these purposes, the keys were considered to be accessory to the building.
[49] D.19.1.17.6.
[50] See p. 190 for the *actio exhibendum*.
[51] If the buyer was aware then, of course, the seller would not be liable. The position may have been different in the Republic: see A Rodger, 'Concealing a Servitude' in Stein and Lewis, *Studies in Justinian's Institutes*.
[52] D.19.1.1.1. On servitudes, see Chapter 13.
[53] D.19.1.2.1.
[54] See *e.g. Welsh v Russell* (1894) 21 R 769.
[55] See pp. 357–8.
[56] D.21.2.2. On the development of guarantee against eviction, see Zimmermann, *Obligations* 293–302.
[57] D.18.1.25.1; D.19.1.11.2.

neighbour. The neighbour successfully sues me for recovery of the land. Following this, however, I agree with the neighbour to buy the disputed area from him. Even though I remain in possession of the property, the neighbour's successful challenge means that I am considered to have been evicted, and accordingly you are liable to compensate me. With the exception of the requirement for double damages, these rules have been received in Scots law, and still apply to sales of land.[58] The requirement for eviction is capable of causing practical difficulties. However, it should be remembered that defects in title would often in Roman law be cured by *usucapio* after a relatively short period of time.[59]

(d) Guarantee against Defects

What if the property sold turned out to be defective in some way? A distinction has to be made first between patent and latent defects. A patent defect is one that should be obvious to the buyer, and for that reason the buyer had no remedy for patent defects. Anyone who was unaware of a patent defect was considered to have 'deceived himself'.[60]

The position with latent (*i.e.* non-obvious) defects was more complicated. Originally, there was no liability for latent defects unless the seller had given an express undertaking of soundness, which undertaking could be either general or specific.[61] Over time, though, greater protection for the buyer was developed.

The first stage in the development of general liability for latent defects arose from the good faith clause in the *actio empti*.[62] As we have seen, the liability of the parties to the contract was to be judged according to the standard of what good faith required. This opened the door to holding the seller liable for failing to disclose something that he or she was aware of, which in good faith ought to have been disclosed. The first case that we know of involved sale of a tenement building on the Caelian Hill[63] by an individual called Titus Claudius Centumalus, to Publius Calpurnius Lanarius.[64] Centumalus failed to disclose that he had been ordered by the augurs[65] to reduce the height of the building, as it interfered with their observations of the flight of birds. Centumalus was held liable for failing to disclose this, which was considered to be a defect which should have been

---

[58] See *e.g. Clark v Lindale Homes Ltd* 1994 SC 210. A different rule applies in sales of moveables: Sale of Goods Act 1979, s. 12.

[59] See pp. 239–43. Similar provision exists in Scots law, though with a longer period and certain further requirements: Prescription and Limitation (Scotland) Act 1973, s. 1.

[60] D.18.1.43.1 (Florentinus). The example Florentinus gives is a slave who has lost his eyes, but who is sold under a guarantee of physical soundness. As the lack of eyes is a patent defect, the guarantee in such a case would be taken to refer to the rest of the slave's body.

[61] In other words, the seller might either guarantee that the property had no defects at all, or else might simply guarantee the absence of some specific defect or defects.

[62] See generally Zimmermann, *Obligations* 308–10.

[63] The Caelian Hill was one of the original Seven Hills of Rome, and lies to the south-east of the Forum.

[64] For an account of this case, see D Liebs, *Summoned to the Roman Courts: Famous Trials from Antiquity* (R L R Garber and C G Cürten trans, University of California Press 2012) 33–42.

[65] These were priests, among whose roles was to determine the will of the gods by observing the flight of birds from the Capitoline Hill. The Capitoline Hill is between 1 and 1.5 miles to the north-west of the Caelian Hill.

disclosed to the buyer. As this case shows, the defect need not be physical. Thus, for example, where a slave was sold who, to the knowledge of the seller, was a thief, that was a defect for which the seller could be held liable.[66] In all of these cases, however, liability was based on a lack of good faith, which implied that the seller would not be liable if he or she was unaware of the defect.

The second stage in the development of general seller's liability for defects came in the edict of the aediles, magistrates who were responsible among other things for the proper management of the marketplace.[67] They made provision requiring sellers to make buyers aware of any defect in slaves or livestock exposed for sale in the marketplace. The relevant provision for slaves comes down to us as follows: 'Those who sell slaves are to make purchasers aware of any disease or defect there may be and whether the slave is a runaway or a loiterer or is subject to undischarged noxal liability . . .'[68] The aediles would grant an action if this was not done. It was irrelevant that the seller was unaware of the defect. Similar provision was made for livestock.[69] If no undertaking was given that the slave or animal was free from defects, the buyer could rescind the contract within two months using the *actio redhibitoria*, even if no defect had appeared. If a defect did appear, then the buyer had six months from that point to rescind using the *actio redhibitoria*,[70] returning the property and reclaiming the price.[71] Alternatively, the buyer could keep the property, but claim the difference between the value of the property as it was and the value that it would have had if free from defects. This was done using the *actio quanti minoris* (the 'action for how much less'), which had to be brought within a year of the defect becoming apparent.[72]

What, then, counted as a defect for these purposes? Certain preliminary points must be made. First, what counted as a defect might differ between slaves and livestock. For example, there are animals for which castration is not uncommon, and this did not count as a defect if the animal's stamina or usability was not reduced; the contrary was true of a slave.[73] Second, the edict was concerned only with latent defects. Patent defects, that is defects which the buyer should have been able to spot, such as blindness or visible scarring, were not covered.[74] Third, where the defect was an illness or disease, the edict could apply even if the condition was temporary.[75]

As a general test, the edict applied to 'any defect or disease which impedes the use and serviceability of the slave' or animal, but not very minor defects.[76] The

---

[66] D.19.1.4pr.
[67] For general discussion, see Zimmermann, *Obligations* 311–19.
[68] D.21.1.1.1. A loiterer is a slave who does not run away, but who wanders aimlessly and wastes time, returning home late from errands: D.21.1.17.14.
[69] D.21.1.38pr.
[70] D.21.1.55.
[71] D.21.1.28; D.21.1.38pr.
[72] D.21.1.38pr.
[73] D.21.1.38.7.
[74] D.21.1.6; D.21.1.14.10.
[75] D.21.1.4–6pr.
[76] D.21.1.1.8 (Ulpian).

texts abound with examples of both. For instance, a slave who could not speak or who could only do so unintelligibly was considered defective; one who merely had difficulty in speaking clearly was not.[77] Short-sightedness counted as a defect in slaves.[78] There was great concern with the fertility of female slaves: a female slave who was sterile[79] or who regularly gave birth to stillborn children[80] was considered to be defective for these purposes, as was a woman who menstruated twice in a month or not at all (unless, in the latter case, this was on account of age).[81] Unsurprisingly, therefore, pregnancy was not considered a defect.[82] Left-handedness was not considered a defect,[83] and nor was bad breath, unless it was a symptom of a more serious complaint.[84] This last example illustrates very well the difficulty of making a clear distinction between those defects that were sufficiently serious and those that were not, for one might have considered very bad breath a more serious defect than mild short-sightedness.

One important limitation to the scope of the aediles' edict was that, in a sale of a slave, character defects did not normally count except to the extent that they were mentioned by the edict itself.[85] For example, a seller did not have to disclose the fact that the slave was a gambler, a drunkard or a liar or was quarrelsome,[86] or the slave was prone to religious fanaticism, frivolity or superstition.[87] Likewise, incontinence in a slave was not a defect, as long as it resulted from deep sleep, drunkenness or laziness, rather than an illness.[88] Some character defects were, however, considered serious enough to come within the edict. For example, a slave who had committed a capital crime[89] or who had attempted suicide[90] was considered defective. Equally, a physical affliction with mental consequences would fall within the edict.[91] Here, though, it is the underlying physical affliction that is the defect, rather than its consequences on the slave's character. A character defect might, though, be something that would give rise to liability under the *actio empti* if known about and not disclosed, so the general exclusion of character defects is less important than might otherwise be thought. After all, a slave-owner would often have been in a position to know of the character defects of the slave, which would then, if they were serious enough, make the owner liable under the *actio empti* for failing to disclose them on sale.

---

[77] D.21.1.9.
[78] D.21.1.10.3.
[79] D.21.1.14.7.
[80] D.21.1.14pr.
[81] D.21.1.15.
[82] D.21.1.14.1.
[83] D.21.1.12.3.
[84] D.21.1.12.4.
[85] D.21.1.4.3. This, says Ulpian here, is why tendency to wander or abscond is expressly included.
[86] D.21.1.4.2.
[87] D.21.1.1.9.
[88] D.21.1.14.4.
[89] D.21.1.1.1; D.21.1.23.2.
[90] D.21.1.23.3.
[91] D.21.1.4.1.

The third and final stage was the extension during the classical period of the rules of the aediles' edict to all sales, not just those of slaves and livestock, on the basis of the good faith clause in the *actio empti*.[92] For example, where a container for holding liquids was sold, there was an implied undertaking that it was sound, even if nothing was expressly agreed.[93] Liability for defects included not just the reduced value of the property, but also consequential losses. For example, if unsound timber was sold and then used to build a house, the seller would be liable for the building's value if it collapsed due to the unsoundness; if diseased animals were sold, the seller would be liable also for the damage caused to any other of the buyer's animals that were infected as a result.[94]

The reception of these ideas in Scots law also has a complex history. We must first distinguish between land and moveable property. As far as moveables are concerned, this and other issues in sale are regulated by a UK statute, the Sale of Goods Act 1979.[95] The question of defective goods is addressed in section 14 of that Act, which imposes an implied term, in sales of goods in the course of a business,[96] that the goods are of 'satisfactory quality'.[97] Although this is a UK statute, it has been said that there is 'every reason to believe' that section 14 was inspired by the writings of the French *ius commune* writer Pothier, and thus ultimately by Roman law.[98] Thus, for all that it is a UK statute, anyone concerned with an issue of fitness of goods could do worse than to explore the Roman and *ius commune* materials on the matter.

As far as land is concerned, although this has been argued to be historically incorrect,[99] it is widely thought in modern Scots conveyancing practice that there is no implied guarantee of fitness in a sale of land or buildings.[100] Such guarantees may be, and commonly are, provided for in respect of specific attributes of the property. However, beyond that, the practice is to rely instead on an examination of the property by a professional surveyor to disclose any defects that may be discovered in that way, and on insurance for any defects that may emerge later. For situations where the seller is in breach of an obligation under the contract of sale, it came to be accepted during the nineteenth century that the *actio quanti minoris* had not been received as part of Scots law, with the result that the buyer could

---

[92] D.21.1.63. For discussion, see Zimmermann, *Obligations* 320–2.
[93] D.19.1.6.4.
[94] D.19.1.13pr.
[95] Originally the Sale of Goods Act 1893. The 1979 Act to a substantial extent re-enacts the 1893 Act.
[96] In this respect, by not restricting these requirements to business sales, Roman law was more protective of the buyer than is the modern law.
[97] Sale of Goods Act 1979, s. 14(2). This was previously 'merchantable quality'. The change was made by the Sale and Supply of Goods Act 1994, s. 1(1).
[98] Zimmermann, *Obligations* 336. According to Zimmermann, the specific source is D.19.1.6.4.
[99] R Black, 'Practice and Precept in Scots Law' 1982 JR 31, 47–50. See also the response of J M Halliday, 'The Scope of Warrandice in Conveyances of Land' 1983 JR 1. Professor Black's views come at the end of an article, the remainder of which should be required reading for any student or practitioner of Scots law.
[100] For discussion, see now C Jayathilaka, *Sale and the Implied Warranty of Soundness* (Edinburgh Legal Education Trust 2019) chapter 4.

not keep the property and recover damages. Instead, the buyer had to rescind the contract and reject the property. This development may have been based on confusion with the Roman rules on *laesio enormis*, which were certainly not accepted.[101] The rule excluding the *actio quanti minoris* in contracts of sale was removed by section 3 of the Contract (Scotland) Act 1997.[102]

(3) Buyer's Duties

The buyer was also subject to a number of duties, enforced by the *actio venditi*. This was in substantially the same wording as the *actio empti*, above, with the obvious change of the property having been sold to the defender rather than having been bought from him or her.

(a) Payment of Price

The buyer's basic duty was to pay the agreed price, with interest payable on failure to do so.[103]

(b) Acceptance on Delivery

Where delivery was offered in accordance with the contract, the buyer was obliged to accept delivery and could be compelled to do so.[104] Failure to accept delivery had the additional consequence that, from that point until delivery was actually made, the seller ceased to be liable for damage to the property except to the extent that the damage resulted from the seller's intentional wrongdoing.[105]

(c) Payment of Expenses

The buyer was obliged to reimburse any necessary, unforeseen expenses in caring for the property. An example might be money caring for a slave who became ill before delivery to the buyer of that slave.[106]

(4) Additional Terms

In addition to these implied obligations, it was common for parties to a sale to agree additional terms. These were fully enforceable as long as they were agreed at the time the contract was entered into.[107] Often these special terms imposed

---

[101] R Evans-Jones, 'The *Actio Quanti Minoris* in Mixed Legal Systems' in J Sondel, J Reszczyński and PŚciślicki eds, *Roman Law as Formative of Modern Legal Systems: Studies in Honour of Wiesław Litewski*, vol 1 (Jagiellonian University Press 2003).

[102] In this respect, the law was catching up with practice, for it had become common for conveyancers expressly to agree that the *actio quanti minoris* would be available. For the position with sales of moveable property, see Sale of Goods Act 1979, s. 53A(2).

[103] D.19.1.13.19–20.

[104] D.19.1.9.

[105] D.18.6.18.

[106] D.19.1.13.22.

[107] D.2.14.7.5. If the special term was agreed later, it was generally not directly enforceable, not being one of the recognised contracts. However, such a term would be considered to be a *pactum*, and as such could be pled as a defence. On *pacta*, see pp. 381–2.

conditions, whether suspensive or resolutive, as for example where one party was given the right to withdraw from the agreement. We saw in Chapter 17 how contractual conditions worked.[108] Other possibilities existed, however. For example, the parties might want to make special provision for the time and place for performance of the contract.

C. Hire *(Locatio Conductio)*

(1) Nature and Classification of Hire

An oddity about the contract of hire was the breadth of situations that it covered. Take, for example, a lease of land, a contract engaging a tradesman to carry out a piece of work and a contract of employment. We would not nowadays particularly consider these arrangements to have anything more in common with each other than they do with other contracts. In Roman law, however, they all fell within the one contract, the contract of hire, without making any clear distinction between them. Modern accounts, though, typically do distinguish between the three: the *locatio conductio rei* (hire of a piece of property), the *locatio conductio operis* (hire of a piece of work, an agreement to perform a specific task in exchange for payment) and the *locatio conductio operarum* (hire of services, in effect a contract of employment).

This brings us to a matter of terminology. The two parties to a contract of hire were called the *locator* and the *conductor*, but this terminology was used in a way that is capable of causing confusion. The term *locator* is related to the verb *locare* (to place, or to place at the disposal), so a *locator* is 'one who places something at the disposal of another'. The *conductor* is the person who accepts responsibility for that something: the verb *conducere* means to carry along or to take with one. In a hire of a piece of property, the property is placed by the lessor in the hands of the lessee, so the lessor is the *locator* and the lessee is the *conductor*. In a hire of services, the employee places his services at the disposal of the employer, so the employee is the *locator* and the employer the *conductor*. In a hire of a piece of work, by contrast, the piece of work is placed in the hands of the workman, so in this case the customer is the *locator* and the workman is the *conductor*. Thus, in a hire of a services, it is the *locator* who is doing the work, while in a hire of a piece of work it is the *conductor* who is doing the work.

(2) Distinguishing Hire from Sale

There are various texts commenting on the similarity of hire and sale.[109] Most obviously, both were subject to similar rules for their constitution, being constituted when the subject matter and the amount payable[110] were agreed. The connection between them went beyond this, though. In some circumstances, it could be difficult to tell into which category the agreement fell.

---

[108] See pp. 335–7.
[109] See *e.g.* D.19.2.2pr.
[110] In the case of hire, the sum to be paid is known as *merx*.

Suppose, for example, that you are a jeweller, and I approach you to make a gold ring for me. Is this a contract of sale of the ring, or is it a contract of hire of the work involved in making the ring? It has characteristics of both. The position that was taken was that the answer depended on who supplied the materials for the ring.[111] If the gold is supplied by me, then the contract is one of hire of a piece of work: it cannot be a sale, as I retain ownership of the gold throughout, and a transfer of ownership is a fundamental part of a sale. By contrast, if you supply the gold, then the contract is a sale. What if a diamond is to be mounted on the ring, the diamond to be supplied by one of us and the gold for the ring itself by the other? This question is not directly addressed, but it would seem reasonable to suppose that the answer would still depend on which of us supplied the gold. According to the principles of accession, which we saw in Chapter 12,[112] the ring is the principal thing. On attachment, the diamond's identity is subsumed into that of the ring. Accordingly, even if I, the customer, supply the diamond, I lose ownership of it when it is attached to the ring that you are making with your own gold.

Again, suppose that you are in the business of supplying slaves to fight in gladiatorial shows. Now in such circumstances, it is likely that some of the gladiators will come back to you more or less unscathed, while others will not, either because they have been killed or they have been so wounded as to be of no further use to you. We might therefore agree that I will pay 20 *sesterces* for each gladiator that is unharmed and 1,000 for each that is maimed or killed. In those circumstances, the view that was reached was that the contract was one of hire of the unharmed gladiators and sale of those who were maimed or killed.[113]

Although the classification of contracts as sale or hire is not as important in modern law, it can still have significance. In appropriate cases, the Roman materials may still be of use. We can see this in *Marjandi Ltd v Bon Accord Glass Ltd*,[114] a case which shows very well the continuing fertility and vitality of Roman and *ius commune* sources.[115] In that case, the defenders were a company which, among other things, supplied and built conservatories. The pursuers were a company which had formerly

---

[111] J.3.24.4; G.3.147; D.19.2.2.1.
[112] See pp. 221–31.
[113] G.3.146. There are practical problems here. If the nature of the contract is not established until after the show has taken place, how is it to be enforced beforehand, for example if you fail to provide the gladiators at all? See A M Prichard, 'Sale and Hire' in D Daube ed, *Studies in the Roman Law of Sale: Dedicated to the Memory of Francis de Zulueta* (Oxford University Press 1959), suggesting that this problem is more academic than real, being intended merely to illustrate the principles involved for the benefit of Gaius' students, and that in reality a *stipulatio* would have been used.
[114] 15 October 2007, Aberdeen Sheriff Court, available at <https://www.scotcourts.gov.uk/search-judgments/judgment?id=432887a6-8980-69d2-b500-ff0000d74aa7> (last accessed 14 September 2020). Mystifyingly, the case has not appeared in any of the law reports.
[115] The case was concerned with the very modern Commercial Agents (Council Directive) Regulations 1993 (SI 1993/3053). These Regulations make certain provisions with regard to commercial agents, a commercial agent being defined for these purposes as 'a self-employed intermediary who has continuing authority to negotiate the sale or purchase of goods on behalf of another person (the principal) or to negotiate and conclude the sale or purchase of goods on behalf of, and in the name of that principal . . .'

been engaged, as agents of the defenders, to negotiate with prospective customers for the supply and building of conservatories. For the purposes of the proceedings in the case, it was necessary to determine whether a contract for the supply and building of a conservatory was a contract of sale of the conservatory, or whether it was, instead, a contract of hire of building services. Following discussion of the views of Gaius, Justinian and the French *ius commune* writer Pothier, as well as of Scottish sources, the sheriff held that this was a contract of hire. The substance of the contract was the performance of work on property belonging to the customer, namely the customer's house and land, with ownership of the components of the conservatory being transferred to the customer by accession, on attachment to the land.[116] As with the customer who supplies gold for the manufacture of a ring, the principal thing here (the land) was supplied by the customer.

(3) Hire of a Thing *(Locatio Conductio Rei)*

(a) Creation

This was a hire of a piece of property, which could be either land or moveable. The lessor was the *locator* and the lessee the *conductor*. The contract was formed when the parties agreed on the subject matter and the rent to be paid. It is generally thought that the rent had to be in money, with the exception of leases of agricultural land, in which case the rent could partly consist of a share of the produce of the land.[117]

Normally the hire would be for a specified period,[118] at the end of which the property had to be surrendered to the lessor. A special rule existed in agricultural leases, however.[119] According to this rule, if the lessee was allowed to remain on the land beyond the agreed end date, the parties were considered to have impliedly agreed a renewal of the lease. This implied renewal is known as 'tacit relocation', and exists also in modern Scots law.[120]

It is important to understand that a hire of a thing was, in Roman law, entirely a contractual arrangement. That is to say, it gave the lessee no right in the property itself. This contrasts with medieval and modern attempts to provide greater protection to tenants of land: in Scots law, for example, a lease of land has been capable of becoming a real right since the Leases Act 1449.[121] In Roman law, the

---

[116] Accession is the attachment of a lesser thing (the accessory) to a greater thing (the principal), with the result that the accessory becomes part of the principal and, if the two were in separate ownership, the owner of the principal acquires ownership of the accessory. See pp. 221–31.

[117] J.3.24.2; J A C Thomas, 'The Nature of Merces' 1958 AJ 191.

[118] Where no fixed term was agreed, either party could terminate the lease at will: Zimmermann, *Obligations* 357–8.

[119] D.19.2.14.

[120] Indeed, the modern law goes further, and applies tacit relocation to leases of land generally, rather than solely to agricultural leases. The modern law also operates somewhat differently on account of the need to comply with the relevant periods of notice to bring the lease effectually to an end, such notice periods being unknown in Roman law. For comparative discussion, see Scottish Law Commission, *Discussion Paper on Aspects of Leases: Termination* (SLC DP No 165, 2018) chapter 2.

[121] For developments in other countries, see Zimmermann, *Obligations* 381–3; P J Conradie, 'The Effect of the Maxim "Hire Goes Before Sale" in Short Leases' (1954) 71 SALJ 369.

position was different. A lessee had only a personal right against the lessor, and no real right in the property itself.[122] The consequence of this was that, if the lessor transferred ownership of the property to someone else, the lessee would not be able to enforce the hire agreement against that acquirer. The lessee would certainly have a remedy against the lessor, who by disposing of the property breached his or her obligations under the hire contract, but the lessee would have no remedy against the third party acquirer.[123] Indeed, so little protection did the lessee have that the lessee was not even considered to possess the property, and so had no access to the possessory interdicts if a third party interfered with the lessee's use of the property.[124]

(b) Duties of Locator

We can identify three specific duties as owed by the *locator* to the *conductor* in a hire of a thing. First, the property had to be delivered to the *conductor* in accordance with the agreement, along with any accessories customary for the type of property in question,[125] and the *locator* had to uphold the *conductor*'s position for the full term of the lease.[126] The *locator* would be in breach of this obligation if, for example, the *conductor* was ejected from the property, whether or not this was the *locator*'s doing.

Second, the property had to be provided by the *locator* in the appropriate condition[127] and maintained in that way through the whole term of the hire. If the *locator* failed to comply with the repairing obligation, the *conductor* could deduct the cost of this from the rent.[128]

Third, the *locator* was responsible for any extraordinary expenses on the property beyond ordinary maintenance costs. For example, the *conductor* was entitled to reimbursement for useful improvements made to land that had been leased.[129]

The obligations of the *locator* were enforced by the *actio conducti*.

(c) Duties of Conductor

The *conductor* was subject to certain obligations, enforceable by means of the *actio locati* (action for a thing let out). The main obligation was of course payment of

---

[122] For the distinction between real and personal rights, see pp. 163–5.
[123] The maxim that is sometimes used to express this is 'sale breaks hire', but this is true only loosely. The contract of hire is still in full effect, but is only enforceable against the lessor (in the form of a claim for damages), not against the third party acquirer.
[124] On possession and its protection, see pp. 172–89.
[125] D.19.2.19.2. For discussion, see *e.g* B W Frier, 'Law, Technology, and Social Change: The Equipping of Italian Farm Tenancies' (1979) 96 ZSS (rA) 204.
[126] D.19.2.24.4.
[127] D.8.5.8.5; D.19.2.19.1; B W Frier, 'Tenant Remedies for Unsuitable Conditions Arising after Entry: A Roman Law Perspective on Modern American Common Law' in R S Bagnall and W V Harris eds, *Studies in Roman Law in Memory of A Arthur Schiller* (Leiden 1986).
[128] D.43.10.1.3.
[129] D.19.2.55.1.

the agreed rent and, as we saw in Chapter 15, where land had been leased out the landlord had an implied security over certain categories of goods on the property.[130] The *conductor* was also obliged to take care of the property,[131] to the standard of the 'most careful *paterfamilias*'.[132]

(4) Hire of Services *(Locatio Conductio Operarum)*
(a) Creation
A hire of services is, in effect, a contract of employment. Here the *locator* is the employee and the *conductor* the employer. The contract was made when there was agreement on the work to be done and the payment to be made.

One important limitation on the scope of the hire of services is that it could only be used for low-status occupations, of a kind commonly carried out by slaves.[133] Thus, one could employ a labourer, a craftsman, a business manager, a schoolteacher or a doctor,[134] but not a lawyer, advocate[135] or philosopher. It was seen as unseemly for high-status Romans to engage in such activities for such a low, mercenary reason as the pursuit of money[136] (which, as high-status individuals, it would be supposed anyway that they did not need).[137] The appropriate contract for such occupations was the contract of mandate, considered below.

(b) Duties of Locator
The *locator* was obliged to carry out the agreed duties with due diligence, to the standard of any professional expertise claimed. Absence of the proper skills counted as fault.[138]

---

[130] See pp. 274–6. The *conductor* might, however, be excused the obligation to pay rent in certain circumstances, *e.g.* where a crop was destroyed by exceptional weather conditions: D.19.2.15.2. This would not be the case, however, with more ordinary hazards of agriculture, such as a crop being destroyed by worms or weeds. This distinction may not have been easy to make in practice.

[131] D.19.2.11.2. On the duty of the *conductor*, see B W Frier, 'Tenant's Liability for Damage to Landlord's Property in Classical Roman Law' (1978) 95 ZSS (rA) 232.

[132] J.3.24.5.

[133] The term used is *operae illiberales*. The contrary term is *operae liberales*. For discussion, see J A C Thomas, 'Locatio and Operae' (1961) 64 BIDR 231, 240–7.

[134] The final two occupations were often carried out by educated Greek slaves. This is a reminder, if one were needed, that values change.

[135] It will be remembered from pp. 30–1. that the primary qualification for advocacy was skill in public speaking, not legal knowledge, hence why lawyers and advocates are listed here separately.

[136] D.50.13.1.4. That such attitudes survive today may be seen in the fact that very many people, who would never dream of appropriating the labour of a plumber, fisherman or builder without payment, will quite cheerfully make illegal copies of books or illegally download music. Presumably the thought process is that musicians, artists and authors do what they do for the love of their art, and should not expect to be paid as well. Still, those who think in that way should reflect that musicians, artists and authors have to eat as well, and taking the fruits of their labour without payment and without permission is taking food from their mouths just as much as it would be with those in occupations not considered to be labours of love.

[137] Arguments of this kind are likely to be self-fulfilling: if it is not possible to provide for an enforceable payment obligation in respect of services of a particular kind, the provision of such services is likely to be restricted to those with private means.

[138] D.50.17.132.

(c) Duties of *Conductor*

The *conductor* was liable for any loss caused by fault, for example by providing an unsafe system of work. The *conductor*'s main obligation, however, was payment of the agreed wage. This had to be paid even if the work was not done, as long as that failure was not the fault of the *locator*.[139]

(5) Hire of a Piece of Work *(Locatio Conductio Operis)*

(a) Nature and Creation

A hire of a piece of work was similar to a hire of services, in that both involved work being done for money, and was likewise constituted as a contract when those matters were agreed. Where, though, a hire of services created essentially an ongoing employment relationship, a hire of a piece of work was concerned with payment for some specific task. For example, if I employ a chauffeur, that is a hire of services; if I book a taxi to the airport, that is a hire of a piece of work. Likewise, if I ask a craftsman to make me a wooden chair, that is a hire of a piece of work; if I set up a workshop for the making of such chairs, those working there are engaged under a hire of services.

Another (perhaps confusing) difference between hire of services and hire of a piece of work is the terminology involved. As we have seen, in a hire of services, the person doing the work is the *locator* and the employer is the *conductor*. In a hire of a piece of work, it is the other way around: the customer is the *locator* and the workman is the *conductor*. We have seen above the reason for this difference of terminology.

(b) Duties of Locator

The *locator* was, of course, obliged to pay the agreed fee, and would be liable for any loss caused by fault on the part of the *locator*.

(c) Duties of Conductor

The *conductor* had the duty to carry out the work to the required standard. This was an objective test, based on the judgement of the hypothetical reasonable man.[140] Accordingly, the *conductor* was liable where failure resulted from inexperience or lack of skill as well as where it resulted from subjective fault.[141] The *conductor* bore the risk of failure to perform the agreed task to the required standard, even where there was no specific fault on the part of the *conductor*.[142] To this rule, there were two exceptions. First, where the failure arose from a defect in materials provided by the *locator*,

---

[139] D.19.2.38pr. Where, however, the *locator* found alternative employment, payment of wages under that contract excluded a claim under the earlier contract: D.19.2.19.9.

[140] D.19.2.24pr. For discussion of the process of approval of the works in construction contracts, see S D Martin, 'A Reconsideration of Probatio Operis' (1986) 103 ZSS (rA) 321.

[141] D.19.2.9.5.

[142] D.19.2.13.6.

the *conductor* was not liable.¹⁴³ Second, the *conductor* was excused liability where the failure arose through *vis maior*, that is some overwhelming event that could not have been guarded against,¹⁴⁴ such as a work in progress being destroyed by earthquake¹⁴⁵ or landslide.¹⁴⁶ Serious adverse weather might be another example.¹⁴⁷

D. Mandate *(Mandatum)*

(1) Nature and Creation of Mandate

The essence of mandate was that it involved a request by one person (the mandator) to another (the mandatary) to carry out some action on behalf of the mandator, and the mandatary's agreement to this. An example might be one person agreeing to go to market to buy goods on behalf of another.

In principle, a contract of mandate was gratuitous, or else it would be a contract of hire.¹⁴⁸ In origin, it was an arrangement by which services were provided out of friendship or as a favour. This, though, became a problem in the Empire, by which time professionals such as advocates expected to be paid for their efforts, yet who, as providers of *operae liberales*, could not enter into a contract of hire for them.¹⁴⁹ The solution was to allow for promises to pay the mandatary a fee, known as an *honorarium*, to be enforceable, but to maintain the distinction with hire by having that promise enforceable only through the *cognitio extraordinaria* procedure.¹⁵⁰

The simplest case of mandate is where the action to be carried out is solely for the benefit of the mandator, for example where the mandatary is requested to buy property or act as cautioner¹⁵¹ for the mandator.¹⁵² However, there were other possibilities. For example, the mandate could be for the benefit of both mandator and mandatary. An example would be where the mandator requested the mandatary to lend money at interest to someone who is to apply the money in the interests of the mandator.¹⁵³ Indeed, the mandate could be solely for the benefit of a third party or the benefit of a third party and the mandatary between

---

[143] D.19.2.13.5: a jewel given to the *conductor* for setting or engraving, which breaks because of a flaw.
[144] For discussion, see S Martin, 'The Case of the Collapsing Watercourse: Builders' Responsibility for Damage in Classical Roman Law' (1986) 4 LHR 423.
[145] D.19.2.59.
[146] D.19.2.62.
[147] There must be noted in passing here the effect of the adoption in Roman law of the *lex Rhodia de iactu*. This was concerned with the case where part of a ship's cargo had to be sacrificed to save the ship. In that case, the loss was shared among the owners whose goods had been lost and those whose goods had been saved. Where carriage was on the basis of a hire of a piece of work, this rule therefore represents an exception to the general position. See D.14.2.1–2pr; Zimmermann, *Obligations* 406–12.
[148] D.17.1.1.4.
[149] Zimmermann, *Obligations* 415–18.
[150] D.50.13.1; C.4.35.1 (late classical).
[151] A cautioner (pronounced 'KAYshunner') is someone who has agreed to act as a guarantor for another's debt. See pp. 277–8.
[152] J.3.26.1.
[153] J.3.26.2.

them.¹⁵⁴ The only possibility that is excluded by Justinian is a mandate that is solely for the benefit of the mandatary.¹⁵⁵ For example, suppose that I advised you how to invest your money. This would be advice rather than a mandate, so I would not be liable to you even if the investment turned out badly.¹⁵⁶ This raises the more general question of whether the mandator had to have an interest in the performance of the mandate. The texts are inconclusive.¹⁵⁷ It is likely that the position was that the mandator had to have some interest in the matter, but that this could be indirect, as for example where the matter was primarily in the interests of the mandatary or a third party, but the mandator was indirectly benefiting from the performance of the mandate.¹⁵⁸

Except for the requirement that the mandate be gratuitous (which we have seen, in any case, was substantially departed from), mandate bears a great deal of similarity to a modern contract of agency. Both, after all, involve one person carrying out some form of transaction on behalf of another. This should not be overstressed, however. Suppose that I have agreed to negotiate the purchase of a horse on your behalf, and I then do so. A contract of sale of the horse is constituted. In modern law, I am seen as acting as your agent here. As long as I act within the authority you have given me, and the seller knows that he is dealing with an agent, I am not a party to the contract of sale and have no liability under it. In a modern agency arrangement, I am merely the means by which you have entered into the contract. The contract is enforceable by and against you, not me.

The Roman contract of mandate was different. In the scenario just described, the contract would be between the seller of the horse and me, the mandatary. It would be enforceable by and against me just as if I was buying the horse for my own benefit. My relationship with you would be none of the seller's concern, and in the first instance ownership of the horse would pass from the seller to me, not to you, because property bought by a mandatary was not owned by the mandator until delivered to the mandator.¹⁵⁹ This simplifies matters somewhat: means were developed for the enforcement, in certain circumstances, of such contracts against the person who instructed their making.¹⁶⁰ In principle, though, it remained always the position that the mandator was not a party to contracts made by the mandatary, and could not normally sue under them unless the rights under such a contract were assigned to the mandator.¹⁶¹

(2) Duties of Mandator

The mandator was obliged to accept the performance of the mandate by the mandatary and to make good any expenses the mandatary had incurred in

---

[154] J.3.26.4–5.
[155] J.3.26.6.
[156] Even here, though, see A Watson, *Contract of Mandate in Roman Law* (Oxford University Press 1961) 123–4.
[157] Compare D.17.1.6.4 and D.17.1.8.6, both attributed to Ulpian.
[158] For discussion, see Birks, *Obligations* 121–3.
[159] D.41.1.59.
[160] See pp. 150–5. The main method was the *actio institoria*, which allowed individuals to be held liable for the actions of their business managers.
[161] On assignation of contractual rights, see p. 323–4.

execution of the mandate. It was disputed between the two classical schools of jurists, the Sabinians and the Proculians, what would happen if the mandatary exceeded the mandate, for example by spending more than the maximum stated by the mandator on buying goods.[162] The Sabinian view was that the mandatary would not be entitled to recover anything from the mandator.[163] The view that prevailed, though, was that of the Proculians that the mandatary would be entitled to recover from the mandator everything spent up to the agreed limit.[164] The mandator's duties were enforced using the *actio mandati contraria*.

(3) Duties of Mandatary

The mandatary's duty, of course, was to carry out the mandate. What if the mandatary carried out the mandate in such a way that loss was caused to the mandator? Certainly, the mandatary would not be liable if the loss arose from circumstances outside his or her control. It is not entirely clear, though, whether the mandatary would be liable for mere negligence in carrying out the mandate, or whether intentional wrongdoing was needed.[165] A remedy for the mandatary's failure was obtained using the *actio mandati directa*.

(4) Termination of Mandate

A mandate could be freely renounced by either party, bringing the contract to an end, as long as this was done before either had changed position in reliance on it.[166] Thus, if the mandatary was to decide to renounce the mandate, this had to be done as soon as possible: if the mandatary renounced without good reason, he or she would be liable to the mandator if the latter was left in a worse position.[167]

A mandate was also brought to an end by the mandator's death.[168] However, Justinian nonetheless allowed the mandatary an action (against the mandator's heir) if the mandate was carried out in ignorance of that death.[169]

E. Partnership *(Societas)*

(1) Nature and Relationship

Stated generally, partnership can be defined as an agreement made by two or more people to share risks and benefits, either generally or in some specific business or activity. Partnership also exists in modern law, but was a much broader idea in Roman law than it is now. Unlike a modern partnership, for example, a Roman partnership was not necessarily a business relationship, and indeed

---

[162] D Nörr, 'Reflections on Faith, Friendship, Mandate' (1990–2) 25–7 Irish Jurist (NS) 302.
[163] G.3.161.
[164] J.3.26.8; D.17.1.3.2; D.17.1.4.
[165] For discussion, see *e.g.* W M Gordon, 'The Liability of the Mandatary' in A Guarino and L Labruna eds, *Synteleia Vicenzo Arangio-Ruiz*, vol 1 (Jovene Editore 1964); A Watson, *Contract of Mandate in Roman Law* (Oxford University Press 1961) 195–216; G MacCormack, 'The Liability of the Mandatary' (1972) 18 Labeo 156.
[166] J.3.26.9.
[167] J.3.26.11.
[168] See though D.17.1.12.17, in which the mandate (to build a monument to the mandator) was not to begin until the mandator's death. This was held to be enforceable against the mandator's heir.
[169] J.3.26.10.

could cover the whole of the partners' property and affairs. This, in fact, was the oldest form of partnership in Roman law. As we saw in Chapter 7, a Roman citizen whose *paterfamilias*[170] was still alive could not own any property.[171] As we saw in Chapter 16, where the *paterfamilias* died intestate, leaving surviving children, the property of the *paterfamilias* would be divided equally among the children.[172] Thus, the first time that the surviving children ever owned property, it would come to them all at once and together through succession. In such cases, the default option could easily be seen as being for the surviving children to continue managing the family property together as a unit. Thus, the siblings formed by implication[173] a partnership to manage the family property rather than dividing it into individual shares. This arrangement was known in early law by the name *ercto non cito*,[174] and continued to be possible through the classical period and beyond. This is very different from a modern partnership, which exists as a business relationship between the partners, separate from their own, personal property and affairs.

Certain features of a Roman partnership can be traced back to this origin of partnership as a family arrangement, not least the fact that breach of partnership obligations had the very serious consequence that the erring partner incurred *infamia*.[175] However, a partnership could also be a more limited relationship. Two or more individuals could make a partnership for some specific purpose, which did not need to be a business transaction. For example, two neighbours might make an agreement to manage together the space between their houses, in which they intended to build a supporting wall, or they might agree together to acquire a neighbouring area of land to prevent obstruction of the light.[176] In both cases, there would be a partnership, and the neighbours would owe each other the duties of partners until the purpose was fulfilled. In the modern business world, such a relationship is known as a joint venture, for example where two businesses combine their efforts to launch a new product or enter a new market.

Where the partnership was a business relationship, it could be for the purposes of a particular business or for all of the partners' business affairs. The latter was presumed in the absence of contrary agreement.[177]

---

[170] *I.e.* the oldest direct ascendant in the male line. In practice, given ancient life expectancy, and given that men did not normally marry until they were into full adulthood, this would most commonly be one's father, but could be one's paternal grandfather or even his father. See pp. 116–17.

[171] Unless he or she had been emancipated from the power of the *paterfamilias*, in which case he or she would have no *paterfamilias*. Inroads were made into the rule that children in power could not own property, but it remained always the position in principle. See pp. 120–1.

[172] See pp. 288–9.

[173] Indeed, at this point, it is probably anachronistic to talk of the co-heirs as making any kind of contract here.

[174] G.3.154a.

[175] For an interesting comparative discussion, see D Daube, '*Consortium* in Roman and Hebrew Law' 1950 JR 71. On *infamia*, see p. 100–1.

[176] D.17.2.52.13.

[177] D.17.2.7. In the modern world, the reverse is the case. For example, in the modern law, a person who becomes a partner in a firm of solicitors does not thereby agree to hand over the profits of any separate, unrelated business dealings, unless otherwise agreed. The Partnership Act 1890, s. 29(1), which limits a partner's obligation to account for private profits, applies only to transactions concerning the partnership or from the partner's use of the partnership's property, name or business connections.

A person could be a member of more than one partnership, and the fact of such membership did not in any way cause the partnerships to combine: 'my partner's partner is not my partner'.[178] As a consequence of this, the assumption of a new member of a partnership needed the agreement of all existing partners.

The default position was that the partners shared profits and losses equally. However, situations might arise where there was a desire to recognise the greater contribution of one or more of the partners by adopting unequal sharing. There was disagreement among jurists as to whether this arrangement was competent, but it was eventually settled that it was.[179] It was even possible to excuse a partner of losses altogether,[180] although this meant net losses: profits first had to be set off against losses.[181] Whatever system of sharing of profit and loss was adopted, though, a partner was entitled to reimbursement from the other partners for expenses incurred in the execution of partnership business.[182]

A partner would be liable to the other partners for causing loss through fault. Negligence was enough for liability. However, the test for negligence here was subjective: it was enough for the partner to show the same level of care shown in that partner's own affairs, 'for someone who assumes a careless partner has only himself to blame'.[183] It was only where the partner's conduct as partner fell below even that standard that the partner would be liable.

(2) Termination

A partnership came to an end in various ways.[184] If the partnership was created for a specific transaction, it came to an end with that transaction.[185] The choice of partner was a personal one, so the death of any partner ended the partnership, unless there was contrary agreement.[186] The heir of the deceased partner should, however, complete any business already begun by the deceased.[187] Where a partner, through insolvency, had had confiscated or had been obliged to surrender his or her assets, this also brought the partnership to an end.[188] If the partners wished

---

[178] D.17.2.20 (Ulpian).
[179] J.3.25.2; D.17.2.29pr. For discussion, see A Watson, 'The Notion of Equivalence of Contractual Obligation and Classical Roman Partnership' (1981) 97 LQR 275. As Watson points out, it is difficult to understand why the point should ever have been seen as controversial unless we bear in mind the origin of partnership as a family arrangement. Unequal sharing could be seen as inconsistent with the nature of that relationship, in much the same way as there is a tendency in the modern law of divorce to divide matrimonial assets equally, regardless of the spouses' actual contributions. For this last point, see pages 281–2 of the Watson article.
[180] D.17.2.29.1.
[181] J.3.25.2.
[182] D.17.2.52.15. It seems, though, that there was some disagreement over the precise extent of the partner's right to reimbursement: D.17.2.60.1–17.2.61.
[183] D.17.2.72; J.3.25.9.
[184] D.17.2.4.1.
[185] J.3.25.6.
[186] J.3.25.5.
[187] D.17.2.40.
[188] J.3.25.7–8. The rationale given is that, in such circumstances, another person has succeeded to the insolvent partner's rights, in a similar way to the death of a partner.

to continue anyway, that was considered to be a new partnership.[189] Finally, the partnership could be brought to an end at any time by any partner's renunciation of it. Care was needed here, though. If a partner renounced in bad faith, to keep an anticipated benefit for himself or herself, he or she could be made to hand over an appropriate share to the other partners.[190] This is an exception to the normal rule that the former partners had no right to anything acquired by each other after the end of the partnership. The important point, though, was the renouncing partner's motive: a partner who happened to receive a windfall after the end of the partnership did not have to share it. This would only be necessary if it was the prospect of that windfall that motivated the renunciation. Similar consequences would ensue if one of the partners renounced in circumstances that resulted in loss to the other partners.[191]

(3) Remedies
The partners' obligations among themselves were enforced by the *actio pro socio*. Breach of partnership obligations also terminated the partnership contract and, as mentioned above, incurred *infamia* as well. As far as third parties were concerned, some practical difficulty was caused by the fact that outsiders could only deal with partners as individuals, not as representative of the whole partnership. It was, though, only in limited circumstances that one partner could be held directly liable for the acts of another partner.[192]

(4) Partnership in Modern Law
The modern Scots law on partnership is primarily contained in the Partnership Act 1890, and includes some fundamental differences from Roman partnerships. For example, unlike a Roman partnership, a modern partnership is a specifically commercial relationship.[193] In a modern partnership, the individual partners are agents for the partnership as a whole and for each other, with the result that the partners are personally liable for each other's acts in pursuance of partnership business.[194] Moreover, a Scottish (though not an English) partnership has legal personality separate from the partners themselves, with the result that it is possible for the partnership itself to enter into contracts and own property.[195]

---

[189] J.3.25.8.
[190] J.3.25.4. The outcome would differ, though, if the inheritance unexpectedly caused loss. There, the partner who had renounced the partnership in bad faith in order not to have to share the inheritance would have to bear all of the loss personally.
[191] D.17.2.65.5.
[192] See *e.g.* D.17.2.82, stating that liability is imposed when money obtained by one partner is paid into a common fund. See also Zimmermann, *Obligations* 467–8.
[193] Partnership Act 1890, s. 1(1).
[194] Partnership Act 1890, s. 5.
[195] Partnership Act 1890, s. 4(2).

Nonetheless, despite these differences, there has been influence from the Roman law on the modern law of partnership, and on occasion the opportunity arises to make use of the Roman sources. An example of this is to be found in *Duncan v MFV Marigold PD145*.[196] That case involved a partnership in the running of a fishing boat. The executors of a deceased partner sought a payment in respect of a deceased partner's share of the firm's capital. It was noted by the court[197] that section 38 of the Partnership Act 1890, which is concerned with the continuation of partnership business following the partnership's dissolution, was inspired by Roman law.

Chapter Summary

The consensual contracts were so called because they were all constituted by agreement. There were four of them: sale, hire, mandate and partnership. Sale is an exchange of identified property for an identified price. Hire is really three different kinds of arrangement, though the distinction is not made explicit in the Roman sources: a hire of a thing (a lease of land or moveable property), a hire of services (essentially a contract of employment) or a hire of a piece of work (an arrangement for a specific task to be performed in exchange for payment). Mandate is a contract by which one person agrees to undertake a task for another. It is gratuitous: if payment was made, the contract would be a hire of a piece of work. A partnership is a contract by which two or more people agree to share profits and losses, either for some particular undertaking or for their whole property and affairs.

The consensual contracts are, of all the Roman contracts, the most like modern contracts and, indeed, they have had the greatest influence on the modern law of contract. Many rules from these contracts have been received into modern law, such as the rule allocating risk in sales. Likewise, the position on liability for defective property in a sale has been influential on later law.

Equally, there are important differences from modern law. For example, although mandate has some similarity to modern agency, it does not have the full consequences of agency. A person acting under mandate cannot bind the principal by his or her acts. Again, unlike a modern partnership, a Roman partnership is not necessarily a commercial arrangement, it has no legal personality, and the partners are not agents of the partnership or of each other.

---

[196] 2006 SLT 975.
[197] At para [36].

Further Reading

G.3.135–62

J.3.22–6

D.17; 18; 19; 21

C.4.35, 37, 38, 45–58, 65

P Birks, *The Roman Law of Obligations* (E Descheemaeker ed, Oxford University Press 2014) chapter 5

D Daube, '*Societas* as Consensual Contract' (1938) 6 Cam LJ 381

D Daube ed, *Studies in the Roman Law of Sale: Dedicated to the Memory of Francis de Zulueta* (Oxford University Press 1959)

B Frier, *Landlords and Tenants in Imperial Rome* (Princeton University Press 1980)

J Mackintosh, *The Roman Law of Sale, With Modern Illustrations* 2nd edn (T & T Clark 1907)

E Metzger ed, *A Companion to Justinian's Institutes* (Duckworth 1998) 150–68

P du Plessis, 'Between Theory and Practice: New Perspectives on the Roman Law of Letting and Hiring' (2006) 65 Cam LJ 423

A Watson, *Contract of Mandate in Roman Law* (Oxford University Press 1961)

A Watson, 'The Origins of Consensual Sale: A Hypothesis' (1964) 32 TvR 245

F de Zulueta, *The Roman Law of Sale: Introduction and Select Texts* (Clarendon Press 1945)

CHAPTER TWENTY-ONE
Other Contractual Arrangements

A. Introduction

In the previous three chapters, we have considered the most important forms of contract recognised by Roman law. In this chapter, we look at some further matters. Unlike the position in modern law, where there is a general law of contract, we have seen that Roman law recognised a range of specific contracts. This required any agreement to be fitted into a specific recognised category of contract if it was to be enforceable. Alongside the contracts already considered, there is a further category to consider, that of the 'literal' contracts. In addition, the limitations of the system of specific contracts had the result that it came to be seen as necessary to give at least some legal recognition to further types of transaction.

As we shall see, not everything covered in this chapter was considered to be a contract, though all had some affinity to contracts. For this reason, the looser term 'contractual arrangements' is used in the title of this chapter, rather than 'contracts'.

B. Literal Contracts *(Obligationes Litteris)*

Alongside the categories of real, verbal and consensual contracts, the institutional scheme also included a fourth category. This was the category of contracts created in writing, often called literal contracts or literal obligations, from the Latin term *obligationes litteris*.

As originally understood, this term did not refer to written contracts generally, in which writing was simply evidence of the terms of the parties' agreement rather than being constitutive of the contract. As long as there has been writing, it has been common for contracting parties to record important agreements in writing, to minimise the risk of later disputes. In that case, though, the writing has purely evidential purposes. Suppose that I agree to sell you a large area of land or a shipment of wine. If we are sensible, for such a contract we will put our agreement in writing. However, that is not essential to the contract, which will be just as enforceable if evidenced in some other way.[1]

---

[1] Although, on this last point, see p. 353 on Justinian's provisions on contracts of sale agreed to be made in writing. In modern law, by contrast, certain matters require writing for their validity: Requirements of Writing (Scotland) Act 1995, s. 1(2).

The true literal contract was different, in that it was the writing in the correct form that actually created the obligation.[2] Literal contracts arose from the custom of a *paterfamilias* to record financial transactions in a household accounts book. If this was done in the correct form, and with the consent of the debtor, it was sufficient to create an obligation that there had been made an entry in the accounts book to the effect that the debtor was indebted to the *paterfamilias*. The contract was unilateral, as obligations were only imposed on one party. It seems to have been commonly used for the purposes of novation.[3] This was very useful to the creditor as this form of contract was *stricti iuris*, with the result that it was not necessary for the creditor to prove the basis of the obligation.

Gaius deals with this matter very briefly,[4] and much is uncertain about the precise details of the operation of this contract. Literal contracts were becoming obsolete in Gaius' day, and had long since become so by Justinian's time. A place is kept for literal contracts in Justinian's *Institutes*,[5] but what is considered is something quite different, namely the recording in writing of a debt's existence. In principle, the person who had made a written statement that he or she owed a debt ought to have been able to avoid liability by showing that no valid contract in fact existed. Justinian held that such an argument could only be made within two years (reduced from the five years of previous imperial pronouncements), introducing an irrebuttable presumption that there was a valid obligation if it had not been challenged during this period. In effect, this introduced a new form of contract created in writing, but it was one with no historical connection to the original literal contract.[6]

C. Innominate Contracts

The innominate contracts are a group with a confusing name, for many of them did in fact have names. What they all had in common was that they were enforceable when one party had performed his or her side of the bargain, but the other had not.[7] As a general principle, the praetor allowed agreements of this kind, where either something had been given[8] by one party to the other or one had performed labour for the other, to be enforced using the *actio praescriptis verbis*.[9]

---

[2] For the distinction, see G.3.131.
[3] *I.e.* the discharge of an existing obligation and its replacement with a new one. See p. 325.
[4] G.3.128–9.
[5] J.3.21.
[6] See also the discussion at pp. 341–2 of *stipulationes* recorded in writing.
[7] For example, a sale (a consensual contract) agreed to be carried out at some later point in time would be enforceable; by contrast a barter (an innominate contract) would not be, until one party had carried out his or her side of the bargain. In other words, in the terminology sometimes used, a sale in Roman law is an executory contract, while barter is not, a characteristic which barter shares with the real contracts (p. 344). For discussion of the nature of the innominate contracts, see G MacCormack, 'Contractual Theory and the Innominate Contracts' (1985) 51 SDHI 131.
[8] Given the example of *transactio* below, this should be understood in a broad sense. Someone compromising an action is, in the sense meant, giving up something in favour of the other party to the action.
[9] This means the 'action on the introductory words', so called because it was necessary to lay out, as an introduction, the particular facts of the case. On the *actio praescriptis verbis*, see D.19.5; J B Thayer, 'Actio Praescriptis Verbis' (1944–5) 19 Tulane LR 62.

Before this, the only remedy was to claim for the restoration of the value of the property using the *condictio*, or else, perhaps, the *actio de dolo*.[10] Various specific examples are worthy of mention.

Permutatio (barter) was an exchange of property, rather than an exchange of property for money:[11] as we saw in Chapter 20, after disagreement among jurists, it was eventually settled that this did not count as a sale.[12] *Permutatio*, however, was very similar to sale, and was governed by many of the same rules. One difference, however, was that in *permutatio* each party guaranteed that ownership would be transferred; there was therefore no need for eviction to found a claim.[13]

Aestimatum was a form of sale or return, in other words where the buyer of goods was given a period of time in which to decide whether to keep them or reject them.[14] In an *aestimatum*, the seller retained ownership until the approval period had expired or the buyer acted in a manner inconsistent with a right of return. Nonetheless, a buyer who sold the goods before the approval period expired was able to give ownership. After all, selling the goods was inconsistent with a right of return, so by doing so the buyer was making the choice not to return them.[15]

Transactio was a compromise of an action,[16] something that remains very common when success in litigation is doubtful. A *transactio* could be made formally, using *stipulatio*, but an informal compromise became binding when the *actio praescriptis verbis* was allowed. After this point, a party to litigation, who abandoned that litigation on the strength of an informal undertaking, could then sue on the basis of that undertaking.

Precarium was a permission to use property belonging to the granter.[17] It differed from a *commodatum*[18] in being of a fixed duration, and from a gift by being temporary. The property was recoverable using the interdict *de precario*, but Justinian classed this also as an innominate contract.[19]

D. Pacts *(Pacta)*

Generally speaking, a pact (*pactum*; plural *pacta*) was an agreement of a kind that could be pled as a defence to a claim, but could not itself be enforced.[20] Such a pact was said to be a 'bare pact' (*nudum pactum*). There were exceptions to this, however, known as 'clothed pacts' (*pacta vestita*). For example, as we saw in Chapter 20, in a contract

---

[10] See p. 423.
[11] D.19.4.
[12] See p. 355. For an interesting discussion of the distinction, even though not everyone will find the analysis convincing as a historical explanation, see D L Hall and F D Raymond, 'Economic Analysis of Legal Institutions: Explaining an "Inexplicable" Rule of Roman Law' (1985) 61 Indiana LJ 401. See also F Atria, 'A Roman Puzzle' (1999) 34 Irish Jurist (NS) 276, 284–7.
[13] D.19.4.1pr. Compare pp. 359–60.
[14] Compare the case where there is a *pactum displicentiae* in a contract of sale, considered at p. 337.
[15] Compare *Brown v Marr* (1880) 7 R 427.
[16] D.2.15.1; M de Villiers, 'Notes on *Transactio* (Compromise of Suit)' (1923) 40 SALJ 261.
[17] D.43.26.1–2pr.
[18] See pp. 347–9.
[19] Zimmermann, *Obligations* 536.
[20] D.2.14.7.4.

of sale a pact could be enforced if agreed on at the time the contract was made.[21] In such a case, the pact could be used to introduce additional terms to the contract. There were also various pacts made enforceable by imperial pronouncement.[22] The most important category of clothed pacts, however, was that of praetorian pacts.

The praetorian pacts were pacts that were made enforceable by the praetor. There were two of these. *Constitutum debiti* was an agreement to pay a debt that already existed.[23] This was not a novation, and so did not extinguish the original debt. Rather, it reinforced the original debt, and was often used to provide personal security for a debt owed by another.[24]

The other praetorian pact was *receptum*, which was the collective name for a category of agreements whereby a person assumed responsibility for something. For example, the *receptum arbitri* was an agreement to act as an arbitrator.[25] Of particular interest is the *receptum* by which innkeepers, stablekeepers and carriers by sea undertook the safekeeping of travellers' property in their care. This, however, has a complex interaction with the quasi-delictual liability imposed on such individuals, and will be considered alongside that matter in Chapter 25.[26]

E. Gift *(Donatio)*

The final category that we need to address is that of gifts (*donationes*). The Romans distinguished two forms of gift, namely the *donatio mortis causa* (the gift on account of death) and the *donatio inter vivos* (the gift between living persons). Although these are often treated together, they are really very different. The *donatio mortis causa* is better considered as part of the law of succession, and is considered along with that in Chapter 16. Here we are concerned only with the *donatio inter vivos*.[27]

A gift was a unilateral donation of something. This was not necessarily an item of corporeal property, as the term 'gift' would normally be understood in the modern world. Rather, a gift could be anything that involved a donor giving up an asset in favour of a donee. For example, the unilateral discharge of a debt could be classified as a gift.

An agreement to make a gift was not considered to be a contract. It had, though, certain characteristics in common with contracts. Thus, an agreement to make a gift was a valid *iusta causa* for *traditio*[28] or *usucapio*.[29] The agreement was not itself enforceable, however, and so the person who promised to make a gift could not be compelled to do so. Under Justinian, though, this changed: an undertaking

---

[21] D.2.14.7.5. See pp. 364–5.
[22] An example was *compromissum*, an agreement to submit a dispute to arbitration. See Zimmermann, *Obligations* 526–7.
[23] D.13.5.1pr.
[24] See Chapter 15 on securities.
[25] D.4.8.13.2.
[26] See pp. 442–3.
[27] For general discussion of gifts, see Zimmermann, *Obligations* 477–98.
[28] See pp. 207–10.
[29] See pp. 241–2.

to make a gift was held to imply an obligation to deliver.[30] In effect, by this change, a promise to make a gift became a form of contract.

From time to time, attempts were made to control the giving of gifts. One prominent attempt was the *lex Cincia* of 204 BC, which prohibited gifts beyond a certain value[31] to anyone outside a statutory list of (mostly) relations. Breach of the *lex* had, however, no direct consequences: there were no criminal sanctions and any transfer of property was valid.[32] There were also long-standing restrictions on gifts between spouses.[33] Under the emperor Constantine,[34] a system of registration[35] of gifts was introduced, with failure to register rendering the gift void.[36] Under Justinian, all gifts over 500 *solidi* in value had to be registered.[37] Higher gifts were void to the extent of the excess, with very limited exceptions.

As a general rule, gifts were irrevocable. Once the gift was given, that was that, although a gift by slave-owner to a former slave that he or she had freed could be revoked for the freedman's ingratitude.[38] Under Justinian, a more general right of revocation for ingratitude was recognised.[39]

Chapter Summary

A system of specific contracts, rather than a general law of contract, leaves gaps where an agreement does not fall within one of the established contract types. In the preceding three chapters, we saw three of the four institutional categories of contract. In this chapter, we saw the fourth, namely literal contracts. In time, though, at least some recognition was given to other forms of agreement. In this chapter, we saw three further categories of agreement that could have legal consequences. These were:

- innominate contracts, which could be enforced by a party who had performed his or her side of the bargain, against a party who had not;
- pacts, which could be used as a defence but which could not be enforced, except where (particularly praetorian) intervention had made them enforceable;
- agreements to make gifts, which became enforceable under Justinian.

---

[30] J.2.7.2.
[31] The exact value is unknown.
[32] In other words, this was a *lex imperfecta*. See pp. 203–4.
[33] These were the *donatio inter virum et uxorem* and the *donatio propter nuptias*. See pp. 144 and 146–7 respectively.
[34] Reigned AD 306–37.
[35] Known as *insinuatio*.
[36] C.Th.8.12.3 (AD 316).
[37] J.2.7.2. This was increased from the earlier sum of 200 *solidi*.
[38] C.8.55.1 (AD 249).
[39] J.2.7.2.

Further Reading

G.3.128–34, 138

J.3.21

P Birks, *The Roman Law of Obligations* (E Descheemaeker ed, Oxford University Press 2014) chapter 3

E Metzger ed, *A Companion to Justinian's Institutes* (Duckworth 1998) 148–50, 168–9

A Watson, *The Law of Obligations in the Later Roman Republic* (Oxford University Press 1965) chapter 3

R Zimmermann, *The Law of Obligations: Roman Foundations of the Civilian Tradition* (Oxford University Press 1996) chapters 16 and 17

CHAPTER TWENTY-TWO

The Law of Delicts and the *Lex Aquilia*

A. Nature and Scope of the Law of Delicts

The law of delicts is concerned with liability for wrongdoing.[1] The same term, 'delict', is used for this area in modern Scots law. In modern law, though, the word is usually used in the singular – 'the law of delict' – whereas in Roman law we tend to talk in the plural – 'the law of delicts'. The reason for this is that the Roman law was not based yet on a general principle of liability for wrongful acts, but rather on specific delicts or wrongs. We have seen the same point in the law of contracts.[2] One consequence of this is that there will often be gaps in the law, where justice demands that a person be held liable but there is no legal basis for this. We shall see in this chapter some of the ways in which the problem of these gaps was addressed.

Another consequence of a law of specific delicts is that there will sometimes be overlap between two different delicts. For example, suppose I were to damage your property out of spite. We shall see in this chapter that you could sue me for the value of the damage to the property. We shall see in the next chapter that you might also be able to sue me for the insult to you that this conduct entails. Thus, the same conduct could have quite different legal consequences depending on the choice of legal basis on which the wrongdoer was sued. No doubt there was often anxious consideration of the tactical implications of the choice. That the choice could exist is certain.[3] However, instead of making the choice, could the victim sue on both grounds? The position seemed to be that this was possible, but that the victim could bring a second action to recover only the excess due under the other delict, rather than the full amount due under both.[4]

In addition to being a law of individual delicts rather than a general law of delict,[5] the Roman law had certain further characteristics that distinguish it from

---

[1] J.4.1pr.
[2] See pp. 325–7.
[3] D.47.10.15.46.
[4] D.44.7.34pr.
[5] In fact, this ideal is not quite reached even in modern law. See *e.g.* the South African case *Chowan v Associated Motor Holdings (Pty) Ltd* 2018 (4) SA 145. On the position in the English legal tradition, see B Rudden, 'Torticles' (1991–2) 6 Tulane European and Civil Law Forum 105.

the modern law. In modern law, generally speaking delictual liability is strictly compensatory. In other words, the purpose of delict is to compensate the victim for losses suffered, rather than to punish the wrongdoer. Punishment is the role of the criminal law. In Roman law, however, the criminal jurisdiction was less well developed,[6] and instead delicts often had a penal element. Because of this, delictual liability was strictly personal. The heir of the wrongdoer could not be bound to pay a penalty arising from a delict.[7] This is quite different from modern law, where a delictual liability is essentially an ordinary debt, to which the deceased's estate is subject just like any other. Again, where there were multiple wrongdoers, each was liable in full. Because liability was penal, payment by one did not free others who participated in the wrong.[8] This is also different from modern law, where the victim is not normally entitled to recover more than has been lost.

In Justinian's account of the law of delicts, four specific delicts are identified.[9] These are: theft; robbery; liability under the *lex Aquilia* for 'loss wrongfully caused'; and liability for insult under the *actio iniuriarum*. This is misleading, however; there were, in fact, several other recognised delicts. There was also a category known as quasi-delicts, which had features in common with delicts but which were thought not to fit into the law of delicts for one reason or another.

In this chapter, we consider one of the two most important delicts, liability under the *lex Aquilia* for loss wrongfully caused. In the next chapter, we consider the other main delict, liability for insult. The other delicts are considered in Chapter 24, and the quasi-delicts in Chapter 26. To keep things as simple as they may be, we will be assuming throughout this chapter and Chapters 23 and 24 that the defender personally is the one alleged to be responsible for the wrongdoing. There are situations in which a person might be held liable for another's wrongdoing, but these have been considered separately.[10]

B. The *Lex Aquilia*

(1) Introduction

The *lex Aquilia* was a statute[11] on the basis of which there was liability for wrongful damage to the property of another. It is not possible to date the *lex Aquilia* with complete certainty,[12] but the traditionally accepted date is around 287 BC. Even if the true date is somewhat later than this, though, it is well before the classical period of Roman law, and extremely early for a statute making major reforms to private law. In its developed form, at any rate, Aquilian liability (as we may

---

[6] On the Roman criminal law and its administration, see A Lintott, 'Crime and Punishment' in D Johnston ed, *The Cambridge Companion to Roman Law* (Cambridge University Press 2015).
[7] D.50.17.38. J.4.3.9 links this rule specifically to the penal element.
[8] D.9.2.11.2.
[9] J.4.1pr.
[10] See pp. 155–6.
[11] Specifically of the *concilium plebis*. On the *concilium plebis*, see pp. 11–12, 13.
[12] See D Ibbetson, 'The Dating of the *Lex Aquilia*' in *Judge and Jurist*.

call liability under the *lex Aquilia*) provided a broad basis for liability for property damage. Thus, as Ulpian explains, it superseded earlier delictual remedies concerned with such damage: 'The *lex Aquilia* derogated from all previous laws concerned with wrongful loss, whether in the Twelve Tables or otherwise. It is not now necessary to refer to these laws.'[13]

A pursuer seeking damages under the *lex Aquilia* would sue using the action called the *actio legis Aquiliae*.[14] This had a special rule that the defender had to pay double damages if he or she denied liability, but was found liable.[15] As we shall see below, the *lex Aquilia* was originally narrower in scope than it came to be. Much of this development came through juristic interpretation, but much also came from the praetor allowing, on special cause shown, an *actio in factum* or *actio utilis*[16] where justice demanded a remedy but the facts did not quite fall within the statutory action on the *lex Aquilia* itself. In time, particular types of fact situation came to be seen as entitling a pursuer to an *actio in factum*, and the practical difference was probably simply that the double damages rule did not apply to an *actio in factum*. It was therefore preferable to use the statutory action where possible.

We are concerned here with the delict that Justinian, above, calls 'loss wrongfully caused' (*damnum iniuria datum*), because it consists of these three elements:

- loss (*damnum*) on the part of the pursuer;
- wrongful conduct on the part of the defender (*iniuria*; sometimes the term *culpa* (fault) is used);
- the loss was caused (*datum*) by that conduct of the defender.

We shall see each of these in more detail below. First, though, we need to take a closer look at the wording of the *lex Aquilia*.

(2) Contents

The *lex Aquilia* was divided into three sections, or 'chapters'.[17] Only the first and third are relevant here. The content of the second chapter was unknown until 1816, when Gaius' *Institutes* were rediscovered, putting to an end centuries of (as it turned out, wildly erroneous) scholarly speculation. The second chapter was

---

[13] D.9.2.1pr.
[14] There is some doubt whether this was a single procedural formula, or whether the pursuer had to choose in advance between suing on one of the two relevant chapters of the *lex* that are outlined below. See P Birks, 'The Model Pleading of the Action for Wrongful Loss' (1990–2) 25–7 Irish Jurist (NS) 311.
[15] G.4.9. Presumably if the defender admitted liability, but disputed the valuation of the loss, this did not apply, or else there would be no reason for having this as a special provision. Instead, the relevant chapters of the *lex Aquilia* could simply define the liability in this way, which, as we shall see, they do not.
[16] On the praetor's jurisdiction to allow these, see p. 51. It is not clear that there is any substantial difference between these two terms. Certainly, the jurists seem to treat them as interchangeable, although J.4.3.16 makes a distinction.
[17] At least, that is what has come down to us. We do not have the statute in its original form, rather only as it is quoted by the jurists. It is not clear where the rule imposing double damages where liability was denied, mentioned above, was found. It is possible that it was in a further chapter.

concerned with the case of an *adstipulator*[18] who wrongfully released a creditor, and therefore has nothing at all to do with the subject matter we are concerned with here.

(a) First Chapter
As it is reported by Gaius, the first chapter of the *lex Aquilia* provided as follows:

> If anyone wrongfully kills a male or female slave belonging to another, or a four-footed animal of the class of cattle, let him be condemned to pay the most that it was worth in the previous year.[19]

Chapter 1, then, is fairly narrow in scope. It is concerned specifically with the killing of a slave or of an animal of a certain class. There seems to have been some debate as to exactly what kinds of animal were included. The settled position was that chapter 1 only included in its scope domestic grazing animals. Thus, bears, lions and panthers were wild, and so were not covered.[20] Gaius considers elephants and camels to be of a problematic 'mixed' nature: they are naturally wild, but are nonetheless used as draught animals. His conclusion is that they are within the scope of chapter 1. There seems also to have been debate about the status of pigs. Partially on the basis of a passage in the Greek poet Homer's *Odyssey*,[21] Justinian classes pigs as grazing animals, and so as within the scope of chapter 1.[22] Domestic animals that did not graze, such as dogs, were not included.[23]

A notable feature of the first chapter is the requirement for the wrongdoer to pay 'the most that [the property] was worth in the previous year'.[24] The jurists consider this as a penal provision of the *lex Aquilia*, sometimes giving the pursuer more than he or she has actually lost. Anything that made the slave or animal more valuable could be included. Various examples are given.[25] For instance, a skilled painter who had lost a thumb in the previous year would be valued as if he still had the thumb. Where a slave had previously had a good character, but his or her character had deteriorated in the previous year, the slave would be valued on the basis of the previous good character. It is more likely, though, that the purpose of this rule was to take into account fluctuations in value over the course of a year. It is likely, for example, that demand pushed up the market value of slaves

---

[18] G.3.215. On *adstipulatio*, see p. 278.
[19] D.9.2.2pr.
[20] D.9.2.2.2.
[21] This poem, probably written around the late eighth century BC, recounts the wanderings and return home of the Greek hero, Odysseus, after the Fall of Troy. As we saw at p. 4, the Fall of Troy was an important part of Rome's foundation myth.
[22] J.4.3.1. See, however, G McLeod, 'Pigs, Boars and Livestock under the *Lex Aquilia*' in J W Cairns and O F Robinson eds, *Critical Studies in Ancient Law, Comparative Law and Legal History* (Hart 2001), who argues that there was never any problem with the inclusion of domestic pigs, and that the controversy was originally over wild boars kept in enclosures.
[23] J.4.3.1.
[24] The year was counted back from the date of the injury that caused the death, even if death did not actually occur until some time later: D.9.2.51.2.
[25] The examples that follow are taken from D.9.2.23.3–6.

for agricultural labour at harvest time. By contrast, in the winter, when there is less work needing done, such a slave's market value would likely be lower.[26]

(b) Third Chapter

As reported by Ulpian, the third chapter of the *lex Aquilia* said:

> In the case of all other things other than slaves or cattle that have been killed, if anyone causes loss to another, by wrongfully burning, breaking or rending his property, let him be condemned to pay as much as that thing will be worth in the nearest thirty days.[27]

There are uncertainties as to the scope and meaning of this provision.

First, in the form in which we have it, the third chapter extends to all property damage that does not fall within the first chapter. It has been suggested, however, that chapter 3 was originally much narrower in scope, either applying at first only to inanimate objects or else only to damage to slaves and livestock that fell short of killing.[28] Numerous different positions have been taken on this issue and on the others mentioned here, each supported by strong arguments but also opposed by strong counter-arguments.

Second, the verbs used for the damage caused – 'burning, breaking or rending' – are quite strong, and perhaps suggest an intention that chapter 3 should only cover quite serious damage, amounting to destruction or near-destruction of the property. By juristic interpretation, however, the scope of the third chapter was broadened substantially. As Gaius says: 'by rending [*ruptum*] we understand spoiling [*corruptum*] in any way'.[29] For example, if I spill your wine on the floor, it is spoiled for human consumption even though it is not physically damaged, and so this falls within the third chapter. Again, Ulpian tells us that, if corn is wrongfully mixed up with something else, such as sand, with the result that separation is difficult, the owner of the corn can recover damages under the third chapter.[30] Indeed, the praetor might be willing to go even further, and grant an *actio in factum*, by analogy with the third chapter, when loss had occurred without anything that could be described as damage to the property. For example, suppose that there is a wild boar caught in my trap. You release the boar with the result that it ceases to be mine.[31] Proculus says that I have an *actio in factum* against you for my loss.[32] Again, suppose that you startle my cattle into running off. As a result of this, the cattle fall into the hands of thieves and so are lost to me. Ulpian says that I can have an *actio in factum* against you.[33]

---

[26] For an alternative view of the purpose of this provision, see Zimmermann, *Obligations* 961–2.
[27] D.9.2.27.5.
[28] See *e.g.* D Daube, 'On the Third Chapter of the *Lex Aquilia*' (1936) 52 LQR 253.
[29] G.3.217.
[30] D.9.2.27.20. In appropriate cases, there could also be an argument that *commixtio* has occurred. See pp. 237–8.
[31] As we saw at p. 220, wild animals are owned only as long as possession is retained, or at least, the animal having escaped, it is pursued with a reasonable chance of success.
[32] D.41.1.55.
[33] D.47.2.50.4.

Third, there are difficulties with the reference to the 'nearest thirty days'.[34] Does the word translated here as 'nearest' (*proximis*) mean 'next' or 'previous'? In other words, are damages to be calculated by reference to the next thirty days or the previous thirty days? On one view, which makes particular sense if the third chapter originally only applied to living things, this is a reference to the next thirty days and links to the first chapter of the *lex Aquilia*.[35] Suppose that I own a slave. The slave is injured through your fault. Even if the slave does not die immediately, he may well die later from the wound. Such things are not predictable. On this view, I need to wait thirty days from the occurrence of the injury. If the slave has died from the wound, I sue you under the first chapter. If not, I sue under the third chapter, on the basis of the reduction in the slave's value measured at the end of the thirty days. It has to be said that this interpretation seems less apt for damage to inanimate property, although of course even there the extent of the damage may not immediately be obvious. For example, suppose that you negligently run your wagon into mine. It may be that there is no immediately apparent damage. However, it is entirely conceivable that the collision has weakened a wheel or an axle, with the result that it breaks a little later. It may have been supposed that thirty days was enough time for any such latent damage to emerge.

An alternative view of the 'thirty-day' rule is that it was intended to refer to the thirty days preceding the damage.[36] In other words, on this view, the thirty-day rule in the third chapter worked in the same way as the one-year rule in the first chapter, except that the highest value in the previous thirty days was taken rather than the highest in the previous year. This was the approach of the classical[37] and Justinianic[38] law, in terms of which damages payable were to be based on the diminution in the property's value from the highest point that it had reached in the previous thirty days.

C. Requirements for Liability

(1) Loss

Both chapter 1 and chapter 3 of the *lex Aquilia* clearly envisage that the pursuer will have suffered loss, and this is indeed a requirement. As we have seen, the pursuer's loss was measured somewhat differently depending on which chapter it fell under.

---

[34] For discussion, see Zimmermann, *Obligations* 963–9.
[35] D Daube, 'On the Third Chapter of the *Lex Aquilia*' (1936) 52 LQR 253.
[36] G MacCormack, 'On the Third Chapter of the Lex Aquilia' (1970) 5 Irish Jurist (NS) 164. If the third chapter was intended originally to cover only destruction or near-destruction of property, this would be the highest value the property had had in the previous thirty days. Otherwise, perhaps it would be only the diminution of value from that high point.
[37] G.3.218.
[38] J.4.3.15.

In both cases, damages were based on the financial loss only, not any sentimental loss.[39] Equally, speculative losses were excluded. For example, if a fisherman's nets were damaged, 'no account is to be taken of the fish which were not caught because of the damage, as it is so uncertain whether they would have been caught'.[40]

Damages, however, were not limited strictly to the valuation of the physical damage. Consequential losses (called *damnum emergens*) were also included. For example, if a slave had been named in someone's will as that person's heir, and that slave was then killed by another's fault, the loss to the master of the inheritance would be recoverable.[41] Where a slave had embezzled from the master, and the slave's death had denied the master power to interrogate the slave to discover his accomplices, this additional loss would be recoverable.[42] If I had agreed to sell a slave, and became liable to pay the purchaser a penalty as a result of the slave's death, I would be able to recover that penalty from the wrongdoer who caused the slave's death.[43] The same might also even be true of the value of other property belonging to the same owner, if its value was reduced. Paul, for instance, gives the example of the case where one of a troupe of actors or musicians or one of a pair of mules is killed. If the slaves or animals had been trained to work together, that would raise the value of all of them. Damages would therefore be recoverable for the reduction in value of the survivors.[44] One thing that is less clear, however, is how or whether account was taken of any residual value of the damaged property. For example, suppose you wrongfully kill my pig, in circumstances where I can nonetheless sell the pig's meat. Is the money I receive for that meat to be deducted from the compensation that I can claim from you? The Roman texts do not directly address this question.[45]

(2) Fault

The *lex Aquilia* did not hold a person liable for damage unless he or she was at fault.[46] It is not completely clear how much fault was required – Ulpian says that 'even the slightest degree of fault' counts,[47] but more commonly only reasonable diligence was said to be required[48] – but on any view there had to be at least

---

[39] This appears to differ from modern Scots law. See *e.g. Lockhart v Cunninghame* (1870) 8 SLR 151; Stair, *Institutions* 2.1.39. Different approaches have been taken in different countries. See A J Verheij, 'Compensation of *Pretium Affectionis* – A Constitutional Necessity?' (2004) 67 THRHR 394.

[40] D.9.2.29.3.

[41] D.9.2.23pr.

[42] D.9.2.23.4. It would, of course, be very hard to prove. In many cases, recovery of this additional loss would require proof of who the accomplices were anyway, in which case the death of the slave has cost nothing extra in this regard.

[43] D.9.2.22pr.

[44] D.9.2.22.1.

[45] H Dondorp, 'Residual Value and Assessment of Damages under the *Lex Aquilia*' (2019) 87 TvR 1.

[46] J.4.3.3. The term used in modern law for fault-free liability is 'strict liability'. For discussion of the Roman requirements for fault, see G MacCormack, 'Aquilian *Culpa*' in A Watson ed, *Daube Noster*: Essays in Legal History for David Daube (Scottish Academic Press 1974).

[47] D.9.2.44pr.

[48] See *e.g.* D.9.2.31.

something that could be described as fault. Thus, there was no liability where the damage was accidental. For example:

> When some people were playing ball, one of them pushed a slave boy when he was trying to pick up the ball, and the slave fell and broke his leg. It was asked, whether the slave's master could sue the one by whose push he had fallen under the *lex Aquilia*. I answered that he could not, because the thing seemed to have happened more by accident than wrongfully.[49]

Equally, self-defence was a complete defence to an action under the *lex Aquilia*.[50] Again, someone who committed damage under great necessity was not considered to be at fault. Thus, Ulpian reports: 'Celsus writes about the one who, to prevent a fire reaching his own house, pulled down his neighbour's house',[51] and was not held liable under the *lex Aquilia*.[52]

What none of this tells us, however, is what fault actually means. It seems certain that the meaning of fault developed over time.[53] In the classical law, there was no single, clear definition of fault.[54] The test for fault, whatever else it may be, is however an objective one. A person cannot plead in defence his or her own weakness or inexperience:

---

[49] D.9.2.52.4 (Alfenus). There was a general view that injuries incurred in sporting contests were not actionable. This did not apply, though, to injuries to spectators or, for example, to a participant in a boxing match who had surrendered: D.9.2.7.4.

[50] D.9.2.4. See also D.43.16.1.27. The right to self-defence did not extend beyond what was necessary to protect oneself and did not exclude liability to a bystander who was accidentally struck: D.9.2.45.4.

[51] D.9.2.49.1.

[52] See also D.9.2.29.3 (freeing of a ship entangled with another's ropes by cutting those ropes, where there was no other way of releasing it). It is interesting to compare the US case *Vincent v Lake Erie Transportation Company* (1910) 109 Minn. 456, 124 N.W. 221. In this case, a storm arose while the defendants' ship was unloading at the plaintiffs' dock, of such severity that the ship could not safely leave. Accordingly, the ship's master kept the ship moored at the dock until the storm abated, with the result that the dock was damaged by being repeatedly struck by the ship. It was held that the master's actions had been entirely appropriate in the circumstances but that, nonetheless, the defendants were liable for the damage. O'Brien J said (at para 17): 'having thus preserved the ship at the expense of the dock, it seems to us that her owners are responsible to the dock owners to the extent of the injury inflicted'. Again, at para 20, he said: 'Theologians hold that a starving man may, without moral guilt, take what is necessary to sustain life; but it could hardly be said that the obligation would not be upon such person to pay the value of the property so taken when he became able to do so.' In other words, the decision proceeds on the basis that a person who does what is necessary does nothing wrong, but is nonetheless obliged to make good any loss resulting from that. Perhaps the difficulty Ulpian and Celsus have here is the quasi-penal nature of the *lex Aquilia*, and the idea of moral wrongdoing at the heart of the idea of fault that this entails. Reasoning rather closer to that in *Vincent v Lake Erie Transportation Company* was to be found in the *lex Rhodia de iactu*, incorporated into Roman law in the late Republic. In terms of this, where goods had to be jettisoned to save a ship, the loss was to be divided between those whose goods had been jettisoned and those whose goods had not been jettisoned. Again, here, a master who has done what is necessary is held not to have done wrong, but the owner of the goods is nonetheless to be compensated. On the *lex Rhodia de iactu*, see Zimmermann, *Obligations* 406–9.

[53] See *e.g.* G MacCormack, 'Aquilian *Culpa*' in A Watson ed, *Daube Noster: Essays in Legal History for David Daube* (Scottish Academic Press 1974); M Floriana Cursi, 'What Did *Occidere Iniuria* in the *Lex Aquilia* Actually Mean?' (2011) 7 Roman Legal Tradition 16.

[54] H Scott, 'Pits and Pruners: *Culpa* and Social Practice in Digest 9.2' in *Judge and Jurist*.

Also if a mule-driver is not able to control his mules because of inexperience, with the result that they run over someone else's slave, he is generally held to be liable for fault. The same is true if he cannot control the mules because of physical weakness: nor does it seem unfair if weakness is counted as fault, for nobody ought to undertake what he knows or ought to know his weakness will cause to be a danger to others.[55]

One test that is found in the texts is based on the idea that a person is liable if damage arises when that person is doing something he or she is not entitled to do. Consider this passage, from Ulpian:

> But if a slave is killed by people throwing javelins for sport, the Aquilian action lies. But if when others were throwing javelins in a field, and a slave crossed that place, the Aquilian action does not lie, because he should not have crossed the javelin practice field at an inopportune moment. However, if someone deliberately aims at him, he is liable under the *lex Aquilia*.[56]

Justinian expands this case somewhat with the additional detail that the person throwing the javelin is a soldier, doing so in a designated practice field.[57] Because the soldier is doing what he has the right to do, he is only liable if he intentionally aims at the slave.[58] We see the same test in another case, in which a man has hired out his mules for the carrying of a fixed maximum weight. The mules were injured when the hirer loaded them with a greater weight than this. It was said that the owner had an action under the *lex Aquilia*.[59] Alan Watson points out:

> it does not necessarily follow that a person acting outside the terms of his contract is negligent or fraudulent. The mules may well, wrongly, appear to a *diligens paterfamilias* able to carry a particular burden which exceeds the limit fixed in the contract.[60]

In other words, the reason that the hirer is held liable is not that he has been careless. Rather, he is liable because he did something that he was not entitled to do, and damage resulted. It may be that this was the original requirement. After all, the part of the phrase *damnum iniuria datum* that relates to fault is the word *iniuria*, which is related to the word *ius* ('law' or 'right'). Something that is *iniuria* is, therefore, something that is not lawful or is not right.

---

[55] D.9.2.8.1 (Gaius).
[56] D.9.2.9.4.
[57] J.4.3.4.
[58] There is in this case also the issue of the slave himself doing something that is dangerous. We shall see this point again below, when we consider causation.
[59] D.19.2.30.2.
[60] Watson, *Obligations* 237. A *diligens paterfamilias* is a careful (i.e. non-negligent) *paterfamilias*.

In other cases, a different test is applied. Paul gives the following case:

> If a pruner threw a branch down from a tree . . . and killed a slave passing underneath, he is liable if it happened in a public place, unless he shouted a warning so that the accident could have been avoided. But Mucius says that, even if it happened on private land, he could be pursued if at fault. He thinks that there is fault when what would have been foreseen by a careful person was not foreseen, or the warning was too late for the accident to be avoided. According to that reasoning, it does not matter much whether the deceased was going through a public or a private place, as people often go through private places. But if there is no path, the defender should only be held liable for deliberate wrongdoing, for he should not throw anything at someone he sees passing by. But he is not to be considered at fault when he could not have predicted that someone was about to pass through that place.[61]

The test here seems to be: was the damage a reasonably foreseeable result of what the defender did? If so, he or she is liable. As we shall see below, this is very similar to the modern test for negligence, and may well have played a role in its development.

(3) Causation

Finally, for there to be liability for the loss, it had to be shown that the defender's misconduct was the cause of the pursuer's loss. This is an idea that is familiar in modern law: regardless of whether I have been careless, I will not be liable if you would have suffered the same loss either way.[62] As in modern law,[63] it was not necessary for the seriousness of the damage to have been foreseeable, as opposed to the occurrence of the accident being foreseeable. For example, suppose that I attack your slave. Unknown to me, the slave is a haemophiliac, and dies from his injuries. I am liable for the death, even though most people would not have died from those injuries: I must take my victim as I find him or her.[64]

The defender's misconduct would usually be a positive action, such as throwing a javelin or a branch that hits someone, but could be an omission where the defender had some form of duty to act but did not do so.[65] For example, a doctor who neglected a patient's aftercare would be liable,[66] as would someone whose

---

[61] D.9.2.31.
[62] See *e.g. Barnett v Chelsea and Kensington Hospital Management Committee* [1969] 1 QB 428 for an (English) example of this principle. I may of course be *criminally* liable for my misconduct, even if it has not led to any injury, but that is a different matter.
[63] See *e.g. Hughes v Lord Advocate* 1963 SC (HL) 31.
[64] D.9.2.7.5. This is sometimes known as the 'thin skull rule', and applies also in modern law. See *e.g. Simmons v British Steel plc* 2004 SC (HL) 94.
[65] For discussion, see D McCusker, 'Liability for Omission under the *Lex Aquilia*' (1999) 50 NILQ 380, especially at 382: 'It is suggested that the jurists did not consider the matter in such distinct terms at all [i.e. distinguishing between acts and omissions], but rather that they sought simply to identify a *blameworthy* source of the loss incurred, irrespective of whether that source strictly acted or omitted to act.'
[66] D.9.2.8pr.

job it was to watch a furnace but failed to do so, with the result that the house caught fire.[67]

There could be evidential difficulties in determining causation. The jurist Paul gives the example of two slaves jumping over some burning straw. They bump into each other and fall into the fire, and one of the slaves is burned to death. If it cannot be determined which slave knocked the other over, liability under the *lex Aquilia* cannot be established.[68]

In earlier law, the requirement for causation was very strict: the damage had to be caused *corpore corpori*, 'by the body to the body'. In other words, the damage had to be inflicted by direct physical force.[69] However, by juristic interpretation and the grant of *actiones in factum* (it is not always clear which is in play in a particular case), the requirement came to be considerably relaxed. For example, the damage might have been caused to the body but not by the body, in other words the property might have been damaged without direct infliction of physical force. Into this category would fall cases where someone shuts up another's slave or animal so that it dies of starvation, overworks a draught animal so that is injured, or induces someone else's slave to climb up a tree, from which the slave falls and is injured or killed.[70] Likewise, if I startled your horse while your slave was riding it, with the result that the slave was thrown off and killed, or I caused your cattle to stampede and run off a cliff, you would have an *actio in factum* against me.[71] In some cases, the Romans made a distinction between killing and furnishing the cause of death.[72] For example, suppose a midwife provided a drug to a woman in her care, from which the woman died. If the drug was directly administered by the midwife, the midwife was liable for having killed. If, however, the midwife only gave the drug to the woman for her to take it herself, the midwife had only furnished the cause of death and was liable only through an *actio in factum*.[73] The distinction made here may appear artificial, but the issue is a real one. All legal systems have to face eventually the problem of when the victim's own voluntary acts should be held to interrupt the chain of causation.[74]

There were also cases where liability was imposed for loss caused by the body but not to the body, in other words where there is direct infliction of bodily force, but the property is not actually physically damaged. Ulpian reports such a case:

> If someone knocks coins from my hand, Sabinus thinks that the action under the *lex Aquilia* applies if they are lost without coming into someone else's hands, for example if they fall into a river or the sea or a drain.[75]

---

[67] D.9.2.27.9.
[68] D.9.2.45.3.
[69] J.4.3.16.
[70] J.4.3.16.
[71] D.9.2.9.3; D.47.2.51.
[72] For discussion, see N H Andrews, '"*Occidere*" and the Lex Aquilia' (1987) 46 Cam LJ 315.
[73] D.9.2.9pr.
[74] For an interesting example, in a different context, see *Khaliq v HM Advocate* 1984 JC 23.
[75] D.9.2.27.21.

The coins themselves are not damaged here, but they are nonetheless irretrievably lost. It is therefore appropriate to hold the person who has caused that loss liable for it.

Finally – and this category was certainly the last one to be recognised – there might sometimes be liability where there was neither direct infliction of force nor physical harm, that is the loss was neither by the body nor to the body. We have already seen two examples of this above, when we considered the scope of the third section of the *lex Aquilia*. These were the release of an animal from a trap, so that it escapes, and the causing of animals to stampede and come into the hands of thieves. Another example would be releasing a slave from his chains and letting him escape.[76]

Situations could arise where there were multiple causes of the same injury. This was straightforward enough where there were two or more assailants acting together: each would be held liable unless it could be clearly determined which of them had caused death.[77] Suppose, though, that a wound is inflicted that is likely to prove fatal but, while the victim is dying, another person independently comes onto the scene and finishes off the job. Ulpian reports the following:

> Celsus writes that, if someone inflicts a mortal wound, and another finishes the victim off, the first of them will not be held liable for having killed, but for having wounded, because he died from the other's wound. The other will be held liable, because he killed. That is how it seems to Marcellus, and it is the more likely opinion.[78]

Compare, though, the following passage from Julian:

> A slave had been injured, such that it was certain that he would die of the wound. In the meantime, he was instituted as someone's heir and then died from another wound. The question was whether both attackers can be pursued under the *lex Aquilia* for having killed him. He [the jurist] answered: he is generally said to have killed if he has furnished the cause of death in any way. But under the *lex Aquilia* he is only held liable if he has caused death by the application of force and, so to speak with his own hand ... On the other hand, under the *lex Aquilia* not only those who have wounded so as to deprive of life immediately, but also those who inflict a wound that is certain to be fatal, are held liable. Therefore, if someone mortally wounds a slave, and then later another wounds him so that he dies earlier than he otherwise would have done, it is settled that both attackers are liable for killing. This is supported by the authority of the ancient jurists who, when a slave had been wounded by a number of people, such that it was not clear which wound killed him, held all of the attackers to be liable under the *lex Aquilia*.[79]

---

[76] J.4.3.16.
[77] D.9.2.51.1.
[78] D.9.2.11.3.
[79] D.9.2.51pr–1. For a short discussion, see H Ankum, 'The Functions of Expressions with *Utilitatis Causa* in the Works of the Classical Roman Lawyers' (2010) 16 Fundamina 5, 8–10.

Julian goes on to tell us that the measure of damages will (or at least may) be different for the two attackers. The reason for this is that damages for killing a slave are, as we have seen, based on the highest value the slave had in the year preceding the injury. If the two injuries happened a significant amount of time apart, that may lead to a different valuation. For example, in the specific facts discussed by Julian, only in the case of the second attacker would the value of the inheritance be included. There is, though, a clear conflict between these two texts. According to the opinion reported by Ulpian, only the second attacker will be liable for killing, and the first only for wounding. According to Julian, both are liable for killing. There is no obvious way of resolving the conflict, and both approaches are defensible on different grounds. On the one hand, the first attacker has simply not, as a matter of fact, caused the death. Ulpian's opinion is therefore preferable from the point of view of strict logic. Equally, Julian's analogy with the case where attackers are acting in concert is far from convincing. Again, there is the difficulty of knowing whether either wound would in fact have proved fatal on its own. On the other hand, if the penal approach of the *lex Aquilia* is borne in mind, it makes sense to hold a person responsible for the natural consequences of his or her actions, and not to excuse that person of those consequences just because a third party has fortuitously intervened.[80]

Another situation that caused difficulty was the case where the injured party's own fault contributed to the loss. Ulpian reports the following case:

> Mela writes that, when some people were playing with a ball, one of them hit it hard and it hit the hand of a barber, such that the throat of a slave that the barber was shaving was cut by the jerking of the razor. On which of them does fault lie, such that he is subject to the *lex Aquilia*? Proculus says that the barber is at fault, and surely it will be imputed to him if he was shaving there, where it was the custom to play or where many were going to and fro. But it is not said badly in reply that, if someone entrusts himself to a barber who has his chair in a dangerous place, he has only himself to blame.[81]

This is a complex case. No clear answer to the question posed is possible, and none is given. It becomes even more difficult if the possibility is added that the person who struck the ball might be liable, as that brings in issues of multiple causes. The approach taken in the quoted passage is the jurists' typical, casuistic style,[82] and in practice everything would depend on the analysis of the facts of the specific case.[83] The point for the present, though, is that the conduct of the injured party is seen as simply part of the causal background of the injury.

---

[80] For discussion of Julian's view, particularly with reference to *Fairchild v Glenhaven Funeral Services Ltd* [2003] 1 AC 32 (discussed below), see H Scott, 'Killing and Causing Death in Roman Law' (2013) 129 LQR 101.
[81] D.9.2.11pr.
[82] See p. 58.
[83] In practice, the outcome of many cases turns on the impression made in court by the parties and their witnesses, and this case would be very likely to fall into that category.

The question is to be answered by asking whose fault caused the injury: the barber's or the slave's? We saw the same approach above, in the case of the slave hit by a javelin while crossing the practice field. There was no liability there to a slave who caused the accident himself, by crossing the field at an inopportune moment.[84] Unlike modern law,[85] what the Romans did not have was a concept of contributory negligence, by which damages could be reduced to reflect the pursuer's contribution to the incident.

D. Extensions to Liability

We have seen that the original scope of the *lex Aquilia* was extended by both juristic interpretation and praetorian intervention. Various further extensions were also made. For example, certain non-owners, such as usufructuaries,[86] were given an analogous remedy for damage to the property.[87] A *paterfamilias* was allowed to sue for injuries to those in his power,[88] just as he could for injuries to his slaves.[89] Such developments were, however, limited to cases where the pursuer's interest in the property was in some way analogous to that of an owner. There was no general development of liability for anything like what in the modern law of delict is known as pure economic loss, where the pursuer's loss does not arise from injury to the pursuer's own property or person.[90]

More problematic is the question of whether a person could ever proceed under the *lex Aquilia* for personal injuries that he or she had suffered. As we have seen, the *lex Aquilia* was specifically directed at property damage. Accordingly, says Ulpian, 'nobody is seen as owner of his own limbs' (*dominus membrorum suorum nemo videtur*).[91] However, the same text says that a free person who has been injured is entitled to an *actio utilis*. This passage, though, has been said to be 'virtually certain' to have been 'generalized by the compilers', and to have originally referred to a person who was injured while believing himself to be a slave.[92] On this view, the extension of Aquilian liability to injuries to free persons was a post-classical development, and texts where personal injuries are considered without reference to the injured party's status were intended to be assumed to refer to slaves.[93]

---

[84] D.9.2.9.4. For general discussion of issues arising from the injured party's own conduct, see J T Laster, 'The Role of the Victim's Conduct in Assessing Fault under the *Lex Aquilia*: Insights into the Analytical Methods of Roman Jurists' (1996) 25 Anglo-Am L Rev 188.
[85] Law Reform (Contributory Negligence) Act 1945, s. 1.
[86] On usufruct, see Chapter 14.
[87] D.9.2.12.
[88] On the power of a *paterfamilias*, see pp. 116–27.
[89] D.9.2.5.3.
[90] An example of such a case is one where the damage to another person's property prevents the pursuer fulfilling a contract obligation, and thus becoming liable in damages, as in *Nacap Ltd v Moffat Plant Ltd* 1987 SLT 221. D Johnston, 'Appointments and Disappointments: *White v Jones* in Rome and Today' (2000) 53 CLP 283 discusses another situation of this kind. In modern law, pure economic loss is generally not recoverable in the law of delict, but there are exceptions.
[91] D.9.2.13pr. See also D.9.3.7 (Gaius).
[92] Zimmermann, *Obligations* 1017.
[93] See *e.g.* D.9.2.7.7; D.9.2.11.5; D.9.2.52.1.

E. The Lex *Aquilia* and Modern Law

The specific rules of the *lex Aquilia* were never directly received into the *ius commune*.[94] For example, the rules for assessing damages contained in the first and third chapters were never received into later law, nor was there any rule of double damages where liability was denied. Instead, the jurists' discussion of issues of principle, such as the meaning of fault and causation, were used as the basis for a more general rule of liability for damage caused through the fault of the defender. This applied both to damage to property and to personal injuries.[95]

The influence of those developments was also felt in Scotland. The law of Scotland in this area was by no means fully developed in the time of the institutional writers.[96] However, it certainly had a foundation on which a principled modern system could be built. Erskine, for example, gives this statement of general principle:

> *Alterum non laedere* is one of the three general precepts laid down by Justinian, which it has been the chief purpose of all civil enactments to enforce. In consequence of this rule, every one who has the exercise of reason, and so can distinguish between right and wrong, is naturally obliged to make up the damage befalling his neighbour from a wrong committed by himself. Wherefore every fraudulent contrivance, or unwarrantable act, by which another suffers damage, or runs the hazard of it, subjects the delinquent to reparation.[97]

The case of *Donoghue v Stevenson*[98] is seen as the foundation of the modern law in this area. In that case, the pursuer had gone with a friend to the Wellmeadow Café in Paisley. The friend bought her a bottle of ginger beer that had been manufactured by the defender. When the pursuer had drunk part of the contents of the bottle, a decomposing snail was allegedly discovered in it. She claimed to have become ill as a result, and sued the defender.[99] In the House of Lords, she was successful by a 3–2 majority.[100]

Stated like this, it is not obvious why the case is so important, why it was necessary to fight it all the way to the House of Lords, or why the pursuer was only successful by such a narrow margin. It seems unlikely on the basis of what has

---

[94] See Chapter 4.
[95] On these developments, see Zimmermann, *Obligations* 1017–49.
[96] See especially Bankton, whose treatment of personal injury focuses on the (now obsolete) native delict of assythment. Although he draws heavily on texts relating to the *lex Aquilia*, he applies them only to damage to property (*Institutes* 1.10.40–9).
[97] Erskine, *Institute* 3.1.13. *Alterum non laedere* can be translated as 'Do not harm another'. See also Stair, *Institutions* 1.9.4 and 1.9.6.
[98] 1932 SC (HL) 31.
[99] She could not have successfully sued the café owner: she had not bought the ginger beer, and so she had no contractual remedy against him; equally, she had no delictual remedy against him because, the bottle being opaque and sealed, he had no way of detecting the presence of the snail. He was not, therefore, at fault.
[100] This was a decision on relevancy. That is to say, it was a decision that, if the pursuer could prove all that she alleged, she would be entitled to the remedy she sought. As the case was then settled out of court, the pursuer was never called on actually to prove that the snail had been there.

been said above that Stair or Erskine would have been altogether surprised by the pursuer's success, and certainly the general principle of liability for injuries caused by fault, based on the principles of the *lex Aquilia*, was well established by the end of the 1700s.[101] What, after all, could be more in accordance with principle than to hold a supplier of goods, whose negligence has introduced a defect into those goods, responsible for injury resulting from that defect?

The answer lies in developments between the 1700s and 1932, when *Donoghue* was decided. During that period, the general principles of liability for loss caused by fault, on which the institutional writers drew in their accounts, had become obscured by the adoption from English law of different special rules for specific situations. If what follows contains criticisms of the English law, these should not be taken to imply criticism of the English system as a whole. Instead, they should be taken as arising from a Scots lawyer's frustration that, at a time when Scots law had the tools to allow it to cope better with these issues, these tools were needlessly cast away in favour of English rules that were – to say the least – no better.

For example, it has long been settled law that an employer is liable to victims of injury caused by the negligence of employees in the course of their employment. In English law, however, a rule developed that this did not apply where the victim was a co-worker of the negligent employee. This was known as the doctrine of common employment. The justification for this doctrine was that, by taking up employment, a person voluntarily accepted the risk that some other person employed, now or in the future, to work over, under or alongside him, might negligently injure him.[102] This justification can only be described as fanciful, but it was happily no part of the law of Scotland, which was able to decide such cases in accordance with general principles. It was, however, imposed on Scotland by the House of Lords in *Bartonshill Coal Co v Reid*.[103] In that case, a mineworker had been killed at work through the negligence of a co-worker. His widow and children sued the employer for damages. After reviewing the English authorities on common employment, Lord Chancellor Cranworth had the following to say:

> but if such be the law of England, on what ground can it be argued not to be the law of Scotland? The law, as established in England, is founded on principles of universal application, not on any peculiarities of English jurisprudence; and unless, therefore, there has been a settled course of decision in Scotland to the contrary, I think it would be most inexpedient to sanction a different rule to the north of the Tweed from that which prevails to the south.[104]

---

[101] See *e.g. Innes v Magistrates of Edinburgh* (1798) Mor 13189, a personal injury case, in which reliance was placed on Roman authorities. For discussion of this whole area, see H MacQueen and W D H Sellar, 'Negligence' in *History of Private Law*, vol II.

[102] In principle, the same would apply to female employees, but the masculine is largely justified here: overwhelmingly, at this time, those vulnerable to workplace accidents were men working in dangerous jobs.

[103] (1858) 3 Macq 266.

[104] At p. 285. The point might well have been made here that, if the law was to be the same in both Scotland and England, it is not obvious why the English rule should necessarily be the one adopted. Unsurprisingly, however, the point was not taken.

Reduced to its essentials, the reasoning here is this: if English law has adopted a rule, then the English rule is presumptively the law of all civilised countries, and so is to be applied unless there is unequivocal authority to the contrary. It would be hard to conceive of a more insular and parochial approach. It took another ninety years for the obvious, that the rule is contrary to justice, principle and common sense, to be realised sufficiently for the rule to be abolished (for both Scotland and England).[105]

Another example is the law of occupiers' liability. In Scots law, where a person was injured while on another's land, the same general principle of liability for fault applied as in other cases. This afforded Scots law the flexibility to deal with each case on its own merits, as justice demanded. Whether a person was a trespasser, for example, would be relevant to questions such as whether it was foreseeable that they would be present, but it would not by itself be conclusive. Sometimes justice would demand reparation for an injury, even when the injured party was a trespasser.[106] In English law, by contrast, it was necessary to categorise injured parties according to a rigid classification into licensees, invitees and trespassers. This approach was imposed on Scots law by the House of Lords in *Dumbreck v Robert Addie & Sons (Collieries) Ltd*.[107] In that case, a four-year-old boy had entered land occupied by the defenders. He was killed when employees of the defenders started up some mining machinery without checking to make sure nobody was in the way. His father sued for damages. The defenders knew that children played on the land, and made few efforts to prevent this. There were gaps in the fencing and the machinery itself was openly accessible. Reversing the Court of Session, the House of Lords held that the four-year-old boy was a trespasser. As such, this four-year-old entered the land at his own risk, and the defenders owed no duty to take care not to injure him. The boy's father was denied damages. In England, this rule was abolished by the Occupiers' Liability Act 1957. This English rule limped on in Scotland for another three years before the UK Parliament saw fit to abolish it there as well.[108] It must be remembered that, at this time, there was no Scottish Parliament, and so Scots legislation had to be fitted into the legislative timetable of the UK Parliament.

A third example, closer to *Donoghue v Stevenson*, is in the area of product liability. In *Mullen v Barr & Co; McGowan v Barr & Co*,[109] on facts indistinguishable from those in *Donoghue v Stevenson*,[110] it was held on the basis of English authority that a manufacturer of goods owed no duty to consumers of the goods, unless he knew the goods to be dangerous and concealed the fact, or else he was a dealer in goods (such as explosives) that were dangerous in nature. In other words, it was held that a manufacturer of soft drinks had no duty to take care not to poison his customers.

---

[105] Law Reform (Personal Injuries) Act 1948, s. 1(1).
[106] For discussion, see *Stair Memorial Encyclopaedia*, vol 15 para 313.
[107] 1929 SC (HL) 51.
[108] Occupiers' Liability (Scotland) Act 1960, ss. 1–2.
[109] 1929 SC 461.
[110] The only difference was that it was a dead mouse in the bottle rather than a snail.

By the time *Donoghue v Stevenson* was decided, therefore, the law of negligence was a patchwork of specific rules, with little reference to general principle. The importance of the case, then, lies in the attempt to distil from all of the different special rules a single general principle, by which a person could be held liable for the consequences of his or her fault. This rule was formulated in *Donoghue* by Lord Atkin, in the following terms:

> The rule that you are to love your neighbour becomes in law, you must not injure your neighbour; and the lawyer's question, Who is my neighbour? receives a restricted reply. You must take reasonable care to avoid acts or omissions which you can reasonably foresee would be likely to injure your neighbour. Who, then, in law, is my neighbour? The answer seems to be – persons who are so closely and directly affected by my act that I ought reasonably to have them in contemplation as being so affected when I am directing my mind to the acts or omissions which are called in question.[111]

In formulating this doctrine, Lord Atkin relied exclusively on English and American authorities. This is a curiosity in what is, after all, a Scottish case. The outcome could have been reached on the basis of Scots authorities. Indeed, there is preserved a judgment by one of the Scottish judges in the majority of the House of Lords, Lord Macmillan, which did exactly that.[112] These were largely dropped from the judgment that he actually delivered, possibly at the instigation of Lord Atkin, who wanted to use the case to settle the point for English law.[113]

Even so, it does appear that there is a hidden debt here to Roman law. It has been suggested that the neighbour principle was in fact drawn from Erskine,[114] and it is possible that the foreseeability requirement was taken from the passage of Paul, referred to earlier, in which a pruner was held liable on the basis of foreseeability.[115] The argument has been summarised in the following terms:

> The 'neighbourhood' principle is now universally regarded as his own [*i.e.* Lord Atkin's] creation. But that is not the case. There can be no doubt that the principle was drawn from the civilian tradition, in particular from the teachings of the

---

[111] At p. 44.

[112] This judgment is contained in an appendix to A Rodger, 'Lord Macmillan's Speech in Donoghue v Stevenson' (1992) 108 LQR 236, which is a commentary on it.

[113] At p. 70 of his judgment, Lord Macmillan gives what could almost be seen as an apology for or protest about the omission: 'The prolonged discussion of English and American cases into which I have been led might well dispose your Lordships to think that I had forgotten that the present is a Scottish appeal which must be decided according to Scots law. But this discussion has been rendered inevitable by the course of the argument at your Lordships' bar, which, as I have said, proceeded on the footing that the law applicable to the case was the same in England and in Scotland.' By contrast, untroubled by the fact that the facts of the case occurred in Paisley rather than in Penzance or Peterborough, Lord Buckmaster (one of the judges in the minority) was quickly able to satisfy himself that 'it is on the English law alone that . . . we ought to proceed' (at p. 35).

[114] R Evans-Jones and H Scott, 'Lord Atkin, *Donoghue v Stevenson* and the *Lex Aquilia*: Civilian Roots of the "Neighbour" Principle' in P J du Plessis ed, *Wrongful Damage to Property in Roman Law: British Perspectives* (Edinburgh University Press 2017) 270.

[115] R Evans-Jones and H Scott, 'Lord Atkin, *Donoghue v Stevenson* and the *Lex Aquilia*: Civilian Roots of the "Neighbour" Principle' in P J du Plessis ed, *Wrongful Damage to Property in Roman Law: British Perspectives* (Edinburgh University Press 2017)271. The passage, quoted earlier, can be found at D.9.2.31.

natural lawyers. On the other hand, the restrictions placed upon it by Lord Atkin appear to have been drawn from the humanist tradition, and perhaps specifically from Donellus. These – both the principle and the restrictions – were expressions of general civilian jurisprudence which had been well known to English lawyers for hundreds of years . . . [T]he debt to the civilian tradition in *Donoghue* is beyond question, but it had to be hidden in order to ensure that the decision of the House of Lords changed English law.[116]

The Roman writings on the *lex Aquilia* remain a fruitful source of ideas today, not by direct application of the *lex Aquilia* but on account of the discussion and ideas that those writings contain. For example, in *Macdonald v Aberdeenshire Council*,[117] reference to Ulpian was made in discussing local authority liability in relation to road maintenance.[118] Another case (in fact, an English one) is *Fairchild v Glenhaven Funeral Services Ltd*.[119] In that case, the claimants were individuals who had developed mesothelioma from workplace exposure to asbestos. As they had been exposed to asbestos with more than one employer, no one employer's negligence could be conclusively proved to have caused the damage. It was held to be enough that the defendants' negligence had materially increased the risk. In support of this conclusion, Lord Rodger of Earlsferry considered[120] the Roman texts (discussed above) on injuries caused by more than one attacker, and found that the jurists considered a departure from strict rules of causation to be justified in some cases.

Chapter Summary

Roman law had a law of delicts rather than a law of delict. In other words, in principle, an injured party had to fit his or her claim into some specific category of recognised wrong, rather than relying on a general principle requiring compensation for loss caused by wrongdoing. In this chapter, we have focused on liability for damage to property, imposed by the *lex Aquilia*. Although the specific rules of the *lex Aquilia* were generally not received into later law, the Roman jurists' discussion of issues of principle, such as the concepts of fault and causation, has had an influence that is still felt in modern law.

---

[116] R Evans-Jones and H Scott, 'Lord Atkin, *Donoghue v Stevenson* and the *Lex Aquilia*: Civilian Roots of the "Neighbour" Principle' in P J du Plessis ed, *Wrongful Damage to Property in Roman Law: British Perspectives* (Edinburgh University Press 2017) 260, 262.
[117] [2013] CSIH 83, 2014 SC 114.
[118] See the Opinion of Lord Drummond Young, at para [57].
[119] [2003] 1 AC 32.
[120] At paras 157–60.

Further Reading

G.3.182, 210–19
J.4.1pr, 4.3
D.9.2; 47.1
C.3.35

P Birks, *The Roman Law of Obligations* (E Descheemaeker ed, Oxford University Press 2014) chapter 9

B W Frier, *A Casebook on the Roman Law of Delict* (Scholars Press 1989)

H MacQueen and W D H Sellar, 'Negligence' in R Zimmermann and K Reid eds, *A History of Private Law in Scotland, Volume II: Obligations* (Oxford University Press 2000)

E Metzger ed, *A Companion to Justinian's Institutes* (Duckworth 1998) 174–5, 184–92

P J du Plessis ed, *Wrongful Damage to Property in Roman Law: British Perspectives* (Edinburgh University Press 2017)

A Watson, *The Law of Obligations in the Later Roman Republic* (Oxford University Press 1965) chapter 16

R Zimmermann, *The Law of Obligations: Roman Foundations of the Civilian Tradition* (Oxford University Press 1996) chapters 29 and 30

CHAPTER TWENTY-THREE

Liability for Insulting Behaviour: The *Actio Iniuriarum*

A. Development and General Nature

The Twelve Tables made provision imposing liability for physical assaults, by way of either retaliation or fixed financial penalties depending on the circumstances. In time, however, the value of the fixed penalties declined to the point of ceasing to be any real deterrent. The story is that this was illustrated by an individual called Lucius Veratius, who amused himself by proceeding through the streets slapping passers-by on the face. He was accompanied by one of his slaves with a purse of money, from which the slave would immediately pay the victim the now-trivial statutory penalty.[1] This caused the praetors to intervene, and to allow the court[2] discretion to set the compensation to be paid according to what seemed appropriate for the particular case.

To say the least, it unfortunately cannot be taken for granted that there is any truth in this story. What is known, though, is that from perhaps around 200 BC, the Twelve Tables rules came to be superseded by praetorian edicts regulating the matter. These edicts in fact went beyond what was provided for by the Twelve Tables, and imposed general liability for wrongfully insulting conduct rather than simply for physical assaults.[3]

B. Requirements for Liability

(1) An Insulting Act

The name *iniuria* literally means something that is wrongful or which is done without right.[4] It has, however, more specific meanings in different contexts. We

---

[1] On the early developments in this area, see P B H Birks, 'The Early History of Iniuria' (1969) 37 TvR 163; A Watson, 'Personal Injuries in the XII Tables' (1975) 43 TvR 213; A K W Halpin, 'The Usage of *Iniuria* in the Twelve Tables' (1976) 11 Irish Jurist (NS) 344; J Plescia, 'The Development of "Iniuria"' (1977) 23 Labeo 271.

[2] In fact a panel of *recuperatores*, rather than the more usual single *iudex*: Cicero, *De Inventione* 2.20.59–60.

[3] There seems to have been a general edictal provision for *iniuria*, together with special provision for particular forms of insulting behaviour. In the late Republic, a *lex Cornelia de iniuriis* introduced a criminal or quasi-criminal remedy for certain types of *iniuria*. For discussion, see J Giltaij, 'The *Lex Cornelia de Iniuriis* and "Hyperlinks" in Roman Law' (2018) 24 Fundamina 21.

[4] J.4.4pr.

saw one of these in Chapter 22, in connection with the *lex Aquilia*.[5] In the area we are concerned with here, the term can reasonably be translated as 'insult'. Ulpian divides these into three categories. Every actionable insult, he says, pertains to one of three things: the body (*corpus*), a person's dignity (*dignitas*) or a person's reputation (*fama*).[6] An insult pertaining to the body would be a physical assault. As an example of an insult to dignity, Ulpian gives the act of leading off a lady's companion, the point being that it was considered improper for a lady to appear in public unescorted. An insult pertained to reputation when it placed the victim in disrepute. Ulpian's example is the making of an attempt on a woman's chastity. This might be done either by what would nowadays be called stalking or by directly propositioning the victim.[7]

Ulpian's examples of both insult to dignity and disrepute draw attention to a difficulty with understanding *iniuria*. This difficulty is that the understanding of words and acts is to a very great extent culturally dependent. There is nowadays of course no stigma in a woman being unescorted in public. Equally, behaviour might still be considered offensive but for different reasons. To us, stalking is objectionable primarily because of the fear and alarm it causes the victim. To the Romans, it was objectionable primarily because it was harmful to the victim's reputation, as implying that the victim might be receptive to the perpetrator's advances. For this reason, to act in this way towards a woman who was dressed as a respectable lady would be considered a much greater offence than to the same towards a woman dressed as a prostitute, a factor which would not seem particularly relevant to us. Viewed from the reputational perspective, however, it is obvious that a prostitute has no reputation for chastity to lose.

Iniuria is a delict of potentially very broad scope. It has to be said that Ulpian's scheme is a little artificial, and individual insults are not always easy to categorise according to it. For example, insults to the body include of course physical assaults, but what about drugging a person to the derangement of their mind? That is certainly physical harm, and it is certainly actionable.[8] Equally, however, it could be seen as inconsistent with the dignity of the victim.

Insults to a person's dignity may in very broad terms be defined as acts and words that involve a lack of proper respect for the victim and his or her social standing. This is not to say that those of low social standing could not experience this form of insult – as Ulpian observes, even slaves have feelings[9] – but it does mean that such insults to those of higher status would be seen as more serious. Treating a freeman as a slave was an insult of this kind,[10] as was interrupting him in an insulting manner as he was speaking in court.[11] Entering a house without the owner's permission was actionable, even if the purpose was to summon the

---

[5] See p. 393.
[6] D.10.1.2.
[7] D.47.10.15.22–3. Pursuing a boy who had not yet come of age would also constitute *iniuria*: G.3.220.
[8] D.47.10.15pr.
[9] D.47.10.15.35. Slaves could not, however, bring an action for *iniuria*.
[10] D.47.10.22.
[11] D.47.10.13.3.

owner to court.[12] Preventing a person selling his or her own slave was *iniuria*.[13] More generally, it was *iniuria* to interfere in a person's going about his or her lawful business, for example by preventing the victim fishing in a place where this was lawful, using the public baths, conducting business, or conversing in a public place.[14] This form of insult could also be committed indirectly, through a member of the pursuer's household. Examples are the debauching of the pursuer's female slave[15] or making his son a laughing stock by taking him into a bar or playing dice with him and, presumably, getting him drunk or causing him to gamble away his money.[16] Other such cases are the damaging of a statue set over the pursuer's father's grave,[17] the detaining or otherwise mistreating of the corpse of a person to whom the pursuer is heir,[18] and the commission of insulting acts at the deceased's funeral.[19]

Insults to reputation would certainly include false accusations of wrongdoing. The accusation might be implied, for example by wearing mourning clothes in sympathy with an accused person, which would be considered an insulting act against the accuser if done by anyone not closely related to the accused.[20] Another example is seizing a person's goods as if that person was refusing to pay his or her debts, the implication being that the victim was unable or unwilling to comply with his or her obligations.[21] We are not concerned here solely with false accusations, however. Anything directed towards another's disrepute fell within the scope of the delict.[22] Accordingly, to reveal true but embarrassing information might constitute *iniuria*, as long as this was done 'contrary to good morals' (*contra bonos mores*). Obviously, what counts as contrary to good morals will vary between different times and places. An example given by Ulpian is a case where a will has been deposited with someone for safekeeping. The depositee then reads the will out while the testator is still alive. This is actionable as *iniuria*, if done with the intention of revealing the testator's 'private judgements'.[23] Again, it was *iniuria* for people to gather together to raise a clamour (*convicium*) against someone, where this was directed *contra bonos mores* to the disrepute or unpopularity of the victim,[24] or for a person to write a lampoon to another's discredit.[25]

---

[12] D.47.10.23.
[13] D.47.10.24.
[14] D.47.10.13.7.
[15] D.47.10.25.
[16] D.47.10.26.
[17] D.47.10.27.
[18] D.47.10.1.4, 6.
[19] D.47.10.1.6. Insults falling into these categories were conceptualised differently depending on whether the heir had yet accepted the inheritance. If the heir had accepted the inheritance, the defender's actions were considered to be an insult to the heir. Otherwise, they were considered to be an insult to the deceased's estate, and only indirectly to the heir.
[20] D.47.10.39.
[21] J.4.1pr.
[22] D.47.10.15.27.
[23] D.16.3.1.38.
[24] D.47.10.15.2–5.
[25] D.47.10.15.27.

While some of these cases involve interference with the victim's property rights, *iniuria* did not protect property rights as such. Damage to or interference with property was only actionable as *iniuria* if it could properly be considered insulting. For example, Javolenus considered the case where the owner of lower premises created smoke that affected his neighbour, or the owner of upper premises threw or poured things down onto those below. This would only be *iniuria* if done with an intention to insult.[26] If property damage was caused by the perpetrator's actions, other remedies were available.[27]

(2) Intention to Insult

Not every insulting act gave rise to liability for *iniuria*. As Ulpian tells us, *iniuria* 'consists in the will of the wrongdoer',[28] so an insane person or a young child could not be held liable for *iniuria*. More generally, there was normally no liability where there was no intention to insult.[29] For example, to strike someone as a joke or during a wrestling match was not *iniuria*.[30] In the example given above, of the defender making a laughing stock of the pursuer's son or slave in a bar or in a game of dice, this was only *iniuria* if done with the intention to insult the pursuer. It was not *iniuria* if it was done without any thought of the pursuer.[31] Where the contents of someone's will were wrongfully read out, as noted above there was only liability for *iniuria* if this was done with the intention of revealing the testator's private judgements, but not otherwise.[32] The wrongful discharge of smoke or water onto a neighbour's property would constitute *iniuria* if done with an intention to insult, but not otherwise.[33] Something properly done by a magistrate was not actionable, even if someone was offended, because it was done not to insult but to vindicate public authority.[34] If I intended to strike my slave, but actually hit you, I would not be liable for *iniuria* as my intention was not to insult you (and, of course, it was perfectly lawful for me to hit my own slave).[35]

On the other hand, it appears that some acts were considered so flagrantly offensive that there would be liability for *iniuria*, even without a specific intention

---

[26] D.47.10.44. See though pp. 439–40 for quasi-delictual liability for things poured or thrown.
[27] Especially the *lex Aquilia*, on which see Chapter 22. See *e.g.* D.47.10.25.
[28] D.47.10.3.1.
[29] This at least is the conventional view. Zimmermann, *Obligations* 1060–1 is more cautious: 'A purely subjective mental element was . . . to put it cautiously, not indispensable for purposes of liability . . . [I]t is obvious from the examples contained in the Digest that the delict of iniuria only covered situations where dolus on the part of the offender could typically be presumed to have been present.' The intention requirement certainly seems to have been part of the medieval law, although there was a rebuttable presumption that insult was intended (except in certain cases of those in positions of authority or those acting in a professional capacity, such as doctors, in which case intention had to be proved) (Zimmermann, *Obligations* 1067–70).
[30] D.47.10.3.3.
[31] D.47.10.26. See though at pp. 422–3 the delict of corruption of slaves, which might be available even where there was no intention to insult.
[32] D.16.3.1.38. There might, however, be contractual liability if this was done by someone with whom the will had been deposited for safekeeping. See pp. 349–50.
[33] D.47.10.44. See also the discussion of the *actio negatoria* at p. 255.
[34] D.47.10.33.
[35] D.47.10.4.

to insult. For example, one text tells us that it was *iniuria* to enter a house without the owner's permission, even if this was done with the intention of summoning the owner to court.[36] It is, of course, highly culturally dependent what kinds of act will reach the necessary level of offensiveness, and the Romans' judgement on this will not always match our own.[37]

(3) Injury to Feelings

It was essential that the victim actually be upset by the insult. A victim who chose to ignore the insult or who came to terms with the perpetrator lost the remedy and could not revive it afterwards.[38]

(4) Lack of Justification

Not every act of the kinds described above would give rise to liability. An act that was justified would not be *iniuria*. For example, force used in self-defence would not be *iniuria*. The disclosure of a person's wrongdoing would not be *iniuria*, as long as it was not done *contra bonos mores*, 'for it is proper that the faults of the guilty be known'.[39] A person who did something authorised by a public authority would not be treated as having done it with a view to insult, 'for there is nothing wrongful in the execution of the law'.[40] We have already seen this in connection with the actions of magistrates. This was not a complete licence to insult, however, and a magistrate who abused his position in order to commit *iniuria*-type acts could nonetheless be liable.[41]

C. Bringing a Claim

(1) The Identity of the Pursuer

The remedy was not necessarily limited solely to the person who was directly insulted. A *paterfamilias* could have an action for *iniuria* for an insult to any of his children[42] or to his daughter-in-law. A husband could have an action where his wife was insulted,[43] in addition to her own action.[44]

The right of the *paterfamilias* was paramount. If the person actually insulted wanted to sue, but his or her *paterfamilias* did not, normally this excluded any remedy. It was only if the *paterfamilias* was 'vile and abject, while the son is a

---

[36] D.47.10.23.
[37] The standard term for describing an act of this kind is to say that it is 'against good morals' (*contra bonos mores*), but what counts as good morals varies from place to place and over time.
[38] J.4.4.12; D.47.10.11.1.
[39] D.47.10.18pr.
[40] D.47.10.13.1.
[41] D.47.10.32.
[42] As long as they were subject to his *potestas*.
[43] Although a wife had no remedy for an insult to her husband: 'It is right that wives should be defended by husbands, not husbands by wives': J.4.4.2.
[44] J.4.4.2; D.47.10.1.9. Where a married woman was insulted, therefore, there could potentially be four actions: by the woman herself, her husband, her own *paterfamilias* and her husband's *paterfamilias*.

decent man',[45] that the *paterfamilias* would not be allowed to value the insult by his own standards. The child in power would then be allowed to proceed. Otherwise, the decision of the *paterfamilias* would stand.

Where an insult was directed at a slave, the master could potentially sue for *iniuria*. Unlike the position with children in power, however, this was not the case for all insults. The master only had a remedy where the insult was directed at a slave 'where something atrocious occurs, manifestly in contempt of the master'.[46] Thus there would be a remedy for a severe beating or flogging, but not simply for verbal abuse or striking with a fist. The slave could not be insulted personally,[47] and so had no remedy even if later freed.[48]

(2) Specification of Claim

When bringing the action for *iniuria*, the pursuer was required to state the precise basis for the claim: 'he who brings an action for *iniuria* must state precisely what has been done that constitutes *iniuria*'.[49] The reason for this was that a person found to have committed *iniuria* thereby incurred *infamia*.[50] The legal and social consequences of this being comparatively severe, the defender was therefore entitled to expect detailed notice of what he or she was alleged to have done in order to be able to defend his or her reputation.

(3) Liability

Liability for *iniuria* was restricted to one year from the alleged insult.[51] Of course, it is highly likely that someone who did not take action before that time would be held to have let the insult go anyway. As we have seen, a victim who lets an insult go is held to have waived the insult.

Damages for *iniuria* were not based on financial loss, but on the nature and seriousness of the insult. Everyone who took part in the insulting behaviour,[52] or who even encouraged it,[53] was separately liable.

The pursuer could claim damages based on his or her own assessment of the insult. The judge, though, was not bound by this, and could award a lower sum if he thought appropriate.[54] In setting the damages payable, the judge was entitled to take into account any aggravating factor. An insult could be aggravated by the identity of the persons involved.[55] For example, an insult was considered more

---

[45] D.47.10.17.12–13.
[46] J.4.4.3.
[47] J.4.4.3.
[48] D.47.10.30pr.
[49] D.47.10.7pr.
[50] On *infamia*, see pp. 100–1.
[51] C.9.35.5 (AD 290, although reflecting existing law).
[52] D.47.10.34.
[53] J.4.4.11.
[54] G.3.224. Sometimes the praetor might impliedly make a lower assessment, by requiring the defender only to provide for a lower sum as security for appearance (*vadimonium*). When this was done, Gaius tells us, the judge would normally follow this assessment 'in deference to the praetor'. On *vadimonium*, see p. 38.
[55] J.4.4.7; G.3.225.

serious if committed against a person of higher status.[56] An insult to a person to whom the defender owed a duty of respect, such as a magistrate, parent or patron,[57] was considered more serious.[58] An assault on a slave holding a responsible position was considered more serious than one on a slave not holding such a position.[59] An insult could also be aggravated by the time or place in which it happened.[60] Thus, an insult committed in a public place was considered more serious.[61] Finally, an insult could be aggravated by its own nature,[62] for example when an assault resulted in a serious wound or was on the pursuer's face rather than body.[63]

D. *Iniuria* in Modern Law

Of the treatments of this area by the Scots institutional writers, those by Stair and Bankton are of the greatest interest.[64] Stair[65] gives an account of delict based on reparation for wrongful damage to certain identified interests. These are:

- 'Life, members and health', seeming to be concerned specifically with financial loss;[66]
- liberty;
- 'fame, reputation, and honour';[67]
- 'our content, delight, or satisfaction' in our property;
- 'goods and possession', concerned with the actual value of property.

The second and third of these seem closest to *iniuria*, and to some extent the first.

Bankton takes a different approach. For the most part, he presents the law of delict as a series of more or less specific wrongs. However, as far as the subject matter of this chapter is concerned, he describes a single, broad delict, called 'injury'.[68] The influence of Roman law is clear, as this is largely based on Roman texts and covers very much the same range of wrongful acts as *iniuria*.[69]

---

[56] J.4.4.9.
[57] On patrons and freedmen, see pp. 113–14.
[58] D.47.10.7.8.
[59] J.4.4.7.
[60] G.3.225.
[61] J.4.4.9; D.47.10.7.8.
[62] G.3.225.
[63] J.4.4.9; D.47.10.7.8, 9. A blow to the face is presumably considered more serious at least partly because a cut or bruise on the face cannot readily be concealed, with the result that the injured party would so to speak have to carry around the disgrace, for all to see, until the wound healed.
[64] Erskine has less to say. His brief account of delict at *Institute* 3.1.13–15 is mostly concerned with acts causing financial loss, although see also *Institute* 4.4.81 on statements about a person's creditworthiness.
[65] Stair, *Institutions* 1.9.4.
[66] This is justified by reference to D.9.1.3: 'the body of a free person is not subject to valuation' (Gaius).
[67] Curiously, the Roman texts cited in support of this (D.42.5.31.5, D.47.10.15.31 and 33, and D.47.10.19 and 20) are particularly focused on slights against the reputation of financial solvency.
[68] Bankton, *Institutes* 1.10.21–39.
[69] See *e.g.* K McK Norrie, 'The Intentional Delicts' in *History of Private Law in Scotland, vol II* 483 describing Bankton's category of injury as being 'directly traceable from the *actio iniuriarum*'.

For example, Bankton's delict of 'injury' includes assaults as well as words wounding a person's character, and also 'composing infamous libels and satires to one's disgrace'.[70] Also falling within the scope of this delict is the 'writing, printing or publishing Pamphlets or Satires, to another's dishonour', with 'the truth of the things objected' no excuse.[71] This is significantly broader than the modern law of defamation, which is specifically concerned with untrue assertions that are harmful to someone's character.

From the eighteenth century onwards, under the influence of English law, the Scots law of delict moved away from this kind of general principle of liability. Instead, the modern law in this area is characterised by a series of narrower, more specific delicts, such as defamation or assault, each with rules of its own dealing with a particular kind of wrongful conduct.[72]

The problem with this is that the range of ways in which a person can be insulted has certainly not shrunk since the days of the Roman jurists, never mind since the eighteenth century. If anything, modern technology has increased the ways in which a person's dignity or reputation can be damaged or affronted. The major shortcoming of a law of specific delicts is that, from time to time, a case comes up in which justice demands a remedy but which does not readily fit into an established category. Sometimes, Parliament can fill a gap, an example being the introduction by statute of a delict of harassment.[73] Even then, though, legislation is not normally retrospective, and so cannot help anyone harmed by the conduct in question before the legislation comes into force. In such cases, there is benefit in having a general principle of liability to fall back on. It is noticeable that the Romans, with a general principle of liability, did not have any trouble fitting harassment-type behaviours within its scope.[74]

The difficulty that the modern law has had in dealing with harassment can be seen in *Cowan v Bennett*.[75] In that case, the pursuer and defender were both members of a business networking club. The pursuer was a painter and decorator, the defender a designer and printer. At club meetings, the defender persistently referred to the pursuer as 'the gay painter', acted in an exaggeratedly 'camp' manner when the pursuer was mentioned, printed the pursuer's business cards on pink card, and said and did various other things intended to suggest that the pursuer was a homosexual (which he was not). This was done with the intention

---

[70] Bankton, *Institutes* 1.10.21.
[71] Bankton, *Institutes* 1.10.32.
[72] On this development, see E Reid, 'Protection of Personality Rights in the Modern Scots Law of Delict' in N R Whitty and R Zimmermann eds, *Rights of Personality in Scots Law: A Comparative Perspective* (Dundee University Press 2009); J Blackie, 'Defamation' in *History of Private Law in Scotland, vol II* 665; K McK Norrie, 'The Actio Iniuriarum in Scots Law: Romantic Romanism or Tool for Today?' in E Descheemaeker and H Scott eds, *Iniuria and the Common Law* (Hart 2013).
[73] Protection from Harassment Act 1997, s. 8.
[74] For discussion of English law in this area in *iniuria* terms, see P Birks, 'Harassment and Hubris: The Right to an Equality of Respect' (1997) 32 Irish Jurist (NS) 1.
[75] 2012 GWD 37–738.

of embarrassing and humiliating the pursuer, for supposedly humorous purposes. The case was not argued as one of harassment.[76] Instead, in the absence of a clear common law principle of liability for affronts to a person's dignity, the case was argued on the basis of defamation. This case could never have succeeded, for two reasons.[77] First, an allegation is only considered defamatory if it lowers the person referred to 'in the estimation of right-thinking members of society'. While an allegation of homosexuality would once have been considered to do so, this is no longer the case. Second, none of the other members of the club took the defender to be seriously suggesting that the pursuer was homosexual. In any case, though, to categorise this as defamation (which means loss of *fama*, or reputation) seems to miss the point. The pursuer was not upset because his reputation had been harmed, because it had not.[78] Instead, he was upset by a persistent course of conduct designed to embarrass and humiliate him. The effect would have been the same if he had in fact been homosexual.[79]

With a law of specific delicts, rather than a law based on broad, general principles, the courts have two options: either refuse the injured party any remedy, or stretch an existing ground of liability so that it will fit. Consider, for example, the English case of *Tolley v J S Fry & Sons Ltd*.[80] In this case, a picture of a well-known amateur golfer was used, without his consent, in an advertisement for a chocolate bar. The golfer sued for defamation, on the grounds that anyone seeing the advertisement would assume that he had been paid for the use of his image. This would be inconsistent with his amateur status, and so it would (he argued) lower him in the estimation of right-minded people. He was successful in this argument. We must ask ourselves, though: is this really what he was most offended by? Perhaps it was – a sportsman's amateur status was more jealously guarded then than it is now – but it is probably fair to suspect that a professional golfer would have been just as annoyed by his image being used without his consent. It is interesting to compare the very similar South African case of *O'Keeffe v Argus Printing and Publishing Co Ltd*.[81] In that case, a photograph of a well-known broadcaster – not an amateur, and so unlike Mr Tolley – was used in an advertisement without her consent. She sued successfully. Because South African law has retained a much greater sense of *iniuria* as a general ground of liability, the court was able to give its decision a much more realistic basis (expressly based on the *actio iniuriarum*), that this was

---

[76] It is not clear why. This conduct would seem, at least arguably, to fall within the 1997 Act.
[77] For discussion of the defamation aspects of this case, see R Whelan, 'Case Comment: Cowan v Bennett' 2013 JR 557.
[78] If anything, it was the defender's own reputation that was harmed by his antics, which other club members seem to have found no wittier than the pursuer did.
[79] It is interesting to compare the decision, in an employment law context, in *English v Thomas Sanderson Ltd* [2008] EWCA Civ 1421, [2009] 2 CMLR 18. In that case, a heterosexual employee was subjected to 'homophobic abuse' by colleagues, apparently because he had been to boarding school and lived in Brighton.
[80] [1931] AC 333.
[81] 1954 (3) SA 244.

an offence against Ms O'Keeffe's dignity rather than her reputation.[82] This may also be the case with other situations where upsetting words or images appear, even where the words are in fact true. An example might be where a person is exposed without warning to insensitive or sensationalist television coverage of the murder of a close relation.[83]

Privacy is an area that has raised particular concerns in recent decades, probably because modern technology makes it much easier to invade someone's privacy. Roman law did not have any specific right to privacy,[84] though we have seen some ways in which *iniuria* could operate to protect privacy. There have been suggestions that *iniuria* could provide the basis for a modern law of privacy.[85] For example, it has been suggested that *iniuria* could provide a basis for liability for the release of 'revenge porn' images, normally by a former romantic partner.[86]

It is interesting here to compare the South African case of *Le Roux v Dey*.[87] In that case, a teenage school pupil downloaded a sexually explicit image of two naked men, and crudely altered the image so that the men's heads were replaced with those of the principal and deputy principal of the school. The image was then circulated among the boy's friends, and a copy appeared on a school notice board. After the boys involved received only minor punishment from the school, the deputy principal sued the boys for damages. He was successful. The case raises a number of difficult issues, and it has been criticised on a number of grounds with which we are not concerned here.[88] For present purposes, what the case boils down to is this: if A creates and circulates pornographic images of B, albeit they are crudely and obviously faked, is this actionable? For the South African Constitutional Court, the answer was 'yes', and it was in part said to be so expressly on the basis of *iniuria*.[89] The effect of the boys' actions was to 'belittle and humiliate' the deputy principal, and 'to represent him as unworthy – or at least less worthy – of respect by the learners of the school'. In other words, the

---

[82] For discussion of the issues in these cases, see D Vaver, 'Advertising Using an Individual's Image: A Comparative Note' (2006) 122 LQR 362.
[83] For discussion of this and other examples, see S C Smith, 'When the Truth Hurts' 1998 SLT (News) 1.
[84] M D Blecher, 'Aspects of Privacy in the Civil Law' (1975) 43 TvR 279.
[85] See *e.g.* J Morgan, 'Privacy, Confidence and Horizontal Effect: "Hello" Trouble' (2003) 62 Cam LJ 444; L Hernández González, 'Habeo Facebook Ergo Sum? Issues around Privacy and the Right to Be Forgotten and the Freedom of Expression on Online Social Networks' (2013) Ent L Rev 82; D Mac Síthigh, 'Beyond Breach of Confidence: An Irish Eye on English and Scottish Privacy Law' 2014 JR 27.
[86] J Brown, '"Revenge Porn" and the Actio Iniuriarum: Using "Old Law" to Solve "New Problems"' (2018) Legal Studies 1.
[87] [2011] ZACC 4, 2011 (3) SA 274. Compare *Charleston v News Group Newspapers Ltd* [1995] 2 AC 65.
[88] For discussion of some of these issues, see M Stubbs, 'In Loco Parentis: Le Roux v Dey (Discussion of Le Roux v Dey (Freedom of Expression Institute and Another as Amici Curiae) 2011 3 SA 274 (CC))' (2013) 24 Stellenbosch L Rev 377; A Fagan, 'The Constitutional Court Loses Its (and Our) Sense of Humour: Le Roux v Dey' (2011) 128 SALJ 395; J Barnard-Naudé and P de Vos, 'The Heteronormative Observer: The Constitutional Court's Decision in Le Roux v Dey' (2011) 128 SALJ 407; L Mills, 'Failing Children: The Court's Disregard of the Best Interests of the Child in Le Roux v Dey' (2014) 131 SALJ 847.
[89] See at para [141] of the decision, where there is direct reference to the tripartite categorisation of interests protected by *iniuria*: body (*corpus*), dignity (*dignitas*) and reputation (*fama*). See also the discussion of the development of Roman-Dutch law in this area at paras [195]–[199].

creation and circulation of the image offended against the dignity of the deputy principal. Viewed this way, it can be seen as very similar to the creation and circulation of revenge porn.

In its current state of development, Scots law gives clear protection to two of the interests covered by *iniuria*, namely body and reputation. Protection for the broad interest called dignity is less clear. There are, though, at least some hints that Scots law may include a general principle protecting dignity, including a person's right to privacy and freedom from interference. *Henderson v Chief Constable, Fife Police*[90] seems to be an example of this, even though *iniuria* was not referred to by name. In that case, a laboratory technician was arrested during an industrial dispute. When being put in a cell, she was required to remove her bra. In the circumstances, this was held to have been unnecessary. She was awarded damages for 'invasion of privacy and liberty'. More recently, in the Outer House decision in *C v Chief Constable of the Police Service of Scotland*,[91] a right to privacy was expressly recognised as forming part of Scots law. Perhaps surprisingly, though, there was no direct reference to Roman or *ius commune* sources. In the Inner House, it was doubted whether there was in fact such a right to privacy, though it was not necessary in the circumstances for the court to decide the point.[92]

There have been some cases also where *iniuria* has been directly referred to. For example, in *Stevens v Yorkhill NHS Trust*,[93] the mother of a baby who had died aged just over one month sued when she discovered that some of the baby's organs had been removed and retained without her consent. It was held that Scots law recognises as a legal wrong the unauthorised removal and retention of organs from a dead body, and this was said expressly to be based on the *actio iniuriarum*.[94] The issue was also raised in *Martin v McGuiness*.[95] This was an action for damages for injuries arising from a road accident. Suspecting that the pursuer's injuries were exaggerated, the defender hired private investigators to undertake surveillance, including calling at his house on false pretences. The pursuer sought declarator that the investigators' activities were unlawful. In the event, the investigators' actions were held to be reasonable and proportionate, taking into account the interests of the defender and of society at large in preventing the presentation of a false case. However, although it was put in 'rather cautious' terms, the court was clearly receptive to the pursuer's argument based on *iniuria*. It has been suggested that the European Convention on Human Rights may lead to further developments in this area, particularly article 8, in terms of which there is a right to respect for private and family life, home and correspondence.[96]

---

[90] 1988 SLT 361.
[91] [2019] CSOH 48, 2019 SLT 875.
[92] [2020] CSIH 61.
[93] [2006] CSOH 143, 2006 SLT 889. For discussion of the issues raised in cases like this, see N R Whitty, 'Rights of Personality, Property Rights and the Human Body in Scots Law' (2005) 9 Edin LR 194.
[94] See paras [62]–[63] of the decision.
[95] 2003 SLT 1424.
[96] See *e.g.* H L MacQueen, 'Protecting Privacy' (2004) 8 Edin LR 249.

Chapter Summary

Liability for the delict of *iniuria* was based on the defender having, contrary to good morals (*contra bonos mores*), injured the pursuer in body, dignity or reputation. The delict was concerned with the pursuer's feelings rather than financial loss: the offensiveness of the conduct complained of was the focus. The insult could be indirect, for example in certain circumstances where the immediate victim was the pursuer's wife, child or slave. This is an area of Roman law that has influenced modern Scots law, but in which the Roman influence has been somewhat lost sight of. It may well have continuing potential as a source of legal ideas.

Further Reading

G.3.220–5

J.4.4

D.47.10

C.9.35

P Birks, *The Roman Law of Obligations* (E Descheemaeker ed, Oxford University Press 2014) chapter 10

J Blackie, 'Defamation' in R Zimmermann and K Reid eds, *A History of Private Law in Scotland, Volume II: Obligations* (Oxford University Press 2000)

J Brown, 'The Defamation and Malicious Publications (Scotland) Bill: an undignified approach to law reform?' 2020 SLT (News) 131

E Descheemaeker and H Scott eds, *Iniuria and the Common Law* (Hart 2013)

B W Frier, *A Casebook on the Roman Law of Delict* (Scholars Press 1989) chapter V part B

E Metzger ed, *A Companion to Justinian's Institutes* (Duckworth 1998) 192–7

N R Whitty and R Zimmermann eds, *Rights of Personality in Scots Law: A Comparative Perspective* (Dundee University Press 2009)

R Zimmermann, *The Law of Obligations: Roman Foundations of the Civilian Tradition* (Oxford University Press 1996) chapter 31

CHAPTER TWENTY-FOUR
Other Delicts

A. Introduction

In Chapters 22 and 23 we considered the two most important of the Roman delicts, liability under the *lex Aquilia* and liability for *iniuria* (insult). These were not the only delicts, however, and in this chapter we consider some others. There is less focus on these, as they have been less influential on later law. As we saw in Chapter 22, by contrast, the scope of the *lex Aquilia* became greatly expanded from its origins imposing liability for wrongful damage to property. Through juristic interpretation and praetorian intervention, it came to include much of the ground covered by the delicts discussed in this chapter.[1] While, as we shall see, there were often good reasons for a Roman litigant to bring (say) an action for theft, these mostly relate to the calculation of damages. In modern law, delictual damages are compensatory rather than penal, so such considerations are now largely irrelevant. Thus, the breadth of Aquilian liability meant that it largely formed the basis of post-Roman developments on delictual liability for financial loss.

B. Theft

We consider first theft. We are concerned here not with criminal liability for theft, but rather with how thieves were dealt with by private law. Although this is one of the four delicts in the institutional account,[2] we may doubt how important it was in practice. Thieves rarely have the financial means to be worth suing nowadays, and it hardly seems likely that the situation was any different with the Romans. Nonetheless, a considerable body of law was built up on theft.

(1) The Definition of Theft

Theft can be defined simply, according to Paul, as 'the fraudulent handling of a thing with a view to gain, whether by the thing itself or by its use or possession'.[3]

---

[1] See p. 398.
[2] See p. 386.
[3] D.47.2.1.3. For discussion of this definition and its elements, see A Watson, 'The Definition of Furtum and the Trichotomy' (1958) 28 TvR 197; B Nicholas, 'Theophilus and Contrectatio' in Stein and Lewis, *Studies in Justinian's Institutes*; D Ibbetson, 'The Danger of Definition: *Contrectatio* and Appropriation' in Lewis and Ibbetson, *Roman Law Tradition*.

Looking at the matter in more detail, from the texts that have come down to us we can identify a number of specific requirements. Theft involves:

- the handling;
- of moveable property;
- belonging to another;
- dishonestly and with an intention to gain;
- contrary to the owner's will.

To take these requirements in order, the first thing we see is that theft does not require actual removal of the property. Although the position was probably otherwise in early law,[4] in classical law theft was committed (assuming all of the other requirements were present) by handling the goods. This included authorised handling done in an unauthorised manner, as where a pledgee or depositee used the thing pledged or deposited, or a borrower used the thing for some other purpose than that for which it had been lent.[5]

If theft is committed by handling, what if the thief removed only part of the property, as for example where part of a heap of corn or a jar of wine is taken? Is the whole heap or the whole of the jar stolen, or only what is taken? The texts are difficult to interpret, but the answer is probably that damages were based on the value of what was actually taken, not of the whole.[6]

The second requirement was that thing stolen be moveable. Land could not be stolen, although anything removed from the land became moveable[7] and could therefore be stolen.[8]

Third, property could only be stolen if it belonged to someone. The idea of belonging had an expanded meaning here: a person *alieni iuris*[9] could be stolen.[10] The requirement that the thing belong to someone meant that ownerless property could not be stolen.[11]

Fourth, the taking had to be dishonest and with a view to gain.[12] A person who took was not a thief if this was done in the honest but mistaken belief that the owner would consent. Likewise, someone who drove off someone's cattle or knocked coins from someone's hand so that they were lost was not a thief, as this was not done with a view to gain.[13]

---

[4] Zimmermann, *Obligations* 927–8.
[5] J.4.1.6.
[6] See *e.g.* D.47.2.21pr; D.47.2.21.8; D.47.2.22.1. As we shall see below, the damages payable would be a multiple of the value of the goods stolen.
[7] See pp. 222–5.
[8] D.47.2.58.
[9] See pp. 96–7.
[10] J.4.1.9.
[11] D.47.2.43.5. This text refers to abandoned property, which can be stolen in modern law: see *e.g. Mackenzie v Maclean* 1981 SLT (Sh Ct) 40. This, though, is because abandoned property does not become ownerless in modern law, whereas it did in Roman law: see pp. 217–18.
[12] D.47.2.52.20.
[13] Such actions might nonetheless give rise to Aquilian liability. See Chapter 22.

Finally, the taking was only theft if done without the owner's consent. This was the case even if the taker was unaware that the owner consented, and the taker intended to steal. If the owner in fact consented, the taking was nonetheless not theft.[14]

As might be expected from the penal nature of this delict, repentance of the thief and return of the thing did not excuse the thief of liability.[15]

(2) The Parties
(a) The Pursuer
Obviously, the pursuer in an action for theft would normally be the owner of the property. This would not always be the case, however. Anyone with 'an interest in the safety of the thing' could bring the action; conversely, an owner with no such interest had no remedy here.[16] In effect, what this means is that, where my property is stolen while it is in your hands, I have no remedy against the thief if I am adequately protected by an action against you. If, though, you are financially damaged by the theft, you can sue the thief. For example, suppose you are a laundryman, washing my clothes. My clothes are stolen. I can sue you on the basis of our contract, so I cannot pursue the thief unless you are insolvent (and so unable to pay me yourself). Because of your contractual liability, you have an interest in the safety of the clothes, and so you can sue the thief.[17] The same was true of a pledgee,[18] if the item pledged was stolen. The pledgee had an interest in the safety of the pledged item, as it gave the pledgee security for the debt owed. Accordingly, the pledgee had an action for theft – even, indeed, if it was the owner of the item who took it.[19] By contrast, a depositee[20] could not pursue the thief, as the depositee was not liable to the owner for the loss of the property. The depositee accordingly did not have the required interest in the safety of the property.[21]

The interest in the safety of the property might be divided. An example would be property held on usufruct,[22] where both the owner and the usufructuary had an interest in the safety of the property. Both could therefore have the action for theft, based on their respective interests.[23]

(b) The Defender
In addition to the thief being personally liable for the theft, anyone by whose advice and assistance the theft was committed was also liable as a thief.[24] Examples given by the texts include: knocking coins from the victim's hand so that another

---

[14] J.4.1.7.
[15] D.47.2.66.
[16] J.4.1.13.
[17] J.4.1.15.
[18] See pp. 271–4.
[19] J.4.1.14.
[20] See pp. 349–50.
[21] J.4.1.17.
[22] See Chapter 14.
[23] D.47.2.46.1.
[24] For discussion, see G MacCormack, 'Ope Consilio Furtum Factum' (1983) 51 TvR 271. For the examples that follow, see J.4.1.12; D.47.2.37.

can take them; obstructing the victim so that another can steal; driving off the victim's animals so that another can take them; placing a ladder for another to climb in and steal; and lending tools for breaking into a building to steal. It was not enough merely to encourage the theft if no actual advice or assistance was given.

(3) Remedies for Theft

(a) Manifest and Non-Manifest Theft

The victim of the theft obtained his or her remedy by bringing the *actio furti*, the action for theft. A distinction was made between two types of theft, manifest and non-manifest. For manifest theft, damages of four times the value of the theft were due; for non-manifest theft, double damages were due.[25] The value of the theft was probably based on its value to the pursuer rather than the value of the property itself.[26] For example, if something was stolen that the pursuer had promised to give to another person on pain of payment of a penalty, the amount of that penalty would be included in the valuation of the theft.[27] The action for theft is described by Justinian as 'entirely penal',[28] meaning that the pursuer is not barred from recovering the property itself in addition to the payment of damages.

As the damages payable depended on whether the theft was manifest or non-manifest, we need now to consider this distinction. The accepted definition of manifest theft was this:[29] a person committed manifest theft if he was 'seen or caught with the stolen thing, whether in public or in private, whether by the owner or by another, before he gets to the place where he intended to put it'.[30] After the thief had got the stolen item to its intended hiding place, the theft was no longer manifest, even if the thief was subsequently seen with the item.

(b) Procedures Supplementary to the Action for Theft

Certain supplementary procedures existed.[31] The Twelve Tables made provision for a formal search of premises before witnesses. If the stolen goods were found in someone's premises during that search, that person was liable for *furtum conceptum*, with liability of three times the value of the property, even if that person was not in fact the thief.[32] If that person was innocent of the theft, he or she had an action for *furtum oblatum*, again for treble value, against the person who planted the goods with, or passed the goods off to, him or her. The praetor introduced actions for preventing a search (*actio prohibiti furti*), with fourfold liability, and for refusing to hand over a stolen thing found during a search (*actio furti non exhibiti*), to make the search provisions more effective.[33]

---

[25] J.4.1.5.
[26] See though D.47.2.50pr.
[27] D.47.2.68.1. See also D.47.2.52.28.
[28] J.4.1.19.
[29] For discussion of early law, see D Pugsley, 'Furtum in the XII Tables' (1969) 4 Irish Jurist (NS) 139.
[30] J.4.1.3. See also D.47.2.7.2.
[31] J.4.1.4.
[32] G.3.186.
[33] G.3.188, 192.

Gaius describes the search procedures:

> An action for preventing a search, for quadruple damages, has been introduced by the praetor's Edict. The Twelve Tables imposed no penalty for this. It simply required that anyone wanting to make a search had to do so naked, wearing a *licium* and carrying a dish. If he finds anything, the law orders that this is manifest theft. It has been asked what a *licium* is. It is probably some kind of cloth for covering the necessary parts.[34] The whole thing is ridiculous. For someone who will not allow you to search while clothed is not going to let you do so naked, especially when, if you find something by searching in this way, a higher penalty will be imposed. Likewise, whether the dish is ordered to be carried to keep the hands occupied, so that nothing can be palmed, or else so that what is found can be placed there, neither explanation works, if that which is searched for is of a size or nature that it can neither be palmed nor placed there. Certainly, it is not doubted, that the law is satisfied whatever material the dish is made from.[35]

The wearing of a loincloth was presumably to avoid the searcher smuggling anything in in order to plant it, or perhaps pocketing anything while there. An alternative interpretation of the role of the dish is that it had eyeholes bored into it, and it was held in front of the searcher's face to save embarrassment (given the searcher's state of comparative undress) if any women were present in the house.[36] Still, there would seem to be more straightforward ways of covering the searcher's face, so this explanation may not convince. A still further possibility that has been suggested is that the dish was used to carry an offering to the household gods.[37] That too perhaps seems doubtful. If that was the explanation, why would the dish be mentioned but not the offering? Certainty is impossible, and it is not implausible that Gaius himself has misunderstood the procedure: it is clear from what he says that the procedure was long obsolete in his day.

(c) *Other Remedies*

An owner whose goods were stolen was not limited to the action for theft. There might also be other delictual remedies, for example. Most importantly, because ownership could not normally be lost against the owner's will, an owner of goods was entitled to recover them from anyone who held them without right, even if that holder was entirely innocent of any wrongdoing.[38] As an alternative, the form of action known as the *condictio*,[39] in this case as the *condictio furtiva*, could be used against the thief.[40] This was useful where the property had been

---

[34] The phrase 'necessary parts' is a literal translation of the Latin used by Gaius. It is hopefully obvious which part of the anatomy he is referring to.
[35] G.3.192–3.
[36] C T Lewis and C Short, *A Latin Dictionary* (Harper 1879), 'licium'.
[37] A J B Sirks, '*Furtum* and *Manus/Potestas*' (2013) 81 TvR 465, 491.
[38] See p. 166.
[39] See pp. 429–32.
[40] The principles of modern Scots law are here essentially the same as in Roman law, although the Roman terminology is little used. The Roman terminology is in wider use in South Africa. See P Pauw, 'Historical Notes on the Nature of the Condictio Furtiva' (1976) 93 SALJ 395; M D Blecher, 'The Owner's Actions against Persons Who Fraudulently Ceased to Possess His Res (Qui Dolo Desierunt Possidere)' (1978) 95 SALJ 341.

destroyed or its location was unknown, as it simply imposed liability for the value of the property.

C. Robbery

Robbery was theft committed using force. It was therefore related to theft, in that every robber was also a thief and could be held liable for theft. However, in 77 BC the praetor introduced a special delictual action, the *actio vi bonorum raptorum* (the action for goods taken by force), to deal specifically with robbery. The action had to be brought within a year, and imposed fourfold liability on the defender.[41] Unlike manifest theft, however, this fourfold liability included the value of the property itself. If the property was recovered, the pursuer would only be entitled to triple damages. If the defender was a manifest thief, therefore, as discussed above, it would be better to bring the action for theft.

In addition to the requirement for force, liability for robbery depended on fraudulent intent, so no liability for robbery was imposed on a person acting in a genuine belief in ownership.[42] Concern that this gave an inducement to violent self-help in property disputes, though, led to imperial pronouncements penalising this kind of action by imposing forfeiture of the property (if the taker owned it) or liability to its value (if not).[43]

The pursuer in an action for robbery did not always have to be owner of the goods. It was enough that the robbery had reduced the pursuer's substance: generally speaking, anyone who could bring an action for theft could, if the theft was committed using force, bring an action for robbery.[44]

D. Corruption of Slaves

Delictual liability arose when a person, with wicked intent, corrupted a slave such that the slave was made worse.[45] There was no liability unless the slave was actually made worse.[46] There was a broad range of ways in which a slave could be corrupted:

> He also makes a slave worse who persuades him to commit an injury or a theft, or to run away, or to stir up another's slave, to mismanage his *peculium*, or to become a lover, or to stray, or to become devoted to evil arts, or to spend too much time at public spectacles, or to become seditious. The same is true if, by money or words, he persuades a factor to tamper with or falsify his master's accounts, or also to confuse accounts that have been entrusted to him . . .[47]
>
> or if he makes him extravagant or argumentative, or he persuades him to submit to sexual immorality.[48]

---

[41] J.4.2pr.
[42] J.4.2.1.
[43] D.4.2.13; D.48.7.7.
[44] J.4.2.2.
[45] D.11.3.1pr. For discussion of certain aspects of the application of this delict, see A A Schiller, 'Trade Secrets and the Roman Law: The Actio Servi Corrupti' (1929–30) 30 Colum L Rev 837.
[46] See though D.11.3.1.4.
[47] D.11.3.1.5 (Ulpian).
[48] D.11.3.2 (Paul).

This could potentially overlap with other delicts. For example, a person who concealed a slave he had persuaded to run away would be liable also for theft of the slave.[49] Depending on what had been done, there might also be liability under the *lex Aquilia*[50] or for *iniuria*.[51]

Liability was for double the loss caused.[52] This was based not just on the reduction in the value of the slave, but on all losses, for example the value of things lost by the corrupted slave's theft.[53] It did not extend, however, to subsequent wrongs, for example where the wrongdoing that had been encouraged became a habit.[54]

E. Deceit and Coercion

These two delicts have in common the fact that they are often applied in the context of property and contract disputes. A property transfer, for example, may be alleged to have been induced by deceit or coercion, or an attempt to enforce a contract may be resisted on the same basis. These aspects of deceit and coercion are dealt with elsewhere.[55] However, they were also free-standing delicts, and are considered here in that context. They both involve a person being led to do something to his or her disadvantage by the actings of another.

(1) Deceit *(Dolus)*

Ulpian gives us our introduction to deceit (*dolus*, often translated as 'fraud'):

> By this edict, the praetor gives help against shifty and deceitful persons who have harmed others by a certain cunning, so that the wickedness of the former is not beneficial to them and the simplicity of the latter harmful. The words of the edict are then these: 'Where something is alleged to have been done by wicked deceit [*dolo malo*], and if there is no other remedy for it and there appears to be a reasonable basis, I will give an action.'[56]

Assuming, as Ulpian reports, the victim of the deceit had no other remedy, the action for deceit (*actio de dolo*) would be allowed. An attempt to enforce an agreement induced by deceit could be met with the defence of deceit (*exceptio doli*).[57]

Deceit can be defined generally as 'any cunning, trickery or manipulation carried out in order to circumvent, mislead or deceive another'.[58] The texts have numerous examples, such as: a person arguing a case in court on behalf of a client deliberately allowing the other party to win;[59] persuading a person to decline an

---

[49] C.6.2.4 (AD 222).
[50] Chapter 22.
[51] Chapter 23.
[52] D.11.3.1pr.
[53] D.11.3.10.
[54] D.11.3.11.1.
[55] See pp. 205–7.
[56] D.4.3.1pr–1.
[57] See *e.g.* D.4.3.40 and, generally, D.44.4.
[58] D.4.3.1.2 (Ulpian, citing Labeo).
[59] D.4.3.7.9.

inheritance on the (false) basis that it is bankrupt;[60] concealing a will so that it cannot be challenged;[61] a debtor sending a forged letter to the creditor, purporting to be from a friend of the creditor, requesting that the creditor release the debtor;[62] and a person falsely defending a case by pretending to possess property whose recovery is sought, so that the true possessor can complete acquisition by *usucapio*.[63]

Deceit was thus a delict that was very broad in scope. There was, however, a major restriction on its availability:

> it will not be given against certain persons, for example children or freedmen against parents or patrons, as it relates to *infamia*. Nor ought it to be given to someone of humble rank against someone of higher rank, for example to a plebeian against a man of consular rank with acknowledged authority, or to a man who is extravagant or a spendthrift or otherwise worthless, against a man of more correct lifestyle.[64]

As we see, the key point is that liability in an action for deceit carried with it *infamia*.[65] It was not thought proper that a person of lower status should be able to inflict that consequence on a person of higher status. If the victim was of lower status, he or she would have to be content with an *actio in factum*, which would give a remedy but which would not inflict *infamia*.

(2) Coercion *(Metus)*

Ulpian tells us: 'The praetor says: "I will not hold to be valid that which is done through coercion."'[66] The victim of coercion could bring the action for coercion (*actio quod metus causa*) within a year, for fourfold damages. If brought outwith that year, only simple damages were due, and even then only if the pursuer had good cause for bringing it after such a delay. An attempt to enforce an agreement extorted by coercion could be met with the defence of coercion (*exceptio metus*). Unlike deceit, liability for coercion did not result in *infamia*.

Coercion occurred when a person was induced to act to his or her disadvantage by force, threats or intimidation. The defender's acts only counted as coercive if they were 'severe' and 'contrary to good morals',[67] and had to be such as would sway 'the most resolute character' rather than a 'weak-minded man'.[68] How severe a threat would have this result would be highly fact-dependent, and so would be determined on a case by case basis.[69] However, the 'contrary to good morals'

---

[60] D.4.3.9.1. On an heir's liability for the debts of the deceased, see pp. 283–8.
[61] D.4.3.9.2.
[62] D.4.3.38.
[63] D.4.3.39. *Usucapio* was a mode of acquisition of ownership by possessing the property for a period of time. See pp. 239–43.
[64] D.4.3.11.1 (Ulpian).
[65] See pp. 239–43.
[66] D.4.2.1.
[67] D.4.2.3.1 (Ulpian). On the introduction of this by the praetor, see Zimmermann, *Obligations* 653.
[68] D.4.2.6 (Gaius).
[69] For general discussion of the requirements, see G Glover, 'Metus in the Roman Law of Obligations' (2004) 10 Fundamina 31, 47–55.

requirement meant, for example, a lawful act of a magistrate would not found an action for coercion.[70] Similarly, fear of a just punishment was not coercion.[71]

F. Liability for Animals

Animals give rise to special issues in the law, by virtue of the fact that they may act in unexpected ways. All legal systems are faced with the problem of how to deal with this.[72] In part, damage caused by animals could be dealt with by other delicts. For example, if your slave was injured by my dog, through my fault, Aquilian liability would be likely.[73] *Iniuria* could certainly be committed using an animal,[74] and a fierce dog might be used to cause enough fear for the purposes of coercion. However, there were also special delicts concerned with animals specifically.

The development of the law on liability for animals is difficult to reconstruct from the available evidence. There seems to have been a variety of actions and remedies, some of which have left little trace.[75] One such, for example, is the *actio de pastu*, an action provided by the Twelve Tables for damage done by livestock grazing on another's land.[76] Two remedies in particular require attention.

(1) Actio de Pauperie

The Twelve Tables imposed liability for *pauperies*, which meant injury done by an animal.[77] Liability was strict, which is to say that the owner of the animal was liable regardless of fault.[78] This was a case of noxal liability,[79] meaning that the owner was liable for the alternatives of paying compensation or handing over the animal.[80]

The texts we have say that the owner is only liable when the animal is of a domestic species and acts 'contrary to nature', meaning the nature of its species.[81] For example, we are told that, if a horse kicks out when it is injured, there is no action for *pauperies* as it is natural for the horse to respond in that way.[82] However, consider this text from Ulpian:

> But this action does not lie in the case of animals that are wild by nature. Accordingly, if a bear escapes and thus causes harm, the former owner cannot be held liable, because he ceased to be owner as soon as the animal escaped.[83]

---

[70] D.4.2.3.1.
[71] D.4.2.21pr.
[72] The current Scots law is contained in the Animals (Scotland) Act 1987.
[73] Chapter 22.
[74] Chapter 23.
[75] B S Jackson, 'Liability for Animals in Roman Law: An Historical Sketch' (1978) 37 Cam LJ 122.
[76] On the reception of this action in South African law, see D L Carey Miller, 'A Restrictive Interpretation of the Actio de Pastu' (1971) 88 SALJ 177.
[77] J.4.9pr. For discussion, see M Polojac, 'Actio de Pauperie: Anthropomorphism and Rationalism' (2012) 18 Fundamina 119.
[78] D.9.1.1.3.
[79] See pp. 155–6.
[80] D.9.1.1pr.
[81] J.4.9pr.
[82] D.9.1.1.7. The person who injured the horse may, however, be liable under an *actio in factum* on the *lex Aquilia*. See pp. 395–6.

There is a clear difficulty here: the word 'Accordingly' is out of place, because the second sentence does not follow from or explain the first. What, for example, would be the position if a wild animal caused damage when it had *not* escaped? As has been said, ' if there is no liability for wild beasts in any case it is unnecessary, and misleading, to add that there is no liability if they escape'.[84] Because of this difficulty, it is widely believed that the 'contrary to nature' requirement is post-classical.

(2) The Edict of the Aediles

The *actio de pauperie* was supplemented by a provision of the edict of the aediles.[85] This provided that a person was forbidden to bring a dog, boar, bear or lion into a place where people came and went. Where a freeman was killed, there was a fixed penalty.[86] Where a freeman was injured, damages were payable according the judge's discretion.[87] For other injuries, double damages were due.[88] There was no requirement to show fault, and the person who brought the animal into a public place would be liable even if the animal had been bound or chained in order not to cause harm.[89]

Chapter Summary

The Romans relied, as we have seen, on a system of discrete nominate delicts rather than on a general principle of liability for wrongdoing. We have considered the most important two delicts, concerned with liability under the *lex Aquilia* and the *actio iniuriarum*, in the previous two chapters. There were numerous others, however. The institutional scheme, which only covers two further delicts, is misleading here. These two, theft and robbery, have been considered together in this chapter on the basis that robbery is essentially theft committed by force. In this chapter, we have also considered a number of other grounds of delictual liability, namely corruption of slaves, deceit, coercion and damage by animals.

---

[83] D.9.1.1.10. On the loss of ownership of animals, see p. 220.
[84] B Nicholas, 'Liability for Animals in Roman Law' 1958 AJ 185, 188. See also A Watson, 'Law out of Context' (2000) 4 Edin LR 147, 151–2.
[85] D.21.1.40–2. The aediles were magistrates with various responsibilities, including responsibility for the public markets. See pp. 10–11.
[86] D.21.1.42.
[87] J.4.9.1.
[88] J.4.9.1.
[89] D.21.1.41.

Further Reading

G.3.183–209

J.4.1.1–19; 4.2

D.9.1; 47.2

C.2.19–20; 6.2

P Birks, *The Roman Law of Obligations* (E Descheemaeker ed, Oxford University Press 2014) chapters 7 and 8

E Metzger ed, *A Companion to Justinian's Institutes* (Duckworth 1998) 175–84, 197

B W Frier, *A Casebook on the Roman Law of Delict* (Scholars Press 1989) chapters IV, V (part A) and VI

G Glover, 'Metus in the Roman Law of Obligations' (2004) 10 Fundamina 31

B S Jackson, 'Liability for Animals in Roman Law: An Historical Sketch' (1978) 37 Cam LJ 122

A J B Sirks, '*Furtum* and *Manus/Potestas*' (2013) 81 TvR 465

A Watson, *The Law of Obligations in the Later Roman Republic* (Oxford University Press 1965) chapters 14 and 17

R Zimmermann, *The Law of Obligations: Roman Foundations of the Civilian Tradition* (Oxford University Press 1996) chapters 28 and 32

CHAPTER TWENTY-FIVE

Quasi-Contractual Liability

A. Scope of Quasi-Contract

In our consideration of the Roman law of obligations, we have looked at contracts – obligations arising through agreement – and delicts – obligations arising from wrongdoing. During the classical period of Roman law, Gaius had said that 'every obligation arises either from contract or from delict'.[1] Despite the apparent exhaustiveness of this statement, however, contracts and delicts do not tell the whole story of obligations. Sometimes the law imposed obligations on a person without that person either having agreed or having committed any kind of wrong. Indeed, Gaius was himself aware of this: in his discussion of contracts, he mentions the situation where someone has paid money that he mistakenly believes himself to owe the recipient. An obligation of repayment is imposed on the recipient, even though the intention was to discharge an obligation rather than to create one.[2] Clearly, then, the law of obligations covered more than just contracts and delicts. In another work, known as the *Golden Words*, Gaius went further: 'Obligations arise either from contract or from wrongdoing or from some special right from various types of cause.'[3]

To say that obligations may arise 'from some special right from various types of cause' is, however, not especially enlightening. The final stage of development in the Roman sources is the fourfold division of obligations in Justinian's *Institutes*, which classified these additional sources of obligation according to whether they have greater similarity to contracts or to delicts. For Justinian, obligations arise 'from a contract, as though from a contract [*quasi ex contractu*], from a wrong or as though from a wrong [*quasi ex maleficio*]'.[4] These two additional categories are accordingly known as quasi-contract and quasi-delict. Quasi-delict is the subject matter of Chapter 26. In this chapter we consider quasi-contract.

---

[1] G.3.88.
[2] G.3.91.
[3] The passage is reproduced in the *Digest* at D.44.7.1pr.
[4] J.3.13.2.

As presented by Justinian, the category of quasi-contracts is quite a miscellaneous group, with no common factor except that they involve obligations, which cannot properly be understood as arising from contract, but which, because they are not based on wrongdoing, are seen as arising 'as though from contract'.[5] The category includes four matters dealt with elsewhere in this book, namely the obligations of guardians towards their wards,[6] the obligations owed by co-owners of property towards each other,[7] the obligations owed by co-heirs of an estate to each other,[8] and an obligation on an heir to make payments from the estate.[9] In this chapter, we will look at the other two areas considered by Justinian, namely *negotiorum gestio* (unauthorised intervention in another's affairs) and, first, the case where a person has been enriched at another's expense without legal justification.

B. Unjustified Enrichment

(1) Nature and Origins: *The Condictio*

The beginnings of unjustified enrichment lie in a form of action called the *condictio*.[10] This form of action was not specific to unjustified enrichment. Rather, it was originally one of a number of pre-classical procedural forms that we met in Chapter 2, called the *legis actiones*, although the *condictio* was a fairly late member of that group.[11]

The *condictio* had a great practical advantage that it was not necessary when raising an action based on it to state the basis of the debt being claimed, only that the debt existed. The *condictio* simply narrated that a debt of a particular amount was being claimed, and directed the judge to condemn or absolve the defender with respect to that in accordance with the evidence. This gave the *condictio* tremendous flexibility, and it was the normal procedural form for a variety of different types of claim. For example, in Chapter 24 we saw it, as the *condictio furtiva*, being used against thieves.[12] Of particular importance here, though, is the use of the *condictio* to enforce repayment of money or property lent under a contract of *mutuum*. As we saw in Chapter 19, this was a loan for consumption, with an equivalent to be repaid by the borrower rather than the original item being given back.[13] As with all of the category of real contracts, in a *mutuum* the contract was

---

[5] J.3.27pr.
[6] J.3.27.2. See pp. 128–32.
[7] J.3.27.3. See pp. 171–2.
[8] J.3.27.4. See pp. 281–317.
[9] J.3.27.5. See pp. 283–4.
[10] As far as Roman law is concerned at least: although the Romans did not use the term 'unjustified enrichment', they were yet capable of grouping together the different cases in which the *condictio* was used to redress unjustified enrichment of one person at the expense of another. As we saw at p. 154, though, the medieval jurists also made use of the *actio de in rem verso* to develop the law of unjustified enrichment.
[11] See pp. 32–7 on the *legis actiones*. The *condictio* was probably introduced by statute in the late third century BC: D Liebs, 'The History of the Roman *Condictio* up to Justinian' in N MacCormick and P Birks eds, *The Legal Mind: Essays for Tony Honoré* (Oxford University Press 1986) 164.
[12] See pp. 421–2.
[13] See pp. 344–7.

not created by the mere agreement of the parties, but instead by the delivery of the property or money that was its subject matter.

The question then arises: what if money or property is handed over, not in order to create an obligation, but to discharge an obligation that is mistakenly believed already to exist? For example, I believe that I owe you a certain sum of money under a contract, so I pay you this sum. In fact, the money is not due. Perhaps I have already paid you, or else maybe the contract under which we believe the money to be due is invalid for some reason. Gaius makes an analogy between this situation and *mutuum*:

> He also is obliged by a real obligation who receives something not due to him from someone who pays in error. For the clause in the *condictio*, 'if it appears that he ought to give', lies against him just as if he had received payment by way of loan.[14]

Thus, he says, the transferee is liable under the *condictio* in such circumstances to make repayment, even though the intention was to discharge an obligation rather than to create one. We may add also (though Gaius did not, having no such category) that this is what justifies classing this situation as quasi-contractual: it looks like *mutuum*, but is not, because the parties did not intend to create a contractual relationship.

(2) Grounds of Enrichment

This claim for repayment of something not due is known to us as the *condictio indebiti*, and is the most straightforward case of unjustified enrichment. In principle, this was only available if the payer believed the payment to be due.[15] A payment could, however, be recovered if it was made on the basis that it would be repaid if it turned out not to be due.[16] This allowed payment to be made provisionally, in circumstances where there was uncertainty as to whether the debt existed. The *condictio indebiti* was excluded where payment had been made towards a liability, in cases where denial of liability increased that liability.[17] The claim under the *condictio indebiti* included any fruits, such as offspring, derived from the property, with deduction for expenses of maintenance.[18]

Gaius and Justinian mention only the *condictio indebiti* in their respective *Institutes*. However, further types of unjustified enrichment claims were developed. One of these was the *condictio causa data causa non secuta*, the claim for something given for

---

[14] G.3.91. See also J.3.27.6; D.44.7.5.3.
[15] D.12.6.1.
[16] D.12.6.2pr. See also C.4.5.11 (AD 530).
[17] J.3.27.7. The main example of this is delictual liability under the *lex Aquilia*, on which see Chapter 22. The purpose of this exclusion is as follows. If you claimed that I was liable to you under the *lex Aquilia*, and I denied that, my liability would be doubled if I was found by the court to be liable. I might therefore decide, rather than denying liability, simply to pay you and then reclaim the payment using the *condictio indebiti*. If the *condictio indebiti* had not been excluded, I could in this way avoid the risk of doubled liability.
[18] D.12.6.65.5.

a cause that had failed. A standard example would be a gift given for a wedding that did not then take place. Ulpian explains this as essentially a variant on the *condictio indebiti*: 'If money is given for a purpose that is not improper, for example that a son be emancipated or a slave manumitted or that court proceedings be abandoned, the right of recovery ceases once the purpose has been achieved.'[19] In other words, the recipient is initially liable to repay, because the money or property given was not in fact due. However, this ceases to be true once the anticipated state of affairs has come about.[20]

Another was the *condictio ob turpem vel iniustam causam*, the claim for something given for a corrupt or unlawful cause. Where something was given for an unworthy purpose, the giver could potentially recover it even if the intended purpose did in fact materialise.[21] Examples might be a kidnapper accepting a ransom to release a victim, or a person intending to commit murder accepting money not to do so. Whether recovery would be possible depended on whether both parties had acted immorally or unlawfully, or only one of them had done so. Where only the receiver had acted wrongfully, recovery was possible; if both were tainted, the loss would be allowed to lie where it fell.[22]

There were, however, always cases that did not readily fit into one of these *condictiones*. The jurists never lost sight of the fact that all of these claims rested on a general principle that, in the words of Pomponius, 'it is by nature fair that nobody should enrich himself at another's expense'.[23] For these cases, there was the *condictio sine causa*, the final two words of that expression meaning 'without legal basis'. Ulpian gives an example:

> A fuller contracts to wash clothes, then, the clothes having been lost, pays the owner their price on being sued under the contract. The owner then finds the clothes. By which action should the fuller recover the price he paid? And Cassius says that he can pursue the owner not only using an action based on the contract, but also using the *condictio*. I think that he can at any rate sue on the basis of the contract. However, it has been questioned whether he can bring the *condictio*, because he did not give something that was not owed, unless perhaps we hold him to bring the *condictio* as where something is given with no basis, for once the clothes are found it seems as though the giving was without any basis.[24]

Another example would be a case in which you requested a loan from me and also from someone else. I told my own debtor to pay you (thus discharging his debt to me), but you believed he was paying on behalf of the other person he asked. There is therefore no contract between us, and no direct payment from

---

[19] D.12.4.1pr.
[20] See Zimmermann, *Obligations* 843–4. The same approach would be, to say the least, unlikely to be taken in modern law.
[21] D.12.5.1.2.
[22] D.12.5.3; D.12.5.8. See further the discussion of the *iusta causa* requirement for transfer at pp. 207–10.
[23] D.12.6.14. See also D.12.6.66.
[24] D.12.7.2.

me to you. Nonetheless, there has in a sense been a transfer of value from me to you, and it is fair that you should have to repay me: after all, you were expecting to have to pay the money back to someone, and there is no good reason why you should get a windfall from your own mistake. I therefore would have the *condictio sine causa* to reclaim the money from you.[25]

(3) Enrichment in Modern Law

Modern Scots law has certainly drawn heavily on Roman law in this area, not least in the use of *condictio*-based terminology. For example, in *Cantiere San Rocco, SA v Clyde Shipbuilding & Engineering Co Ltd*,[26] a contract had been made in May 1914 by which a Scottish firm of engineers was to supply marine engines to an Austrian firm of shipbuilders. After payment of the first instalment, but before the engines had been supplied, war broke out and rendered performance of the contract legally impossible. After hostilities ended, it was held that the shipbuilders were entitled to repayment. This was said, with copious citation of Roman texts and the Scots institutional writers drawing on them, to be based on the *condictio causa data causa non secuta*.[27] At the same time, though, unjustified enrichment does not appear in the Scots institutional writers as a discrete category,[28] and modern enrichment law includes certain claims that would not have been covered by the *condictiones* of Roman law.[29] The major task of modern unjustified enrichment law is to break away from the specific *condictiones* and develop a general principle for the reversal of unjustified enrichment, while still drawing on the Roman tradition.[30]

Another example of a case in which considerable use was made of Roman and *Ius Commune* thinking in this area was *Morgan Guaranty Trust Co of New York*

---

[25] D.12.1.32.
[26] 1923 SC (HL) 105.
[27] Notably, the court here rejected Erskine's view (*Institute* 3.1.10) that recovery was only possible if the recipient was in some way at fault, even though Erskine's view has support in the Roman texts. See D.12.4.5.4; C.4.6.10 (AD 294). G D MacCormack, 'The *Condictio Causa Data Causa Non Secuta*' in Evans-Jones, *Civil Law Tradition* 258–9 discusses this issue, noting that only Erskine among the institutional writers actually cites the Digest. The others seem to draw on views of *ius commune* writers.
[28] See *e.g.* Stair, *Institutions* 1.7, which includes both certain enrichment claims and the obligation to restore another's property under the general heading of restitution. For a general account of the development of Scots enrichment law, see R Evans-Jones, 'Unjustified Enrichment' in *History of Private Law in Scotland, vol II*; N R Whitty, 'Some Trends and Issues in Scots Enrichment Law' 1994 JR 127; H MacQueen, 'The Future of Unjustified Enrichment in Scotland' (2017) 25 Restitution L Rev 14; R Evans-Jones, 'From "Undue Transfer" to "Retention without a Legal Basis"' (The *Condictio Indebiti* and *Condictio ob Turpem vel Iniustam Causam*)' in Evans-Jones, *Civil Law Tradition*.
[29] The major example of this is the right of a good faith improver of another's property to recompense, which exists in Scots law. In Roman law, as we saw at p. 224, the good faith improver's right is simply to retain the property until compensated. Another example is the expansion of the *actio de in rem verso* to apply to unjustified enrichment situations, as we saw at p. 154.
[30] For a South African perspective on these issues, see J du Plessis, 'Labels and Meaning: Unjust Factors and Failure of Purpose as Reasons for Reversing Enrichment by Transfer' (2014) 18 Edin LR 416; H Scott, 'Rationalising the South African Law of Enrichment' (2014) 18 Edin LR 433.

v Lothian Regional Council.³¹ In this case, there had been an agreement between Lothian Regional Council and a firm of merchant bankers involving payments of money between the two. This agreement was subsequently held to be void, so the bankers sought the return of sums paid on the basis of the *condictio indebiti*. The question was whether sums paid under an error of law were reclaimable. In fact, in classical Roman law, they probably were, no distinction being made between errors of fact and errors of law for these purposes, though Justinian altered this position.³² In *Morgan Guaranty*, it was noted that the question had been a matter of dispute from the time of the Glossators,³³ but that the position received in Scots law was that such payments were recoverable.³⁴ This had been thrown into doubt in the nineteenth century, under English influence.³⁵ As a result of its historical investigations, the court in *Morgan Guaranty* was able to restore the position of the institutional writers and, with it, that of the classical Roman law.

Probably the most important case in modern Scots enrichment law has been *Shilliday v Smith*.³⁶ In that case, the parties had been in a cohabiting relationship. They had become engaged. The pursuer had paid for materials and repair work for the defender's property, with a view to living there together as husband and wife. Following their separation, the pursuer was held to be entitled to recover his expenditure on the basis of the *condictio causa data causa non secuta*. The Lord President (Rodger) made this statement of principle: 'a person may be said to be unjustly enriched at another's expense when he has obtained a benefit from the other's actings or expenditure, without there being a legal ground which would justify him in retaining that benefit'.³⁷ The individual *condictiones* are not separate remedies, but rather each is used 'to describe one particular group of situations in which the law may provide a remedy because one party is enriched at the expense of the other'.³⁸ In other words, they are specific examples of the application of a more general principle.

In *Shilliday*, the parties were engaged to be married. It is less clear, though, that unjustified enrichment is of much use in cohabitation situations more generally. Unjustified enrichment is not an apt tool for disentangling the financial affairs of separating cohabitants. The *condictio indebiti* is clearly not appropriate, as contributions by each party are not intended to discharge a supposed legal

---

31 1995 SC 151.
32 Zimmermann, *Obligations* 850–1; R Evans-Jones, 'From "Undue Transfer" to "Retention without a Legal Basis" (The *Condictio Indebiti* and *Condictio ob Turpem vel Iniustam Causam*)' in Evans-Jones, *Civil Law Tradition* 225.
33 As we saw at pp. 74–5, the Glossators were medieval jurists, who began the study of the *Corpus Iuris Civilis*.
34 Erskine, *Institute* 3.3.54.
35 Bell, *Principles* s. 532; *Wilson & McLellan v Sinclair* (1830) 4 W & S 398.
36 1998 SC 725.
37 1998 SC 725, 727. The reference to a need for a legal ground to justify retaining the benefit may strike the reader as odd. Why should I need to demonstrate a special ground to justify retaining my own property? The difficulty disappears when focus is placed on the manner in which I acquired the benefit. That is what must be justified.
38 1998 SC 725, 728.

obligation. As for the *condictio causa data causa non secuta*, if the parties were not intending to marry then it will often be difficult to identify any definite outcome that has failed to transpire, and which has made retention of the contributions unjust.[39] If a disappointed expectation of continued cohabitation is enough for this, then it is not fanciful to imagine a financially vulnerable cohabitant being coerced into continuing the relationship by the threat of financial ruin if the party who has made the greater financial contribution must be repaid following separation. That the court might, on equitable grounds, exclude such a claim does not entirely remove the risk.[40]

C. Negotiorum Gestio

Negotiorum gestio can be translated as 'management of affairs'. It is concerned with the situation where one person (the *gestor*) intervenes, without agreement, in the affairs of another (the principal). This situation gave rise to possible actions on both sides: the principal could pursue the *gestor* for compensation for any damage the *gestor* had done; the *gestor* could pursue the principal to recover his or her expenses. This principle has entered modern systems,[41] including Scots law.[42] We can consider this also to be a quasi-contractual situation, as the intervener is acting as if under a contract of mandate[43] even though no such contract exists. Indeed, there was some tendency for the boundary between mandate and *negotiorum gestio* to become blurred.

The *gestor* was allowed to claim for recovery of expenditure and for relief of any obligations the *gestor* had entered into in the interest of the principal.[44] To justify this claim, the *gestor* had to show three things: first, that the intervention was reasonable; second, that the intervention was beneficial; and, third, that the *gestor*'s intentions were not inconsistent with a right to recompense.

As to the first of these, it would be difficult to see the intervention as reasonable if the principal could have acted but chose not to do so. *Negotiorum gestio* has never been intended to be a licence to interfere in another person's business without proper cause. For this reason, *negotiorum gestio* claims would normally arise where

---

[39] Although such a claim succeeded in *Satchwell v McIntosh* 2006 SLT (Sh Ct) 117. For discussion of the case, taking a different view from the one expressed here, see R Evans-Jones, 'Causes of Action and Remedies in Unjustified Enrichment: *Satchwell v McIntosh*' (2007) 11 Edin LR 105. For a comparative perspective on the issue, see A Sanders, 'Cohabitants in Private Law: Trust, Frustration and Unjust Enrichment in England, Germany and Canada' (2013) 62 ICLQ 628.

[40] Alongside the common law of unjustified enrichment, note that the Family Law (Scotland) Act 2006, s. 28, makes provision for financial awards between separating cohabitants. The existence of a claim under this provision, however, does not exclude a potential remedy under the law of unjustified enrichment: *Pert v McCaffrey* [2020] CSIH 5, 2020 SLT 225. For a review of the whole area, see Scottish Law Commission, *Aspects of Family Law: Discussion Paper on Cohabitation* (SLC DP No 170, 2020).

[41] T W Dornis, 'The Doctrines of Contract and *Negotiorum Gestio* in European Private Law: Quest for Structure in a No Man's Land of Legal Reasoning' (2015) 23 Restitution LR 73.

[42] Stair, *Institutions* 1.8.3–5; Erskine, *Institute* 3.3.52–3. Indeed, it would not be too much of an exaggeration to describe these passages as little more than a commentary on the Roman law.

[43] See pp. 371–3.

[44] D.3.5.2.

the principal was mentally incapable[45] or absent, especially if the intervention took place in an emergency.[46] This was not absolutely required, however, and several texts deal with the situation where the *gestor* was not acting in an emergency.[47]

As noted, the intervention had to have been beneficial for the *gestor* to be entitled to be compensated. This was judged at the time of the intervention. Thus, it was not relevant that the benefit was subsequently lost due to events outwith the control of the *gestor*. Examples include the *gestor* shoring up a building to prevent collapse, but the building then burning down; and taking care of a sick slave, who then dies anyway.[48] In neither case would the fact that the benefit was subsequently lost prevent the *gestor* recovering his or her expenses.

The final requirement, as noted, related to the intention with which the *gestor* acted. A person intending to make a gift would not be entitled to recompense, and nor would someone acting out of a sense of family obligation (unless there was an intention to be compensated).[49]

In intervening, the *gestor* had to exercise a degree of care. Justinian tells us that the *gestor* had to exercise *exactissima diligentia*, 'the most exact diligence'. It was not enough just to apply the normal standard of care that the *gestor* exercised in his or her own affairs.[50] In fact, though, we find out elsewhere that the position was more complicated than that. The standard of care varied depending on the situation. Thus, where the *gestor* had, out of friendship, intervened in an emergency situation, the *gestor* would be liable only for intentional wrongdoing.[51] By contrast, where the *gestor* involved the principal in business that he or she did not normally undertake, the *gestor* would have to bear losses that arose even in the absence of fault.[52]

Chapter Summary

Quasi-contractual liability is an umbrella term for various situations in which the law holds a person liable without there being a contract between the parties, but where the situation is in some sense analogous to a contractual one. We have considered two such cases in this chapter: unjustified enrichment, where a person is enriched at another's expense without proper legal justification; and *negotiorum gestio*, which is relevant where a person acts reasonably on another's behalf, but without authority to do so. The law in both of these areas has influenced modern Scots law.

---

[45] As in *e.g. Fernie v Robertson* (1871) 9 M 437.
[46] As in *e.g. Kolbin & Sons v Kinnear & Co* 1930 SC 724.
[47] See *e.g.* D.3.5.10; D.3.5.45pr. Indeed, *negotiorum gestio* may even have initially arisen in non-emergency cases: Zimmermann, *Obligations* 436–8.
[48] D.3.5.9.1.
[49] C.2.18.11 (AD 227); C.2.18.15 (AD 239).
[50] J.3.27.1.
[51] D.3.5.3.9.
[52] D.3.5.10.

Further Reading

J.3.27
D.3.5; 12.4–7
C.2.18; 4.5–9
P Birks, *The Roman Law of Obligations* (E Descheemaeker ed, Oxford University Press 2014) chapter 11
R Evans-Jones, 'From "Undue Transfer" to "Retention without a Legal Basis" (The *Condictio Indebiti* and *Condictio ob Turpem vel Iniustam Causam*)' in R Evans-Jones ed, *The Civil Law Tradition in Scotland* (Stair Society 1995)
G D MacCormack, 'The *Condictio Causa Data Causa Non Secuta*' in R Evans-Jones ed, *The Civil Law Tradition in Scotland* (Stair Society 1995)
E Metzger ed, *A Companion to Justinian's Institutes* (Duckworth 1998) 169–71
R Zimmermann, *The Law of Obligations: Roman Foundations of the Civilian Tradition* (Oxford University Press 1996) chapters 14 and 26

CHAPTER TWENTY-SIX

Quasi-Delictual Liability

A. Nature and Scope of Quasi-Delictual Liability

The final part of the law of obligations is the law of quasi-delictual liability, the law concerned with obligations arising 'as though from wrongdoing'.[1] We do at least know the content of this category: Roman law imposed certain special liabilities on judges, occupiers of buildings, carriers by sea, innkeepers and stablekeepers. What is less clear is the basis for their categorisation together. This is a rather enigmatic category of obligations, fairly miscellaneous in its content. It is much more so than quasi-contract, and much ink has been spilt on the question of what binds the quasi-delicts together as a coherent category.[2] The theories usually focus on the aspects of strict liability or vicarious liability that are undoubtedly present in the quasi-delicts, though that is rather forced in the case of judges' liability. Perhaps, though, it is a mistake to approach things in this way. A better approach may be simply to say that the quasi-delicts all involve some element of wrongfulness, but each of the quasi-delicts, for one reason or another, does not fit within the law of delicts.

B. The Judge Who Made the Case His Own

In a system of litigation, some individual[3] is empowered by the state to determine the rights of disputing parties. Inevitably, at least one party is going to be disappointed by the decision reached.[4] On occasion, that party will have good reason to be disappointed, because the judge, whether through corruption, carelessness or inadvertence, has reached the wrong decision. Mistakes are inevitable in any human system, and the most that can be done is to minimise how often they

---

[1] J.3.13.2.
[2] For discussion, see P Stein, 'The Nature of Quasi-Delictal Obligations in Roman Law' (1958) 5 Revue Internationale des Droits de l'Antiquité (3rd series) 563; E Descheemaeker, *The Division of Wrongs: A Historical Comparative Study* (Oxford University Press 2009) chapters 3 and 4; E Descheemaeker, 'Obligations Quasi Ex Delicto and Strict Liability in Roman Law' (2010) 31 J Leg Hist 1.
[3] Or, of course, group of individuals, when two or more judges sit as a panel.
[4] Sometimes both parties will be disappointed, if the decision reached is not fully in either party's favour.

occur. One way of attempting to do this is to have a system of appeals, whereby a judge's decision can be reviewed by a higher court.

At the same time, though, in the interests of certainty and finality, there must be some limitation on the review of judges' decisions. In particular, there are dangers if the whole merits of the case can be reargued:

> To have allowed any reopening of a case on the pure merits of the matter would have been to destroy the system. We can be clear about that. To have done so would necessarily have been to pave the road to infinite rearguing of effectively the same point before a series of different judges.[5]

It is largely for this reason that the modern law on the whole excludes appeals on questions of fact.[6] Given that perfection cannot be attained by any human efforts, any system of review of judicial decisions must balance these considerations: the search for truth on the one hand, and certainty and finality on the other.

Under the *legis actiones* system of procedure, and subsequently the formulary system, used through the Republic and into the Early Empire, there was no system of appeals against judges' decisions.[7] Indeed, as we saw in Chapter 2,[8] judges under the *legis actiones* and formulary systems were not professional judges or (normally)[9] trained lawyers; instead, they were private individuals chosen by the parties to arbitrate on their dispute. As we also saw in Chapter 2, a disappointed litigant could not bring further proceedings against the same person on the same facts.[10] Accordingly, defeat in litigation was final.

The solution adopted during the Republic was to allow the disappointed litigant to sue the judge who, by giving the wrong decision, had 'made the case his own'. A new judge would be appointed who would, if the original judge was found liable, award damages according to his own discretion.[11]

Was the judge liable for any mistake, or was it necessary to show some degree of fault? The scope of this quasi-delict has long been a matter of controversy.[12] It seems certain at least that, in classical law under the formulary procedure, a judge would be liable for exceeding the authority given to him by the *formula* approved by the praetor, which gave the judge his instructions on what he was to

---

[5] D N MacCormick, 'Iudex Qui Litem Suam Facit' 1977 AJ 149, 151.
[6] *Stair Memorial Encyclopaedia* Civil Procedure (Reissue) para 264.
[7] See pp. 36 and 41. A system of appeals developed in the Empire, under the *cognitio* system.
[8] See p. 31.
[9] That is to say, there was no barrier to a trained lawyer acting as a judge, but equally there was no effort to ensure that the judge had legal expertise of his own.
[10] See pp. 35, 40. This is because, once the stage of *litis contestatio* had been reached (which happened in the *legis actiones* and formulary systems once the issues had been agreed before the praetor), the pursuer's cause of action was consumed.
[11] J.4.5pr.
[12] For a sample of the literature, see D Pugsley, '*Litem Suam Facere*' (1969) 4 Irish Jurist (NS) 351; D N MacCormick, 'Iudex Qui Litem Suam Facit' 1977 AJ 149; P B H Birks, 'A New Argument for a Narrow View of Litem Suam Facere' (1984) 52 TvR 373; O F Robinson, 'The "Iudex Qui Litem Suam Fecerit" Explained' (1999) 116 ZSS (rA) 195.

decide.[13] An example might be awarding 50 or 150 when the *formula* directed the judge either to award 100 or to absolve the defender, or else failing to give a valid decision at all. Equally, it seems probable that the judge would be liable for actual corruption, on the basis of this comment attributed to Ulpian:

> A judge is understood to make himself liable, when he deceitfully [*dolo malo*] gives a decision in fraud of the law (he is seen as having done this deceitfully if he is clearly shown to be guilty of bias, enmity or even corruption), and he is held liable for a fair estimation of the value of the action.[14]

By implication, though, this excludes liability for mere negligence. Partiality is one thing; a litigant who complained of judicial incompetence would likely be met with the retort that he or she had agreed on the identity of the judge, and should have picked better. In any case, the question of liability for negligence would generally be academic: as judges did not have to give reasons for their decisions, there would be no basis for attacking their findings of law or fact. The position may have been different under Justinian, though. He refers to judges incurring liability *per imprudentiam*, in other words by ignorance or carelessness,[15] though that may simply be intended as a reference to carelessness in understanding the extent of their authority rather than carelessness in applying the law or determining the facts.

It is likely that this quasi-delict declined in importance once a system of appeals was developed. This is certainly true in modern Scots law: while there are some older cases establishing the principle as applicable,[16] none is later than 1712.[17] A disappointed litigant would nowadays appeal rather than attempt to sue the judge.

C. Things Poured or Thrown

If the late first/early second century writer Juvenal is to be believed, merely to walk in the streets of Rome was a risky business:

> What extreme height to the lofty roofs from which a piece of pot falls down on my head, how often a broken vessel is shot from the upper windows, with what a force it strikes and dints the cobblestones! If you go out to dinner without long since

---

[13] See also G.4.52.
[14] D.5.1.15.1.
[15] J.4.5pr. See also D.44.7.5.4; D.50.13.6.
[16] See *e.g. Leitch v Fairy* (1711) Mor 13946, in which a judge was found liable for sitting in a case in which he had an interest. See also the striking case of *Stewart v Sinclair* (1694) 4 Bro Sup 195. In this case a clerk of the court was sued because his actions, later held to be wrongful, deprived the pursuer of the possibility of recovering a debt owed to her. He had acted on the instructions of one of the judges of the Court of Session, himself with the advice of other judges. The judges 'thought it unworthy to allow the clerk to suffer for what he did by their authority and warrant', and so they 'offered to pay the sum out of their own pockets'.
[17] *Lewars v Hay* (1712) 4 Bro Sup 894, in which it was held that a judge would not be liable simply for making a mistake. This is not to say that the conduct of members of the judiciary has ever after been entirely above reproach. See R S Shiels, 'The Ordeal of Advocates in 1896' 2006 SLT (News) 209.

having made a will, you'll be thought a fool, reckless of fate and sudden disaster; for as many sure deaths are lying in wait in the night as the open windows you pass in the street. So you hope and plaintively pray they may be content to treat you to showers of no more than what's in their full slop jars.[18]

The picture Juvenal paints is no doubt exaggerated. Nonetheless, it is also true that a great many Romans lived in high tenement buildings, without direct access to sewerage or means of waste disposal. For many, the easy option of disposal via the window would have been much more tempting than the long trip downstairs for proper disposal.

In this context, it is easy to understand why the occupier of premises was made quasi-delictually liable when anything caused damage by being poured or thrown from those premises. This was the case whether the premises were the defender's own, they were rented, or they had been provided gratuitously to the defender.[19] It was not necessary to prove that the occupier was responsible for the pouring or throwing: this was an example of vicarious liability, meaning liability for another person's acts. Accordingly, the victim might have a choice: either sue the actual thrower in delict or, if that person could not be identified, sue the occupier of the premises in quasi-delict.[20] Where property (including slaves) was damaged, liability was for double the value of the damage. Where a free man was killed, Justinian stated a fixed penalty of 50 *aurei*.[21] If a free man was injured, damages were in accordance with the judge's discretion, taking into account medical expenses and lost earnings.[22]

As noted, it was the occupier of the premises who was liable. Difficulties could arise with houses in multiple occupancy. Certainly, a guest was not liable under this quasi-delict, even if something was poured or thrown from the part of the house occupied by that guest.[23] A lodger might, however, be liable. Depending on the circumstances, the lodger, the owner or both might be liable.[24]

The status of this quasi-delict in modern Scots law is uncertain.[25] The institutional writer Bankton indeed tells us that it was received.[26] There is, however, a lack of modern authority.

---

[18] Adapted from Juvenal, *The Satires of Juvenal* (H Creekmore trans, Mentor 1963) lines 268–77.
[19] J.4.5.1.
[20] If the occupier was successfully sued, he or she could then recover from the actual thrower by an *actio in factum* or, in the case of a tenant, in an action on the lease: D.9.3.5.4.
[21] This was a popular action, which is to say that it could be brought by anyone. Preference was given, however, to one with a special interest in the matter or who was related by blood or marriage to the deceased: D.9.3.5.5.
[22] J.4.5.1; D.9.3.1pr.
[23] D.9.3.1.9.
[24] D.9.3.1.10; D.9.3.5pr–2.
[25] For discussion of this quasi-delict and its treatment in Scots law, see P Stein, 'The Actio de Effusis vel Dejectis and the Concept of Quasi-Delict in Scots Law' (1955) 4 ICLQ 356.
[26] Bankton, *Institutes* 1.4.31. The sheriff's contrary interpretation of this passage in *Gray v Dunlop* 1954 SLT (Sh Ct) 75 was rejected by the Inner House of the Court of Session in *McDyer v The Celtic Football and Athletic Co Ltd* 2000 SC 379, 389.

D. Things Hung or Suspended

Similarly to liability for things poured or thrown, there was also liability for leaving something 'placed or hanging where people come and go, which could harm someone if it fell'.[27] There was a fixed penalty for this,[28] imposed on the occupier of the premises or the person responsible for the placing or hanging.[29] This is therefore a further example of vicarious liability imposed on the occupier of premises.[30] There was no need for actual damage to occur.

The application of this quasi-delict in modern Scots law was considered in *McDyer v The Celtic Football and Athletic Co Ltd*.[31] In that case, the pursuer was a spectator at a sports stadium during the opening ceremony of the European Special Olympic Games, and was injured when a piece of wood fell from the stadium roof. He sued the owners of the stadium and the organisers of the event, in part on the basis of the quasi-delict. In the event, the quasi-delict was held not to apply, because it was concerned with harm to those outside the building rather than to those, like the pursuer, inside the building. This distinction has been criticised as not reflecting Roman law.[32]

E. Carriers by Sea, Innkeepers and Stablekeepers

Finally, special liability was imposed on carriers by sea,[33] innkeepers and stablekeepers for theft of or damage to goods in their care or on their premises (or, in the case of carriers by sea, the ship). This was in fact subject to two overlapping regimes, one of which is contractual rather than quasi-delictual, but which is dealt with here as a complete picture of the situation cannot otherwise be given.[34]

(1) Quasi-Delictual Liability

First, carriers by sea, innkeepers and stablekeepers were of course liable for thefts committed by themselves, but also for thefts committed by the members of the ship's crew,[35] staff of the inn or stable, or permanent residents of the inn.[36] This,

---

[27] J.4.5.1; D.9.3.5.6.
[28] The penalty stated at J.4.5.1 was 10 *aurei*.
[29] D.9.3.5.8.
[30] It is disputed, however, whether in this case the occupier had to be aware of the placing or hanging in order to be liable. Compare W M Gordon, 'The Actio de Posito Reconsidered' in Stein and Lewis, *Studies in Justinian's Institutes* and A Watson, 'Liability in the *Actio de Positis ac Suspensis*' in *Mélanges Philippe Meylan: Recueil de travaux publiés par la Faculté de droit*, vol 1 (Imprimerie Centrale de Lausanne 1963).
[31] 2000 SC 379. Consideration of the quasi-delict is at 387–91.
[32] T Wallinga, '*Effusa Vel Deiecta* in Rome and Glasgow' (2002) 6 Edin LR 117.
[33] The word used in the texts, *nauta*, has the ordinary meaning of 'sailor'. However, it was settled that, in this context, the word was to be understood as referring to those in charge of ships rather than to ordinary sailors: D.4.9.1.2.
[34] For discussion of the distinction between these two actions, see D S Bogen, 'Ignoring History: The Liability of Ships' Masters, Innkeepers and Stablekeepers Under Roman Law' (1992) 36 Am J Leg Hist 326.
[35] D.47.5.1pr.
[36] D.47.5.1.6.

said Justinian, was quasi-delictual because the party held liable might not be personally responsible for the theft, but was nonetheless 'in a sense guilty of fault for having used the services of bad people'.[37] This then is another example of vicarious liability. This liability did not extend to thefts by passengers on a ship or passing travellers at an inn or stable.[38] Liability was for double the value of the property stolen.[39]

(2) Edictal Liability for *Receptum*

The second ground of liability here is derived from a provision in the praetor's edict: 'The praetor says: "I will give an action against ships' masters, innkeepers and stablekeepers in respect of what they have received and undertaken to keep safe."'[40] Here liability was strict: the carrier, innkeeper or stablekeeper would be liable for theft or damage,[41] by whichever person it was committed.[42] Thus, liability extended to the acts of passengers on ships and passing travellers in the cases of inns and stables.[43] Absence of personal fault on the part of the carrier, innkeeper or stablekeeper was no defence; only unforeseeable events or superior force, such as a shipwreck or an attack by pirates, would absolve the defender.[44]

With this edictal liability, then, the carrier, innkeeper or stablekeeper was held responsible for a broader range of wrongdoers than with the quasi-delictual liability, as well as being responsible for damage as well as theft. Did the edictal liability then render the quasi-delictual liability redundant? The answer is that it did not, because the edictal liability was in another respect much more limited in scope. The key is in the words of the edict itself: carriers, innkeepers and stablekeepers were liable 'in respect of what they have received and undertaken to keep safe'. In other words, for edictal liability, it was not enough just that the stolen or damaged property was on the ship or in the inn or stable. Instead, the carrier, innkeeper or stablekeeper had to have made an undertaking, in the course of business,[45] to keep it safe. In other words, this was a form of contractual liability; specifically, we are concerned here with *receptum*, one of the innominate contracts considered in Chapter 21.[46] As such, liability could be excluded at the outset by agreement.[47] The carrier, innkeeper or stablekeeper would only be liable if the property had been entrusted to the care of someone in a position of authority. Thus, on a ship, it would not be enough to entrust the property to an ordinary sailor, unless the captain had directed this to be done.[48]

---

[37] J.4.5.3.
[38] D.47.5.1.6.
[39] D.47.5.1.2.
[40] D.4.9.1pr (Ulpian).
[41] For inclusion of both theft and damage, see D.4.9.5.1.
[42] The carrier, innkeeper or stablekeeper could, however, then pursue the actual wrongdoer: D.47.5.1.4.
[43] D.4.9.1.8–4.9.2.
[44] D.4.9.3.1.
[45] D.4.9.3.2.
[46] See p. 382.
[47] D.4.9.7pr.
[48] D.4.9.1.2–3. For the equivalent position with inns and stables, see D.4.9.1.5.

(3) Summary
Taken together, then, the result of these grounds of liability is the following:

- The carrier, innkeeper or stablekeeper was liable for thefts committed by employees and, in the case of an inn, permanent residents.
- If the carrier, innkeeper or stablekeeper had actually accepted responsibility for an item of property, strict liability was imposed for any theft of or damage to that property, even where the theft or damage was carried out by a passenger of a ship or a passing traveller using a stable or inn.

(4) Carriers, Innkeepers and Stablekeepers in Modern Law

There can be no doubt that this form of liability was received in Scots law.[49] Thus, for example, in *Mustard v Paterson*,[50] a stablekeeper was held strictly liable for injury to a horse entrusted to his care, unless he could show that it was the result of 'inevitable accident, or from the action of the King's enemies'.[51] Equally, carriers by sea are liable in the same way. Indeed, liability has been extended to carriers by land,[52] as long as they fall into the category of 'common carrier'.[53]

Most of the case law on this form of liability is concerned with innkeepers. From the authorities on innkeepers' liability, it appears that the two grounds of liability in Roman law – *receptum* and quasi-delict – have in Scots law been merged into a single ground of liability.[54] Thus, in *Scott v Yates*,[55] an innkeeper was held liable when items were stolen from a guest, even though the items in question had not been entrusted to the innkeeper's care. In *Williamson v White*,[56] the innkeeper was held liable even though the parcel from which money was later stolen was handed to a member of staff rather than to the innkeeper personally. There has been some question as to whether lodging houses are inns for these purposes. It was held that they were inns in *May v Wingate*[57] and *Watling v McDowall*,[58] although

---

[49] For a general account of the law as received, see J Mackintosh, '*Nautae Caupones Stabularii*: Special Liabilities of Shipmaster, Innkeepers, and Stablers' (1935) 47 JR 54.
[50] 1923 SC 142.
[51] 1923 SC 142, 148 (Lord Justice-Clerk).
[52] Though, in fact, it has been suggested that this is actually an extension of innkeeper's liability, arising from the close connection in the eighteenth century between the trades of innkeeping and carriage of goods by land: A Rodger, 'The Praetor's Edict and Carriage by Land in Scots Law' (1968) 3 Irish Jurist (NS) 175.
[53] A common carrier is one who 'undertakes for hire to transport the goods of all who choose to employ him in the business which he professes to ply' (W M Gloag and R C Henderson, *The Law of Scotland* 14th edn, H L MacQueen and Rt Hon Lord Eassie eds (W Green, 2017) para 21.02). In practice, most commercial carriers of goods contract out of the status of common carrier. Liability of a common carrier by land is now limited by the Carriers Act 1830, s. 1. In terms of that provision, such a carrier will only be liable, in the case of certain items with a value above £10, if the nature and value of the item are declared when the item is delivered to the carrier. The carrier may then charge a higher fee for carriage.
[54] Compare, though, R Zimmermann and P Simpson, 'Strict Liability' in *History of Private Law in Scotland, vol II* 570–2, where it is argued that *receptum*-liability alone, and not the quasi-delictual liability, was received in Scots law.
[55] (1800) Hume 207.
[56] 21 June 1810, FC.
[57] (1694) Mor 9236.
[58] (1825) 4 S 83.

in the latter case the fact of the theft being committed by a housebreaker was held to constitute *vis maior* ('superior force') excluding liability. By statute, this liability is now excluded as far as innkeepers are concerned unless the establishment is a hotel within the meaning of the Hotel Proprietors Act 1956.[59] In *Drake v Dow*,[60] it was held that a bed and breakfast establishment was not an inn, but that was partly on the basis of a concession by the pursuer that it was not a hotel within the meaning of the 1956 Act.[61]

Chapter Summary

The basis of Justinian's classification of certain grounds of liability as quasi-delictual is unclear. In each of four cases, however, this label is applied to situations in which a special liability is imposed on a person, but that liability is for some reason not thought of as property delictual. These situations are the liability of a judge who 'makes the case his own' by deciding wrongfully; the liability of an occupier of premises for damage caused by things poured or thrown from those premises; a similar liability for things hung or suspended from premises; and the liability of a carrier by sea, innkeeper or stablekeeper for theft of or damage to goods left in their care. Each of these has to some extent been received into Scots law, but their current scope and status is in each case a matter of some doubt.

Further Reading

J.4.5
D.4.9; 9.3
P Birks, *The Roman Law of Obligations* (E Descheemaeker ed, Oxford University Press 2014) chapter 11
E Metzger ed, *A Companion to Justinian's Institutes* (Duckworth 1998) 197–200
R Zimmermann, *The Law of Obligations: Roman Foundations of the Civilian Tradition* (Oxford University Press 1996) 15–20 and 1126–30

---

[59] Hotel Proprietors Act 1956, s. 1(1). Section 1(3) of this Act defines 'hotel' as meaning 'an establishment held out by the proprietor as offering food, drink and, if so required, sleeping accommodation, without special contract, to any traveller presenting himself who appears able and willing to pay a reasonable sum for the services and facilities provided and who is in a fit state to be received'. Further limitations on liability are contained in s. 2.

[60] 2006 SCLR 456. For discussion of the case, see P du Plessis, 'Innkeeper's Liability for Loss Suffered by Guests: *Drake v Dow*' (2007) 11 Edin LR 89.

[61] This concession was certainly unwise, given that it entirely undermined the pursuer's case. It may also have been unfounded: while the defenders stated that they did not hold themselves out as offering accommodation to travellers, the truth of that would have needed to be established by consideration of the evidence.

APPENDIX 1:

Roman Sources

A. Finding and Citing Roman Sources

Any study of Roman law that goes beyond a very basic level will require working directly with the primary sources of Roman law, the legal texts produced by the Romans themselves. To be able to do this, it will be necessary to learn how to find these, and for this it will be necessary to learn to understand how Roman sources are cited.

The purpose of this appendix is twofold. First, it explains how the main Roman sources are found and cited. Second, it lists all of the Roman legal sources referred to in the book, together with where they are found in the book. This will allow those with an interest in a particular Roman text to find any passages in the book where it is discussed.

To explain the standard system of citation for Roman texts, let us take an example. Suppose we see the following on the page: 'D.7.1.68.2'. What is this referring to? First, the letter at the beginning shows which work is being referred to. In this case, the letter 'D' indicates that we need to look at the work called the *Digest* of Justinian. Other works are indicated by other letters. References to Justinian's *Institutes* begin 'J' (or sometimes 'Inst' or 'J Inst'). References to Justinian's *Codex* begin 'C', and references to the *Novels* begin 'Nov'. Where the reference begins 'G', this is a reference to Gaius' *Institutes*. 'C.Th.' is a reference to the *Codex Theodosianus*.

After the initial letter or letters, there will be one or more numbers. These indicate where exactly in the work there is to be found the passage referred to. We have seen that D.7.1.68.2 is in the *Digest*. The *Digest* is divided into fifty books, and the first number shows that this passage is from book 7. Each book is further divided into one or more titles, and this is the next number.[1] In this case, then, the passage is from book 7, title 1.

As we saw in Chapter 3,[2] each title of the *Digest* is made up of a number of extracts from different Roman jurists. These extracts are called *leges* (singular *lex*),

---

[1] In those books containing only a single title, this number may be omitted.
[2] See p. 65.

and each is numbered. Each *lex*, except for very short ones, is further subdivided into numbered paragraphs. These are the final two numbers.

Taking all this together, D.7.1.68.2 can then be found by looking up book 7, title 1, *lex* 68, paragraph 2.

There is a final complication to mention in this system. The first paragraph in a *lex* has no number. Instead, it is marked with *pr* (for *principium*, 'beginning'). The first paragraph in D.7.1.68 is, therefore, D.7.1.68pr.[3] D.7.1.68.2 is the third paragraph, not the second.

References to other Roman legal literature work on essentially this system, though some have fewer numbers. For example, Justinian's *Institutes* lack the division of titles into *leges*, so a reference to a passage in the *Institutes* will have at most three numbers. In Gaius' *Institutes*, there is no division into titles. There is only a division into book and paragraph, so a reference to Gaius' *Institutes* will have at most two numbers.

B. Texts from the *Corpus Iuris Civilis*

(1) The *Digest*

The standard English translation of the *Digest* is A Watson ed, *The Digest of Justinian* (4 vols, University of Pennsylvania Press 2009). In addition to the text of the *Digest* itself, three important imperial pronouncements are included. These are the *Constitutio Deo auctore*, which instructed the compilation of the *Digest*; and the *Constitutio omnem* and *Constitutio tanta*, which announced its completion.

Constitutio Deo auctore, 65, 66	D.1.4.2, 53	D.2.13.1pr, 29, 37
7, 65	D.1.5.3, 96	D.2.14.1.3, 326
9, 65	D.1.5.4.1, 103	D.2.14.7.4, 327, 381
10, 65	D.1.5.9, 97	D.2.14.7.5, 364, 382
Constitutio omnem, 66	D.1.5.12, 122, 123	D.2.15.1, 381
Constitutio tanta, 66	D.1.5.18, 104	D.3.2.1, 101
1–8c, 68	D.1.6.2, 108	D.3.4.1pr, 95
15, 68	D.1.6.6, 123	D.3.4.7.1, 95
D.1.1.7.1, 51	D.1.6.9, 117	D.3.5.2, 434
D.1.2.2.6, 55	D.1.7.15pr, 125	D.3.5.3.9, 435
D.1.2.2.7, 55	D.1.7.15.3, 124, 125	D.3.5.9.1, 435
D.1.2.2.35, 55	D.1.7.16, 124	D.3.5.10, 435
D.1.2.2.43, 31	D.1.7.28, 127	D.3.5.45pr, 435
D.1.2.2.48, 56	D.1.7.40pr, 125	D.4.2.1, 205, 424
D.1.2.2.49, 57	D.1.7.40.1, 124	D.4.2.3.1, 424, 425
D.1.4.1pr, 53	D.2.2.47, 56	D.4.2.6, 424
	D.2.4.5, 122	D.4.2.9.8, 206

---

[3] Note that there is no full stop between the *lex* number and *pr*.

D.4.2.13, 189, 422
D.4.2.14.3, 206
D.4.2.14.5, 206
D.4.2.21pr, 425
D.4.3.1pr, 205
D.4.3.1pr–1, 423
D.4.3.1.2, 423
D.4.3.7.9, 423
D.4.3.9.1, 424
D.4.3.9.2, 424
D.4.3.11.1, 424
D.4.3.38, 424
D.4.3.39, 424
D.4.3.40, 423
D.4.4.1, 130
D.4.5.2.2, 322
D.4.5.11, 95, 97
D.4.8.13.2, 382
D.4.9.1pr, 442
D.4.9.1.2, 441
D.4.9.1.2–3, 442
D.4.9.1.5, 442
D.4.9.1.8–4.9.2, 442
D.4.9.3.1, 442
D.4.9.3.2, 442
D.4.9.5.1, 442
D.4.9.7pr, 442
D.5.1.15.1, 439
D.5.2.1, 310
D.5.2.2, 310
D.5.2.3, 311
D.5.2.4, 311
D.5.2.5, 310
D.5.2.8.14, 310
D.6.1.5pr, 238
D.6.1.5.1, 237
D.6.1.5.2, 228
D.6.1.6, 232
D.6.1.9, 189
D.6.1.23.2, 228
D.6.1.23.3, 229
D.6.1.23.5, 227, 230
D.6.1.23.6, 225
D.6.1.23.6–7, 225

D.6.1.27.3, 190
D.6.1.27.5, 185
D.6.1.33, 190
D.6.1.37, 183, 224
D.6.1.38, 185, 224
D.6.1.41pr, 205
D.6.1.48, 224
D.6.1.61, 228
D.6.1.67, 239
D.6.1.68, 43
D.6.2.16–17, 186
D.7.1.1, 259
D.7.1.7.2, 264
D.7.1.9pr, 264
D.7.1.10, 262
D.7.1.12.2, 261
D.7.1.13pr, 264
D.7.1.13.2, 263
D.7.1.13.5, 263
D.7.1.13.6, 263
D.7.1.13.7, 264
D.7.1.15.4, 261
D.7.1.22, 261
D.7.1.44, 265
D.7.1.68pr, 261
D.7.1.68.2, 264
D.7.1.69, 264
D.7.2.8, 259
D.7.4.3.3, 267
D.7.4.5.2, 267
D.7.4.10.1, 267
D.7.7.6.1, 262
D.7.8.2pr, 260
D.7.8.2.1–7.8.7, 261
D.7.9.1pr, 263
D.7.9.1.2, 263
D.7.9.1.3, 263
D.7.9.5pr, 263
D.7.9.7pr, 264
D.8.1.1, 244
D.8.1.2, 171
D.8.1.5.1, 252
D.8.1.7, 248
D.8.1.8pr, 246

D.8.1.9, 252, 254
D.8.1.14pr, 253
D.8.1.15pr, 247
D.8.1.15.1, 246
D.8.1.16, 255
D.8.2.2, 249
D.8.2.6, 257
D.8.2.10, 169
D.8.2.16, 249
D.8.2.30pr, 257
D.8.2.31, 251
D.8.2.33, 246
D.8.2.38, 246
D.8.3.1.2, 251
D.8.3.3.1–2, 248
D.8.3.3.3, 252
D.8.3.5.1, 246, 247
D.8.3.6pr, 247
D.8.3.6.1, 252
D.8.3.7pr, 248
D.8.3.7.1, 246
D.8.3.8, 248
D.8.3.12, 248
D.8.3.13.1–3, 252
D.8.3.15, 254
D.8.3.23.3, 254
D.8.3.25, 254
D.8.3.29, 247
D.8.3.34pr, 171
D.8.3.36, 251
D.8.4.1.1, 245
D.8.4.3, 251
D.8.4.5, 251
D.8.4.6, 251
D.8.4.6pr, 246
D.8.4.6.3a, 252
D.8.4.7.1, 254
D.8.4.8, 252
D.8.4.11, 254
D.8.4.12, 245
D.8.4.14, 252
D.8.5.2pr, 255
D.8.5.4.2, 255
D.8.5.4.5, 255

D.8.5.6.2, 246
D.8.5.8.5, 169, 249, 368
D.8.5.10pr, 254, 257
D.8.5.17pr, 249
D.8.5.17.2, 249
D.8.6.1, 245, 257
D.8.6.6.1, 257
D.8.6.8pr, 257
D.8.6.11pr, 252
D.8.6.13, 254
D.8.6.17, 252
D.8.10pr, 260
D.9.1.1pr, 425
D.9.1.1.3, 425
D.9.1.1.7, 425
D.9.1.1.10, 426
D.9.1.3, 411
D.9.2.1pr, 387
D.9.2.2pr, 388
D.9.2.2.2, 388
D.9.2.4, 392
D.9.2.5.3, 398
D.9.2.7.4, 392
D.9.2.7.5, 394
D.9.2.7.7, 398
D.9.2.8pr, 394
D.9.2.8.1, 393
D.9.2.9pr, 395
D.9.2.9.3, 395
D.9.2.9.4, 393, 398
D.9.2.11pr, 397
D.9.2.11.2, 386
D.9.2.11.3, 396
D.9.2.11.5, 398
D.9.2.12, 398
D.9.2.13pr, 398
D.9.2.22pr, 391
D.9.2.22.1, 391
D.9.2.23pr, 391
D.9.2.23.2, 301
D.9.2.23.3–6, 388
D.9.2.23.4, 391
D.9.2.23.7, 448
D.9.2.27.5, 389

D.9.2.27.9, 395
D.9.2.27.20, 389
D.9.2.27.21, 395
D.9.2.29.3, 391, 392
D.9.2.29.7, 195
D.9.2.31, 391
D.9.2.44pr, 391
D.9.2.45.3, 395
D.9.2.45.4, 392
D.9.2.49.1, 392
D.9.2.51pr–1, 396
D.9.2.51.1, 396
D.9.2.51.2, 388
D.9.2.52.1, 398
D.9.2.52.4, 392
D.9.3.1pr, 440
D.9.3.1.9, 440
D.9.3.1.10, 440
D.9.3.5pr–2, 440
D.9.3.5.4, 440
D.9.3.5.5, 440
D.9.3.5.6, 441
D.9.3.5.8, 441
D.9.3.7, 398
D.9.4.7pr, 155
D.10.1.2, 406
D.10.1.2.1, 170
D.10.1.3, 170
D.10.1.5–6, 170
D.10.1.8pr, 170
D.10.1.13, 170
D.10.2, 172
D.10.2.17, 172
D.10.3.3pr, 172
D.10.3.14.2, 171
D.10.3.28, 171
D.10.4.1–2, 190
D.10.4.3.7, 190
D.10.4.3.14, 228
D.10.4.12.3, 234
D.10.4.19, 190
D.11.3.1pr, 422, 423
D.11.3.1.4, 422
D.11.3.1.5, 422

D.11.3.2, 422
D.11.3.10, 423
D.11.3.11.1, 423
D.11.7.14.8, 287
D.12.1.2.2, 345
D.12.1.3, 345
D.12.1.18pr, 206, 208
D.12.1.18.1, 208, 329
D.12.1.32, 330, 432
D.12.2.1, 38
D.12.4.1pr, 431
D.12.4.5.4, 432
D.12.5.1.2, 431
D.12.5.3, 431
D.12.5.8, 431
D.12.6.1, 430
D.12.6.2pr, 430
D.12.6.14, 431
D.12.6.19pr, 347
D.12.6.64, 448
D.12.6.65.5, 448
D.12.6.66, 431
D.12.7.2, 431
D.13.5.1pr, 382
D.13.6.3.1, 348
D.13.6.3.2, 347
D.13.6.3.6, 347
D.13.6.4, 47
D.13.6.5.2, 272
D.13.6.5.10, 348
D.13.6.17.3, 348
D.13.6.18pr, 347, 348
D.13.6.18.2, 348
D.13.6.18.3, 348
D.13.7.1pr, 270
D.13.7.8pr, 272
D.13.7.9.3, 272
D.13.7.11.6, 175
D.13.7.18.3, 253
D.13.7.24.3, 272
D.14.1.1.20, 150
D.14.1.6pr, 155
D.14.2.1–2pr, 371
D.14.3.5.11, 151

D.14.4.1.2, 155
D.14.6.1pr, 346
D.14.6.2, 121
D.14.6.3pr, 347
D.14.6.7.15, 347
D.14.6.7.16, 347
D.15.1.4pr, 152
D.15.1.4.1, 153
D.15.1.4.2, 449
D.15.1.5.4, 152, 153
D.15.1.7.4, 152
D.15.1.7.6, 152
D.15.1.8, 153
D.15.1.21pr, 153
D.15.2.1pr–1, 153
D.15.3.1.1, 154
D.15.3.3.3–4, 154
D.15.4.1.1, 151
D.15.4.1.6, 151
D.16.1, 98
D.16.1.2.1, 98
D.16.1.2.2, 98
D.16.3.1.1, 349
D.16.3.1.4, 349
D.16.3.1.8, 349
D.16.3.1.23, 349
D.16.3.1.38, 407, 408
D.16.3.5–6, 177
D.16.3.5.1, 350
D.16.3.12pr, 349
D.16.3.17.1, 449
D.16.3.23, 449
D.16.3.26.1, 350
D.16.3.28, 350
D.16.3.32, 349
D.17.1.1.4, 371
D.17.1.3.2, 373
D.17.1.4, 373
D.17.1.6.4, 372
D.17.1.8.6, 372
D.17.1.12.17, 373
D.17.2.4.1, 375
D.17.2.7, 374
D.17.2.20, 375

D.17.2.29pr, 375
D.17.2.29.1, 375
D.17.2.40, 375
D.17.2.52.13, 374
D.17.2.52.15, 375
D.17.2.60.1–17.2.61, 375
D.17.2.65.5, 376
D.17.2.72, 375
D.17.2.82, 376
D.18.1.1.1, 355
D.18.1.1.2, 352
D.18.1.2.1, 355
D.18.1.3, 337
D.18.1.4–6pr, 335
D.18.1.7.1, 355
D.18.1.8pr, 354
D.18.1.8.1, 354
D.18.1.9, 331
D.18.1.9pr, 329
D.18.1.9.1, 329
D.18.1.9.2, 330
D.18.1.11.1, 331
D.18.1.14, 331
D.18.1.15pr, 353
D.18.1.18pr, 203
D.18.1.25.1, 359
D.18.1.34.3, 354
D.18.1.35.5, 356
D.18.1.35.7, 353
D.18.1.38, 355
D.18.1.40.1, 252
D.18.1.41.1, 331
D.18.1.43.1, 360
D.18.1.57pr, 354
D.18.1.67, 353
D.18.1.69, 226
D.18.1.74, 211
D.18.2.1, 336
D.18.2.2pr, 336
D.18.2.2.1, 336
D.18.3.2, 337
D.18.3.5, 336
D.18.3.6pr, 337
D.18.4.11, 354

D.18.5.5.1, 325
D.18.6.1.2, 210
D.18.6.2–3, 358
D.18.6.2.1, 358
D.18.6.8pr, 356
D.18.6.15.1, 210
D.18.6.18, 364
D.19.1.1.1, 358, 359
D.19.1.2.1, 359
D.19.1.4pr, 361
D.19.1.6.1, 355
D.19.1.6.4, 363
D.19.1.9, 364
D.19.1.11.2, 359
D.19.1.13pr, 363
D.19.1.13.19–20, 364
D.19.1.13.22, 364
D.19.1.17pr, 359
D.19.1.17.6, 190, 359
D.19.1.21.3, 358
D.19.1.31pr, 358
D.19.1.36, 358
D.19.2.2pr, 365
D.19.2.2.1, 366
D.19.2.9.5, 370
D.19.2.11.2, 369
D.19.2.13.5, 371
D.19.2.13.6, 370
D.19.2.14, 367
D.19.2.15.2, 369
D.19.2.19.1, 368
D.19.2.19.2, 368
D.19.2.19.9, 370
D.19.2.21, 205, 358
D.19.2.22.3, 355
D.19.2.24pr, 370
D.19.2.24.4, 368
D.19.2.24.5, 283
D.19.2.30.2, 393
D.19.2.38pr, 370
D.19.2.52, 329
D.19.2.55.1, 368
D.19.2.59, 371
D.19.2.62, 371

D.19.4, 381
D.19.4.1pr, 381
D.19.5, 380
D.19.5.5pr, 104
D.19.5.11, 51
D.20.1.4, 275
D.20.1.6, 275
D.20.1.8, 275
D.20.1.11.1, 272
D.20.1.21.2, 272
D.20.2.2, 274
D.20.2.3, 274
D.20.2.4pr, 274
D.20.2.7pr, 274
D.20.2.7.1, 274
D.20.4.11pr, 275
D.21.1.1.1, 361, 362
D.21.1.1.8, 361
D.21.1.1.9, 362
D.21.1.4–6pr, 361
D.21.1.4.1, 362
D.21.1.4.2, 362
D.21.1.4.3, 362
D.21.1.6, 361
D.21.1.9, 362
D.21.1.10.3, 362
D.21.1.12.3, 362
D.21.1.12.4, 362
D.21.1.14pr, 362
D.21.1.14.1, 362
D.21.1.14.4, 362
D.21.1.14.7, 362
D.21.1.14.10, 361
D.21.1.15, 362
D.21.1.17.14, 361
D.21.1.23.2, 362
D.21.1.23.3, 362
D.21.1.28, 361
D.21.1.38pr, 361
D.21.1.38.7, 361
D.21.1.40–2, 426
D.21.1.41, 426
D.21.1.42, 426
D.21.1.55, 361

D.21.1.63, 363
D.21.2.2, 359
D.22.1.29, 346
D.22.1.45, 184
D.22.2.1, 345
D.22.2.3, 345
D.22.2.5pr–1, 346
D.22.3.2, 191
D.22.3.19pr, 191
D.22.3.29.1, 122
D.22.6.1.2, 122
D.23.1.4, 137
D.23.1.5, 137
D.23.1.10, 137
D.23.1.11, 137
D.23.1.12, 137
D.23.1.14, 137
D.23.1.15, 141
D.23.1.18, 137
D.23.2.2, 120
D.23.2.5, 140
D.23.2.8, 139
D.23.2.12.1–2, 137
D.23.2.12.4, 140
D.23.2.17pr–1, 139
D.23.2.17.2, 139
D.23.2.19, 120, 145
D.23.2.23, 141
D.23.2.24, 141
D.23.2.30, 140
D.23.2.31, 141
D.23.2.44pr, 141
D.23.2.57a, 137
D.23.3.7pr, 145, 146
D.23.3.17pr, 146
D.23.3.39pr, 106
D.24.1.1, 144
D.24.1.31.8, 144
D.24.1.31.9, 144
D.24.1.32.13, 140
D.24.2.3, 145
D.24.2.9, 145
D.25.3.1, 123
D.25.3.5pr, 119

D.25.3.5.1, 120
D.25.3.5.2, 119
D.25.3.5.4, 119
D.25.3.5.7, 120
D.25.3.5.11, 120
D.25.3.6.1, 113
D.25.4.10, 123
D.25.7.1pr, 116, 136
D.25.7.1.1, 136
D.25.7.3pr, 136
D.25.7.3.1, 136
D.26.1.1pr, 128
D.26.7.1pr, 128
D.26.7.7, 129
D.26.7.12.3, 129
D.26.8.9pr, 128, 129
D.26.8.9.1, 128
D.26.8.9.3, 129
D.26.10.3.18, 129
D.27.1, 128
D.27.10.1pr, 100
D.27.10.5, 41
D.27.10.7pr, 100
D.27.10.10pr, 100
D.28.1.18pr, 296
D.28.1.18.1, 101
D.28.1.2, 296
D.28.1.3, 295
D.28.1.6pr, 295
D.28.1.6.1, 296
D.28.1.7, 296
D.28.1.12, 106
D.28.1.21.3, 298
D.28.1.26, 101
D.28.1.27, 299
D.28.2.2, 309
D.28.2.11, 284
D.28.2.12pr, 305
D.28.3.12pr, 309
D.28.5.1pr, 300, 301
D.28.6.2pr, 302
D.28.7.1, 301
D.28.7.3, 301
D.28.7.11, 301

D.28.7.14, 301, 308
D.28.7.27pr, 301
D.29.1.1pr, 298
D.29.1.3, 316
D.29.1.4, 296
D.29.2.37, 283
D.29.2.57pr, 285
D.29.2.99, 285
D.29.5.1, 106
D.30.1.44.2, 233
D.31.87.3, 312
D.31.88.15, 315
D.32.1.88pr, 233
D.34.2.33, 307
D.34.3.11, 307
D.34.7.1pr, 308
D.34.7.2, 308
D.34.9.1, 306
D.34.9.9pr, 306
D.34.9.9.1, 306
D.35.1.3, 308
D.35.1.7pr, 308
D.35.1.14, 301
D.35.1.15, 140
D.35.1.17.1, 329
D.35.1.18, 308
D.36.1.1.2, 315
D.36.1.14, 117
D.36.1.69.2, 285
D.36.2.7pr, 307
D.37.1.3.9–37.1.5, 292
D.37.12.5, 119
D.37.13.1.1, 297
D.38.1.15pr, 114
D.38.1.27, 114
D.38.1.31, 113
D.38.1.38pr, 114
D.38.6.1.8, 302
D.38.8.1.3, 291
D.38.8.1.4, 292
D.38.15.1pr, 290
D.38.15.2pr, 291
D.38.16.3.11, 123
D.38.16.3.12, 123

D.38.16.14, 284
D.39.1.20pr, 168
D.39.2.2, 168
D.39.2.4.1, 168
D.39.2.5pr, 168
D.39.2.6, 168
D.39.2.43pr, 168
D.39.3.1.2, 169
D.39.3.1.3–7, 169
D.39.3.1.23, 169
D.39.3.2.1, 169
D.39.3.24pr, 169
D.39.5.6, 212
D.39.5.25, 205
D.39.5.27, 267
D.39.5.31.2, 127
D.39.6.2, 313
D.39.6.25pr, 312
D.39.6.35pr, 313
D.39.6.35.3, 313
D.39.6.37pr, 313
D.40.2.15.1, 110
D.40.4.24, 110
D.40.4.29, 122, 284
D.40.7.3.16, 110
D.40.9.10, 109
D.41.1, 68
D.41.1.1, 68
D.41.1.2, 228
D.41.1.3, 68
D.41.1.3.2, 220
D.41.1.4, 220
D.41.1.5, 68, 221
D.41.1.5pr, 220
D.41.1.5.1, 220
D.41.1.5.3, 228
D.41.1.7, 68, 233, 234
D.41.1.7.1, 225
D.41.1.7.10, 225
D.41.1.7.10–11, 225
D.41.1.7.12, 224, 225
D.41.1.7.13, 223
D.41.1.7.2, 226
D.41.1.7.3, 226

D.41.1.7.6, 226
D.41.1.7.7, 233, 234
D.41.1.7.8, 237
D.41.1.7.8–9, 237
D.41.1.9, 68
D.41.1.9pr, 224
D.41.1.9.1, 228
D.41.1.9.2, 228, 231
D.41.1.9.5, 212
D.41.1.9.6, 211
D.41.1.9.7, 212
D.41.1.12pr, 226
D.41.1.12.1, 237
D.41.1.13, 175
D.41.1.14pr, 196
D.41.1.14.1, 197
D.41.1.20pr, 202
D.41.1.20.2, 210
D.41.1.24, 233
D.41.1.26pr, 228, 233
D.41.1.26.1, 225
D.41.1.26.2, 233
D.41.1.27.2, 228
D.41.1.30.1, 170
D.41.1.30.3, 226
D.41.1.31pr, 208
D.41.1.31.1, 239
D.41.1.36, 208
D.41.1.48, 185
D.41.1.48pr, 184
D.41.1.50, 196, 197
D.41.1.51.1, 218
D.41.1.55, 219, 389
D.41.1.58, 217
D.41.1.59, 175, 372
D.41.2, 178
D.41.2.1.3, 177, 181
D.41.2.1.15, 174
D.41.2.1.21, 211
D.41.2.3pr, 176, 256
D.41.2.3.1, 173, 174
D.41.2.3.5, 174, 177
D.41.2.3.6, 180
D.41.2.3.8, 181

D.41.2.3.11, 180
D.41.2.3.13, 180
D.41.2.3.14, 219
D.41.2.3.17, 174
D.41.2.3.19, 179
D.41.2.3.20, 180
D.41.2.6.1, 181
D.41.2.7, 181
D.41.2.8, 180
D.41.2.10.1, 178
D.41.2.12.1, 173
D.41.2.13pr, 181
D.41.2.18pr, 180, 213
D.41.2.18.2, 175, 211
D.41.2.19pr, 180
D.41.2.24pr, 207
D.41.2.26, 207
D.41.2.30pr, 175
D.41.2.41, 175
D.41.2.51, 211
D.41.3.4.6, 240
D.41.3.4.28, 257
D.41.3.16, 174
D.41.3.24pr, 240
D.41.3.41, 175
D.41.7.2pr, 217
D.41.7.2.1, 217
D.42.1.15.2, 44
D.42.1.15.3, 44
D.42.1.15.5, 270
D.42.1.31, 43, 44
D.42.5.31.5, 411
D.42.6.1pr, 288
D.42.6.1.13, 288
D.42.6.1.18, 286
D.42.8.5, 218
D.43.2.1, 293
D.43.2.2, 293
D.43.3.1.1, 182
D.43.7.1, 197
D.43.7.3pr, 193
D.43.8.2pr, 197
D.43.8.2.21–4, 195
D.43.8.2.24, 195

D.43.8.3.1, 196
D.43.10, 195
D.43.10.1.3, 368
D.43.11.2, 195
D.43.12.1.3, 195
D.43.16.1.27, 187, 392
D.43.16.1.30, 188
D.43.16.3.2–4, 189
D.43.16.3.13, 267
D.43.16.3.17, 267
D.43.17.4, 267
D.43.19, 257
D.43.19.3.11, 246, 254
D.43.19.3.14, 246, 254
D.43.19.7, 256
D.43.20, 257
D.43.22, 257
D.43.24.4, 169
D.43.26.1pr, 177
D.43.26.1–2pr, 381
D.43.26.2pr–2, 177
D.43.26.2.3, 256
D.43.26.6.2, 267
D.43.26.20, 205
D.43.27.1.8–9, 170
D.43.28.1, 170
D.43.30.1pr, 119
D.43.30.1.3, 119
D.43.30.1.5, 144
D.43.30.3pr, 119
D.43.30.3.4, 119
D.43.30.5, 119
D.43.40.3.4, 119
D.44.4, 423
D.44.4.4.31, 206
D.44.4.4.33, 206
D.44.7.1pr, 323, 428
D.44.7.3pr, 322
D.44.7.5.3, 430
D.44.7.5.4, 439
D.44.7.34pr, 385
D.44.7.39, 120
D.44.7.54, 205
D.45.1.1.2, 341

D.45.1.1.6, 340, 341
D.45.1.5pr, 340
D.45.1.5.1, 339
D.45.1.13, 341
D.45.1.26–7pr, 334
D.45.1.38.17, 328, 340
D.45.1.38.20, 328
D.45.1.83pr, 321
D.45.1.103, 334
D.45.1.134pr, 137
D.45.1.137, 335
D.45.1.137pr, 340
D.45.3.39, 59
D.46.2.1pr, 325
D.46.3.70, 337
D.46.3.78, 203
D.46.3.79, 175, 211
D.46.3.107, 325
D.47.2.1.3, 417
D.47.2.7.2, 420
D.47.2.15.2, 276, 349
D.47.2.21pr, 418
D.47.2.21.8, 418
D.47.2.22.1, 418
D.47.2.37, 419
D.47.2.43.5, 418
D.47.2.46.1, 419
D.47.2.50pr, 420
D.47.2.50.4, 389
D.47.2.51, 395
D.47.2.52.20, 63, 418
D.47.2.52.28, 420
D.47.2.55pr, 272
D.47.2.58, 418
D.47.2.62.8, 274
D.47.2.66, 419
D.47.2.68.1, 420
D.47.5.1pr, 441
D.47.5.1.2, 442
D.47.5.1.4, 442
D.47.5.1.6, 441, 442
D.47.7.6.2, 170
D.47.10.1.4, 407
D.47.10.1.6, 407

D.47.10.1.9, 98, 409
D.47.10.3.1, 408
D.47.10.3.3, 408
D.47.10.4, 408
D.47.10.7pr, 410
D.47.10.7.8, 411
D.47.10.7.8–9, 411
D.47.10.11.1, 409
D.47.10.13.1, 409
D.47.10.13.3, 406
D.47.10.13.7, 196, 219, 407
D.47.10.15pr, 406
D.47.10.15.2–5, 407
D.47.10.15.22–3, 406
D.47.10.15.24, 137
D.47.10.15.27, 407
D.47.10.15.31, 411
D.47.10.15.33, 411
D.47.10.15.35, 406
D.47.10.15.46, 385
D.47.10.17.12–13, 410
D.47.10.18pr, 409
D.47.10.19, 278

D.47.10.19–20, 411
D.47.10.22, 406
D.47.10.23, 407, 409
D.47.10.24, 407
D.47.10.25, 407, 408
D.47.10.26, 407, 408
D.47.10.27, 407
D.47.10.30pr, 410
D.47.10.32, 409
D.47.10.33, 408
D.47.10.34, 410
D.47.10.39, 407
D.47.10.44, 408
D.48.5.2.2, 135
D.48.5.6.1, 135
D.48.5.12.13, 146
D.48.5.21–2, 118
D.48.5.24, 118
D.48.5.25pr–1, 135
D.48.5.30pr, 135
D.48.5.39.8, 135
D.48.6–7, 189
D.48.7.7, 189, 422

D.48.8.2, 118
D.48.8.4.2, 108
D.48.9.5, 118
D.48.15.6.2, 103
D.49.15.8, 106
D.49.15.12.4, 106
D.49.15.14.1, 106
D.49.17.10–11, 121
D.50.13.1, 371
D.50.13.1.4, 369
D.50.13.6, 439
D.50.16.110, 117, 350
D.50.16.176, 324
D.50.16.195.2, 116
D.50.17.2, 97
D.50.17.38, 386
D.50.17.54, 203
D.50.17.73.2, 169
D.50.17.132, 369
D.50.17.133, 150
D.50.17.185, 334

(2) Justinian's *Institutes*

There are numerous English translations of the *Institutes*. A very useful one is a parallel Latin and English text, with introduction: P Birks and G McLeod, *Justinian's Institutes* (Duckworth 1987).

J.1.1.2, 69
J.1.2.2, 103
J.1.4pr, 104, 112
J.1.5.1, 109
J.1.5.2, 109
J.1.5.3, 113
J.1.6pr, 109
J.1.6.2, 110
J.1.6.3, 109
J.1.6.4–6, 109, 110
J.1.7, 110
J.1.9pr, 116
J.1.9.1, 134

J.1.9.2, 117
J.1.9.3, 116
J.1.10pr, 138, 140
J.1.10.1, 139
J.1.10.2, 139
J.1.10.3, 139, 140
J.1.10.4, 139
J.1.10.6–7, 140
J.1.10.8, 140
J.1.10.10, 139
J.1.10.12, 116, 137
J.1.10.13, 126
J.1.11.2, 125

J.1.11.10, 124
J.1.11.12, 112
J.1.12.6, 127
J.1.12.8, 125
J.1.19, 128
J.1.22pr, 129
J.1.22.6, 129
J.1.23.2, 130
J.1.24pr, 129
J.1.25, 128
J.2.1.2, 195
J.2.1.3, 196
J.2.1.4, 195, 196

J.2.1.5, 196
J.2.1.8, 195
J.2.1.9, 195
J.2.1.12, 219, 220
J.2.1.13, 220
J.2.1.13–14, 221
J.2.1.14, 219, 228
J.2.1.15, 219, 220
J.2.1.16, 219
J.2.1.17, 218
J.2.1.18, 217
J.2.1.20, 170, 226
J.2.1.21–4, 170
J.2.1.22, 226
J.2.1.22–3, 170
J.2.1.23, 226
J.2.1.24, 226, 233, 236
J.2.1.25, 231, 233, 236
J.2.1.25–8, 231
J.2.1.26, 228, 231
J.2.1.27, 237
J.2.1.28, 238
J.2.1.29, 222, 224, 225
J.2.1.29–32, 166
J.2.1.30, 183, 185, 224, 225
J.2.1.31–2, 223
J.2.1.32, 224
J.2.1.33, 228, 230
J.2.1.34, 229
J.2.1.35, 184
J.2.1.36, 261
J.2.1.37, 167, 261
J.2.1.38, 264
J.2.1.39, 239
J.2.1.41, 358
J.2.1.43, 164, 231
J.2.1.44, 212
J.2.1.45, 211
J.2.1.46, 212
J.2.2.1, 197
J.2.2.2, 197, 323
J.2.3pr, 248
J.2.3.1, 247, 248, 249
J.2.3.2, 248, 249

J.2.3.4, 251
J.2.4pr, 259, 267
J.2.4.1, 260
J.2.4.2, 260
J.2.4.3, 259, 267
J.2.5pr–1, 260
J.2.5.1, 261, 262
J.2.5.2, 260
J.2.5.3, 260
J.2.6pr, 239, 241, 242
J.2.6.1, 240
J.2.6.2, 240
J.2.6.4, 240
J.2.6.5, 240
J.2.6.7, 240, 241
J.2.6.9, 240
J.2.6.11, 242
J.2.6.12, 241, 242
J.2.7, 312, 313
J.2.7.1, 312
J.2.7.2, 383
J.2.7.3, 147
J.2.8pr, 146, 203
J.2.8.1, 164, 203
J.2.8.2, 129
J.2.9pr, 176
J.2.10.6, 296
J.2.13.5, 309
J.2.14.10, 301
J.2.15, 301
J.2.16, 302
J.2.17.2, 302
J.2.18pr, 310
J.2.18.1, 310
J.2.18.2, 311
J.2.19.6, 287
J.2.20.23, 307
J.2.20.25, 305
J.2.20.29–30, 305, 307
J.2.20.29–31, 305
J.2.20.31, 305
J.2.20.36, 308
J.2.21, 305
J.2.23.1, 314

J.2.23.2, 315
J.2.23.3, 315
J.2.23.4, 315
J.2.23.7, 316
J.2.25pr, 314, 316
J.2.25.1, 316
J.2.25.2, 316
J.3.1.2b, 285
J.3.1.6, 284, 289
J.3.1.9, 291
J.3.1.13, 290
J.3.3, 290
J.3.4, 290
J.3.7.4, 112
J.3.9pr, 306
J.3.12.1, 105
J.3.13pr, 163, 322
J.3.13.2, 323, 428, 437
J.3.14pr, 345
J.3.14.1, 272
J.3.14.2, 345, 347
J.3.14.3, 349
J.3.14.4, 269, 272
J.3.15pr, 342
J.3.15.1, 350
J.3.15.4, 336
J.3.19.3, 337
J.3.19.12, 340, 341
J.3.21, 380
J.3.23pr, 353
J.3.23.1, 355
J.3.23.2, 355
J.3.23.3, 357
J.3.23.3a, 357
J.3.24.2, 367
J.3.24.4, 366
J.3.24.5, 369
J.3.25.2, 375
J.3.25.4, 376
J.3.25.5, 375
J.3.25.6, 375
J.3.25.7–8, 375
J.3.25.8, 376
J.3.25.9, 375

J.3.26.1, 371
J.3.26.2, 371
J.3.26.4–5, 372
J.3.26.6, 372
J.3.26.8, 373
J.3.26.9, 373
J.3.26.10, 373
J.3.26.11, 373
J.3.27pr, 429
J.3.27.1, 435
J.3.27.2, 429
J.3.27.3, 172, 429
J.3.27.4, 429
J.3.27.5, 429
J.3.27.6, 430
J.3.27.7, 430
J.4.1pr, 385, 386, 407
J.4.1.3, 420
J.4.1.4, 420
J.4.1.5, 420
J.4.1.6, 418
J.4.1.7, 419
J.4.1.9, 418

J.4.1.12, 419
J.4.1.13, 419
J.4.1.14, 419
J.4.1.15, 419
J.4.1.17, 419
J.4.1.19, 420
J.4.2pr, 422
J.4.2.1, 422
J.4.2.2, 422
J.4.3.1, 388
J.4.3.3, 391
J.4.3.4, 393
J.4.3.9, 386
J.4.3.15, 390
J.4.3.16, 387, 395, 396
J.4.4pr, 405
J.4.4.2, 98, 409
J.4.4.3, 410
J.4.4.7, 410, 411
J.4.4.9, 411
J.4.4.11, 410
J.4.4.12, 409
J.4.5pr, 438, 439

J.4.5.1, 440, 441
J.4.5.3, 442
J.4.6.1, 163
J.4.6.3–5, 186
J.4.6.20, 171
J.4.6.32, 143
J.4.7.4, 153
J.4.7.4a, 154
J.4.7.5a, 155
J.4.8.3, 155
J.4.8.5, 155
J.4.8.7, 155
J.4.9pr, 425
J.4.9.1, 426
J.4.15.2, 187
J.4.15.4, 176, 180, 182, 187
J.4.15.4a, 187, 188
J.4.15.6, 189
J.4.17.2, 189
J.4.17.5, 171
J.4.17.6, 170

(3) The *Codex*

A translation of the *Codex* is available: F H Blume *et al*, *The Codex of Justinian: A New Annotated Translation, with Parallel Latin and Greek Text* (3 vols, Cambridge University Press 2016).

C.2.3.20, 210
C.2.18.11, 435
C.2.18.15, 435
C.2.19.2, 208
C.2.30.3pr, 110
C.2.81.1, 272
C.3.28.27, 310
C.3.28.28pr, 311
C.3.28.28.2, 311
C.3.28.30, 311
C.3.29.1, 312
C.3.29.7, 312
C.3.29.8, 312

C.3.33.4, 264
C.3.33.7, 264
C.3.34.1, 253
C.3.34.2, 253
C.3.34.13, 257
C.3.34.14pr, 252, 257
C.3.37.3.1, 172
C.3.37.5, 171
C.3.42.8, 328
C.4.5.11, 430
C.4.6.10, 432
C.4.21.17pr, 353
C.4.21.17.2, 353

C.4.24.1, 272
C.4.24.6, 272
C.4.24.7.1, 272
C.4.24.9, 272
C.4.32.26.2, 346
C.4.35.1, 371
C.4.43.1, 105
C.4.43.2, 105, 117
C.4.44.2, 355
C.4.44.8, 355
C.5.1.1, 137
C.5.4.9, 141
C.5.4.16, 122

C.5.4.22, 141
C.5.4.23.7, 141
C.5.4.24, 138
C.5.13.1b, 146
C.5.17.5, 144
C.5.17.8, 145
C.5.24.1, 119
C.5.26.1, 136
C.5.27.10, 126
C.5.27.11, 126
C.5.31.1, 130
C.5.31.6, 130
C.5.32.2, 128
C.5.32.3, 128
C.5.35.1, 128
C.5.59.5.2, 75
C.6.2.4, 423
C.6.6.1, 113
C.6.11.2, 300
C.6.23.15, 300
C.6.23.19, 300
C.6.23.21, 300
C.6.23.21.3, 300
C.6.23.21.4, 300
C.6.23.21.6, 303
C.6.23.27.2, 303
C.6.24.3, 295
C.6.24.14, 295
C.6.24.14.1, 295
C.6.26.9, 302
C.6.28.4, 309
C.6.30.17, 287

C.6.30.18, 129
C.6.30.22, 287
C.6.30.22.13a, 286
C.6.36.8.3, 316
C.6.37.21, 305
C.6.37.26.1, 305
C.6.43.1, 305
C.6.43.3.1, 307
C.6.48.1, 315
C.6.48.1.2, 306
C.6.51.1, 306
C.6.54.7, 264
C.6.60.1, 121
C.6.61.8, 121
C.7.6.1c, 112
C.7.6.2, 112
C.7.6.3–3a, 112
C.7.6.5, 112
C.7.6.9, 112
C.7.6.11–11a, 112
C.7.16.1, 105
C.7.16.3, 105
C.7.24, 105
C.7.30.1, 242
C.7.31.1, 242
C.7.31.1.3, 241
C.7.31.1.5, 199
C.7.32.1, 175
C.7.39.2, 241
C.7.39.3, 241
C.7.54.2–3, 43
C.8.4.7, 189

C.8.13.14, 275
C.8.14.1, 275
C.8.16.4, 324
C.8.26.1.2, 272
C.8.27.4, 273
C.8.27.8, 273
C.8.33.1, 273
C.8.33.2, 273
C.8.33.3, 273
C.8.34.3, 273
C.8.37.1, 341
C.8.37.10, 341
C.8.37.15, 335
C.8.40.28, 278
C.8.41.3, 324
C.8.47.11, 125
C.8.48.5, 127
C.8.51.2, 119
C.8.51.3, 122
C.8.53.1, 210
C.8.53.28, 278
C.8.53.33, 324
C.8.53.35.5, 213
C.8.55.1, 383
C.8.56.2, 313
C.8.56.4, 313
C.8.58.2, 290
C.9.9.18, 138
C.9.15.1, 119
C.9.17.1, 118
C.9.35.5, 410
C.12.30.1, 121

(4) The *Novels*

For the *Novels*, the best option is F H Blume's translation, available online at <http://www.uwyo.edu/lawlib/blume-justinian/ajc-edition-2/novels/index.html> (last accessed 14 September 2020).

Nov.4, 278
Nov.12.3, 126
Nov.18.1, 311
Nov.18.11, 126
Nov.22.7, 106
Nov.53.3, 43

Nov.78.4, 126
Nov.92, 312
Nov.107, 300
Nov.115.3, 311
Nov.118, 290
Nov.118.5, 128

Nov.119.2, 110
Nov.127, 290
Nov.134.8, 99
Nov.140, 145
Nov.159, 315

C. Other Sources

(1) The Twelve Tables
A reconstruction of the Twelve Tables can be found in M H Crawford ed, *Roman Statutes* (2 vols, Institute of Classical Studies 1996).

Table III.1, 36
Table V.6, 48
Table X.1, 48
Table X.8, 48
Table XI.1, 49

(2) Gaius' *Institutes*
Gaius' *Institutes* can be found in translation in W M Gordon and O F Robinson trans, *The Institutes of Gaius* (Duckworth 1988) or F de Zulueta trans, *The Institutes of Gaius* (Oxford University Press 1946).

G.1.5, 53	G.1.103, 124	G.2.6, 195
G.1.7, 57	G.1.104, 124	G.2.7–7a, 195
G.1.9, 96	G.1.107, 125	G.2.8, 195
G.1.12, 113	G.1.111, 142	G.2.9, 195
G.1.13–15, 113	G.1.112, 142	G.2.11, 195
G.1.17–18, 110	G.1.113, 142	G.2.13, 197
G.1.17–19, 109	G.1.115a, 98	G.2.14, 197, 249
G.1.20, 109	G.1.117, 117	G.2.14a, 198
G.1.21, 110	G.1.119, 199, 200	G.2.15, 198
G.1.27, 113	G.1.121, 200	G.2.16, 198
G.1.37, 109	G.1.122, 200	G.2.17, 247
G.1.38, 109	G.1.134, 125	G.2.20, 202
G.1.38–40, 110	G.1.137, 143	G.2.21, 198
G.1.42–3, 110	G.1.137a, 143	G.2.24, 200
G.1.45, 111	G.1.144, 98, 131	G.2.29, 251
G.1.46, 111	G.1.144–6, 128	G.2.31, 251
G.1.52, 107, 108	G.1.155, 128	G.2.38, 324
G.1.55, 117	G.1.157, 132	G.2.39, 324
G.1.59, 139	G.1.160, 97	G.2.40, 201
G.1.61, 139	G.1.161, 97	G.2.41, 201
G.1.62, 139	G.1.165, 128	G.2.59–61, 241
G.1.63, 140	G.1.166, 128	G.2.64, 164
G.1.64, 138	G.1.173–4, 132	G.2.73, 222
G.1.76, 96	G.1.185, 128	G.2.74–5, 223
G.1.77–8, 96	G.1.190, 98	G.2.76, 224
G.1.84, 105	G.1.190–1, 132	G.2.77, 228, 230
G.1.101, 125	G.1.196, 138	G.2.78, 228, 231
G.1.102, 125	G.2.2, 195	G.2.79, 234, 235

G.2.93, 267
G.2.95, 175
G.2.103, 297, 298
G.2.111, 297
G.2.117, 300
G.2.119–21, 298
G.2.123, 300
G.2.129, 309
G.2.130–1, 305
G.2.130–4, 309
G.2.144–5, 302
G.2.151, 302
G.2.154, 286
G.2.155, 286
G.2.157, 284
G.2.158, 285
G.2.164, 286
G.2.165, 286
G.2.166, 287
G.2.167, 287
G.2.170, 287
G.2.193, 304
G.2.197, 304
G.2.199, 306
G.2.202, 303
G.2.204, 303
G.2.206–8, 306
G.2.209–14, 304
G.2.217, 304
G.2.221, 304
G.2.222, 304
G.2.225–6, 313
G.2.235–7, 308
G.2.238, 305
G.2.241, 306
G.2.254, 303
G.2.257, 316
G.2.285, 315
G.2.285–6a, 315
G.2.287, 315
G.3.40, 114
G.3.41, 114
G.3.78, 38
G.3.79, 41

G.3.80, 41
G.3.88, 322, 428
G.3.90, 345
G.3.91, 428, 430
G.3.92, 340
G.3.93, 340
G.3.95a, 339
G.3.96, 339
G.3.97, 334
G.3.97a, 334
G.3.98, 308, 334
G.3.100, 337
G.3.102, 341
G.3.104, 120
G.3.105, 296
G.3.117, 278
G.3.121, 278
G.3.128–9, 380
G.3.131, 380
G.3.136, 352
G.3.137, 352
G.3.139, 353
G.3.140, 355
G.3.141, 355
G.3.146, 366
G.3.147, 366
G.3.154a, 374
G.3.161, 373
G.3.169, 325
G.3.170, 325
G.3.180, 325
G.3.186, 420
G.3.188, 420
G.3.192, 421
G.3.192–3, 421
G.3.199, 119
G.3.215, 388
G.3.217, 389
G.3.218, 390
G.3.220, 406
G.3.224, 410
G.3.225, 410
G.4.9, 387
G.4.11, 32

G.4.12, 33
G.4.13, 33
G.4.14, 33
G.4.15, 34
G.4.16, 29
G.4.16–17, 33
G.4.17–20, 34
G.4.17a, 34
G.4.17b, 29
G.4.20, 35
G.4.21, 36
G.4.23, 204
G.4.26–9, 37
G.4.31, 168
G.4.36, 186
G.4.40, 39
G.4.41, 38
G.4.42, 29, 39
G.4.43, 39
G.4.44, 39
G.4.48, 39
G.4.49, 39
G.4.50, 39
G.4.52, 439
G.4.53–53d, 40
G.4.61, 325
G.4.70, 151
G.4.71, 151
G.4.72, 155
G.4.72a, 153, 154
G.4.73, 152
G.4.74, 152
G.4.74a, 155
G.4.75–6, 155
G.4.77, 155
G.4.141, 187
G.4.143, 187
G.4.147, 275
G.4.151, 188
G.4.152, 188
G.4.153, 176, 180
G.4.154, 189
G.4.155, 189
G.4.160, 187

(3) Codex Theodosianus
A translation of the *Codex Theodosianus* is available in C Pharr, *The Theodosian Code and Novels, and the Sirmondian Constitutions* (Princeton University Press 1952).

C.Th.2.19.1, 310
C.Th.2.33.4, 346
C.Th.4.4.1, 316
C.Th.4.4.6, 302

C.Th.4.12.2, 105
C.Th.8.12.3, 383
C.Th.8.16.1, 297
C.Th.8.17.2, 297

(4) Other Sources
Cicero, *De Amicitia* 1.1, 57
Cicero, *De Inventione* 2.20.59–60, 405
Cicero, *De Legibus* 2.59, 48
Cicero, *Pro Caecina* 11.33, 82
Vatican Fragments 90, 267

APPENDIX 2:

Timeline of Major Events from the Foundation of Rome to Justinian I

Note that dates given for kings and emperors are the dates of their reigns, rather than dates of their births or deaths, unless otherwise indicated. To avoid undue repetition of the abbreviations 'BC' and 'AD', these are only given for the first date listed that falls within each. The letter 'c' (*circa*, 'around') before a date indicates that the date is approximate.

Monarchy

753 BC	Foundation of Rome (traditional date)
753–716	Reign of Romulus, Senate established
715–672	Reign of Numa Pompilius
672–642	Reign of Tullus Hostilius
642–616	Reign of Ancus Marcius
616–579	Reign of Tarquinius Priscus
579–534	Reign of Servius Tullius
534–509	Reign of Tarquinius Superbus

Earlier Republic

509	Overthrow of Monarchy, establishment of Republic
451–450	Twelve Tables compiled
443	Establishment of office of Censor
390	Sack of Rome by Gauls
367	Praetorship and Aedileship established, *leges Liciniae Sextiae* enacted
287	*Lex Hortensia* makes *plebiscita* of *concilium plebis* binding

Later Republic

264–241	First Punic War
242	Praetorship divided into two (Urban and Peregrine)
218–201	Second Punic War
214–148	First to Fourth Macedonian Wars

149–146	Third Punic War
133	Tiberius Gracchus elected tribune
123	Gaius Gracchus elected tribune
91–88	Social War
60	Julius Caesar elected consul
60–53	First Triumvirate (Caesar, Pompey and Crassus)
58–50	Conquest of Gaul
49–45	Civil War between Caesar and Pompey
44	Assassination of Caesar
43–33	Second Triumvirate (Octavian, Marcus Antonius and Marcus Lepidus)
33–31	Civil War between Octavian and Marcus Antonius

Principate

27	Octavian awarded title of Augustus
c. 4	Birth of Jesus
AD 14	Death of Augustus
14–37	Reign of Tiberius
c. 33	Crucifixion of Jesus
37–41	Reign of Caligula
41–54	Reign of Claudius
43	Invasion of Britain, leading to creation of province of Britannia
54–68	Reign of Nero
69	Year of Four Emperors
83/84	Battle of Mons Graupius
117–138	Reign of Hadrian
122	Construction of Hadrian's Wall begins
138–161	Reign of Antoninus Pius
142	Construction of Antonine Wall begins
161–180	Reign of Marcus Aurelius
212	*Constitutio Antoniniana*: general grant of Roman citizenship
c. 235	Beginning of Crisis of the Third Century
238	Year of Six Emperors
270–275	Reign of Aurelian

Dominate

284	Beginning of reign of Diocletian
293	Establishment of the Tetrarchy and first division of Empire into East and West
305	Abdication of Diocletian
306	Constantine I proclaimed western emperor
313	Edict of Milan, establishing official toleration of Christianity

324	Constantine I becomes sole emperor, Constantinople established as capital
337	Baptism and death of Constantine I
361–363	Reign of Julian the Apostate, last non-Christian emperor
379–395	Reign of Theodosius I as eastern emperor (western emperor from 392)
402–450	Reign of Theodosius II (alone from 408, with regent 408–416)
410	Sack of Rome by Visigoths, Romans abandon Britannia
426	Law of Citations
438	*Codex Theodosianus*
c. 440s	Arrival of Anglo-Saxons in former Roman Britannia
476	Last western emperor, Romulus Augustulus, deposed
527–565	Reign of Justinian I
533	*Digest* and *Institutes* of Justinian
534	*Codex* of Justinian

Index

acceptilatio, 324–5
accession, 216, 218n, 221–31
   land to land, of, 225–7
   modern law, in, 231
   moveables to land, of, 165n, 198n, 222–5, 367
   moveables to moveables, of, 227–31, 237n, 366
   nature and scope, 221–2
Accursian Gloss see Glossa Ordinaria
Accursius, 75
Acquisition
   civil law and natural law modes of, 194
   derivative, 194–215
   original, 216–43
actio (action)
   ad exhibendum, 190, 224–5, 230, 359
   ad supplendam legitimam portionem, 311
   adiecticiae qualitiatis, 150–5
   aquae pluviae arcendae, 169, 227
   bonae fidei, 334n
   bonorum raptorum, 422
   communi dividundo, 171–2
   commodati, 347
   commodati contraria, 349
   conducti, 368
   confessoria, 255, 257, 266
   de dolo, 381, 423
   de in rem verso, 153–4
   de pastu, 425
   de pauperie, 425–6
   de peculio, 153
   de tigni iniuncto, 225
   depositi, 349
   depositi contraria, 349
   empti, 358, 359, 360, 362, 363
   ex stipulatu, 342
   exercitoria, 151
   familiae erciscundae, 172
   fiduciae, 271
   finium regundorum, 170
   furti (action for theft), 190, 417–22
   furti non exhibiti, 420
   in factum, 51, 230, 264, 387, 389, 395, 424, 440n
   iniuriarum see iniuria
   institoria, 151, 372n
   iudicati, 36, 41
   legis Aquiliae, 387; *see also* Aquilian liability
   locati, 368
   mandati contraria, 373
   mandati directa, 373
   metus, 206–7, 424
   negatoria, 169, 255, 257, 266, 408n
   personal, 161–3
   pigneraticia, 272
   praescriptis verbis, 344n, 380
   pro socio, 376
   prohibiti furti, 420
   Publiciana, 185–6, 201, 239, 243
   quanti minoris, 361, 363, 364
   quod iussu, 151
   quod metus causa, 424
   real, 161–3
   redhibitoria, 361
   rei uxoriae, 146
   Serviana, 275

actio (action) (*cont.*)
   stricti iuris, 334n
   tributoria, 154–5
   utilis, 51, 231n, 255n, 285n, 387, 398
   venditi, 364
   vi bonorum raptorum, 422
actions, law of, 29–45, 60, 86, 93;
   see also actio; institutional scheme
adiudicatio, 38, 39
adoptio see adoption
adoption, 123–5, 139–40, 285
adpromissio, 277–8
adrogatio see adoption
adstipulatio, 278, 388
advocate (Roman), 30–1, 32, 43, 369, 371
advocate (Scots), 57, 84, 85, 88, 89
aedile, 10–11, 55, 361–3, 426; *see also* edict, aediles'
aemulatio vicini, 167–8
aestimatum, 381
affectio maritalis, 140–1, 145
affront *see iniuria*
ager publicus, 16
alieni iuris, 96–7, 116–27, 140, 144n, 152n, 148
alluvion, 225–7
animal
   as *res mancipi/nec mancipi*, 198
   defects in, 361–2, 363
   domestic and wild, 218–19
   liability for injury caused by, 425–6
   liability for injury to, 388–90; *see also* Aquilian liability, theft
   ownership of, 167, 228, 217–21, 261
   sacrifice of, 8n
antichresis, 272
Antoninus Pius, 21, 108
appeals, 36, 41, 42, 44, 58–9; *see also* quasi-delictual liability, judge who made the case his own
apud iudicem, 30, 32
Aquilian liability, 386–404, 418n, 423, 425n, 430n
   causation, 394–8
   extensions to, 398
   fault, 391–4

   first chapter, 388–9
   loss, 390–1
   modern law and, 399–403
   requirements for, 386–7, 390–8
   scope, 387–90
   third chapter, 389–90
arbitrator, 252, 382
   similarity of judge to, 33, 42
arra, 352–3
assemblies, 7, 8–9, 11, 13, 19–20, 49–50, 52, 297; *see also comitia calata, comitia centuriata, comitia curiata, concilium plebis*
assignation *see* right, personal
Augustus, 18–20, 37, 42, 52, 56, 57, 109, 110, 111, 118n, 120, 121, 314, 316
   marriage legislation of, 132, 134n, 135, 145, 146, 296–7
avulsion, 225–7
Azo, 75

Baldus de Ubaldis, 76
Bankton, 187, 399n, 411–12, 440
barter *see permutatio*
Bartolus of Sassoferrato, 76
Bell, George Joseph, 88–9, 227–8, 229–30, 337
beneficium abstinendi, 285
beneficium divisionis, 278
beneficium excussionis vel ordinis, 278
beneficium inventarii, 287
betrothal, 136–7
Bluhme, 65
bonitary ownership *see* ownership
bonorum possessio, 290, 291–3, 298, 302, 306, 309n, 310n
bonorum venditio, 41
Britain, Britannia, 20–1, 25, 73

Caesar, Julius, 17–18, 139n, 297–8, 307n
canon law, 30, 76–8, 79, 80, 84, 85, 116n, 126, 140, 144n, 145n, 187, 283n, 327; *see also* Christianity; Reformation, Protestant
capacity, legal, *see* slave, women, children, *traditio*
capitis deminutio, 97, 302

Carthage, 4n, 14, 15
cautio
   damni infecti, 168
   Muciana, 308
   usufructuaria, 263–4
censor, 10, 13, 107–8, 145n
cessio bonorum, 42
children, legal capacity of, 99–100
Christianity, 21, 24–5, 61, 67, 76, 95, 108, 145, 195, 297; *see also* canon law; Reformation, Protestant
Cicero, 12n, 31, 48, 57, 182, 186
citizenship, 4, 14, 16, 22, 96, 97, 100
Claudius, emperor, 20, 112, 131, 139, 145n
Codex, 69–70; *see also First Codex*
Codex Gregorianus, 63
Codex Hermogenianus, 63
Codex Theodosianus, 63, 73
codicil, 305, 314, 316
coemptio, 98, 142, 144n, 296
coercion, 205–7, 333–4, 423, 424–5; *see also actio metus*
cognitio, procedure 30, 42–4
collatio bonorum, 291, 293
comitia calata, 124, 297
comitia centuriata, 8–9, 10, 13
comitia curiata, 7, 8, 9
Commentators, 76, 80
commixtio, 216, 237–8
commodatum, 347–9, 381
   borrower's duties, 347–8
   lender's duties, 348–9
   nature and development, 347
common employment, 400–1
Common Law (English), 79, 81n, 82, 83, 314n, 323n; *see also* English law
compensatio, 325
compromise (of an action) *see transactio*
concilium plebis, 11–12, 13, 50
concubine, 136
condemnatio, 38, 39, 43
condictio, 34–5, 231, 313, 342, 353, 381, 421, 429–34
   causa data causa non secuta, 430–1
   furtiva, 421
   indebiti, 430

   ob turpem vel iniustam causam, 431
   sine causa, 431–2
conditio si testator sine liberis decesserit, 309–10
condition *in diem addictio*, 336
conditions, suspensive and resolutive *see* contracts; *traditio*
confarreatio, 142, 143, 144n
confusio
   acquisition of ownership by, 216, 237–8
   extinction of obligations by, 325
   extinction of praedial servitudes by, 257
Constantine, 24–5, 273, 297, 300, 304–5, 383
constitutio Antoniniana, 22
constitutio see pronouncement, imperial
constitutum debitum, 382
consul, 9, 10, 11, 13, 14
contracts, 325–84
   bonae fidei, 326
   causa, role of, 327–8
   conditions in, suspensive and resolutive, 335–7
   consensual, 352–78; *see also* sale, hire, mandate, partnership
   error in, 328–33
   formation of, 328–35
   grounds of invalidity of, 328–35, 337
   illegal and immoral, 334
   impossible, 334–5
   innominate, 380–1
   invalid, implement of, 337
   literal, 379–80
   nature of, 325–7
   perfection of, 336
   real, 344–51; *see also mutuum, commodatum, depositum*, pledge
   stricti iuris, 326
   verbal *see stipulatio*
   written, 341–2, 353, 379–80
conubium, 96, 138
convicium, 407
co-ownership, 39, 171–2, 207
Corpus Iuris Canonici, 77
Corpus Iuris Civilis, 64–70
Court of Session, 85, 87–8, 299, 439n

Crassus, Marcus Licinius, 17, 18
cretio, 286–7
Crisis of the Third Century, 22–3, 62
Cujas, Jacques, 87
culpa in contrahendo, 331–3
culpa see Aquilian liability
cura minorum, 130–1
curator *see cura minorum*

damnum
  emergens, 391
  fatale, 358–9
  infectum, 168
  see also Aquilian liability
deceit, 205–7, 334, 423–4; *see also actio de dolo, exceptio doli*
Decretum (of Gratian) *see Corpus Iuris Canonici*
decretum see pronouncement, imperial
dediticii, 113
delicts, law of, 385–427
  nature and scope of, 385–6
  see also Aquilian liability; *iniuria*; theft; robbery; slave, corruption of; deceit; coercion; animal, liability for
delivery *see traditio*
demonstratio, 39
depositum, 349–50
  irregulare, 350
dictator, 11, 17n, 18
dies, 337
diffareatio, 143
Digest, 65–70
  compilation of, 65–6
  contents of, 68–9
  interpolations in, 66–8
dignity, 406–7
Diocletian, 23–4, 25, 63, 125
disinheritance, 308–12; *see also querela inofficiosi testamenti*
divorce, 142–3, 144–5
dolus see deceit
Dominate, 23–7
dominium see ownership
Domitian, 108
donatio
  inter virum et uxorem (between husband and wife), 144
  inter vivos, 382–3
  mortis causa, 312–13
  propter nuptias, 146–7
dos see dowry
dotis dictio, 339n
dowry, 145–6
duress *see* coercion

edict
  aediles', 361–3, 426
  of emperor, 53, 62
  on prices, 24
  praetorian, 32, 38, 51–2, 58, 59, 60, 68, 405, 421, 423, 442
  see also ius honorarium
Edict of Milan, 25
Edictum Perpetuum, 52
emphyteusis, 192
Empire, 18–27
England, 20, 21n, 26, 73n, 85n, 87
English law, 79, 82, 99, 236n, 314n, 327–8, 400–3, 412; *see also* Common Law (English)
equestrian, 23
ercto non cito, 374
Erskine, John, 88, 137n, 183, 196, 212, 216n, 224n, 225, 229, 230, 265, 312, 399, 402, 411n, 432n
Etruscans, 6–7
exceptio, 40
  doli, 185n, 206, 210n, 224, 235n, 276, 293n, 325, 334, 423
  metus, 334, 424
execution of judgements, 36–7, 41–2, 43–4
extranei see heredes

Faculty of Advocates *see* advocate (Scots)
familiae emptor, 298
fideicommissum, 314–16
fideiussio, 277–82
fidepromissio, 277
fiducia, 271
Fifty Decisions, 64, 70
filiusfamilias, 150–6, 116–27

First Codex, 64, 65, 70
fishing, right of, 195–6
foreshore, public rights over, 196–7
formula see formulary procedure
formulary procedure, 37–42
France, 17n, 73n, 80, 84, 99, 209
fraud *see* deceit
freedman, 100, 112–14
furiosi, 100

Gaius (jurist), 59–60, 63; *see also*
    institutional scheme
Gaius Gracchus, 16
Germany, 17n, 81, 99, 209, 278n, 332
gift *see donatio*
Glossa Ordinaria, 75
Glossators, 74–5
good faith *see* possession; *usucapio*;
    contracts, *bonae fidei*
Gratian, 77
Great Gloss see Glossa Ordinaria
Greek (language) , 21, 26, 67, 72, 303, 340
Grotius, 81, 82n
guardianship
    of children, 128–9
    of women, 131–2

habitatio, 260
Hadrian, 21, 52, 53, 57, 98, 104, 105,
    108, 118, 239, 278, 290, 296, 315
heirs *see heredes*
heredes, 284–8
    conditional institution of, 301
    extranei, 286–8
    institution of, 300–2
    necessarii, 285–6
    pupillary substitution of, 302
    substitution of, 301–2
    sui, 284–5, 288–9
    sui et necessarii, 284–5
hereditatis petitio, 288, 293
    possessoria, 293
Hexabiblos, 73
hire, contract of, 365–71
    distinguished from sale, 365–7
    locatio conductio operarum (hire of
        services), 369–70

locatio conductio operis (hire of a piece of
    work), 370–1
locatio conductio rei (hire of a thing), 367–9
nature and classification of, 365
House of Lords, 87n, 88, 99n, 399–403
Humanism, Legal, 80–1
hypothec, 274–6

imperium, 10
in iure, 30, 33–5, 38–40
in iure cessio, 198, 200–1, 251
in ius vocatio, 33, 38
infames see infamia
infamia, 41, 42, 113, 129n, 100–1, 138,
    349, 374, 376, 410, 424
iniuria, 101, 137, 196n, 255, 278n, 386,
    405–16, 423, 425
    identity of the pursuer, 137,
        409–10
    injury to feelings, 409
    insulting act, 405–8
    intention to insult, 408–9
    lack of justification, 409
    liability, basis of and restrictions on,
        410–11
    modern law, in, 411–15
    requirements for liability for, 405–9
    specification of claim, 410
insanity *see furiosi*
Institutes of Gaius, 59n, 60, 73
Institutes of Justinian, 69
institutional scheme, 59–60, 69, 197,
    323, 379
insult *see iniuria*
intentio, 38–9
interdictum (interdict) , 40
    de itinere actuque privato, 257
    de precario, 381
    de vi/de vi armata, 186, 189
    possessory, 187–9, 257, 266–7, 293;
        see also possession, protection of
    quod vi aut clam, 169
    quorum bonorum, 293
    Salvianum, 275
    uti possidetis, 187–8
    utrubi, 188
intestabiles, 101

Irnerius, 74
iudex see judge
iudicis postulatio, 34
ius capiendi, 296
ius civile Flavianum, 55n
ius commune, 78–9, 81, 82, 84–7, 88, 89, 91, 154, 167–8, 363, 399, 432
ius gentium, 68, 96, 103, 104, 194
ius honorarium, 50–2, 322
ius liberorum, 132, 290
ius quaesitum tertio, 327–8
ius respondendi see jurists
ius tollendi, 223, 224, 225n
iusiurandum liberti, 339n
iusta causa see traditio; usucapio
iustum pretium, 355–6

Jhering, 178–9, 182, 332
judge, 31, 32, 35–6, 41
   liability of, 437–9
   selection of, 35
Junian Latin, 111–13
jurists, 54–60
   emergence of, 54–6
   ius respondendi and, 56–7
   references of Scottish courts to, 89–91
   roles of, 57–9
   schools of, 56
   see also Sabinians, Proculians, Gaius
just cause *see iusta causa*
Justinian, 26–7, 63–70; *see also* Corpus Iuris Civilis

laesio enormis, 355–6
Latin rights, 96n, 111
Law of Citations, 63
lawyers, role of, 30–1
legacy *see legatum*
legatum, 303–8
   conditional, 307–8
   debiti, 307
   identification of, 306–7
   incertae personae, 305–6
   joint, 306
   optionis, 307
   partitionis, 303
   per damnationem, 303

   per praeceptionem, 304
   per vindicationem, 303, 304
   revocation of, 304
   sinendi modo, 304
leges Liciniae Sextiae, 12
leges regiae, 47
legis actiones, 32–7
legislation, 49–50, 52–4
legitim, 312
legitimation, 126
legitimi, 291
lenocinium, 135
Lepidus, Marcus Aemilius, 18
lex, 49–50, 52
   Aebutia, 37n
   Aelia Sentia, 109, 110, 112, 113
   Aquilia, 386–404, 408n, 423, 425n, 430n; *see also* Aquilian liability
   Atinia, 240
   Calpurnia, 34n
   Cincia, 204, 209, 383
   Cornelia de iniuriis, 405n
   commissoria, 337
   Falcidia, 301, 313, 315
   Fufia Caninia, 110–11
   Furia, 277
   Furia testamentaria, 301, 313
   Hortensia, 12
   imperfecta, 203–4; *see also* contracts, invalid, implement of
   Iulia de adulteriis coercendis, 118, 135
   Iulia de maritandis ordinibus, 132n, 297
   Iulia de vi privata aut publica, 189
   Iulia et Plautia, 240n
   Iunia, 111
   Laetoria, 130
   Minicia, 96
   minus quam perfecta, 203–4; *see also* contracts, invalid, implement of
   Papia Poppaea, 132n, 297
   perfecta, 203–4; *see also* contracts, invalid, implement of
   Petronia, 108
   Plaetoria, 130
   Poetelia, 36, 270
   Rhodia de iactu, 371n, 392n
   Romana Visigothorum, 73

Scribonia, 253, 256, 257
Silia, 34n
Voconia, 296, 301, 313
liberi, 291
liberty, 95; *see also* slavery; slave
licence *see precarium*
litis contestatio, 35, 40, 183, 277–8, 325, 438n
longi temporis praescriptio, 241, 253, 256
longissimi temporis praescriptio see longi temporis praescriptio
Louisiana, 79, 82

Macedonian Wars, 15
mancipatio, 199–200
mandate, contract of, 371–3
   duties of mandatary, 373
   duties of mandator, 372–3
   nature and creation of, 371–2
   termination, 373
mandatum of emperor *see* pronouncement, imperial
mandatum, contract of *see* mandate, contract of
manumission, 108–12
manus iniectio, 36
manus marriage *see* marriage
Marcus Antonius, 18
Marcus Aurelius, 130, 144n, 189n
Marius, Gaius, 17n
marriage, 134–48
   cum manu, 142–3
   formation of, 136–41
   legal consequences of, 142, 144
   sine manu, 143–5
   termination of *see* divorce
metus see coercion
missio in possessionem, 38, 40, 41
mixed legal systems, 82
Modestinus, 63
Monarchy, 6–10
mutuum, 344–7
   borrower's duties, 344–5
   moneylending and, 346–7
   nature and development of, 344–5

Natural Law, 81
navigation, right of, 195–6

negotiorum gestio, 434–5
Nero, 20n, 21, 138n, 304, 315
Netherlands, 17n, 82, 84, 88n; *see also* Roman-Dutch law
nexum, 270
nominatio, 38, 39
novatio, 324, 325
Novels, 70
noxal liability, 155–6, 425

obligations, law of, 319–444
   civil law, 322
   natural, 322
   nature and structure of, 321–3
   praetorian, 322
   see also right, personal
obsequium, 113, 311
occupatio, 217–21
   scope, 217–19
   acquisition by, 219–20
   modern law, in, 220–1
Octavian *see* Augustus
operae liberales, 369n, 371
operis novi nuntiatio, 168–9
Optimates and *Populares*, 12n
ownership; nature of, 165–6
   acquisition of *see* acquisition
   bonitary, 192, 201–2
   loss of, 217–18, 220
   proof of, 190–1
   recovery based on, 166, 189–91
   relationship with possession, 173, 186–7
   restrictions on, 167–71
   rights arising from, 166–7
   shared *see* co-ownership
   see also vindication, property

pacta (pacts), 381–2
   displicentiae, 337, 381
   legis commissoriae, 273; *see also lex commissoria*
   nuda, 381–2
   praetorian, 382
   vestita, 381–2
Papinian, 63, 65n
pars legitima see portio legitima

partnership, contract of, 373–7
  modern law, in, 376–7
  nature of, 373–5
  remedies of partners, 376
  termination, 375–6
paterfamilias
  liability of, 121–2, 149–157
  rights over property, 120–2
  rights over the person, 117–20
  see also patria potestas; paternity, proof of
paternity, proof of, 122–3
patria potestas, 116–27
  creation of, 122–5
  nature of, 116–7
  termination of, 127
  see also legitimation, adoption, *paterfamilias, peculium*
patricians and plebeians, 11–12, 13, 47–8, 49, 50
patron *see* freedman
Paul (jurist), 63, 68
pauperies see actio de pauperie
peculium, 106–7, 120–1, 151–5
  adventitium, 121, 125n
  castrense, 121
  content of, 152–3
  liability based on, 151–5
  of *filiusfamilias*, 120–1
  of slave, 106–7
  quasi castrense, 121
  see also paterfamilias
permutatio, 381
personality, legal, 95
persons, law of, 93–157; *see also* institutional scheme
pignoris capio, 37
pignus see pledge
plebeians *see* patricians and plebeians
plebiscitum, 11, 12, 50; *see also concilium plebis*
pledge, 271–4, 350
  nature of, 271–2
  parties' rights, duties and liabilities in, 272
  enforcement of, 273–4
Pompey (Gaius Pompeius Magnus), 17–18

pontifex, 12, 55, 297
pontifex maximus, 55n, 124, 297n
Populares see Optimates and *Populares*
portio legitima, 311, 312
possession, 172–89, 242
  civil, 178
  elements of, 173–80
  good faith, in, 183–6
  loss of, 180–1
  mental element of, 176–80
  natural, 178
  nature of, 172–4
  of incorporeals *see* quasi-possession
  physical element of, 174–6
  protection of, 181–3, 187–9
  relationship with ownership, 173, 186–7
  through another, 175–6
  see also traditio, interdict, *usucapio*
postliminium, 105
postulatio see iudicis postulatio
postumi, 305–6, 309–10
potestas see patria potestas
Pothier, 363, 367
practicks, 85
praescriptio, 40n
praetor, 11, 14
  fideicommissarius, 314
  peregrine, 14
  remedies granted by, 40; *see also interdictum*
  role in litigation, 30; *see also legis actiones*, formulary procedure
  urban, 14
  see also ius honorarium, edict
precarium, 381
priests, 5n, 7–8, 11, 12, 54–5, 142, 195n, 360n; *see also pontifex, pontifex maximus*
princeps see Principate
Principate, 18–23
privacy, 414–15
Proculians *see* jurists, schools of
procuratio in rem suam, 324
procurator, 36, 40, 324
prodigi, 100
pronouncement, imperial, 53–4, 61, 62–3; *see also Codex*

property
  abandoned, 217–18
  corporeal, 197
  divini iuris, 194–5
  enemy, 218
  fungible, 199
  humani iuris, 194–5
  immoveable, 198
  incorporeal, 197
  law of, 159–279
  moveable, 198
  public, 195
  types of, 194–9
  see also res, ownership, vindication
Punic Wars, 15

quaestor, 10, 14
quasi-contractual liability, 428–36
  scope of, 428–9
  see also unjustified enrichment;
    negotiorum gestio
quasi-delictual liability, 156,
    437–44
  carriers by sea, innkeepers and
    stablekeepers, 441–4
  judge who made the case his own,
    437–9
  nature and scope of, 437
  things hung or suspended, 441
  things poured or thrown, 439–40
quasi-possession, 176, 256–7,
    266–7
Quebec, 79, 82, 99, 246n
querela inofficiosae donationis, 311–12
querela inofficiosi testamenti, 310–12
Quintus Mucius Scaevola, 31, 57

Reception of Roman Law, 72–91
receptum, 382, 442–3
Reformation, Protestant, 80, 84
Regiam Majestatem, 83, 84, 312n
regula Catoniana, 308
rei vindicatio see vindication
replicatio, 40
Republic, 10–18
reputation, 406, 407
res iudicata, 325

res
  mancipi, 198–9, 199–202
  nec mancipi, 198–9, 202–14; *see also*
    property
  religiosae, 195
  sacrae, 195
  sanctae, 195
rescriptum see pronouncement, imperial
restitutio in integrum, 40
retention, 276
right, personal, 163–5
  extinction of, 324–5
  transfer of, 323–4
right, real, 163–5
rights in security, 269–79
  nature and function of, 269–70
  see also security, real; security,
    personal; *nexum*; *fiducia*; pledge;
    hypothec; retention; *adpromissio*;
    sponsio; *fidepromissio*; *fideiussio*;
    adstipulatio
river
  ownership of, 226–7
  public, 195–6
  see also alluvion, right of fishing
robbery, 422
Roman-Dutch law, 82, 88, 179n, 314n,
    414n; *see also* Netherlands, South
    Africa, Sri Lanka
Romano-canonical procedure, 30, 77
Romulus, 5, 7, 9, 142

Sabinians *see* jurists, schools of
sacramentum, 33–4
St Paul, 108
sale, contract of, 352–65
  additional terms in, 364–5
  aestimatum, 381
  buyer's duties, 364
  chance, of, 354
  expected thing, of, 354
  formation of, 352–8
  guarantee against defects, 360–4
  guarantee against eviction, 359–60
  price in, 355–6
  risk in, 356–7
  seller's duties in, 358–64

sale, contract of (*cont.*)
   seller's obligation to deliver with vacant possession, 359
   seller's obligation to take care of property, 358–9
   subject matter of, 353–4
   transfer of ownership in, 357–8; *see also traditio, mancipatio, in iure cessio*
Savigny, 178–9, 182
Scotland, 21, 80n; *see also* Scots law, Union of the Crowns, Union of Parliaments
Scots law, 82–92, 99
   influence of English law on, 82, 83, 85 87–90, 276n, 400–3, 433
   institutional writers of, 60, 88–9; *see also* Bankton, Bell, Erskine, Stair
   Reception of Roman law into, 82–91
sea and seabed, public rights over, 196
security, personal, 277–8; *see also* rights in security; security, real; *adpromissio; sponsio; fidepromissio; fideiussio; adstipulatio*
security, real, 270–6; *see also* rights in security; security, personal; *nexum; fiducia;* pledge; hypothec; retention
Senate, 7, 12–13, 14, 16, 17, 18, 19n, 20, 23, 24, 50, 53; *see also senatusconsultum*
senatusconsultum, 20, 50, 53
   Claudianum, 105
   Macedonianum, 150n, 346–7
   Neronianum, 304
   Orphitianum, 290
   Pegasianum, 315
   Silianum, 106n
   Tertullianum, 290
   Trebellianum, 315–6
   Velleianum, 98–9
separatio bonorum, 286, 288
sequester see sequestratio
sequestratio, 177, 350
services of slaves and animals, 260
servitude, personal *see* usufruct
servitude, praedial, 244–58
   creation of, 250–4
   establishing or denying, 255
   exercise of, 254
   extinction of, 257

   modern law, in, 244–5, 258
   nature of, 244–5
   positive, 248; negative 248
   possessory protection of, 256–7
   protection of, 255–7
   recognised types of, 247–50
   restrictions on creation of, 245–7
slave
   corruption of, delictual liability for, 422–3
   legal capacity of, 106–7
   treatment of, 107–8, 408
   see also slavery, *peculium*
slavery, 103–15
   imposition of, 104–6
   nature of, 103–4
   role of, 104
   end of *see* manumission
   see also slave
Social War, 16
solutio, 324
South Africa, 82, 88; *see also* Roman-Dutch law
spatium deliberandi, 286, 287
specificatio, 216, 231–7
   compensation, and, 235
   good faith and, 234–5
   Justinianic law of, 233–4
   modern law, in, 236–7
   nature of, 231–2
   Sabinian/Proculian dispute concerning, 232–3
sponsio, 277
Sri Lanka, 82
Stair, Viscount, 85–7, 129, 130–1, 154, 179, 182–3, 196, 221, 230, 234, 238, 278, 327, 331, 400, 411
stipulatio, 339–43
   enforcement, 342
   nature and development of, 339–40
   requirements for, 340–4
   writing, use of, 341–2
Struggle of the Orders, 11–12
stuprum, 135, 136, 138
succession, 281–317
   agnates, by, 289, 291
   cognates, by, 291

gens, by, 289
heirs and *see heredes*
intestate, 288–93
liberi, by, 290–1, 297
legitimi, by, 291
praetorian order of, 290–1; *see also* will
sui heredes, by, 288–9
testate, 294–312
Twelve Tables, intestate succession under, 288–9
universal, 283–4
sui iuris, 127–32
Sulla, Lucius Cornelius, 17n
superficies, 191–2

testamenti factio, 96, 295
theft, 417–22
   definition of, 417–9
   furtum conceptum, 420
   furtum oblatum, 420
   identity of the defender, 419–20
   identity of the pursuer, 419
   manifest and non-manifest, 420
   remedies for, 420–2
Theodosius II, 63
thesaurus see treasure
things, law of, 159–444; *see also* institutional scheme
Tiberius Gracchus, 16
traditio, 202–14
   brevi manu, 212
   by permission to take possession, 211–12
   capacity, requirement for, 203–4
   clavium, 211
   conditions, suspensive and resolutive, 205
   consent, requirement for, 205–7
   constitutum possessorium, by, 212–13
   direct, 211
   general nature of, 210
   general requirements for, 202–10
   identification, requirement for, 207
   in Scots law, 213–14
   incertae personae, 212
   iusta causa, requirement for, 207–10
   longa manu, 211
   operation of, 210–14
   symbolical, 210, 211, 213
   title, requirement for, 202–3
   see also possession
Trajan, 119, 301
transactio, 16
treasure, 238–9
Tribonian, 65, 69, 70
tribune, 11, 16
tutela see guardianship
Twelve Tables, 47–9

Ulpian, 63, 68
Union of the Crowns, 87
Union of Parliaments, 87
United States of America, 79, 82n, 104; *see also* Louisiana
unjustified enrichment, 429–34
   grounds of, 430–2
   modern law, in, 432–4
usucapio, 239–43
   good faith and, 241
   iusta causa and, 241–2
   modern law, in, 242–3
   nature and scope of, 239–41
   possession and, 242
usufruct, 259–68
   creation of, 260
   exercise of, 260–6
   extinction of, 267
   fruits, right to, 261–2
   modern law, in, 265–6
   nature of, 259–60
   owner's remedies in, 263–5
   preservation of substance of property, and, 262–3
   protection of, 266–7
   use, right to, 261
usureceptio, 241n
usus, constitution of *manus* marriage by, 142, 143
usus, personal servitude of, 260
Usus Modernus Pandectarum, 81

vadimonium, 38, 410n
Vatican Fragments, 267
vindex, 33, 36, 38

vindication, 162, 189–90
vis maior, 371, 444

Wars of Independence, 83–4
will
  comitial, 297
  holograph, 300
  in procinctu, 297
  institution of heir in, 300–2
  mancipatory, 298
  praetorian, 298–9
  public, 300
  revocation of, 302–3
  soldier's, 297–8
  tripartite, 300
  will, capacity to make, 295–7, *see also testamenti factio*
  will, nature and role of, 294–5
  see also legatum; disinheritance
women
  adoption of, 124
  guardianship of *see* guardianship
  legal capacity of, 97–9
  succession rights of, 289, 290